IRISH TRADE UNION LAW

To Lui and in memory of Edward

IRISH TRADE UNION LAW

by

TONY KERR
M.A., LL.M.
College Lecturer, University College, Dublin

and

GERRY WHYTE
B.C.L., M.A., LL.M.
Barrister-at-Law, Lecturer, Trinity College, Dublin

with a

FOREWORD

by

The Honourable Mr. Justice BRIAN WALSH
M.A. (N.U.I.), LL.D. (h.c.) (Dublin)
Senior Ordinary Judge of the Supreme Court of Ireland
Judge of the European Court of Human Rights

PROFESSIONAL BOOKS LIMITED
1985

*Published in 1985 by
Professional Books Limited,
Milton Trading Estate, Abingdon, Oxon.
Typeset and printed in Great Britain
by Photobooks (Bristol) Ltd.*

ISBN: Hardback: 0 86205 051 0
Paperback: 0 86205 093 6

All rights reserved. No part of this publication may be reproduced or transmitted in any form or by any means, electronic, mechanical, photocopying, recording or otherwise, or stored in any retrieval system of any nature, without the written permission of the publishers.

©

A. KERR and G. WHYTE
1985

FOREWORD

Irish trade union law has many facets. In this excellent work they are all exposed to the reader and many of them are ones which only infrequently come to the attention of the public or, indeed, of the judges and lawyers. Trade union activities can have their impact upon the criminal law and upon constitutional law. They also can create problems in the area of public law as well as in the area of private law. Trade unions have come a very long way from the days when they were outlawed for being conspiracies in restraint of trade to the position of great economic, social, political and legal power which they enjoy today. The development of trade union law reflects the history of the development of the power of trade unionism. It has reflected the progress from the repression of the eighteenth and nineteenth centuries to the more liberal and enlightened attitude at the beginning of the twentieth century, and now at the end of the twentieth century the law is tending to reflect the problems of controlling the concentration of power which trade unions now enjoy in western democracies.

Unfortunately, the public perception of trade unions tends to be conditioned by particular experiences. It varies from those who see trade unions as the defenders and protectors of the underprivileged to those who see them as tyrants who have no regard for anything but their own immediate advantage and dedicated to restrictive practices to an extent that they are felt to represent a grave threat to economic progress and prosperity. The oft-expressed desire of trade unions to keep the law out of industrial relations is seen in a similar light. These very subjective perceptions tend to be those of the principal protagonists, the unions and the employers. Yet it cannot be denied that trade unions have conferred immense social and economic benefits on millions of workers who previously had been suffering grave injustices. However, it must be recognised that trade union activities, particularly in the field of industrial action, no longer concern only workers and employers but tend more and more to draw in the general public and the Government. This is particularly so in the Ireland of today, where so many fields of employment are in the public utilities, the public transport systems and the many companies in which the State plays an active direct or indirect role. In simple terms, the regulation of employment conditions can be properly regarded as a problem of human and social relationships. Yet in the modern State the involvement of the public at large and public authorities in particular gives a whole new dimension to the problem. This in its turn is bound to produce its own effect on the laws dealing with trade unions. Excessive concentration of economic power or excessive group power over individuals become problems of public law. Laws can frequently reflect political reactions against the growth of such power within the State because individual freedom must be protected against power groups. Yet the law must acknowledge and indeed protect the ideological motive in freedom of association.

The freedom to associate with others is one which the trade union movement is as much entitled to benefit from as are political and industrial groups. The many cases referred to in this work illustrate not only the emergence of these questions but how they have been dealt with by the law itself and by those whose task it is to administer the law. It is clear that in many respects trade unions enjoy a privileged position under the law. Some of their activities are prevented from being unlawful, as they would be if they had been engaged in by other persons or bodies of persons. Certain immunities against suit are available which are not available to other persons or bodies. Ireland has a written Constitution which in general leans against inequality and discrimination. Consequently there must be a question mark over the idea that any person or body of persons can be above the law. This is particularly so in respect of activities which would bring any other person or body of persons into conflict with the criminal law.

The right to work is a natural right and is therefore a fundamental human right. While that does not mean that work must necessarily be provided for somebody where in fact no work exists, it does mean that a person cannot properly be excluded from exercising his right to work if work which he is willing to do is available and on offer. The right to associate with other persons for the same purpose is also a fundamental human right. This right is matched by the correlative right to abstain from association. That recalls for the reader the cases which have arisen in the Irish courts on the question of the closed shop and the cases which have arisen in other jurisdictions on the same point. While it is easy to perceive the motive which originally lay behind the institution of the closed shop and the advantage it conferred on unions, even the advantages which employers frequently found in such arrangements, yet it is difficult to understand the shock and surprise which was created in Irish trade union circles by the decision in *The Educational Company of Ireland* v. *Fitzpatrick* which effectively declared the closed shop to be unconstitutional for being an infringement of the individual freedom guaranteed by the Constitution. More than a decade earlier, Article 20 of the Universal Declaration of Human Rights had already proclaimed that "no one may be compelled to belong to an association". When the European Convention on Human Rights was being drawn up those engaged in that task were very conscious of this but nevertheless, for reasons of political expediency rather than conviction, elected to omit from the Convention any express statement of that right. Yet in 1981 the European Court of Human Rights found itself in the same position and, in effect, arrived at the same conclusion as the Irish Supreme Court did in considering an almost identically worded provision of basic law in *Educational Company* v. *Fitzpatrick*.

It is well known that after the *Educational Company* decision trade unions made many representations to the Government of the day and subsequent Governments to find some way of avoiding the effects of that decision. However, there was no way out of it. The displeasure of the trade unions, however, did find its reflection in the Unfair Dismissals Act 1977, which lists as an unfair dismissal, a dismissal grounded upon union membership but not one based on non-membership. Yet the Bill for that law when first circulated also listed dismissal for refusal to join a trade union as unfair dismissal but that was caused to disappear during the legislative process. The unfortunate result is that an employee who is dismissed for that particular reason is left to find his remedy by bringing a constitutional action in the High Court with all the attendant expense which will ultimately fall upon the loser of the action. However, the reality is that notwithstanding the Constitution closed shops continue to exist in practice in many areas with the result that exclusion from a controlling union can often amount to what has been described as "a sentence of industrial death". That raises the point which has been twice referred to in Irish decisions, namely whether one has a right to join a trade union. The courts have held that there is no right guaranteed by the Constitution to join a trade union in the sense that a trade union may be compelled to accept as a member someone whom it does not want as distinct from the constitutional right to form a trade union or indeed to join one when that union is prepared to accept the applicant.

To many persons it may be regarded as somewhat anomalous that trade unions are regarded as private associations when, in the present era, trade union activities affect not only individual persons but also the public at large and often even the State. Recent British legislation, in what is essentially a closed-shop context, has sought to provide against unreasonable exclusion from a trade union. In the Irish context, however, it is very doubtful if the law could take any formal cognisance of the existence of the closed shop which is in effect contrary to the Constitution. Therefore if the law is to approach the problem at all it must do so on the basis of whether, in the circumstances of the particular case, exclusion from membership of a union effectively prevents a person from lawfully marketing his labour or skills. Where the circumstances warrant it the courts have ample power to make whatever orders they deem to be necessary to defend the constitutional rights of the injured citizen.

The courts in Ireland probably have had relatively greater experience in dealing with cases concerning industrial disputes than the courts in most countries. Many of the cases concerning trade disputes which arrive in the courts arise from picketing. In Ireland the sanctity conferred on the picket line, or what has been called the *piseóg* or magic of the picket, is one which may have its roots deep in the Irish character. It recalls the practice of distraining on the opponent's doorstep which proved so potent in the era of the Brehon laws. It is often suggested that the intervention by courts in trade disputes is unhelpful and that they are undertaking a role for which they are not suited. This is to overlook the fact that the courts do not of their own motion intervene in trade disputes, nor do they intervene for the purpose of settling a trade dispute. When the jurisdiction of the courts is invoked in respect of some matter arising out of, or in the course of, a trade dispute it is because some party to the dispute or some person affected by the dispute is seeking to protect his legal rights. It is unfortunate that on occasion parties to an industrial dispute appear not to countenance any judicial decision which they see as curbing their actions. This arises most frequently in connection with what might be called the "labour injunction". In Ireland this is frequently resorted to. Indeed it has not been always clear that every interim or interlocutory "labour" injunction granted has been justified. However, the courts are in danger of being brought into disrepute by the way in which some injunctions, properly granted, are subsequently used by the persons who obtained them. Frequently they are simply used as bargaining counters and the person who has obtained the injunction will often stand by and allow the order of the court to be openly flouted without any effort to refer the matter back to the court. While it may prove expedient in some cases for such persons not to refer the matter back to court, yet that is to act with great disrespect to the court. As the ultimate sanction for disobedience to a court injunction can be imprisonment, the court which grants an injunction should adopt the position of *dominus litis* from the moment it grants an injunction. Indeed there is a strong case for providing that any such injunction should be granted only upon an undertaking being given by the person obtaining it immediately to report to the court any breach of that injunction and to seek the appropriate sanction. Alternatively there should be built into the injunctions some self-discharging mechanism. Injunctions cannot be allowed to be flouted with impunity. To many persons engaged in industrial disputes the term "court" arouses feelings of hostility. It is somewhat ironic that the Labour Court should be so called when in fact it bears no resemblance to a court. It really functions as a body which, in the words of Professor Charles McCarthy, offers a third opinion on a dispute. The title of the body is misleading to persons who are not familiar with its limited functions and procedures.

The authors have written on the relationship of the social welfare system to industrial disputes. It is perhaps not always fully appreciated by the general public that the funds of the social welfare and social insurance systems are frequently used in a manner which benefits both the employers and the trade unions. If a group of workers in a business take industrial action in which the greater part of the other workers is not engaged, the employers are frequently only too happy to accede to the requests of these other workers who are thus left without work to lay them off officially so that they then become a charge on the social insurance fund. Indeed there have been instances where persons so laid off and in receipt of tax-free pay-related benefit have demanded compensation for going back to work to earn taxable wages. Another interesting aspect of this type of situation is where members of the management team are laid off in breach of their contracts of employment because of some industrial dispute to which they are not parties. They find themselves unwillingly quartered on the social insurance fund instead of being allowed to draw their salaries at least until the expiration of the period necessary to terminate their contracts.

The authors also draw attention to the effects of European Communities law on Irish work contracts. It is regrettable that the Brussels Private International Law Convention on Contractual Obligations and which incorporates special conflict rules relating to employment contracts is, like its sister Convention, the Judgments Convention, still awaiting ratification in Ireland.

The learned authors have presented a very careful and absorbing analysis of every aspect of Irish trade union law. Many areas of this rarely, if ever, come before the courts. In the result most judges and practitioners have not very much experience in these particular fields. These areas include the difficult problems which can arise in respect of collective agreements and in respect of the internal structures of trade unions and the relationship between the trustees of trade unions and the use of trade union property and funds.

Trade unions remain essential elements of a free society and as such have their rights and their corresponding obligations. As trade unionism and trade unions evolve, so also must the law which provides the protection of those rights and the enforcement of those obligations. The essential function of the law is to afford protection and to provide for the peaceful resolution of justiciable disputes.

Students of this book will find themselves greatly indebted to the authors for their erudite exposition of how the law now stands and for the great wealth of knowledge concerning trade unions which they have made available to lawyers and others concerned with Irish trade union law.

BRIAN WALSH
The Supreme Court
September 1985

PREFACE

Trade union law in Ireland has not been subject to the kind of "bewildering changes of pace and direction" that have occurred in Britain, and to a lesser extent, Northern Ireland, over the last two decades. Whilst what might be described as *individual employment law* has been transformed with the enactment of legislation regulating the individual employment relationship, no comparable changes have taken place in the area of *collective labour law*. This should not be taken to imply, however, that no changes are needed, or looked for. For many years there has been considerable dissatisfaction expressed from all quarters with the law governing Irish industrial relations. Demands for reform and rationalisation have been frequently and forcefully made and, at the time of writing, the Minister for Labour is co-ordinating discussions on reform of the law relating to industrial relations.

In order to appreciate fully the proposed reforms, it is necessary to comment briefly on the evolution of trade union law in this jurisdiction. The legislation which Ireland inherited from Britain was designed to remove the legal obstacles from workers' ability to organise and act collectively. In both respects it is possible to see, in Irish trade union law, a marked divergence from this common heritage. This divergence became particularly apparent in the 1940s with the enactment of two major pieces of legislation – the Trade Union Act 1941 and the Industrial Relations Act 1946 – which had no equivalent in Britain or Northern Ireland. The 1941 Act, as subsequently amended, is concerned primarily with the problem of multiplicity of unions, seeking to tackle it by discouraging the formation of new trade unions and encouraging the merger of existing ones. The 1946 Act, as the name implies, is concerned more generally with industrial relations and enshrines the principle of free collective bargaining, ensuring that the State's role in the collective bargaining system remains an auxiliary one, confined to assisting the parties to resolve their differences voluntarily through the provision of representative industrial relations machinery.

Finally, in this brief summary of the development of Irish trade union law, sight should not be lost of Article $40.6.1^0$ (iii) of the Constitution, which expressly guarantees "liberty for the exercise . . . subject to public order and morality . . . [of] the right of the citizens to form associations and unions". This guarantee transforms the nature of trade union law in this jurisdiction and ensures that it is no mere clone of British law.

By the late 1970s, dissatisfaction with this statutory framework had reached such a level that the Government established, in May 1978, a Commission of Inquiry into Industrial Relations. The Commission's terms of reference were to consider and report on industrial relations generally and in particular on:

1. the practices of employers and their organisations and of workers in their trade unions under the system of free collective bargaining;
2. the relevance of statute law to industrial relations; and
3. the operation of institutions, structures and procedures.

The Commission, as McCarthy and von Prondzynski have pointed out ("The Reform of Industrial Relations" (1982) 29 *Administration* 220) was the first to inquire into the area of industrial relations since the foundation of the State, and there were high hopes, not only for useful proposals, but also for a substantial increase in our knowledge of the Irish system of industrial relations. On both counts, unfortunately, these expectations were not realised. On the first count, the Commission was hamstrung by the withdrawal, in July 1979, of the I.C.T.U. representatives. In their absence, the remaining members were "reluctant to formulate specific proposals" in the area of reform of trade union structures, and, in the area of reform of the law on industrial conflict, the lack of any direct trade union involvement effectively deprived the Commission of any chance of searching out a consensus on which reform could be built. On the second count, a majority of the members considered that the Commission's immediate task "could best be served by utilising the evidence submitted . . . and the information that was readily available, rather than initiating our own research programme."

The Commission concluded, in its Report published in July 1981, that voluntary means alone were incapable of importing the required degree of order to the collective relations between unions and management, and that the many serious consequences of the failure of existing voluntary arrangements made it imperative that some alternative source of order be established (para. 651). A majority of the Commission felt that the law could make an effective contribution towards curbing the undesirable consequences (as they saw them) of Irish industrial relations. Accordingly, the Commission, as well as recommending considerable institutional changes (the abolition of the Labour Court and the Employment Appeals Tribunal and their replacement by a Labour Relations Board and a Labour Relations Court), made a number of specific recommendations concerning the law on industrial conflict, namely that workers would be required to comply with certain procedures, including a ballot, before taking industrial action and that certain limitations be placed on the type of issues over which industrial action could be taken. Sympathetic and secondary action should also be outlawed. As Kelly and Roche have observed ("Institutional Reform in Irish Industrial Relations" (1983) LXXII *Studies* 221), the underlying philosophy is one which "unambiguously seeks a central role for legal regulation", a philosophy which is totally incongruent with the Irish tradition of industrial relations and which represents "a fundamental departure from all that has gone before". The writers share Kelly and Roche's belief that the Commission was mistaken in its views on the likely merits of this new legal framework and we question whether the Commission's preoccupation with the regulation of disputes through a mandatory procedural sequence would have the desired effect of introducing greater order into industrial relations.

The status of the recommendations was of course affected by the absence of the I.C.T.U. representatives and by the very strong dissent expressed on the part of two of its independent members and, as McCarthy and von Prondzynski predicted, it was necessary to go through the whole process again as the Commission's recommendations did not provide an adequate basis for reform. In October 1983, the Department of Labour published a *Discussion Document on Industrial Relations Reform*. The purpose of the document was to set out for consideration by the F.U.E. and the I.C.T.U. the "routes of inquiry and the range of options" which were to be pursued. These included possible reform of the law governing collective bargaining, a review of the existing institutional arrangements, minimum wage fixing machinery, industrial relations practices and procedures including codes of practice, and the structure of trade union and employer organisations. The *Discussion Document* does not make the mistake of over-estimating the importance of law in industrial relations. Its theme is not that law has no place here but that legislation will not automatically lead to fewer strikes and an improved economic performance. In the Department's view any increase in the incidence of strikes indicated inadequacies in the industrial relations dispute-settling machinery rather than defects in the law. Following discussions between Department officials and representatives of the F.U.E. and the I.C.T.U., the Minister announced a number of proposals.

1. The form and content of all aspects of trade dispute law would be the subject of an immediate examination which would actively explore the feasibility of replacing the system of immunities from legal liabilities by a system which would give workers a positive right to strike.
2. A Labour Relations Commission, charged with statutory responsibility for the promotion of good industrial relations, would be established as an independent agency. The specific services and functions for which it would have responsibility were (i) a conciliation service; (ii) an advisory service; (iii) the equality officer service; (iv) the Rights Commissioner Service; (v) a research function; (vi) an industrial relations review and monitoring function; (vii) the preparation of codes of practice. The Labour Court would retain responsibility for the investigation of disputes, appeals from Rights Commissioners and Equality

Preface xiii

    Officers, and existing or proposed functions in respect of Registered Employment Agreements, Joint Industrial Councils and Joint Labour Committees. The Employment Appeals Tribunal would retain jurisdiction in cases involving redundancy, minimum notice, unfair dismissal and maternity protection.

3. The existing policy of discouraging the formation of new unions and facilitating the amalgamation of existing ones would be retained and improved by the introduction of amending legislation providing for the payment of grants for feasibility studies and exploratory research carried out in contemplation of a merger regardless of whether it finally took place. The Minister also indicated that the minimum membership level and financial deposit normally required for the granting of a negotiation licence would be reconsidered "with a view to establishing if increases are desirable". Overall it is clear that the Minister accepts that responsibility for rationalisation of the trade union structure rests with the trade unions themselves.

4. Amendments would be made to the minimum wage-fixing machinery. At present Joint Labour Committees which establish minimum rates of pay and conditions of employment for the trades or industries covered by the Committee comprise an equal number of employer and trade union representatives plus three independent members. The Minister proposed to have only one independent member; to allow the Committee to seek an assessor's report on the economic condition of the trade or industry; to allow for greater flexibility in amending orders regulating pay and conditions of employment; and to increase the penalties for breaches of such orders.

While welcoming this review of the law, the authors would hope that the Minister would not confine his reforms to the foregoing proposals, far-reaching as they may be. Our research indicates that a number of areas need to be examined, even if only, in certain instances, to eradicate technical defects in the legislation. The operation of political funds; the treatment of strikers who wish to claim social security; and the liability of union trustees are just some areas which are in need of reform. Hopefully this book may be of some assistance to those whose responsibility it is to decide such matters, as well as to all those involved in Irish industrial relations generally.

    The authors are indebted to many people for their comments, help, interest and encouragement. We are most grateful to Mr. Justice Walsh for agreeing to write a foreword at embarrassingly short notice. We would like particularly to thank Dr. Robert Clark, G.W. Hogan and Declan Madden for their invaluable suggestions on sections of the book; Roy Parker who did an immense amount of work preparing the table of cases and table of statutes; Geraldine Doyle, Bernadette

Bradley, Ann Coughlan, Ann Kelliher, Margot Aspel, Amanda McConnell who at various stages provided sterling secretarial service; Esther Semple and Tony Eckloff of the U.C.D. Law Library and Elizabeth Gleeson, the T.C.D. Law Librarian, for all their help; Maeve Kane of the Central Office for her assistance with unreported High Court decisions; various officials in the Department of Labour, the Department of Trade and Industry, the Labour Court and the Office of the Registrar of Friendly Societies for their information on specific queries; our students who endured earlier drafts of chapters disguised as lectures; all those at Harborne Hall for their kindness and hospitality; and not least Caitriona McKeever and Mary Bergin, both of whose tolerance fortunately knew no end. We would also like to take this opportunity to record our gratitude to Professor J.C. Wylie, without whose steady stream of blue envelopes this book would still be months away from publication and who was nearly tried beyond endurance over the course of the last three years. We would also like to record our intellectual indebtedness to all those whose works we have plundered, in particular Citrine, Kahn-Freund and Wedderburn.

We have endeavoured to state the law as it was on July 31, 1985, except we have been able to make the briefest of references to the decision of Barrington J. in *Aughey* v. *Ireland* which was handed down on August 29, 1985. Here the constitutionality of section 13 of the Garda Síochána Act 1924 (as inserted by section 1 of the Garda Síochána Act 1977) was called into question during proceedings concerning proposed changes in the system of promotion for the Gardaí. Section 13 authorises the establishment of one association for all ranks below the rank of surgeon or of a number of associations for one or more of those ranks. Pursuant to the powers contained in this section the Garda Representative Association and the Association of Garda Sergeants and Inspectors were established. The plaintiffs had been refused permission to form a new association for the purpose of representing members assigned to the Detective branch on the ground that section 13 did not authorise the establishment of more than one association for any particular rank. The plaintiffs submitted that section 13 violated their right of freedom of association guaranteed by Article 40.6.1° (iii) in that it compelled them, if they wished to belong to any association, to be members of either of the existing associations. The right to form associations and unions, however, is expressly stated to be subject to "public order". Since the Garda Síochána is "intimately concerned with the security of the State", it appeared to Barrington J. that the Oireachtas was justified in imposing limitations on the extent to which members of the Garda Síochána may organise and concluded: "Because of their close connection with the security of the State, gardaí may have to accept limitations on their right to form associations and unions which other citizens would not have to accept." We would also like to refer here to a group of E.A.T. decisions which, although delivered in August and October 1984, we have only recently been able to obtain. They all concern the dismissal of C.I.E. employees because of incidents occurring during a strike. In the main they support the proposition in the text (p. 209) that an employer is free to dismiss for grave misconduct during the course of a strike (see *Grogan* v. *C.I.E.* U.D. 28/1984; *McCarthy* v. *C.I.E.* U.D. 172/1984; *Moore* v. *C.I.E.* U.D. 355/1984) but they demonstrate that the misconduct must be grave. An isolated incident, such as breaking a car windscreen, might not justify dismissal (see *Tierney* v. *C.I.E.* U.D. 26/1984; *Dalton* v. *C.I.E.* 81/1984). These cases also illustrate that the employer even though there is a strike, is still under a duty to fully investigate the circumstances surrounding the alleged offence and to allow the employee an opportunity to defend the charge. This was emphasised by Judge Clark in *Kelly* v. *C.I.E.* Circuit Court, unreported, 11 February 1985.

Responsibility for the whole book is shared between us jointly and severally but the first named writer assumed primary reponsibility for chapters 6, 7, 8, 9, 10, 11 and 12 and the second named writer assumed primary responsibility for chapters 1, 2, 3, 4 and 5. Chapter 13 was truly collaborative.

Tony Kerr
Gerry Whyte
Harborne Hall
St. John Chrysostom's Day, 1985.

TABLE OF CONTENTS

	Page
Foreword	v
Preface	x
Table of Statutes	xviii
Table of Statutory Instruments	xxxi
Table of Constitutional Provisions	xxxiv
Table of European Community Legislation	xxxiv
Table of Labour Court Recommendations/Determinations/Orders	xxxv
Table of Social Welfare Tribunal Adjudications	xxxvi
Table of Decisions of the Registrar of Friendly Societies	xxxvii
Constitution of the Irish Congress of Trade Unions	xxxvii
Table of Cases	xxxviii
CHAPTER 1 Freedom of Association	1
CHAPTER 2 Trade Unions: The Legal Framework	38
CHAPTER 3 Amalgamation and Dissolution of Unions	70
CHAPTER 4 Property, Trustees and Union Funds	82
CHAPTER 5 Internal Trade Union Affairs	99
CHAPTER 6 Collective Bargaining	143
CHAPTER 7 Legal Support for Collective Bargaining	166
CHAPTER 8 Liability in Respect of Industrial Action	204
CHAPTER 9 Statutory Protection in Trade Disputes	249
CHAPTER 10 Picketing	282
CHAPTER 11 The Labour Injunction	316
CHAPTER 12 Disputes Resolution	337
CHAPTER 13 Strikers and Social Welfare	361
Index	377

TABLE OF STATUTES

(i) Statutes of the Parliament of Ireland
1775 Tumultuous Risings Act
    s.2 294

(ii) Statutes of the Parliament of the United Kingdom of Great Britain and Ireland
1824 Arbitration Act 337
1825 Combination Laws Repeal Act Amendment Act................ 214
1831 Truck Act 96, 97
    s.2 96
    s.3 96
1842 Dublin Police Act
    s.14(13)... 293
1859 Molestation of Workmen Act.. 214
1863 Telegraph Act
    s.45... 219
1871 Trade Union Act 38, 48, 63, 79, 83, 99, 137, 223
    s.3 .... 82, 129
    s.4 .... 81, 102, 123–133, 153
    s.4(1) 123, 128
    s.4(2) 123, 128
    s.4(3) 123, 124, 127, 129, 130
    s.4(4) 64, 123, 128
    s.5 .... 40, 62, 64
    s.6 .... 42, 43, 44
    s.7 .... 48, 64, 82, 83
    s.8 .... 48, 64, 82, 83, 84, 85
    s.9 .... 49, 64, 84, 85, 86–88, 89, 138, 252, 253, 256
    s.10... 49, 83, 86, 137
    s.11.. 49, 83, 85, 88, 137, 138
    s.12.. 47, 49, 83, 89, 111, 138
    s.13.. 45
    s.13(1)... 42, 136
    s.13(2)... 43
    s.13(3)... 43
    s.13(4)... 88
    s.13(5)... 43, 44, 45
    s.14.. 99, 108, 110, 118
    s.14(2).. 110
    s.15.. 50, 138
    s.16... 50, 86, 88, 110, 136, 138, 139
    s.18.. 50, 139
    s.23.. 40, 153
    Sched. 1, para. 4 .... 83, 134, 136
    Sched. 1, para 5 88

Criminal Law Amendment Act................................. 214, 215
1875 Conspiracy and Protection of Property Act
          214, 215–218, 219, 223, 249
    s.3 .... 215, 216, 257
    s.4 .... 29, 206, 209, 216, 217, 218
    s.5 .... 29, 206, 209, 216, 217, 218
    s.7 .... 215, 285, 286, 287, 289–293, 315
    s.16 .... 219, 285
    s.17 214
  Employers and Workmen Act 216
  Friendly Societies Act.. 138
1876 Trade Union Act Amendment Act............................ 63–64
    s.3 .... 48, 82, 83, 85
    s.4 .... 46, 49, 83, 84
    s.5 .... 49, 89
    s.6 42
    s.8 .... 43, 44, 45, 46, 47, 48, 79, 94
    s.9 .... 84, 109, 134, 136
    s.10 .... 49, 109, 110
    s.12 70
    s.14 .... 80, 109
    s.15 .... 80, 139
    s.16 .... 38, 89, 153
1877 Supreme Court of Judicature (Ireland) Act
    s.28(8)... 84, 316–317
1883 Provident Nominations and Small Intestacies Act
    s.3 .... 49, 110
    s.7 49
1887 Truck Amendment Act
    s.2 96
1890 Partnership Act
    s.1 40–41
1893 Trustee Act
    s.2 85
    s.3 85
    s.4 85
    s.5 85
    s.10 84
    s.24 .... 86, 137
    s.25 84
1894 Merchant Shipping Act 172, 219
    s.225 29
1896 Conciliation Act.. 337
  Truck Act
    s.1 96
1906 Trade Disputes Act 8–11, 19, 42, 44, 56, 87, 245, 247,

xx *Irish Trade Union Law*

	248, 249–281, 311, 314, 321, 326, 327, 343
s.1	137, 250, 257–258, 327
s.2	40, 61, 137, 250, 280, 283, 284, 285, 287, 289, 293, 297–310, 311, 320, 327
s.3	40, 61, 90, 137, 239, 250, 258–261, 280, 281
s.4	40, 43, 44, 61, 63, 66, 87, 88, 139, 250–257
s.4(1)	87, 252, 253, 254, 255, 256, 257
s.4(2)	49, 87, 88, 252, 253, 256, 257
s.5(3)	1, 265, 306, 310, 327

1908 Post Office Act
s.56	29
s.57	29

1913 Trade Union Act 7, 67, 72, 78, 79, 89–95, 99–100, 136
s.1	89, 153
s.1(1)	82, 83
s.2	153
s.2(1)	39, 43, 44, 45, 47, 49
s.2(2)	44, 45, 46
s.2(3)	41, 45, 46
s.2(4)	42, 45
s.2(5)	41, 45, 47
s.3	89
s.3(1)	46, 78, 89, 92, 93, 94, 95, 134
s.3(2)	47, 48, 94, 95, 110
s.3(3)	90–92
s.3(4)	93
s.3(5)	90
s.4	89, 108
s.4(1)	46, 92
s.4(2)	47, 92, 110
s.5	89
s.5(1)	93
s.5(2)	94
s.6	89, 93

1917 Trade Union Amalgamation Act 74
s.1	70

1919 Constabulary and Police (Ireland) Act
s.3	219

(iii) Statutes of the Parliament of the Irish Free State

1924 Garda Siochána Act
s.13(3)	219
s.14	29

Railways Act
s.55	16, 19, 160

1925 Shop Hours (Drapery Trades, Dublin and Districts) Act 65

1927 Electricity Supply Act

Table of Statutes xxi

    s.110 220
1933 Railways Act
    s.10 .... 12, 160
1935 Trade Union Act 1, 48, 82
1936 Conditions of Employment Act
    s.50 146
    Insurance Act
        s.6(c) 49
        s.6(e) 49
        s.25 54

(iv) Statutes of the Oireachtas

1939 Offences against the State Act
    s.9 29
    s.9(2) 218
    s.9(3) 218
    s.28(1) 284
    s.36 290
1941 Trade Union Act 3, 5, 27–29, 40, 50, 53, 79, 100, 103, 113, 143
    s.6 .... 29, 40, 51, 61
    s.6(1) 18, 41, 51, 60
    s.6(2) 139
    s.6(3) 51
    s.6(3)(a) 41
    s.6.(3)(f) 185
    s.6.(6) 51
    s.6(7) 51
    s.6(8) 60
    s.7 .... 53, 54
    s.7(1) 55
    s.7(1)(a) 53, 56, 57
    s.7(1)(b) 57, 83
    s.8 .... 53, 55
    s.9 58
    s.10 58
    s.11 .... 29, 40, 42, 43, 44, 49, 60, 61, 66, 87
                                                          88, 250, 251, 283, 301
    s.12 .... 59, 66, 100, 109, 139
    s.12(1)(a) 113
    s.12(1)(b) 113
    s.12(1)(c) 109, 110
    s.12(2) 111, 139
    s.12(4) 59, 110
    s.13 .... 59, 60, 100, 109, 139
    s.13(1) 5, 111
    s.13(1)(c) 113
    s.13(1)(d) 109, 110

xxii *Irish Trade Union Law*

    s.13(2) 47, 60, 111, 136
    s.13(4) 110
    s.14 .... 53, 55, 83
    s.15 .... 53, 55, 60
    s.15(1) 53, 55, 110
    s.15(2) 53, 66, 111, 139
    s.16 .... 54, 55
    s.17 .... 58, 100
    Sched. 55, 57
    Local Government Act 171

1942 Trade Union Act
    s.2 .... 51, 60, 62
    s.3 .... 51, 52
    s.4 59

1946 Industrial Relations Act 2, 19, 146, 151, 158, 160, 166,
                                                                                                                                    183, 311, 338, 343
    s.3 .... 62, 147
    s.10(8) 338
    s.10(10) 339
    s.10(11) 338
    s.10(12) 339
    s.17 .... 353, 354
    s.20(3) 353
    s.20(4) 353
    s.20(6) 346, 347
    s.21 345
    s.24 .... 213, 351, 352
    s.25 147
    s.27 147
    s.27(3)(a) 147
    s.27(3)(b) 148
    s.27(3)(c) 147
    s.27(3)(d) 149
    s.27(3)(e) 148
    s.27(4) 148
    s.27(5)(a) 148
    s.27(5)(b) 148
    s.28 150
    s.28(1) 150
    s.28(2)(a) 150
    s.28(2)(b) 150
    s.28(2)(c) 150
    s.29(1) 149, 150
    s.29(2) 150
    s.29(3) 150
    s.29(4)(a) 149

s.29(4)(b)	150
s.30	146
s.30(2)	151
s.30(3)	151
s.31(2)	150
s.32(2)	152
s.32(2)(b)(i)	151
s.32(2)(b)(ii)	151
s.32(4)	151
s.33	152
s.36	185
s.37(a)	185
s.37(b)	185
s.38	186
s.38(c)	186
s.38(d)	186
s.39(1)	186
s.39(2)	186
s.40	186
s.42	185, 188
s.43	188
s.43(1)(d)	191
s.44	185, 188
s.44(2)	192
s.45(2)	191
s.45(3)(b)	191
s.45(7)	192
s.46	192
s.47(1)	191
s.47(2)	192
s.49	193
s.49(2)	193
s.56	40, 51, 52, 185
s.57	192
s.57(2)	192
s.57(3)	192–193
s.64	357
s.65	40, 51, 52
s.65(1)	191
s.65(3)	191
s.67	342, 343, 344
s.67(1a)	341
s.67(1b)	341
s.68(2)	351
s.69	342
s.69(2)	342

s.70 .... 351, 354
s.71 .... 350, 351, 355
s.72 350
Sched. 2 186
para. 2(2) 187
para. 6(3) 187
para. 7 187
para. 9 187

1950 Transport Act
s.46 .... 12, 19, 160

1955 Factories Act
s.73 62
s.77 62

1956 Civil Service Commissioners Act 356
Civil Service Regulation Act 342, 356

1957 Married Women's Status Act
s.8 .... 124, 130

1958 Trustee (Authorised Investments) Act 85, 137
Civil Service Regulation (Amendment) Act 356

1959 Apprenticeship Act
s.7(1) 52

1961 Road Traffic Act
s.98 293
Courts (Supplemental Provisions) Act
s.8(2) 317
s.48(3) 317
Electricity (Temporary Provisions) Act 217

1963 Companies Act
s.17 201
s.47 201
s.125 201
s.195 201
s.370 201
Sched. 5 201

1965 Mines and Quarries Act
s.98 62
s.101(e) 62

1966 Electricity (Special Provisions) Act 217

1967 Income Tax Act
s.336 49
Redundancy Payments Act 143
s.6 205

1968 Road Traffic Act
s.44(2)(a) 47
s.60 293

1969 Industrial Relations Act

Table of Statutes xxv

    s.3 339
    s.4(1) 343
    s.4(2) 339
    s.4(5) 339
    s.6 341
    s.6(2) 341
    s.7 .... 153, 353
    s.8 344
    s.8(2) 344, 346
    s.10(1) 151
    s.10(1)(b) 151
    s.10(2) 151
    s.11 353
    s.13 356
    s.13(3)(a)(ii) 357
    s.13(4) 356
    s.13(5) 356
    s.13(6) 356
    s.13(8) 356
    s.13(9)(a) 357
    s.17 .... 171, 342
    s.17(3) 342
    s.18 .... 341, 344
    s.18(1)(b) 352
    s.19 .... 347, 348
    s.20(1) 22, 344, 347, 348
1971 Prohibition of Forcible Entry and Occupation Act   313–315, 336
    s.1(4) 314
    s.2 313
    s.3 .... 313, 314
    s.4 313
    s.6 314
    s.7 314
    s.9 314
    Trade Union Act 3, 53, 56
    s.2 .... 54, 56, 79
    s.2(1)(a)(iii) 83
    s.2.(1)(b) 54
    s.2(2) 54, 79
    s.2(3) 55
    s.3 56
    s.3(1) 56
    s.3(2) 56
    Sched. 55, 56
1973 Minimum Notice and Terms of Employment Act 37, 205

xxvi *Irish Trade Union Law*

s.9	159
Sched. 1, para. II	206
Regulation of Banks (Remuneration and Conditions of Employment) Act	143
1974 Anti-Discrimination (Pay) Act	340
s.1	153
s.5	143, 149
1975 Regulation of Banks (Remuneration and Conditions of Employment) Act	143
Trade Union Act	3, 53, 70, 74, 78
s.1(2)	71
s.2	72, 74, 100, 110
s.2(2)	47
s.2(4)	74
s.3	74, 100
s.3(1)	46, 73, 75
s.3(1)(d)	47
s.3(2)	73, 74
s.3(3)	47, 73
s.3(4)	73
s.4	74, 100, 110
s.5	100, 110, 149
s.6	74, 75, 78, 79, 100, 110
s.7	74, 76, 100, 110
s.8	74, 76, 100, 108, 110, 137
s.9	71, 72
s.10	46, 47, 75, 76, 110
s.10(1)	46
s.10(2)	75
s.10(3)	75
s.10(4)	75
s.10(5)	75
s.10(6)	75
s.10(8)	76
s.10(9)	47, 76
s.10(10)	46, 76
s.10(11)	76, 77
s.10(12)	46, 76
s.11	83
s.11(1)	77
s.11(2)	77
s.11(3)	77
s.11(4)	77
s.12	43, 78
s.14	70
s.15	77

Table of Statutes xxvii

    s.17 .... 61, 72, 100, 112, 136
        s.17(2) 57
        s.17(3) 57
        Sched. para 1 76
            para 2 76
            para 3 76
1976 Criminal Law (Jurisdiction) Act
    s.10 315
    Industrial Relations Act
        s.2 343
        s.5 187
        s.6 51
        s.6(1) 52
        s.7 193
        s.8 338
        s.8(3) 339
    Regulation of Banks (Remuneration and Conditions of
    Employment) Act 143
1977 Worker Participation (State Enterprises) Act 166, 195
        s.1 196
        s.6(1)(b) 196
        s.7(1) 197
        s.7(3) 197
        s.8(a) 197
        s.8(b) 197
        s.9(3) 196
        s.10 196
        s.10(2) 197
        s.10(4) 196
        s.11 196
        s.11(1) 198
        s.11(2) 198
        s.11(3) 198
        s.11(4) 198
        s.11(5) 198
        s.11(6) 19, 198
        s.11(7) 199
        s.12(1) 199
        s.12(3) 199
        s.12(4) 200
        s.13 200
        s.13(3)(e) 200
        s.13(5) 200
        s.13(6) 200
        s.16.... 198
        s.16(1) 200

s.17	200
s.17(3)	200
s.18(2)	200
s.22	199, 200
s.23(2)	196
Protection of Employment Act	61, 166, 167, 169–179, 180
s.1	20, 133, 172
s.2	61
s.6	169, 170
s.6(3)(a)	171
s.6(3)(c)	171
s.7(1)	171
s.7(2)	171
s.8	170
s.9	172
s.9(3)	172
s.10	174
s.10(2)	172
s.10(3)	172
s.11	175, 176
s.12	174, 176
s.13	175
s.14	176
s.14(1)	176
s.14(2)	176
s.15(1)	175
s.17(1)	178–179
s.17(2)	178
s.17(3)	179
s.18	179
s.18(4)	179
s.19	176
s.21(1)	179
s.22	176
Protection of Young Persons (Employment) Act	61–62
s.1	62
s.6	61
s.17	61
s.23	62
Unfair Dismissals Act	61, 140, 205, 210, 213
s.1	37, 61
s.2	34
s.3	34
s.4	34
s.5	100, 210
s.5(2)	210–213, 247

Table of Statutes xxix

s.6	213
s.6(1)	34
s.6(2)(a)	33, 34, 35, 36, 37, 166
s.6(7)	33
s.7(1)(i)	37
s.15	140

Employment Equality Act 136, 340
- s.5 ..... 102, 134
- s.9 ..... 149, 218
- s.20(c) 218

1978 Industrial and Provident Societies (Amendment) Act 28–29

1980 Safety in Industry Act
- s.35 ..... 181, 182
- s.35(1) 62
- s.35(3) 182
- s.35(5) 182
- s.36 182–183
- s.36(4)(a) 181, 182
- s.36(4)(g) 182
- s.36(6) 182
- s.36(7) 182
- s.37(2) 182

1981 Social Welfare (Consolidation) Act
- s.17 361
- s.35 363
- s.35(1) 360, 362, 365, 371
- s.35(2) 364
- s.35(6) 363
- s.142(3) 361, 363, 365, 372
- s.142(4) 364
- s.203 363
- s.203(1) 361, 362, 370
- s.203(2) 365
- s.203(3) 363, 364
- s.204 363
- s.213(1) 370
- s.232B 371
- s.301A 372
- s.301 A(1) 372
- s.301 A(2)(a) 372
- s.301 A (2)(c) 376
- s.301 B 372

Social Welfare (Amendment) Act
- s.17 364

1982 Trade Disputes (Amendment) Act 56, 61, 263, 275, 343
Social Welfare (No. 2) Act 362, 371

s.1 .... 372, 376
1983 Postal and Telecommunications Services Act
    s.34 .... 166, 195
    s.64 252
    s.84 .... 29, 219
1984 Social Welfare Act
    s.13 371
1985 Age of Majority Act
    s.2(3) 84, 109, 136
    Social Welfare Act
    s.4 371

(v) Northern Ireland legislative provisions
1927 Trade Disputes and Trade Unions Act (Northern Ireland) .. 89
    s.4(1) 93
    s.4(5) 92
1965 Trade Union (Amalgamations *etc.*) Act (Northern Ireland)
    s.5(4) 78
    Contract of Employment and Redundancy Payments Act
    s.21 144
1976 Fair Employment (Northern Ireland) Act
    s.21 102
    Industrial Relations (Northern Ireland) Order
    Art.2 .... 40, 52
    Art.3(3) 276
    Art.22(4) 35
    Art.23 210
    Art.26 144
    Art.57 144
    Part IV 167
    Industrial Relations (No. 2) (Northern Ireland) Order
    Art.8 144
    Art.37 166
    Art.38 166
    Art.50 .... 166, 203
    Art.51 203
    Art.52 203
    Art.53 203
    Art.54 203

TABLE OF STATUTORY INSTRUMENTS

1941 Emergency Powers (No. 83) Order
    (S.R. & O. No. 195 of 1941).................................... 143, 337
1942 Trade Union Act 1941 (Application for Negotiation
    Licence) Regulations (S.R. & O. No. 106 of 1942)............ 58
    Trade Union (Inspection of Register of Members)
    Regulations (S.R. & O. No. 156 of 1942) 59
1946 Emergency Powers (No. 83) Order 1941 (Revocation Order)
    (S.R. & O. No. 303 of 1946).. 143
1950 The Rules of the Circuit Court (S.I. No. 279 of 1950)
    0.6 r.10 63
1957 Trade Union Act 1941 (Exclusion from Section 6) Order
    (S.I. No. 221 of 1957)... 51
1960 Trade Union Act 1941 (Exclusion from Section 6) Order
    (S.I. No. 17 of 1960)... 51
    Trade Union Act 1941 (Exclusion from Section 6)
    (No. 2) Order (S.I. No. 233 of 1960)............................... 51
1962 The Rules of the Superior Courts (S.I. No. 72 of 1962)
    0.15 r.8.. 253
    0.15 r.9.. 62
    0.44 r.1.. 334
    0.44 r.3.. 334
    0.44 r.7.. 334
    0.47 r.2.. 312
    0.50 r.6.. 84
1963 Trade Union Act (Exclusion from Section 6) (No. 2) Order
    (S.I. No. 63 of 1963)... 51
1965 Trade Union Act 1941 (Exclusion from Section 6)
    (No. 2) Order (S.I. No. 55 of 1965) 51
    Trade Union Act 1941 (Exclusion from Section 6)
    (No. 3) Order (S.I. No. 56 of 1965) 51
1969 Trade Union Act 1941 (Exclusion from Section 6)
    (No. 1) Order (S.I. No. 227 of 1969)............................... 51
    Trade Union Act 1941 (Exclusion from Section 6)
    (No. 2) Order (S.I. No. 228 of 1969)............................... 51
    Trade Union Act 1941 (Exclusion from Section 6)
    (No. 3) Order (S.I. No. 229 of 1969)............................... 51
    Trade Union Act 1941 (Exclusion from Section 6)
    (No. 4) Order (S.I. No. 230 of 1969)............................... 51
    Trade Union Act 1941 (Exclusion from Section 6)
    (No. 5) Order (S.I. No. 231 of 1969)............................... 51
    Trade Union Act 1941 (Exclusion from Section 6)
    (No. 6) Order (S.I. No. 232 of 1969)............................... 51
1971 Trade Union Act 1941 (Exclusion from Section 6)
    (No. 1) Order (S.I. No. 296 of 1971)............................... 51

xxxii *Irish Trade Union Law*

1972 Trade Union Act 1971 (Notice of Intention to apply for
  Negotiation Licence) Regulations (S.I. No. 158 of 1972)..   55
  Offences Against the State (Scheduled Offences)
    (No.2) Order (S.I. No. 282 of 1972)   290
1973 Trade Union Act 1941 (Revolution of Negotiation Licence)
    (No. 1) Order (S.I. No. 54 of 1973) 58
  Trade Union Act 1941 (Revocation of Negotiation Licence)
    (No. 2) Order (S.I. No. 55 of 1973)   58
  Trade Union Act 1941 (Revocation of Negotiation Licence)
    (No. 3) Order (S.I. No. 56 of 1973)   58
  Trade Union Act 1941 (Revocation of Negotiation Licence)
    (No. 4) Order (S.I. No. 89 of 1973)   58
1976 Trade Union Amalgamations Regulations
    (S.I. No. 53 of 1976)   73
  European Communities (Non-Life Insurance) Regulations
    (S.I. No. 115 of 1976)   49
1977 Protection of Employment Act 1977 (Notification of
  Proposed Collective Redundancies) Regulations
    (S.I. No. 140 of 1977)   174–175
1978 Trade Union Act 1941 (Revocation of Negotiation Licence)
    (No. 1) Order (S.I. No. 258 of 1978)   58
1980 Trade Union Act 1941 (Revocation of Negotiation Licence)
    (No. 1) Order (S.I. No 295 of 1980)   58
  European Community (Safeguarding of Employees' Rights
  on Transfer of Undertakings) Regulations
    (S.I. No. 303 of 1980)   158–159
  European Community (Safeguarding of Employees' Rights
  on transfer of Ownership) Regulations
    (S.I. No. 306 of 1980) 166, 179
    Reg. 7   179–180
    Reg. 7(2)   180
1981 Trade Union Act 1941 (Revocation of Negotiation Licence)
    (No. 2) Order (S.I. No. 187 of 1981)   58
  Trade Union Act 1941 (Revocation of Negotiation Licence)
    (No. 1) Order (S.I. No. 192 of 1981)   58
  Trade Union Act 1941 (Revocation of Negotiation Licence)
    (No. 3) Order (S.I. No. 194 of 1981)   58
  Trade Union Act 1941 (Revocation of Negotiation Licence)
    (No. 5) Order (S.I. No. 313 of 1981)   58
  Trade Union Act 1941 (Revocation of Negotiation Licence)
    (No. 6) Order (S.I. No. 396 of 1981)   58
  Trade Union Act 1941 (Revocation of Negotiation Licence)
    (No. 7) Order (S.I. No. 397 of 1981)   58
1982 Trade Union Act 1941 (Revocation of Negotiation Licence)
    (No. 1) Order (S.I. No. 14 of 1981)   58
  Trade Union Act 1941 (Revocation of Negotiation Licence)

(No. 2) Order (S.I. No. 249 of 1982)... 58
Social Welfare (Social Welfare Tribunal) Regulations
  (S.I. No. 309 of 1982) 375
  Art. 4.. 375
  Art. 6(1) 375
  Art. 6(2) 375
  Art. 7.. 375
  Art. 12(1).. 376
  Art. 17.. 375
  Art. 19.. 376
1983 Trade Union Act 1975 (Section 17) (Commencement) Order
  (S.I. No. 177 of 1983) 57
  Trade Union (Fees) Regulations (S.I. No. 292 of 1983)... 42, 73
1984 Button Making Joint Labour Committee (Abolition) Order
  (S.I. No. 39 of 1984).. 186
  Messengers (Cork City) Joint Labour Committee
    (Abolition) Order (S.I. No. 40 of 1984)........................... 186
  Messengers (Limerick City) Joint Labour Committee
    (Abolition) Order (S.I. No. 41 of 1984)........................... 186
  Messengers (Waterford City) Joint Labour Committee
    (Abolition) Order (S.I. No. 42 of 1984)........................... 186
  European Communities (Life Assurance) Regulations
    (S.I. No. 57 of 1984)... 49
  Contract Cleaning (City and County of Dublin) Joint
    Labour Committee (Establishment) Order
    (S.I. No. 105 of 1984) 184
  Social Welfare (Family Income Supplement) Regulations
    (S.I. No. 278 of 1984)
    Art. 3(1)(a) 371
    Art. 3(2) 371
    Art. 20(1).. 361, 363, 364
  European Communities (Stock Exchange) Regulations
    (S.I. No. 282 of 1984)
    Reg. 13 201

TABLE OF CONSTITUTIONAL PROVISIONS

Constitution of the Irish Free State 1922 .... 8, 66
   Art. 73 .... 9, 42
Constitution of Ireland 1937 .... 3, 8, 87, 93, 111, 246, 255
   Art. 12.6.3° 91
   Art. 29.3 91
   Art. 34 47
   Art. 34.1 58
   Art. 34.3.1° 47–48
   Art. 34.4.3° 333
   Art. 37 .... 47, 48, 58
   Art. 40 .... 8, 31, 247, 248
   Art. 40.3 .... 5, 9, 246, 248
   Art. 40.6 .... 4, 9, 10, 12, 246
   Art. 40.6.1° 4, 28, 90
   Art. 40.6.1°(i) 9, 284
   Art. 40.6.1°(ii) 284
   Art. 40.6.1°(iii) .. 3, 4, 5, 7, 8, 11, 12, 15, 18, 23, 24, 26, 27, 28, 29
   Art. 40.6.2° 4, 27, 28
   Art. 50 .... 8, 256

TABLE OF EUROPEAN COMMUNITY LEGISLATION

Directives
73/238/EEC 49
75/129/EEC 167–169, 170, 171, 173, 177
   Art. 1 167
   Art. 2 167–168
   Art. 3 168
   Art. 4 168
77/187/EEC 179–180
78/660/EEC 201
79/267/EEC 49
Regulations
1612/68 .... 101, 112, 134
312/76 .... 112, 134

TABLE OF LABOUR COURT RECOMMENDATIONS/ DETERMINATIONS/ORDERS

Abbot (Ireland) Ltd. and Irish Transport and General
  Workers' Union, Recommendation no. 6720 96
Bimeda Chemicals Ltd. and Amalgamated Union of
  Engineering Workers (T.A.S.S.), Recommendation no. 9679   21
Brady (John) and Son Ltd. and Two Workers, Determination
  no. 2/1983 192
Caltex (Ireland) Ltd. and Irish Transport and General
  Workers' Union, Recommendation no. 500 20
Construction Industry Federation v. Barry Brothers, R.E.A.
  Order no. 2/1975 151
Cork Milling Co. Ltd. and Amalgamated Transport and
  General Workers' Union, Recommendation no. 358 20
Crane (Robert J.) and One Worker, Determination no. 1/1980   192
De Beer Industrial Diamond Division and Irish Transport
  and General Workers' Union, Recommendation no. 7508..... 96
Dehymeats Ltd. and Amalgamated Union of Engineering
  Workers, Recommendation no. 9142 22
Guinness (Arthur), Son and Co. Ltd. and Workers Union of
  Ireland, Recommendation no. 1853 21
Hospitals' Trust Ltd. and Workers Union of Ireland (1982) 1
  J.I.S.L.L. 84 (Recommendation no. 381) **20–21**
Krups Engineering Ltd. and Association of Scientific
  Technical and Managerial Staffs, Recommendation no. 9385   22
North-Western Health Board and North-Western Hospitals'
  Employees Association (1982) 1. *J.I.S.L.L.* 92
  (Recommendation no. 6021) **22–23**
O'Connor & Co. Ltd. and Irish Distributive and
  Administrative Trade Union, Recommendation no. 9851...... 96
Pantry Franchise (Ireland) Ltd, and Irish Transport and
  General Workers' Union (1982) 1 *J.I.S.L.L.* 95
  (Recommendation no. 5338) 21
Roadstone Ltd. and Association of Scientific Technical and
  Managerial Staffs (1982) 1 *J.I.S.L.L.* 105
  (Recommendation no. 6707) **21–22**
Royal Liver Friendly Society and Irish Liver Assurance
  Employees' Union (1983) 2 *J.I.S.L.L.* 118
  (Recommendation no. 912) 20
St. Vincent's Hospital and Local Government and Public
  Service Union, Recommendation no. 5545 96

TABLE OF SOCIAL WELFARE TRIBUNAL ADJUDICATIONS

Brennan v. Comer International Ltd. A1/1982 374
Collins v. European Printing Corp. Ltd. A10/1984 .... 373, 374
Comer v. Clery & Co. (1941) Ltd. A5/1983 372
Coveney v. Blackwater Ltd. A8/1984 373
Cox v. Hanley Meats Group A3/1985 374
D'Alton v. Longford Printing & Publishing Co. Ltd.
A1/1984 .... 373, 374
Donohue v. Whessoe (Ireland) Ltd. A2/1983 .... **373–374**
Dunphy v. Nacanco (Ireland) Ltd. A2/1985 373
Enright v. Trust House Forte (Ireland) Ltd. A2/1983 374
Galvin v. North-Western Cattle Breeding Society Ltd. A1/1985   372
Hannon v. Becton Dickinson & Co. Ltd. A3/1984 374
Harris v. I. S. Varian & Co. Ltd. A2/1984 .... 213, 373
Kelly v. Becton Dickinson & Co. Ltd. A8/1984 375
Loughnane v. Roscrea Meat Products Ltd. A4/1983 373
McGuigan v. Trust House forte (Ireland) Ltd. A9/1984 375
McNamara v. Nissan Datsun Ltd. A7/1984 .... **375**
O'Neill v. Alfa Cavan Rubber Manufacturing Co. Ltd. A3/1983 **374**
Saunders v. Cahir Meat Packers Ltd. A5/1984 373
Sheridan v. Heritage Knitwear Ltd. A6/1984 .... 364, 375

Note: The mode of citation adopted by the authors is based on the sequence in which the adjudications are issued in a particular year rather than the sequence in which the applications are received by the Tribunal.

TABLE OF DECISIONS OF THE REGISTRAR OF FRIENDLY SOCIETIES

Forster and National Amalgamated Union of Shop Assistants,
 Warehousemen and Clerks (1925) Report of the Registrar 92
McCafferty and Irish Transport and General Workers Union
 (1952) Report of the Registrar (Irl.) **94–95**
McCarthy and National Association of Theatrical and Kine
 Employees (1957) Report of the Registrar 91
Wilson and Amalgamated Engineering Union (1958) Report
 of the Registrar 93

CONSTITUTION OF THE IRISH CONGRESS OF TRADE UNIONS

cl. 2(b)(ii) 57
cl. 46 102
cl. 47(d) 6, 7, 17, 102–106

TABLE OF CASES

(Reference to a case in the text, as distinct from the footnotes, is indicated by **heavy type**)

Abbott v. Sullivan [1952] 1 KB 189; [1952] 1 T.L.R. 133; [1952] 1 All E.R. 226 101

Abbot and Whelan v. Irish Transport and General Workers Union and the Southern Health Board (1982) 1 *J.I.S.L.L.* 56 .... **5, 16–18, 103**

Acrow (Automation) Ltd. v. Rex Chainbelt Ltd. [1971] 1 W.L.R. 1676; [1971] 3 All E.R. 1175 .... **242, 244**

Acton and Jordan Ltd. v. Duff; High Court, unreported, 12 July 1982 .... **311**

Adderly v. Florida (1966) 385 U.S. 39 282

Ahern v. Molyneux (1965) Ir. Jur. Rep. 59 69

Aikens v. Wisconsin (1904) 195 U.S. 194 225

Aitken v. Association of Carpenters and Joiners of Scotland (1885) 12 R. (Ct. of Sess) 1206; 22 S.L.R. 796 .... 123, 127

Aksjeselskapet Jatul v. Waterford Ironfounders Ltd.; High Court, unreported, 8 November 1977 322

Albert and Le Compte v. Belgium (1983) 5 E.H.R.R. 533 14

Alfin v. Hewlett (1902) 18 T.L.R. 664 127

Allen v. Flood [1898] A.C. 1, 14 T.L.R. 125 **224–225, 226, 227, 232, 234, 242, 245, 249, 258**

Allen v. Thorn Electrical Industries Ltd. [1968] 1 Q.B. 487; [1967] 3 W.L.R. 858; [1967] 2 All E.R. 1137 161

Allied Amusements v. Reaney (1936) 3 W.W.R. 129 291

Allied Irish Banks Ltd. v. Lupton (1984) 3 *J.I.S.L.L.* 107 .... **159**

Allied Irish Banks Ltd. v. Tuite and Kirwan High Court unreported, 2 February 1981 .... **300–301**

Amalgamated Food Employees' Union, Local 590 v. Logan Valley Plaza Inc. (1968) 391 US 308 .... 304, 305

Amalgamated Society of Carpenters v. Braithwaithe [1922] 2 AC 440; 38 T.L.R. 879 .... **128**, 133

Amalgamated Society of Railway Servants v. Osborne [1910] A.C. 87; 26 T.L.R. 177 .... 64, 67, **89**

American Cyanamid Co. v. Ethicon Ltd. [1975] 1 All E.R. 504 .... 319, 322, 323, 324, 326

American Express Co. v. British Airways Board [1983] 1 W.L.R. 701; [1983] 1 All E.R. 557 .... **252**

Amos, In re; Carrier v. Price [1891] 3 Ch. 159; 7 T.L.R. 559 ... **82**

Annamunthodo v. Oilfield Workers' Trade Union [1961] A.C. 945; [1961] 3 W.L.R. 650; [1961] 3 All E.R. 621 117

Ardmore Studios Ltd. v. Lynch [1965] I.R. 1 .... **154**

Armour (Receiver of Barry Staines Ltd.) v. Association of

Table of Cases xxxix

Scientific, Technical and Managerial Staffs [1979]
I.R.L.R. 24 .... **177–178**
Artane Service Station v. O'Byrne; High Court, unreported
13 June 1984 284
Associated Newspapers Group Ltd. v. Flynn (1970) 10 K.I.R. 17 **274**
Associated Newspapers Group Ltd. v. Wade [1979] I.C.R. 664;
[1979] 1 W.L.R. 697 .... 244, **277**, 306
Associated Provincial Picture Houses Ltd. v. Wednesbury
Corporation [1948] 1 K.B. 223; [1947] 2 All E.R. 680 355
Association of Patternmakers and Allied Craftsmen v.
Kirvin Ltd. [1978] I.R.L.R. 318 .... **175**
Association of Scientific, Technical and Managerial Staffs v.
Parkin [1984] I.C.R. 127; [1983] I.R.L.R. 448 .... 89, 90, 92
Atkinson v. Newcastle and Gateshead Waterworks Co. (1877)
2 Ex. D. 441 220
Attorney General v. Cunningham [1932] I.R. 28 295
Attorney General v. Kissane (1893) 32 L.R. Ir. 220 313
Attorney General's Reference (No. 3 of 1983) [1985] Q.B. 242;
[1985] 2 W.L.R. 253 1 All E.R. 501 294
Aughey v. Ireland; High Court, unreported, 29 August 1985 29

Baker v. Ingall [1912] 3 K.B. 106; 105 L.T. 934 .... **132, 133**
Baldwin v. Lett; High Court, unreported, 1 February 1977 .... **154**
Ballymun Inns Ltd. v. Fagan; High Court, unreported,
11 January 1980 284
Banton v. Alcoa Minerals of Jamaica Ltd. (1977) 17 W.I.R. 275   17
Barrett v. Markham (1872) L.R. 7 C.P. 405; 27 L.T. 313 138
Barrett v. Tipperary (North Riding) County Council [1964]
I.R. 22 294
Barthorpe v. Exeter Diocesan Board of Finance [1979] I.C.R.
900; (1979) 123 S.J. 585 140
Barton v. Harten [1925] 2 I.R. 37 270
Beaudesert Shire Council v. Smith (1969) 120 C.L.R. 145 .... **221**
Beaverbrook Newspapers Ltd. v. Keys [1978] I.C.R. 582;
[1978] I.R.L.R. 34 .... **274**, 277, 306
Becton Dickinson & Co. Ltd. v. Lee [1973] I.R. 1 ..   13, 18, 19, 31,
32–33, 207–209, 212, 240, 241, 242, **246**, 258, 259, **271**, 308, **310**, 327
Beddow v. Beddow (1878) 9 Ch. D. 89 .... **317**
Beekman v. Masters (1907) 80 N.E. 817 233
Beetham v. Trinidad Cement Ltd. [1960] A.C. 132;
[1960] 2 W.L.R. 77; [1960] 1 All E.R. 274 19
Bents Brewery Co. Ltd. v. Hogan [1945] 2 All E.R. 570 276
Bermingham v. Murphy (1931) 65 I.L.T.R. 73 69
Best v. Butler [1932] 2 K.B. 108; 48 T.L.R. 481 138
Bettel v. Yim (1979) 88 D.L.R. (3d) 543 239
Bheolain (Ni) v. City of Dublin Vocational Education

Committee High Court, unreported, 28 January 1983............ 69
Birch v. National Union of Railwaymen [1950] Ch. 602;
[1950] 2 All E.R. 253 .... **95**, 134
Bird v. O'Neal [1960] A.C. 907; [1960] 3 W.L.R. 584; [1960]
3 All E.R. 254 .... 264, 265
Blackhall v. National Union of Foundry Workers (1928)
39 T.L.R. 431 .... 128, 130
Blake v. Attorney General [1982] I.R. 117; [1981] I.L.R.M. 34   255
Bligh v. Rathangan Drainage Board [1898] 2 I.R. 205;
32 I.L.T.R. 73 220
Bonsor v. Musicians' Union [1956] A.C. 101; [1955]
3 W.L.R. 788; [1955] 3 All E.R. 518 .... 62, 64, 100, 101,
128, **130**, 139
Boulting v. Association of Cinematograph, Television and Allied
Technicians [1963] 2 Q.B. 606; [1963] 2 W.L.R. 529;
[1963] 1 All E.R. 716 .... **100**, 101, 106, 253, 254
Bourne v. Colodense Ltd. [1985]I.C.R. 291; [1985] I.R.L.R. 339   108
Bowen v. Hall (1881) 6 Q.B.D. 333; 44 L.T. 75 .... **231**
Bowes and Partners Ltd. v. Press [1894] 1 Q.B. 202; 10 T.L.R. 55 **206**
Bowles (F.) and Sons Ltd. v. Lindley [1965] 1 Lloyd's Rep. 207   253
Booth v. Amalgamated Marine Workers' Union [1926]
Ch. 904; 42 T.L.R. 580 .... 70, 75
Boyd v. Sinnamen; Northern Ireland Court of Appeal,
unreported, 17 June 1974 .... **332**
Boyne v. British American Optical Co. U.D. 951/1982 211
Bradbury (J.) Ltd. v. Duffy (1984) 3 *J.I.S.L.L.* 86 .... **270**, 280
Braithwaite v. Electrical, Electronic and Telecommunication
Union- Plumbing Trades Union [1969] 2 All E.R. 859;
6 K.I.R. 169 117
Brand v. London County Council, *The Times*, October 28th 1967   162
Branigan v. Keady [1959] I.R. 283 .... 111, 115, **135**, **354**
Breen v. Amalgamated Engineering Union [1971] 2 Q.B. 175;
[1971] 2 W.L.R. 742; [1971] 1 All E.R. 1148 .... 101, 117, 135
Brendan Dunne Ltd. v. Fitzpatrick [1958] I.R. 29 .. **246**, 265, 266,
271, **282–283**, **299**, 309
Brennan v. Attorney General [1983] I.L.R.M. 449 .... **256**
Brennan v. Glennon; Supreme Court, unreported,
26 November 1975 .... 281, **321**, 331
Brentall v. Hetrick (1928) N.Z.L.R. 788 .... 57, 83, 113
Brimelow v. Casson [1924] 1 Ch. 302; 130 L.T. 725 .... **239**
British Actors' Equity Association v. Goring [1978] I.C.R.
791, H.L.; reversing in part [1977] I.C.R. 393, C.A. 107, 133
British Airports Authority v. Ashton [1983] I.C.R. 696;
[1983] 1 W.L.R. 1079; [1983] 3 All E.R. 6 303
British Broadcasting Corporation v. Hearn [1977] 1 W.L.R.
1004; [1977] I.C.R. 685 .... **261–262**, **272**, **332**

British Columbia Government Employees' Union and Attorney
  General for British Columbia [1983] 6 W.W.R. 640; 2 D.L.R.
  (4th) 705; 48 B.C.L.R. 5 295
British Homes Stores Ltd. v. Mitchell; High Court, unreported,
  18 April 1984 312
British and Irish Steampacket Co. v. Branigan [1958] I.R. 128 ... 263
British Leyland (U.K.) Ltd. v. McQuilken [1978]
  I.R.L.R. 245 ...... **164–165**
British Motor Trade Association v. Salvadori [1949] Ch. 556;
  [1949] 1 All E.R. 208 64
Brittain Smith Manufacturing Ltd. v. Fitzpatrick High Court,
  unreported, 13 March 1969 307
Brodie v. Bevan [1922] 1 Ch. 276; 38 T.L.R. 172 ...... 127, 130
Broome v. Director for Public Prosecutions [1974] A.C. 587;
  [1974] 2 W.L.R. 58; [1974] 1 All E.R. 314 ...... **298–299**, 310
Brophy v. Mapstone (1985) 56 A.L.R. 135 141
Brown v. Amalgamated Union of Engineering Workers
  (Engineering Section) [1976] I.C.R. 147; (1975) 119 S.J. 709   136
Bruce v. Donaldson (1918) 53 I.L.T.R. 24 63
Bryanston Finance Ltd. v. de Vries (No. 2) [1976] Ch. 63;
  [1976] 2 W.L.R. 41; [1976] 1 All E.R. 25 326
Buckley v. Rooney [1950] Ir. Jur. Rep. 5 ...... **8**
Burke v. Amalgamated Society of Dyers [1906] 2 K.B. 583 108
Burke v. Minister for Labour [1977] I.R. 354 ...... **187, 188–189**
Burke v. Smith (1888) 37 N.W. 838 226
Burn v. National Amalgamated Labourers Union of Great
  Britain and Ireland [1920] 2 Ch. 364; 123 L.T. 411 ...... **113–114**
Burroughs Machines Ltd. v. Timmoney [1977] I.R.L.R. 404   **163–164**
Burton Group Ltd. v. Smith [1977] I.R.L.R. 351 161
Bussy v. Amalgamated Society of Railway Servants (1908)
  24 T.L.R. 437 137
Butler v. M.B. (Ireland) Ltd. U.D. 1058/1982 210

Callaghan v. Loughlin U.D. 5221/1980 35
Calvin v. Carr [1980] A.C. 574; [1979] 2 W.L.R. 755;
  [1979] 2 All E.R. 440 119
Camden Exhibition and Display Ltd. v. Lynott [1966]
  1 Q.B. 555, [1965] 3 W.L.R. 763; [1965] 3 All E.R. 28   **164, 254,** 259
Camden Nominees Ltd. v. Forcey [1940] Ch. 352; 56 T.L.R. 445   235
Camellia Tanker Ltd. S.A. v. International Transport Workers'
  Federation [1976] I.C.R. 274; [1976] I.R.L.R. 183, 190 259
Campus Oil Ltd. v. Minister for Industry and Energy, (No. 1)
  [1983] I.L.R.M. 258 323
—— v. —— (No. 2) [1983] I.R. 88; [1984] I.L.R.M. 45   **323, 325, 326**
Canada Cement LaFarge Ltd. v. British Columbia Lightweight
  Aggregate Ltd. [1983] I.S.C.R. 452; [1983] 6 W.W.R. 685;

xxxxii *Irish Trade Union Law*

145 D.L.R. (3d) 385	**221**
Carey v. Joinwood Manufacturing Ltd. U.D. 382/1981	34
Carlin Music Corporation v. Collins [1979] F.S.R. 348	242
Carpendale v. Barry (1984) 3 *J.I.S.L.L.* 116	162
Carrington v. Therm-A-Stor Ltd. [1983] I.C.R. 208; [1983] 1 All E.R. 796	**36**
Carroll v. Irish Biscuits Ltd. (1982) 1 *J.I.S.L.L.* 63	161
Carty v. Dublin County Council; High Court, unreported 6th April 1984	329
Cattle Express Shipping Corporation of Liberia v. Cheasty; High Court, unreported, 19 April 1983	235, 317
Central Canada Potash Co. Ltd. v. Government of Saskatchewan (1978) 88 D.L.R. (3d) 609	**241**
Chamberlain's Wharf Ltd. v. Smith [1900] 2 Ch. 605; 16 T.L.R. 514	127
Chappell v. Times Newspapers Ltd. [1975] I.C.R. 145; [1975] 1 W.L.R. 482; [1975] 2 All E.R. 233	142
Charnock v. Court [1899] 2 Ch. 35; 80 L.T. 564	287, 292
Chant v. Aquaboats Ltd. [1978] I.C.R. 643; [1978] 3 All E.R. 102	35
Cheall v. Association of Professional Executive Clerical and Computer Staff [1983] 2 A.C. 180; [1983] 2 W.L.R. 679; [1983] I.C.R. 398; [1983] 1 All E.R. 1130, H.L.; reversing [1983] Q.B. 126; [1982] 3 W.L.R. 685; [1982] I.C.R. 543; [1982] 3 All E.R. 855, C.A.	7, 100, 102, **104–105**
City of Birmingham District Council v. Beyer [1977] I.R.L.R. 211	33
Clark and Ontario Securities Commission, In re [1966] 2 O.R. 277; 56 D.L.R. (2d) 585	119
Clarke v. Chadburn [1985] 1 W.L.R. 78; [1985] 1 All E.R. 211	108, **335**
Clarke v. Ferrie [1926] N.I. 1	113, 130
Clarke v. Heathfield [1985] I.C.R. 203	84
Clarks of Hove Ltd. v. Bakers' Union [1978] I.C.R. 1076; [1978] 1 W.L.R. 1207; [1979] 1 All E.R. 152	177
Cleary v. Coffey; High Court, unreported, 30 October 1979	**269,** 270, 307–308
Clegg Parkinson & Co. v. Early Gas Co. [1896] 1.Q.B. 592	223
Cleminson v. Post Office Employees Union [1980] I.R.L.R. 1	93
Coal Distributors Ltd. v. McDaid; High Court, unreported, 17 October 1980	326
Coates and Venables v. Modern Methods and Materials Ltd. [1983] Q.B. 192; [1982] 3 W.L.R. 764; [1982] I.C.R. 763; [1982] 3 All E.R. 946	**212–213**
Coleman v. Post Office Employees Union [1981] I.R.L.R. 427	92
Collier v. Hicks (1831) 2B. & Ad. 663	117
Collins v. Cork Vocational Education Committee; Supreme Court, unreported 8th March 1983	12, 69

Collins v. Locke (1879) 4 App. Cas. 674; 41 L.T. 292.............. **125**
Collymore v. Attorney General [1970] A.C. 538; [1970]
2 W.L.R. 233; [1969] 2 All E.R. 1207................................. **23**
Commission of the European Communities v. Italy [1982]
E.C.R. 2133.. **168**
Condon v. Minister for Labour; High Court, unreported
11 June 1980... 143
Connolly v. McConnell [1983] I.R. 172; (1983) 2 J.I.S.L.L. 101   26,
66, 111, **112**, 115, 129, 140
Conway v. Wade [1909] A.C. 509, 25 T.L.R. 779   265, **266**, **276**, 277
Cooper v. Millea [1938] I.R. 749; 72 I.L.T.R. 209.................... 240
Cope v. Crossingham [1909] 2 Ch. 148; 25 T.L.R. 593   81, **83**, 113, 127
Córas Iompar Éireann v. Darby; High Court, unreported
16 January 1980... 16, **262**, 322
Córas Iompar Éireann v. Hennessy; High Court, unreported
13 June 1983 306
Corboy v. McInerney and Sons Ltd. UD 279/1981................... 34
Corry v. National Union of Vintners, Grocers and Allied
Trades Assistants [1950] I.R. 315; 85 I.L.T.R. 190.............. **252**,
254, 317
Cory Lighterage Ltd. v. Transport and General Workers Union
[1973] I.C.R. 339; [1973] 1 W.L.R. 792; [1973] 2 All E.R. 558   **271**
Cotter v. Ahern; High Court, unreported, 25 February 1977....... 12
Cotter v. National Union of Seamen [1929] 3 Ch. 58;
45 T.L.R. 352... 64, 68, 122
Cowan v. Scargill [1984] I.C.R. 646; [1984] 3 W.L.R. 501;
[1984] 2 All E.R. 750 .... **85**
Cox v. Louisiana (1965) 379 U.S. 559 284
Cox v. National Union of Foundry Workers (1928)
44 T.L.R. 345.. 68, 108
Craddock v. Davidson (1929) S.R. Qd. 328............................. 135
Crazy Prices (Northern Ireland) Ltd. v. Hewitt [1980] N.I. 150;
[1980] I.R.L.R. 396 .... **267–268**, 276
Crofter Hand Woven Harris Tweed Co. v. Veitch [1942]
A.C. 345; [1942] 1 All E.R. 142..................... 23, **229**, 239, 242
Crosspan Developments Ltd. v. Bridgeman High Court,
unreported, 23 October 1979 307
Crowley v. Cleary [1968] I.R. 261 .... 8, **265**
Crowley v. Ireland [1980] I.R. 102 .... 10, **30**, 248
Cullen v. Elwin (1904) 90 L.T. 840; 20 T.L.R. 490.................... 108
Cummins v. British Leyland Cars Ltd. (1982 No. 4326P) *Irish
Times* July 19, 1984.. 158
Cunard SS Co. v. Stacey [1955] 2 Lloyd's Rep. 247......... **219–220**
Cunliffe v. Goodman [1905] 2 K.B. 237................................. **238**
Cunningham v. McGrath Bros. [1964] I.R. 209; 99 I.L.T.R. 183   **293**
Cunningham Bros. Ltd. v. Kelly High Court, unreported

xxxiv   *Irish Trade Union Law*

18 November 1974 270
Curle v. Lester (1893) 9. T.L.R. 480 .... 87, 253
Curran v. Treleaven [1891] 2 Q.B. 545 215

Daily Mirror Newspapers Ltd. v. Gardner [1968] 2 Q.B. 762;
    [1968] 2 W.L.R. 1239; [1968] 2 All E.R. 163 242
Dallimore v. Williams (1913) 29 T.L.R. 67 .... **266**
Dalton v. Irish Pharmaceutical Union U.D. 137/1984 140
Danchevsky v. Danchevsky [1975] Fam. 17; [1974]
    3 W.L.R. 709; [1974] 3 All E.R. 934 335
Daniels v. Daniels [1978] Ch. 406; [1978] 2 W.L.R. 73; [1978]
    2 All E.R. 89 68
Dansk Metalarbejderforbund and Specialarbejderforbund
    I. Denmark v. Nielsen, E.C.J., February 12, 1985 .... 170, 177
Darby v. Leonard (1973) 107 I.L.T.R. 82 .... 67, **300**, 317
Datsun Ltd. v. Mooney; High Court, unreported, 25 June 1979   307
Datsun Ltd. v. O'Loughlin; High Court, unreported,
    20 December 1983 305
Davidson v. Gilbert Ash Construction Ltd. U.D. 441/1981   34
Deerpark Ltd. v. Leonard; High Court, unreported, 10 June 1983   326
Denton v. Auckland City [1969] N.Z.L.R. 256 119
De Francesco v. Barnum (1890) 45 Ch. D. 430 141
De Verteuil v. Knaggs [1918] A.C. 557 119
Devlin v. Player Wills (Ireland) Ltd. U.D. 901/1978   18
Dickson v. Pharmaceutical Society of Great Britain [1967]
    1 Ch. 708; [1967] 2 W.L.R. 718; [1967] 2 All E.R. 558 (CA)
    [1970] A.C. 403; [1968] 2 All E.R. 686 101
Dillon v. Dunnes' Stores; Supreme Court, unreported,
    20 December 1968 .... **227**
Director of Public Prosecutions v. Smith [1961] A.C. 290;
    [1960] 3 All E.R. 161 238
Dixon and Shaw v. West Ella Developments Ltd. [1978] I.C.R.
    856; [1978] I.R.L.R. 151   35
Dodd v. Amalgamated Marine Workers' Union [1924]
    1 Ch. 116, 39 T.L.R. 379 109
Doe d. Rochester v. Bridges (1831) 1 B & Ad. 847 220
Dolphin Delivery Ltd. v. Retail etc. Union (1984)
    10 D.L.R. (4th) 198 .... 23, 24
Dooley v. Attorney General [1977] I.R. 205 313
Doran v. Lennon and O'Kelly [1945] I.R. 315 .... 264, **265**
Doyle v. Beirne; High Court, unreported, 22 August 1977 307
Doyle v. Griffin and Others [1937] I.R. 93   69
Doyle v. Trustees of Irish Glaziers' and Glass Workers' Trade
    Union (1926) 60 I.L.T.R. 78 .... **126**, 128
Drennan v. Beechey [1935] N.I. 74 .... 87, 253
Drew v. St. Edmundsbury Borough County Council [1980]

I.C.R. 513 [1980] I.R.L.R. 459 36
Dublin Colleges Academic Staff Association v. City of Dublin
   Vocational Education Committee (1982) 1 *J.I.S.L.L.* 73 17
Dublin Glass and Paint Co. Ltd. v. Collinge; High Court,
   unreported, 22 July 1977 311
Duffy v. Tara Mines Ltd. U.D. 50/1980 210
Duggan v. Galco Steel Ltd. U.D. 507/1980 .... **36–37**
Duke v. Littleboy (1880) 43 L.T. 216; 49 L.J. Ch. 802 127
Dudfield v. Ministry of Works, *The Times*, January 4, 1964 162
Dunne v. Marks; High Court, unreported, 30 May 1968 47, 70, 73, 74
Dunnes' Stores (Clonmel) Ltd. v. Butler; High Court,
   unreported 7 November 1972 311
Duport Steel Ltd. v. Sirs [1980] I.C.R. 161; [1980]
   1 W.L.R. 142; [1980] 1 All E.R. 529 .... **278**, 307, 332
Durham Miners' Association, In re; Watson v. Cann (1900)
   17 L.T.R. 39 127

E. v. E. [1982] I.L.R.M. 497 3
East Donegal Co-Operative Livestock Mart Ltd. v. Attorney
   General [1970] I.R. 317; 104 I.L.T.R. 81 .... 58, 255
Eastern Health Board and Social Services Board v. Deeds and
   Currie; Northern Ireland Court of Appeal, unreported,
   5 April 1984 .... 36, 37
Edinburgh Master Plumbers' Association v. Munro 1928
   S.C. 565 .... **132–133**
Educational Co. of Ireland Ltd. v. Fitzpatrick [1961]
   I.R. 323 .... **319–320, 322, 323, 324**, 327
Educational Company of Ireland Ltd. v. Fitzpatrick (No. 2)
   [1961] I.R. 345, 97 I.L.T.R. 16.... **8–11, 12, 13, 15**, 246, 247, 248
                                                          255, 282, **288**, 317
Edwards v. Halliwell [1950] 2 All E.R. 1064 .... 68, 122
Edwards v. Skyways Ltd. [1964] 1.W.L.R. 349; [1964]
   1 All E.R. 494 156
Edwards v. Society of Graphical and Allied Trades [1971]
   Ch. 354; [1970] 3 W.L.R. 713; [1970] 3 All E.R. 689.... 101, **118**
Egan v. Shop, Distributive and Allied Employees' Federation
   of Australia; New South Wales (1979) 143 C.L.R. 325 ..... 75, 79
Eglantine Inn v. Smith [1948] N.I. 29 .... 137, 251
E.I. & Co. Ltd. v. Kennedy [1969] I.R. 69 .... 17, 327, 331
Electrical and Engineering Staff Association v. Ashwell Scott
   Ltd. [1976] I.R.L.R. 319 .... 175, 176
Electricity Supply Board v. Gormley Supreme Court,
   unreported, 21 March 1985 .... **255–256**
Elliott v. Society of Graphical and Allied Trades [1983] I.R.L.R. 3 93
Ellis v. Wright [1976] I.R. 8 .... **279–280, 306–307**
Elston v. State Services Commission (No. 3) [1979]

1 N.Z.L.R. 218 271
Emerald Construction Co. v. Lowthian [1966] 1 W.L.R. 691;
  [1966] 1 All E.R. 1013 .... **233, 237,** 258
Employment Equality Agency v. Irish Transport and General
  Workers' Union EE14/1984.. 218
Enderby Town Football Club v. Football Association [1971]
  Ch. 591; [1971] 1 All E.R. 215.. 117, 346
Esplanade Pharmacy Ltd. v. Larkin [1957] I.R. 285;
  92 I.L.T.R. 149 .... 250, **266,** 269, **272, 276,** 283, 317
Esso Petroleum Co. (Ireland) Ltd. v. Fogarty [1965] I.R. 531   320, **324**
Esterman v. National and Local Government Officers'
  Association [1974] I.C.R. 625; 118 S.J. 596 .... 107, **120**
Evans v. Bartham [1937] A.C. 473 .... **332**
Evans (Joseph) and Co. v. Heathcote, [1918] 1 K.B. 418;
  [1918–19] All E.R. Rep. 279; 34 T.L.R. 247 127
Examite Ltd. v. Whitaker [1977] I.R.L.R. 312 .... **264**
Express Newspapers Ltd. v. MacShane [1980] A.C. 672;
  [1980] 2 W.L.R. 89; [1980] I.C.R. 42; [1980] 1 All E.R.
  65, H.L.; reversing [1979] I.C.R. 210; [1979] 1 W.L.R. 390;
  [1979] 2 All E.R. 360, C.A............................. **277–279,** 306, 307

Fairbairn Wright & Co. v. Levin and Co. Ltd. (1914) 34
  N.Z.L.R. 1.. 242
Faramus v. Film Artistes' Association [1964] A.C. 925;
  [1964] 2 W.L.R. 126; [1964] 1 All E.R. 25 ..... 100, 101, 107, 118
Farrer v. Close (1869) L.R. 4 Q.B. 602; 20 L.T. 802 38
Federation of Irish Rail and Road Workers v. Great Southern
  Railway Co. [1942] Ir. Jur. Rep. 33... **16**
Feeney and Shannon v. MacManus [1937] I.R. 23 81
Fellowes and Son v. Fisher [1976] Q.B. 122; [1975] 3
  W.L.R. 184; [1975] 2 All E.R. 829... 326
Fennely v. Assicurazioni Generali S.P.A. Supreme Court,
  unreported 16 April 1985; varying High Court, unreported,
  12 March 1985 141
Ferguson Ltd. v. O'Gorman [1937] I.R. 620 .... 264, **288–289,**
  300, 302
Ford Motor Co. Ltd v. Amalgamated Union of Engineering
  and Foundry Workers [1969] 2 Q.B. 303; [1969] 1 W.L.R.
  339; [1969] 2 All E.R. 481.. **155, 156, 157**
Forde v. Fottrell (1930) 64 I.L.T.R. 89 69
Forster v. National Amalgamated Union of Shop Assistants,
  Warehousemen and Clerks [1927] 1 Ch. 539; [1927] All
  E.R. Rep. 618.. 91
Foss v. Harbottle (1843) 2 Hare 461; 106 L.J. 611 .... **5, 50,**
  67–69, 121–122
Fowler v. Kibble [1922] 1 Ch. 487; [1922] All E.R. 626 286

Table of Cases xxxxvii

Fraser v. Mudge [1975] 1 W.L.R. 1132; [1975] 3 All E.R. 78 ... 117, 346

G. v. An Bord Uchtála [1980] I.R. 32 .... 26, **31–32**, 118, 247
Gaffney v. Stericord Ltd. U.D. 594/1981 35
Galland v. Mineral Underwriters Ltd. [1977–78] W.A.R. 116 .. 227
Galt v. Philp 1984 S.L.T. 28 .... **292–293**, 315
Gannon v. Duffy; High Court, unreported, 4 March 1983 .... 30, 248, 326
Garvey v. Ireland [1981] I.R. 75 105
Gascol Conversions Ltd. v. Mercer [1974] I.C.R. 420; [1974] I.R.L.R. 155 160
Geraghty (Stephen) and Co. Ltd. v. Whelan High Court, unreported, 19 September 1979 270
General Aviation Services (U.K.) Ltd. v. Transport and General Workers' Union [1976] I.R.L.R. 224 223
General and Municipal Workers' Union (Managerial, Administrative, Technical and Supervisory Association Section) v. British Uralite Ltd. [1979] I.R.L.R. 406 ...... 172, 175
General Union Society of Operative Carpenters and Joiners (Belfast Branch) v. O'Donnell and Todd (1877) 11 I.L.T.S.J. 282 .... **124**
Gibbons v. Associated British Ports, *The Times*, February 27, 1985 163
Giblan v. National Amalgamated Labourers Union of Great Britain & Ireland, [1903] 2 K.B. 600; 89 L.T. 368; 19 T.L.R. 708 .... 139, **223–224**
Gibson v. British Transport Docks Board [1982] I.R.L.R. 228   209
Gibson v. Lawson [1891] 2 Q.B. 545 .... **215**
Glover v. B.L.N. Ltd. (No. 2) [1973] I.R. 388 .... 105, 111, **135**
Goggin v. Fenney (1949) 83 I.L.T.R. 180 69
Gordon v. Dealgan Amusement Enterprise Ltd. U.D. 221/1981 .... **34–35**
Gordon et al and Nova Scotia Teacher's Union, Re (1984) 1 D.L.R. 4th 676 .... 63, 69
Goulding Chemicals Ltd. v. Bolger [1977] I.R. 211   40, 60, **61, 156,**
   161, 162, 250, 264, 269–270, 280, 301, 308–310, 317
Gouriet v. Union of Post Office Workers [1978] A.C. 435; [1977] 3 W.L.R. 306; [1977] 3 All E.R. 70 .... 219, **333–334**
Gozney v. Bristol Trade and Provident Society [1909] 1 K.B. 901; 25 T.L.R. 370 .... **125–126**, 133
Grad v. Finanzamt Traunstein [1970] E.C.R. 825; [1971] C.M.L.R. 1 169
Grassick v. T.P. O'Connor & Sons Ltd. U.D. 114/1979 35
Griffin v. Kelly's Strand Hotel High Court, unreported, 24 January 1980 322
Guinness and Mahon Ltd. v. Cunningham and Whelan High

Court, unreported, 22nd May 1984 .... 307, 329
Gunton v. Richmond-Upon-Thames London Borough Council
  [1981] Ch. 448; [1980] I.C.R. 755; [1980] 3 W.L.R. 714;
  [1980] 3 All E.R. 577 141

Hadmor Productions Ltd. v. Hamilton [1983] 1 A.C. 191;
  [1982] I.C.R. 114; [1982] 2 W.L.R. 322, H.L.; reversing [1981]
  I.C.R. 690; [1981] 3 W.L.R. 139; [1981] 2 All E.R. 724,
  CA **259–260**, 261, **331–332**
Hardie and Lane Ltd. v. Chiltern [1928] 1 K.B. 663; 43 T.L.R.
  709 .... 63, 137
Harrison v. Carswell (1975) 62 D.L.R. (3d) 68 .... **304–305**
Harrison v. Duke of Rutland [1893] 1 Q.B. 142; 9 T.L.R. 115 **288**
Haselhorst v. Finanzamt Düsseldorf-Altstadt [1970] E.C.R. 881 169
Hawkins v. Rogers [1951] I.R. 48; 85 I.L.T.R. 128 225
Hayes, Conyngham and Robinson Ltd. v. Kilbride [1963]
  I.R. 185 333
Health Computing Ltd. v. Meek [1981] I.C.R. 24; [1980]
  I.R.L.R. 437 .... 265, 276
Heath v. J.F. Longman (Meat Salesman) Ltd [1973] I.C.R. 407;
  [1973] 2 All E.R. 1228 210
Heaton's Transport (St. Helens) Ltd. v. Transport and General
  Workers' Union [1973] A.C. 15; [1972] I.C.R. 308;
  [1972] 3 W.L.R. 73; [1972] 3 All E.R. 101 ..... 108, 133, 136, 223
Hewlett v. Allen [1984] A.C. 383 .... **96–97**
Hickman v. Massey [1900] 1 Q.B. 752 .... **288**
Hill v. C.A. Parsons and Co. Ltd. [1972] Ch. 305; [1971]
  3 W.L.R. 995; [1971] 3 All E.R. 1345 141
Hodges v. Webb [1920] 2 Ch. 70; 36 T.L.R. 311 241
Hodgson v. National and Local Government Officers
  Association [1972] 1 W.L.R. 130; [1972] 1 All E.R. 15 62, 68, 69
Holland v. London Society of Compositors (1924) 40 T.L.R. 440 153
Hornby v. Close (1867) L.R. 2 Q.B. 153; 15 L.T. 563 38
Hounslow London Borough Council v. Twickenham Garden
  Developments Ltd. [1971] Ch. 233; [1970] 3 W.L.R. 538;
  [1970] 3 All E.R. 326 329
Housing (Private Rented Dwellings) Bill 1981, In re, [1983]
  I.R. 181; [1983] I.L.R.M. 246 255
Howden v. Yorkshire Miners' Association [1903] 1 K.B. 308 .. 122
Howman and Son v. Blyth [1983] I.C.R. 416 163
Hubbard v. Pitt [1976] Q.B. 142; [1975] I.C.R. 308; [1975] 3
  W.L.R. 201; [1975] 3 All E.R. 1 .... 286, **293**, 326
Huljich v. Hall. [1973] 2 N.Z.L.R. 279 240
Huntley v. Thornton [1957] 1 W.L.R. 321; [1957] 1 All E.R. 234 **268**
Hutchinson v. Aitchison (1970) 9 K.I.R. 69 263
Hynes v. Conlon [1939] Ir. Jur. Rep. 49 .... **7–8**

Inspector of Taxes' Association v. Minister for the Public
 Service; High Court, unreported, 24 March 1983....... 17, **155**, **359**
Intacta Investments Ltd. v. Power; Supreme Court, unreported,
 7 April 1974 331
International Brotherhood of Teamsters, Local 695 v.
 V. Vogt Inc. (1957) 354 U.S. 284 284
Irani v. Southampton and South-West Hampshire Health
 Authority [1985] I.C.R. 203 141
Irish Aviation Executive Staff Association v. Minister for
 Labour [1981] I.L.R.M. 350.................................... **56**
Irish Biscuits Ltd. v. Miley; High Court, unreported, 3 April 1972 310
Irish Dunlop Ltd. v. Power; High Court, unreported, 10 and
 23 September 1981 305
Irish National Teachers' Organisation v. St. Olcan's
 Maintained School Committee No. 1/79 F.T.C............... 175
Irish Shell Ltd. v. Burrell; High Court, unreported, 17 June 1981 322
Irish Shell Ltd. v. Elm Motors Ltd [1984] I.L.R.M. 595 .... **323,
 325, 326**, 329
Irish Transport and General Workers' Union v. Green and
 Transport and General Workers' Union [1936] I.R. 471   42, 43, 86
 250, 254
Island Records Ltd., ex parte [1978] Ch. 122; [1978] 3 All E.R.
 824 .... **220, 243**, 334

Jackson v. Barry Railway Co. [1893] 1 Ch. 238; 9 T.L.R. 90 .. 117
Jenkins and Government of Prince Edward Island, In re (1983)
 150 D.L.R. (3d) 43; 43 Nfld. & P.E.I.R. 114 119
Jervis St. Hospital v. Fagan; High Court, unreported,
 3 March 1980.. 263
Joel v. Cammell Laird (Ship Repairers) Ltd. [1969] I.T.R. 206 **162**
John v. Rees [1970] Ch. 345; [1969] 2 W.L.R. 1294; [1969]
 2 All E.R. 274............................... 63, **81, 105–106**, 113
John Paul & Co. Ltd. v. Martin; Supreme Court, unreported,
 21 June 1979 331
Johnstone v. Associated of Ironmoulders of Scotland 1911
 2 S.L.T. 478 89
Jordan v. Walter D. McKenna Ltd. U.D. 577/1982.................. **211**
Journeymen Tailors' case (1721) 8 Mod. Rep. 10...................... 38
Junior Books Ltd. v. Veitchi Co. Ltd. [1983] A.C. 520; [1982]
 3 W.L.R. 477; [1982] 3 All E.R. 201............................. **222, 223**

Kamara v. Director of Public Prosecutions see R. v. Kamara
Kantoher Co-Operative Agricultural and Dairy Society Ltd. v.
 Costello; High Court, unreported, 23 and 24 August 1984...... 263
Kavanagh v. Hiscock [1974] Q.B. 600; [1974] I.C.R. 282;
 [1974] 2 All E.R. 177 .... **295, 296**

l Irish Trade Union Law

Kayfoam Woolfson Ltd. v. Woods; High Court, unreported,
  4 June 1980 .... **310–311**
Kearney v. Lloyd (1890) 26 L.R. Ir. 268 227
Kearney v. Rose Hill House Hotel Ltd. U.D. 816/1982 34
Keeble v. Hickeringill (1705) 11 East 547n., 103 E.R. 1127 ...... **242**
Keenan Brothers Ltd. v. Córas Iompair Éireann [1963] 97
  I.L.T.R. 54 320
Kelly, Kane and McGee v. McWilliams U.D. 77, 78 and 79/1977 35
Kelly v. National Society of Operative Printers (1914)
  31 T.L.R. 32; 113 L.T. 1055 .... 127, 129
Kennedy v. Cowie [1891] 1 Q.B. 771; 7 T.L.R. 474 289
Kenny v. O'Reilly (1927) 61 I.L.T.R. 137 281
Kenny v. Vauxhall Motors Ltd (1985) 283 I.R.L.I.B. 154
Keys v. Boulter [1971] 1 Q.B. 300; [1971] 1 All E.R. 289;
  9 K.I.R. 127 86
——v.—— (No. 2) [1972] 1 W.L.R. 642; [1972] 2 All E.R. 303 **80**
Kiely v. Minister for Social Welfare [1977] I.R. 267 117
Kilkenny v. Irish Engineering and Foundry Workers' Union
  [1939] Ir. Jur. Rep. 52 .... 26, **111–112**, 115, 130
King v. University of Saskatchewan (1968) W.W.R. 745;
  6 D.L.R. (3d) 120 119
Kire Manufacturing Co. Ltd. v. O'Leary High Court,
  unreported, 29 April 1974 .... 240, **310**
Kirk v. Eustace U.D. 693/1982 .... 35, 37
Kirwan v. Harris; High Court, unreported, 29 November 1976 .. 104
Knight v. Whitmore (1885) 1 T.L.R. 550; 53 L.T.233 138

Lamb Brothers (Dublin) Ltd. v. Davidson; High Court,
  unreported, 4 December 1978 .... **264**
Land v. West Yorkshire Metropolitan County Council [1979]
  I.C.R. 452; [1979] I.R.L.R. 174 159
Landers v. The Attorney-General (1975) 109 I.L.T.R. 1 30
Larkin v. Belfast Harbour Commissioners [1908] 2 I.R. 214;
  42 I.L.T.R. 52 .... **292**, **298**, **303**, 311
Larkin v. Long [1915] A.C. 814; 31 T.L.R. 405 .... 250, 263, **265**
Larkins v. National Union of Mineworkers; High Court,
  unreported, 18 June 1985 84
Latham v. Singleton [1981] N.S.W.L.R. 843 238
Lawlor v. Union of Post Office Workers [1965] Ch. 712;
  [1965] 1 All E.R. 353 .... **121**
Leadmore Ice Cream Ltd. v. Cummins; High Court, unreported,
  9 July 1984 284
Leary v. National Union of Vehicle Builders [1971] Ch. 34;
  [1970] 3 W.L.R. 434; [1970] 2 All E.R. 713 ... 117, **119–120**, **142**
Lee v. Showmen's Guild of Great Britain [1952] 2 Q.B. 329;
  [1952] 1 All E.R. 1175 .... 101, 107, 119, **121**

Table of Cases li

Leigh v. National Union of Railwaymen [1970] Ch. 326; [1970]
 2 W.L.R. 60; [1969] 3 All E.R. 1249 .... 119, **134–135**
Lewis v. Heffer [1978] 1 W.L.R. 1061; [1978] 3 All E.R. 354 .. 326
Linaker v. Pilcher (1901) 17 T.L.R. 256; 84 L.T. 421 67, **86–87**, 253
Liptrott v. National Union of Mineworkers (Nottingham Area)
 [1985] I.R.L.R. 286 108
Lloyd Corporation Ltd. v. Tanner (1972) 407 U.S. 551 304
Loftus v. The Attorney-General [1979] I.R. 221 27
Longdon-Griffiths v. Smith [1951] 1 K.B. 295; [1950] 2 All E.R. 662 87
Lonhro Ltd. v. Shell Petroleum Ltd. (No. 2) [1982] A.C. 173;
 [1981] 3 W.L.R. 33; [1981] 2 All E.R. 456 .... **220, 221, 222,
 227, 228**
Love. v. Amalgamated Society of Lithographic Printers of Great
 Britain and Ireland 1912 S.C. 1078; (1912) 2 S.L.T. 50 **130, 131**
Lowdens v. Keaveney [1903] 2 I.R. 82; 36 I.L.T.R. 163 .... **294**
Lumley v. Gye (1853) 2 E & B 216; 118 E.R. 749 **231, 233, 234**, 235
Lupovich v. Shane [1944] 3 D.L.R. 193; 62 C.C.C. 341 285
Lynch v. Fitzgerald (No. 2) [1938] I.R. 382; 71 I.L.T.R. 212 ... 296
Lyons v. Wilkins [1899] 1 Ch. 255 ..... **286, 287, 288, 291, 297, 298**

M. v. An Bord Uchtála [1977] I.R. 287 .... **32**
McC. v. An Bord Uchtála [1982] I.L.R.M. 159 31
McCarthy v. Amalgamated Transport and General Workers'
 Union Northern Ireland; High Court, unreported, 14 January
 1976 .... 102, 107
McCarthy v. Association of Professional Executive Clerical and
 Computer Staff [1980] I.R.L.R. 335 .... 91, 92
Macauley v. Minister for Posts and Telegraphs [1966] I.R. 345 112, 255
McClelland v. Northern Ireland General Health Services Board
 [1957] N.I. 100; [1957] 1 W.L.R. 594; [1957] 2 All E.R. 129 141
McCobb v. Doyle [1938] I.R. 444 .... **280–281**
McConnell v. Eastern Health Board; High Court, unreported,
 1 June 1983 117
McCormac v. P.H. Ross Ltd. U.D. 206/199 36
McCormick v. Horsepower Ltd. [1981] I.C.R. 535; [1981]
 1 W.L.R. 993; [1981] 2 All E.R. 746 .... **212**
McCormick MacNaughton Ltd. v. Brangan High Court,
 unreported, 26 June and 18 July 1980 318
McCusker v. Smith [1918] 2 I.R. 432; 52 I.L.T.R. 29 .... **303–304**
McDona v. Croker and Power [1941] Ir. Jur. Rep 61 .... **126**
McDonagh v. Turmec Teo. U.D. 104/1982 .... **209**
McDonald v. Bord na gCon [1965] I.R. 217 255
McDonald v. Feely; Supreme Court, unreported, 23 July 1980 .. 332
McDougall v. Gardiner (1875) 1 Ch. D. 13 .... 67, 122
McElhinney v. Neil Sheridan and Sons (Creeslough) Ltd. U.D.
 626/1980 33

McElroy v. Mortished; High Court, unreported, 17 June 1949 .. 338, 346–347
McF. v. G. [1983] I.L.R.M. 32 31
McGourty v. Córas Iompair Éireann U.D. 215/1981 34
McGowan v. Murphy; Supreme Court, unreported, 10 April 1967 229
McGrane v. Louth County Council; High Court, unreported, 9 December 1983 63
McGrath and O'Rourke v. Trustees of Maynooth College; Supreme Court, unreported, 1 November 1979 117
McHenry Brothers v. Carey (1984) 3 *J.I.S.L.L.* 86 .... **270**
McHugh v. Kileen Paper Mills (1982) 1 *J.I.S.L.L.* 91 161
McInnes v. Onslow-Fane [1978] 1 W.L.R. 1520; [1978] 3 All E.R. 211 .... **106–107**
McKay v. Oliver (1967) 15 F.L.R. 39 141
McKernan v. Fraser (1931) 46 C.L.R. 343 .... **228, 230**
M'Kernan v. United Operative Masons' Association of Scotland (1874) 1 R. (Ct. of Sess.) 453; 11 S.L.R. 219 .... 64, 123
McLaren v. Miller (1880) 7 R. 867 127
MacLean v. Worker's Union [1929] 1 Ch. 602; 45 T.L.R. 256 . 118
McLelland v. National Union of Journalists [1975] I.C.R. 116 117
McLuskey v. Cole [1922] 1 Ch. 7; 127 L.T. 269 .... 69, **128**
McMahon v. Minister for Finance; High Court, unreported, 1962 .... **155, 359**
McManus v. Bowes [1938] 1 K.B. 98 233
McPherson v. Hilberg (1912) 14 W.A.R. 48 86
McQuade v. Scotbeef Ltd. [1975] I.R.L.R. 332 36
McQualie v. Heeney and O'Connor [1959] Ir. Jur. Rep. 32 63
Madden v. Rhodes [1906] 1 K.B. 534; 22 T.L.R 356 .... 87, 89, 138
Maher v. Attorney-General [1973] I.R. 140 47
Mark Fishing Ltd. v. United Fishermen and Allied Workers' Unions (1972) 24 D.L.R. (3d) 385 242
Marley Tile Co. Ltd. v. Shaw [1980] I.C.R. 72; [1985] I.R.L.R 25 .... 36, 37
Martell v. Victorian Miners' Association (1903) 29 V.L.R. 475 226, 241
Martin v. Scottish Transport and General Workers' Union [1952] 1 All E.R. 691; [1952] 1 T.L.R. 677 107
Maynard v. Osmond [1977] Q.B. 240; [1976] 3 W.L.R. 711; [1977] 1 All E.R. 64 117
Mayor of Bradford v. Pickles [1895] A.C. 587 .... **225**
Meade v. London Borough of Haringey [1979] 1 W.L.R. 637; [1979] 2 All E.R. 1016 .... **245**
Merchants Warehousing Co. Ltd. v. McGrath High Court, unreported, 22 April 1974 310
Mercury Communications Ltd. v. Scott-Garner [1984] Ch. 37; [1984] I.C.R. 74; [1983] 3 W.L.R. 914; [1984] 1 All E.R. 179 269
Merkur Island Shipping Corporation v. Laughton [1983]

2 A.C. 570; [1983] I.C.R. 178; [1983] 2 W.L.R. 45; [1983]
1 All E.R. 334; [1983] I.R.L.R. 218 .... **237**
Mersey Dock and Harbour Co. v. Verrinder [1982] I.R.L.R.
152 .... **287–288**
Meskill v. Córas Iompair Éireann [1973] I.R. 121.... **11–12, 13, 15**
Midland Cold Storage Ltd. v. Steer [1972] Ch. 630; [1972] 3 All
E.R. 941 .... **232**
Miller v. Amalgamated Engineering Union [1938] Ch. 669;
[1938] 2 All E.R. 517 .... **44, 45, 128**
Mineral Water Bottle Exchange and Protection Society v.
Booth (1887) 26 Ch. D. 465; 57 L.T. 573............................ **123**
Mintuck v. River Valley Band No. 63A [1977] 2 W.W.R. 369;
75 D.L.R (3d) 589... **63, 242**
Monaghan Urban District Council v. Alf-A-Bet Promotions Ltd.;
Supreme Court, unreported, 24 March 1980....................... **55**
Monk v. Warbey [1936] 1 K.B. 75... **220**
Moore v. Attorney General for Saorstát Éireann (No. 2) [1930]
I.R. 471 .... **63**
Moran v. Attorney General [1976] I.R. 400 .... **120**
Moran v. Workers' Union of Ireland [1943] I.R. 485 **114–115, 118, 130**
Morgan v. Fry [1968] 2 Q.B. 710; [1967] 3 W.L.R. 65; [1968]
3 All E.R. 452 .... **207, 242, 259, 261**
Morgan v. Park Developments [1983] I.L.R.M. 156................. **256**
Morris v. C.H. Bailey Ltd. [1969] 2 Lloyd's Rep. 215.............. **163**
Morris v. Redland Bricks Ltd. [1970] A.C. 652; [1969] 2 W.L.R.
1437; [1969] 2 All E.R. 576... **329**
Moss v. McLachlan [1985] I.R.L.R. 76 .... **296**
Mothercare Ltd. v. Robson Books Ltd [1979] F.S.R. 466........ **326**
Moynihan v. Greensmyth [1977] I.R. 55 .... **255**
Mullen v. Midland Meats Ltd. U.D. 424/1982......................... **35**
Mullett v. United French Polishers' London Society (1904) 20
T.L.R. 595; 91 L.T. 133 .... **123, 127**
Murphy v. Attorney-General [1982] I.R. 241 .... **32**
Murphy v. Stewart [1973] I.R. 97; 107 I.L.T.R. 117   **3, 5–6, 13, 17, 26,
30, 31, 101, 102, 108, 109, 113**
Murtagh Properties Ltd. v. Cleary [1972] I.R. 330.............. **8, 30**
Myerscough & Co. Ltd. v. Kenny; High Court, unreported,
18 April 1975 .... **269**

Nagle v. Feilden [1966] 2 Q.B. 633; [1966] 2 W.L.R. 1027;
[1966] 1 All E.R. 689 .... **101, 102**
National Association of Local Government Officers v. Bolton
Corporation [1943] A.C. 166 .... **265**
National Belgian Police Union v. Belgium (1975) 1 E.H.R.R. 578 **18**
National Coal Board v. Galley [1958] 1 W.L.R. 16; [1958]
1 All E.R. 91 .... **206**

National Engineering and Electrical Trade Union v. McConnell
(1983) 2 *J.I.S.L.L.* 97 .... 26, 115, 129
National Labour Relations Board v. Fruit and Vegetable
Packers Union, Local 760 (1964) 377 U.S. 58 309
National and Local Government Officers' Association v.
National Travel (Midlands) Ltd. [1978] I.C.R. 598............... 177
National Seamen's and Firemen's Union of Great Britain and
Ireland v. Reed [1926] Ch. 536; 42 T.L.R. 513 120
National Union of General and Municipal Workers v. Gillian
[1946] K.B. 81; [1945] 2 All E.R. 593 .... 64, 66, 250
National Union of Gold, Silver and Allied Trades v. Albury
Bros. Ltd. [1979] I.C.R. 84; [1978] I.R.L.R. 504, C.A.;
affirming [1978] I.C.R. 62, E.A.T. 161, **173–174**
National Union of Mineworkers (Kent Area) v. Gormley,
The Times, October 20, 1977... **108**
National Union of Public Employees v. General Cleaning
Contractors Ltd. [1976] I.R.L.R. 362.................................... 175
National Union of Railwaymen v. Sullivan [1947] I.R. 77; 81
I.L.T.R. 55 .... **3, 9, 10, 11, 27–28,** 103
National Union of Ships' Stewards, Cooks, Butchers and
Bakers, In re [1925] Ch. 20; 132 L.T. 628; 40 T.L.R. 871 42
National Union of Tailors and Garment Workers' v. Charles
Ingram and Co. Ltd. [1977] I.C.R. 530; [1978] 1 All E.R. 1271 **174**
National Union of Teachers v. Avon County Council [1978]
I.C.R. 626; [1978] I.R.L.R. 55... 176
Nelson v. National Union of Seamen (1978) 128 *N.L.J.* 24 134
Newbridge Industries Ltd. v. Bateson; High Court, unreported,
7 and 15 July 1975 .... 270, **309**
Newbridge Industries Ltd. v. Bateson; Supreme Court,
unreported, 31 July 1975... **330**
Nicolau v. Attorney-General [1966] I.R. 567; 102 I.L.T.R. 1 31
Niven v. Galleria Ltd. U.D. 409/1982.. 34
Nolan v. Fagan; High Court, unreported, 8 May 1985.................. 62
Nolan v. South Australian Laborers' Union [1910] S.A.L.R. 85 139,
223, 230
Norbrook Laboratories Ltd. v. King [1984] I.R.L.R. 200 268, 311
Norey v. Keep [1909] 1 Ch. 561; 25 T.L.R. 289 109
Norris v. Attorney-General; Supreme Court, unreported,
22nd April 1982 3
North London Railway v. Great Northern Railway (1883) 11
Q.B.D. 30.. 317
N.W.L. Ltd. v. Nelson [1979] I.C.R. 755; [1979] 2 Lloyd's Rep. 317 **328**
N.W.L. Ltd v. Woods [1979] I.C.R. 867; [1979] 1 W.L.R. 1294;
[1979] 3 All E.R. 614 .... 265, **267, 269,** 317, **327–328,** 332

O'Brien v. Bord na Móna [1983] I.R. 2551 [1983] I.L.R.M. 314 106

Table of Cases lv

O'Brien v. Keogh [1972] I.R. 144 255
O'Bryan v. National Amalgamated Society of Operative
  House Decorators (1900) 1 N.I.J.R. 160 .... **124**
O'Byrne v. Eastern Health Board; High Court, unreported,
  14 May 1980 245
O'Callaghan v. The Commissioners of Public Works in
  Ireland [1985] I.L.R.M. 364 9
O'Connor v. Martin [1949] Ir.Jur. Rep. 9 280
O'Connor v. Waldron [1935] A.C. 76 355
O'Dea v. O'Connor (1937) 71 I.L.T.R. 169 69
O'Donoghue v. Veterinary Council [1975] I.R. 398 116
O'Donovan v. Goggin (1892) 30 L.R.Ir. 579 84
O Laighleis, In re [1960] I.R. 93; 95 I.L.T.R. 92 3
O Monocháin v. An Taoiseach; Supreme Court, unreported,
  16 July 1982 255
O'Neill v. Transport and General Workers' Union
  [1934] I.R. 633 .... 68, 108, **113–114**, 130, 140, 251
Orchard v. Tunney [1957] 8 D.L.R. [2d] 273 251
O'Reilly v. Antigen Ltd. U.D. 433/1983 34
O'Rourke v. Talbot [Ireland] Ltd. [1984] I.L.R.M. 587 **156–158, 159**
Osborne v. Amalgamated Society of Railway Servants [1911]
  1 Ch. 540 .... 81, 127, **129**, 133

Pantry Franchise (Ireland) Ltd. v. Castlemahon Frozen
  Foods Ltd.; High Court, unreported, 27 March 1977 313
Pantry Franchise (Ireland) Ltd. v. Macken; High Court,
  unreported, 5 April 1979 331
Parke v. Daily News Ltd. [1962] Ch. 927; [1962] 3 W.L.R.
  566; [1962] 2 All E.R. 929 193
Parker v. Camden London Borough Council [1985]
  3 W.L.R. 47; [1985] 2 All E.R. 141 329
Parker v. South Helton Coal Co. Ltd. (1907) 97 L.T. 98 206
Parkin v. Association of Scientific, Technical and Managerial
  Staffs [1980] I.C.R. 662; [1980] I.R.L.R. 188 90
Parr v. Lancashire and Cheshire Miners' Federation [1913]
  1 Ch. 366; 29 T.L.R. 235 .... 44, 62, 251
Partington v. National and Local Government Officers'
  Association [1981] I.R.L.R. 537; 1981 S.L.T. 184 .... **120**, 164
Pattison v. Institute for Industrial Research and Standards;
  High Court, unreported, 31 May 1979 .... **161**
Payne v. Electrical Trades Union, *The Times*, April 14, 1960... 117
Pender v. Lushington (1877) 6 Ch.D. 70 68
Penney's Ltd. v. Kerrigan; High Court, unreported,
  7 February 1977 .... 284, **300**
People (Attorney General) v. Conmey [1975] I.R. 341 255
People (D.P.P.) v. Douglas and Hayes [1985] I.L.R.M. 25 238

Pete's Towing Services Ltd. v. Northern Industrial Union
 of Workers [1970] N.Z.L.R. 32 238
Pett v. Greyhound Racing Association (No. 1) [1969] 1 QB
 125 [1968] 2 All E.R. 545 .... 117, 346
Pett v. Greyhound Racing Association (No. 2) [1969] 1 Q.B.
 125; [1968] 2 W.L.R. 1471; [1968] 2 All E.R. 545 117
Piddington v. Bates [1961] 1 W.L.R. 162; [1960] 3 All E.R. 660 **295**
Pillai v. Singapore City Council [1968] 1 W.L.R. 1278 119
Pitman v. Typographical Association, *The Times*,
 September 22, 1949 153
P.M.P.A. Insurance Co. Ltd. v. Walsh; High Court,
 unreported, 4 August 1977 306
P.M.P.S. Ltd. and Moore v. Attorney-General [1983] I.R. 339 **28–29**
Porter v. National Union of Journalists [1979] I.R.L.R. 404.... **121**
Posluns v. Toronto Stock Exchange (1966) 53 D.L.R. [2d]
 193; affirming (1964) 46 D.L.R. [2d] 210 238
Post Office v. Union of Post Office Workers [1974] I.C.R.
 378; [1974] 1 W.L.R. 89; [1974] 1 All E.R. 229 36
Post Office Workers' Union v. Minister for Labour [1981]
 I.L.R.M. 355 .... **56**
Power v. National Corrugated Products U.D. 336/1980 .... **211**
Presho v. Department of Health and Social Services [1984]
 A.C. 310; [1984] I.C.R. 463; [1984] 1 All E.R. 97, H.L.;
 reversing [1983] I.C.R. 595; [1983] I.R.L.R. 295, C.A. . **368–369**
Printers' and Transferrers' Amalgamated Trades Protection
 Society, In re [1899] 2 Ch. 184; T.L.R. 394 .... 81, 129
Prudential Assurance Co. Ltd. v. Lorenz (1971) 11 K.I.R. 78 **245**, 259
Public Service Alliance of Canada v. The Queen in Right of
 Canada (1984) 11 D.L.R. (4th) 337 .... **23–24**
Publico Ministerio v. Tulli Ratti [1979] E.C.R. 1629; [1980]
 1 C.M.L.R. 96 169
Publishers' Book Delivery Service v. Filkins [1979] I.R.L.R.
 356 .... 277, 306
Punton v. Ministry of Pensions and National Insurance
 (no. 2) [1964] 1 W.L.R. 226; [1964] 1 All E.R. 448 368
Pye (Ireland) Ltd. v. Tuamley; Supreme Court, unreported,
 23 March 1969 331

Queen (The) in Right of Canada v. Saskatchewan Wheat Pool
 [1983] 1 S.C.R. 205; 143 D.L.R. (3d) 9 .... 220, 222
Quigley v. Beirne [1955] I.R. 62 .... 264, **269**, 317
Quinn v. Leathem [1901] A.C. 495; 17 T.L.R. 749
 223, 225, **226**, 227, 231, 232

R. v. R. and the Attorney-General; High Court, unreported,
 16 February 1984 48

Table of Cases   lvii

R. v. Brent London Borough Council, *ex parte* Gunning,
   The Times, April 30 1985 119
R. v. British Broadcasting Corporation, *ex parte* Lavelle [1983]
   I.C.R. 99 [1983] 1 W.L.R. 23; [1983] 1 All E.R. 241 141
R. v. Bunn (1872) 12 Cox C.C. 316.. **214–215**
R. v. Central Arbitration Committt, *ex parte* B.T.P. Tioxide Ltd.
   [1981] I.C.R. 843; [1982] I.R.L.R. 60 174
R. v. Cole (1891) 113 C.C.C. Sess.Cas. 622................................. 219
R. v. Druitt, Lawrence and Adamson (1867) 10 Cox C.C 592;
   16 L.T. 855.. 285
R. v. Duffield (1851) 12 Cox C.C. 316 .... **214**
R. v. Eccles (1873) 1 Leach 274; 99 E.R. 684 38
R. v. Hibbert (1875) 13 Cox C.C. 82 285
R. v. Jones [1974] I.C.R. 310; [1974] I.R.L.R. 177 .... **216**
R. v. Kamara [1974] A.C. 104; [1973] 2 All E.R. 1242 .... **216**
R. v. Louth Justices [1900] 2. I.R. 714; 34 I.L.T.R. 131............. 96
R. v. Lynch [1898] 1 Q.B. 61... 289
R. v. McNaughten (1881) 14 Cox C.C. 576 294
R. v. Moloney [1985] 1 All E.R. 1025 238
R. v. Post Office ex.p. Association of Scientific, Technical
   and Managerial Staffs (Telephone Contracts Officers'
   Section) [1981] I.C.R. 76; [1981] 1 All E.R. 139................... **19**
R. v. Registrar of Friendly Societies (1872) L.R. 7 Q.B. 741..... **43**
R. v. Selsby (1847) 5 Cox C.C. 495 n 285
R. v. Shepherd (1868) 11 Cox C.C. 325....................................... 285
R. v. Stainer (1870) L.R. 1 C.C.R. 230 11 Cox 483; 21 L.T. 758   38
R. v. Wall (1890) 113 C.C.C. Sess. Cas. 880.............................. 219
R. v. Wall (1907) 21 Cox C.C. 401 .... **292**
R. and Attorney-General of the Commonwealth v.
   Associated Northern Collieries (1911) 14 C.L.R. 387 230
R [Irish Union of Distributive Workers and Clerks] v.
   Rathmines Urban District Council [1928] I.R. 260 ..... **64–66**, 67
R (Martin) v. O'Mahony [1910] 2 I.R. 695................................. 47
R (Webster) v. Recorder of Londonderry (1901) 2 N.I.J.R. 26   **124**
Rachich v. Mastrovich (1937) 273 N.W. 660 226
Radford v. National Society of Operative Printers, Graphical
   and Media Personnel [1972] I.C.R. 484 .... 108, 118
Rae v. Plate Glass Merchants' Association 1919 S.C. 426;
   56 S.L.R. 315 .... **128**
Rainsford v. McMahon Confectionaries Ltd. U.D. 178/1980 ...   36
Raymond v. Doherty (1965) 49 D.L.R. (2d) 99; [1965]
   1 O.R. 593.. 83, 113
Read v. Friendly Society of Operative Stonemasons
   of England, Ireland and Wales [1902] 2 K.B. 732;
   87 L.T. 493; 19 T.L.R. 20 239
Reeves v. Transport and General Workers' Union [1980]

I.C.R. 728; [1980] I.R.L.R. 307 .... 93, 94
Reg Armstrong Motors v. Córas Iompair Éireann; High
   Court, unreported, 2 December 1975 .... 213, **235–236**, 331
Rex Pet Foods Ltd. v. Lamb Brothers (Dublin) Ltd.;
   High Court, unreported, 26 August 1982 323
Richards v. National Union of Mineworkers [1981] I.R.L.R. 247   90
Rigby v. Connol (1880) 14 Ch.D. 482; 42 L.T. 139..   121, 123, 127
Riordan v. Butler [1940] I.R. 347; 74 I.L.T.R. 152 .... **240**
Roadstone Ltd. v. Bailie; High Court, unreported,
   10 November 1982 313
Rochford v. Storey; High Court, unreported, 4 November
   1982 69
Rodgers v. Irish Transport and General Workers' Union;
   High Court, unreported, 15 March 1978 .... 6, **24–26**, 30,
                                                                                                68, 101, 112
Roebuck v. National Union of Mineworkers
   (Yorkshire Area) [1977] I.C.R. 573 120
Roebuck v. National Union of Mineworkers
   [Yorkshire Area]; (no. 2) [1978] I.C.R. 676 .... 16, 117
Rogers v. Moore [1931] I.R. 23; 65 I.L.T.R. 49 .... 67, 69
Rookes v. Barnard [1964] A.C. 1129; [1964] 2 W.L.R. 269;
   [1964] All E.R. 367, H.L.; reversing [1963] 1 Q.B. 623;
   [1962] 3 W.L.R. 260; [1962] 2 All E.R. 579, C.A.: restoring
   [1961] 3 W.L.R. 438; [1961] 2 All E.R. 825
                                            164, **240**, 247, 243, 244, 257, 258, **259**
Rooney v. Trustees of Textiles Operatives Society of Ireland
   (1913) 47 I.L.T.R. 303 .... **124, 126, 130**
Ross and Co. Ltd. v. Swan [1981] I.L.R.M. 416   **314–315, 335–336**
Rothwell v. Association of Professional, Executive, Clerical
   and Computer Staff [1976] I.C.R. 211;
   [1975] I.R.L.R. 375 .... 75, 103, **104**
Roundabout Ltd. v. Beirne [1959] I.R. 423 .... **264, 266, 305–306**
Royal Aquarium and Summer and Winter Garden Society Ltd.
   v. Parkinson [1892] 1 Q.B. 431; 66 L.T. 513; 8 T.L.R. 352 ..   355
Royal London Mutual Insurance Society Ltd. v. Williamson
   (1921) 37 T.L.R. 742 259
Russell v. Amalgamated Society of Carpenters and Joiners
   [1912] A.C. 421; [1911–13] All E.R. 550; 28 T.L.R. 276 126
Russell v. Duke of Norfolk [1949] 1 All E.R. 109; T.L.R. 225   101
Ryan v. Attorney-General [1965] I.R. 294 .... 247, 257
Ryan v. Cooke and Quinn [1938] I.R. 512 .... **265, 273, 309**

S. v. Eastern Health Board; High Court, unreported,
   28 February 1979 31
S.A.C.E. v. Ministry for Finance of the Italian Republic [1970]
   E.C.R. 1212; [1971] C.M.L.R. 123 .... **169**

Table of Cases   lix

Sakals v. Transport and General Workers' Union (1985) 280
 I.R.L.I.B. 12... 94
Salt v. National Graphical Association, *The Times*, May 15, 1978 108
Santer v. National Graphical Association [1973] I.C.R. 60;
 (1972) 14 K.I.R. 193.. 130
Sansom v. London and Provincial Union of Licensed Vehicle
 Workers (1920) 36 T.L.R. 666 127
Saunders v. Smith (1837) 3 My. Cr. 710............................... 326
Sayer v. Amalgamated Society of Carpenters' and Joiners
 (1902) 19 T.L.R. 122.. 123
Scala Ballroom (Wolverhampton) Ltd. v. Ratcliffe
 [1958] 1 W.L.R. 1057; [1958] 3 All E.R. 220 272
Schmidt and Dahtstrom v. Sweden (1976) 1 E.H.R.R. 637 .... **18**
Schwartz-Torrence Investment Corporation v. Bakery and
 Confectionary Workers' Union, Local 31 (1964) 394 P. 2d 921 304
Scott v. Avery (1856) 5 H.L.C. 811; 10 E.R. 1121.................. 119
Scott v. Jess (1985) 56 A.L.R. 379.. 108
Seaboard World Airlines Inc. v. Transport and General
 Workers' Union [1973] I.C.R. 458; [1973] I.R.L.R. 300........ 213
Secretary of State for Employment v. Amalgamated Society
 of Railway Servants (No 2) [1972] 2 Q.B. 455; [1972]
 2 All E.R. 949 213
Service Employees' International Union, Local 204 and
 Broadway Manor Nursing Home, Re (1984) 4 D.L.R.
 (4th) 231; 44 O.R. (2d) 392 .... 16, **23**
Shanks v. Plumbing Trades Union, unreported,
 November 15, 1967 .... **140**
Shanks v. United Operative Mason's Association of Scotland
 (1841) 1 R (Ct. of Sess.) 823; 11 Sc. L. R. 356.................. 123
Sheet Iron workers' and Light Platers' Society v.
 Boilermakers' and Iron and Steel Shipbuilders' Society
 (1924) 40 T.L.R. 294 70
Shelbourne v. Oliver (1866) 13 L.T. 630................................ 214
Shepherd Homes Ltd. v. Sandham [1971] Ch. 340; [1970]
 3 All E.R. 402 .... **329–330**
Sherard v. Amalgamated Union of Engineering Workers
 [1973] I.C.R. 421; [1973] I.R.L.R. 188 .... **274**
Sheriff v. McMullen [1952] I.R. 236; 91 1 L.T.R. 60
                              242, 258, **260**, **265**, **268**, **273–274**
Sherrard v. Ulster Pension Trustees Ltd. Northern Ireland;
 High Court, unreported, 22 February 1971 207
Shiels v. Joe Bonner Engineering Ltd. U.D. 67/1977................ 36
Shinwell v. National Seaman's and Fireman's Union (1913)
 2 S.L.T. 83 .... 87, 254
Sick and Funeral Society of St. John's Sunday School, Golcar,
 In re [1973] 1 Ch. 51; [1972] 2 W.L.R. 962; [1972] 2 All E.R.

lx   *Irish Trade Union Law*

439 .... 81, 113, **118**
Silver Tassie Co. Ltd. v. Cleary (1958) 92 I.L.T.R. 27   264, **279**, 300, 317
Silvester v. National Union of Printing, Bookbinding and
   Paper Workers (1966) 1 K.I.R. 679; (1966) 166 *N.L.J.* 1489   117
Simmons v. Hoover Ltd. [1977] Q.B. 284; [1977] I.C.R. 61;
   [1976] 3 W.L.R. 901; [1977] 1 All E.R. 775; [1976] I.R.L.R.
   266 .... **207, 210**
Singh v. British Steel Corporation [1974] I.R.L.R. 131   **162–163**
Sinnott v. Quinnsworth Ltd. [1984] I.L.R.M. 523 156
Skinner v. Kitch (1867) L.R. 2 Q.B. 393 214
Slade and Stewart Ltd. v. Haynes (1969) 5 D.L.R. (3d) 736 239
Smith v. Beirne (1954) 89 I.T.L.R. 24 .... 263, 265, **275**, 317
Smith v. Scottish Typographical Association 1919 S.C. 43;
   56 Sc.L.R. 46; 2 S.L.T. 250 .... **127**, 133
Smith v. Thomasson (1890) 16 Cox C.C. 470 292
Sorrell v. Smith [1926] A.C. 700; [1925] All E.R. Rep. 1;
   41 T.L.R. 529 .... **225, 227, 242–243**
South Wales Mines' Federation v. Glamorgan Coal Co.
   [1905] A.C. 239; [1904–7] All E.R. 211; 21 T.L.R. 441   **231–232**
Spring v. National Amalgamated Stevedores and Dockers
   Society [1956] I.W.L.R. 585; [1956] 2 All E.R. 221   113, **103–104**, 113
Springhead Spinning Co. v. Riley (1868) L.R. 6 Eq 551
   19 L.T. 64 .... 214, 221
Squibb United Kingdom Staff Association v. Certification
   Officer [1979] I.C.R. 235; [1979] 1 W.L.R. 523; [1979]
   2 All E.R. 452 52
Star Sea Transport Corporation of Monrovia v. Slater [1978]
   I.R.L.R. 507; (1979) 1 Lloyd's Rep. 26 277
State (Byrne) v. Frawley [1978] I.R. 326 .... **32**
State (Casey) v. Labour Court [1984] 3 *J.I.S.L.L. 135* **345**
State (Cole) v. Labour Court [1984] 3 *J.I.S.L.L.* 128 .... 346, 350
State (Commins) v. McRann [1977] I.R. 78 335
State (Elm Park Developments Ltd.) v. An Bord Pleanala
   [1981] I.L.R.M. 108 75
State (Furey) v. Minister for Defence; Supreme Court,
   unreported, 2nd March 1984 111
State (Gleeson) v. Minister for Defence [1976] I.R. 280 .... 30, 32
State (Graham) v. Racing Board; High Court, unreported,
   22 November 1983 117
State (Hardy) v. O'Flynn [1948] I.R. 343 290
State (Horgan) v. Exported Live Stock Insurance Board and
   Committee of Assessors [1943] I.R. 581 47
State (Kearns) v. Minister for Social Welfare; High Court,
   unreported, 10 February 1982 .... **364–365**, 371
State (Lynch) v. Cooney [1982] I.R. 337 29
State (McCarthy) v. O'Donnell [1945] I.R. 126 47

Table of Cases lxi

State (Quinn) v. Ryan [1965] I.R. 70; 100 I.L.T.R. 105............ 30
State (Shannon Atlantic Fisheries Ltd.) v. McPolin [1976] I.R. 93 355
State (Smullen) v. Duffy; High Court, unreported,
   21 March 1980 .... 117, 346
State (St. Stephen's Green Club) v. Labour Court [1961]
   I.R. 85 .... 343, **355**
State (Williams) v. Army Pensions Board [1983] I.R. 308;
   [1983] I.L.R.M. 331 .... 106, 117
Steele v. South Wales Miners' Federation [1907] I.K.B. 361
   23 T.L.R. 228; 96 L.T. 260... 68, 123
Stephen [Harold] and Co. Ltd. v. Post Office [1977] I.W.L.R.
   1172; [1978] 1 All E.R. 939... **330**
Stevenson v. United Road and Transport Union [1977] I.C.R.
   893; [1977] 2 All E.R. 941... 140, **141**
Stratford [J.T.] Co. v. Lindley [1965] A.C. 269 [1964] 3 All
   E.R. 102; [1964] 3 W.L.R. 541 H.L.; reversing [1964]
   2 W.L.R. 1002; [1964] 2 All E.R. 209; C.A.; restoring [1964]
   1 Lloyd's Rep. 138 .... 238, 241, 258, **259**, **261**, **262–263**, 265
Strick v. Swansea Tin Plate Co. [1887] 36 Ch. D. 588;
   57 L.T. 392.. 131
Stuart v. Clarkson 1894 22 R. 5; 32 S.L.R. 4; 2 S.L.T. 246...... 290
Swaine v. Wilson (1890) 24 Q.B.D. 252; 6 T.L.R. 121 .... 38, **125**
Swedish Engine Drivers' Union v. Sweden (1976) 1 E.H.R.R. 617 **18**
Sweeney v. Coote [1906] I.R. 428 .... **227**
Syndicat Catholique des Employes de Magasin de Quebec
   Inc. v. Compagnie Pacquet Ltee. [1959] S.C.R. 206 145

Tadd v. Eastwood [1983] I.R.L.R. 320...................... 164, **355–356**
Taff Vale Railway Co. Ltd. v. Amalgamated Society of
   Railway Servants [1901] A.C. 426; 83 L.T. 474
                                         64, 86, 87, 153, **223–224**, 249
Talbot [Ireland] Ltd. v. Merrigan; Supreme Court,
   unreported, 30 April 1981 .... 243, **247–248**, **260**, 331
Talke Fashions Ltd. v. Amalgamated Society of Textile
   Workers and Kindred Trades [1977] I.C.R. 833; [1977]
   I.R.L.R. 309; [1978] 2 All E.R. 649 .... **179**
Taylor v. National Union of Mineworkers (Derbyshire Area)
   [1985] I.R.L.R. 99 .... 68, 108, 109, **122–123**
Taylor v. National Union of Mineworkers (Yorkshire Area)
   [1984] I.R.L.R. 445 .... 107–108, **120**
Telling v. National Association of Operative Plasterers,
   The Times, July 4, 1953... 129
Temperton v. Russell [1893] 1 Q.B. 715 [1891–4] All E.R.
   Rep. 724; 9 T.L.R. 393.. 226, **232**
Thomas v. National Union of Mineworkers (South Wales
   Area) [1985] 2 W.L.R. 1081; [1985] I.R.L.R. 136; [1985]

2 All E.R.I. 68, 298, **299–300**
Thomas v. Portsmouth 'A' Branch of the Ship Constructors
 and Shipwrights' Association (1912) 28 T.L.R. 372 64
Thomson [D.C.] and Co. Ltd. v. Deakin [1952] Ch. 646;
 [1952] 2 All E.R. 361; [1952] 2 T.L.R. 105 .... 233, 235,
 236, 237, 259
Thornhill v. Alabama [1940] 310 U.S. 88 284
Tierney v. Amalgamated Society of Woodworkers [1959]
 I.R. 254 .... **4–5**, 6, **26**, 30, **59**, **68**, 101, **106**, 109
Tierney v. Tough [1914] I.I.R. 142 81
T.M.G. Group Ltd. v. Al Babtain Trading and Contracting
 Co. [1982] I.L.R.M. 349 322
Toppin v. Feron (1909) 43 I.L.T.R. 190 309
Tormey v. Ireland [1985] I.L.R.M. 375 .... **48**
Torquay Hotel Co. Ltd. v. Cousins [1969] 32 Ch. 106, [1969]
 1 All E.R. 522; [1969] 2 W.L.R. 289
 233, **234**, 235, **242**, **254–255**, 259, 261
Tramp Shipping Corporation v. Greenwich Marine Inc.
 [1975] I.C.R. 261; [1975] 2 All E.R. 989 212
Transport and General Workers' Union v. Dyer [1977]
 I.R.L.R. 93; (1976) 12 I.T.R. 113 174
Trapp v. Mackie [1979] I.W.L.R. 377; [1979] 1 All E.R. 489 ... **355**
Transport Salaried Staffs Association v. Córas Iompair
 Éireann [1965] I.R. 180; 100 I.L.T.R. 189 .... 19, 65, **160**
Tuttle v. Buck (1909) 119 N.W. 946 .... **226**
Twist v. Randwick Municipal Council (1976) 51 A.L.J.R. 193 119
Tynan v. Balmer [1967] 1 Q.B. 91; [1966] 2 W.L.R. 1181
 [1966] 2 All E.R. 133 293

Unident Ltd. v. Delong (1982) 131 D.L.R. 3d 225 233
Union of Shop Distributive and Allied Workers v. Leancut
 Bacon Ltd. [1981] I.R.L.R. 295 177
Union of Shop Distributive and Allied Workers v. Sketchley
 Ltd. [1981] I.C.R. 644; [1981] I.R.L.R. 291 .... **174**
United Biscuits (U.K.) Ltd. v. Fall [1979] I.R.L.R. 110 276
United Kingdom Association of Professional Engineers v.
 Advisory, Conciliation and Arbitration Service [1980]
 I.C.R. 201; [1980] I.R.L.R. 124, H.L., reversing [1979]
 I.C.R. 303, C.A. 355
United States of America v. Hill (1918) 248 U.S. 420 .... **28**
Universe Tankships Inc. of Monrovia v. International
 Transport Workers Federation [1983] 1 A.C. 366; [1982]
 I.C.R. 262; [1982] I.R.L.R. 200; [1982] 2 All E.R. 67 ... **251–252**
University College Galway v. Conlon; High Court,
 unreported, 17 January 1977 263

Vacher and Sons Ltd. v. London Society of Compositors
[1913] A.C. 107 [1911-13] All E.R. Rep. 241; 29 T.L.R. 73 . **252**
Valentine v. Hyde [1919] 2 Ch. 129; 35 T.L.R. 301;
120 L.T. 653 267
Van Camp Chocolates Ltd. v. Aulsebrooks Ltd. [1984] 1
N.Z.L.R. 354 242
Van Duyn v. Home Office [1975] 1 C.M.L.R. [1974] E.C.R.
1337 169
Van Gend en Loos v. Nederlandse Administratie der
Belastingen [1963] E.C.R. 1; [1963] C.M.L.R. 105 169
Vella v. Morelli [1968] I.R. 11 .... **332-333**
Volkswagen (Canada) Ltd. v. Spicer (1978) 91 D.L.R. (3d) 42   243
Von Colson and Kamann v. Land Nordrhein-Westfalen
[1984] E.C.R. 1891 169
Voyager Explorations Ltd. v. Ontario Securities Commission
(1970) 8 D.L.R. (3d) 135; [1970] 1 O.R. 237; 60 C.P.R. 153.   106

Walker v. Amalgamated Union of Engineering and Foundry
Workers 1969 S.L.T. 150 117
Walker v. Nolan U.D. 563/1981 36
Wall v. Morrissey [1969] I.R. 10; 105 I.L.T.R. 57 .... **294**
Walsh v. Amalgamated Union of Engineering Workers
The Times, July 15, 1977 104
Walsh v. Kilkenny County Council High Court, unreported,
23 January 1978 220
Waltham Electronics (Ireland) Ltd. v. Doyle High Court,
unreported, 15 November 1974 310
Ward, Lock and Co. v. Operative Printers' Assistants' Society
(1906) 22 T.L.R. 327 .... **286, 287, 297, 298**
Ware and de Freville Ltd. v. Motor Trade Association [1921] 3
K.B. 40; [1920] All E.R. Rep. 387 .... **254**
Wark and Green, In re (1985) 15 D.L.R. (4th) 577;
58 N.B.R. (2d) 229 117
Waterford Co-operative v. Griffin High Court, unreported,
8th May 1977 307
Watson v. Smith [1941] 2 All E.R. 725; 57 T.L.R. 552 129
Watt v. Lord Advocate [1979] S.L.T. 137 .... **368**
Western Health Board v. Greaney High Court, unreported,
9 June 1982 263
Whellan v. Rodgers (1887) 3 T.L.R. 450 130
White v. Kuzych [1951] A.C. 585; [1951] 2 All E.R. 435 .... **117**
White v. Riley [1921] 1 Ch. 1 267
Wigoder (H.) and Co. Ltd. v. Moran [1977] I.R. 112;
111 I.L.T.R. 105 .... **333**
Wilkie v. King 1911 S.C. 1310; 48 Sc. L.R. 1057 .... **131-132**
Wilkinson v. Downton [1897] 2 Q.B. 57 .... **224**

Williams v. Butlers Ltd. [1975] 1 C.R. 208; [1975] 2 All E.R.
 889; [1975] I.R.L.R. 120... 97
Williams v. Gleeson U.D. 272/1978... 34
Williams v. Western Mail and Echo Ltd. [1980] I.C.R. 366;
 [1980] I.R.L.R. 222... 213
Willis and London Society of Compositors v. Brooks [1947]
 1 All E.R. 191 62 T.L.R. 745... 64
Wilson v. Renton 1909 S.C.(J.) 32; 47 Sc.L.R. 209 292
Winder v. Kingston-Upon-Hull Corporation for the Poor
 (1888) 20 Q.B.D. 412; 58 L.T. 583.............................. 123, 131
Winter v. United Society of Boilermakers (1909) 26 Sh.
 Ct. Rep. 320.. 276
Wolfe v. Matthews (1882) 21 Ch.D. 194; 47 L.T. 158.............. 127
Wooley v. Dunford [1972] 3 S.A.S.R. 243.................................. 237
Woolworth (F.W.) Ltd. v. Haynes High Court, unreported,
 19th July 1984.. 312

X. v. Belgium, Application 4072/69 yearbook v. 13 p. 708....... 14
X. v. Ireland, Application 4152/69... 54

Yeates v. Minister for Posts and Telegraphs; High Court,
 unreported, 21st February 1978 30
Yorkshire Miners' Association v. Howden [1905] A.C. 256;
 21 T.L.R. 431... 127
Young v. Ladies' Imperial Club Ltd. [1920] 2 K.B. 523;
 36 T.L.R. 392... 117
Young, James and Webster v. United Kingdom [1981]
 I.R.L.R. 408... 13–14, 32
Yule Inc. v. Atlantic Pizza Delight Franchise (1968) Ltd.
 (1979) 80 D.L.R. (3d) 725... 321

Zucker v. Astrid Jewels Ltd. [1978] I.C.R. 1088; [1978]
 I.R.L.R. 385... 36

Chapter 1

FREEDOM OF ASSOCIATION

One of the most pressing problems facing Irish trade unionism since Independence has been the need to rationalise the trade union movement by reducing the number of trade unions operating in Ireland. Indeed it is significant that all *post*-1922 trade union legislation, with only one exception,[1] is designed to tackle this problem in one fashion or another.

But despite repeated efforts[2] to resolve the problem, it continues to create serious difficulties for the Irish trade union movement. In the first place, multiplicity of unions prevents decision-making power moving to the top of the trade union leadership, encouraging instead a decentralised way of negotiating wages by individual groups of workers. According to Schregle, the shifting of decision-making power to the top of the trade union movement is vital if workers' interests are to be adequately protected in times of economic crises.[3] Secondly, many small unions competing among themselves cannot afford to provide those services to their members which one larger union representing the same workers would be in a position to provide. Consequently, multiplicity of unions affects the quality of services provided for trade union members.[4] Thirdly, the existence of competition for members between rival unions can result in inter-union disputes which are costly and damaging to the public image of a trade union movement, for example the Ferenka dispute in 1978. It is clear, therefore, that the problem of multiplicity of unions is one of considerable magnitude for the Irish trade union movement.[5]

A number of solutions to this problem could be suggested. First, as recommended by the Commission of Inquiry on Industrial Relations, the statutory definition of "trade dispute"[6] in section 5(3) of the Trade Dispute Act 1906 could be amended to exclude disputes between workmen and workmen, thus depriving inter-union disputes of the protection of the 1906 Act.[7]

---

[1] Trade Union Act 1935.
[2] For an account of such efforts see McCarthy, *Trade Unions in Ireland (1894–1960)* (Dublin, 1977), esp. chs. 4, 9 and 10; Schregle, *Restructuring of the Irish Trade Union Movement* Memorandum submitted to the I.C.T.U. (1975), pp. 15–20.
[3] *Op. cit.*, pp. 25–26. See also Fogarty, "Trade Unions and the Future" in Nevin ed., *Trade Unions and Change in Irish Society* (Dublin, 1980) at p. 146.
[4] Though *cf.* Elias, "Trade Union Amalgamations: Patterns and Procedures" (1973) 2 *I.L.J.* 125 at p. 125.
[5] See Report of Commission of Inquiry on Industrial Relations (Pl. 114), paras. 64 *et seq.*
[6] See *infra*, pp. 261 *et seq.*
[7] Report of the Commission of Inquiry on Industrial Relations (Pl. 114) at para. 683. Such a change has been effected in Britain by s.18(2)(*b*) of the Employment Act 1982. On inter-union

This proposal, however, suffers from a number of shortcomings. There is the problem of definition. Should the concept of inter-union dispute be extended to embrace a situation where the supposedly neutral employer favours one of the parties to the dispute, a situation which arises in many of these cases? Moreover it deals only with the symptoms of the problem and does not go to the root of the malaise – *viz.* the excessive number of unions operating in this country.

Secondly, on a more positive note, one could encourage co-operation among existing unions in an attempt to avoid inter-union disputes.[8] This co-operation could take a number of different forms:

1. Discussion of common interests under the auspices of bodies like trades or workers' councils.
2. Inter-union agreements as to the areas in which particular unions will operate or the class of worker they will organise.
3. Group negotiation – common action by the unions in a particular industry for the purpose of carrying on negotiations. Fogarty indeed calls for the establishment of a single works committee for every organisation, along German lines.[9]

The great advantage of this approach is that it is a voluntary policy emanating from the trade union movement itself. As such it has been accepted by most Irish trade unions[10] and has a direct effect on the symptoms caused by multiplicity of unions. It is rather cautious, however, and again does not attempt to tackle the source of the problem.

Finally, one could restructure the trade union movement and reduce the number of unions operating in the Republic. The authors agree with the Commission of Inquiry on Industrial Relations that, in reality, "the necessary improvements in trade union structures can be brought about only by the trade unions themselves."[11] In the past, however, the Government has attempted to force this issue through legislative intervention. Two strategies were adopted:

1. Radical restructuring of the trade union movement co-ordinated by a Government agency empowered to make binding decisions

---

disputes over representation and demarcation generally, see the Commission of Inquiry's Report at paras. 299–318.

[8] See the discussion in the Report of the Royal Commission on Trade Unions and Employers' Associations 1965–1968 (Cmnd. 3623), paras. 683–695.

[9] Fogarty in Nevin ed., *op. cit.*, pp. 149–150. For legislative provisions encouraging the development of similar bodies, see the Industrial Relations Act 1946, Part V, which deals with Joint Industrial Councils.

[10] The decision of the I.T.G.W.U. in *Murphy* v. *Stewart* [1973] I.R. 96 to abide by the ruling of the I.C.T.U. Disputes Committee in that particular case is a good example of this.

[11] Report of Commission of Inquiry on Industrial Relations (Pl. 114), para. 76.

in this respect. This was attempted in Part III of the Trade Union Act 1941 but was held to be unconstitutional by the Supreme Court in *National Union of Railwaymen.* v. *Sullivan.*[12]

2. A more gradual process of restructuring by discouraging the formation of new unions and facilitating the amalgamation of existing ones. In the aftermath of the Supreme Court decision in *N.U.R.* v. *Sullivan,* successive Irish Governments have adopted this strategy which is contained in Part II of the Trade Union Act 1941, as amended by the Trade Union Act 1971, and the Trade Union Act 1975.

Central to Government policy in this area is the concept of freedom of association.[13] This is guaranteed by Article 40.6.1°(iii) of the Constitution. In addition, Ireland has also incurred international obligations under the European Convention on Human Rights,[14] the European Social Charter and Conventions Nos. 11, 87 and 98 of the International Labour Organisation.[15] The European Communities have not yet tackled directly the legal relationship that exists between the social partners, though some measures adopted pursuant to Articles 48 and 49 of the Treaty of Rome – dealing with freedom of movement of workers – do restrict the right of trade unions to reject applications for membership from foreign nationals.[16]

In the remainder of this chapter, we will examine the manner in which the Constitution and legislation guarantees freedom of association, referring, where relevant, to Ireland's international obligations in this area.[17] This examination will take place largely against a backdrop

---

[12] [1947] I.R. Hereafter referred to as *N.U.R.* v. *Sullivan.* See *infra,* pp. 27–28.

[13] On an important point of terminology, some commentators have argued for the application to the Constitution of the Hohfeldian distinction between "freedoms" and "rights", the former designating the benefit derived from the absence of legal constraints imposed on the person who enjoys the freedom, while the latter entails a positive claim coupled with a corresponding legal duty on others to respect that claim. The language of the Constitution, however, does not facilitate the application of this distinction to the subject matter of Article 40.6.1°(iii) which guarantees liberty for the exercise of the right of the citizens to form associations and unions. Furthermore the distinction can often be confusing given that in many cases the liberty to do something will be accompanied by the existence of a right. The authors therefore have used the word "right" in its conventional sense as designating a claim enforceable at law, and the phrase "freedom of association" in its conventional sense as referring to the legal concept protected by Article 40.6.1°(iii).

[14] Though Ireland has ratified the European Convention on Human Rights it has failed to incorporate it into domestic law and accordingly Irish courts for the most part refuse to entertain arguments based directly on the Convention – see *e.g. In re O'Laighleis* [1960] I.R. 93; *Norris* v. *Attorney General* Supreme Court, unreported, 22 April 1982 and *E.* v. *E.* [1982] I.L.R.M. 497. It is arguable, however, that Article 29.3 of the Constitution requires the Irish courts to give effect to the Convention notwithstanding the absence of incorporation. For further on this see Whyte, "The application of the European Convention on Human Rights before the Irish Courts" (1982) 31 *I.C.L.Q.* 856.

[15] See Forde, "The European Convention on Human Rights and Labour Law" (1983) 31 *A.J.C.L.* 301.

[16] See *infra,* pp. 101, 112–113.

[17] For an earlier version of this chapter, see Whyte, "Industrial Relations and the Constitution" (1981) 16 *Ir. Jur. (n.s.)* 35.

of the problem of multiplicity of unions. However, it should also be borne in mind that the guarantee of freedom of association is highly significant in relation to the contract of employment and to the union-member relationship insofar as it has the potential to strengthen the position of the individual employee in both these contexts. Furthermore, the guarantee is also relevant to the union–employer relationship, particularly in the context of recognition disputes where there is no statutory provision for securing recognition for trade unions.

FREEDOM OF ASSOCIATION: ELEMENTS OF THE RIGHT

Article 40.6.1° of the 1937 Constitution provides:

"The State guarantees liberty for the exercise of the following rights, subject to public order and morality:-
(i) . . . .
(ii) . . . .
(iii) The right of the citizens to form associations and unions. Laws, however, may be enacted for the regulation and control in the public interest of the exercise of the foregoing right."

Article 40.6.2° provides:

"Laws regulating the manner in which the right of forming associations and unions and the right of free assembly may be exercised, shall contain no political, religious or class discrimination."

Right to form

The use in Article 40.6.1°(iii) of the verb "to form" instead of "to join" is not without significance for our understanding of the constitutional guarantee of freedom of association. For these two verbs, though similar, are not identical. The right to join is a singular right in the sense that it may be exercised by an individual acting alone, and does not require the consent of those members of the organisation to which the individual attaches himself. The right to form, in contrast, is a collective right which can only be exercised when at least two individuals decide to act together. It is only this latter concept which is protected by Article 40.6.1°(iii), a point borne out in the case of *Tierney v. Amalgamated Society of Woodworkers*.[18]

In this case the plaintiff, a carpenter, applied for membership of the defendant union. The union decided at one of its meetings to refuse him admission on the grounds that he was not a genuine carpenter and

---

[18] [1959] I.R. 254. See also de Blaghd, "The problem of the reluctant non-union worker" (1973) 107 *I.L.T.S.J.* 11.

could not present any proof of apprenticeship. The plaintiff brought an action seeking, *inter alia*, an order directing the defendants to accept his application for membership, to submit such application to a meeting of the Galway branch of the union, and to take all necessary and proper steps for the holding of an election on such application.

Budd J. dismissed his action in the High Court, holding that the Trade Union Act 1941 did not create a right to join a trade union. Nor did the union rule book constitute a continuing offer to any interested member of the public to join because the union did not intend to become contractually bound. Even assuming that the plaintiff had a right to join the union, nevertheless the court could not entertain his claim because of the rule in *Foss* v. *Harbottle*.[19] Further, assuming that the rule in *Foss* v. *Harbottle* did not apply, still the plaintiff failed, as the decision of the union was made honestly and in good faith, and did not violate the rules of natural justice.

Counsel for the plaintiff had argued that the plaintiff had a right to work under Article 40.3, and that the creation of a statutory right to join a trade union in the 1941 Act vindicated this right. Budd J. accepted that the right to work was a personal right of the citizen but he felt unable to hold that section 13(1) of the 1941 Act, which obliged authorised trade unions to include in their rule book provisions specifying the conditions of entry and cesser of membership of such unions, was intended to create a statutory right to join a trade union in order to vindicate that right to work. In his opinion, that section could have several other possible objects and, furthermore, he felt that it would be unlikely that the legislature would introduce such a revolutionary change into the law in such a devious fashion.

The plaintiff appealed to the Supreme Court, but his appeal was unanimously dismissed. In relation to the constitutional arguments, Maguire C.J., with whom the other members of the court concurred, stated simply that he agreed with the views of Budd J. that no support for the plaintiff's case could be got from the Constitution.

The basis for the decision in this case was, therefore, that the citizen's constitutional right to work under Article 40.3 did not include as a corollary a right to join a trade union. In *Murphy* v. *Stewart*[20], the Supreme Court went further and held that such a right was not included in Article 40.6.1°(iii). The plaintiff here was a member of the defendant union, the National Union of Vehicle Builders (N.U.V.B.), who wished to transfer to the I.T.G.W.U. The latter union accepted him as a member, despite the objections of the defendant union, but subsequently restored him to membership of N.U.V.B. pursuant to the re-

---

[19] But *cf*. "Admissions to non-statutory associations" (1967) 30 *M.L.R.* 389, at pp. 395–396, where Rideout argues that *Foss* v. *Harbottle* is inapplicable to an action based on rejection of an application for membership.
[20] [1973] I.R. 97, followed by McWilliam J. in *Abbot and Whelan* v. *I.T.G.W.U.* (1982) 1 *J.I.S.L.L.* 56. See also de Blaghd, (1974) 108 *I.L.T.S.J.* 71.

commendation of the Disputes Committee of the Irish Congress of Trade Unions (I.C.T.U.). The I.T.G.W.U. refused to accept the plaintiff's further application for membership because of the refusal of the defendant union to consent to the transfer, which consent was required by the terms of clause 47(d) of the I.C.T.U. Constitution. That clause provided:

> "Where any grade, group or category of workers, or the workers in any establishment, form a negotiating unit and their wages or conditions of work are determined by negotiations conducted by a single union of which the majority, or a substantial proportion of the workers concerned are members, no other union shall organise or enrol as members any workers within that negotiating unit . . . save only with the consent of the union concerned."[21]

The plaintiff then brought an action in which he claimed that the refusal of the defendant union to consent to his becoming a member of the I.T.G.W.U. was an infringement of his constitutional rights.

Murnaghan J., in the High Court, decided in favour of the plaintiff but the defendant union appealed and the appeal was allowed by a unanimous Supreme Court. Walsh J., with whom Ó Dálaigh C.J. and Fitzgerald, Butler and Budd JJ. concurred, disagreed with the trial judge's holding that the defendant union was infringing the plaintiff's right to join the I.T.G.W.U. First, the Constitution did not guarantee citizens the right to join the union of their choice, but merely the right to form unions or associations. Secondly, the reason why the plaintiff could not join the I.T.G.W.U. was because the I.T.G.W.U. refused to accept him without the consent of the defendant union, pursuant to the provisions of clause 47(d), not because the defendant union would not give him permission. The I.T.G.W.U. had a right to accept the plaintiff into membership without having to have regard to the wishes of any third party, but it voluntarily surrendered that right when it affiliated to Congress by agreeing to be bound by clause 47(d). It was suggested, *obiter*, that if the plaintiff could establish that the defendant union was refusing consent solely out of a desire to injure the plaintiff, or if it was employing unlawful means, the decision would be set aside and the union could be compelled to give the matter proper consideration.[22]

It is now quite clear therefore that, subject to certain qualifications, there is no constitutional right to join a trade union.[23] An immediate

---

[21] This provision was subsequently amended at the 1982 Annual Conference of the I.C.T.U. by the addition of the following passage "except that such consent shall not be withheld where there is evidence that 80% or more of the workers in that grade, group, category or establishment wish to transfer in the case of a firm where representation rights have been established more than two years before the date of application to transfer."

[22] *Per* Walsh J., [1973] I.R. 97, 118–119.

[23] The authors are inclined to regard judicial references to a right to join trade unions, in subsequent cases such as *Rodgers* v. *I.T.G.W.U.* High Court, unreported, 15 March 1978 and *Abbot and Whelan* v. *I.T.G.W.U.* (1982) 1 *J.I.S.L.L.* 56, as a regrettable example of laxity in terminology rather than as a conscious attempt to undermine the principle in *Tierney*.

implication of this is that the trade union movement can continue to regulate inter-union transfers by means of devices such as clause 47(d). The foregoing, however, must be read in the light of the individual's constitutional rights, in particular his right to work.[24] If membership of a particular union was a precondition to obtaining work then, in order to vindicate the individual's right to work, it is possible that the union may be compelled to accept him into membership.[25] Finally, it should be noted that there is some statutory restriction on a union's powers in relation to applications for membership. By virtue of section 3(1)(*b*) of the Trade Union Act 1913, a union with a political fund cannot insist that contribution to the fund be a pre-condition for admission to the union.[26] Nor can unions discriminate on grounds of sex, marital status, and in certain cases, nationality, in relation to eligibility for union membership.[27]

Right to dissociate

A second question which arises from an examination of Article 40.6.1°(iii) is whether the Constitution protects not only freedom of association but also the right to dissociate. If the latter right is protected, it will have considerable implications for the legitimacy of agreements between employers and unions whereby jobs are only to be obtained or retained if the individual is, or becomes and remains, a member of a specified union. Such agreements are commonly referred to as "closed shop" agreements and industrial relations practitioners draw a distinction between "pre-entry" and "post-entry" agreements. Under the former the individual has to be a union member before he can be engaged; under the latter, the employer is free to engage a non-unionist provided he agrees to join immediately or shortly after engagement.[28]

There are two recorded instances of cases decided after the enactment of the Constitution, where an Irish court upheld a pre-entry closed shop agreement. In *Hynes* v. *Conlon*,[29] the defendants, who were trade union officials, secured the dismissal of the plaintiff on the grounds that his employment amounted to a breach of a closed shop agreement negotiated between the union and the employer. The plaintiff brought an action in tort against the defendants for inducing breach of contract and for interfering with his right to dispose of labour. Hanna J., who took the view that the case could be decided on the basis of the common law alone, dismissed the plaintiff's action

---

[24] Which is not the most specific of constitutional rights. See Whyte, *loc. cit.*, pp. 68–71. On the legal implications of cl. 47(d) see *infra*, pp. 102–106.
[25] *Per* Walsh J. in *Murphy* v. *Stewart* [1973] I.R. 97, 117. See also the similar remarks of Lord Diplock in *Cheall* v. *A.P.E.X.* [1983] 2 A.C. 180, 191.
[26] See *infra*, p. 94.
[27] See *infra*, p. 101.
[28] See McCarthy, *The Closed Shop in Britain* (Oxford, 1964), p. 16. See also Hanson, Jackson and Miller, *The Closed Shop* (Hants., 1982).
[29] [1939] Ir. Jur. Rep. 49.

because the defendants had not threatened or used violence against the employers. In *Buckley* v. *Rooney*[30], the plaintiff was dismissed because he was not a member of the I.T.G.W.U., there being an agreement between that union and the defendant employers that the latter would employ only members of the I.T.G.W.U. at their workplace. The plaintiff claimed damages for wrongful dismissal, but Judge O'Connor, in the Circuit Court, held that his claim failed because the employer had given the requisite period of notice of dismissal under the contract of employment. The judge, without elaboration, briefly commented that, in his opinion, the closed shop agreement did not violate the provisions of Article 40 of the Constitution.

The leading authority in relation to post-entry closed shops is the decision of the Supreme Court in *Educational Co. of Ireland Ltd.* v. *Fitzpatrick (No. 2).*[31] The facts of this case were briefly as follows: certain employees of the plaintiff companies, having been organised by the Irish Union of Distributive Workers and Clerks (I.U.D.W.C.), decided that they would refuse to work with employees who were not members of the union. When management refused to compel the non-union employees to join the union, the defendant employees went on strike and picketed the plaintiffs' premises. The plaintiffs sought an injunction to restrain the picketing.

In the High Court, Budd J. took the view that Article 40.6.1°(iii) protected the right to dissociate; that the provisions of the Trade Disputes Act 1906 must be read subject to the Constitution; and that, consequently, the picketing in this case, which violated the constitutional rights of the non-union employees, was unlawful. An injunction restraining the picketing was issued.

This decision was appealed to the Supreme Court, but the appeal was dismissed by a majority. The leading opinion here was delivered by Kingsmill Moore J., with whom Ó Dálaigh J. agreed. The earlier part of Kingsmill Moore J.'s judgment dealt with the legality of picketing at common law and on this point he concluded that the picketing was illegal unless conducted in furtherance of a trade dispute within the ambit of the Trade Disputes Act 1906. Furthermore, Kingsmill Moore J. was prepared to hold that, prior to the enactment of the Free State Constitution, a dispute similar to the dispute in the instant case would be protected by the provisions of the 1906 Act. However, the Act now had to be interpreted in the light of the present Constitution as Article 50 thereof only carried over the laws in force in *Saorstát Éireann* to the extent to which they were not inconsistent with

---

[30] [1950] Ir. Jur. Rep. 5.
[31] [1961] I.R. 345. For an application of the *Educational Co.* decision, see *Crowley* v. *Cleary* [1968] I.R. 261; also *Murtagh Properties Ltd.* v. *Cleary* [1972] I.R. 330 at 334. For an account of the effect of this decision on industrial relations, see McCartney, "Strike Law and the Constitution" (1964) 30 *Ir. Jur.* 54 at pp. 59 *et seq.*; de Blaghd, "How closed can my shop be?" (1972) 106 *I.L.T.S.J.* 67 at pp. 98, 103–104.

the 1937 Constitution. Article 73 of the 1922 Constitution had in turn provided for the continued validity of pre-1922 law only to the extent to which it complied with the Free State Constitution.

In Kingsmill Moore J.'s opinion, the 1937 Constitution guaranteed, by necessary implication, the right of citizens not to join associations or unions if they did not so desire. He based this conclusion on the fact that Article 40.6.1°(i), which guarantees the right to express freely convictions and opinions, must include the right not to be forced to join a union or association professing, forwarding and requiring its members to subscribe to, opinions to which they are opposed. It is submitted that the reasoning here is not particularly cogent. Citizens are not prevented from holding certain opinions or indeed obliged to hold stipulated beliefs, simply because they are compelled to join a union. A closed shop policy works to strengthen unions in industrial relations and does not automatically extend to the realm of politics. Indeed the existence of a separate political fund respects the political beliefs of union members.[32]

Kingsmill Moore J. also pointed out that Article 40.3, to the extent that it protected property rights, arguably included an undertaking to protect the citizen's right to dispose of his labour as he willed, and impliedly protected the right of the citizen not to be forced into an association which exacted from him a regular payment. The answer to this is, of course, that property rights under the Constitution are not absolute and may be overridden in the interests of social justice.[33]

Lastly, Kingsmill Moore J. felt that a guarantee of a right to form associations or unions was only intelligible where there was an implicit right to abstain from joining associations or unions.[34] In support of this conclusion, he relied on a statement of Murnaghan J. in *N.U.R.* v. *Sullivan*,[35] to the effect that depriving a citizen of the choice of persons with whom he could associate amounted to a denial of his constitutional right of association. He conceded that certain forms of pressure, for example social ostracism or economic pressure motivated by legitimate interests, though designed to prevent a citizen from exercising his constitutional rights, could not be restrained by law. However, the law could prevent the legislature from authorising or facilitating coercion by attempting to legalise acts, directed to preventing a citizen from exercising his constitutional rights, which previously were illegal. Consequently, the law could prevent the

---

[32] On the political fund, see *infra*, pp. 89–95.
[33] See Casey, "Freedom of Association in Labour Law" (1972) 21 *I.C.L.Q.* 699 at p. 707 and more recently the decision of the Supreme Court in *O'Callaghan* v. *The Commissioners of Public Works in Ireland* [1985] I.L.R.M. 364.
[34] Casey argues, *loc. cit.* at pp. 707–708, that the existence of a right to dissociate depends on the purpose and policy of the guarantee of freedom of association. If Article 40.6 is regarded as a protection against the State and employers of the right of unions to exist, then such a right can stand on its own, and there is no need to imply a right to dissociate.
[35] [1947] I.R. 77, 102.

legislature from legalising an unlawful act – picketing – for the purpose of interfering with a citizen's constitutional rights. On this last point it is submitted that the distinction between activity which is lawful at common law, and which would be tolerated by the courts, and activity which is not so lawful and therefore liable to be injuncted, is no longer sustainable in the context of an interference with the constitutional rights of the citizen. And indeed the Supreme Court itself recognised as much in the subsequent case of *Meskell* v. *Córas Iompair Éireann*[36], when it rejected the contention that because the plaintiff had been lawfully dismissed at the common law there was no violation of his constitutional rights. It is submitted, therefore, that the court will restrain interference in the exercise of a citizen's constitutional rights in all cases, except where the exercise of that right will in fact infringe the constitutional right of another.[37] This qualification covers the position of an employer who is reluctant to employ an employee who refuses to join a union. Here the employee's right to dissociate must be read subject to the employer's right to dissociate from an individual whose employment is likely to give rise to certain difficulties.

In the event, Kingsmill Moore J. concluded that the 1906 Act could not be relied upon to protect picketing which was designed to prevent citizens from exercising their constitutional rights, and he dismissed the appeal.

Haugh J., concurring with Kingsmill Moore J., based his decision on the positive right of the non-unionists to associate together so as to resist pressure imposed on them by the I.U.D.W.C., rather than on their negative right to refuse to join the union. He examined the concept of freedom of association in the light of the judgment of the Supreme Court in *N.U.R.* v. *Sullivan* and concluded that the right of the citizen to associate with whomsoever he wished was limited in two ways only: (i) it had to be exercised subject to public order and morality – this was not relevant in the instant case; (ii) it had to be read subject to the legislature's power of regulation and control. Haugh J. felt unable to hold that the 1906 Act was an Act continued in existence in order to regulate or control the rights of citizens to form unions and associations. Consequently, he took the view that the nine non-union members of the plaintiff's staff had individually and collectively an unqualified constitutional personal right to associate together.[38] The actions of the defendants were designed to interfere with the exercise of the constitutional rights of the non-unionists and, to the extent to which the 1906 Act afforded protection for this interference, it was inconsistent with the Constitution. He also adopted statements from

---

[36] [1973] I.R. 121. See *infra*, pp. 11–12.
[37] As in *Crowley* v. *Ireland* [1980] I.R. 102.
[38] Casey argues, *loc. cit.* at p. 708, that Article 40.6 does not protect an association to resist trade unionism, as that Article specifically mentions the right to form unions. It is submitted that the better view is that such an association is protected by the Article, which recognises the right to form associations generally.

N.U.R. v. *Sullivan* to the effect that one could not legislate to compel citizens to join unions or associations.

Maguire C.J., dissenting,³⁹ pointed out that, prior to the adoption of the Constitution, a dispute similar to that in the present case would have come within the scope of the 1906 Act. He failed, therefore, to see how a provision of the Constitution, designed to protect trade unions, could in fact reduce the legitimate activities in which a union could engage. Nor did he consider the decision in *N.U.R.* v. *Sullivan* to be relevant. That decision was authority for the proposition that legislation depriving citizens of the choice of persons with whom they could associate was unconstitutional; in this case the trade union was merely trying to persuade the non-unionists to join in. Furthermore, the logical result of the plaintiffs' position was that any step taken with a view to compelling the non-unionists to join the union would be unconstitutional, whereas in fact the plaintiffs conceded that only the act of picketing was unconstitutional.⁴⁰ The Chief Justice concluded that the defendants in this case were merely exercising their freedom of association and that consequently the picketing was not unlawful.

Any doubts which might have existed as to whether Article 40.6.1°(iii) included a right to dissociate were dissipated by the decision of a unanimous Supreme Court in *Meskell* v. *C.I.E.*⁴¹ This case arose out of an attempt by C.I.E. and four trade unions⁴² to improve the level of union membership in C.I.E. It was agreed that C.I.E. would terminate the contracts of employment of all their employees and would offer each employee immediate re-employment upon the same terms as before if they agreed, as an additional condition of employment, to be "at all times" a member of one of the four trade unions. The plaintiff, who was a bus conductor in C.I.E., refused to accept re-employment on these terms because he objected, on principle, to having to join a union under duress, and he brought an action in which he claimed damages for violation of his constitutional rights.

He failed in the High Court, Teevan J. holding that the object of the combination between the defendants and the trade unions had been to advance their own interests rather than to injure the plaintiff. The plaintiff appealed, and his appeal was allowed by the Supreme Court. Walsh J., with whom Ó Dálaigh C.J. and Budd J. concurred, pointed out that a constitutional right carries with it its own right to a remedy or for the enforcement of it and therefore the fact that the plaintiff's action did not fit into any of the ordinary forms of action in either common law or equity was not fatal to his claim. In this case, the trial

---

³⁹ Lavery J. dissented also, identifying himself with the views expressed by the Chief Justice.
⁴⁰ A point accepted by the Supreme Court in *Meskell* v. *C.I.E.* [1973] I.R. 121. See *infra*, p. 12.
⁴¹ [1973] I.R. 121. See also de Blaghd, (1974) 108 *I.L.T.S.J.* 71.
⁴² The unions involved were I.T.G.W.U., W.U.I., A.T.G.W.U. and N.A.T.E.

judge had held that there was no actionable conspiracy because the object of the agreement was not unlawful. Walsh J. pointed out, however, that a conspiracy may be actionable if the means used are unlawful, even though the object of the conspiracy is lawful. The infringement of another's constitutional right or coercing him into abandoning or waiving those rights would amount to unlawful means in this context. Walsh J. concluded that the agreement infringed the plaintiff's right to dissociate which was protected by Article 40.6.1°(iii). The defendant's right at common law to dismiss the plaintiff had to be read subject to the Constitution and therefore the fact that the plaintiff was lawfully dismissed at common law was irrelevant to the outcome of the plaintiff's appeal. Nor could the defendants rely on section 10 of the Railways Act 1933, as applied by section 46 of the Transport Act 1950, to justify the agreement. Those sections provided that rates of pay, hours of duty and other conditions of service of the road transport employees should be regulated in accordance with agreements made or to be made from time to time between trade union representatives of such employees and the defendant company. Walsh J. did not think that these sections extended to cover questions of compulsory membership of unions. Even if they could be so construed, they would have to be read in the light of the Constitution and could not validate unconstitutional activity. Consequently, the plaintiff's appeal was allowed and he was awarded such damages as he could prove were sustained by him.[43]

It would appear, therefore, that the right not to join a trade union is protected by Article 40.6 of the Constitution.[44] This right was recognised by the majority of the Supreme Court in *Educational Co. of Ireland Ltd.* v. *Fitzpatrick (No. 2)* as a corollary of the constitutional freedom of association which is protected by Article 40.6.1°(iii), but it submitted that there is a fatal flaw in the "shallow legalism"[45] of this reasoning.

As we have already seen, the Constitution refers only to a right to *form* associations or unions, and not to a right to *join* such bodies.[46] The right to form unions is of its very nature a collective right, so it is difficult to see how its corollary can be a right not to join unions, which

---

[43] See also *Cotter* v. *Ahern* High Court, unreported, 25 February 1977, where Finlay P. held, applying *Meskell* v. *C.I.E.*, that attempts of the defendant to prevent the appointment or promotion of a national teacher as part of a general campaign to try and ensure that he and all other national teachers in any particular area or in the whole country would become and remain members of a trade union, was an actionable conspiracy in as much as it sought to coerce that person into waiving his constitutional right to dissociate. It is interesting to note that in awarding damages, Finlay P. only took into account loss actually suffered by the plaintiff and did not award him any aggravated damages for breach of constitutional rights *per se*.

[44] Non-unionists, however, have no constitutional right to refuse to meet with trade union members during the course of their employment – *Collins* v. *Cork V.E.C.* Supreme Court, unreported, 8 March 1983.

[45] Kahn-Freund, *Labour and the Law* 2nd ed. (London, 1977) p. 196.

[46] See *supra*, p. 4.

is an individual right.⁴⁷ It would be more accurate to say that the corollary of this constitutional right is a right not to form unions. Thus, even if one wishes to rely on this process of symmetrical reasoning, so heavily criticised by Kahn-Freund,⁴⁸ one is not led to the conclusion that the Constitution protects a right not to join trade unions. However, this essential distinction between a right not to form, and a right not to join, trade unions, has not yet been recognised by the Irish judiciary, who have made it quite clear, in the cases cited above, that every citizen has a constitutional right not to join trade unions.⁴⁹

Leaving aside the analytical objections, one must read the cases carefully in order to ascertain the precise effect of these decisions. It is important to note that what is protected is the right of an *existing* employee to refuse to join specified unions. Thus it may still be open to employers to request prospective employees to join specified unions.⁵⁰ Furthermore, neither *Educational Co. of Ireland Ltd.* v. *Fitzpatrick (No. 2)* nor *Meskell* v. *C.I.E.* is authority for the proposition that workers have the right to refuse to join trade unions generally, as in both cases the workers involved were being compelled to join specific unions. Arguably, therefore, workers might be compelled to become trade union members though their right to select the union of their choice must be respected.

This would also appear to be the position in relation to Article 11 of the European Convention on Human Rights. The case of *Young, James and Webster* v. *U.K.*⁵¹ arose out of the dismissal of the three applicants from their employment with British Rail, because they had refused to join specified trade unions pursuant to a collective agreement negotiated between British Rail and the National Union of Railwaymen (N.U.R.), the Transport Salaried Staffs' Association (T.S.S.A.), and the Associated Society of Locomotive Engineers and Firemen (A.S.L.E.F.). They contended, *inter alia*, that the provisions of the Trade Union and Labour Relations Act 1974 (T.U.L.R.A.) and the Trade Union and Labour Relations (Amendment) Act 1976, infringed Article 11 of the Convention insofar as these permitted the dismissal of

---

⁴⁷ For recent judicial recognition of this argument, see the dissenting judgment of Judge Sorenson in *Young, James and Webster* [1981] I.R.L.R. 408.

⁴⁸ *Op. cit.*, pp. 193–196.

⁴⁹ Though they have recognised the distinction between the positive right to form and the positive right to join: see *Murphy* v. *Stewart* [1973] I.R. 97. For further criticism of the judicial recognition of the right to dissociate, based on the Hohfeldian distinction between "rights", and "freedoms", see Redmond, "Towards an Hohfeldian View of the Rights and Freedoms in the Irish Constitution" (1979-80) *D.U.L.J.* 52 at p. 55.

⁵⁰ See the remarks of Henchy J. in *Becton Dickinson & Co. Ltd.* v. *Lee* [1973] I.R. 1 at 47–48. Though see *infra*, pp. 31–33.

⁵¹ Judgment handed down on August 13, 1981 and reported at [1981] I.R.L.R. 408. See Forde, "The 'Closed Shop' Case" (1982) 11 *I.L.J.* 1; von Prondzynski, "Freedom of Association and the Closed Shop: the European Perspective" (1982) 41 *C.L.J.* 256; Whyte, "The European Convention on Human Rights and the Closed Shop" (1981) 75 *Gazette of the Incorporated Law Society of Ireland* 237.

workers who objected on reasonable grounds to joining a trade union.

The European Court of Human Rights, in a judgment marked by caution and restraint, held that Article 11 did afford some protection to the right to dissociate.[52] However, the Court was not prepared to consider the effect of Article 11 on the closed shop system in general but instead confined its attention to the issues raised by the application before it. Here existing employees had been dismissed for refusing to join particular trade unions and the Court, while conceding that compulsion to join a particular trade union might not always be contrary to the Convention, took the view that this amounted to a violation of the applicant's rights not to be compelled to join a trade union or association under Article 11. The Court continued by suggesting that the restriction of the applicants' choice of unions also infringed Article 11: "An individual does not enjoy the right to freedom of association if in reality the freedom of action or choice which remains available to him is either non-existent or so reduced as to be of no practical value."[53] The implications of this line of reasoning for industrial relations in Ireland are very significant. In particular, it suggests that, though workers may be compelled to become trade unionists, their freedom to select the union of their choice must be respected. This calls into question the validity of the practice of requiring potential employees to join specified trade unions as a pre-condition to obtaining employment, though it is arguable that it merely anticipates a similar decision by Irish courts, given recent Supreme Court pronouncements on waiver of constitutional rights.[54]

The Court strengthened still further the right to dissociate by reading Article 11 in the light of Articles 9 and 10, which protect freedom of belief and freedom of expression respectively. The Court was of the opinion that the protection of personal opinion afforded by Articles 9 and 10 was also one of the purposes of association as guaranteed by Article 11. Consequently, it was contrary to that Article to exert pressure of the kind applied to the applicants in order to compel the applicants to join a trade union contrary to their convictions.

The European Social Charter and the International Labour Organisation's Conventions Nos. 87 and 98 are silent on this point of the legitimacy of the closed shop, though in relation to I.L.O.

---

[52] A decision anticipated by the Commission in the case of *X* v. *Belgium*, Application 4072/69, Yearbook, vol. 13, p. 708. And yet *cf.* the subsequent decision of the Court in the case of *Albert and Le Compte* v. *Belgium* (1983) Series A, no. 58; 5 E.H.R.R. 533, where the Court held that, on the facts of the case, there was no reason to determine whether the Convention recognises the freedom not to associate. Does this mean, by implication, that the decision in *Young, James and Webster* still leaves the matter open?
[53] Judgment of the Court, para. 56.
[54] See *infra*, pp. 31-33. *Quaere* whether current legislative policy with regard to formation of unions is compatible with this principle of freedom of choice.

Convention No. 87, the Committee of Experts did say that it required the possibility of trade union pluralism to remain open.[55]

Finally, it should be noted that the right to dissociate, like all constitutional rights, is a qualified right only,[56] and may be regulated in the public interest, though such legislation cannot go so far as to deny freedom for the exercise of that right.[57] Arguably, therefore, non-unionists might be obliged to contribute financially to the negotiating union, as is the practice in the United States.[58] Conversely, non-unionists might be deemed not to be entitled to benefits negotiated by unions for their members. Casey concluded, however, that the legal position in Ireland of such a practice would entail great practical difficulties for the employer and ran counter to the tradition among trade unions of representing all workers in a particular employment and not merely those who are "in benefit" trade union members.[59]

In summary, therefore, the reasoning of the Supreme Court in *Educational Co. of Ireland Ltd.* v. *Fitzpatrick (No. 2)* and *Meskell* v. *C.I.E.* prohibits the imposition of a closed shop on existing employees. The practice of requiring prospective employees to join specified unions is not affected by these decisions but may be contrary to our international obligations and cannot be guaranteed immunity from constitutional attack in all cases.

Right to have one's union recognised

Collective bargaining presupposes that both unions and employers are willing to bargain collectively. If an employer is willing to bargain with a particular union then the employer is said to recognise that union. It is generally recognised that "an essential prerequisite for an effective and harmonious system of collective bargaining is the recognition of the right of trade unions to represent employees."[60] Most employers do recognise the trade unions, or some of them, that their employees have joined, realizing that more is to be gained in terms of efficiency and satisfaction, when the employees, through their union representative, have some say in the determination of their terms and conditions. An important question, therefore, in the absence of any general statutory provision on recognition,[61] is whether the Constitu-

---

[55] See *General Survey on the application of the Conventions on Freedom of Association and on the Right to Organise and Collective Bargaining*, Report 3, Part 4b (1973) at p. 85.
[56] See Casey, *(1972) 7 Ir. Jur (n.s.)* 1 at pp. 15–16. Though *cf.* de Blaghd, (1974) 108 *I.L.T.S.J.* 71 at p. 84.
[57] See Robinson and Temple-Lang, "The Constitution and the Right to Reinstatement after Wrongful Dismissal" (1977) 71 *Gazette of the Incorporated Law Society of Ireland* 78.
[58] Though *cf.* Kingsmill Moore J. in *Educational Co. of Ireland* v. *Fitzpatrick* [1961] I.R. 345 at 395.
[59] (1972) 21 *I.C.L.Q.* 699 at pp. 708–710.
[60] *Industrial Relations in Northern Ireland* Report of the Review Body 1971–1974 (Belfast, 1974) p. 59.
[61] Casey, in an article in (1972) 7 *Ir. Jur. (n.s.)* 1 entitled "Reform of Collective Bargaining Law", concludes, at pp. 7–8 thereof, that Article 40.6.1°(iii) would not give rise to a right to bargain collectively, because of the practical difficulties involved, but he did consider that the Oireachtas could create a statutory duty to negotiate.

tion guarantees workers the right to have their union recognised for the purposes of collective bargaining.

In *Federation of Irish Rail and Road Workers* v. *Great Southern Railway Co.*,[62] the plaintiff union sought an order by way of injunction, *mandamus*, or otherwise, to compel the defendant unions, who represented other workers of the defendant company, to enter into negotiations for a new agreement governing conditions of service of employees, or alternatively, to compel the defendant company to enter into negotiations with the plaintiff union, without the concurrence of the defendant unions. Gavan Duffy J. granted the plaintiff union a declaration that it was a trade union representative of railway employees within the meaning of section 55 of the Railways Act 1924,[63] but held that he was unable to grant it any relief entitling it to enter into negotiations with either the defendant union or the defendant company.

It would appear from this case, therefore, that unions do not have a constitutional right to enter into negotiations. It must be pointed out that the Constitution was not cited before Gavan Duffy J. and consequently the decision may not be of much weight. In *Abbott and Whelan* v. *I.T.G.W.U. and the Southern Health Board*,[64] however, McWilliam J. in the High Court ruled that the Constitution does not protect a right to have one's trade union recognised.

The plaintiffs, who were employees of the defendant Board, resigned from the I.T.G.W.U. and joined the A.T.G.W.U., being dissatisfied with the former union. The ensuing inter-union dispute was referred to the Disputes Committee of the I.C.T.U., which decided that the A.T.G.W.U. should not organise or seek to represent members concerned in the dispute and should actively encourage them to resume membership of the I.T.G.W.U. In the interim period a trade dispute had arisen between a member of the A.T.G.W.U. and the Southern Health Board. The defendant Board refused to negotiate with the A.T.G.W.U. over this dispute because it feared that such a course of action would provoke the I.T.G.W.U. into taking industrial action. As a result of the Board's refusal to negotiate with the A.T.G.W.U., the plaintiffs commenced industrial action and also brought proceedings

---

[62] [1942] Ir. Jur. Rep. 33, and cited in *C.I.E.* v. *Darby* High Court, unreported, 16 January 1980.
[63] Which provides: "From and after the passing of this Act the rates of pay, hours of duty and other conditions of service of railway employees shall be regulated in accordance with agreements made or to be from time to time made between the trade union representatives of such employees of the one part and the railway companies and other persons by whom they are employed of the other part." For an interesting view of this section, see Labour Court Recommendation No. 371, reported in (1982) 1 *J.I.S.L.L.* 65. See also *infra*, p. 19.
[64] (1982) 1 *J.I.S.L.L.* 56. See Whyte, "The Right of Workers to Choose their Collective Bargaining Agents" (1981) 75 *Gazette of the Incorporated Law Society of Ireland* 53. See also Labour Court Recommendations nos. 5962 and 6021 reported in (1982) 1 *J.I.S.L.L.* at pp. 101 and 92 respectively. For an interesting contrast to the decision in *Abbot and Whelan*, see *Re Service Employees' International Union, Local 204 and Broadway Manor Nursing Home* (1984) 4 D.L.R. (4th) 231.

in the High Court claiming, *inter alia*, an order restraining the defendants from interfering with the exercise of the plaintiffs' rights to join the trade union of their choice and to be represented by such union in the conduct of negotiations concerning wages and conditions of employment.

McWilliam J. rejected the view that workers had a constitutional right to select their negotiating unit:

> ". . . the suggestion in the pleadings that there is a constitutional right to be represented by a union in the conduct of negotiations with employers has not been pursued and, in my opinion, could not be sustained. There is no duty placed on any employer to negotiate with any particular citizen or body of citizens."[65]

Nor was the Southern Health Board obliged to negotiate with the A.T.G.W.U. in order to respect fully the plaintiffs' right to dissociate.[66] With reference to clause 47(d) of the I.C.T.U. Constitution, McWilliam J. felt that he was not obliged to consider the constitutionality of this clause under the circumstances, but he did state that ". . . there may be a distinction between placing a statutory embargo upon any person doing or refraining from doing something and a voluntary agreement between parties that they will or will not do something which they are entitled to do or not to do at their discretion."[67]

McWilliam J. held that it followed from the decision of the Supreme Court in *Murphy* v. *Stewart*[68] that the refusal of the I.T.G.W.U. to consent to the transfer of its former members to the A.T.G.W.U. did not infringe the constitutional rights of the plaintiffs, even where, as in the present case, the transferee union had received the workers into membership. This last factor constituted an essential difference between this case and *Murphy* v. *Stewart*, and consequently McWilliam J. felt obliged to consider the relevance of the absence of the facility to negotiate on the plantiffs' position. He concluded, however, that the A.T.G.W.U. had as little right as the I.T.G.W.U. to negotiate with the Board and that there was nothing unconstitutional in one union endeavouring to obtaining better terms for its members than those

---

[65] *Ibid.* at p. 59. A view which he had earlier expressed during the course of an application by former members of the I.T.G.W.U. seeking an injunction restraining that union from entering into negotiation with Telecommunications Ltd. without informing the company as to the number of employees represented by the union – see the *Irish Times*, November 20, 1979. See also *Dublin Colleges A.S.A.* v. *City of Dublin V.E.C.* (1982) 1 *J.I.S.L.L.* 73; *Inspector of Taxes Association* v. *Minister for the Public Service* High Court, unreported, 24 March 1983. These decisions were anticipated by Walsh J. in *E.I. Co. Ltd.* v. *Kennedy* [1968] I.R. 69, wherein he stated, at 89; "In law an employer is not obliged to meet anybody as the representative of his workers, nor indeed is he obliged to meet the worker himself for the purpose of discussing any demand which the worker may take." A similar approach was also taken by the Jamaican courts in *Banton* v. *Alcoa Minerals of Jamaica Ltd.* (1971) 17 W.I.R. 275.
[66] *Ibid.*, p. 60.
[67] *Ibid.*, p. 60.
[68] [1973] I.R. 79. See *supra*, pp. 5–7.

obtained by any other union, whether by obtaining special negotiation rights or otherwise. Consequently the plaintiffs' claim failed.

It would appear, therefore, that Article 40.6.1°(iii) does not guarantee workers the right to be represented by the union of their choice. This statement must be qualified, however, by reference to Ireland's obligations under the European Convention on Human Rights.

From the decisions of the European Court of Human Rights in *National Belgian Police Union* v. *Belgium*,[69] *Swedish Engine Drivers Union* v. *Sweden*,[70] and *Schmidt and Dahlstrom* v. *Sweden*,[71] it would appear that freedom of association under the Convention includes the right to have one's union make representations on one's behalf, though not the right to compel employers to negotiate with that union. However, the right to represent one's members cannot be regarded as a blanket right to represent them in all situations – arguably a distinction can be drawn between representing members in relation to individual grievances, which is protected by Article 11 of the European Convention, and representing members in negotiations on general terms and conditions of employment which may not be so protected. It is interesting to note that such a distinction has been recognised by the Labour Court in a number of recommendations.[72] And the Employment Appeals Tribunal has held that the denial of trade union representation to an employee facing disciplinary proceedings in relation to allegations of a serious nature, *e.g.* theft, is an "unfair industrial practice".[73]

It is submitted, therefore, that there is no authority supporting the proposition that the constitutional guarantee of freedom of association includes the right to select one's negotiating unit, and it would appear to be open to employers and trade unions to agree that the employer would negotiate with certain designated unions only, on terms and conditions of employment. Individual workers may have the right to select the union with whom they wish to associate[74] and may even insist that the union represent them in relation to their own individual grievances, but it would appear that they have no constitutional right to have their chosen union participating in collective bargaining with management.

---

[69] Judgment of the Court delivered on October 27, 1975; 1 E.H.R.R. 578.
[70] Judgment of the Court delivered on February 6, 1976; 1 E.H.R.R. 617.
[71] Judgment of the Court delivered on February 6, 1976; 1 E.H.R.R. 637.
[72] See Recommendations Nos. 381, 5070 and 5338, reported in (1982) 1 *J.I.S.L.L.* at pp. 84, 110 and 95 respectively.
[73] *Devlin* v. *Player Wills (Ireland) Ltd.* U.D. 90/1978. In this context it is worth noting that making representations on behalf of individual workers arguably does not fall within the scope of s. 6(1) of the Trade Union Act 1941 as it does not amount to the carrying on of negotiations for "the fixing of wages or other conditions of employment". See *infra*, pp. 50–51.
[74] See Henchy J.'s reference, in *Becton Dickinson & Co. Ltd.* v. *Lee* [1973] I.R. 1 at 48, to a "workers' constitutionally guaranteed right to choose whom he shall join in union with." See also Recommendation No. 371 of the Labour Court, reported in (1982) 1 *J.I.S.L.L.* 65.

While the courts have held that there is no legal obligation to bargain with a trade union they have held that a dispute over whether a trade union be recognised is a trade dispute within the meaning of that phrase as defined by the Trade Disputes Act 1906 and the Industrial Relations Act 1946.[75] Industrial action can, therefore, be taken in contemplation or furtherance of such a dispute without incurring the risk of civil liability. This is significant because studies of trade union growth in Britain reveal that the size of a union and its willingness to engage in industrial action has been the major factor encouraging employers to recognise a union.[76]

A rare example of the direct use of the law in this area is found in section 55 of the Railways Act 1924, as amended by section 46 of the Transport Act 1950, which provides that the rates of pay, *etc.* of C.I.E. employees are to be regulated in accordance with agreements entered into between C.I.E. and appropriate trade unions.[77] The provisions confer a wide discretion on C.I.E. in selecting the unions with which it will negotiate but the discretion is not absolute. C.I.E. must consider the appropriateness of the organisation and the desirability of consulting it. If C.I.E. acts honestly, in good faith and on reasonable grounds, the courts will not interfere. This is well illustrated by *R. v. Post Office, ex parte Association of Scientific, Technical and Managerial Staffs (Telephone Contracts Officers' Section)*,[78] where the union seeking recognition only represented a small number of employees, its main membership being in a different industry. The other recognised unions objected to A.S.T.M.S. being recognised and the Post Office took the view that the intrusion of A.S.T.M.S. would upset stable collective bargaining arrangements. The Court of Appeal refused to grant relief to A.S.T.M.S., commenting that, in their opinion, the recognition of A.S.T.M.S. would fragment, complicate and conflict with the existing structure and would thus be detrimental to orderly and effective collective bargaining. It would appear from this decision that a union, denied recognition by such a public corporation, would have to show, in order to succeed, that its members' interests were not being protected adequately by the existing collective bargaining structure, and even then the Court may find that the corporation's decision was reasonable in the light of other circumstances.

There are two situations where important trade union rights hinge on the question of whether the union has been recognised. First, section 11(6) of the Worker Participation (State Enterprises) Act 1977,

---

[75] *Becton Dickinson & Co. Ltd. v. Lee* [1973] I.R. 1; *Beetham v. Trinidad Cement Ltd.* [1960] A.C. 132.
[76] Bain, *Trade Union Growth and Recognition* Royal Commission on Trade Unions and Employers' Associations Research Paper No. 6 (H.M.S.O., 1967) pp. 68 *et seq.*
[77] On which see *T.S.S.A. v. C.I.E.* [1965] I.R. 180.
[78] [1981] I.C.R. 76. Paragraph 11 of Schedule 1 to the Post Office Act 1969 provided that it should be the duty of the Post Office to seek consultations with any organisation "appearing to it to be appropriate."

which defines the bodies qualified to nominate candidates for election as worker directors, provides that such a body must be recognised for the purposes of collective bargaining negotiations. Secondly, the operation of the provisions of the Protection of Employment Act 1977 as to compulsory consultation on collective redundancies hinges on there being, on the part of the employer, a practice of conducting collective bargaining negotiations with a union.[79]

Recognition disputes and the Labour Court

The Labour Court has always accepted that employers in general are under no legal obligation to enter into negotiations over pay and conditions of employment with their employees, either directly or through a trade union acting on their behalf.

> "The question whether it is desirable and expedient for employers to recognise workers' trade unions and negotiate with them [is] a matter not of legal obligation but of good industrial relations, general public policy and social morals."[80]

Where there has been no practice of trade union recognition and a union refers a dispute over recognition to the Court, the Court invariably recommends that, in the interests of promoting the best possible level of industrial relations, the employer should agree to negotiate a collective agreement with the union and agree to enter into meaningful negotiations forthwith.[81] The Court will recommend this even where the trade union in dispute has not secured a majority of the employees in membership. Different considerations arise however if the employer does recognise a trade union and is resisting the attempts of another union to secure recognition. The Labour Court's consistent view here has been that, while it would be desirable on grounds of convenience that there should be only one body representing the staff in regulations with management, the right of an employee to be represented by the organisation of his own choice ought not to be restricted unless there are strong reasons for imposing some limitation. "The convenience of the employer is not in itself a sufficiently strong reason."[82]

In *Hospitals' Trust Ltd. and Workers' Union of Ireland*,[83] the union was seeking negotiation rights on behalf of "rather less than 1/3rd" of

---

[79] S. 1.

[80] *Caltex (Ireland) Ltd. and Irish Transport and General Workers' Union* L.C.R. 500 (1951), para. 4. See also *Cork Milling Co. Ltd. and Amalgamated Transport and General Workers' Union* L.C.R. 358 (1949), para. 6.

[81] See the cases reported in volumes 1, 2 and 3 of the *Journal of the Irish Society for Labour Law*.

[82] *Per* the Labour Court in *Hospitals Trust Ltd. and Workers' Union of Ireland* (1982) 1 *J.I.S.L.L.* 84 at p. 86. See also *Royal Liver Friendly Society and Irish Liver Assurance Employees' Union* (1983) 2 *J.I.S.L.L.* 118 at pp. 119–120.

[83] (1982) 1 *J.I.S.L.L.* 84.

the total number of office workers employed by the company. Most of the employees, including some W.U.I. members, belonged to a House Association with which management indicated they would be prepared to negotiate. The company, however, was not prepared to negotiate with a second body which represented a minority of the staff. The Court in its recommendation referred to the "marked difference" in the character of the two organisations.

> "One is a house association, whose ability and effectiveness in negotiation may be thought to be affected by the limited membership and by the fact that they would be represented in negotiations by persons in the same employment and therefore not sufficiently independent of management. The other is an ordinary trade union, able to place the resources and experience of a trade union at the services of its members in this employment as in other employments."[84]

The Court went on to say that the choice between the two was a matter for the employees to make "in the light of what they consider to be their relative advantages." If the number of employees who decided to join the union was "very small" then, "though it might nevertheless be wise for the management to meet their representatives, negotiations could hardly be of much practical value and the management might reasonably object to the loss of time and inconvenience they would cause." If, however, "any considerable number" had joined, then the union would have "a clear right to be heard and to receive such consideration as the weight of its members and its arguments might warrant." The Court accordingly recommended that the Company should recognise and negotiate with the union, in addition to the house association, on condition that the union demonstrated that a "substantial proportion" of the staff desired to be represented by it and not the association.[85]

The Court is reluctant, however, to disturb existing collective bargaining arrangements that have been working satisfactorily. In *Roadstone Ltd. and A.S.T.M.S.*[86], the union was in dispute over its right to negotiate on behalf of certain executive employees employed by the company. The company already negotiated with twelve trade unions, including two which had a substantial number of the clerical and executive staff in membership. The Court pointed out, at the outset of

---

[84] At p. 86.
[85] See however *Arthur Guinness, Son & Co. Ltd. and Workers' Union of Ireland* L.C.R. 1853 (1965) where only 11.9% of the senior foremen, in respect of whom the union sought negotiating rights, were members of the union; *Pantry Franchise (Ireland) Ltd. and Irish Transport and General Workers' Union* (1982) 1 *J.I.S.L.L.* 95 where union membership represented only 7% of the entire workforce employed by the company.
[86] (1982) 1 *J.I.S.L.L.* 105. See also *Bimeda Chemicals Ltd. and A.U.E.W. (T.A.S.S.)* L.C.R. 9679 (1985).

its recommendation, that this case did not involve the principle of recognition "as the company is perfectly willing to have the salaries and conditions of these employees determined through collective bargaining with an already recognised trade union." What was in issue before the Court was the need to balance the desire of some members of the executive grades to be represented through a different union to other workers and the desire of the company to limit the number of unions with which it must negotiate. The Court referred to the fact that the unions which represented other employees in the same grades were "fully independent and effective instruments for representing the interests of these employees", noted that having to deal with another union would pose difficulties for the company and concluded that it could not recommend that the company recognise a third union to represent the same grade of workers.

In *Dehymeats Ltd and A.U.E.W. (T.A.S.S.)*[87] the union was in dispute with the company over negotiating rights for three of the technical staff. The company already recognised I.T.G.W.U., in respect of factory employees, and N.E.E.T.U., in respect of craftsmen, and maintained that, in the event of the technical staff deciding to join a trade union, the appropriate union was I.T.G.W.U. A.U.E.W. (T.A.S.S.) referred the matter to the Labour Court under section 20(1) of the Industrial Relations Act 1969 (thus agreeing in advance to accept the terms of the recommendation). At the hearing the company argued that because of its size (50 employees) two unions were more than adequate to meet the employees' needs and demands. The Court considered that the interests of the three employees concerned could be equally well served by being in membership of I.T.G.W.U. as it would be by being in membership of A.U.E.W. (T.A.S.S.). The Court therefore recommended that if the three employees wished to be represented by a trade union it should be the I.T.G.W.U. and that the company should recognise the I.T.G.W.U. for negotiating purposes for them.

Another case where the Court did not recommend recognition was *North Western Health Board and North West Hospitals' Employees Association.*[88] The employees concerned in the claim were non-nursing personnel employed by the Board. They had resigned from membership of a union with which it was the Board's normal practice to negotiate, and now had formed an association. The Association then wrote to the Board seeking the right to negotiate on behalf of the employees that it

---

[87] L.C.R. 9142 (1984). *Cf. Krups Engineering Ltd. and Association of Scientific, Technical and Managerial Staffs* L.C.R. 9385 (1984). Here the union had recruited 42% of the salaried staff grade but the company resisted the claim for recognition on the grounds that it already recognised two unions, one of which (I.T.G.W.U.) had members in that grade, and that recognition of a third union would have an adverse effect on industrial relations stability. The Court, on the understanding that the I.T.G.W.U. had no objection to the union recruiting in the salaried staff grade, recommended, however, that the company recognise the union on behalf of its members in that grade.

[88] (1982) 1 *J.I.S.L.L.* 92.

represented. The Board refused, and their decision so to do was upheld by the Labour Court, who commented that the Association did not command the necessary resources to give adequate representation to the workers concerned. The Court felt that it would be "far more conducive" to good industrial relations if the employees concerned made a more determined effort to realise the full potential of their position as union members in an effectively organised section.

Right to take industrial action[89]

The Irish courts have not yet considered whether the constitutional guarantee of freedom of association also provides constitutional protection for activities undertaken in furtherance of the lawful objects of the association. It could be argued that freedom of association, if it is to be a meaningful freedom, must include the freedom to strike. In the absence of binding conciliation and arbitration, the ability to strike is the only substantial economic weapon available to employees.[90] Without it the association, as a practical matter, is a "barren and useless thing". As Galligan J. said in *Re Service Employees' International Union and Broadway Manor Nursing Home*:[91] "Freedom of association includes within it the sanction that makes it a worthwhile freedom. If that sanction is removed the freedom is valueless because there is no effective means to force an employer to recognise the workers' representatives and bargain with them."[92] If this reasoning were to be adopted here, an obvious implication would be that any legislative restriction on the ability to take industrial action would have to be justified in terms of the proviso to Article 40.6.1°(iii).[93]

This reasoning, however, was not accepted by the Judicial Committee of the Privy Council in *Collymore* v. *Attorney General*,[94] a case in which a law of Trinidad and Tobago abolishing strikes was upheld. There the view was taken that freedom of association meant no more than "freedom to enter into consensual arrangements to promote the common interest objects of the associating group"[95] and, therefore, an Act which abridged the freedom to strike did not leave the right of free Association empty of content. This was also the view of Reed J. in *Public Service Alliance of Canada* v. *The Queen in right of Canada*.[96] She said:

---

[89] See *infra*, pp. 246–248.
[90] See Lord Wright in *Crofter Hand Woven Harris Tweed Co. Ltd.* v. *Veitch* [1942] A.C. 435, 463: "The right of workmen to strike is an essential element in the principle of collective bargaining."
[91] (1984) 4 D.L.R. (4th) 231, a decision of the Ontario High Court of Justice. *Cf.* the subsequent decision of the British Columbia Court of Appeal, in *Dolphin Delivery Ltd.* v. *Retail etc. Union* (1984) 10 D.L.R. (4th) 198, which is critical of the reasoning in *Broadway Manor*.
[92] At 249. See also O'Leary J. at 284: "To take away an employee's ability to strike so seriously detracts from the benefits of the right to organise as to make [that right] virtually meaningless."
[93] As to which see *infra*, pp. 27–29.
[94] [1970] A.C. 538.
[95] At 547.
[96] (1984) 11 D.L.R. (4th) 337.

"In my view, the clause 'freedom of association' guarantees to trade unions the right to join together, to pool economic resources, to solicit other members, to choose their own internal organizational structures, to advocate to their employees and the public at large their views and not to suffer any prejudice or coercion by the employer or State because of such union activities. But it does not include the economic right to strike."[97]

This is reinforced somewhat by reference to the fact that the guarantee of freedom of association does not relate solely to trade unions. The guarantee is intended to protect the right of everyone to associate as they please and to form associations of all kinds "from political parties to hobby clubs".[98]

Right to participate in the decision-making processes of the union

Before leaving this question of the *ratione materiae* of Article 40.6.1°(iii), reference must be made to the decision of the High Court in *Rodgers* v. *I.T.G.W.U.*[99] which is authority for the proposition that the right to join (*sic*) and form associations has, as a corollary, the right to take part in the democratic processes provided by the union and, in particular, the right to take part in the decision-making processes within the rules of the trade union. This case arose out of a decision of the I.T.G.W.U. Dockers' Section, No. 5 Branch, Cork to retire compulsorily members of the section reaching 65 years of age. The Docks Section Committee decided to recommend to the Docks Section a resolution for the introduction of a compulsory retirement pension scheme at the age of 65. This resolution was adopted at a meeting convened to discuss the terms of the national wages agreement. The plaintiff, who was nearing retirement age, arrived at the meeting after it had begun and after this resolution had been adopted. He had no notice of the fact that the issue of compulsory retirement was to be raised at that meeting. The union subsequently informed the plaintiff's regular employer that dockers would not accept employment from his foreman, the plaintiff, as the latter had refused to comply with the provisions of the retirement scheme. As a result of this, the plaintiff's solicitors wrote to the union threatening the institution of proceedings in the High Court. Following on from this letter, a general meeting of the Docks Section was summoned to discuss the pension scheme. The Court found that the plaintiff was aware of the fact that it was proposed to discuss the compulsory retirement scheme at this meeting. Nevertheless, the plaintiff failed to attend. A resolution relating to the introduction of the scheme was again put to the union members at this

---

[97] At 358.
[98] *Per* Esson J. in *Dolphin Delivery Ltd.* v. *Retail etc. Union* (1984) 10 D.L.R. (4th) 198, 209.
[99] High Court, unreported, 15 March 1978.

meeting and, after debate, was accepted by an overwhelming majority. The union subsequently informed the plaintiff's employer that the dockers would not work under him after a specified date.

The plaintiff then brought a case to the High Court seeking a declaration that the decision was invalid and an injunction restraining the union from implementing it. He argued, first, that his fundamental right to natural justice and fair procedures in relation to meetings of the Docks Section of the defendant union was violated because he was not given notice of the fact that the question of compulsory retirement was to be discussed at either meeting; and secondly, that the decision to enforce a rule of compulsory retirement infringed his constitutional right to work. In the context of the present discussion the authors will confine themselves to an examination of the decision on the first claim.

Finlay P. (as he then was) held that it was "a necessary corollary to the right to join and become a member of a trade union that the right must extend to taking part in the democratic processes provided by it and in particular to taking part in the decision-making processes within the rules of trade union."[1] In this case, the decision arrived at during the first meeting was invalid because the plaintiff was not made aware of the fact that it was proposed to discuss compulsory retirement and therefore his right to participate in the decision-making processes of the union was infringed. However, the same could not be said of the decision reached at the second meeting, for Finlay P. was satisfied that there was no want of fair procedures in the method of summoning and announcing the meeting of the 3rd August. Consequently the plaintiff's claim on this ground failed.[2]

An interesting feature of the judgment of Finlay P. is that he appears to suggest that the plaintiff's right to participate in the decision-making processes of the union could be restricted by the terms of the union rule book:

> "It would clearly be open to a trade union so to formulate its rules so that in regard to certain matters, or even in regard to all matters, that decision making would be in the hands of the delegates or elected officers and specified members of the union and a person who joined under those terms could not complain of being excluded in accordance with the rules of the union which he joined from the making of any particular decision."[3]

In this case, however, the union rule book did not so restrict the plaintiff's right.

The view that a citizen's constitutional rights might be limited by what is, in effect, the unilateral imposition of restrictions by a second party is surprising and led to suggestions that this might be implied

---
[1] *Ibid.* at p. 14.
[2] The plaintiff also failed to establish that the scheme violated his constitutional right to work.
[3] *Ibid.* at p. 15.

support for the waiver of constitutional rights theory.[4] It is submitted that this is not so. First, it is clear from the latest pronouncements of the Supreme Court on the matter that a citizen's constitutional rights can only be waived if the citizen voluntarily and knowingly consents to such a waiver.[5] The judgment of Finlay P. does not suggest that the validity of restrictions in the rule book on constitutional rights depends on the free and full consent of the potential member to such restrictions being obtained. In fact the tenor of the remarks cited above appears to suggest that the only option open to a potential member who objects to the restriction of decision-making powers to a handful of individuals is either not to join the union – which hardly says much for the effect of the constitutional "right to join" – or to join and accept the consequences. Secondly, it is submitted, with respect, that there is a more serious flaw in this judgment, which goes to the root of the finding that union members have a constitutional right to participate in the decision-making processes of the union. Finlay P. based this right on the right of citizens to join established unions, but it is clear from the decisions of the Supreme Court in *Tierney* v. *A.S.W.* and *Murphy* v. *Stewart* that citizens do not have a right to join established unions, except, possibly, in cases where membership of the union is a pre-requisite to obtaining employment in a particular firm.

If one does not have a constitutional right to join a union, then, *a fortiori*, one does not have a constitutional right to participate in the decision-making processes of that union. If an individual is accepted into membership by a union, then he has contractual rights against that union, which rights are contained in the rule book. The right to participate in the decision-making processes of the union is, therefore, a contractual right and not a constitutional right.

Rejection of this part of Finlay P.'s judgment does not mean, however, that union members do not have a right to fair procedures. The right to natural justice at common law exists independently of any concept of freedom of association and in at least three Irish cases it has been held that procedures relating to the expulsion of members must comply with these rules[6] – in other words, fair procedures must be adopted.

FREEDOM OF ASSOCIATION: THE QUALIFICATIONS

Thus far we have been examining the elements of the constitutional freedom of association guaranteed by Article 40.6.1°(iii). It is now proposed to examine those circumstances in which that freedom may be lawfully restricted.

---

[4] Kerr, (1978) *D.U.L.J.* 61 at p. 63.
[5] *G.* v. *An Bord Uchtala* [1980] I.R. 32. See *infra*, pp. 31–32.
[6] *Kilkenny* v. *I.E.F.U.* (1939) Ir. Jur. Rep. 52; *N.E.E.T.U.* v. *McConnell* (1983) 2 *J.I.S.L.L.* 97; *Connolly* v. *McConnell* [1983] I.R. 172. See also de Blaghd, (1973) 107 *I.L.T.S.J.* 11.

Article 40.6.1°(iii)

The first qualification is expressly provided for by the Constitution itself. After establishing freedom for the right to form associations, Article 40.6.1°(iii) goes on to provide: "Laws may be enacted for the regulation and control in the public interest of the exercise of the foregoing right." Such laws, however, shall contain no political, religious, or class discrimination.[7]

This constitutional proviso was considered for the first time in the case of *N.U.R.* v. *Sullivan*.[8] The background to this case was as follows: the Government proposed, in Part III of the Trade Union Act 1941, to establish a trade union tribunal with power to grant a determination that a specified union or unions alone should have the right to organise workers or a particular class. The I.T.G.W.U. applied to the tribunal for a determination that it should have the sole right to organise workmen employed in the road passenger service of C.I.E. Before the hearing of such application, the N.U.R. and several workmen affected by the application brought an action in the High Court, claiming a declaration that Part III of the 1941 Act was unconstitutional because it violated Article 40.6.

In the High Court, Gavan Duffy J. held that the 1941 Act did not violate any provision of the Constitution. In relation to the Constitution, the plaintiffs had argued that the Act provided for the conscription of labour, contrary to the guarantee of freedom to form associations or unions; that the Government's power of regulation and control, conferred by Article 40.6.1°(iii), did not include a power to veto the exercise of the right of association; that the Act involved political discrimination in as much as the organising trade union might apply part of its general funds in furtherance of political objects, and that this discrimination was unconstitutional; and, finally that the Act delegated the determination of the public interest to a subordinate body, whereas the Constitution had conferred regulatory powers on the Oireachtas.

In the opinion of Gavan Duffy J. the Act was a regulatory one within the scope of the proviso to Article 40.6.1°(iii). In answer to the plaintiffs' first contention, he held that the fact that the legislation made some unions more attractive to workers than others did not make it unconstitutional. Although he did not expressly say so, by implication he appeared to reject the view that Part III of the 1941 Act provided for conscription of labour. In reply to the second contention, Gavan Duffy J. took the view that the power to regulate included the power to veto, basing his opinion on American case law,

---

[7] Article 40.6.2°.
[8] [1947] I.R. 77. It was also considered, in the context of registration of political parties, in *Loftus* v. *Attorney General* [1979] I.R. 221 at 241-2. See Anon, "The Constitutionality of the Trade Union Act 1941" (1942) 76 *I.L.T.S.J.* 15.

particularly *U.S.A.* v. *Hill*,⁹ and on the textual arrangement of freedom of association together with the right of assembly in Article 40.6.2°, it being accepted that the Government might veto the exercise of the right of assembly. The third objection failed because there was no trace of political discrimination in the Act, and the court could not invalidate a measure in advance because of an anticipated impropriety in its administration. Lastly, he held that the Constitution did not forbid the Oireachtas from delegating the power of determining the public interest to the tribunal, so that the fourth objection failed also.

The plaintiffs appealed against this decision to the Supreme Court and succeeded. Murnaghan J., delivering the judgment of the Court, began by emphasising the constitutional limitations on the power of the Oireachtas and the role of the courts in ensuring that these limitations were respected.¹⁰ Then, after quoting the relevant passages in Article 40.6.1°, he continued: "This language means that, subject to public order and morality, each citizen is free to associate with others of his choice for any object agreed upon by him and them."¹¹ The qualification to this, contained in Article 40.6.1°(iii), did not protect Part III of the Trade Union Act 1941, which purported to limit the right of the citizen to join certain trade unions, because the Act did not control the exercise of freedom of association, but denied it altogether. *U.S.A.* v. *Hill* was distinguished on the grounds that the American Constitution had conferred a power on Congress to regulate inter-state commerce, whereas, in the present case, the Irish Constitution had conferred a right on Irish citizens. Bearing in mind that the Irish Constitution then conferred a power on the Oireachtas to regulate the exercise of this right, it is difficult to see how the distinction can be drawn between the two jurisdictions.

The decision of the Supreme Court in *N.U.R.* v. *Sullivan* was criticised for being crude and unsophisticated and led to predictions that the reasoning involved might eventually be rejected by the present Supreme Court.¹² These predictions would appear to have been fulfilled in *P.M.P.S. Ltd. and Moore* v. *Attorney General*.¹³ The plaintiffs, a limited company and one of its shareholders, argued that the Industrial and Provident Societies (Amendment) Act 1978 infringed, *inter alia*, their constitutional guarantee of freedom of

---

⁹ (1918) 248 U.S. 420.

¹⁰ To be contrasted with the approach of Gavan Duffy J. at first instance who stressed the limitations on the powers of the courts in relation to matters of policy, this being "emphatically" within the legislative domain.

¹¹ [1947] I.R. 77 at 101.

¹² See Whyte, *loc. cit.* at p. 67; Kelly, *The Irish Constitution* 2nd edn. (Dublin, 1984) at p. 597. For general commentary on the decision see Casey, "Reform of Collective Bargaining Law" (1972) 7 *Ir. Jur (n.s.)* at pp. 11–15. See also the Report of the Committee on the Constitution (1967) (Prl. 9817) at p. 42, for a reference to proposed legislation which was intended to circumvent this decision. This legislation (the Trade Union Bill 1966) was never enacted, however.

¹³ [1983] I.R. 339. See Whyte, (1983) 5 *D.U.L.J. (n.s.)* 273.

association because the effect of the legislation was to make it virtually impossible for the shareholders to associate together for the purpose of carrying on a banking business. This contention was rejected by the Supreme Court which stated, in a judgment delivered by O'Higgins C.J.:

> "Mr. Moore's right to associate with others has not been interfered with. The exercise of such a right is not prevented by a law limiting and controlling in the public interest what such an association may do. In this instance the law which is impugned does no more than to regulate what the Society or association may do and this is not an infringement of Article 40.6.1°(iii) of the Constitution."[14]

Bearing in mind the drastic effect which the 1978 Act had on the plaintiffs' activities,[15] a cogent argument could now be advanced in support of the validity of legislation akin to Part III of the Trade Union Act 1941.[16] It can certainly be argued that existing legislation which restricts union rights in the public interest is in a stronger position now as a result of the *P.M.P.S.* case.[17] However, this decision is not without its own difficulties. In particular the terse, almost perfunctory, nature of the judgment affords very little guidance as to the full extent of the State's regulatory powers and indeed suggests an excessively deferential attitude on the part of the courts to the Oireachtas in this matter. It is submitted that legislation which cannot reasonably be related to the public interest or which is arbitrary or capricious in its operation should not be afforded the protection of the proviso.[18] Beyond that, however, one can only speculate as to where the line may be drawn.

Constitutional rights of others

The second qualification of freedom of association is also furnished by the Constitution itself, though this time impliedly – that freedom can only be exercised in so far as it does not infringe the constitutional rights of others.

---

[14] *Ibid*. at 361–362.
[15] In the High Court, Mr. Moore had testified that the Society would have to wind down business and go into liquidation in the event of the legislation being upheld.
[16] Which did not force unions out of existence but merely prevented them acting on behalf of their members if some other union had obtained a Tribunal determination conferring upon it sole negotiation rights in relation to those members.
[17] For example, the Conspiracy and Protection of Property Act 1875, ss. 4, 5; the Merchant Shipping Act 1894, s. 225; the Post Office Act 1908, ss. 56, 57; the Garda Síochána Act 1924, s. 14; the Offences against the State Act 1939, s. 9; the Postal and Telecommunications Act 1983, s. 84; all of which impose restrictions on the taking of industrial action by certain categories of workers. Ss. 6 and 11 of the Trade Union Act 1941 would also benefit from this new approach in as much as they seek to regulate the activities of unauthorised trade unions, as would legislation enacted in the interests of national security, on which see *Aughey* v. *Ireland* High Court, unreported, 29 August 1985 at pp. 20–21 of Barrington J.'s judgment.
[18] *State (Lynch)* v. *Cooney* [1982] I.R. 337.

Generally

In *Crowley* v. *Ireland*,[19] McMahon J. stated:

"The character of an act depends on the circumstances in which it is done and the exercise of a constitutional right *for the purpose of infringing the constitutional rights of others* is an abuse of that right which, in my opinion, can be restrained by the courts."[20]

The right to work

In *Murphy* v. *Stewart*,[21] Walsh J. suggestion, *obiter*, that a union might not be allowed to refuse to admit a person to membership if this was done solely to prevent that person from exercising his or her right to work.[22] He said:

"... if the right to work was reserved exclusively to members of a trade union which held a monopoly in this field and the trade union was abusing the monopoly in such a way as to effectively prevent the exercise of a person's constitutional right to work, the question of compelling that union to accept the person concerned into membership (or, indeed, of breaking the monopoly) would fall to be considered for the purpose of vindicating the right to work."[23]

This begs the question as to what amounts to a right to work. Walsh J. did not elaborate on this, merely observing that the question of whether that right is being infringed must depend upon the particular circumstance of any given case. Indeed, though the right to work, or similar rights, have been referred to in a number of Irish cases,[24] it is submitted that it is still a vague, almost abstract, entity and, as such, constitutes an uncertain limitation on a union's power to determine membership. In *Rodgers* v. *I.T.G.W.U.*,[25] however, Finlay P. held, *inter alia*, that a compulsory retirement scheme did not infringe the plaintiff's right to work, so that it is arguable, by analogy, that a trade union can refuse to admit persons to, or retain members in,

---

[19] [1980] I.R. 102.
[20] At 110 (emphasis added). The deliberate infringement of a person's constitutional rights can, in certain circumstances, also amount to contempt of Court – see *State (Quinn)* v. *Ryan* [1965] I.R. 70.
[21] [1973] I.R. 97.
[22] If, however, the refusal is in pursuance of proper and *bona fide* trade union objectives, such as compliance with an I.C.T.U. Disputes Committee ruling, and has the incidental effect of interfering with the applicant's constitutional right to work then, clearly, different considerations apply. See Kerr and Whyte, "Trade Disputes and the Constitution" (1984) 6 *D.U.L.J. (n.s.)* 187.
[23] [1973] I.R. at 117.
[24] *Tierney* v. *A.S.W.* [1959] I.R. 354; *Murtagh Properties Ltd.* v. *Cleary* [1972] I.R. 330; *Landers* v. *Attorney General* (1975) 109 I.L.T.R. 1; *State (Gleeson)* v. *Minister for Defence* [1976] I.R. 280; *Moran* v. *Attorney General* [1976] I.R. 400; *Yeates* v. *Minister for Posts and Telegraphs* High Court, unreported, 21 February 1978; *Rodgers* v. *I.T.G.W.U.* High Court, unreported, 15 March 1978; *Gannon* v. *Duffy* High Court, unreported, 4 March 1983. See Whyte, *loc. cit.*, pp. 68–71.
[25] High Court, unreported, 15 March 1978.

membership in persuance of "proper and *bona fide*" trade union objectives.

Waiver and forfeiture

Finally, freedom of association is further qualified by the fact that it may be waived or forfeited by the individual citizen. The question of whether a citizen can waive his constitutional rights has only been finally decided in recent times.[26] Heretofore, members of the judiciary had suggested, in a number of *obiter dicta*, that constitutional rights might be legally waived,[27] but the issue was unsettled[28] until the decision in *G.* v. *An Bord Uchtála*,[29] which arose in the context of an unmarried mother's constitutional right to the custody of her child. Here, a majority of the Supreme Court[30] decided that it was possible to waive one's constitutional rights.

According to the Chief Justice, waiver required "a free consent on the part of the mother given in the full knowledge of the consequences which follow upon her placing her child for adoption."[31] A similar approach was adopted by Parke J., who made the additional point that one could not waive one's constitutional rights if such waiver infringed the constitutional rights of another.

The remaining judge of the majority on the Supreme Court – Walsh J. – stated that before any constitutional rights could be waived, there would have to be a "fully informed, free and willing surrender or an abandonment of these rights." He continued:

> "However, I am also of the opinion that such a surrender or abandonment may be established by her conduct when it is such as to warrant the clear and unambiguous inference that such was her fully informed, free and willing intention. In my view, a consent motivated by fear, stress or anxiety, or consent or conduct which is

---

[26] *G.* v. *An Bord Uchtála* [1980] I.R. 32. See McCann. "*G.* v. *An Bord Uchtála* – the best interests of the child and constitutional rights in adoption" (1979) 73 *Gazette of the Incorporated Law Society of Ireland* 203. See also Redmond, (1979–80) *D.U.L.J.* 104.

[27] In *Nicolau* v. *Attorney General* [1966] I.R. 567, Walsh J. suggested, at 644, that personal rights guaranteed by Article 40 might be surrendered, abdicated, or transferred by the person entitled to them; see also Henchy J.'s remarks in *Becton Dickinson & Co. Ltd* v. *Lee* [1973] I.R. 1 at 48; In both *Becton Dickinson* and *Murphy* v. *Stewart*, Walsh J. was prepared to assume that arrangements restricting or waiving constitutional rights were not unconstitutional. See also *Glover* v. *BLN Ltd.* [1973] I.R. 388, 425, where he expressed a similar sentiment.

[28] See Temple-Lang, "Private Law Aspects of the Constitution" (1972) 7 *Ir. Jur. (n.s.)* 257, where it is suggested that waiver of constitutional rights is contrary to public policy. For contrary opinion, *cf.* Robinson and Temple-Lang, *loc. cit.* at p. 79; Mathews, "Tort of Conspiracy in Irish Labour Law" (1973) 8 *Ir. Jur. (n.s.)* 252 at p. 266; Kelly, *op. cit.*, pp. 438–440.

[29] [1980] I.R. 32. See also *S.* v. *Eastern Health Board* High Court, unreported, 28 February 1979; *McC.* v. *An Bord Uchtála and St. Louis Adoption Society* [1982] I.L.R.M. 159; *McF.* v. *G.* [1983] I.L.R.M. 228.

[30] O'Higgins C.J., Walsh and Parke JJ. Henchy and Kenny JJ. did not have to consider this as they took the view that the unmarried mother had no constitutional right to her child.

[31] [1980] I.R. 32, 57.

dictated by poverty or other deprivations does not constitute a valid consent."[32]

He summarised the legal position thus:

"Before anybody may be said to have surrendered or abandoned his constitutional rights it must be shown that he is aware of what the rights are and of what he is doing. Secondly, the action taken must be such as could reasonably lead to the clear and unambiguous inference that such was the intention of the person who is alleged to have either surrendered or abandoned the constitutional rights."[33]

Germane to the topic under discussion is the suggestion of Walsh J. that consent to the waiver of rights induced by poverty or other deprivations will not be effective in law. Arguably, therefore, if a worker agrees to join a union in order to obtain employment, he may, at a later stage, reassert his constitutional right to dissociate from the union involved on the grounds that it was never validly waived. The implications of this for the legal position of closed shops in Ireland are significant – it calls into question the validity of closed shop agreements negotiated with prospective employees. It is submitted, however, that no other legal conclusion is possible, given the exalted status of constitutional rights in our legal policy. The decision in *G. v. An Bord Uchtála*, therefore, arguably complements the threat to this species of closed shop which stems from certain pronouncements of the European Court of Human Rights in *Young, James and Webster*.[34]

The possibility that constitutional rights might be forfeited by the citizen has been accepted by at least one member of the present Supreme Court – Henchy J. In his opinion, the failure of the respective plaintiffs in *State (Byrne) v. Frawley*,[35] *M. v. An Bord Uchtála*[36] and *Murphy v. Attorney General*[37] to exercise their constitutional rights resulted in the forfeiture of those rights.[38] In as much as forfeiture is based on acquiescence, it does not differ greatly from waiver of constitutional rights, which is based on consent, and indeed in many cases it may be difficult to know whether a litigant has waived his rights or forfeited them. However, it is submitted that the distinction is not without practical significance. Consider a situation similar to that which arose in *Becton Dickinson & Co. Ltd. v. Lee*,[39] where the workers had signed an agreement, prior to taking up employment, which, *inter*

---

[32] *Ibid.* at 74. Emphasis added.
[33] *Ibid.* at 80.
[34] See *supra*, pp. 13–14.
[35] [1978] I.R. 326.
[36] [1977] I.R. 287.
[37] [1982] I.R. 241.
[38] See also O'Higgins C.J. in *G. v. An Bord Uchtála* [1980] I.R. 32, 55; Butler J. in *State (Gleeson) v. Minister for Defence* [1976] I.R. 280, 289.
[39] [1973] I.R. 1.

alia, obliged them to join and remain members of specified unions. Arguably, the workers in that type of situation do not validly waive their rights if they are obliged to join the respective unions under the threat of economic deprivation. However, if having secured employment, they then fail to assert their constitutional right to dissociate, they may later be held to have forfeited that right through acquiescence.

STATUTORY PROTECTION OF FREEDOM OF ASSOCIATION

Statutory protection for the employee's freedom of association may be found in section 6(2)(*a*) of the Unfair Dismissals Act 1977 which provides that a dismissal shall be deemed to be unfair if it results wholly or mainly from –

> "the employee's membership, or proposal that he or another person become a member of, or his engaging in activities on behalf of, a trade union or excepted body under the Trade Union Acts, 1941 and 1971,[40] where the times at which he engages in such activities are outside his hours of work or are times during his hours of work in which he is permitted pursuant to the contract of employment between him and his employer so to engage."

Section 6(2)(*a*) merely protects employees who have been dismissed on account of union membership or activities; it does not otherwise secure any preferential treatment for trade union members or protect them against discriminatory action which falls short of dismissal.[41] Nor does it protect the trade union member who has been refused employment because of his union membership.[42] On the other hand, section 6(7) does extend the statutory protection against dismissal for a reason specified in section 6(2)(*a*) to employees who are not otherwise covered by the Unfair Dismissals Act 1977, *viz.* employees with less than twelve months continuous service; employees who have reached retirement age; employees on probation or undergoing training during a period starting with the commencement of their employment; and finally apprentices dismissed within six months of the commencement of the apprenticeship or within one month of its termination. Unlike other cases of unfair dismissal, however, the burden of proving that the dismissal was unfair rests on those employees relying on section 6(2)(*a*) who are not otherwise protected by the Unfair Dismissals Act 1977.[43]

---

[40] For the difficulties with this definition, see *infra*, at p. 61.
[41] *Cp*, in Britain, s. 23 of the Employment Protection (Consolidation) Act 1978 as amended by s. 14 of the Employment Act 1980. Though if a trade union member is dismissed for misconduct or poor performance, the dismissal will be unfair if the same conduct would have been tolerated in the case of other non-union employees. *McElhinney* v. *Neil Sheridan & Sons (Creeslough) Ltd.* U.D. 626/1980.
[42] *City of Birmingham District Council* v. *Beyer* [1977] I.R.L.R. 211.
[43] S. 6(7) provides: "Where it is shown that a dismissal of a person referred to in paragraph (a) or (b) of section 2(1) or sections 3 or 4 of this Act results wholly or mainly from one or more of the matters referred to in subsection (2)(a) of this section, then subsections (1) and (6) of this section

This burden is rather onerous[44] and an essential ingredient in the employee's proofs would be showing that the employer was aware of the claimant's union membership or of the fact that he was engaging in activities on behalf of the union on the date of dismissal.[45] Conversely, in the case of dismissal for trade union membership, it will be virtually impossible for the claimant to succeed if the employer establishes that he hired the claimant in the knowledge that he was a member of the union in question.[46]

Dismissal for union membership

The first limb of section 6(2)(a) only protects employees who are dismissed because of their union membership or because they propose to join a union – it does not protect employees who are dismissed because they refuse to join a union.[48] Such employees can, no doubt, rely on the general terms of section 6(1) unless they are in those categories of employment not ordinarily covered by the Act.[49] In the latter case, the employee has no statutory alternative to his constitutional or common law action for wrongful dismissal.[50]

Statutory protection does extend to non-unionists who wish to join a union. In *Niven* v. *Galleria Ltd.*[51], it was stated that such claimants must show that they are "actively engaged in making an application for membership or encouraging others to do so." So a claimant who had simply made inquiries about union membership from a friend of hers did not come within the scope of the section. It is submitted, with respect, that such a standard is not warranted by the wording of the section as it places a premium, from the employer's point of view, on nipping potential trade union organisation in the bud and leaves unprotected employees who are merely considering their options. The better view is to be found in *Gordon* v. *Dealgan Amusement Enterprise Ltd.*[52], where the claimant, a non-unionist, was held to be unfairly

---

... shall not apply in relation to the dismissal." This is not a very happy piece of drafting; in particular one would have thought that the use of the word "alleged", rather than "shown", in the opening phrase, would more accurately reflect the intentions of the draftsperson.

[44] See, *e.g.*, *Carey* v. *Joinwood Manufacturing Ltd.* U.D. 382/81. In *O'Reilly* v. *Antigen Ltd.* U.D. 433/1983, the E.A.T. observed, in this context, that ". . . one would normally expect a trade union activist who was victimised to be supported by his trade union," so that the absence of union representation in this case strengthened the E.A.T. in its view that here the claimant had not been dismissed because of trade union activity.

[45] *McGourty* v. *C.I.E.* U.D. 215/1981; *Corboy* v. *McInerney & Sons Ltd.* U.D. 279/1981.

[46] See *Davidson* v. *Gilbert Ash Construction Ltd.* U.D. 441/1981.

[47] See, *e.g. Kearney* v. *Rose Hill House Hotel Ltd.* U.D. 816/1982; *Williams* v. *Gleeson* U.D. 272/78.

[48] *Cp.*, in Britain, s. 58(1)(c) of the Employment Protection (Consolidation) Act 1978.

[49] Ss. 2, 3 and 4 of the Act.

[50] And yet this distinction is probably not unconstitutional because it is arguable that, in the interests of effective collective bargaining, the Oireachtas is entitled to discriminate in favour of those employees who wish to join a union as opposed to those who wish to remain non-unionists.

[51] U.D. 409/1982.

[52] U.D. 221/1981.

dismissed where he threatened to consult a union about his complaint against the employer.[53]

Dismissal for union activity

Two questions arise in connection with the second limb of section 6(2)(*a*), viz. what constitutes union activity for the purpose of the sub-section and during what times is an employee permitted to engage in such activity?

With regard to the first question, such E.A.T. decisions as there are in this area give little guidance on the point. Clearly institutional activity such as recruiting members, organising ballots and elections, *etc.* is covered.[54] It is virtually impossible, however, to construct an exhaustive definition of union activity and each case must be examined on its merits. Certain guidelines can be deduced, however, from an analysis of the sub-section, read in the light of E.A.T. decisions and also in the light of the experience in the U.K. with its comparable legislation.[55] First, the activity must be taken on behalf of the union. This means, at the very least, that there must be some union involvement, or anticipation of union involvement, in the activity before section 6(2)(*a*) will apply, so that individuals acting on their own accord are not protected, even though the activity may be similar to that engaged in by trade unions.[56] However, such involvement does not actually have to have occurred for section 6(2)(*a*) to apply – anticipation of involvement will suffice. So complaining[57] or threatening to complain[58] to a union about alleged grievances at the workplace constitutes union activity for the purpose of the Act.[59] In relation to the requirement that the activity be taken "on behalf of" the union, it is submitted that implied authorisation by the union would satisfy this aspect of the Act.[60] Secondly, industrial action does not

---

[53] See also *Kirk v. Eustace* U.D. 693/1982 where the claimant was held to have been unfairly dismissed when she was let go for presenting to the employer a list of five demands concerning improved conditions and wages and trade union membership.

[54] See, *e.g. Callaghan v. Loughlin* U.D. 522/1980.

[55] Employment Protection (Consolidation) Act 1978, s. 58(1); Industrial Relations (Northern Ireland) Order 1976, art. 22(4).

[56] See, *e.g. Chant v. Aquaboats Ltd.* [1978] I.C.R. 643.

[57] *Mullen v. Midland Meats Ltd.* U.D. 424/1982. See also *Dixon and Shaw v. West Ella Developments Ltd.* [1978] I.C.R. 856.

[58] *Kelly, Kane and McGee v. McWilliams* U.D. 77, 78 and 79/1977.

[59] However, applying to the union office for wet-time insurance claim forms does not constitute trade union activity – *Grassick v. T.P. O'Connor & Sons Ltd.* U.D. 114/1979.

[60] *Quaere* whether non-unionists can ever act "on behalf of" a union. Kidner thinks not – see *Trade Union Law* 1st ed. (London, 1979) p. 103 – however, it is not inconceivable that non-unionists might engage in activities on behalf of a union, particularly in relation to recruitment campaigns. See *Gaffney v. Stericord Ltd.* U.D. 594/1981, where the E.A.T. highlighted the fact that the claimant, a non-unionist, had discussed joining a union with her co-workers during a tea break. The limitation with regard to time only applies in the case of dismissal for engaging in trade union activity, and is inapplicable in the case of dismissal for proposing to join a union, so by implication the E.A.T. regarded this case as coming with the former category of claim. Nevertheless the claim succeeded.

constitute union activity for the purposes of section 6(2)(*a*) if only because it is not the sort of activity which can be engaged in during permitted times.[61] Thirdly, it would appear that action taken by a union on behalf of its members, and in which they have taken no part, does not constitute trade union activity for the purposes of section 6(2)(*a*). In a British decision, *Carrington* v. *Therm-A-Stor Ltd.*,[62] the employer's response to the union's request for recognition was to make twenty employees, including the claimants, redundant. Because the individual claimants had not actually done anything in relation to the request for recognition, the Court of Appeal held that they were not dismissed for participating, or proposing to participate, in union activities. This decision reveals a large lacuna in the statutory protection available to trade union members inasmuch as it leaves them vulnerable to the consequences of union action taken on their behalf but without their actual participation. Such a result was hardly envisaged by the Oireachtas and, if *Carrington* correctly represents the legal position in this jurisdiction, immediate steps should be taken to rectify the situation. Finally, the fact that the employee is engaged in union activity does not give him a licence to misbehave so that the manner in which he engages in such activity may furnish a justifiable reason for dismissal.[63]

Statutory protection against dismissal for engaging in trade union activity only exists if the activity takes place outside the hours of work or at times during the hours of work in which he is permitted by the employer to engage in such activity. It would appear that lunch or tea breaks are outside the hours of work for the purpose of section 6(2)(*a*).[64] If the employee wishes to engage in union activity during hours of work, the employer's consent must be obtained. Such a consent can be implied. In *Duggan* v. *Galco Steel Ltd.*,[65] a collective agreement provided that shop stewards will "represent their members

---

[61] Though *cf. Rainsford* v. *McMahon Confectioneries Ltd.* U.D. 178/1980 where a claimant who had been dismissed for supporting an official strike won his case under s. 6(2)(*a*). For British authorities to the contrary see, *e.g., Drew* v. *St. Edmundsbury Borough Council* [1980] I.R.L.R. 459; *McQuade* v. *Scotbeef Ltd.* [1975] I.R.L.R. 332.

[62] [1983] I.C.R. 208. In an earlier Irish decision, *Walker* v. *Nolan*, U.D. 563/1981, the E.A.T. held that the sending of a letter by the union to the employer seeking a rise in the claimant's pay did not constitute trade union activity for the purpose of s. 6(2)(*a*). However, it seems to have been the nature of the activity, rather than any lack of participation by the claimant, which led to the dismissal of the claim.

[63] See, *e.g., Shiels* v. *Joe Bonner Engineering Ltd.* U.D. 67/1977, where the claimant, who had assaulted two of his co-workers in the course of a recruitment campaign, was held to have been fairly dismissed.

[64] See *McCormac* v. *P.H. Ross Ltd.* U.D. 206/1979. See also *Post Office* v. *Union of Post Office Workers* [1974] I.C.R. 378.

[65] U.D. 507/1980. See also *Marley Tile Co. Ltd.* v. *Shaw* [1980] I.C.R. 72, and more recently *Eastern Health Board and Social Services Board* v. *Deeds and Currie* N.I. Court of Appeal, unreported, 5 April 1984. In *Zucker* v. *Astrid Jewels Ltd.* [1978] I.R.L.R. 385, it was stated that if employees are permitted to converse upon anything they like with fellow employees nearby, to the extent that it does not cause disruption, they may be deemed to have implied consent to discuss union activities.

fairly and effectively in all matters in accordance with the procedures contained in this agreement" and "have reasonable facilities provided by the company to carry out their functions." This was held to amount to a consent on the part of the employer for the claimant to discuss serious problems with employees during working hours. However, silence on the part of the employer when informed of proposed union activity during hours of work does not necessarily amount to consent.[66]

Finally, the adequacy of the remedies available to a claimant who succeeds under section 6(2)(*a*) has to be questioned. A recent survey has indicated that less than 5% of claimants are awarded re-employment by the E.A.T.[67] In *Kirk* v. *Eustace*[68], for example, the employer saw the submission of five demands concerning improved conditions and wages and trade union membership as "a gift from the gods" and dismissed the claimant without notice. Notwithstanding this flagrant violation of the claimant's statutory, and indeed constitutional, rights, the E.A.T., having decided to award compensation, were constrained by the terms of section 7(1)(i) of the 1977 Act, which limits compensation to "such financial loss incurred by [the claimant] and attributable to the dismissal as is just and equitable having regard to all the circumstances," and so were only able to award compensation of £218.00 under that Act, together with a further sum of £40 under the Minimum Notice and Terms of Employment Act 1973.

---

[66] *Marley Tile Co. Ltd* v. *Shaw* [1980] I.C.R. 72. Though *cf. Eastern Health and Social Services Board* v. *Deeds and Currie* N.I. Court of Appeal, unreported, 5 April 1984.
[67] See Joyce and Murphy, "Restoring Management Prerogative: The Unfair Dismissals Act 1977 in Practice" (1984) 6 *I.B.A.R.* 21.
[68] U.D. 693/1982.

Chapter 2 - is outdated by 1990 Act Pt 2

TRADE UNIONS: THE LEGAL FRAMEWORK

The Trade Union Acts 1871-1982 recognise various types of association ranging from temporary combinations, such as unofficial strike committees, to permanent trade unions. Permanent trade unions in turn range from unregistered unions through unregistered certified unions to registered unions. An alternative and overlapping classification of trade unions would be –

(a) those unions which can lawfully engage in collective bargaining, *i.e.* "excepted bodies" and authorised trade unions;
(b) those which cannot.

In this chapter we will examine the statutory definition of a trade union and then proceed to examine the legal provisions relating to the various types of permanent combinations. The chapter will conclude with an examination of the legal status of trade unions.

STATUTORY DEFINITION

Section 23 of the Trade Union Act 1871 defined "trade union" as "such combination, whether temporary or permanent, for regulating the relations between workmen, or between masters and masters, or for imposing restrictive conditions on the conduct of any trade or business as would, if this Act had not been passed, have been deemed to be an unlawful combination by reason of some one or more of its purposes being in restraint of trade." Implicit in this definition was the view that trade unions could not exist as lawful organisations at common law because their operations would invariably be in restraint of trade.[1] Shortly after the enactment of the 1871 Act however, this view was felt to be erroneous.[2] Trade unions could exist as lawful organisations at common law provided their purposes were not in restraint of trade. Section 16 of the Trade Union Act Amendment Act 1876 consequently amended the statutory definition to take this development into account.

The statutory definition was further amplified, in response to the House of Lords decision in *Osborne* v. *Amalgamated Society of Railway*

---

[1] See *Hornby* v. *Close* (1867) L.R. 2 Q.B. 153; *Farrer* v. *Close* (1869) L.R. 4 Q.B. 602. There were conflicting judicial views as to whether membership of a trade union was an offence at common law. In favour of this proposition are the decisions in *R.* v. *Eccles* (1873) 1 Leach 274 and the *Journeymen Tailors case* (1721) 8 Mod. Rep. 10, while *R.* v. *Stainer* (1870) 11 Cox 483 favours the alternative view.
[2] The first judicial recognition of this can be seen in *Swaine* v. *Wilson* (1890) 24 Q.B.D. 252.

Servants,[3] by section 2(1) of the Trade Union Act 1913 which provides:

"The expression 'trade union' for the purpose of the Trade Union Acts 1871 to 1906, and this Act, means any combination, whether temporary or permanent, the principal objects of which are under its constitution statutory objects, provided that any combination which is for the time being registered as a trade union shall be deemed to be a trade union as defined by this Act so long as it continues to be so registered."

The resultant definition, therefore, is as follows:

The expression 'trade union', for the purpose of the Trade Union Acts 1871–1982 means any combination, whether temporary or permanent, the principal object of which are under its constitution the regulation of the relations between workmen and masters, or between workmen and workmen, or between masters and masters, or the imposing of restrictive conditions on the conduct of any trade or business, and also the provision of benefits to members, whether such combination would or would not, if the Trade Union Act 1871 had not been passed, have been deemed to have been an unlawful combination by reason of some one or more of its purposes being in restraint of trade –

provided that the Acts shall not affect:
1. Any agreement between partners as to their own business;
2. Any agreement between an employer and those employed by him as to such employment;
3. Any agreement in consideration of the sale of the goodwill of a business or of instruction in any profession, trade, or handicraft;

and provided that any combination which is for the time being registered as a trade union shall be deemed to be a trade union as defined by the Trade Union Acts so long as it continues to be so registered.

This definition does not appear to have been the subject of judicial pronouncement by any Irish judge. It does give rise, however, to a number of points. First, the definition is so sweeping that it includes bodies which are not regarded as trade unions in the general sense. It is clear from the definition that the criterion for determining whether an association is a union is the objective of the body, not its membership. Thus employers' associations can be trade unions within the meaning of the legislation, provided they have as their primary objects the stautory objects set out in the 1871 Act as amended.[4] Likewise associations of

---
[3] [1910] A.C. 87.
[4] Approximately two dozen employers' associations are registered as trade unions with the Registrar of Friendly Societies, including the C.I.I., and sixteen of them, including the F.U.E. and the C.I.F., hold negotiation licences.

self-employed persons,[5] manufacturing associations and trade protection societies would appear to be within the statutory definition. Indeed it has been argued in relation to the United Kingdom that many trade associations, being within the definition of "trade union", have been wrongfully registered as companies or industrial and provident societies.[6] Joint Industrial Councils and Joint Labour Committees also apparently come within the scope of the definition.[7] A federation of unions may also be a trade union.[8]

Secondly, a combination may be temporary or permanent. Thus unofficial strikers could form a trade union for the purposes of the Trade Union Acts, though before this can happen, the combination must be "sufficiently stable and well defined".[9] This is a situation which is fraught with some danger for unofficial strikers, because if they act in such a way as to suggest that they have implicitly resigned from their trade union and now constitute a new trade union, they could be found guilty of an offence if they engage in collective bargaining with more than one employer,[10] and furthermore will be deprived of the protection of sections 2-4 of the Trade Disputes Act 1906.[11] If they remain within an authorised trade union, they are at least guaranteed the protection of sections 2 and 3 of the 1906 Act.[12]

Thirdly, certain subsisting combinations are expressly excluded from the scope of the definition.[13] These are:

(1) Agreements between partners as to their own business. The Partnership Act 1890 defines partnership as "the relation which

---

[5] Note the position in Britain where "trade union" is defined by s.28(1) of T.U.L.R.A. 1974 as meaning, *inter alia*, an organisation consisting wholly or mainly of workers, and "worker" is defined in s.30 as including the self-employed. This is also the position in Northern Ireland, Industrial Relations (Northern Ireland) Order 1976, art. 2. A number of professional bodies are expressly exempted from the application of s.6 of the Trade Union Act 1941, so by implication they are regarded as coming within the statutory definition of a trade union. See *infra*, p. 51.

[6] See Hickling, "Trade Unions in Disguise" (1964) 27 *M.L.R.* 625. S. 5 of the 1871 Act provides, *inter alia*, that the registration of any trade union under the Friendly Societies Acts, the Industrial and Provident Societies Acts and the Companies Acts shall be void. The converse proposition does not necessarily follow, however, so that bodies which may not be trade unions may yet avail of some, at least, of the benefits of the Trade Union Acts. In particular there does not appear to be any reason to prevent such bodies acquiring the status of "excepted bodies" for the purposes of the Trade Union Act 1941. See, for example, the Irish Nurses' Organisation which is a limited company under the Companies Acts and an "excepted body" for the purposes of the 1941 Act.

[7] Ss. 56 and 65 of the Industrial Relations Act 1946 provide, respectively, that J.L.C.'s and J.I.C.'s are excepted bodies under the Trade Union Acts.

[8] In this respect it is interesting to note that the Irish Congress of Trade Unions does not hold a negotiation licence, nor indeed has it ever registered as a trade union.

[9] See Hickling (ed.), *Citrine's Trade Union Law*, 3rd ed. (London, 1967) at p. 396.

[10] Trade Union Act 1941, s. 6. See *infra*, pp. 50-51.

[11] Trade Union Act 1941, s. 11. See *infra*, p. 61.

[12] *Gouldings Chemicals Ltd.* v. *Bolger* [1977] I.R. 211. See p. 280.

[13] 1871 Act, s. 23.

exists between persons carrying on business in common with a view to profit."[14]

(2) Any agreement between an employer and those employed by him as to such employment. This exception is further bolstered by the wording of section 6(1) of the Trade Union Act 1941 from which it is clear that it is not unlawful for a single employer to engage in negotiations for the fixing of wages and other conditions of employment, and also by section 6(3)(*a*) of the same Act which provides that an "excepted body" includes a body which carries on negotiations for the fixing of the wages or other conditions of employment of its own (but no other) employees.[15]

It is clear from all the foregoing that the statutory definition of "trade union" is very sweeping. Satisfying the statutory definition, however, merely places a combination at the base of the legal framework created for trade unions and before such a body can lawfully operate as an effective entity in industrial relations, it must advance through other stages of this framework. It is now proposed to examine these stages in order of ascendancy.

CERTIFIED TRADE UNIONS

A body which satisfies the statutory definition of trade union and is not a registered trade union may apply to the Registrar of Friendly Societies[16] in compliance with section 2(3) of the Trade Union Act 1913 for a certificate that it is a union within the meaning of the Trade Union Acts 1871-1982. If the Registrar is satisfied, having regard to the constitution and practice of the union, that the principal objects of the union are statutory objects, he is obliged to grant the certificate. The sub-section refers to the fact that the Registrar must have regard to the "mode in which the union is being carried on" – by implication the union must already have been functioning for some time before it can apply for a certificate. The granting of such a certificate does not affect the legal status of the body in question, nor does it confer any additional benefits or powers on the union. However, as long as it remains in force it is conclusive evidence that the Union is a trade union.[17]

Section 2(3) also provides that any person may apply to the Registrar to have the certificate withdrawn. The Registrar must afford the union an opportunity of being heard, but if he is satisfied that the certificate is no longer justified he may withdraw it. It is arguable that the only

[14] Partnership Act 1890, s. 1.
[15] See *infra*, p. 51.
[16] Whose office is at 13 Hume St., Dublin 2.
[17] 1913 Act, s. 2(5). As to the constitutionality of this provision, see *infra*, p. 47.

grounds for holding that the certificate is no longer justified is where, having regard to its constitution or the mode in which it is being carried out, the union's principal objects are no longer statutory objects.[18] An appeal against refusal to certify or withdrawal of a certificate lies to the High Court.[19]

At present there are only two certified trade unions in Ireland.[20] The only advantage of being a certified trade union is that one does not have to prove one's status in litigation. However, the value of this has diminished since 1913, given that section 11 of the 1941 Act restricts the protection of the 1906 Act to authorised trade unions only, and that the advantages conferred on trade unions by the employment legislation of the 1970s are almost invariably restricted to authorised trade unions.

REGISTERED TRADE UNIONS

By way of contrast there are several advantages[21] attached to the status of registered trade union and therefore, although registration is not obligatory, 100 unions operating in the Republic were registered with the Registrar of Friendly Societies, as at December 31, 1984.

Process of registration

The process of registration is governed by provisions of pre-Independence legislation. Section 6 of the 1871 Act provides that any seven or more members of a trade union might

"by subscribing their names to the rules of the union and otherwise complying with the provisions of the Act with regard to registry, register such trade union under the Act, provided that if any one of the purposes of such trade union be unlawful, such registration shall be void."[22]

Such a union must be in existence before an application for registration will be entertained by the Registrar,[23] though unlike applicants for certification, it does not have to have been functioning for any period of time.

Section 13(1) of the 1871 Act provides that an application to register a trade union and printed copies of its rules, together with a list of the titles and names of the officers, should be sent to the Registrar of Friendly Societies.

---

[18] Citrine, *op. cit.*, p. 415.
[19] 1913 Act, s. 2(4).
[20] Irish Nurses Union; E.S.B. Staff Association. The former body is not to be confused with the Irish Nurses' Organisation, on which see fn. 6 *supra*.
[21] See *infra*, pp. 48–50. S.I. No. 292 of 1983 sets out the appropriate fee for registration.
[22] S. 6 of the Trade Union Act Amendment Act 1876 provided for the "recording" of the rules and amendments thereto of a registered trade union in the other component jurisdictions of the United Kingdom. However, this provision was not carried over by Article 73 of the Irish Free Constitution into the laws of the new State – *I.T.G.W.U.* v. *Green* [1936] I.R. 471.
[23] *Re National Union of Ships' Stewards* [1925] Ch. 20.

Limitations on the power to register

Having duly received the application and accompanying documents, the Registrar is obliged to register the union and its rules except in the following four situations:

(1) If the Registrar discovers that one of the union's purposes is unlawful, he can not register that union.[24] If he has already registered such a union, however, the registration remains effective until actually withdrawn.[25]

(2) If the union has failed to comply with the appropriate trade union regulations, the Registrar shall not register it.[26]

(3) A union cannot be registered under a name identical to that of any existing registered union, or so nearly resembling it as to be likely to deceive members of the public.[27] In *R. v. The Registrar of Friendly Societies*[28] it was held that the Registrar was also justified in refusing to register a trade union under a name identical to that of an existing unregistered trade union. Certain difficulties arise where a union is inadvertently registered under a name similar to or identical with that of a registered union. The common law remedy available to the latter union would be an injunction to restrain the tort of passing off. However, this remedy is not available against authorised trade unions[29] and, in such a case, one has to proceed against individual tortfeasors.[30] Alternatively one could seek a declaration that the new union is using a name identical to that of the existing union or so similar as to be likely to deceive the public. There is no statutory procedure for resolving this problem. One could request the Registrar to cancel the registration of the new union on the grounds of mistake.[31] However, this procedure may not be entirely satisfactory since at least two months' notice must be given to the union before cancellation. Provision is made for allowing a union to change its name,[32] but there is no statutory power to compel it to do so.

(4) The principal objects of the union must be statutory objects before it can be registered under the Trade Union Acts. In determining the principal objects of a trade union, the Registrar

---

[24] 1871 Act, s. 6.
[25] 1871 Act, s. 13, para. 5; 1913 Act, s. 2(1).
[26] 1871 Act, s. 13, para. 2.
[27] S. 13, para. 3.
[28] (1872) L.R. 7 Q.B. 741.
[29] Trade Disputes Act 1906, s. 4 as amended by the Trade Union Act 1941, s. 11. See also *I.T.G.W.U. v. Green* [1936] I.R. 471. On the constitutionality of this immunity, see *infra*, pp. 255–257.
[30] See *infra*, p. 251.
[31] 1876 Act, s. 8.
[32] Trade Union Act 1975, s. 12.

looks to both the constitution of the union and to its actual practice.[33]

Effect of certificate of registration

A certificate of registration, once issued by the Registrar, is conclusive evidence that the union has complied with the statutory regulations with respect to registry,[34] and, as long as it continues in force,[35] is deemed by virtue of section 2(1) of the Trade Union Act 1913 to be conclusive evidence of the fact that the holder is a trade union within the meaning of the Trade Union Acts.[36] The value of this latter provision used to lie in the fact that, by virtue of section 4 of the Trade Disputes Act 1906, possession of a certificate of registration was a defence to any tortious action. However, this is no longer so, given that the immunities conferred on trade unions by the 1906 Act have been restricted to authorised, rather than registered, trade unions.[37] Furthermore, the sweeping nature of section 2(1) renders it susceptible to constitutional attack.[38]

Power of withdrawal or cancellation

A certificate of registration, once granted, may only be withdrawn or cancelled in a number of specified situations.[39] Section 8 of the 1876 Act provides that such a certificate may be withdrawn by the Registrar, at the request of the trade union, on proof to his satisfaction that a certificate of registration has been obtained by fraud or mistake or that the registration of the union is void under section 6 of the 1871 Act because one of the union's purposes is unlawful or that such trade union has wilfully, and after notice from the Registrar, violated any of the provisions of the Trade Union Acts, or has ceased to exist.

This must now be read in the light of section 2(2) of the 1913 Act, which provides that the Registrar may withdraw the certificate of registration if the constitution of the union has been altered in such a way that, in his opinion, the principal objects of the union are no longer statutory objects, or if, in his opinion, the principal objects for which the union is actually carried on are not statutory objects.

The effect of withdrawal or cancellation of a certificate of registration is that the union involved ceases to enjoy the privileges of a

---

[33] 1913 Act, s. 2(2).
[34] 1871 Act, s. 13, para. 5.
[35] Registration of a union continues in force until the certificate is actually withdrawn – *Parr* v. *Lancashire and Cheshire Miners Federation* [1913] 1 Ch. 366.
[36] See *Miller* v. *A.E.U.* [1938] Ch. 669.
[37] 1941 Act, s. 11. See *infra*, p. 61.
[38] See *infra*, p. 47.
[39] An examination of the Registrar's files on "dead" trade unions revealed that 13 unions had been de-registered as a result of amalgamations or transfers of engagements, 7 were de-registered on request or because they had been dissolved by the members, a further 7 were listed as having "ceased to exist" and finally 2 unions were de-registered because of a failure to make the annual returns.

Trade Unions: The Legal Framework 45

registered trade union. However, any liability incurred by the union is deemed to be unaffected.[40]

Right of appeal against decisions of the Registrar

Section 2(4) of the 1913 Act provides for a right of appeal to the High Court against specified decisions of the Registrar. These are:

(1) A refusal to register a combination as a trade union.
(2) A refusal to grant a certificate under section 2(3) of the 1913 Act that an unregistered trade union is a trade union within the meaning of the Act.
(3) A withdrawal under section 2(2) of the 1913 Act of a certificate of registration.
(4) A withdrawal under section 2(3) of the 1913 Act of a certificate that an unregistered trade union is a trade union within the meaning of the Act.

Section 2(4) is defective in one respect, however, in that it fails to provide for a right of appeal against a decision of the Registrar to cancel registration under section 8 of the 1876 Act.[41]

Constitutionality of the Registrar's powers

It is clear from the foregoing that the Registrar of Friendly Societies has considerable powers in relation to certain aspects of trade union law. In particular, he has:

(1) Power to register a trade union.[42] As mentioned above,[43] a certificate of registration, once granted, is conclusive evidence that the union has complied with the regulations of the Trade Union Acts with regard to registration[44] and also (as long as the union continues to be registered) that the association is a union within the meaning of the Trade Union Acts.[45]
(2) Power to certify that an unregistered trade union is a trade union within the meaning of the Trade Union Acts. Section 2(5) of the 1913 Act provides that such a certificate (as long as it remains in force) is conclusive evidence of this fact.

---

[40] 1876 Act, s. 8.
[41] It has been argued that s. 2(4) does not necessarily cover a right of appeal against a refusal to register under the 1871 Act on the grounds, *inter alia*, that it would be anomalous to give an appeal against a refusal to register under the 1871 Act but not against cancellation of registration under s. 8 of the 1876 Act – see Citrine, *op. cit.*, p. 225. One would have thought, however, that the literal meaning of a statutory provision should not be qualified by reference to legislative oversight (as opposed to legislative action) even if that does result in some anomalies.
[42] 1871 Act, s. 13.
[43] See *supra*, p. 44.
[44] 1871 Act, s. 13, para. 5.
[45] 1913 Act, s. 2(1). See *Miller* v. *A.E.U.* [1938] Ch. 669.

(3) Limited powers to cancel a certificate of registration.[46] It appears that no appeal lies against such a decision of the Registrar made pursuant to section 8 of the 1876 Act.[47]

(4) Power to withdraw a certificate of status from an unregistered trade union.[48]

(5) Limited power to transfer stock in public funds vested in union trustees.[49]

(6) Jurisdiction to hear complaints arising out of the administration of the political fund of a trade union. Section 3(2) of the 1913 Act provides that the Registrar's decisions here are binding and conclusive, without appeal, not removable into any court of law or restrainable by injunction.[50]

(7) Jurisdiction to hear specified complaints arising out of trade union amalgamations,[51] *viz.* whether the matter in which the vote on the resolution, approving the instrument of amalgamation or transfer, satisfied the conditions in section 3(1) of the Trade Union Act 1975 or whether the votes recorded in relation to the resolution had the effect of passing it. An appeal against the decision of the Registrar in such a case may be taken on points of law only to the High Court[52] and the Registrar may state a case for the opinion of the High Court on a question of law arising in the proceedings.[53] Furthermore, the validity of a resolution approving an instrument of amalgamation or transfer cannot be questioned in any legal proceedings (except those taken pursuant to section 10 of the 1975 Act) on any ground on which a complaint could have been made to the Registrar under section 10. The effect of this is to give the Registrar sole original jurisdiction to entertain complaints on the grounds specified in section 10(1) of the 1975 Act.

(8) Power to withhold approval from the political fund provisions in a union rule book required by the 1913 Act[54] and from the provisions in the union rule book relating to the holding of a ballot for the purpose of that Act.[55] Furthermore, where he certifies that such rules have been approved by a majority of the union members or by a majority of the delegates of such union voting at a meeting called for the purpose, such rules have effect notwithstanding a failure to comply with the provisions of the

---

[46] 1876 Act, s. 8; 1913 Act, s. 2(2).
[47] See *supra*, p. 45.
[48] 1913 Act, s. 2(3).
[49] 1876 Act, s. 4.
[50] See *infra*, pp. 47–48.
[51] 1975 Act, s. 10(1).
[52] 1975 Act, s. 10(12).
[53] S. 10(10).
[54] 1913 Act, s. 3(1).
[55] S. 4(1).

rules of the union as to the alteration of existing rules or the making of new rules.[56]

(9) Power to withhold approval from the statutory notice, and method of its communication to union members, and the instrument of transfer or amalgamation required by the 1975 Act.[57]

Though the powers of the Registrar in this context are, by and large, unobjectionable, it is submitted that some are constitutionally suspect. In particular it is submitted that section 2(1) and (5) of the 1913 Act, which provide that the certificate of registration of a registered trade union and a certificate of status of an unregistered trade union constitute conclusive evidence of the status of the respective bodies, have to be read subject to Articles 34 and 37 of the Constitution, which, *inter alia*, prohibit the administration of justice in criminal[58] cases by persons other than judges appointed under the Constitution.[59] So, for example, in relation to offences under sections 12(2) and 13(2) of the Trade Union Act 1941, the courts cannot be precluded from investigating the status of the bodies before them merely because those bodies possess a certificate of registration or status from the Registrar.

Similar arguments apply to section 10(9) of the Trade Union Act 1975 in so far as it purports to preclude an investigation into the validity of a resolution approving an instrument of amalgamation or transfer in any legal proceedings other than those initiated before the Registrar pursuant to section 10 of the Act.[60] If the validity of such a resolution became an issue, for example, in the prosecution of an offence under section 12 of the 1871 Act, section 10 would have to submit to the terms of Article 34 and Article 37 of the Constitution.

Finally, certain difficulties arise in relation to section 3(2) of the 1913 Act, in so far as it attempts to protect the decisions of the Registrar on complaints arising out of the administration of the political fund of a trade union from challenge in the courts. The protection of section 3(2) is probably only available if the decision is taken within jurisdiction[61], but, even if the sub-section has this limited effect, is it consistent with Article 34.3.1° of the Constitution which provides that the High Court

---

[56] S. 4(2).

[57] 1975 Act, s. 3(3), s. 3(1) (*d*) and s. 2(2) respectively.

[58] Article 37 does permit the exercise of limited functions and powers of a judicial nature in *civil* matters by persons other than judges appointed under the Constitution. Arguably, therefore, it is still permissible to rely on the certificate in civil actions.

[59] See *Maher* v. *Attorney-General* [1973] I.R. 140 where the Supreme Court struck down s. 44(2) (*a*) of the Road Traffic Act 1968 which provided that a certificate, stating that a specimen of a person's blood contained a specific concentration of alcohol, was to be *conclusive* evidence of that fact.

[60] *Quaere* – whether this provision is a reaction to an attempt in 1968 to challenge the validity of an amalgamation in the High Court. See *Dunne* v. *Marks* High Court, unreported, 30 May 1968.

[61] See *R. (Martin)* v. *O'Mahony* [1910] 2 I.R. 695; *State (Horgan)* v. *Exported Livestock Insurance Board* [1943] I.R. 581, 609; *State (McCarthy)* v. *O'Donnell* [1945] I.R. 126, 161–162.

shall have "full original jurisdiction in and power to determine all matters and questions whether of law or fact, civil or criminal"? If Article 34.3.1° were to be read literally and in isolation from the rest of the Constitution then it would follow that section 3(2) was unconstitutional in that it assigns justiciable issues to the Registrar to the exclusion of the High Court.[62] In *Tormey* v. *Ireland*,[63] however, the Supreme Court held that the full original jurisdiction of the High Court referred to in Article 34.3.1° must be deemed to be full in the sense that all justiciable matters and questions, save those removed by the Constitution itself from the High Court's original jurisdiction, shall be within the original jurisdiction of the High Court "in one form or another". If, in exercise of its powers under Article 37, the Oireachtas entrusts certain limited matters (other than criminal matters) exclusively to a person such as the Registrar, then the Oireachtas is not to be taken as having ousted the jurisdiction of the High Court. While the High Court will not hear and determine the matter, its full jurisdiction is there to be invoked in proceedings such as *certiorari*, prohibition, *mandamus*, *quo warranto*, injunction or declaratory action, "so as to ensure that the hearing and determination will be in accordance with the law."[64]

Advantages of registration

The major advantages enjoyed by a registered trade union, and its members, are as follows:

(1) Originally under the 1871 Act only registered trade unions and branches thereof could purchase or lease buildings in the name of their trustees and sell, exchange, mortgage or let same. Unregistered trade unions now are impliedly empowered to do this by virtue of the 1913 Act. Registered trade unions, however, still enjoy the additional advantage that purchasers, assignees, mortgagees, or tenants are not bound to enquire into the authority of the trustees to sell, exchange, mortgage or let the property in question.[65]

(2) Real and personal estate of a registered trade union is vested in the union trustees by virtue of section 8 of the 1871 Act as amended by section 3 of the 1876 Act. On the death or removal of such trustees the property vests in succeeding trustees without the need for any conveyance or assignment, except in the case of public stocks and securities. Provision is also made for the transfer of stock to trustees of registered trade unions in

---

[62] See Gannon J. in *R.* v. *R. and the Attorney General* High Court, unreported, 16 February 1984. See also Hogan, "Constitutional Aspects of the Distribution and Organisation of Court Business" (1984) 6 *D.U.L.J. (n.s.)* 40.
[63] [1985] I.L.R.M. 375.
[64] *Ibid.* at 380.
[65] 1871 Act, s. 7 as amended by the Trade Union Act 1935. See *infra*, p. 82.

the case of absence, bankruptcy, death, or removal from office of preceding trustees.[66]

(3) Trustees or other appropriate officers of a registered trade union may bring or defend any action concerning the property, right, or claim to property of the trade union.[67]

(4) The responsibility of trustees of a registered trade union is limited to moneys actually received by them on account of the trade union.[68]

(5) Treasurers and other officers of a registered trade union are legally bound to render accounts and to deliver up to the trustees all property in their hands on being required to do so.[69]

(6) The legislation also provides special summary remedies wherever any person (a) obtains possession of any moneys, securities, books, papers or other effects of the registered trade union by false representation or imposition, or (b) wilfully withholds or fraudulently misapplies same, or (c) wilfully applies same to purposes other than those authorised by the rule book.[70]

(7) The Insurance Acts 1909-1983 are inapplicable to registered trade unions.[71]

(8) Members over the age of 16 may nominate persons to whom the sum of not more than £100 may be payable by the union on the death of the nominee.[72]

(9) The certificate of registration is conclusive proof that a combination is a trade union.[73]

(10) A registered trade union is entitled to an exemption from income tax.[74]

(11) Registered trade unions benefit from the provisions of the Provident Nominations and Small Intestacies Act 1883.[75]

---

[66] 1876 Act, s. 4. See *infra*, p. 84.
[67] 1871 Act, s. 9 as amended by the Trade Disputes Act 1906, s. 4(2) and the Trade Union Act 1941, s. 11. See *infra*, pp. 86-88.
[68] 1871 Act, s. 10. See *infra*, p. 86.
[69] 1871 Act, s. 11. See *infra*, pp. 137-138.
[70] 1871 Act, s. 12 as amended by the 1876 Act, s. 5.
[71] Insurance Act 1936, s. 6(c). Very limited provision was made in 1936 for exempting unregistered trade unions who, *inter alia*, were lawfully carrying on an insurance business on October 31, 1935 – see 1936 Act, s. 6(e). It appears, however, that no advantage was taken of this provision. *Quaere* whether the provisions of Council Directives 73/238 (O.J.L. 228, 16.8.73, p. 3) and 79/267 (O.J.L. 63, 13.3.79, p. 1) which were implemented in Ireland by S.I. Nos. 115 of 1976 and 57 of 1984 respectively are applicable to trade unions, see Preamble to 73/238 and Art. 2(3) of 79/267.
[72] 1876 Act, s. 10, as amended by s. 3 of the Provident Nominations and Small Intestacies Act 1883. See *infra*, p. 110.
[73] 1913 Act, s. 2(1). See *supra*, pp. 44-47.
[74] Income Tax Act 1967, s. 336.
[75] S. 7 of the Provident Nominations and Small Intestacies Act 1883 provides that "[i]f any member of a registered trade union, entitled from the funds thereof to a sum not exceeding £100, dies intestate and without having made any nomination which remains unrevoked at his death, such sum shall be payable, without letters of administration, to the person who appears to a majority of the directors, upon such evidence as they may deem satisfactory, to be entitled by law to receive the same."

(12) A registered trade union may sue in its registered name.
(13) Registration is a *sine qua non* for Irish unions who wish to obtain the advantages enjoyed by authorised trade unions.[76]

On the other hand registration also entails a number of obligations for trade unions:

(1) The rules of a registered trade union must contain provisions in respect of various matters stipulated in the legislation.[77]
(2) A registered trade union must have a registered office to which all communications and notices may be addressed.[78]
(3) A registered trade union must make annual returns to the Registrar showing assets and liabilities at the date of return, and receipts and expenditure during the preceding year, and such other particulars as the Registrar may require. The Registrar must also be notified of any alterations to the union rulebook. Each member of the trade union is entitled to receive a free copy of this statement.[79] Any person who wilfully makes, or orders to be made, any false entry in, or omission from, these returns, is liable to a penalty up to £50 for each offence. Furthermore, section 18 provides that circulating false copies of the rules of a registered trade union or representing that the rules of an unregistered trade union are those of a registered trade union, with intent to mislead or defraud, is a misdemeanour.
(4) Registered trade unions may be sued in their registered names, except in the case of tortious actions, and even here their trustees can be sued except where the tort was committed in contemplation or furtherance of a trade dispute.[80]
(5) Registered trade unions are subject to the doctrine of *ultra vires* and to the rule in *Foss* v. *Harbottle*,[81] unlike their unregistered counterparts, though this distinction may be more apparent than real.

AUTHORISED TRADE UNIONS AND EXCEPTED BODIES

Trade unions can be further classified into those which are entitled to engage in collective bargaining and those for whom participation in such activity would be an offence.

The Trade Union Act 1941, which is part of an overall legislative policy of reducing the number of trade unions in Ireland, provides that it is an offence for any body of persons to carry on negotiations for the

---

[76] See *infra*, pp. 53, 54.
[77] See *infra*, at pp. 108–109.
[78] 1871 Act, s. 15.
[79] 1871 Act, s. 16. See *infra*, p. 110.
[80] See *infra*, pp. 86–88.
[81] (1843) 2 Hare 461. See *infra*, pp. 66–69.

Trade Unions: The Legal Framework 51

fixing of wages or any other conditions of employment unless such body is the holder of a negotiation licence or is an excepted body.[82]

Excepted bodies

"Excepted body" is defined in section 6(3) of the Trade Union Act 1941, as amended,[83] and includes:

(1) A body which carries on negotiations for the fixing of the wages or other conditions of employment of its own (but no other) employees. This provision covers, for example, members of a board of directors, or a partnership, who wish to negotiate with their employees – individual employers in negotiating with their work force do not have to possess a negotiation licence as they are not a "body of persons" under section 6(1).

(2) Civil service staff associations recognised by the Minister for Finance.

(3) Teachers' organisations recognised by the Minister for Education.

(4) Joint labour committees established under the Industrial Relations Acts 1946–1976.[84]

(5) A body in respect of which an order under section 6(6) is for the time being in force. The Minister may, by order made pursuant to section 6(6), exempt from the provisions of section 6 any particular body or persons.[85] Such an order may be revoked by the Minister under section 6(7). It would appear from the *Dáil*

---

[82] 1941 Act, s. 6. It is certainly arguable that the I.C.T.U., which is neither an authorised trade union nor an excepted body, comes within the ambit of this provision as no distinction is drawn, for the purposes of the section, between negotiations carried on at national level which establish basic guidelines in relation to wages, *etc.*, and negotiations at a more localised level which fix the specific terms of employment.

[83] Section 6 has been amended by ss. 2 and 3 of the Trade Union Act 1942, ss. 56 and 65 of the Industrial Relations Act 1946 and s. 6 of the Industrial Relations Act 1976. The resultant definition includes bodies which are not trade unions, see fn. 85 *infra*.

[84] Industrial Relations Act 1946, s. 56.

[85] In relation to bodies under this sub-section it was initially felt that exemption could be effected by simple Ministerial Order. Subsequently, this policy was abandoned in favour of the use of Statutory Instruments. The bodies exempted are:
Irish Nurses Organisation – Ministerial Order dated 7 May 1942;
Banks Staffs Relations Committee – Ministerial Order dated 24 November 1942;
The Institute of Clerks of Works in Ireland – S.I. No. 221 of 1957;
County and City Managers' Association – S.I. No. 17 of 1960;
Association of Hospital and Public Pharmacists – S.I. No. 233 of 1960;
Irish Dental Association – S.I. No. 63 of 1963;
Incorporated Law Society of Ireland – S.I. No. 54 of 1965;
Royal Institute of Architects of Ireland – S.I. No. 55 of 1965;
Veterinary Medical Association of Ireland – S.I. No. 56 of 1965;
Chartered Society of Physiotherapy – S.I. No. 227 of 1969;
Irish Association of Chiropodists – S.I. No. 228 of 1969;
Association of Occupational Therapists of Ireland – S.I. No. 229 of 1969;
Association of Clinical Biochemists in Ireland – S.I. No. 230 of 1969;
Institute of Chemistry in Ireland – S.I. No. 231 of 1969;
Agricultural Science Association – S.I. No. 232 of 1969;
Irish Association of Speech Therapists – S.I. No. 296 of 1971.

Debates that this provision is intended to cover those bodies which occasionally have to negotiate about wages and conditions with their employers but which do not regard the strike weapon as a normal part of their armoury – (*i.e.* professional associations, County Councils, industrial councils, conciliation councils.)[86]

(6) A body, all the members of which are employed by the same employer, and which carries on negotiations for the fixing of wages or other conditions of employment of its own workers but of no other employees. It is difficult to understand why this provision was inserted as it affords some protection for "house unions" and this surely runs contrary to the stated legislative policy of reducing the number of unions in Ireland. Furthermore, this legislative provision might infringe Article 2, section 2 of the I.L.O. Convention No. 98 on the principles of the right to organise and to bargain collectively which provides that acts designed to promote the establishment of workers' organisations under the domination of employers' organisations, or to support workers' organisations by financial or other means so as to place such organisations under the control of employers or their organisations, are acts of interference prohibited by Article 2, section 1.[87]

By virtue of section 3(1) of the 1942 Act as amended,[88] a body which negotiates on a board to which that section applies, is not, by reason only of so negotiating, required to have a negotiation licence. The boards referred to are:

(1) A joint industrial council recognised by the Minister, a joint conciliation or arbitration board so recognised, or any similar body so recognised.[89]
(2) A joint labour committee established under the Industrial Relations Acts 1946–1976.

Apart from the foregoing, all other bodies who wish to engage in negotiations concerning wages or conditions of employment must be authorised trade unions.

---

[86] See 84 *Dáil Debates* cc. 88 and 148 (24 June 1941).
[87] *Cp.* the U.S. National Labor Relations Act 1935, s. 8(2)(*a*) of which provides that it is "an unfair labor practice for an employer to dominate or interfere with the formation or administration of any labor organisation or contribute financial or other support to it." *Cp.* also Article 2 of the Industrial Relations (Northern Ireland) Order 1976 which defines an "independent" trade union as one which is neither under the domination or control of an employer nor liable to interference by an employer, arising out of the provision of financial or material support or by any other means whatsoever, tending towards such control. See *Squibb United Kingdom Staff Association* v. *Certification Officer* [1979] I.C.R. 235.
[88] Industrial Relations Act 1946, s. 56; Industrial Relations Act 1976, s. 6(1) and Apprenticeship Act 1959, s. 7(1).
[89] This includes Joint Industrial Councils registered under the Industrial Relations Act – Industrial Relations Act 1946, s. 65.

Authorised trade unions

The 1941 Act refers to authorised trade unions as bodies of persons entitled to be granted or to hold a negotiation licence.[90]

(a) *Conditions of entitlement*

Restrictions on the granting and retention of such licences, which are designed to hinder attempts to create new unions, are contained in section 7 of the 1941 Act as amended by the Trade Union Acts of 1971 and 1975. It would appear that these restrictions vary in accordance with the category of union to which the applicant union belongs. In this context unions can be grouped into four different categories.

(1) Irish-based unions which obtained negotiation licences prior to the enactment of the Trade Union Act 1971, or any union resulting from an amalgamation of two or more such unions. Such a union must:
 (i) be registered under the Trade Union Acts;[91]
 (ii) have kept deposited with the High Court a sum of money determined in accordance with the Schedule to the 1941 Act.[92] The size of the deposit varies in accordance with the size of the union from a minimum of £1,000 where the membership does not exceed 500 persons, to an overriding maximum of £10,000 where the membership exceeds 20,000. However, the Minister is empowered to reduce the deposit by up to 75 per cent.[93] Section 14 of the 1941 Act provides for the methods whereby a deposit may be made, dealt with or withdrawn. Pursuant to this section, a depositor may request that the deposit be invested in such authorised securities as the depositor shall specify, and the income derived from such investment is payable to the depositor. Section 15 of the 1941 Act provides that an authorised trade union is obliged, "on or within one month after every third anniversary of the making of a deposit", to send to the Minister a statement of the number of its members on such anniversary[94] and, if necessary, to increase or apply for the reduction of such deposit, as the case may require.

---

[90] 1941 Act, s. 7.

[91] 1941 Act, s. 7(1)(*a*). On registration, see *supra*, pp. 42–50.

[92] In the fourth volume of their Conclusions, at p. 39, the Committee of Experts who monitor the European Social Charter concluded that the requirement of a deposit, in excess of what was needed to cover minimal administrative costs, as a prerequisite to obtaining negotiating powers was contrary to Article 5 of the Charter.

[93] 1941 Act, s. 8, as amended by the Trade Union Acts 1947–52. Sixteen unions benefit from the terms of this section, though it has not been invoked at all in recent years, the last order having been made in 1961.

[94] Failure to comply or wilfully sending a false statement is an offence punishable, on summary conviction, by a fine of up to £100 – s. 15(2).

Section 16 of the 1941 Act enables a judgment creditor of an authorised trade union to have his debt satisfied out of the deposit placed in the High Court by the union. The union then has three months in which to make up any deficiency after which time, if it fails to pay the balance, it will lose its negotiation licence. The then Minister for Industry and Commerce quoted section 25 of the Insurance Act 1936 as a precedent for this measure.[95] It is submitted, however, that section 16 of the 1941 Act is much wider than section 25 of the 1936 Act, which is limited to claims arising out of policies issued by insurance companies. The ordinary creditors of an insurance company cannot have resort to the deposit lodged by that company, whereas the ordinary creditors of a union can be satisfied out of the deposit lodged pursuant to section 7, while at the same time endangering the union's right to a negotiation licence. Nor does there seem to be any obligation on the creditor, under section 16, to use the ordinary means of enforcing a court order for payment of money before proceeding against the deposit.

(2) Irish-based unions which make their first application for a negotiation licence after 1971. Unions in this category must:
   (i) register under the Trade Union Acts;
   (ii) show to the satisfaction of the Minister that, both at a date not less than eighteen months before the date of application and at the date of application, it had not less than 500 members resident in the State;[96]
   (iii) comply with the residual conditions of section 2 of the 1971 Act,[97] which provides that a body of persons[98] wishing to obtain a negotiation licence must, at least eighteen months before the date of application for the licence,

---

[95] See 84 *Dáil Debates* c. 571 (1 July 1941).

[96] Section 2(1)(*b*). *Quaere* whether this requirement of a minimum number of 500 members is compatible with the Constitution? In *X. v. Ireland*, Application 4125/69, the European Commission on Human Rights stated that freedom of association included the right of workers' and employers' organisations "to elect their representatives in full freedom" and "to organise their administration". This suggests that any attempt by the Government to rationalise the trade union movement by denying smaller unions the right to protect the interests of their members is *prima facie* contrary to Article 11 of the European Convention on Human Rights, so that s. 2(1)(*b*) of the 1971 Act could be challenged in Europe. Section 2(1)(*b*) is also arguably inconsistent with Article 2 of the I.L.O. Convention concerning freedom of association and protection of the right to organise (No. 87), which provides that "workers and employers, without distinction whatsoever, shall have the right to establish; and, subject only to the rules of the organisation concerned, to join organisations of their own choosing without previous authorisation." The Committee of Experts monitoring this Convention concluded that a minimum number of 100 was "exceptional" - see *General Survey on the Application of the Conventions on Freedom of Association and on the Right to Organise and Collective Bargaining*, Report 3, Part 4b (1972) at p. 27.

[97] On this Act, see Asmal (1972) 1 *I.L.J.* 164.

[98] Other than a union resulting from the amalgamation of two or more existing authorised trade unions – s. 2(2). See *infra*, p. 79.

(a) notify the Minister for Labour, the Irish Congress of Trade Unions (I.C.T.U.) and any trade union of which members of the new body are members, of its intention to make the application;
(b) cause to be published, in at least one daily newspaper in the State, a notice in the prescribed form of its intention to make the application;[99] and
(c) deposit and keep deposited with the High Court, during this eighteen month period, the appropriate sum set out in the Schedule to the 1971 Act. The size of the deposit again varies in accordance with the size of the union, in this case from a minimum of £5,000 where the membership does not exceed 2,000 to an overriding maximum of £15,000 where the membership exceeds 20,000.

Section 2(3) provides for the application to this deposit of sections 14, 15 and 16 of the 1941 Act.[1]

As far as the retention of the negotiation licence is concerned, it has been departmental practice to require such unions to keep deposited with the High Court a sum of money determined in accordance with the Schedule to the 1971 Act. However, the legislative provisions on this matter are far from clear. Section 2 of the 1971 Act refers only to the conditions which have to be satisfied for the *granting* of a negotiation licence, whereas section 7(1) of the 1941 Act refers to the conditions which have to be satisfied for the granting and *holding* of a negotiation licence. It could be argued, therefore, that the deposit required for retention of a negotiation licence is that calculated in accordance with the Schedule to the 1941 Act. In other words, a union need only keep deposited the larger sum, calculated in accordance with the Schedule to the 1971 Act, for the duration of the eighteen month period pending the grant of the negotiation licence, and, once the negotiation licence is granted, the union would be entitled to apply to the High Court under section 14 of the 1941 Act for return of part of this deposit. On the other hand, section 2(3) of the 1971 Act makes applicable to deposits under that Act, *inter alia*, section 15(1) of the 1941 Act the terms of which, as transposed to the 1971 Act, do not appear to envisage such an alteration in the deposit.

These provisions would appear to have been extremely successful in curtailing the establishment of new trade unions in Ireland as only 14

---

[99] For the prescribed form, see S.I. No. 158 of 1972. The directions specified in this Statutory Instrument are mandatory and arguably, failure to comply with them will nullify an application for a negotiation licence. *Cp. Monaghan U.D.C.* v. *Alf-A-Bet Promotions Ltd.* Supreme Court, unreported, 24 March 1980.

[1] It is interesting to note that s. 8 of the 1941 Act, as amended, which empowers the Minister to reduce the size of the deposit, is not applicable to such deposits.

have obtained negotiation licences since 1971 and of these, 9 were obtained by public service unions who changed their status from "excepted bodies" to authorised trade unions in order to avail of the protection of the Trade Disputes Act 1906, following the enactment of the Trade Disputes (Amendment) Act 1982.[2] In order to facilitate this changeover, many of these unions relied on section 3 of the 1971 Act. That section provides that a body of persons which satisfies section 7(1)(a) of the 1941 Act, *i.e.* is either a registered or a foreign based union, and which has deposited the appropriate sum of money pursuant to Schedule 1 of the 1971 Act with the High Court, but which fails to satisfy any one of the other conditions specified in section 2 of the 1971 Act, may apply to the High Court for a declaration that the granting of a negotiation licence to the applicant would not be against the public interest.[3] The High Court may, at its discretion, and after hearing evidence adduced by the applicant, the Minister, the I.C.T.U. and any other trade union, grant such declaration, in which event the Minister must grant the negotiation licence. Section 3 has been invoked on at least thirteen occasions since its enactment[4] and written judgments have been delivered by Carroll J. in relation to two of these applications: *Irish Aviation Executive Staff Association* v. *Minister for Labour*[5] and *Post Office Workers' Union* v. *Minister for Labour.*[6]

Three points emerge from her judgments. First, this machinery is to be relied on only as a last resort and unions should explore all possible avenues compatible with the legislative policy of reducing the number of trade unions operating in the country before applying to the High Court pursuant to section 3. Secondly, section 3(1) refers to a failure to comply with "a condition" specified in section 2 of the 1971 Act, so an applicant union cannot rely on its application under section 3 in order to excuse failure to comply with two or more of the conditions stipulated in section 2. Thirdly, in order to ensure that the evidential requirements specified in section 3(2) are satisfied, the applicant union should apply to the High Court for directions in relation to the evidence to be adduced prior to the hearing.

(3) *Foreign based unions which obtained negotiation licences prior to the enactment of the 1971 Act.* A foreign based, or

---

[2] See *infra*, pp. 61, 263.
[3] The practical wisdom of this arrangement is questioned by Asmal in Nevin ed., *Trade Unions and Change in Irish Society* (Dublin, 1980) at p. 107, fn 10a. See also Casey, "The Constitution and the Legal System" (1979) 14 *Ir. Jur. (n.s.)* 14 at p. 30. The Commission of Inquiry on Industrial Relations, however, saw s. 3 as a safeguard against possible objections to the 1971 Act generally on constitutional grounds – see Report of the Commission (Pl.114) para. 777.
[4] Twelve of the thirteen applications were successful, and of these twelve, two were brought by existing unions in order to replace negotiating licences which had previously been withdrawn, while the remaining ten reflect the extension of the Trade Disputes Act 1906 to the public sector by the Trade Disputes (Amendment) Act 1982.
[5] [1981] I.L.R.M. 350.
[6] [1981] I.L.R.M. 355.

"amalgamated", union in this category does not have to register with the Registrar of Friendly Societies. If it is not so registered, it must be a trade union under the law of the country in which its headquarters control is situated.[7] In either event, it must have deposited and kept deposited with the High Court a sum of money determined by reference to the Schedule of the 1941 Act,[8] and comply with section 17(2) of the Trade Union Act 1975 by having a controlling authority, every member of which is resident in the State or Northern Ireland, which authority is empowered by the union rule book "to make decisions in matters of an industrial or political nature which arise out of and are in connection with the economic or political condition of the State or Northern Ireland, are of direct concern to members of the trade union resident in the State of Northern Ireland and do not affect members not so resident."[9]

The foregoing conditions would also apply to unions which are the product of an amalgamation of two foreign based unions or an amalgamation of an Irish union and a foreign based union, provided all amalgamating unions, immediately before the amalgamation, held negotiation licences.

(4) Foreign based unions which make their first application for a negotiation licence after 1971. Again, such a union does not have to register with the Registrar of Friendly Societies.[10] If it is not so registered, it must be a trade union under the law of the country in which its headquarters control is situated. In either event, unless it makes an application under section 3 of the 1971 Act, it must satisfy section 2 of the 1971 Act and section 17(2) of the 1975 Act in order to obtain a negotiation licence. In order to retain the negotiation licence it must not only continue to comply with section 17(2) but must also keep deposited with the High Court a sum of money. However, similar difficulties arise here, as with Irish based unions who made their first application after 1971, in determining pursuant to which Act this deposit is to be calculated.[11]

---

[7] 1941 Act, s. 7(1)(a). Irish trade union legislation clearly authorises foreign based unions to operate branches in this country. However, even in the absence of such authorisation, there would not appear to be any valid legal objections to foreign based unions organising Irish workers. See the remarks of Adams J. in *Brentall* v. *Hetrick* [1928] N.Z.L.R. 788 at 793.
[8] 1941 Act, s. 7(1)(b).
[9] This puts in legislative form the position of Art. 2(b)(ii) of the I.C.T.U. Constitution. By virtue of s. 17(3) of the 1975 Act, a Ministerial Order was required to fix the date on which s. 17(2) should apply to existing holders of negotiation licences. S.I. No. 177 of 1983 fixed this date as July 1, 1983.
[10] 1941 Act, s. 7(1)(a).
[11] See *supra*, p. 55.

(b) *Procedure*

Having satisfied these various conditions a union, other than a section 3 applicant, must then apply to the Minister for Labour for a negotiation licence. The application must be on the prescribed form containing the requisite particulars and must be accompanied by the prescribed documents and a fee of £1.[12] Where the Minister is satisfied that the applicant is an authorised trade union (*viz.* that it has satisfied the various statutory conditions)[13] he must grant the licence.[14] However, he is empowered by section 17 of the 1941 Act to revoke any negotiation licence if he is satisfied that the holder has ceased to be an authorised trade union.[15] It is unlikely that the granting of a negotiation licence could be regarded as an "administration of justice" attracting the attention of Article 34.1 of the Constitution which provides that justice shall be administered by judges appointed under the Constitution.[16] But even if it could, it is submitted that the Minister is protected by Article 37 of the Constitution which authorises the exercise of limited functions and powers of a judicial nature in matters other than criminal matters, by persons other than judges. In making this decision, however, the Minister is bound to act judicially, *i.e.* in accordance with natural justice.[17]

---

[12] Trade Union Act 1941, s. 9. See also S.R. 20. No. 106 of 1942.

[13] See 84 *Dáil Debates* c. 157 (24 June 1941), where the then Minister for Industry and Commerce stated: "... when the conditions prescribed in s. 7 are fulfilled the Minister must of necessity grant the licence." Professor McCarthy has referred to this as the principle of automaticity – "Industrial Relations: Some Strategies for Change" (1979) 27 *Administration* 294 at p. 303.

[14] Trade Union Act 1941, s. 10. The Commission of Inquiry on Industrial Relations rejected proposals to introduce "normative criteria" to determine whether a union should be granted or allowed to retain a negotiation licence on the grounds, *inter alia*, that, as individual employers did not require a negotiation licence, the operation of such criteria would be seen as anomalous and inequitable – See Report, para. 781.

[15] The Minister cannot revoke a licence for any other reason so the potential of this section to act as a control mechanism is very limited. Indeed it would appear that this power is usually exercised when a union has ceased to exist or been de-registered by the Registrar of Friendly Societies. The following bodies have had their licences revoked:
National Union of Insurance Workers (Composite Section) – S.I. No. 54 of 1973;
Irish Union of Scalemakers – S.I. No. 55 of 1973;
Union of Insurance Staff – S.I. No. 56 of 1973;
Wireless Dealers' Association – S.I. No. 89 of 1973;
Irish Veterinary Union – S.I. No. 258 of 1978 – though this body subsequently obtained a new licence through a s. 3 application, see *supra*, p. 56.
Building Workers' Trade Union – S.I. No. 295 of 1980;
Irish Shoe and Leather Workers' Union – S.I. No. 187 of 1981;
Irish Actors' Equity Association – S.I. No. 192 of 1981;
Federation of Rural Workers – S.I. No. 194 of 1981;
National Society of Brushmakers – S.I. No. 313 of 1981;
Irish National Union of Woodworkers – S.I. No. 397 of 1981;
Irish Society of Woodcutting Machinists – S.I. No. 397 of 1981;
Irish Racecourse Bookmakers Assistants' Association – S.I. No. 14 of 1982;
Guild of Irish Journalists – S.I. No. 249 of 1982;

[16] On this point generally, see Kelly, *The Irish Constitution* 2nd ed., (Dublin, 1984) at pp. 210–232.

[17] *East Donegal Co-Op Livestock Mart Ltd.* v. *Attorney General* [1970] I.R. 317.

(c) *Obligations*

Authorised trade unions have certain statutory obligations imposed on them by virtue of the fact that they hold a negotiation licence. Section 12 of the 1941 Act provides that, in the case of an authorised trade union registered under the Trade Union Acts, such trade union must:

(1) include in its rules, provisions specifying the conditions of entry into, and cesser of membership of, such trade union. In *Tierney* v. *Amalgamated Society of Woodworkers*[18] it was held that this provision merely imposes an obligation on trade unions and does not confer any right to join a trade union on anyone satisfying the conditions.

(2) maintain at its office a register of its members containing certain information about each member.[19] This register must be kept open for inspection, in accordance with Ministerial regulations,[20] at union offices by any interested person who pays the requisite fees. "Interested person" includes:

   (i) any person having an interest in the funds of the trade union;
   (ii) any officer of the Minister authorised by the Minister in writing to inspect the register;[21]
   (iii) any person who has obtained an authorisation from the Minister to inspect the register.[22]

Failure on the part of the union to comply with this section is an offence and the union and such officers thereof as consent to or facilitate the failure are each liable on summary conviction to a fine not exceeding £5 together with a further fine not exceeding £1 for every day during which the offence is continued.[23]

Similar obligations are imposed on foreign based unions who do not register under the Trade Union Acts.[24] In addition, such a union must:

(1) maintain an office within the State and notify the Minister in writing of the situation of such office and of any change of address;

---

[18] [1959] I.R. 254. See *supra*, pp. 4–5.
[19] Name and address; the date of commencement of membership; where membership has ceased, the date of cessation and whether it was caused by resignation, suspension, expulsion or otherwise, and where membership has ceased by suspension or expulsion, the date of the order directing, and a reference to the rule or other provision authorising such suspension or expulsion. A person who ceases, otherwise than by death, to be a member of such a trade union shall be deemed, for the purposes of the Act, to continue to be a member thereof for one month after such cessation.
[20] S.R. & O. No. 156 of 1942.
[21] And who, incidentally, does not have to pay the stipulated fees – Trade Union Act 1942, s. 4.
[22] 1941 Act, s. 12(4).
[23] 1941 Act, s. 12(2).
[24] 1941 Act, s. 13.

(2) notify the Minister in writing of the name of a person ordinarily resident in the State whom it considers suitable for accepting service of documents on its behalf; and
(3) notify the Minister in writing of each of the following changes within three weeks of the change having taken place:
  (i) every change in its rules or constitution;
  (ii) every change in its committee of management or other controlling authority;
  (iii) every change in its trustees;
  (iv) every change in its secretary or other principal officer.

Fines for non-compliance with this section can only be imposed on those officers and members who consent to or facilitate the offence.[25]

Authorised trade unions are also obliged to file a statement of the number of its members with the Minister "on or within one month after every third anniversary of the making ... of a deposit" and, if necessary, to reduce or increase the amount of money on deposit not later than 4 months after the anniversary.[26] Authorised Irish trade unions have additional statutory obligations imposed on them by virtue of their status as registered trade unions.[27] Furthermore, by obliging Irish unions to register in order to obtain a negotiation licence, the legislation makes them more amenable to legal proceedings.[28]

(d) *Advantages*

Certain advantages adhere to authorised trade unions by virtue of the fact that they hold a negotiation licence. First, they are able to negotiate over terms and conditions of employment. Section 6 of the Trade Union Act 1941 makes it an offence for anyone, other than excepted bodies and authorised trade unions, to carry on negotiations for the fixing of wages or other conditions of employment. A particular problem which arises here relates to the position of unofficial strike committees. Such a body may be entitled to the protection of the Trade Disputes Act 1906 if it consists of members or officials of authorised trade unions.[29] However, it cannot lawfully negotiate for the resolution of any dispute concerning wages or other conditions of employment unless all its members are employed by the same employer and it is negotiating on behalf of its members only.[30]

---

[25] 1941 Act, s. 13(2). Presumably because such unions, not being registered under the Trade Union Acts, do not constitute legal entities distinct from their members. See *infra*, pp. 62–63.
[26] 1941 Act, s. 15.
[27] See *supra*, p. 50. Similar obligations are, of course, imposed on foreign based unions who choose to register with the Registrar of Friendly Societies.
[28] See *infra*, pp. 63–69.
[29] 1941 Act, s. 11. See *Gouldings Chemicals Ltd.* v. *Bolger* [1977] I.R. 211.
[30] 1942 Act, s. 2. S. 6(8) of the 1941 Act had exempted from the scope of s. 6(1) of the Act "any person or group of persons (who sought) to mediate in a trade dispute or to bring together the parties in a trade dispute with a view to reaching an amicable settlement" but this was repealed in 1942.

Secondly, authorised trade unions, and their members and officials, are entitled to the protection of the Trade Disputes Act 1906. Section 11 of the 1941 Act restricts the application of sections 2, 3 and 4 of the 1906 Act to authorised trade unions, which for the time being are holders of negotiation licences, and their members and officials.[31] The phrase "for the time being" could be of some significance in the case of a new trade union which has satisfied the various statutory conditions, has applied for a negotiation licence, but is still awaiting the grant of that licence, as it may be that such a union cannot rely on the 1906 Act. On a different point, in *Goulding's Chemicals Ltd.* v. *Bolger*[32] the Supreme Court held that members and officials of authorised trade unions engaged in unofficial action were covered by section 11 of the 1941 Act.

With the Trade Disputes (Amendment) Act 1982 the protection of the 1906 Act was extended to all employees, save members of the Defence Forces and the Gardai, who were members of authorised trade unions. One consequence of this was that public service unions became entitled to the protection of the 1906 Act provided they had a negotiation licence. Inevitably, many of these unions, which had formerly been excepted bodies, became authorised trade unions.[33]

Thirdly, certain advantages under employment protection legislation accrue to authorised trade unions and their members. For the purposes of the Unfair Dismissals Act 1977 a dismissal for trade union membership or activity will be deemed to be unfair only if the union in question is an authorised trade union or an excepted body under the Trade Union Acts 1941–1971.[34] Similarly, section 2 of the Protection of Employment Act 1977 defines the employees' representatives with whom an employer must negotiate in cases of collective redundancies as officials of an authorised trade union under the Trade Union Acts 1941–1971[35] or of a staff association with whom it has been the practice of the employer to conduct collective bargaining negotiations – presumably an excepted body under section 6 of the 1941 Act.[36] In relation to the Protection of Young Persons (Employment) Act 1977, representatives of employees with whom the Minister must consult before exercising his powers under sections 6 and 17 of the Act, means

---

[31] There must be some doubt as to whether this provision is compatible with our international obligations, particularly under I.L.O. Convention No. 87. See *General Survey on the Application of the Convention on Freedom of Association and on the Right to Organise and Collective Bargaining* (1973), Report 3, Part 4b at para. 109.

[32] [1977] I.R. 211. See *infra*, pp. 250 fn. 11, 280.

[33] 9 out of 11 unions which registered with the Registrar since January 1983 are public service unions and all of the 9 unions which were granted negotiation licences since January 1982 are public service unions.

[34] Unfair Dismissals Act 1977, s. 1. *Quaere* whether the omission, in the statutory definition, of any reference to s. 17 of the Trade Union Act 1975 excludes foreign based unions from the scope of the Act?

[35] For difficulties with this definition of "trade union", see fn. 34, *supra*.

[36] As amended by s. 2 of the Trade Union Act 1942. On the Protection of Employment Act 1977 generally, see *infra*, pp. 167–179.

either such authorised trade unions as represent the employees concerned or, where there is no such union, representatives of the employees.[37] Furthermore, authorised trade unions are entitled to initiate prosecutions on behalf of their members in relation to an offence committed under that Act.[38] Finally note must be taken of the fact that for the purposes of the Industrial Relations Acts 1946-1976, trade union means a holder of a negotiation licence granted under the Trade Union Acts.[39]

Finally, authorised Irish trade unions holding negotiation licences enjoy the minor advantages of being registered under the Trade Union Acts.[40]

THE LEGAL STATUS OF TRADE UNIONS

Perhaps the most complex legal issue which stems from the trade union legislation enacted since 1871 is one that is not dealt with expressly in any of the Acts – *viz.* what is the legal status of a trade union?[41] To answer this question one must distinguish between registered and unregistered trade unions.

Unregistered trade unions

The legal position of the unregistered trade union is comparatively straightforward – it is an unincorporated voluntary association of individuals similar in legal nature to a social club.[42] The union has no legal personality itself and consequently any action concerning the union, its property or activities must be brought or defended by way of representative action.[43]

R.S.C., O. 15, r. 9 provides that: "Where there are numerous persons having the same interest in one cause or matter, one or more of such persons may sue or be sued, or may be authorized by the Court to defend, in such cause or matter, on behalf, or for the benefit, of all persons so interested." Before a representative action can be brought

---

[37] Protection of Young Persons (Employment) Act 1977, s. 1.
[38] *Ibid.*, s. 23.
[39] Industrial Relations Act 1946, s. 3. On the other hand, it is interesting to note that authorised trade unions are not afforded any special privileges under industrial safety legislation – see for example, the Factories Act 1955, ss. 73 and 77; the Mines and Quarries Act 1965, ss. 98, 101 (*e*) (*v*); the Safety in Industry Act 1980, s. 35(1).
[40] See *supra*, pp. 48-50. See also Henry Rothschild II, "Government Regulation of Trade Unions in Gt. Britain" (1938) 38 *Col. L.R.* 1 at pp. 30-34.
[41] S. 5 of the 1871 Act does provide, *inter alia*, that trade unions may not incorporate themselves under the Companies Acts. For an examination of the differing approaches to the question of the legal status of trade unions in the U.S.A. and the U.K., see Newell, "The Status of British and American Trade Unions as Defendants in Industrial Dispute Litigation" (1983) 32 *I.C.L.Q.* 380.
[42] For an account of the general principles of law applicable to such a club, see Geldart, "The status of trade unions in England" (1911-1912) 25 *Harv. L.R.* 579 at pp. 581-4; also Lord MacDermott in *Bonsor* v. *Musician's Union* [1956] A.C. 101 at 134.
[43] See, *e.g., McLuskey* v. *Cole* [1922] 1 Ch. 7; *Parr* v. *Lancashire and Cheshire Miners' Federation* [1913] 1 Ch. 366; *Hodgson* v. *N.A.L.G.O.* [1972] 1 W.L.R. 130; *Nolan* v. *Fagan* High Court, unreported, 8 May 1985 (see *Irish Times,* May 9, 1985).

under O. 15, r. 9, however, the interests of the prospective litigants must be the same – it is not sufficient that the interests be similar.[44] This requirement of common interest severely restricts the availability of the representative action. According to Professor Lloyd:

> "It seems clear, therefore, that if the representative parties are plaintiffs their rights must derive from an identical source *e.g.* a common contract or grant. If they are defendants their position *vis à vis* the claim must be identical in the sense that there must not be different defences available to each or any of them. This would appear to exclude an action based on tort or contract, whether brought on behalf of or against representative parties; in the former case because each individual would have to prove the damage personal to himself and in the latter, because separate defences might be available to the various defendants."[45]

In *Moore and Others* v. *Attorney General for Saorstát Éireann*[46] Kennedy C.J., with whom Fitzgibbon J. agreed, stated that "no such thing is possible as an action of tort against representative defendants."[47] In this respect, it is interesting to note that O. 6, r. 10 of the Circuit Court Rules 1950 provides for representative actions "save in actions founded on tort." There is authority, however, for the proposition that when a body corporate or association engages in activity which is *ultra vires* that body, all members of the body are aggrieved and a representative action lies.[48]

Registered trade unions

The passing of the Trade Union Acts 1871 and 1876 gave rise to a

---

[44] Consequently, in *Hardie & Lane Ltd.* v. *Chiltern* [1928] 1 K.B. 663, the plaintiffs were not entitled to sue the defendants in a representative capacity for all members of the Motor Trade Association as that body had a shifting membership with some members coming in and some leaving and as a result the defendants did not have a common interest with the persons to be represented.

[45] Lloyd, "Actions instituted by or against unincorporated bodies" (1949) 12 *M.L.R.* 409 at p. 414. For the practical difficulties involved in suing an unregistered trade union by way of representative action, see Grunfeld, *Modern Trade Union Law* (London, 1966) at pp. 41–44; also *The Report of the Royal Commission on Trade Unions and Employers' Associations 1965–68*, at p. 208.

[46] [1930] I.R. 471. See also *Mintuck* v. *Valley River Band No. 63A* (1977) 75 D.L.R. (3d) 589.

[47] *Ibid.* at 499. In *McGrane* v. *Louth County Council* High Court, unreported, 9 December 1983, however, the High Court did entertain a representative action in which the plaintiffs sought a *quia timet* injunction to restrain the defendant from committing a nuisance. No reference was made, though, to the suitability of the representative action for this type of case.

[48] See *Re Gordon et al and Nova Scotia Teachers' Union* (1984) 1 D.L.R. (4th) 676; see also *John* v. *Rees* [1970] Ch. 345. So in *Bruce* v. *Donaldson and Others* (1918) 53 I.L.T.R. 24 an order was made authorising the three first named defendants to defend, on behalf of all members of the union, an action arising out of the expulsion of the plaintiff from an unregistered trade union; see also *McQualie* v. *Heeney and O'Connor* [1959] Ir. Jur. Rep. 32 where a similar order was made in relation to ejectment proceedings involving an unincoporated members' club. However, even if one could sue in tort in representative actions, unregistered, authorised trade unions would still have the benefit of the immunity conferred by s. 4 of the Trade Disputes Act 1906 – see *infra*, p. 88.

new type of trade union – the registered trade union – and it is the precise legal status of this type of union which has generated most discussion.[49] In the light of the ambiguity of the 1871 and 1876 Acts on this point, the views of the judiciary assumed great importance. It was common ground that registered unions were not corporations in the strict sense[50] but that did not by any means conclude the case. In Britain there were two conflicting views as to the precise effect of registration. On the one hand, there was the view that a registered trade union, though not a corporation, was nevertheless a new legal entity, distinct from its members – a quasi or near corporation.[51] The contrary view was that registration did not affect the essential quality of a union as an unincorporated association but merely provided a *procedural* alternative to suing a union by way of representative action by permitting litigants to sue it in its registered name.[52] The matter has been considered only once by the Irish courts. In *R. (I.U.D.W.C.)* v. *Rathmines U.D.C.*,[53] the plaintiff union sought a writ of *mandamus* to

---

[49] It would appear from the Minority Report to the Royal Commission of 1867 that, in order to minimise legal intervention in union affairs, it was not intended to confer corporate status on trade unions. This is borne out by the Trade Union Act 1871, s. 5, which provides, *inter alia*, that the Companies Acts 1862 and 1867, which established machinery for incorporating business associations, should not apply to any trade union. Furthermore, s. 9 provides that actions touching or concerning the property, right or claim to property of a registered trade union should be brought or defended by the trustees of the union, not by the union itself, while s. 7 empowers unions to purchase or lease land in the names of the union trustees. On the other hand, s. 4, para. 4, of the 1871 Act refers to any agreement made between one trade union and another, so by implication trade unions have the capacity to enter into contracts and, therefore, must be some kind of legal entity distinct from the members. Further support for this viewpoint can be found in s. 8 which provides that union property shall be held in trust by union trustees for the benefit of the union and its members. As is pointed out at p. 209 of *the Report of the Royal Commission on Trade Unions and Employers Associations 1965-1968*, "if the union was not itself a legal entity, then the trustees would have to hold the property for the benefit of the members only." Furthermore, ss. 15 and 16 provide for the imposition of fines on trade unions, as opposed to representatives of the union members, for failure to comply with the sections.

[50] Thus the opinion of Farwell J. in *Taff Vale Railway Co. Ltd.* v. *Amalgamated Society of Railway Servants* [1901] A.C. 426 that a union was not a corporation, whatever else it might be, was accepted by all members of the Court of Appeal and the House of Lords in the subsequent appeal. Though for evidence of an early difference of opinion on this, see the Lord Justice-Clerk in *M'Kernan* v. *United Operative Masons' Association of Scotland* (1874) 1 R. 453 in which he said that the legislature gave trade unions "a legal incorporation and the power of legal action for certain purposes." See also the judgment of Pickford J. in *Thomas* v. *Portsmouth "A" Branch of the Ship Construction and Shipwrights Association* (1912) 28 T.L.R. 372.

[51] See the speeches of the Earl of Halsbury, Lords Shaw and Brampton in *Taff Vale*; the *dictum* of Lord Atkinson in *A.S.R.S.* v. *Osborne* [1910] A.C. 87 at 102; the decisions of the Court of Appeal in *Cotter* v. *N.U.S.* [1929] 2 Ch. 58 and *N.U.G.M.W.* v. *Gillian* [1946] K.B. 81; the decision of Oliver J. in *Willis* v. *Brooks* [1947] 1 All E.R. 191; *B.M.T.A.* v. *Salvadori* [1949] 1 Ch. 556 and the speeches of Lords Morton and Porter in *Bonsor* v. *Musicians' Union* [1956] A.C. 104. For academic comment on the *Taff Vale* case, see the contemporary case note at (1901) 15 *Harv. L.R.* 310; also Henry Rothschild II, *op. cit.*, at pp. 1343-5.

[52] See the speeches of Lords MacNaghten and Lindley in *Taff Vale* and those of Lords MacDermott, Somerville and Keith in *Bonsor*. See also Lloyd, "Damages for Wrongful Expulsion from a Trade Union" (1956) 19 *M.L.R.* 121; Thomas, "Trade Unions and their members" (1956) 14 *C.L.J.* 67; Wedderburn, "The Bonsor Affair: Postscript" (1957) 20 *M.L.R.* 105.

[53] [1928] I.R. 260.

compel the defendant council to enforce the provisions of the Shop Hours (Drapery Trades, Dublin and Districts) Act 1925. A preliminary issue was whether a registered trade union could have sufficient interest in the subject matter of the dispute to have standing to obtain a writ of *mandamus*. The High Court held that it could, but on the facts of the case, decided, in the exercise of its discretion, against granting an absolute order of *mandamus*. The union appealed to the Supreme Court where it was held, by a majority, that the union did not have a sufficient interest to support an application for *mandamus*. However, on the more general question of the legal nature of a registered trade union, the Supreme Court was unanimous in holding that such a union was a legal entity distinct from its members. Kennedy C.J. said:

"... a trade union which has been registered with a name, an address, a constitution and rules is a legal person, at least analagous to a statutory corporation, having an existence apart from the individuals aggregated in the combination. In my opinion a trade union is as such capable of suing in its registered name in pursuance of its defined objects. It is not my view that the union, suing in its registered name, would do so in a representative capacity representing its members as separate individuals, and asserting their common but separate individual rights as in the ordinary case of litigation where one of a number of individuals having the same interest in the proceedings, is allowed to represent his class . . .

It follows, therefore, that, in my opinion, in as much as the union would take any proceedings in its own right as a legal integer, it must show for the purpose of applying for an order of mandamus a specific interest *as a union* apart from any specific interest which may be vested in its individual members who, aggregated in the union, do not lose their individuality in the combination."[54]

It was on this last point that the Chief Justice disagreed with his brethren in the Supreme Court, for he believed that the union *per se* did have sufficient interest in the dispute to bring an application for mandamus. Murnaghan J., with whom Fitzgibbon J. agreed, denied that a trade union had sufficient interest in the subject matter of the application to maintain the writ because the rule book did not authorise the union to institute legal proceedings for this purpose.[55] Furthermore even if the rule book did contain such a power, the union would have to show, before it could maintain the action, that the interests of its affected members were somehow merged with the interests of the union itself. This it could not do, according to the majority of the Supreme Court, because the true view of the position in

---
[54] *Ibid.* at 300.
[55] *Cp.* the subsequent Supreme Court decision in *T.S.S.A.* v. *C.I.E.* [1965] I.R. 180.

66   Irish Trade Union Law

the eye of the law was that it was an entity distinct from the individuals who might together form an association.[56] Furthermore the Constitution (of the then Free State), which protected the right of individual liberty, impliedly prohibited the merging of the individual's rights with those of his union. Murnaghan J. continued:

> "The individual joining an association or Union remains in the eye of the law the possessor of the rights, and is subject to the duties, of a citizen, and no part of these rights is translated to the entity know [sic] as his Union. Once a trade union is recognised as a legal entity, distinct from the personalities of the individuals who happen to be members, it must be considered quite as distinct from these individuals as is an incorporated company from its shareholders."[57]

It would appear, therefore, that in Ireland,[58] a registered trade union is regarded as a quasi-corporation, with a legal personality distinct from its members, rather than as an unincorporated association of individuals. Indeed this position has been impliedly recognised by the Oireachtas, for sections 12 and 13 of the Trade Union Act 1941 distinguish between registered and unregistered trade unions for the purpose of imposing penalties for non-compliance with statutory obligations. The basis of the distinction is that a registered trade union, being a separate legal entity, can have penalties imposed on itself as well as on the union officer, whereas in the case of an unregistered trade union, the officers only can be punished for the infringement of the Act.

The legal status of trade unions is of more than academic interest for the fact that registered trade unions are regarded as quasi-corporations does have some practical implications. The funds of such unions become susceptible to statutorily imposed penalties[59] and to awards of damages in actions other than those sounding in tort.[60] Such unions have sufficient legal personality to maintain actions for defamation,[61] and their status as quasi-corporations arguably facilitates the application to registered trade unions of two doctrines having their origin

---

[56] See Murnaghan J., [1928] I.R. at 304.
[57] *Ibid.* at 306. Emphasis added.
[58] The legal status of a registered trade union in Britain is now governed by s. 2(1) of T.U.L.R.A. 1974 which provides *inter alia*, that a trade union shall not be, or be treated as if it were, a body corporate. S. 2(2) provides that any registration of a trade union under the Companies Acts shall be void. Provision is made, however, for the voluntary incorporation of employers' associations and professional bodies. Furthermore, though unions are not to be treated as if they were incorporated, they can make contracts and sue or be sued in their own names. There is no equivalent to T.U.L.R.A. s. 2 in Northern Ireland, so that, as in the Republic, a registered trade union in Northern Ireland is regarded as a quasi-corporation. See Wood ed., *Encyclopaedia of Northern Ireland Labour Law and Practice* Vol. 2, sect. 5A.
[59] See, *e.g.,* Trade Union Act 1941, see. 12, 15(2).
[60] See, *e.g.,* Connolly v. McConnell [1983] I.R. 172. Note, however, that the immunity in tort conferred by s. 4 of the Trade Disputes Act 1906 is confined, by virtue of s. 11 of the Trade Union Act 1941, to authorised trade unions holding a negotiation licence.
[61] See, *e.g., National Union of General and Municipal Workers* v. *Gillian* [1946] K.B. 81.

in company law, *viz.* the doctrine of *ultra vires* and the Rule in *Foss* v. *Harbottle*, though virtually identical principles also apply to voluntary associations.

The quasi-corporate status of registered unions did cause certain judges to suggest that the doctrine of *ultra vires* applicable to unions was analogous to that applicable to companies[62] and, at the turn of the century, the doctrine of *ultra vires* was applied to trade union activity at two different levels – union activity might be *ultra vires* the general trade union legislation or the particular union rule book.[63]

The Trade Union Act 1913 freed unions from the constraints of the former application of the doctrine, while the second was superseded by the view that union members have a contractual right to ensure that the union's business is carried on in accordance with the rule book, with the consequence that members of unregistered as well as registered unions may have recourse to the courts in order to restrain a breach of the union rule book.[64]

The Rule in *Foss* v. *Harbottle*[65] is a principle of company law designed to restrict judicial intervention in the company's internal affairs for minor infringements of the company rules by requiring the company, and not individual shareholders, to sue whenever the duty to be enforced is one owed to the company. One implication of the rule is that the courts will not entertain litigation arising out of some irregularity which can be ratified by the general meeting, unless the general meeting consents to the bringing of the litigation. The reason for this is that:

"If the thing complained of is a thing which in substance the majority of the company are entitled to do, or if something has been done irregularly which the majority of the company are entitled to do regularly, or if something has been done illegally which the majority of the company are entitled to do legally, there can be no use in having a litigation about it, the ultimate end of which is only that a meeting has to be called and ultimately the majority gets its wishes."[66]

---

[62] See, *e.g.*, Mathew J. in *Linaker* v. *Pilcher* (1901) 17 T.L.R. 256; Lord Atkinson in *A.S.R.S.* v. *Osborne* [1910] A.C. 87, 102. For a comment on the changes wrought in Britain by T.U.L.R.A. s. 2 see Wedderburn, (1985) 14 *I.L.J.* 127.

[63] For the former see *A.S.R.S.* v. *Osborne* [1910] A.C. 87 and for the latter see *R. (I.U.D.W.C.)* v. *Rathmines U.D.C.* [1928] I.R. 240.

[64] For an example of judicial intervention in the internal affairs of Irish unions in order to secure compliance with the rule book, see *Darby* v. *Leonard* (1973) 107 I.L.T.R. 82. See also the remarks of Fitzgibbon J. in *Rogers* v. *Moore* [1931] I.R. 23 at 37, where he states, "the members of a club . . . may contract to be bound *inter se* by any rules – not actually illegal – which they please to make, and other parties may agree by contract to be bound by these rules also. It is not a question of *ultra vires* but of agreement to be bound."

[65] (1843) 2 Hare 461.

[66] *Per* Mellish L.J. in *McDougall* v. *Gardiner* (1875) 1 Ch. D. 13 at 25. For a detailed account of this aspect of trade union law see Grunfeld, *op. cit.*, pp. 95–111; also Wedderburn, "Shareholder Rights and the Rule in *Foss* v. *Harbottle*" (1957) 15 *C.L.J.* 194 and (1958) 16 *C.L.J.* 93.

It is clear from the case law[67] that the Rule applies, not only to companies, but also to registered[68] trade unions. In *Tierney* v. *A.S.W.*,[69] the plaintiff brought an action seeking, *inter alia*, an order directing the defendants to accept him for membership of the union. Budd J. held that the plaintiff had no constitutional or statutory right to join the trade union but went on to state that, even assuming that legal relations had existed between the plaintiff applicant and the union, the court had no jurisdiction in the matter of the complaint, because the Rule in *Foss* v. *Harbottle* applied.[70]

There are four exceptions to the Rule in *Foss* v. *Harbottle* where individuals are allowed to bring suit in place of the legal entity and indeed these exceptions are so sweeping that it may be difficult to imagine situations where the original rule still applies. The exceptions are:

(1) where the act complained of is *ultra vires*. This would include the very important category of actions arising out of wrongful expulsions.[71]
(2) where the act complained of can only be effective if a special or extraordinary resolution has been passed and such resolution has not been validly passed.[72]
(3) where the personal rights of the individual, including his right to vote,[73] are being infringed.[74]
(4) where those who control the union are perpetrating a fraud on the minority.[75]

---

[67] *Steele* v. *South Wales Miners' Federation* [1907] 1 K.B. 361; *Cox* v. *National Union of Foundry Workers* (1928) 44 T.L.R. 345; *Cotter* v. *N.U.S.* [1929] 2 Ch. 58; *Hodgson* v. *N.A.L.G.O.* [1972] 1 W.L.R. 130; *Taylor* v. *N.U.M. (Derbyshire Area)* [1985] I.R.L.R. 99.

[68] In *Cotter* v. *N.U.S.* [1929] 2 Ch. 58, Lord Hanworth M.R. held that *Foss* v. *Harbottle* was applicable to registered trade unions because they were, on the authority of *Taff Vale*, legal entities which work though agents and are governed by the rule book. Note also the remarks of Vinelott J., in *Taylor* v. *N.U.M. (Derbyshire Area)* [1985] I.R.L.R. 99, where he said at 102, referring to the application by the Court of Appeal in *Cotter* v. *N.U.S.* of the rule in *Foss* v. *Harbottle* to a trade union: "The principle so laid down [in *Taff Vale*] was . . . an essential step in the reasoning . . . The trade union was treated as analogous to a company for the purposes of the rule in *Foss* v. *Harbottle* because as regards its property it was to be treated as a separate legal entity governed by the code constituted by its rules and could be sued and be made liable to the extent of its property in its name."

[69] [1959] I.R. 254. See *supra*, pp. 4–5.

[70] See also the remarks of Finlay P. in *Rodgers* v. *I.T.G.W.U.* High Court, unreported, 15 March 1978, at p. 19 of the transcript. *Cf. Thomas* v. *N.U.M. (South Wales Area)* [1985] I.R.L.R. 136 where Scott J. held that if a union or its officers breached the union rules the members could sue irrespective of the rule in *Foss* v. *Harbottle*. This decision would appear to be at odds with existing authorities on this point.

[71] *E.g., O'Neill* v. *T.G.W.U.* [1934] I.R. 634.

[72] See *Edwards* v. *Halliwell* [1950] 2 All E.R. 1064.

[73] *Pender* v. *Lushington* (1877) 6 Ch. D. 70.

[74] See *Edwards* v. *Halliwell* [1950] 2 All E.R. 1064.

[75] In *Daniels* v. *Daniels* [1978] Ch. 406, Templeman J. extended this exception to cover cases where the company directors negligently, though without fraud, benefitted themselves at the expense of the company.

The Rule in *Foss* v. *Harbottle* does not apply to unregistered unions because such a union is not a legal entity capable of suing in its own name.[76] However, such bodies are afforded virtually identical protection by the "majority principle" which is applicable to all unincorporated associations.[77] The effect of this principle is that courts will not interfere in the internal affairs of an unincorporated association on the ground of mere irregularity in form in the conduct of those affairs, but will intervene to correct defects of substance.[78] It would appear from Irish case law on this point that such intervention is warranted if the association has acted in excess of its powers under the rules;[79] or the rules of natural justice have not been observed;[80] or the association has acted *mala fide*.[81]

One possible distinguishing feature between this approach and the Rule in *Foss* v. *Harbottle* which has been suggested is that a defect of substance in the internal affairs of an unincorporated association might not be open to a vote by the association's general meeting.[82] The point is still moot.[83]

---

[76] *Hodgson* v. *N.A.L.G.O.* [1972] 1 W.L.R. 130.
[77] See Citrine, *op. cit.*, p. 387; Grunfeld, *op. cit.*, pp. 106-111. See also the remarks of MacKeigan C.J.N.S. in *Re Gordon et al and Nova Scotia Teachers' Union* (1984) 1 D.L.R. (4th) 676 at 681.
[78] See, *e.g., Doyle* v. *Griffin* [1937] I.R. 93 at 112, where Murnaghan J. refers to the fact that the plaintiff "is entitled that these rules should be observed in all matters of substance."
[79] See *Forde* v. *Fottrell* (1930) 64 I.L.T.R. 89; *Ahern* v. *Molyneux* [1965] Ir. Jur. Rep. 59; *Bermingham* v. *Murphy* (1931) 65 I.L.T.R. 73; *Rogers* v. *Moore* [1931] I.R. 24.
[80] See *Forde* v. *Fottrell* (1930) 64 I.L.T.R. 89; *Ahern* v. *Molyneux* [1965] Ir. Jur. Rep. 59; *Goggin* v. *Fenney and Others* (1949) 83 I.L.T.R. 181. Irish courts have also applied the rules of natural justice to procedures leading to decisions to suspend pending more detailed enquiries. See *Ní Bheolain* v. *City of Dublin V.E.C.* High Court, unreported, 28 January 1983; *Collins* v. *Cork V.E.C.* Supreme Court, unreported, 8 March 1983. Though *cf. Rochford* v. *Storey* High Court, unreported, 4 November 1982.
[81] *Forde* v. *Fottrell* (1930) 64 I.L.T.R. 89; *Ahern* v. *Molyneux* [1965] Ir. Jur. Rep. 59.
[82] See Grunfeld, *op. cit.*, p. 111.
[83] In *O'Dea* v. *O'Connor* (1937) 71 I.L.T.R. 169, Gavan Duffy J. did state, at 175, that, notwithstanding the absence from the rules of an express power of alteration, the contract between the members could be altered if all concerned agreed to the change. This is not quite the same, however, as saying that the majority could ratify a defect of substance notwithstanding the wishes of the minority.

Chapter 3

AMALGAMATION AND DISSOLUTION OF UNIONS

AMALGAMATIONS AND TRANSFERS OF ENGAGEMENTS

Statutory provision for the amalgamation of trade unions dates back to the Trade Union Act Amendment Act 1876, section 12 of which provided that:

"Any two or more trade unions may, by the consent of not less than two-thirds of the members of each or every such trade union, become amalgamated together as one trade union, with or without any dissolution or division of the funds of such trade unions or either or any of them; but no amalgamation shall prejudice any right of a creditor of either or any union party thereto."

Section 12 of the 1876 Act was amended by the Trade Union (Amalgamation) Act 1917, section 1 of which provided that henceforth, before an amalgamation could take place, the votes of at least 50% of the members of each amalgamating union must be recorded and of the votes recorded, those in favour of the proposal must exceed by 20% or more the votes against the proposal.[1]

These conditions were onerous and not a little confusing and in order to facilitate the voluntary amalgamation of unions in Ireland, the Oireachtas, at the behest of the trade union movement,[2] replaced the earlier legislation with the Trade Union Act 1975.[3]

This Act provides two different methods whereby two or more unions[4] may merge:

(i) *Amalgamation* – Here the various unions come together to form a new union.

(ii) *Transfer of engagements* – A transfer of engagements occurs whenever a union (the transferor union) officially transfers its obligations and assets to another union (the transferee union). As the transferee union retains its separate existence, this does

---

[1] For cases arising under pre-1975 legislation, see *Booth* v. *Amalgamated Marine Workers' Union* [1926] Ch. 904; *Sheet Iron Workers' and Light Platers' Society* v. *Boilermakers' and Iron and Steel Shipbuilders' Society* (1924) 40 T.L.R. 294, and in the Irish context, *Dunne* v. *Marks* High Court, unreported, 30 May 1968.

[2] For an indication of how active Congress was in assisting in the drafting of the Trade Union Act 1975, see the address of R. Roberts to the 16th Annual Conference of the I.C.T.U., reported in the 16th Annual Report of the I.C.T.U. (1973–74), at pp. 445–447.

[3] Amalgamations, transfers of engagements or changes of name pending at the date of the commencement of the Act were excluded from its provisions – s. 14. The Irish Act appears to have been modelled on the British equivalent, the Trade Union (Amalgamations, *etc.*) Act 1964.

[4] Thus the 1975 Act arguably does not apply to a merger between a trade union and a non-union body, a not inconceivable situation given that some "excepted bodies" care not trade unions. To effect such a merger, one would have to ensure that it was *intra vires* the constituent bodies and thereafter complied with the provisions of the relevant rule books.

not result in the creation of a new union. This fact carries with it a number of advantages[5] which possibly explains why there have been more transfers of engagements under the 1975 Act than amalgamations.[6]

An initial point to note about the Act is its definition of union member. Section 1(2) defines "member", in relation to a trade union, as

> "a member for the time being entitled to any benefits provided out of the funds of the trade union but, where the rules of a trade union specify the person (or class of persons) entitled to vote on a particular matter (or class of matter) 'member' means those persons."

As in Canada, a significant proportion of the national workforce are members of trade unions which have their head office abroad. The situation is further complicated by the fact that trade unions in Ireland are organised on a 32 county basis. This presents obvious difficulties in the case of amalgamations or transfers involving unions whose operations straddle the various jurisdictions. Section 9 of the 1975 Act deals with one aspect of this problem by providing that a majority of the members of a foreign based union who are resident in the State and Northern Ireland may decide to amalgamate with or transfer their engagements to another trade union whereupon, for the purposes of the 1975 Act, such a majority are regarded as a separate trade union from the date of this decision and may, on subsequently complying with the requirements of the 1975 Act, effect such amalgamation or transfer. This section thus enables the 32 county membership of a British based union to amalgamate with or transfer their engagements to another Irish trade union, or the Irish branch of another British based union, or even another British based union[7] without having to have recourse to their fellow members resident in Britain.

---

[5] See *infra*, pp. 78–79.

[6] To date there appears to have been only three amalgamations under the 1975 Act – the Irish Hairdressers' Association with the National Hairdressers' Federation in 1976; the Irish Union of Woodworkers with the Irish Society of Woodcutting Machinists in 1979; and Irish Graphical Society with the Irish Bookbinders' and Allied Trades Union and the Electrotypers and Stereotypers Society, Dublin and District in 1984. In contrast there have been six transfers of engagements – the Irish Shoe and Leather Workers' Union to the I.T.G.W.U. in 1977; the Irish Actors' Equity to the I.T.G.W.U. in 1979; the Federation of Rural Workers to the Workers' Union of Ireland in 1979; the Irish Racecourse Bookmakers, *etc.* to the I.T.G.W.U. in 1981; the Irish Federation of Musicians to the I.T.G.W.U. in 1982; and the Irish Women Workers' Union to the Federated Workers' Union of Ireland in 1984.

[7] Opposition suggestions that section 9 be restricted to amalgamations with or transfers to "another trade union based in the State or Northern Ireland" were rejected by the Minister for Labour on the ground that the Constitution would not permit such a limitation of the right of association – See 79 *Seanad Debates* cc. 1067–1068 (25 March 1975).

Section 9, however, does not cover the converse situation, *viz.* where a British based union is considering an amalgamation or transfer, which move would affect the position of its Irish members. As far as the authors are aware, this situation has not yet arisen with any of the British based unions operating here. If it were to occur, a ballot of both Irish and British members would have to approve the proposal before it could have legal effect.[8] This would give rise to the following possible scenarios:

(a) An overall majority in both sections of the union in favour of the proposal, in which case the amalgamation or transfer will have legal effect in both jurisdictions.
(b) A majority of Irish members in favour, but a majority of British members opposed. It is submitted that this situation would be covered by section 9 so that the Irish members now constitute a separate trade union and may effect the amalgamation or transfer if the other parties agree and the 1975 Act is satisfied.
(c) A majority of Irish members opposed, but a majority of British members in favour. Insofar as section 9 refers only to a situation where the Irish members of a foreign based union make a *positive* decision to amalgamate or transfer engagements, it would not appear to be applicable here. Nor is this situation necessarily covered by section 17 of the 1975 Act,[9] as the issue here is one which does affect members of the union resident outside the State or Northern Ireland and as such does not have to come within the jurisdiction of the committee of management envisaged by section 17. It may be, of course, that such a move on the part of the Irish members could be construed as an act of secession from the parent union, if the rule book provides for secession.[10] *Absent* such a provision, the alternatives for the Irish members, if they are not prepared to accept the overall majority's decision, are to resign or to bring themselves within section 9 by deciding to effect an amalgamation or transfer with another union.

Effecting amalgamations or transfers of engagements

Section 2 of the 1975 Act, which permits unions to effect amalgamations or transfers of engagements, is peremptory in nature in relation to the method to be used, permitting only amalgamations or transfers effected in the particular way there described.

In order to effect an amalgamation, each amalgamating union must draw up (a) an instrument of amalgamation, and (b) a notice in writing

---

[8] See the Trade Union (Amalgamations, *etc.*) Act 1964, s. 2(3). It is interested to note that in relation to the operation of those provisions of the Trade Union Act 1913 relating to the holding of a ballot for the purposes of establishing a political fund, the Chief Registrar in Britain ruled, in an application by the Amalgamated Society of Lithographic Printers in 1938, *inter alia*, that

to members pursuant to section 3(3). The next step is to satisfy the Registrar[11] on three different points:

(a) that, in accordance with section 3(2), the union has taken all reasonable steps to ensure that, not less than seven days before voting on the resolution begins, every member of the union has received a section 3(3) notice;
(b) that the section 3(3) notice satisfies the conditions of that subsection, *viz.*
   (i) it sets out in full the instrument of amalgamation or gives sufficient account of it to enable a recipient of the notice to form a reasonable judgment of the main effects of the proposed amalgamation;
   (ii) if it does not set out the instrument in full, it states where copies of the instrument may be inspected;
   (iii) it complies with any regulations under the Act;[12]
(c) that the instrument complies with the requirements of any regulations under the Act for the time being in force and relating thereto.[13]

Once the instrument of amalgamation and the section 3(3) notice have been approved by the Registrar, the unions may proceed with the holding of a vote on a resolution approving the instrument of amalgamation. The voting must be taken in a manner satisfying the conditions specified in section 3(1) *viz.*:

(a) every member of the union must be entitled to vote on the resolution and the voting must be by secret ballot;
(b) every member of the union must be allowed to vote without interference or constraint and, so far as is reasonably possible, must be given a fair opportunity of voting[14] – this condition might oblige the union concerned to provide a system of postal voting in certain cases;
(c) the method of voting must consist of the marking of a voting paper by the person voting;

---

the ballot must also be extended to cover Irish based members of the union – see Ewing, *Trade Unions, the Labour Party and the Law* (Edinburgh, 1982) at p. 99.

[9] See *supra*, p. 57.
[10] As to which, see *infra*, p. 81.
[11] The constitutionality of the Registrar's statutory powers in relation to amalgamations is considered *supra*, at p. 47.
[12] The relevant regulation is S.I. No. 53 of 1976. S.I. No. 292 of 1983 contains, *inter alia*, a table of the fees involved in effecting amalgamations, transfers of engagements, and changing the union's name.
[13] S. 3(4).
[14] In *Dunne* v. *Marks* High Court, unreported, 30 May 1968, Teevan J. ruled that denial of participation merely by reason of accident in postal communication or by office mistake of a minor character in an insignificant number of cases would not invalidate a ballot.

(d) the union must take reasonable steps to ensure that, at least seven days before voting begins, every member of the union receives a notice in writing which complies with section 3(3);

(e) the union must publish, at least seven days before the voting on the resolution begins, in at least one daily newspaper published in the State, notice of the holding of the vote.

By virtue of section 5, the resolution may be passed by a simple majority of the votes recorded[15] in each of the ballots organised by the various trade unions, notwithstanding anything in the union rule books. Section 6 provides that the amalgamation itself will not have legal effect until the instrument of amalgamation is registered and the earliest this can take place, in the absence of a complaint being lodged with the Registrar challenging the validity of the resolution, is six weeks after the date of application for registration.[16] Any union wishing to effect a transfer of engagements must go through the same procedure with an instrument of transfer and must, in addition, obtain an undertaking from the transferee union to fulfil the engagements.[17] A significant difference between effecting an amalgamation and effecting a transfer is that in the latter case, one need only obtain a ballot of the members of the transferor union whereas in the former case one requires separate ballots of the members of all the unions involved and in each ballot there must be a majority in favour of the resolution. In this context it should be noted that the legislation goes quite far in overriding the union rule book in order to facilitate amalgamations and transfers. Section 7 provides that sections 2 to 6 of the Act shall apply to every amalgamation or transfer of engagements, notwithstanding anything in the union rule book and section 8 empowers the governing body of a transferee union to alter the union rule book by memorandum in writing so far as may be necessary to give effect to the instrument of transfer, notwithstanding anything in the rules.[18]

Complaints procedure

The instrument of amalgamation or transfer does not take effect until it has been registered by the Registrar under the Act[19] and it

---

[15] In *Dunne* v. *Marks, supra* fn 14, Teevan J. held that spoiled votes did not constitute recorded votes for the purposes of the 1917 Act. This reasoning would appear to be equally applicable to the 1975 Act.

[16] It would appear to be open to the parties, on the wording of s. 6, to provide that the amalgamation should take effect at some date after the registration of the instrument of amalgamation.

[17] Ss. 2(4), 3(2), 4, 5.

[18] However, the union rule book may expressly exclude the application of s. 8 to that union – s. 8(3).

[19] Given that the 1975 Act is peremptory as to the method of effecting an amalgamation of transfer, and, in the absence of an express provision that registration of the relevant instrument is to be conclusive evidence of the validity of the amalgamation or transfer for all

cannot be so registered until six weeks after application for registration has been made to the Registrar.[20] The purpose of the six-week delay is to give any union member, who may have a complaint about the amalgamation or transfer, an opportunity to lodge an appeal with the Registrar, pursuant to section 10. That section entitles trade union members to complain to the Registrar if they have a grievance in respect of the manner in which a resolution approving an instrument of amalgamation or transfer was passed by their union. The complainant must base his claim either on the ground that the conditions specified in section 3(1) were not satisfied, or that the votes recorded in relation to the resolution did not have the effect of passing it. Presumably what is in issue is whether the votes cast in favour of the resolution constituted a simple majority of all the votes recorded in the ballot.

Section 10(2) provides that the complaint must be lodged within six weeks after an application for registration of the instrument of amalgamation or transfer is lodged under section 6 and once a complaint is made the Registrar may not register the relevant instrument until the complaint has been finally determined.[21] The Registrar may, after having given the complainant and the trade union concerned an opportunity of being heard, either dismiss the complaint or find it justified.[22] In the latter case he has to make an order specifying what steps he requires to be taken before he will consider an application for registration of the instrument under section 6 of the Act[23] and, in either case, he is obliged to furnish to the complainant and the trade union concerned a statement of the reasons for his decision.[24] The Registrar is entitled to vary an order made under sub-section (5) and where he had made an order under that sub-section he cannot entertain any application to register the instrument unless he is satisfied that the steps specified by him have been taken.

---

purposes, it is submitted that registration cannot validate an invalid amalgamation or transfer. Cp. Booth v. *Amalgamated Marine Workers' Union* [1926] Ch. 904; *Egan v. Shop, Distributive and Allied Employees Federation of Australia, N.S.W.* (1979) 143 C.L.R. 325.

[20] S. 6. In *Rothwell v. A.P.E.X.* [1979] I.C.R. 211, it was suggested that the registration of an instrument earlier than six weeks after application for registration had been made to the Certification Officer was valid as the corresponding (and virtually identical) provision to s. 6 in the British legislation was directory rather than mandatory. It is submitted, however, that the use of the word "shall" in s. 6 of the 1975 Act indicates that the section is mandatory. In *State (Elm Developments Ltd.) v. An Bord Pleanala* [1981] I.L.R.M. 108, Henchy J. said, at 110:

> "Whether a provision in a statute or statutory instrument, which on the face of it is obligatory (for example, by use of the word 'shall'), should be treated by the courts as truly mandatory or merely directory depends on the statutory scheme as a whole and the part played in that scheme by the provision in question."

It is submitted that, in the present case, s. 6 should be construed as mandatory rather than directory in order to afford adequate protection to the rights of individual trade union members affected by an amalgamation or transfer of engagements.

[21] S. 10(3).
[22] S. 10(4).
[23] S. 10(5).
[24] S. 10(6).

Section 10(8), read in conjunction with the Schedule to the Act, outlines the procedure to be followed in relation to complaints made under section 10. Paragraph 1 of the Schedule details the powers of the Registrar in relation to the hearing of a complaint under section 10. He may, *inter alia*, compel the complainant or any officer of the trade union concerned to attend the hearing, and may also require the attendance of any person as a witness; he may require the production of documents relating to the matter complained of and may administer oaths and take affirmations, and require witnesses to be examined on oath; furthermore he can order that the whole or any part of the expenses of hearing the complaint be paid either out of the trade union funds or by the complainant and may order either party to pay the costs of the other.[25] Paragraph 3(1) makes it an offence for any person to refuse to comply with a requisition of the Registrar made under paragraph 1(*a*), (*b*) or (*c*), or with any order made in pursuance of paragraph 1(*d*). However, he cannot be convicted of any offence by reason of failure to attend as a witness unless he has already been compensated by the person calling him.[26] Paragraph 3(3) provides for taxation of costs and paragraph 3(4) provides for recovery of sums payable under paragraph 1(*e*) or 1(*f*).

The validity of a resolution approving an instrument of amalgamation or transfer cannot be questioned in any legal proceedings, other than those brought before the Registrar under section 10 or proceedings arising out of such proceedings, on any ground on which a complaint could be, or could have been, made to the Registrar under this section.[27] The Registrar may, however, at the request of the complainant or of the trade union, state a case for the opinion of the High Court on a question of law arising out of the proceedings and the decision of the High Court on a case stated under this subsection shall be final.[28]

The effect of the foregoing provisions would appear to be that once six weeks have elapsed from the date of application for registration it is not possible to challenge the validity of a resolution approving an instrument of amalgamation or transfer on the grounds set out in section 10. By implication, challenges based on other grounds, *e.g.* that the merger was between a union and a non-union with the result that sections 7 and 8 could not legitimate any violation of the relevant rule book, could still, even within the terms of the Act, be entertained by the courts, subject to the normal rules of limitation of actions. Alternatively an appeal against a decision of the Registrar under this section[29] may be taken to the High Court on a point of law and of course the

---

[25] Paragraph 2 provides for the reimbursement of any witness required to attend before the Registrar by the person calling him as witness.
[26] Paragraph 3(2).
[27] S. 10(9). On the constitutionality of this provision, see *supra*, p. 47.
[28] S. 10(10).
[29] S. 10(12).

Registrar is also subject to judicial review by means of the stateside orders.

Finally, section 10(11) provides that, for the purposes of the section, a complaint which is withdrawn shall be deemed to be finally determined at the time when it is withdrawn.

Disposition of property on amalgamation or transfer

Section 11(1) provides for the vesting of property belonging to an amalgamating or transferor union in the appropriate trustees after the instrument of amalgamation or transfer has taken effect or the trustees have been appointed, whichever is the later. No conveyance, assignment or assignation is required. The instrument of amalgamation or transfer may, however, except property from the effect of this subsection.[30] If registered land is affected by the amalgamation or transfer, then the Land Registry shall, upon payment of the appropriate fee, register the appropriate trustees as owners of the land.[31] Section 11(4) defines "appropriate trustees" as being either trustees of the branch of the amalgamated or transferee union, where the property is to be held for the benefit of that branch and the union rule book does not provide for the vesting of that property in the national trustees, or, in all other cases, the national trustees.

The Minister for Labour may, with the consent of the Minister for Finance, make a grant of an amount of money to a union to cover such expenses as he is satisfied were exceptional and were incurred by the union as a result, in the course, or in contemplation, of such amalgamation or transfer.[32] It would appear that this is designed to compensate trade union officials who lose their jobs as a result of amalgamation[33] and also to cover printing, postage and general voting expenses. Amalgamation or transfer must have taken place, however, and in this respect it is interesting to note that the Commission of Inquiry on Industrial Relations suggested that financial assistance be made available to unions to cover exploratory research into the feasibility of proposed amalgamations or transfers, whether the anticipated merger actually takes place or not.[34]

---

[30] S. 11(3).
[31] S. 11(2).
[32] S. 15.
[33] See 276 *Dáil Debates* c. 335 (27th November 1974).
[34] See the Report of the Commission of Inquiry on Industrial Relations (Pl. 114), paragraph 87. Significantly certain Congress officials appear to have been under the impression that grants could be obtained even where the merger did not take place. See the remarks of R. Roberts at the 16th Annual Conference of the I.C.T.U., reported at p. 446 of the 16th Annual Report (1973–74). The Minister for Labour in his *Discussion Document on Industrial Relations Reform* (1985) stated, at para. 15, that s. 15 of the 1975 Act would be amended to provide that grants may be paid for expenses incurred in connection with proposed amalgamations or transfers regardless of whether the proposed amalgamation or transfer eventually took place. Furthermore, in para. 16 it was stated that the operation of s. 15 would be reviewed with a view to establishing what improvements were necessary and feasible in the grants currently payable for expenses incurred in connection with amalgamations or transfers.

Change of name

Section 12 permits trade unions to change their name.[35] The union may act either in accordance with its rules or, if they do not expressly provide a method whereby the name can be changed, by altering the provision in the rule book which gives the union its name. The change of name shall not take effect until registered by the Registrar of Friendly Societies under the 1975 Act and the new name cannot be identical to or resemble a name by which any other existing trade union has been registered. Furthermore the change in name cannot affect any right or obligation of the union or of any of its members, nor can it prejudice any pending legal proceedings instituted by or against union trustees or officers.

Political Fund[36]

A significant feature of the Trade Union Act 1975 is the absence of any provision dealing with the political fund of the new entity resulting from amalgamation. Section 5(4) of the British Trade Union (Amalgamations, *etc*) Act 1964[37] provides that where two or more unions are amalgamating and all of them before the amalgamation had political funds, they shall be treated as having passed a resolution for the purpose of authorising the establishment of a political fund, so long as the political fund rules have been included in the new rule book. The 1975 Act contains no comparable provision and it is clear that, before the new entity could operate a political fund, it must satisfy the conditions of the Trade Union Act 1913[38] notwithstanding that all the constituent bodies may have had such funds prior to amalgamation. It would be very convenient if one could make provision for a political fund in the instrument of amalgamation and then treat the ballot on amalgamation as being in addition a ballot on the political fund for the purposes of the 1913 Act.[39] It is not clear, however, that such a practice would be permitted by the legislation. Section 3(1) of the 1913 Act requires a ballot of the "members of the union", not its prospective members. The amalgamated union, however, will not exist until at least six weeks after the ballot on amalgamation has taken place as that is the earliest date upon which the Registrar could register the instrument of amalgamation.[40] It would appear, therefore, that a vote

---

[35] A recent example here is the decision of the Irish Union of Distributive Workers and Clerks to change its name to the Irish Distributive and Administrative Trade Union.
[36] See *infra*, pp. 89–94.
[37] See also s. 5(4) of Trade Union (Amalgamations, *etc.*) Act (Northern Ireland) 1965.
[38] Namely having the expenditure of money on "political" objects approved as an object of the "new" union by a resolution passed on a ballot of the members of the "new" union and having rules providing for the payment of monies in furtherance of "political" objects out of a separate fund approved by the Registrar. See the comments of the Minister for Labour at 276 *Dáil Debates* cc. 338–339 (27 November 1974) and 79 *Seanad Debates* c. 1081 (25 March 1975).
[39] As happened recently when the Irish Graphical Society, the Electrotypers and Stereotypers Society and the Irish Bookbinders and Allied Trades Union amalgamated to form the Irish Print Union.
[40] 1975 Act, s. 6.

taken on the political fund when the new entity has yet to come into existence and has yet to acquire actual members, does not comply with the requirements of the Trade Union Act 1913 and that a second ballot, involving additional expense, is required. Not does the legislation refer, in this context, to the legal position which obtains after a transfer of engagements. However, the position here is more straight-forward. It is submitted that the legal position of the transferee union would determine the issue for, if that union operated a political fund prior to the transfer, then the members of the transferor union would have to contribute to it unless they contracted out.[41] If, on the other hand, the transferee union did not previously operate a political fund, it could not do so after the transfer unless it complies with the provisions of the 1913 Act.

Negotiation Licences

Where two or more unions amalgamate, they lose their separate existence. Consequently, the act of amalgamation results in the revocation of any negotiation licences held by the constituent unions and the new entity has to apply for a new licence. Where each of the amalgamating unions had been the holder of a negotiation licence immediately before the amalgamation, section 2(2) of the Trade Union Act 1971 provides that an application from the newly formed entity is to be processed by reference to the original conditions for holding a licence contained in the Trade Union Act 1941, so that the new entity does not have to comply with the more onerous conditions of the 1971 Act, even where all the amalgamating unions originally had to satisfy the provisions of that Act in order to obtain their respective negotiation licences. The act of amalgamation will have the further consequence that, under section 8 of the Trade Union Act Amendment Act 1876, the Registrar is empowered to cancel the registration of any registered amalgamating unions on the ground that they have ceased to exist. Such unions must be given at least two months notice in writing of the Registrar's intention to cancel registration so that there can be a delay of up to two months between registration of the newly formed entity and deregistration of its constituent parts. It is important to note that registration of the instrument of amalgamation, pursuant to section 6 of the 1975 Act, does not have the effect of registering the new entity under the 1871 Act.[42]

---

[41] An opposition amendment, which would have provided that, where there was a merger of a union which had a political fund with a union which did not, members of the latter should not have to contribute to the political fund unless they contracted in, was defeated – see 276 *Dáil Debates* cc. 1069–1093 (27 November 1974) and 79 *Seanad Debates* cc. 335–356 (25 March 1975).

[42] *Egan v. Shop, Distributive and Allied Employees' Federation of Australia*, N.S.W. (1979) 143 C.L.R. 325 at 334, 352, 363 (*per* Barwick C.J., Gibbs and Stephen JJ. respectively). *Cf.* Murphy J., dissenting, at 371. For registration under the 1871 Act see *supra*, pp. 42–50.

Conclusion

The legislation here is clearly facilitative and cannot be regarded as responsible for the low number of amalgamations and transfers since 1975. Nevertheless, certain reforms of a technical nature could be effected. In particular it might be advisable to introduce legislation along the lines of section 5(4) of the Trade Union (Amalgamations, *etc.*) Act 1964 in order to provide for the continuity of political funds after amalgamations. In addition, the authors feel that some thought should be given to the difficulties which could arise in the event of an amalgamation or transfer of engagements between unions in Britain, where those unions also have an Irish membership.

DISSOLUTION[43]

Method of dissolution

Section 14 of the Trade Union Act Amendment Act 1876 provides, *inter alia*, that the rules of every registered[44] trade union shall provide for the manner of dissolving the union and that notice of such dissolution, signed by the secretary and seven members, must be forwarded to the Registrar within fourteen days of dissolution.[45]

Where the rules do not provide for a manner of dissolution, as for example, in the case of unregistered trade unions, the union may rely on the inherent jurisdiction of the High Court to dissolve voluntary associations whenever it appears "just and equitable" to do so. In *Keys v. Boulter (No. 2)*[46] Megarry J. in the Chancery Division opined that the court had an inherent jurisdiction to order the dissolution of a union where no appropriate machinery existed for securing its proper winding up. In the instant case an amalgamation of two unions into a federally structured union failed and the amalgamated union was left without an executive for a considerable period of time. The union rules did provide for dissolution but only on the basis of a division of assets among all the members of the union. This was somewhat inappropriate where the two constituent unions continued to function separately with property under the control of the executive council so Megarry J., exercising the inherent jurisdiction of the Court, ordered that the union be dissolved and the funds restored to the two constituent unions.

Distribution of assets

The assets of a union will be distributed, on dissolution, in

---

[43] For an enlightening article on this topic, see Green, "The Dissolution of Unincorporated non-Profit Associations" (1980) 43 *M.L.R.* 626.
[44] The section actually refers to "every trade union" but the section has always been treated as applying to registered trade unions only. See Grunfeld, *Modern Trade Union Law* (London, 1966) at p. 57.
[45] Failure to send the notice results in penalties being imposed under s. 15 of the 1876 Act.
[46] [1972] 1 W.L.R. 642.

accordance with any provision of the rule book governing the matter.[47] The law is unclear as to how such assets are to be distributed in the absence of such a provision. On the one hand it is suggested that the concept of resulting trust should be applied to the assets and that the funds be divided in proportion to the amount contributed by each member.[48] The difficulty with this view is that it fails to explain why past members do not share in the distribution of a union's assets on dissolution. The alternative view is that funds should be distributed between members existing at the date of winding up on the basis of membership of the union rather than on the basis of a resulting trust. Normally such funds would be distributed equally among the members though if the rules recognised different classes of members this would not necessarily be the case.[49]

SECESSION

Secession entails a substantial section of a union resigning en masse. Indeed at one stage it was felt that secession was simply a collective exercise of the individual right to resign,[50] but in *John* v. *Rees*,[51] however, the analogy with the individual right to resign was rejected. It now appears that the specific power to secede must be conferred by the union rule book, and in the absence of such a provision, attempts to secede could be restrained by injunction. In the event of a secession being authorised, the property of the seceding section must be distributed in accordance with the union rule book.[52]

---

[47] Union members may bring legal proceedings to enforce their share in the assets on a winding up, as this does not fall within the scope of s. 4 of the Trade Union Act 1871. See Buckley L.J. in *Osborne* v. *A.S.R.S.* [1911] 1 Ch. 540, 567.
[48] *Re Printers and Transferrers' Amalgamated Trades Protection Society* [1899] 2 Ch. 184;
[49] *Tierney* v. *Tough* [1914] 1 I.R. 142; *Feeney and Shannon* v. *MacManus* [1937] I.R. 23; *Re Sick and Funeral Society* [1973] 1 Ch. 51. Green suggests, *loc. cit.* at p. 640, that, in the absence of an express provision in the contract of membership dealing with division of assets, all the members of an unincorporated association should be regarded as tenants in common and that the division of assets should only be on the basis of equality where the individual member's contributions are equal or where it is impossible to quantify such contributions.
[50] See, *e.g.*, Grunfeld, *op. cit.*, p. 207.
[51] [1970] Ch. 345.
[52] *Cope* v. *Crossingham* [1909] 2 Ch. 148.

Chapter 4

PROPERTY, TRUSTEES AND UNION FUNDS

Because the objects of many trade unions were in unlawful restraint of law at common law, any trust for such objects was void and would not be enforced by the Courts. Consequently unions could not vest their property in trustees. Parliament tackled this problem by expressly providing that the purposes of a trade union should not be regarded as unlawful so as to render void or voidable any agreement or trust, merely because they were in restraint of trade,[1] and by giving registered unions statutory powers to hold property by way of trust.[2]

Registered trade unions

Section 7 of the Trade Union Act 1871, as amended,[3] provided that every registered trade union[4] can purchase or take upon lease, in the name of its trustees, any land and guarantees the authority of such trustees to sell, exchange, mortgage, or let the same.

In *Re Amos, Carrier* v. *Price*[5] North J. held that the word "purchase" in section 7 was used in the ordinary sense of "buy for money", not in the technical sense of "acquire otherwise than by descent or escheat" and so ruled that a union could not validly accept testamentary gifts of property. This decision must now be read in the light of section 1(1) of the Trade Union Act 1913 and unions may accept a valid gift or devise of land if authorised to do so by the rule book.[6] But because of this interpretation of the word "purchase", it appears that the authority of trustees of registered unions to sell, exchange, mortgage or let union property is only guaranteed in those cases where the land was purchased for money or money's worth.[7] Thus in the case of land of an unregistered union or in the case of land of a registered union acquired otherwise than by money or money's worth, the prospective purchaser, assignee, mortgagee or tenant will have to satisfy himself that the trustees have authority to enter into the particular transaction involved.[8]

---

[1] Trade Union Act 1871, s. 3.
[2] 1871 Act, s. 8 as amended by the Trade Union Act Amendment Act 1876, s. 3.
[3] Trade Union Act 1935. See fn. 4 below.
[4] S. 7 also provides that, for the purpose of the section, every branch of a trade union shall be considered a distinct union. This was, no doubt, an important provision when trade unions were restricted to holding land not exceeding one acre but this limitation has since been abolished by the Trade Union Act 1935, thirteen years after a similar reform had been enacted in the U.K. – s. 106 of the Law of Property Act 1922.
[5] [1891] 3 Ch. 159.
[6] *Citrine's Trade Union Law*, 3rd ed. (London, 1967) at pp. 159–162.
[7] *Quaere* – where land is acquired for peppercorn rent.
[8] Citrine, *op. cit.* at pp. 161–162.

Property, Trustees and Union Funds 83

All real and personal estate of a registered union is vested in the trustees for the time being of that union[9] and the real and personal estate of any branch is vested in the trustees of such branch, though the trustees of the union may hold the real and personal estate of any branch if the rules so provide.[10] In the event of a change of trustees of a registered trade union, the law provides for the automatic vesting of union property, with the exception of public stock and securities,[11] in the new trustees.[12]

Although the 1871 Act envisages that branch property may be vested in branch trustees, this does not mean that the branch can deal with the property as it wishes. The matter is governed by the union rule book. Thus in *Cope* v. *Crossingham*,[13] an action in which an injunction was sought to restrain a union branch from seceding from the union and distributing its funds among the branch members, it was held that the funds of the branch should be treated as funds of the association, so that the union trustees were entitled to their injunction.[14]

Unregistered trade unions

Sections 7 to 12 of the Trade Union Act 1871 do not apply to unregistered trade unions. However, such bodies may hold property if so authorised by the rule book.[15]

TRUSTEES[16]

Appointment

Registered unions are required to provide in their rule book for the appointment and removal of union trustees.[17] Unregistered trade

---

[9] Authorised trade unions must deposit and keep deposited with the High Court a sum of money determined in accordance with the size of the membership, though the union does have the right to have the deposit vested in such authorised securities as the union shall specify – Trade Union Act 1941, ss. 7(1)(*b*) and 14; Trade Union Act 1971, s. 2(1)(*a*)(iii). See *supra*, pp. 53, 55, 57.

[10] 1871 Act, s. 8 as amended by the 1876 Act, s. 3. The trustees are bound by the doctrine of *ultra vires* and a union member may obtain an injunction to prevent them dealing with union property in a manner which is *ultra vires* the rules. See *supra*, p. 67, *infra*, pp. 121–123.

[11] S. 4 of the 1876 Act empowers the Registrar to transfer public stock held in the name of a trustee where that trustee is absent from Ireland, or becomes a bankrupt, or files a petition for his own bankruptcy, or executes any deed for liquidation of his affairs or composition with his creditors, or becomes a lunatic or is dead or has been removed from his office as trustee or is not known to be living or dead.

[12] 1871 Act, s. 8. The Trade Union Act 1975, s. 11, provides for the automatic vesting of union property in the new trustees and in the case of registered land, for the registration of the new trustees as owners of the land, in the event of amalgamation or transfer of engagements.

[13] [1902] 2 Ch. 148.

[14] In most cases the central authority will be deemed to have sufficient interest in branch funds to prevent their dissipation. See Kidner, *Trade Union Law* 2nd ed. (London, 1983) at p. 66. For similar Commonwealth decisions, see *Brentell* v. *Hetrick* [1928] N.S.L.R. 788; *Raymond* v. *Doherty* (1965) 49 D.L.R. (2d) 99.

[15] Trade Union Act 1913, s. 1(1).

[16] For a comprehensive account of the law applicable to trustees generally, see Wylie, *Irish Land Law* (Oxon, 1975), Ch. 10.

[17] 1871 Act, Sch. 1, para. 4.

unions do not have any similar obligation and the trustees of such unions may be appointed in the ordinary way, *viz.* by deed of appointment or pursuant to the statutory powers of appointment.[18]

As a matter of last resort, the trustees of either registered or unregistered trade unions could be appointed by the High Court, as "equity will not permit a trust to fail for want of a trustee". The Court has also a statutory power of appointment whenever it is otherwise inexpedient, difficult or inpracticable to make such an appointment.[19]

Both registered and unregistered unions are debarred from appointing as trustees persons under 18 years of age.[20]

Whenever a new trustee of an unregistered trade union is appointed, the trust property must be vested in him in accordance with the law relating to trusts generally.[21] Special provision is made for the vesting of trust property in the trustees of registered trade unions. All such property, with the exception of public stocks and securities, is automatically vested in the new trustee.[22]

A trustee's appointment can be terminated by death, retirement[23] or removal from office. A trustee may be removed from office by the beneficiaries provided they are all *sui juris*, or under an express power in the trust instrument. In addition, the High Court has an inherent power to remove trustees where that is required by the welfare of the beneficiaries.[24] Where stock in public funds is vested in a union trustee and that trustee leaves the jurisdiction, or becomes bankrupt or insane or dies or disappears or is removed from office, the Registrar is empowered to direct the transfer of that stock into the names of any other persons as union trustees.[25]

Powers

(i) *Trustees of unregistered trade unions* – The powers of union trustees are determined primarily by the union rule book. With

---

[18] Trustee Act 1893, s. 10. This power can only be exercised in order to replace existing trustees and not to make additional appointments.

[19] 1893 Act, s. 25.

[20] 1876 Act, s. 9, as amended by s. 2(3) of the Age of Majority Act 1985.

[21] As to which, see Wylie, *op. cit.*, pp. 495–496.

[22] 1871 Act, s. 8. S. 9 of the 1871 Act provides for the continuance of litigation affecting union property and to which union trustees were a party, notwithstanding any change of trustees.

[23] Not to be confused with resignation for once a trustee has taken up his office, he cannot resign. See Wylie, *op. cit.*, pp. 496–499.

[24] A power exercised on an *ex parte* application to Mervyn Davies J. in the Chancery Division of the English High Court by sixteen miners in an action against the trustees of the National Union of Mineworkers. An appeal against the order removing the trustees and appointing a receiver of the income, assets, property and effects of the union was dismissed by the Court of Appeal, see *Clarke* v. *Heathfield* [1985] I.C.R. 203. For a detailed account of this and subsequent proceedings, see *Larkins* v. *National Union of Mineworkers* High Court, unreported, 18 June 1985 (Barrington J.). In this jurisdiction, the High Court may appoint a receiver by interlocutory order in all cases in which it appears to the Court to be "just and convenient" so to do, Supreme Court of Judicature Act 1877, s. 28(8) and R.S.C., O.50, r.6(1). See *O'Donovan* v. *Goggin* (1892) 30 L.R. Ir. 579.

[25] 1876 Act, s. 4.

regard to the power of investment, however, the union trustee can also rely on statutory powers of investment conferred by sections 2–5 of the Trustee Act 1893 and the Trustee (Authorised Investments) Act 1958.[26] Furthermore, such trustees are also empowered at common law to bring or defend actions concerning the trust property.

(ii) *Trustees of registered trade unions* – In addition to their powers under the union rule book and the Acts of 1893 and 1958, trustees of registered trade unions have certain statutory powers under the Trade Union Act 1871.[27]

Duties of union trustees

Union trustees have the same general duties as ordinary trustees, and in particular, they must exercise their powers in the best interests of the beneficiaries of the trust, a point emphasised in the recent case of *Cowan* v. *Scargill*.[28] A pension scheme for mineworkers employed by the National Coal Board was administered by ten trustees, five appointed by the National Coal Board and five appointed by the National Union of Mineworkers. When the latter trustees refused to approve an investment plan for the scheme because it permitted overseas investment and also investment in energy industries which were in direct competition with coal, the Board's appointees succeeded in getting a declaration that the union appointees were acting in breach of their fiduciary duties as trustees. Megarry V.-C. said:

"In considering what investments to make trustees must put on one side their own personal interests and views. Trustees may have strongly held social or political views. They may be firmly opposed to any investment in South Africa or other countries, or they may object to any form of investment in companies concerned with alcohol, tobacco, armaments or many other things . . . yet under a trust, if investments of this type would be more beneficial to the beneficiaries than other investments, the trustees must not refrain from making the investments by reasons of the views that they hold."[29]

In addition to the general duties of trustees, union trustees also have a specific statutory duty under section 11 of the Trade Union Act 1871

---

[26] As to which, see Wylie, *op. cit.*, pp. 512–515.
[27] Ss. 7, 8, 9 and 11 (as amended by the 1876 Act, s. 3). For the effect of these sections, see *supra*, pp. 48, 49; *infra*, pp. 86–89, 137.
[28] [1984] I.C.R. 646. See also Schuller and Hyman, "Trust Law and Trustees: Employee Representation in Pension Schemes" (1983) 12 *I.L.J.* 84; Nobles, "Conflicts of Interests in Trustees' Management of Pension Funds – An Analysis of the Legal Framework" (1985) 14 *I.L.J.* 1.
[29] *Ibid.* at 659.

to have the accounts of union monies audited by some "fit and proper person or persons".[30]

Liability

A union trustee is personally liable to the beneficiaries for any breach of trust he commits. He is not liable for breaches by his co-trustees unless he himself is guilty of "wilful default" in the matter.[31] Furthermore, a trustee of a registered trade union is liable only for monies actually received by him on account of such union, notwithstanding his signing any receipt for the sake of conformity.[32]

Union trustees can be sued by way of representative action brought against the union. However, the scope of such action is severely curtailed by the requirement that the interests of all the representative parties be identical.[33] In addition, trustees can also defend actions involving the trust property. The liability of trustees in such actions varies in accordance with whether the union is registered, unregistered or authorised.[34]

(i) *Registered but not authorised:–* In order to allow unions to protect their property rights, trustees or other authorised offices of registered trade unions are authorised by section 9 of the 1871 Act to bring or defend "any action, suit, prosecution or complaint in any court of law or equity, touching or concerning the property, right or claim to property of the trade unions".[35] Furthermore, such action shall not abate or be discontinued by the death or removal from office of the trustees, but shall be continued by the trustee's successor.[36]

Section 9 only applies to trustees or properly authorised officers of registered trade unions,[37] and it only applies to actions which touch or concern the property, right or claim to property of the union. Two conflicting lines of authority exist as to the scope of this section. On the one hand, it was suggested in *Linaker* v. *Pilcher*[38] that it covers any

---

[30] See *infra*, pp. 88–89. S. 16 of the 1871 Act imposes a duty on the union to make detailed annual returns to the Registrar concerning, *inter alia*, union funds, liabilities, membership, *etc*. Though no specific officer is referred to in s. 16, it may be that the trustees are the most appropriate persons to discharge this function.

[31] Trustee Act, 1893, s. 24.

[32] 1871 Act, s. 10; 1893 Act, s. 24.

[33] See *supra*, pp. 62–63.

[34] See R.S.C. O.15, r.8.

[35] Including actions arising prior to registration – see *McPherson* v. *Hilberg and Others* (1912) 14 W.A.R. 48. Notwithstanding the fact that the section continues to provide that the trustees shall "sue and be sued . . . in their proper names, without other description than the title of their office," it appears that trustees can act under s. 9 whenever the union is sued in its own registered name – *Keys* v. *Boulter* [1971] 1 Q.B. 300.

[36] The same privilege is not extended to trustees of unregistered trade unions so in the event of their death, retirement or removal from office, the action would have to be commenced again by the new trustees.

[37] See Meredith J. in *I.T.G.W.U.* v. *Green* [1936] I.R. 471, 480.

[38] (1901) 17 T.L.R. 68. See also Lord Lindley in *Taff Vale Ry. Co.* v. *A.S.R.S.* [1901] A.C. 426, 443.

action which is likely to add or take from the assets of the society. This would cover, for example, all actions for damages for torts committed by or on behalf of the union including those which did not involve property vested in the trustees, *e.g.* defamation. The contrary view is that it only extends to actions directly involving property vested or alleged to be vested in the trustees,[39] *e.g.* actions arising in the context of occupiers' liability. This was the view taken by the Northern Ireland Court of Appeal in *Drennan v. Beechy*.[40] The plaintiff had sued the defendants, trustees of the Amalgamated Transport and General Workers' Union, for wrongfully and maliciously (i) inducing certain persons not to work for him; (ii) interfering with his lawful trade or business; (iii) interfering with certain contracts entered into by him; (iv) conspiring to induce certain persons not to work for him and to interfere with his lawful trade or business. Section 4 of the Trade Disputes Act 1906 precluded the bringing of an action in tort against the union itself, so the plaintiff sued the union's trustees pursuant to section 9. The Northern Ireland Court of Appeal dismissed the claim. According to Best L.J. the liability of the trustees under section 9 was confined to matters in which some question is raised directly involving the property, real or personal, vested in the trustees or which they allege ought to be vested in them or where the property vested in the trustees has been instrumental in injuring the plaintiff.

The attraction of this line of reasoning is that it would avoid the effects of the approach adopted in *Linaker* on trustees' immunity from tort actions under section 4(2) of the 1906 Act, which is virtually to destroy that immunity, a result which does not appear to have been intended by the legislature. However, in view of the possibility that the presumption of constitutionality applies to the provisions of the 1906 Act and that the Act should be interpreted, if possible, in such a way as to accord with the provisions of the Constitution, it may be that Irish courts will have to adopt the *Linaker* approach so as to avoid any unjustified limitation on the individual's right to have access to the courts, or more specifically, his right to a good name.[41]

(ii) *Registered and authorised* – In the case of trustees of unions which are both registered and authorised, one must read section 9 in the light of section 4(1) of the Trade Disputes Act 1906 and section 11 of the Trade Union Act 1941. The effect of these sections read together is to abolish the liability of the trustees of such unions under section 9 in the case of torts committed by or on behalf of the union in contemplation or furtherance of a trade dispute and to abolish the liability of other

---

[39] Including recovery of liquidated sums. See *Madden v. Rhodes* [1906] 1 K.B. 534; *Curle v. Lester* (1893) 9 T.L.R. 480.
[40] [1935] N.I. 74. See also *Shinwell v. National Seamen's and Firemen's Union* (1913) 2 S.L.T. 83; Farwell J. in *Taff Vale Railway Co. v. A.S.R.S.* [1901] A.C. 426; and Slade J. in *Longdon-Griffiths v. Smith* [1951] 1 K.B. 295.
[41] On this possibility see *infra*, pp. 255–257.

union officers under section 9 in respect of all torts committed by or on behalf of the union.

(iii) *Unregistered*:– The common law liability of trustees of unregistered trade unions in respect of actions concerning the trust property was modified by section 4(2) of the Trade Distputes Act 1906 which conferred immunity on such trustees in relation to all tortious actions committed by or on behalf of the union irrespective of whether they were committed in contemplation or furtherance of a trade dispute.[42] This immunity was subsequently withdrawn from the trustees of unauthorised trade unions by section 11 of the Trade Unions Act 1941, but as we have already noted,[43] certain procedural difficulties attach to the bringing of a representative action against unregistered unions.

(iv) *Unregistered and authorised*:– The cumulative effect of section 4 of the 1906 Act and section 11 of the 1941 Act is to render the trustees of such unions[44] totally immune from actions in tort alleged to have been committed by or on behalf of the union.

ACCOUNTS AND RETURNS

Registered[45] unions are required to make annual returns to the Registrar of Friendly Societies.[46] These must detail the assets and liabilities of the union on the date of the return and the receipts and expenditure during the year preceding the date to which the returns are made out. Members are entitled to receive a free copy of this statement from the union secretary or treasurer.[47]

The trustees of registered trade unions are also required to have an audit of funds taken by some "fit and proper person" appointed by them at such times as the rule book provides or whenever the treasurer is requested to furnish details of the union's finances to the trustees or union members.[48] The Registrar has pointed out that the trustees are

---

[42] 1906 Act, s. 4(2), only preserved the liability of trustees of *registered* trade unions under s. 9 of the 1871 Act in respect of torts committed other than in contemplation or furtherance of a trade dispute.

[43] See *supra*, pp. 62–63.

[44] It is theoretically possible for such unions to exist but they must, of necessity, be foreign based unions. See *supra*, pp. 56–57.

[45] A union which has been in operation for more than a year prior to the date of application for registration must submit a similar statement to the Registrar prior to its registration – 1871 Act, s. 13, para. 4.

[46] 1871 Act, s. 16; Sch. 1, r.5. Failure to make these returns, or the wilful making of any false entry or omission from the statement, is punishable by penalties of £5 and £50 respectively.

[47] See *infra*, p. 110.

[48] 1871 Act, s. 11. It would appear to be open to the union members, on the wording of s. 11, to request details of the union's finances and thereby cause an audit to be taken. It is submitted that the union members would also have standing to obtain an injunction restraining the appointment of a particular auditor, if the appointment of that auditor was not a *bona fide* exercise of the trustees' powers. Union members also have a right to inspect the books of the trade union to which they belong. See *infra*, pp. 109, 110.

not legally required to employ a qualified accountant or public auditor for this purpose but has indicated that such a practice is desirable as the standard of accuracy of accounts required under the Act is not less than the "true and fair view" standard required by the Companies Acts 1963-1983.[49] The trustees' duty to have an audit taken is complemented by their statutory power to sue the union treasurer for the recovery of any union property held by him.[50] In addition, it is an offence under section 12 of the 1871 Act for any person to obtain any union property by false representation or having obtained same, to withhold it or to apply it either fraudulently or for purposes other than those listed in the rule book.

POLITICAL FUND

There is one aspect of the law relating to the use of union property which on occasion proves controversial, though more so in Britain than in this jurisdiction, *viz.* the use of union funds for political activities.[51]

The doctrine of *ultra vires* was originally applied to trade unions so as to restrict their activities in two different ways – they could not engage in activity which was *ultra vires* general trade union legislation or *ultra vires* the individual rule books. The House of Lords decision in *Amalgamated Society of Railway Servants* v. *Osborne*[52] granting an injunction to the plaintiff to restrain the defendant union from applying its funds in furtherance of political objects provoked an immediate reaction on the part of the trade union movement which led ultimately to the passing of the Trade Union Act 1913. Under this Act, unions were permitted to have objects other than the statutory objects listed in section 16 of the 1876 Act.[53] However, it was felt that the expenditure of funds on certain political objects[54] should not be left totally unregulated and to this end, sections 3-6 of the 1913 Act were enacted. The importance of these provisions in this jurisdiction[55] is

---

[49] *Report of the Registrar of Friendly Societies* (1983) at pp. 20-21.
[50] 1871 Act, s. 12, as amended by the 1876 Act, s. 5. The trustees could also bring an action under s. 9 of the 1871 Act – see *Madden* v. *Rhodes* [1906] 1 K.B. 534.
[51] For a comprehensive and authoritative examination of this branch of the law, see Ewing, *Trade Unions, The Labour Party and the Law* (Edinburgh, 1982), reviewed by Kerr, (1982) 2 *J.I.S.L.L.* 143. Also, by the same author, "Company Political Donations and the *Ultra Vires* Rule" (1984) 47 *M.L.R.* 57. See also Kidner, "Trade Union Political Fund Rules" (1980) 31 *N.I.L.Q.* 3.
[52] [1910] A.C. 87. See also *Johnstone* v. *Associated Ironmoulders of Scotland and Others* 1911 2 S.L.T. 478. *Quaere* whether the reasoning in this case could be applied to political donations by companies?
[53] S. 1.
[54] In *A.S.T.M.S.* v. *Parkin* [1984] I.C.R. 127, the E.A.T. drew a broad distinction between political activity directed towards securing representation by a candidate in Parliament and other political purposes, the former type of activity only falling within the terms of the 1913 Act.
[55] The position in Northern Ireland is governed by the provisions of the 1913 Act as amended by the Trade Disputes and Trade Unions Act (Northern Ireland) 1927, (though note that Part III) of the Trade Union Act 1984 applies in Northern Ireland but not in relation to any union

undoubtedly increased by virtue of the fact that sections 3, 5 and 6 thereof can be regarded as vindicating the members' constitutional right to freedom of belief, a right not expressly mentioned in the Constitution but clearly implied by Article 40.6.1° which guarantees freedom of expression, freedom of assembly and freedom of association. Section 3(1) of the 1913 Act imposes certain conditions on the application of union funds[56] either directly or indirectly, in furtherance of the political objects enumerated in section 3(3).[57] An objective test is used in order to determine whether the objects upon which the money has been spent are, in fact, political objects.[58] It has been suggested that an indirect application of union funds would arise whenever the union was aware that the payment of monies to another body was likely to be used for political purposes or whenever the union was able to control the use of the funds of the body to which the money was paid.[59] The political objects affected by the Act are listed in section 3(3) thereof. Once a union proposes to engage in any activity covered by that subsection, and assuming that the union is authorised to do so by its rule book, any money expended thereon must come from the union's political fund. If the activity is not within the scope of section 3(3), the union can[60] rely on its general fund for finance, again provided that the union is authorised to engage in the activity by its rule book.

The political objects enumerated in subsection (3) are the expenditure of money on:

(a) The payment of any expenses incurred either directly or indirectly by a candidate or prospective candidate for election to the Oireachtas or to any public office, before, during or after the election in connection with his candidature or election. "Public Office" is defined[61] as "the office of member of any county,

---

which has its head or main office in Northern Ireland – see *infra* fn 69). The major difference between the two jurisdictions is that, in the North, union members do not automatically contribute to their unions' political fund, but rather have to "contract in", whereas in this jurisdiction they are deemed to have agreed to contribute unless they "contract out".

[56] This also applies to the funds of associations or combinations of unions, s. 3(5). *Quaere* whether this could cover the I.C.T.U. On this issue, see Ewing, *op. cit.*, pp. 72–73. (In fact, the I.C.T.U. does not operate a political fund).

[57] Once the conditions are satisfied, the affiliation of the union to one political party cannot prevent union branches from making donations to rival political parties – *Parkin v. A.S.T.M.S.* [1980] I.C.R. 662.

[58] *Richards v. N.U.M.* [1981] I.R.L.R. 247.

[59] Kidner, *Trade Union Law*, 2nd ed. (London, 1983) at pp. 216–217. In *A.S.T.M.S. v. Parkin* [1984] I.C.R. 127, it was held that the provision of property by way of a commercial investment for the use of a political party amounted to expenditure in furtherance of the statutory political objects.

[60] Indeed Ewing argues that the union *must* rely on its general fund to finance such activity, on the ground that the political fund can only be used in respect of activities covered by s. 3(3) – *op. cit.* pp. 93–96.

[61] S. 3(3).

county borough, district or parish, council or board of guardians or of any public body who have power to raise money, either directly or indirectly, by means of a rate". This definition does not appear to cover the position of the Presidency of Ireland or membership of the European Parliament and, consequently, election campaigns to either of these offices may be financed out of a union's general fund, subject to paragraph (e) below.

(b) The holding of any meeting or the distribution of any literature or documents in support of any such candidate or prospective candidate. It has been suggested that "distribution" does not include writing, preparing, printing or publishing.[62] The implication of this view of the word "distribution" is that it is only the costs of the actual distribution of the material and not the additional costs of writing, preparing, printing or publishing it which must come from the political fund.[63] This, however, restricts the scope of the paragraph to cases of free distribution of material thus depriving it of substantial effect. It is submitted that consideration should be given towards closing off this gap in the law.

(c) The maintenance of any person who is a member of the Oireachtas or who holds a public office. This paragraph only precludes the maintenance out of the general fund of members of the Oireachtas or holders of public office as such and does not prohibit a union from continuing to employ and remunerate a union official who also occupies one of these positions, nor from paying a fee in return for services rendered in the Oireachtas. Given the definition of "public office", it is arguable that this paragraph does not prohibit the payment from a union's general fund of sums of money to the President. However, such payments are no doubt prohibited by Article 12.6.3° of the Constitution.[64] There does not appear to be any comparable prohibition in the case of M.E.P.s. Consequently, it would appear that the latter may be sponsored out of a union's general fund.

(d) In connection with the registration of electors or the selection of a candidate for the Oireachtas or any public body. Again, it would appear that unions can vote monies from their general funds in connection with the selection of candidates for the Presidency of Ireland and the European Parliament, subject to paragraph (e) below.

---

[62] *Forster* v. *N.A.U.S.A.W.C.* [1927] 1 Ch. 539; *McCarthy* v. *A.P.E.X.* [1980] I.R.L.R. 335. *Cf.* Ewing, *op. cit.*, p. 90.

[63] See the British case of *McCarthy* and *The National Association of Theatrical and Kine Employees* (1957), Report of the Registrar. For the difficulties with this case, see Ewing, *op. cit.*, pp. 85–86.

[64] Article 12.6.3° provides that "the President shall not hold any other office or position of emolument."

(e) On the holding of political meetings of any kind, or on the distribution of political literature or political documents of any kind, unless the main purpose of the meetings or of the distribution of the literature or documents is the furtherance of statutory objects[65] within the meaning of the 1913 Act. This is a very sweeping clause which encompasses activities not covered by the preceding paragraphs, *e.g.* the financing of selection conventions or election campaigns for the offices of Presidency of Ireland or membership of the European Parliament. In Britain, however, the Registrar has limited the scope of the phrase "political meetings of any kind" by construing "political" as "party political".[66] "Party political" has been further defined as relating to literature or meetings held by a party which has or seeks to have members in Parliament.[67] Consequently a campaign opposing Government cuts in public spending was not "political" for the purposes of the 1913 Act. A final limitation on the scope of this paragraph stems from the fact that if the main purpose of the meeting or distribution is the furtherance of statutory objects it does not come within the statutory definition of political objects even though the meeting or distribution might be regarded as political activity.

If a union wishes to expend money on any of the above objects, it must have the object approved as an object of the union by a "resolution for the time being in force passed on a ballot of the members of the union taken in accordance with the Act for the purpose by a majority of the members voting".[68] The rules providing for the ballot must be approved by the Registrar who shall only do so if he is satisfied that every member has "an equal right and, if reasonably possible, a fair opportunity of voting and that the secrecy of the ballot is properly secured."[69] The resolution, if passed, takes effect as if it

---

[65] Securing the election of a Government favourably disposed towards the trade union movement is not regarded as being in furtherance of a trade union's statutory objects:– *McCarthy* v. *A.P.E.X.* [1980] I.R.L.R. 335. In determining whether a meeting was in furtherance of the statutory objects one has to have regard to the intentions of the organisers of the meeting, and not to the purpose of the union in associating itself with the meeting – *Coleman* v. *P.O.E.U.* [1981] I.R.L.R. 427. For an examination of the statutory objects, see *infra*, pp. 38–41.

[66] *Forster* and *The National Amalgamated Union of Shop Assistants, Warehousemen and Clerks* (1925), Report of the Registrar. In *A.S.T.M.S.* v. *Parkin* [1984] I.C.R. 127, however, the E.A.T. warned that the use of the phrase "party political" in this context did not mean that the support of a Parliamentary or other candidate who was not a member of a party fell outside the definition of "political object".

[67] *Coleman* v. *P.O.E.U.* [1981] I.R.L.R. 427. A decision criticised by Ewing, *op. cit.*, at p. 88.

[68] S. 3(1).

[69] S. 4(1). Once approved and certified by the Registrar, those rules take effect as rules of the union, notwithstanding that the provisions of the rule book as to the alteration of rules or the formulation of new ones have not been complied with – s. 4(2). The comparable provisions for Northern Ireland are to be found in s. 4(5) of the Trade Disputes and Trade Unions Act (Northern Ireland) 1927. British based unions operating in the North and who do not have their head office there are subject now to the provisions of Part III of the Trade Union Act 1984 which

were a rule of the union and may be rescinded in accordance with the union rule book.⁷⁰

Secondly, it must send out a notice to each member informing them of their right to be exempt from contributing to the political fund.⁷¹ Finally it must have rules,⁷² approved by the Registrar,⁷³ providing:

(a) That the payment of monies in furtherance of the political objects shall be made out of a separate fund, known as the political fund, and that any member⁷⁴ who gives notice in accordance with the Act shall be exempt from any obligation to contribute.⁷⁵ The Schedule to the Act contains a form of exemption notice, but the use of this particular formula is not mandatory and an objector may use any form having a "like effect".⁷⁶ Such exemption notice only takes effect as from the first day of January next after it was given, unless it was given within one month of the notice sent to members on approval of

---

widens the definition of political objects and requires unions to renew their objects resolutions at least once every ten years in a ballot of *all* the members – 1984 Act, s. 17(4). Though s. 13(7) allows that, when a British based union currently has a resolution on a political fund in force, it may formulate rules which may provide for "overseas members" of the union not to be allowed to vote in the ballot. For an analysis of Part III of the Trade Union Act 1984 see Ewing, "Trade Union Political Funds: The 1913 Act Revisited" (1984) 13 *I.L.J.* 227. For a note on the implications for Northern Ireland, see Black, "Trade Union Democracy and Northern Ireland" (1984) 13 *I.L.J.* 243 at pp. 245-250.

⁷⁰ S. 3(4).

⁷¹ S. 5(1). This does not appear to impose an obligation on unions to embody such a notice in their rule books. However, most unions do adopt this practice. This can be misleading for members of foreign based unions as a number of such unions fail to publish separate rule books for their Irish members. Consequently, the latter will find themselves advised, when seeking exemption from the obligation to contribute to the political fund, to contact the Certification Officer, Hide Place, London SW1P 4NG.

⁷² S. 3(1).

⁷³ And governed by s. 4(2). See fn. 69 above.

⁷⁴ Prospective members are not covered by the terms of s. 3(1)(a), so that where a prospective member requested an exemption from the political fund on a form proposing him for membership, the Registrar in Britain held that he had not validly contracted out of the obligation to contribute and so was liable to contribute to the political fund until such time as he had been properly exempted *as a member* – Wilson and A.E.U. (1958), Report of the Registrar. It is doubtful, however, whether this conclusion represents good law in this jurisdiction as such an individual would surely be able to rely on his/her constitutional right to freedom of belief.

⁷⁵ *Cp.* 1927 Act, s. 4(1). Effect may be given to the exemption either by requiring non-exempt members to contribute to a separate political fund or by relieving exempt members from the payment of the whole or any part of the periodical subscriptions to the union – s. 6. It would appear that a refunding of the amount of money involved satisfies the statute where an automatic check off system of union contributions is in operation – *Reeves* v. *T.G.W.U.* [1980] I.R.L.R. 307. However, where a union has opted, in its rule book, for a separate levy, the separate levy is mandatory and exempted members should not have to contribute in the first place. Consequently the practice of refunding exempted members in arrears fails to protect their rights in this instance – *Elliott* v. *S.O.G.A.T.* [1983] I.R.L.R. 3. In *Cleminson* v. *P.O.E.U.* [1980] I.R.L.R. 1 the Certification Officer suggested that the best solution is an arrangement enabling exempt members to be relieved from payment of the political contribution through the check-off system. For a general comment on this issue, see Ewing, *op. cit.*, pp. 106-109.

⁷⁶ S. 5(1). On this, see Ewing, *op. cit.*, pp. 103-105.

the political objects, in which case the exemption notice has effect from the date on which it was given.[77]

(b) That an exempted member shall not be excluded, by reason of being so exempt, from any benefits of the union, or placed in any respect either directly or indirectly under any disability or disadvantage[78] as compared with other members of the union except in relation to the control and management of the political fund. Furthermore, contribution to the political fund shall not be made a condition for admission to the union.[79]

Members aggrieved by a breach of the above rules may complain to the Registrar of Friendly Societies, who may make such order for remedying the breach as he thinks just under the circumstances.[80] This jurisdiction can only be invoked by persons who are in membership on the date the complaint was received by the Registrar.[81] Consequently, prospective members cannot complain to the Registrar if, for example, the union makes admission conditional upon contributing to the political fund. The appropriate remedy in such cases would appear to be to apply for a declaration from the High Court that the imposition of the condition was unlawful. And, of course, if it could be shown that the prospective member's constitutional rights were being infringed, the Court could be asked to grant an order restraining the union from insisting on the imposition of this condition.

There is one recorded instance of a complaint being made to the Irish Registrar pursuant to section 3(2).[82] In *McCafferty and Irish Transport and General Workers' Union*,[83] the plaintiff, who was exempt from the obligation to contribute to the political fund, was notified by the secretary of his branch of the union, acting with the approval of the National Executive Council, that he would have to contribute a sum of money, equivalent to the political levy, to the local branch fund. The plaintiff refused to do so and was marked in the books of the union as being in arrears for having failed to pay this special levy. He complained to the Registrar who upheld his complaint on the ground that he was placed at a disadvantage as compared with other members of the union because –

(i) he was required, for the same advantages and without additional benefits, to make a contribution to local branch funds which

---

[77] S. 5(2). *Quaere* whether the delayed effect of the exemption notice amounts to a failure on the part of the state to defend, pursuant to Article 40.6.1°, the member's personal right to freedom of conscience.

[78] The disadvantage must be "material . . . a disadvantage of substance". *Reeves* v. *T.G.W.U.* [1980] I.C.R. 728 at 741, *per* Slynn J.

[79] S. 3(1)(*b*). On the protection afforded to the exempted member, see Ewing, *op. cit.*, pp. 109–121.

[80] S. 3(2). Violation of these rules or indeed of the general provisions of the 1913 Act could, in the case of a registered union, lead to cancellation of registration – 1876 Act, s. 8.

[81] See *Sakals* v. *Transport and General Workers' Union* Decision of the Certification Officer delivered 18 January 1985 (see IRLIB 280 at p. 12).

[82] For possible reasons as to why there are so few appeals, see *infra*, p. 98.

[83] (1952) Report of the Registrar of Friendly Societies at pages 37–40.

other members, who contributed to the political fund, were not obliged to make;
(ii) failure to pay said levy rendered him liable to the various fines, disabilities and penalties accruing under the rules to members who are in arrears, whereas the other members did not incur such arrears.

Consequently, the Registrar ordered the union to strike out the arrears from the plaintiff's union cards and from the union books, to make all payments of benefit necessary to relieve the plaintiff from the penalties, disabilities or disadvantages incurred by him because of failure to pay and to refrain from demanding of the plaintiff that he contribute to this special local levy.

A decision of the Registrar made pursuant to section 3(2) is binding and conclusive on all parties without appeal and cannot be removed into a court of law.[84] It is submitted, however, that this does not completely oust the jurisdiction of the ordinary courts in the case of disputes arising out of the operation of political funds. In the first place, it is unlikely that it precludes the High Court from exercising its traditional power of judicial review of administrative actions.[85] Secondly, the statutory grievance procedure only applies to disputes arising from the alleged breach of union rules made pursuant to section 3 and clearly the courts can entertain the residual category of disputes. In *Birch v. National Union of Railwaymen*[86] the plaintiff was removed from office as chairman of the union branch under a rule passed pursuant to section 3 of the 1913 Act, which rule had been approved by the Registrar of Friendly Societies and which rendered non-contributors to the political fund ineligible for any office or position involving control or management of the political fund. Danckwerts J. noted that section 3(1) of the 1913 Act did not provide that such approval was to be conclusive of the validity of the rules and he therefore felt able to examine those rules in the light of the provisions of the 1913 Act.[87] He held that to the extent that the rules allowed the union to exclude exempted members from control of the affairs of the union *dehors* the administration of the political fund, they did not satisfy section 3(1)(*b*) of the 1913 Act and consequently the statutory prohibition on the application of the union funds for specified political purposes still existed.

---

[84] Provided that the decision is taken within jurisdiction. For consideration of this and the constitutionality of s. 3(2) see *supra*, pp. 47–48. *Cp.* the Employment Protection (Consolidation) Act 1978, s. 136(2), which allows for an appeal to be taken on any question of law against a decision of a Certification Officer in relation to, *inter alia*, political funds to the Employment Appeals Tribunal.
[85] See Citrine, *op. cit.* p. 434. This is borne out by the fact that the Registrar's order in *McCafferty's* case was stated to be a "speaking order", an approach which facilitates judicial review.
[86] [1950] Ch. 602.
[87] *Ibid.* at 612.

THE CHECK-OFF

Finally something should be said about the arrangements which many employers in Ireland have entered into with trade unions representative of their employees relating to the deduction by the employer from the wages of his employees of their weekly contributions to the union of which they are members. Such arrangements are dubbed the "check-off" system. In June 1973 the Employer-Labour Conference (E.L.C.) reported on the check-off system for trade union contributions.[88] The report stated that the E.L.C. was "impressed" by the willingness of many employers, both in the private and public sector, to respond favourably to requests for check-off facilities, and concluded that "there would be advantages to employers and trade unions if the practice became more prevalent."[89] Accordingly the E.L.C. recommended that employers should give sympathetic and favourable consideration to such requests[90] and that they should not make any charge for operating a check-off facility. The E.L.C. did point out, however, that problems might arise on the introduction of the check-off system in employments where there was more than one union. In such circumstances the onus lay on the trade unions concerned to reach agreement or an understanding on the matter.

The E.L.C. also stated that each employee must agree to the deduction of the trade union contribution before the employer can legally make the deduction. This is certainly the case with employees covered by the Truck legislation.[91] Section 2 of the Truck Act 1831, as amended, provides that if, in any contract between any workman and his employer, any provision shall be made directly or indirectly respecting the place where, or the manner in which, or the person or persons with whom, the whole or any part of the wages due to or to become due to any such workman shall be laid out or expended, such contract shall be "illegal, null and void". This provision does not invalidate the check-off agreement itself because it is clear, following *Hewlett* v. *Allen*[92], that, if an employer deducts part of the wages of an employee for the purpose of paying them over to a third party and does so with the consent and by the authority of the employee, there is no contravention of the 1831 Act. Lord Herschell L.C. said:

> "[A] payment made by an employer at the instance of a person employed to discharge some obligation of the person employed, or

---

[88] *Report on Check-Off System for Trade Union Contributions* (1973).
[89] *Ibid*, para. 3.
[90] See *De Beer Industrial Diamond Division and I.T.G.W.U.* L.C.R. 7508; *St. Vincent's Hospital and L.G.P.S.U.* L.C.R. 5545 and *O'Connor & Co. Ltd. and I.D.A.T.U.* L.C.R. 9581. Cf. however, *Abbot (Ireland) Ltd. and I.T.G.W.U.* L.C.R. 6720.
[91] Truck Acts 1831, 1887, 1896. The legislation generally applies to "workmen", defined in s. 2 of the Truck Amendment Act 1887 as being limited to those who engage in manual labour. See *R. v. Louth Justices* [1900] 2 I.R. 114. S. 1 of the Truck Act 1896 applies however to shop assistants.
[92] [1894] A.C. 383.

to place the money in the hands of some person in whose hand the person employed desires it to be placed, is in the sense and meaning of [ss. 2 and 3 of the 1831 Act] a payment to the person employed as much as if the current coin of the realm had been placed in his or her hands."[93]

This principle was applied to a situation directly in point in *Williams v. Butlers Ltd.*[94] Here, Butlers Ltd. had entered into an agreement with the Transport and General Workers' Union as to the deduction of union dues. The agreement contained a clause to the effect that such deductions were to be terminated on receipt of written instructions from the union. One of their employees, who had previously authorised them to make the deductions, now requested them to cease making the deductions. However Butlers Ltd. received no written instructions from the union in respect of the employee's contributions and continued to deduct them. They were then prosecuted for contravening the 1831 Act. The Queen's Bench Divisional court[95] dismissed the complaint. They firmly stated that there was no contravention of the 1831 Act when an employee entered into a contract under which he authorised his employer to deduct from his weekly wage the amount of his trade union dues and that there was nothing in the Truck Acts or the general law of contract which rendered illegal, null or void an agreement that the employee would notify the withdrawal of his consent through the trade union. The employee was well aware of the procedures to be followed before the deductions would cease and chose not to go through them. The correct view, in Michael Davies J.'s judgment, was that:

> "The employee lawfully gave to the defendants authority to make the appropriate deductions from his wages, which authority was freely revocable by him during his employment if he followed the procedure to which he had again lawfully agreed. I emphasise the word 'freely' because there is no suggestion that the employee was irrevocably committed to a continuation of the deductions – only to an agreed procedure for terminating them."[96]

Michael Davies J. further emphasised that there was not "a scrap of evidence" to suggest that the union would in fact disobey any request from the employee to forward the withdrawal of authority to deduct.

Finally, the E.L.C. said that trade unions must be responsible for the collection of any arrears of contributions that may be outstanding in the introduction of the check-off in any employment and that employers must not be expected to accept responsibility for collecting

---

[93] At 389.
[94] [1975] I.C.R. 208.
[95] Lord Widgery C.J., Ashworth and Michael Davies JJ.
[96] [1975] I.C.R. at 210.

such arrears except insofar as individual employees may request them to arrange for appropriate deductions from their pay to meet such arrears.

CONCLUSION

The law relating to the use of union property is largely non-controversial, though certain technical reforms could be effected. In particular, the liability of trustees as representatives of their union should be clarified. The present situation favours unregistered trade unions, a position which is inconsistent with the general legislative policy of encouraging trade union registration. Secondly, the Oireachtas should also clarify the meaning of the phrase "touching or concerning the property, right or claim to property" in section 9 of the 1871 Act.

Nor has the operation of political funds by Irish trade unions generated much controversy since 1913. In particular, there has been a positive dearth of appeals taken to the Registrar. This would appear to be partly because the amount of money involved is not very great[97] and consequently, workers are very apathetic about the whole issue. Currently only nine unions registered in this jurisdiction have political funds[98] and, according to annual returns submitted to the Registrar in respect of the year ended 31st December 1982, the balance in such funds was £30,387.[99] Indeed the only political significance of union political funds in this country of late seems to be as a method of censure of the Irish Labour Party through threats of withdrawal of union finance from that Party.[1]

---

[97] According to the Registrar, political fund levies range from 5p to 26p per member per annum – 1983 Report, p. 25.

[98] Irish Print Union; Bakery and Foodworkers' Amalgamated Union; Operative Plasterers' and Allied Trades Society of Ireland; Irish Distributive and Administrative Trade Union; Federated Workers' Union of Ireland; Irish Transport and General Workers' Union; Irish Municipal Employees' Trade Union; National Association of Transport Employees; Irish National Teachers' Organisation. It should be noted, however, that while O.P.A.T.S.I. has a political fund no members contribute to it. See Table 16 in the Registrar's Report for 1983.

[99] A decrease during 1982 from £61,800, due no doubt to the two General Elections held that year.

[1] See *Irish Times*, 11 February 1983, 19 March 1983, 8 December 1984.

Chapter 5

INTERNAL TRADE UNION AFFAIRS

At present there is little statutory regulation of internal trade union affairs. The clear intent of the legislature when it enacted the Trade Union Act 1871 was that the law should not interfere in the internal affairs of trade unions.[1] Section 4 probably expresses best this policy of non-interference by declaring that certain contracts, including ones for the payment of subscriptions or the provision of benefits, would not be directly enforceable.[2] One also sees this policy reflected in the provisions of the 1871 Act relating to trade union rules.[3] All the 1871 Act did was to require the union to have rules in respect of a very limited range of matters[4] and did not even require these particular rules to take any particular form.

As far as the form and structure of the internal government of a trade union is concerned, that is for the union itself to decide. Whilst the 1871 Act requires registered trade unions to have a rule in respect of the appointment and removal of a general committee of management and other officers, it is not necessary, for instance, that the rules make provision for the election of a governing body, and for its re-election at reasonable intervals, or for the establishment of a particular body authorised to call industrial action on behalf of a trade union.[5]

This policy of non-interference in internal trade union affairs was continued in the subsequent trade union legislation, with the notable exception of the Trade Union Act 1913 which requires the rule books

---

[1] The 1871 Act, while legalising trade unions, expressly refrained from according them corporate status almost certainly in order to minimise legal intervention into relations between trade unions and their members.
[2] See *infra*, pp. 123–124.
[3] S. 14, Sched. 1.
[4] See *infra*, pp. 108–109.
[5] The Committee of Inquiry on Industrial Relations, while recommending (in paras. 239–263) a mandatory dispute procedure, including a ballot, for industrial action, did not advert to the issue of trade union democracy. There is no evidence to suggest that Irish trade unions, in the main, are not internally democratic and, furthermore, the writers would agree that it is "impracticable, or at least inadvisable, for the law to lay down minimum rules of democracy to be followed by all unions" (*per* Kahn Freund in *Labour and the Law* (London, 1977) at p. 212). It should be noted that, because the present British government believes that few trade union members can be confident that their union's electoral arrangements are such that those who take decisions are properly representative of, and accountable to, the membership as a whole, legislation has been enacted to ameliorate the position. Part 1 of the Trade Union Act 1984 requires that voting members of the union's principal executive committee be elected by ballot to their positions and be re-elected at least every five years: see Kidner, "Trade Union Democracy: Election of Trade Union Officers" (1984) 13 *I.L.J.* 193. This part of the 1984 Act does not extend to Northern Ireland but Black has pointed out that the position of the Northern Ireland membership of trade unions with headquarters in Great Britain with respect to such ballots is "both confused and unsatisfactory" – see "Trade Union Democracy and Northern Ireland – A Note" (1984) 13 *I.L.J.* 243.

of those unions with a political fund to contain specific provisions regulating the operation of such funds.[6] The Trade Union Act 1941, however, does require authorised unions to include provisions concerning the conditions of entry and cesser of membership[7] and the Trade Union Act 1975 requires foreign based unions who wish to obtain a negotiating licence to provide in their rules for a controlling authority consisting of members resident in the State or Northern Ireland and empowered to make decisions affecting members in that area.[8]

THE LEGAL RELATIONSHIP BETWEEN A TRADE UNION AND ITS MEMBERS

The legal relationship between the members of a trade union and, in the case of a registered trade union, between the members and the trade union undoubtedly commences in contract, the terms of that contract being contained in the union rule book.[9] But it is a contract of a special kind – a contract of adhesion[10] – and, as Rideout has observed, it is misleading to regard the whole subsequent course of that relationship as a matter of agreement. "The rules of a trade union resemble local laws rather than terms of a contract."[11] Not only is there a complete absence of any bargaining as to the incidents which are to be included in the union-member relationship but also many incidents of that relationship are based on sources other than contract, specifically statute, the Constitution and, to a lesser extent, European Community law.[12]

This has led some British judges, particularly Lord Denning, to say that the union-member relationship is not really founded on contract at all. In *Boulting* v. *Association of Cinematograph, Television & Allied Technicians*[13], Lord Denning stated that the rules of a trade union were not a "mere contract", they were more like "bye-laws" binding on the members whether they liked them or not, and, as such, would only be binding as far as they were reasonable or certain.[14] This attempt to

---

[6] See *supra*, pp. 89–95.
[7] Ss. 12 and 13.
[8] S. 17. Moreover s. 7 of the 1975 Act provides that ss. 2–6 of the Act apply to every amalgamation or transfer of engagements notwithstanding anything in the rules of the trade unions concerned. See also s. 8 which empowers the committee of management to alter the union rule book in order to give effect to a transfer of engagements, notwithstanding anything in the rules, provided the rules do not *expressly* exclude the application of s. 8 to the union.
[9] "True it is that the whole of the rules of the [union] here constitute a contract between the members": *per* Lord Evershed, *Faramus* v. *Film Artistes' Association* [1964] A.C. 925, 941.
[10] As it was described by Donaldson L.J. in *Cheall* v. *A.P.E.X.* [1982] I.C.R. 543, 563.
[11] *Rideout's Principles of Labour Law*, 4th ed. (London, 1983), p. 399.
[12] See *infra*, pp. 112–113.
[13] [1963] 2 Q.B. 606, 627. See also his earlier judgment in *Bonsor* v. *Musicians' Union* [1954] 1 Ch. 479 at 485.
[14] *Cheall* v. *A.P.E.X.* [1982] I.C.R. 543, 555–556.

allow the courts to exercise greater control over the substance of the rules than the law of contract would permit must be seen in context. Davies and Freedland have shown[15] how Lord Denning in the 1950s and 1960s was preoccupied with the need to subject the processes, whereby private associations, such as trade unions, exercised coercive powers against individuals, to the controls appropriate to public bodies. Where a closed shop operated, expulsion from a trade union was not like expulsion from a private club, because loss of union membership would result in the person being excluded from his livelihood. There was, therefore, in Lord Denning's view, greater need for a trade union's rules to be reasonable both in substance and in application.[16] In the main, however, Lord Denning's approach has not been endorsed by his colleagues[17] who have adhered to the view that the primary incidents of the union-member relationship are founded on contract and that the courts' control of the internal affairs of trade unions is through the law of contract. It would appear, however, that the Irish courts are prepared to intervene in internal trade union affairs in order to protect constitutional rights.[18] In no case, however, has an Irish court explicitly considered the judicial basis of judicial intervention in internal union affairs.[19]

Formation of union-member relationship

In line with the view of unions as voluntary associations, the common law did not interfere with a union's discretion to determine conditions of eligibility for membership. In recent times, however, this discretion has been fettered by statutory regulation and constitutional interpretation. Section 5 of the Employment Equality Act 1977 prohibits, *inter alia*, trade unions from discriminating against individuals on the basis of sex or marital status.[20] Nor can unions refuse to accept, as members, nationals of other member states of the E.E.C., merely on the basis of their nationality.[21] This apart, unions are not prohibited by statute from discriminating against individuals on

---

[15] In their chapter on Labour Law in Jowell and McAuslan eds., *Lord Denning: The Judge and the Law* (London, 1984), pp. 368–377.
[16] See the development of this view through his judgments in *Russell* v. *Duke of Norfolk* [1949] 1 All E.R. 109; *Abbot* v. *Sullivan* [1952] 1 K.B. 189; *Lee* v. *Showmen's Guild* [1952] 2 Q.B. 329; *Bonsor* v. *Musicians' Union* [1954] 1 Ch. 479; *Faramus* v. *Film Artistes' Association* [1963] 2 Q.B. 527; *Boulting* v. *A.C.T.A.T.* [1963] 2 Q.B. 606; *Nagle* v. *Feilden* [1966] 2 Q.B. 633; *Dickson* v. *Pharmaceutical Society* [1967] 1 Ch. 708 (upheld by the House of Lords, [1970] A.C. 403); *Edwards* v. *S.O.G.A.T.* [1971] 1 Ch. 354; *Breen* v. *A.E.U.* [1971] 2 Q.B. 175.
[17] See the decisive rejection by the House of Lords, in *Faramus* [1964] A.C. 925, of Lord Denning's view that union rules could be declared invalid if they were unreasonable.
[18] See *Tierney* v. *A.S.W.* [1959] I.R. 254; *Murphy* v. *Stewart* [1973] I.R. 97; *Rodgers* v. *I.T.G.W.U.* High Court, unreported, 15 March 1978.
[19] Although Budd J., in *Tierney* v. *A.S.W.* [1959] I.R. 254, did advert to some of the various bases for intervention without deciding in favour of any one.
[20] And so the Irish Women Workers' Union had to change its rule book to permit males to join.
[21] Regulation 1612/68. See *infra*, pp. 112–113.

grounds such as race, religion or political belief.[22] It is arguable, however, that such discriminatory practices might be restrained by the courts as being contrary to the constitutional guarantees of equality and freedom of conscience.[23] Furthermore, in *Murphy* v. *Stewart*,[24] Walsh J. suggested that the courts might compel a union to accept an individual into membership if union membership was necessary to vindicate the individual's right to work.[25]

Trade unions which are affiliated to the Irish Congress of Trade Unions[26] have voluntarily restricted their freedom to accept new members by agreeing to the provisions of the I.C.T.U. Constitution, in particular clause 47 (d). That clause now reads:

"Where any grade, group or category of workers, or the workers in any establishment, form a negotiating unit and their wages or conditions of work are determined by negotiations conducted by a single union of which the majority or a substantial proportion of the workers concerned are members, no other union shall organise or enrol as members any workers within that negotiating unit (that is workers within that grade, group, category or establishment) save only with the consent of the union concerned, except that such consent shall not be withheld where there is evidence that 80% or more of the workers in that grade, group, category or establishment wish to transfer in the case of a firm where representation rights have been established more than two years before the date of application to transfer."

Clause 47(d) constitutes a voluntary agreement between unions to restrict their right to take on new members, in order to tackle the twin problems of trade union multiplicity and inter-union rivalry. The agreement is morally binding[27] and is enforced by the I.C.T.U. Disputes Committee[28] whose decisions are reviewable by the High

---

[22] Though in the United Kingdom unions cannot discriminate on grounds of race – Race Relations Act 1976, s. 11 – and in Northern Ireland unions cannot discriminate on grounds of religious or political beliefs – Fair Employment (Northern Ireland) Act 1976, s. 21.

[23] *Cf.* Kelly, *The Irish Constitution* 2nd ed. (Dublin, 1984), p. 447. As to the effect of the Constitution on private law relationships, see *infra*, p. 111, fn. 88.

[24] [1973] I.R. 97, 117.

[25] See also the decision of the Court of Appeal in *Nagle* v. *Feilden* [1966] 2 Q.B. 633 where the plaintiff was challenging the Jockey Club's policy of refusing to give training licences to women. Lord Denning said that whereas a man who is "blackballed" in a social club had no cause of action because the members can admit or refuse him as they please, different considerations arose with "an association which exercises a virtual monopoly in an important field of human activity." This was because, by refusing or withdrawing a licence, the stewards of the Jockey Club "can put a man out of business."

[26] At the time of writing there were 82 unions affiliated to the I.C.T.U.

[27] See the remarks of Lowry J. in relation to the comparable T.U.C. provision in *McCarthy* v. *A.T.G.W.U.* Northern Ireland High Court, unreported, 14 January 1966 at p. 9. See also Lord Diplock in *Cheall* v. *A.P.E.X.* [1983] 2 A.C. 180, 187. Moreover the I.C.T.U. Constitution is a contract between trade unions and, as such, is unenforceable because of s. 4 of the Trade Union Act 1871, on which see *infra*, p. 123.

[28] The applicable procedures are set out in cl. 46.

Court, on the same grounds as the decisions of any voluntary association, *viz.* if they *ultra vires*, in breach of natural justice or motivated by *mala fides*.[29] There would be a further ground of review if the decision infringed a person's constitutional rights.

In view of the similarity between clause 47 (d) and Part III of the Trade Union Act 1941, which was held to be unconstitutional in *National Union of Railwaymen* v. *Sullivan*,[30] it is not surprising that the constitutionality of the clause has been questioned. But in both *Murphy* v. *Stewart*[31] and *Abbot and Whelan* v. *I.T.G.W.U.*,[32] the Supreme Court and High Court, respectively, were able to decide the cases without dealing with this question. In *Abbot and Whelan*, McWilliam J. did observe, however, that "there may be a distinction between placing a statutory embargo upon any person doing or refraining from doing something and a voluntary agreement between parties that they will or will not do something which they are entitled to do or not to do at their discretion."[33] In *Murphy* v. *Stewart*, the Supreme Court ruled that the refusal of one I.C.T.U. affiliate to accept into membership members of another I.C.T.U. affiliate, where that latter union had refused to consent to the transfer, did not infringe any of the plaintiff's constitutional rights.

If the Disputes Committee finds that an affiliated union had violated clause 47 (d) by "poaching" members, it may rule that the membership of those recruited in violation of the clause must be terminated. If the union complies with the ruling and expels those persons, can they challenge their expulsion in the courts? Since there is no inherent power to expel a member at common law, no unincorporated association can take such action without authority. The courts, certainly in Britain, have been insistent that the power to expel must be found in the rule book and have refused to *imply* any power to expel. This is vividly and pertinently illustrated by Stone V.-C.'s decision in *Spring* v. *National Amalgamated Stevedores' and Dockers' Society*.[34] Here the union purported to expel the plaintiff from membership to comply with an award of the T.U.C. Disputes Committee. The plaintiff sought an injunction to restrain it from so doing on the ground, *inter alia*, that there was no express provision in the union rules permitting it to expel members for this reason. The union argued that it was an implied term of the plaintiff's contract of membership that the union should have the power to do all things which may be necessary and proper to comply with its lawful and proper agreements. Stone V.-C. found, however, for the plaintiff, pointing out that the British equivalent of

---

[29] See *Rothwell* v. *A.P.E.X.* [1976] I.C.R. 211. See *supra*, p. 69.
[30] [1947] I.R. 77.
[31] [1973] I.R. 97.
[32] (1982) 1 *J.I.S.L.L.* 56.
[33] At p. 60.
[34] [1956] 1 W.L.R. 585.

clause 47 (d) was concerned only with the admissions of new members and that nothing was laid down about getting rid of them. In consequence the great majority of T.U.C. affiliates adopted a 'model rule' giving themselves an express power to expel members in order to comply with Disputes Committee rulings. Very few, if any, Irish trade union rule books contain such a rule.

Adoption of a rule empowering the union to terminate the membership of any member in order to comply with a decision of the I.C.T.U. Disputes Committee would only be of assistance, however, where there was a formal ruling of the Committee. It would not cover, for instance, a situation where, as a result of an agreement with another union, the recruiting union seeks to terminate the membership of workers improperly recruited.[35] Moreover, it is clear that where a union terminates membership in order to comply with a Disputes Committee ruling, it must adhere to its own rules with regard to termination, otherwise the termination will be void.[36]

The mere possession of a power to terminate membership in order to comply with a Disputes Committee decision will not necessarily prevent legal challenges from expelled members. In *Rothwell* v. *Association of Professional Executive Clerical and Computer Staff*,[37] the plaintiff successfully resisted expulsion, which the union claimed was necessary to comply with a T.U.C. Disputes Committee ruling. Foster J. found, as a fact, that the British equivalent of clause 47 (d) had not been infringed and therefore the Committee's ruling was *ultra vires* and void. A challenge might also be mounted on the basis that the procedures which resulted in expulsion did not comply with the provisions of natural or constitutional justice. This challenge could be directed either toward the decision of the Disputes Committee itself, or toward the decision of the union to comply with the Committee's ruling. In either instance, the question must be asked as to whether the member has a right to be heard. In *Rothwell*, Foster J. stated that the fact that the plaintiff was not allowed to be present and to speak at the Disputes Committee hearing did not make the hearing so unfair "as to bedevil the award".[38] Similarly, in *Cheall* v. *Association of Professional Executive Clerical and Computer Staff*[39], it was held that the plaintiff, whose union membership had been terminated on compliance with a Disputes Committee ruling, was a third party to the inter-union dispute which the Disputes Committee had to resolve. The fact that he would be affected by the outcome of the dispute could not be regarded

---

[35] See *Walsh* v. *A.U.E.W.*, The Times, July 15, 1977.
[36] See *Kirwan* v. *Harris* High Court, unreported, 29 November 1976 (Hamilton J.). The same judge gave a similar decision in a subsequent case involving the I.T.G.W.U., see the *Irish Times*, February 26, 1977.
[37] [1976] I.C.R. 211.
[38] At 223.
[39] [1983] 2 A.C. 180.

by the courts as entitling him to participate in its resolution. Lord Diplock[40] said:

> "The only parties to the dispute that was before the disputes committee were the trade unions concerned. They, and only they, were entitled to make representations, written or oral, to the committee. Decisions that resolve disputes between the parties to them, whether by litigation or some other adversarial dispute-resolving process, often have consequences which affect persons who are not parties to the dispute; but the legal concept of natural justice has never been extended to give such persons as well as the parties themselves rights to be heard by the decision-making tribunal before the decision is reached."[41]

In *Cheall*, the plaintiff also argued that his expulsion was invalid because he had not been afforded a hearing by the executive council prior to their decision to terminate his membership. The House of Lords held that there was no legal obligation on the union to hear the plaintiff since nothing he could have said would have affected the outcome. In reality, there was no other decision at which the union could arrive.[42] The authors doubt whether the Irish courts would find the reasoning *on this point* compelling, particularly since he had not been allowed to make representations to the Disputes Committee. Cheall could have persuaded the executive council to postpone any decision to expel pending the outcome of legal proceedings against the Disputes Committee. He could have made representations to the effect that the union should not comply with the Disputes Committee ruling, however unlikely it might have been that it would risk expulsion from the T.U.C. Nor can it be seriously contended, in the context of constitutional justice, that a hearing was not required because giving a hearing would make no difference.[43] As Megarry V.-C. said in *John* v. *Rees*:[44]

> "As everybody who has anything to do with the law well knows, the path of the law is strewn with examples of open and shut cases which, somehow, were not; of unanswerable charges which, in the event, were completely answered; of inexplicable conduct which was fully explained; of fixed and unalterable determinations that, by discussion, suffered a change. Nor are those with any knowledge of human nature who pause to think for a moment likely to underestimate the feelings of resentment of those who find that a

---

[40] In whose speech Lords Edmund-Davies, Fraser, Brandon and Templeman concurred.
[41] At 190.
[42] See Bingham J. at [1982] I.C.R. 231, 250.
[43] See Walsh J. in *Glover* v. *BLN Ltd.* [1973] I.R. 388, 429 and Henchy J. in *Garvey* v. *Ireland* [1981] I.R. 75, 102.
[44] [1970] Ch. 345, 402.

decision against them has been made without their being afforded any opportunity to influence the course of events."

It has also been suggested[45] that it would be open to the courts to treat the implementation of a Disputes Committee ruling as a ministerial or administrative act rather than a disciplinary or judicial act and as such not subject to the rules of natural justice. Although the distinction between administrative acts and judicial acts is "almost as elusive as the Scarlet Pimpernel",[46] the Irish courts have insisted that even persons carrying out administrative acts are under an obligation to act "judicially".[47] In other words, the application of fair procedures does not depend on the classification of the act but on the amount of prejudice that the individual would suffer in their absence.

Apart from the statutory restrictions relating to discrimination on grounds of sex or marital status and discrimination against E.E.C. nationals and the obligations incurred by affiliation to the I.C.T.U., unions are otherwise free to determine both conditions of membership and admissions procedure and a person who is refused membership of a trade union cannot compel the union to accept him into membership.[48] As Budd J. put it in *Tierney* v. *Amalgamated Society of Woodworkers*:[49]

> "[W]hat right of property or of contract or what existing right of any sort, one must ask, is a person, who is not a member of a trade union, deprived of by not being permitted to join such union? He is certainly not deprived of any right or property, nor is he deprived of any other right, be it work or otherwise, which he had before. He is, at most, only deprived of acquiring a right."

It would also seem to follow that the union could not be compelled, at least by the disappointed applicant, to obey its own rules as to admission. The applicant could possibly obtain a declaration of his eligibility for membership under the rules,[50] if such was the reason for refusal. A more difficult issue is whether the courts will impose a duty to give proper consideration to the application and subject the admissions procedure to the requirements of natural justice or constitutional fairness. In *McInnes* v. *Onslow-Fane*[51], Megarry V.-C. accepted that bodies, such as trade unions, were under a duty to reach

---

[45] See Elias, Napier and Wallington, *Labour Law: Cases and Materials* (London, 1980), at p. 338.
[46] *Per* Pennel J., *Voyager Explorations Ltd.* v. *Ontario Securities Commission* (1970) 8 D.L.R. (3d) 135, 139.
[47] See, for example, *State (Williams)* v. *Army Pensions Board* [1983] I.R. 308 and *O'Brien* v. *Bord na Mona* [1983] I.R. 255. See also Kelly, *The Irish Constitution* 2nd ed. (Dublin, 1984), p. 222; Coffey, (1984) 6 *D.U.L.J. (n.s.)* 152.
[48] See Rideout, *The Right to Membership of a Trade Union* (London, 1963), pp. 3-40.
[49] [1959] I.R. 254, 259.
[50] This possibility was recognised by Lord Denning and Upjohn L.J. in *Boulting* v. *A.C.T.A.T.* [1963] 2 Q.B. 606 at 629 and 643 respectively.
[51] [1978] 1 W.L.R. 1520.

an honest conclusion, without bias, in relation to applications for membership but he emphatically rejected that they were under any duty either to inform the applicant of the case against him, or give him an oral hearing, or give the reasons for rejection.

> "The courts must be slow to allow any implied obligation to be fair to be used as a means for bringing before the courts for review honest decisions of bodies exercising jurisdiction over . . . activities which those bodies are far better fitted to judge than the courts."[52]

Incidents of the relationship

Contract

The two principal categories of the incidents based on contract are the express terms contained in the union rule book and the terms inserted into the rule book by statute. In relation to the former, the parties' freedom to contract is subject to certain restrictions. In particular, it must be read subject of the common law doctrine of illegality[53] (though not the doctrine of restraint of trade[54]), various pieces of legislation,[55] the Constitution and European Community Law. Within these constraints, however, the union is free to include in its rule book whatever it wishes. Typical provisions would include a statement of the union's objectives; a description of the union's governmental structure; a statement of the conditions of eligibility for membership and for holding union office; provisions regulating the levying of subscriptions and the holding of union property; disciplinary provisions; and standing orders for the conduct of meetings. Obviously, the courts can exercise a certain amount of control over union rule books by interpreting the rules to produce "reasonable" results,[56] and by insisting that the union must observe the principles of natural justice before expelling members.[57] But this power is limited. The courts cannot strike out rules merely because they believe them to be unreasonable.[58]

In the main, the courts have insisted that the terms of the contract are to be found exclusively in the union rule book,[59] and have refused

---

[52] *Ibid.* at 1535.
[53] As to which see Clark, *Contract* (London, 1982), Ch. 13.
[54] See *supra*, p. 82.
[55] See *infra*, pp. 108–111.
[56] See *Lee v. Showmen's Guild of Great Britain* [1952] 2 Q.B. 329, 342–345, *per* Denning L.J.; *Esterman v. National and Local Government Officers' Association* [1974] I.C.R. 625.
[57] See *infra*, pp. 115–121.
[58] See *Faramus v. Film Artistes' Association* [1964] A.C. 925; *British Actors' Equity Association v. Goring* [1977] I.C.R. 393.
[59] See *Martin v. Scottish Transport and General Workers' Union* [1952] 1 All E.R. 691, where the House of Lords refused to imply a rule allowing the union to admit temporary members; *McCarthy v. Amalgamated Transport and General Workers' Union* Northern Ireland High Court, unreported, 14 January 1966, where Lowry J. refused to imply into the rule book an obligation on the union to negotiate on behalf of all its members; *Taylor v. N.U.M. (Yorkshire*

to imply terms into the contract, particularly in relation to disciplinary provisions.[60] More recently, however, the British courts have indicated that not all terms of the agreement between the members and the union are to be found in the rule book and that the union rule book may be *supplemented* by rules derived from custom and practice, particularly as respects the discretion conferred by the members on committees or officials of the union as to the way in which they may act on the members' behalf,[61] and, in *National Union of Mineworkers (Kent Area)* v. *Gormley*,[62] the Court of Appeal readily implied a power to hold a secret ballot of members on a proposed national productivity incentive scheme.

The terms inserted into the rule book by statute include, in the case of registered trade unions:[63]

(1) the name and place of meeting for business of the trade union;
(2) the objects for which the union is to be established, the purposes for which the funds thereof shall be applicable and the conditions under which any member may become entitled to any benefit assured thereby and the fines and forfeitures to be imposed on any member;
(3) the manner of making, altering and rescinding rules;[64]

Area) [1984] I.R.L.R. 445 where Nicholls J. refused to imply a power enabling the union to postpone local branch elections; *Taylor* v. *N.U.M. (Derbyshire Area)* [1985] I.R.L.R. 99 where Vinelott J. refused to imply a provision for allowances to be paid to members on "unofficial" strike; *Liptrott* v. *N.U.M. (Nottingham Area)* Q.B.D. unreported, 25 May 1985 (see I.R.L.R. 285). where Nolan J. refused to imply a term exempting members on strike from paying contributions, even though its absence could lead to absurd results and was obviously an oversight. See, however, Walsh J. in *Murphy* v. *Stewart* [1973] I.R. 97, 119. On implied terms in union rule books generally, see Gray J. in the Industrial Division of the Federal Court of Australia in *Scott* v. *Jess* (1985) 56 A.L.R. 379, 400.

[60] See *O'Neill* v. *Transport and General Workers' Union* [1934] I.R. 633; *Radford* v. *National Society of Operative Printers, Graphical and Media Personnel* [1972] I.C.R. 484.

[61] *Heaton's Transport (St. Helens) Ltd.* v. *Transport and General Workers' Union* [1973] A.C. 15. See also *Salt* v. *National Graphical Association, The Times*, May 15, 1978; *Bourne* v. *Colodense Ltd.* [1985] I.C.R. 291. Of course, if the rules are clear, custom and practice cannot be given effect if they conflict with the rules; see *Taylor* v. *N.U.M. (Derbyshire Area)* [1985] I.R.L.R. 99, 105.

[62] *The Times*, October 20, 1977.

[63] By virtue of s. 14 of the Trade Union Act 1871 and the First Schedule thereto.

[64] In *Burke* v. *A.S.D.* [1906] 2 K.B. 583, the union altered the rule as to sick benefit to the prejudice of a member, while that member was suffering from insanity, and it was held that the alteration was binding on the member if made in accordance with the rule authorising and regulating the alteration of rules of the union. In *Cox* v. *N.U.F.W.* (1928) 44 T.L.R. 352, Astbury J. held that a resolution which reduced the amount of benefit payable under certain rules in the rule book did not amount to alterations of these rules, even though the amount payable was expressly provided for therein. See also *Cullen* v. *Elwin* (1904) 90 L.J. 840. Alterations of the rule book which comply with the provisions of the rule book are nevertheless null and void, if made in defiance of a court order – *Clarke* v. *Chadburn* [1985] 1 All E.R. 211, 213–214. Finally, in this context, one should note that provisions in a union rule book relating to the making, altering, or rescinding of rules can be ignored where the union is (i) adopting political fund rules (Trade Union Act 1913, s. 4) or (ii) effecting an amalgamation or transfer of engagements, unless the rule book *expressly* provides to the contrary (Trade Union Act 1975, s. 8).

(4) provision for the appointment and removal of a general committee of management, of a trustee or trustees, treasurer and other officers;
(5) provision for the investment of funds, and for an annual or periodical audit of accounts;
(6) provision for the inspection of books and names of members of the trade union by every person having an interest in the union funds;[65]
(7) provision for the dissolution of the union.[66]

Authorised trade unions must also outline, in their rule books, the conditions of entry and cesser of membership,[67] and foreign based unions wishing to obtain a negotiation licence must provide in their rule books for a controlling authority consisting of members resident in the State or Northern Ireland and empowered to make decisions affecting members in that area.[68]

Finally, one should note that section 9 of the Trade Union Act Amendment Act 1876[69] permits a person between the age of 16 and 18 to join a trade union, if the rules so provide, but prohibits him from being a member of a committee of management, a trustee or a treasurer of the union.[70]

Statute

The incidents of the union-member relationship based on statute differ from the incidents inserted into the rule book by statute in that the former do not take effect as contractual provisions but rather confer statutory rights on the parties to the relationship. The incidents[71] referred to are:

---

[65] In *Norey* v. *Keep* [1909] 1 Ch. 561, it was held that a member wishing to inspect the books is entitled to employ accountants to do this, although the accountants can be obliged to give an undertaking that the information received will only be used for the purpose of advising their client. See also *Taylor* v. *N.U.M. (Derbyshire Area)* [1985] I.R.L.R. 65. If the union can prove *mala fides* on the part of the member seeking the inspection, the court may refuse to allow him to employ an accountant – *Dodd* v. *A.M.W.U.* [1924] 1 Ch. 116. A statutory right to inspect the register of members of authorised trade unions is also conferred on "any interested party" by ss. 12 (1) (*c*) and 13 (1) (*d*) of the Trade Union Act 1941.
[66] Trade Union Act Amendment Act 1876, s. 14. See *supra*, pp. 80–81.
[67] Trade Union Act 1941, ss. 12 and 13. In *Murphy* v. *Stewart* [1973] I.R. 97, 119, Walsh J. indicated that legal proceedings could be mounted by a member on foot of the failure of his union to include such rules in the rule book.
[68] Trade Union Act 1975, s. 17.
[69] As amended by the Age of Majority Act 1985.
[70] One implication of s. 9 is that persons under the age of 16 may not become members. S. 10, however, confers a right "on any member of a trade union not being under the age of 16 years" to nominate a person to receive a sum of money on the death of that member. The implication here is that there may be members under 16, although perhaps s. 10 should be read in the context of a situation where there may have been trade union members under the age of 16 at the time of its enactment in 1876.
[71] In *Tierney* v. *A.S.W.* [1959] I.R. 254, Budd J. rejected the argument that the right to join a trade union was one such incident.

(a) the right of a member to complain to the Registrar of Friendly Societies about alleged breaches of the union rules relating to political funds;[72]
(b) the right of members, when adopting political fund rules, to override provisions in the rule book relating to alteration of rules;[73]
(c) the right of all parties to an amalgamation or transfer of engagements between two or more unions to rely on various provisions of the Trade Union Act 1975 in order to effect the amalgamation or transfer, notwithstanding anything in the rule books;[74]
(d) the right of a member to complain to the Registrar about the manner in which a resolution approving an instrument of transfer or amalgamation was passed;[75]
(e) the right of a member to receive a copy of the annual returns filed with the Registrar;[76]
(f) the right of a member over the age of 16 to nominate certain persons to whom any monies not exceeding £100 payable on the death of such member shall be paid at his decease;[77]
(g) the right of members of authorised trade unions to inspect the register of members:[78]
(h) the right of any member[79] to receive, on demand and on payment of a sum not exceeding 5p,[80] a copy of the union rules.

Conversely, the legislation also imposes certain obligations on union members *qua* members. In particular, union members who fraudulently obtain possession of union money, securities, books, papers or other effects or who wilfully withhold or fraudulently misapply the same or who wilfully apply any part of the same for purposes which are *ultra*

[72] Trade Union Act 1913, s. 3 (2). See *supra*, pp. 94–95.
[73] Trade Union Act 1913, s. 4 (2).
[74] Thus s. 7 provides that ss. 2–6 of the 1975 Act, which set out the procedure for effecting an amalgamation or transfer of engagements between two or more unions, shall take precedence over anything in the rule book of the unions concerned. Similarly, s. 5 provides that a simple majority of votes cast shall be sufficient to pass a resolution approving an instrument of amalgamation or transfer, notwithstanding anything in the union rule book, while s. 8 empowers the governing body of a transferee union to alter the rule book by memorandum in writing in order to give effect to the instrument of transfer.
[75] Trade Union Act 1975, s. 10.
[76] Trade Union Act 1871, s. 16.
[77] Trade Union Act Amendment Act 1876, s. 10 as amended by s. 3 of the Provident Nominations and Small Intestacies Act 1883.
[78] Trade Union Act 1941, ss. 12 (1) (c), 12 (4), 13 (1) (d), 13 (4). This right is distinct from the contractual right of a member of any registered trade union to inspect the register of members and the books of the union, pursuant to s. 14 of the 1871 Act. See *supra*, p. 109.
[79] The obligation imposed by s. 14 (2) of the 1871 Act applies not only to members but also to prospective members and to any other person, whether having an interest in the union or not.
[80] It is submitted in *Citrine's Trade Union Law* 3rd ed. (London, 1966), p. 235 that if the rules are supplied by post the cost of packing and postage may be added even though this brings the total above 5p per copy. It is also submitted that there is nothing to prevent the union making different charges to different applicants, provided the statutory maximum is not exceeded. "For example, members may be charged less than outsiders."

vires the union rule book, may be ordered to restore the property and to pay, at the court's discretion, a fine not exceeding £20.[81] Specified members of authorised trade unions, who fail to send a statement of the union's numbers to the Department of Labour pursuant to section 15 (1) of the Trade Union Act 1941, or who send a wilfully false statement, are guilty of an offence and can be fined up to £100.[82] Members of unregistered authorised unions,[83] who consent to or facilitate a failure to comply with section 13 (1) of the 1941 Act[84] are likewise guilty of an offence punishable by fine not exceeding £5 together with a further fine not exceeding £1 for every day during which the offence continues.[85]

The Constitution

The impact of the Constitution on the union-member relationship has been principally in the context of disciplinary proceedings,[86] in relation to which it guarantees those affected by such proceedings the right to fair procedures.[87] In the United Kingdom such proceedings are subject to the rules of natural justice and, arguably, these rules have been subsumed under the concept of constitutional justice and the right to fair procedures.[88] Two important incidents of these concepts are:

1. *Audi alteram partem*, which was applied in *Kilkenny* v. *Irish Engineering and Foundry Workers' Union*[89] where Gavan Duffy J.

---

[81] Trade Union Act 1871, s. 12. Non-compliance with such an order is punishable by up to three months' imprisonment.

[82] Trade Union Act 1941, s. 15 (2).

[83] Members of authorised trade unions are not so liable, although the union itself and such of its officers as consent to or facilitate such failure can be prosecuted – Trade Union Act 1941, s. 12 (2).

[84] See *supra*, p. 59.

[85] Trade Union Act 1941, s. 13 (2).

[86] See *infra*, pp. 113-121.

[87] On which see, *inter alia*, *Glover* v. *BLN Ltd.* [1973] I.R. 388.

[88] The precise relationship between the principles of natural justice and the individual's right to fair procedures has never been definitively established by the courts. Speaking of the role of the right to fair procedures in the context of criminal justice, Kelly states that ". . . it is perhaps best to look at it as a sort of fine-mesh catch-all notion, intended to fill with the general notion of fair play whatever interstices may be left between more traditional rules and principles of criminal justice. . .": *The Irish Constitution* 2nd ed. (Dublin, 1984) at p. 387. It is submitted that the right to fair procedures fulfils a similar function in relation to natural justice. See, *e.g.* the remarks of Walsh J. in *Glover* v. *BLN Ltd.* [1973] I.R. 388, 425 that "the dictates of constitutional justice require that statutes, regulations or agreements setting up machinery for taking decisions which may affect rights or impose liabilities should be construed as providing for fair procedures." See also the comments of McWilliam J. in *Connolly* v. *McConnell* (1983) 2 *J.I.S.L.L.* 104, 110 that ". . . natural justice is nothing more or less than fairness and its requirements must depend on the circumstances of each particular case and the subject matter under consideration"; and the comments of McCarthy J., O'Higgins C.J. concurring, in *State (Furey)* v. *Minister for Defence* Supreme Court, unreported, 2 March 1984 that the concept of constitutional justice was one which "subsumes and assimilates natural justice." In *Furey*, McCarthy J. also said that he did not hold to the view that natural justice was something independent of the Constitution. "In my view the two principles of natural justice as they pre-existed the Constitution are now part of the human rights guaranteed by the Constitution."

[89] [1939] Ir. Jur. Rep. 52. *Cp. Branigan* v. *Keady* [1959] I.R. 293, where the plaintiff's expulsion was declared valid because he had received the "fullest notice" of the various charges against him and was given "every opportunity" to make his defence.

granted a declaration that a resolution which purported to expel the plaintiffs from membership of the defendant union was null and void because it was passed without affording the plaintiffs an opportunity to be heard in their defence; and,

2. *Nemo iudex in causa sua*, which was applied in *Connolly* v. *McConnell*[90] where the Supreme Court held that the suspension of a union official by the union's executive council was null and void because certain members of the council had a personal interest in the charges made against the official.

Apart from the guarantee of fair procedures, one other incident of the union-member relationship based exclusively on the Constitution recognised by the courts is a right to participate in the decision making processes of the union.[91] The reasoning leading to the recognition of this right is not without its difficulties and the authors have argued above that its inclusion in the union-member relationship is not warranted by reference to the Constitution.[92] Another constitutional right, which does have serious implications for the union-member relationship, is the individual's right of access to the courts.[93] Such a right, unless properly waived, would render void any provisions in the rule book which purported to oust the jurisdiction of the courts.[94]

Law of the European Communities

The union-member relationship has also been affected by certain European Community measures made pursuant to Article 48 (2) of the Treaty of Rome.[95] These measures are designed to ensure equality of treatment in respect of representation of the interests of migrant workers by trade unions and other representative bodies. Chief of these is Regulation 1612/68[96], which guarantees for Community nationals "equality of treatment as regards membership of trade unions and the exercise of rights attaching thereto, including the right to vote." Regulation 312/76[97] guarantees Community nationals the right to equality of treatment as regards eligibility to posts in the management or administration of trade unions. Despite Kidner's suggestion[98] that qualifications of residence are contrary to these regulations, it would appear that section 17 of the Trade Union Act 1975, which requires all members of the management committee of foreign based unions to be

---

[90] [1983] I.R. 172.
[91] *Rodgers* v. *I.T.G.W.U.* High Court, unreported, 15 March 1978. Noted by Kerr, (1978) *D.U.L.J.* 61.
[92] See *supra*, pp. 24–26.
[93] *Macauley* v. *Minister for Posts and Telegraphs* [1966] I.R. 345.
[94] See *infra*, p. 119.
[95] See, generally, Evans, "Development of European Community Law regarding the trade union and related rights of migrant workers" (1979) 28 *I.C.L.Q.* 354.
[96] O.J. L257/2, 19.10.1968.
[97] O.J. L39/2, 14.2.1976.
[98] *Trade Union Law* 1st ed. (London, 1979), pp. 45–46.

Termination of the union-member relationship

By the member

A union member may terminate the union-member relationship by resigning or retiring in accordance with the union rule book. Authorised trade unions are required by statute[99] to include in their rule books, provisions specifying the conditions of cesser of membership.[1] Furthermore, the fact of cesser, the reason for same and the date upon which it took effect must be noted in the union's register of members for a period of five years after the former member has left.[2]

Resignation will be deemed to have occurred if "the member has sufficiently manifested his decision to be a member no more"[3] so that non-payment of dues over a period of time could justify the union in treating the defaulter as having resigned.

It would appear that a branch of union members can only secede from the union, taking their share of the union's assets, if secession is provided for in the rule book[4] and if the assets involved belong to the branch as a separate organisation rather than as a constituent of a larger unit.[5]

By the union

The union may terminate the union-member relationship by expelling the member. There have been relatively few Irish cases[6] arising out of the expulsion of trade union members. Certain judicial trends are discernible, however.

First, the courts adopt a strict interpretation of provisions of the rule book conferring the power to expel, and indeed general disciplinary powers, on the trade union authority. So in *O'Neill* v. *Transport and General Workers' Union*[7] there was no express provision in the rule

---

[99] Trade Union Act 1941, ss. 12 (1) (*a*) and 13 (1) (*c*).

[1] The 1941 Act does not expressly imply into every contract of membership a right to resign on giving reasonable notice. See Walsh J., in *Murphy* v. *Stewart* [1973] I.R. 97, 119.

[2] Trade Union Act 1941, ss. 12 (1) (*b*) and 13 (1) (*c*). Where the member has been expelled or suspended, the register must also contain the date of the order directing the expulsion or suspension and a reference to the rule or other provision authorising such expulsion or suspension.

[3] Megarry J. in *In Re the Sick and Funeral Society of St. John's Sunday School, Golcar* [1973] Ch. 51, 62.

[4] *John* v. *Rees* [1970] Ch. 345; *Cope* v. *Crossingham* [1909] 2 Ch. 148. See *supra*, p. 81.

[5] *Cope* v. *Crossingham* [1909] 2 Ch. 148; *Brentall* v. *Hentrick* [1928] N.Z.L.R. 788; *Raymond* v. *Doherty* (1965) 49 D.L.R. (2d) 99.

[6] By comparison to Britain.

[7] [1934] I.R. 633. See also *Clarke* v. *Ferrie* [1926] N.I. 1, where it was held that the phrase "to deal with a member as may be deemed fit" did not include the power to expel; *Spring* v. *N.A.S.D.A.* [1956] 1 W.L.R. 585, on which see *supra*, pp. 103–104, and *Burn* v. *National Amalgamated Labourers'*

book authorising the removal from their positions of honorary officers and Johnston J. refused to imply such a power. He said that "penal powers, if they are conferred at all, must be conferred by express and specific enactment and it is idle to seek to establish their existence by implication from rules of a general character...."[8] This strict approach to the construction of disciplinary provisions can also be discerned in the judgments in the case of *Moran* v. *Workers Union of Ireland*.[9] The plaintiffs had fallen into arrears in the payment of their weekly contributions to the union and eventually were notified by the union that, by virtue of Rule 12 (a) of the rule book which provided, *inter alia*, that if a member failed to pay his contributions, levies, special levies and fines "in respect of a period of 26 weeks, he shall thereupon lapse from membership of the union", they were no longer considered to be union members. They brought an action claiming a declaration that this notification was null and void and that each of the plaintiffs was a member of the union.

Gavan Duffy J., in the High Court, held for the plaintiffs. He held that Rule 12 referred to a period of 26 consecutive weeks; that when the plaintiffs were in default for 26 consecutive weeks, the union failed to take any action but instead continued to treat them as members; and that when the union finally sought to exclude them, they had paid off sufficient of the arrears to avoid the operation of Rule 12 (a). Apparently automatic lapse was subject to the right of the union to waive its right to enforce Rule 12, which altered the contract between the union and these particular members. Furthermore, the plaintiffs were also entitled to succeed on the issue of estoppel.

The case was appealed to the Supreme Court where, in judgments which are not a little confusing, a majority decided that the union's appeal against one of the plaintiffs should be allowed while a differently constituted majority decided to dismiss the appeal in relation to the second plaintiff.

Sullivan C.J. decided that the period of 26 weeks, mentioned in Rule 12 (a), was not necessarily consecutive, and that, on the wording of the rule, lapse was automatic. However, on the facts, the plaintiffs had been re-admitted to membership and since that date, as they had not fallen into arrears for a period of 26 weeks, they could not be excluded from membership under Rule 12. O'Byrne J. agreed, holding that, on the union pleadings, the union was estopped from denying that the plaintiffs had been re-admitted to membership.

Murnaghan J., however, held that lapse was not automatic and said

---

Union of Great Britain and Ireland [1920] 2 Ch. 364 where it was held that a rule empowering the executive committee to suspend, expel or prosecute members acting contrary to the rules did not imply a power to inflict penalties of a different kind, namely suspending part of the member's rights and privileges.

[8] At 646.
[9] [1943] I.R. 485.

that the union would have to act on the fact of non-payment before the plaintiffs could be excluded from membership, so that the plaintiffs continued in membership until notified to the contrary by the union. At that point the first plaintiff was in arrears for 34 consecutive weeks, taking into account his earlier defaults and consequently could be excluded under Rule 12. The second plaintiff, however, had paid off so much of his arrears that he was only in default for 25 consecutive weeks, and so Rule 12 was inapplicable.

Meredith J. allowed the appeal on the technical ground that, on the pleadings, the plaintiffs were not entitled to rely on the fact that, on each payment in 1939, sixpence should be apportioned to the week of payment. Consequently they could not disprove 26 weeks of continuous non-payment and were automatically excluded from membership under Rule 12.

Finally, Geoghegan J. allowed the appeal on the grounds that the plaintiffs had forfeited membership under Rule 12 and had not been re-admitted in accordance with the rule book.

Because of the number and variety of the judgments handed down it is difficult to extract any general principle of law from this case. It is interesting to note, however, that of the six judges involved, four construed the phrase "period of 26 weeks" in Rule 12, to mean a period of 26 consecutive weeks, thereby limiting the effect of the rule. Furthermore, while five of the judges held that lapse of membership under the rule was automatic, no arguments were addressed to the Court on the legality of such a clause. British courts have subsequently held that rules providing for automatic forfeiture of membership without the necessity of a charge and hearing are *ultra vires* and void,[10] so that the decision in *Moran* on this point is of doubtful authority.

The validity of automatic forfeiture clauses brings us to the second general point about judicial construction of union disciplinary provisions. As noted above,[11] the courts have insisted that, before expelling members or dismissing officials, trade unions must abide by the common law rules of natural justice and must respect the individual's constitutional right to fair procedures. In other words, the member or official is entitled to receive full notice of the various charges and to be given every opportunity of making a defence.[12] Moreover, that person is entitled to be heard by an impartial tribunal. The application of these two principles is illustrated by two cases arising out of attempts to dismiss the same trade union official.[13] In 1977, N.E.E.T.U.'s executive council passed a resolution removing the union's Financial General Secretary from his position. The official

---

[10] See *Edwards* v. *S.O.G.A.T.* [1971] Ch. 354.
[11] *Supra*.
[12] Compare *Kilkenny* v. *Irish Engineering and Foundry Workers' Union* [1939] Ir. Jur. Rep. 52 with *Branigan* v. *Keady* [1959] I.R. 283.
[13] N.E.E.T.U. v. *McConnell* (1983) 2 *J.I.S.S.L.* 97 and *Connolly* v. *McConnell* [1983] I.R. 172.

argued successfully before Hamilton J. that the procedure adopted by the council was unfair and contrary to the principles of natural justice in that he was not informed of the charges against him and was not given an adequate opportunity of answering the said charges. Hamilton J. held that the essentials of natural justice required at least that, in considering and reaching a decision on disciplinary matters, the accused party must have an opportunity of defending himself and, in order to do so, that he be made aware of the charges or allegations which he has to meet. From the facts it appeared that the official had been summoned by letter to attend a meeting of the union's resident executive council to answer various charges. The defendant received a copy of the letter shortly before he was due to go away on holiday, but, because it did not in any way state or indicate that, in the event of his failing to attend and make satisfactory answers, he would be suspended forthwith, the official did not treat it as a matter of urgency and did not attend the meeting at which he was suspended. Under the terms of the rule book he had a right of appeal against this decision to the union's executive council but, as he was not informed of the decision to suspend him, he did not exercise that right. At the following meeting of the executive council, therefore, he was removed from office without having been afforded an opportunity of defending himself. On these facts Hamilton J. concluded that there had been a breach of natural justice and that the resolution dismissing the official was therefore null and void.[14]

Subsequently the union executive again sought to dismiss the same official, who, at this stage, had become the union's permanent Financial General Secretary, having been re-elected to that office by the members of the union. He was notified of a number of complaints against him, was invited to attend a meeting at which these matters would be discussed and was warned that a decision could be made to dismiss him. He duly attended the meeting and replied to the charges. Nevertheless he was dismissed. He unsuccessfully contended before McWilliam J. that the proceedings were tainted by bias but succeeded on appeal to the Supreme Court. Griffin J., with whom Henchy and Hederman JJ. concurred, found that, as various members of the executive council had an interest in the charges,[15] correct procedures were not adopted and natural justice was not accorded to the official,

---

[14] See (1983) 2 *J.I.S.L.L.* at p. 104.

[15] Among the reasons which led to his purported dismissal were (a) his refusal to pay the salary of the Assistant General Secretary (AGS) and (b) his refusal to pay expenses to the AGS and one M. Notwithstanding, the AGS and M were allowed to take part in the discussion of the executive council immediately before the vote on whether to dismiss and the AGS actually voted in the motion to dismiss. The union's general president also acted as "prosecutor and judge." On determining whether a tribunal is impartial, see Kenny J. in *O'Donoghue* v. *Veterinary Council* [1975] I.R. 398, 405: "a member is not impartial if his own interest might be affected by the verdict, or he is so connected with the complaint that a reasonable man would think that he would come to the case with prior knowledge of the facts or that he might not be impartial."

with the result that his purported dismissal was null and void.[16]

While the case undoubtedly affirms the *nemo iudex in causa sua* principle, it does not demand of those who take part in disciplinary decisions "the icy impartiality of a Rhadamanthus."[17] Viscount Simon put it well in *White v. Kuzych*[18] when he said that what was required of those who consider the charges and decide to expel was "a will to reach an honest conclusion after hearing what was urged on either side, and a resolve not to make up their minds beforehand on his personal guilt, however firmly they held their conviction as to union policy."[19]

The individual's rights to fair procedures encompasses more than merely the two principles of *audi alteram partem* and *nemo iudex in causa sua*. It is a general guarantee that, having regard to all the circumstances of the case, the procedure adopted will be fair. So a member is entitled to receive in good time particulars of the charge made against him, including a reference to the specific rule which he is alleged to have infringed;[20] he must be given an opportunity to controvert evidence adduced by the other side[21] and may also have the right to call and cross-examine witnesses;[22] he has a right to hear about the penalty to be imposed;[23] he is entitled to have observed the procedural requirements laid down in the rules,[24] particularly with regard to internal appeals.[25] Further possible rights include a right to be represented, though not necessarily legally,[26] and a right to receive reasons.[27]

The constitutional guarantee of fair procedures calls into question therefore the validity of union rules which expressly exclude the

---

[16] See [1983] I.R. at 180. See also *Roebuck v. N.U.M. (Yorkshire Area) (No. 2)* [1978] I.C.R. 676.
[17] Per Bowen L.J. in *Jackson v. Barry Railway Co.* [1893] 1 Ch. 238, 248.
[18] [1951] A.C. 585.
[19] At 596. See also *McGrath v. Trustees of Maynooth College* Supreme Court, unreported, 1 November 1979.
[20] *Annamunthodo v. Oilfield Workers' Trade Union* [1961] A.C. 945.
[21] *Kiely v. Minister for Social Welfare* [1977] I.R. 267; *Williams v. Army Pensions Board* [1983] I.R. 308.
[22] *Payne v. Electrical Trades Union, The Times*, April 14, 1960.
[23] *Graham v. Racing Board* High Court, unreported, 22 November 1983.
[24] *Silvester v. National Union of Printing, Bookbinding and Paper Workers* (1966) 1 K.I.R. 679. Indeed any irregularity in convening a meeting to consider the disciplining of a member will render the purported decision void, see *Young v. Ladies' Imperial Club* [1920] 2 K.B. 323; *Leary v. National Union of Vehicle Builders* [1971] Ch. 34; *McLelland v. National Union of Journalists* [1975] I.C.R. 116.
[25] *Braithwaite v. Electrical Electronic and Telecommunication Union* [1969] 2 All E.R. 859.
[26] The authorities conflict on whether natural justice necessarily involves a right to legal representation. It would appear that there is, at most, only a qualified right to be legally represented where an adverse decision could "ruin" the individual concerned. See *Collier v. Hicks* (1831) 2 B. & Ad. 663; *Walker v. Amalgamated Union of Engineering and Foundry Workers* 1969 S.L.T. 150; *Pett v. Greyhound Racing Association (No. 1)* [1969] 1 Q.B. 125; *Pett v. Greyhound Racing Association (No. 2)* [1970] 1 Q.B. 46; *Enderby Town F.C. v. Football Association* [1971] Ch. 598; *Maynard v. Osmond* [1977] Q.B. 240; *Fraser v. Mudge* [1975] 1 W.L.R. 1132; *State (Smullen) v. Duffy* High Court, unreported, 21 March 1980; *McConnell v. Eastern Health Board* High Court, unreported, 1 June 1983; *Re Wark and Green* (1985) 15 D.L.R. (4th) 577.
[27] See Lord Denning in *Breen v. Amalgamated Engineering Union* [1971] 2 Q.B. 175.

principles of natural justice or which impliedly exclude them by providing for the automatic forfeiture of membership on the occurrence of a particular event. There is some early British authority supporting the view that the principles of natural justice can be expressly excluded by the union,[28] but the modern view is that any such rule will be void.[29] In *Edwards* v. *Society of Graphical and Allied Trades*[30], the plaintiff's expulsion from the defendant union was purportedly carried out under a rule which provides for automatic termination of membership for arrears of subscription,[31] and Lord Denning M.R. declared the rule invalid. "No union can stipulate for a power to expel a man unheard. . . . No union can stipulate for automatic expulsion of a man without giving him the opportunity of being heard."[32] At the very least, a union wishing to uphold automatic forfeiture clauses will have to show that the member concerned freely and willingly waived his constitutional right to put his side of the case. To do this, it will have to be proved that when the member assented to be bound by the rules he was actually aware of the fact that he was waiving his right to fair procedures.[33] It could also be argued, at least in the context of automatic forfeiture clauses for non-payment of dues, that payment of dues is a condition precedent to the retention of membership. A "more realistic and less doctrinal"[34] argument was put forward by Megarry J. in *In re the Sick and Funeral Society of St. John's Sunday School, Golcar*,[35] in the case of a person who had "disregarded all his obligations as a member for several years" and subsequently asserted that he was still a member because the correct procedure to terminate his membership had not been followed. Megarry J. was of the opinion that every member had the unilateral right, not dependent on acceptance, to resign his membership. He continued:

> "There can be no magic in the word 'resign', nor in whether the resignation is written or oral. The essence of the matter seems to me to be whether the member has sufficiently manifested his decision to be a member no more. I cannot see why such a manifestation should not be by conduct instead of by words. . . ."[36]

Megarry J. made it clear, however, that he was not talking of a situation where a member had failed to pay his subscriptions for a few

---

[28] *Maclean* v. *Workers' Union* [1929] 1 Ch. 602, 623–4.
[29] *Edwards* v. *S.O.G.A.T.* [1971] Ch. 354, 376; *Radford* v. *N.A.T.S.O.P.A.* [1972] I.C.R. 484, 496.
[30] [1971] Ch. 354.
[31] Similar to that in *Moran* v. *W.U.I.* [1943] I.R. 485.
[32] [1971] Ch. at 376–377, citing the speeches of Lords Pearce and Evershed in *Faramus* v. *F.A.A.* [1964] A.C. 925.
[33] *G.* v. *An Bord Uchtála* [1980] I.R. 32, 80. See also *supra*, pp. 31–32. See also s. 14 of the Trade Union Act 1871 which requires registered unions to make express provision in the rules for, *inter alia*, "the fines and forfeitures to be imposed on any member of such trade union."
[34] *Per* Rideout, *Rideout's Principles of Labour Law* 4th ed. (London, 1983), p. 415.
[35] [1973] Ch. 51.
[36] At 62.

weeks and the union was "snatching" at some trivial or short-lived breach of rules by a member to deny him membership.[37]

Provisions in the rule book which seek to oust the jurisdiction of the courts in relation to disciplinary matters are void[38] and furthermore cannot be read as a valid requirement that internal remedies must be exhausted before the member resorts to the courts.[39] From the British cases on this matter, two other basic propositions can be advanced:

1. The court is not absolutely precluded by an express requirement in the rules that internal remedies should be exhausted before resort to the courts, because its jurisdiction cannot be ousted. In such a situation, however, the member will have to demonstrate that the circumstances justify disregarding the contractual position.
2. Where there is no such express requirement the courts may more readily intervene but may require the member first to exhaust internal remedies.

In relation to internal appeals the question has arisen as to whether the prejudice suffered by the individual member can be corrected or removed by a fair hearing on appeal. No clear and absolute rule has been laid down as to whether defects in natural justice at the "trial" stage can be cured by the presence of fair procedures at the "appellate" stage.[40] In some cases the courts have adopted the approach of seeing whether the procedure as a whole gave the individual a fair hearing;[41] in other cases the courts have accepted the contention that to allow a sufficiency of natural justice at the "appellate" stage to cure any defects at the "trial" stage has the effect of depriving the individual of his right of appeal if the original decision is upheld.[42] This was the approach adopted by Megarry J., in the context of trade union disciplinary proceedings, in *Leary* v. *National Union of Vehicles Builders*.[43] He said:

> "If the rules and the law combine to give the member the right to a fair trial and the right of appeal, why should he be told that he ought

---

[37] *Id.*
[38] *Scott* v. *Avery* (1856) 5 H.L.C. 811. See also *Lee* v. *Showmen's Guild of Great Britain* [1952] 2 Q.B. 329.
[39] *Leigh* v. *N.U.R.* [1970] Ch. 326.
[40] See Evans ed., *de Smith's Judicial Review of Administrative Action* (London, 1980), pp. 242–243.
[41] *De Verteuil* v. *Knaggs* [1918] A.C. 557; *Pillai* v. *Singapore City Council* [1965] 1 W.L.R. 1278; *Re Clark and Ontario Securities Commission* (1966) 56 D.L.R. (2d) 585; *King* v. *University of Saskatchewan* (1969) 6 D.L.R. (3d) 120; *Twist* v. *Randwick Municipal Council* (1976) 51 A.L.J.R. 193; *Calvin* v. *Carr* [1980] A.C. 574; *Re Jenkins and Government of Prince Edward Island* (1983) 150 D.L.R. (3d) 43.
[42] *Denton* v. *Auckland City* [1969] N.Z.L.R. 256; *R.* v. *Brent London Borough Council, ex parte Gunning, The Times*, April 30, 1985.
[43] [1971] Ch. 34. See also, *per* Lord Wilberforce in *Calvin* v. *Carr* [1980] A.C. 574, 593: "Movement solidarity and dislike of the rebel, or renegade, may make it difficult for appeals to be conducted in an atmosphere of detached impartiality and so makes a fair trial at the first – probably branch – level an essential condition of justice."

to be satisfied with an unjust trial and a fair appeal? . . . As a general rule . . . I hold that a failure of natural justice in the trial body cannot be cured by a sufficiency of natural justice in an appellate body."[44]

Thus, at the procedural level, the courts are able to exercise a high level of supervision over trade union disciplinary provisions. Provided fair procedures are followed, the courts will not interfere with the decision unless they consider it to be plainly unreasonable. This is crucial where the expulsion is for conduct detrimental to the union's interests, or conduct which renders the person unfit for membership, since "what is or is not to the detriment of the interests of the union is a matter which is essentially within the knowledge of the members and officers of the union."[45] One clear substantive control that has emerged from the British case law is that, if a member has refused to participate in industrial action which has not been called for in accordance with the union's rule book, the courts will not uphold any disciplinary action taken against him. So, in *Taylor* v. *National Union of Mineworkers (Derbyshire Area)*,[46] Nicholls J. declared that the strike called by the union, so far as it related to the Derbyshire area, was in contravention of the rules and constitution of the union, that the plaintiff members were lawfully entitled to disregard directions to strike or not to cross picket lines and that the union was not entitled to discipline the plaintiffs for disregarding such directions and instructions.

Similarly, in *Esterman* v. *National and Local Government Officers' Association*,[47] Templeman J. (as he then was) held that no reasonable trade union committee could arrive at the finding that the plaintiff had been guilty of conduct rendering her unfit to be a member of the union by refusing to obey the order of the national executive council to take industrial action when, under the rules, the council did not have the power to issue that order. A Scottish decision – *Partington* v. *National and Local Government Officers' Association*[48] – takes this slightly further. The union had entered into an agreement with a company whereby the latter had the right to require certain employees to remain at work in the interests of safety. The plaintiff went on strike on the instructions of the union but returned to work when the company invoked the safety provisions. The plaintiff was subsequently expelled for conduct which, in the opinion of the branch committee, rendered him unfit for membership and for disregarding a regulation of the branch. The Outer House of the Court of Session held that on neither

---

[44] At 49. *Leary* was approved in *Moran* v. *Attorney General* [1976] I.R. 400.
[45] *Per* Templeman J. in *Roebuck* v. *National Union of Mineworkers* [1977] I.C.R. 573.
[46] [1984] I.R.L.R. 445.
[47] [1974] I.C.R. 625. See also *National Seamen's and Firemen's Union of Great Britain and Northern Ireland* v. *Reed* [1926] Ch. 536, where Astbury J. said that it would be unlawful to discipline a member who refused to participate in a strike which was not in contemplation or furtherance of a trade dispute, as defined in the Trade Disputes Act 1906.
[48] [1981] I.R.L.R. 537.

ground could the plaintiff's expulsion be upheld because requiring employees such as the plaintiff to remain on a strike was a breach, not of the union rules, but of an agreement existing outside the rule book. This decision sits uneasily alongside the earlier decision in *Porter* v. *National Union of Journalists*[49], where the argument that unions cannot discipline a member who refuses to take industrial action because that action would involve a breach of his contract of employment was emphatically rejected by the English Court of Appeal.[50]

Basis for judicial intervention

The original basis of judicial intervention in the purely domestic affairs of a trade union was the need to protect the members' proprietary rights.[51] The more modern view was expressed by Denning L.J. (as he then was) in *Lee* v. *Showmen's Guild of Great Britain*.[52]

> "The power of this court to intervene is founded on its jurisdiction to protect rights of contract. If a member is expelled by a committee in breach of contract, this court will grant a declaration that their action is *ultra vires*. It will also grant an injunction to prevent his expulsion if that is necessary to protect a proprietary right of his; or to protect him in his right to earn a livelihood."

Even if loss of membership of the union does not mean loss of a job and so the disadvantage is not of a financial character, the disadvantage is more than merely social. This was recognised by Ungoed-Thomas J. in *Lawlor* v. *Union of Post Office Workers*:[53]

> "The expulsion does affect the expelled member in his work. It affects his standing with and relation to other members. The trade union is concerned with members in their capacity as workers in their jobs, and expulsion excludes from the advantages which such membership confers. Trade unions, to their honour, also develop strong ties of loyalty among their members, and loss of membership, particularly among members of standing . . . strikes deep, and not the less so because it may not strike at the pocket."

Notwithstanding the broader basis for judicial intervention, there are certain constraints placed on the power of the judiciary to intervene in a trade union's domestic affairs. First there is the rule in *Foss* v. *Harbottle*,[54] which bars the right of an individual member of an association to maintain an action in respect of a wrong alleged to be done to the association where the alleged wrong is a transaction which might be made binding on the association and on all its members by a

---

[49] [1979] I.R.L.R. 404.
[50] See Shaw L.J. at 407.
[51] See *Rigby* v. *Connol* (1880) 14 Ch. D. 482.
[52] [1952] 2 Q.B. 329, 341–342.
[53] [1965] Ch. 712.
[54] (1843) 2 Hare 461. For a detailed examination of the rule, and the four exceptions thereto, in the context of internal trade union affairs, see *supra*, pp. 67–69.

simple majority of members. This rule only applies to protect a trade union and its officials against claims by individual members in respect of matters *intra vires* the union which are capable of being ratified by a simple majority. As *Taylor* v. *National Union of Mineworkers (Derbyshire Area)*[55] illustrates, however, the rule in *Foss* v. *Harbottle* does not bar the right of a member to maintain an action to prevent or remedy an application of the funds of the union which is outside the powers conferred by its constitution. Being *ultra vires*, such a transaction cannot be ratified by any majority of the members. Here the relief sought was an injunction restraining the union from "using, procuring or permitting the use of" union funds for the purposes of a strike, which it was held was in breach of the union's rules. The injunction was sought by two "working miners", but the members of the union had not been consulted on the question of whether proceedings should be brought against the union and the individual defendants (the president, the treasurer and the secretary of the Derbyshire Union), so the question immediately arose as to whether the plaintiffs were in a position to maintain an action against the defendants. Vinelott J. said that it was clear from the authorities[56] that the protection of the rule in *Foss* v. *Harbottle* did not extend to cases where the plaintiff sought to prevent the application of funds which is *ultra vires*. Any member, he said, was entitled to insist that the union's funds were used *exclusively* in furtherance of its objects as contained in its constitution. Every member had an interest in preserving the funds of the union and, since the union's rules did not provide for allowances to be made to members on a strike called in breach of the union's rules, the plaintiffs were entitled to prevent the funds from being used in that way.

It is interesting that Vinelott J., while granting an injunction restraining further application of the union's funds in support of the strike, declined to give summary judgment on the plaintiffs' claim for damages for breach of trust. He said:

> "Although the misapplication of the funds of a [trade union] cannot be ratified by any majority of the members, however large, it is open to a majority of the members, if they think it is right in the interests of the [union] to do so, to resolve that no action should be taken to remedy the wrong done to the [union] and such a resolution, if made in good faith and for the benefit of the [union], will bind the majority. . . . In the instant case there is an impressive body of evidence filed on behalf of the individual defendants which is designed to establish that the overwhelming majority of members approves the expenditure in question. . . . It is common ground that the defendants do not have any substantial resources. The benefit to

---

[55] [1985] I.R.L.R. 99.
[56] *MacDougall* v. *Gardiner* (1875) 1 Ch. D. 13; *Howden* v. *Yorkshire Miners' Association* [1903] 1 K.B. 308 and [1905] A.C. 256; *Cotter* v. *N.U.S.* [1929] 2 Ch. 58; *Edwards* v. *Halliwell* [1950] 2 All E.R. 1064.

the union of recovering everything that could be extracted from them is likely to prove wholly insignificant in contrast with the very large sums in issue. I see no immediate advantage to the union in obtaining a judgment or perhaps taking steps to bankrupt these defendants."[57]

The second restriction is statutory. Section 4 of the Trade Union Act 1871 provides that:

"Nothing in this Act shall enable any court to entertain any legal proceeding instituted with the object of directly enforcing or recovering damages for the breach of any of the following agreements, namely:

1. Any agreement between members of a trade union as such concerning the conditions on which any members for the time being of such trade union shall, or shall not, sell their goods, transact business, employ or be employed.
2. Any agreement for the payment by any person of any subscription or penalty to a trade union.
3. Any agreement for the application of the funds of a trade union –
    a) to provide benefits to members; or
    b) to furnish contributions to any employer or workman not a member of such trade union in consideration of such employer or workman acting in conformity with the rules and resolutions of such trade union; or
    c) to discharge any fine imposed upon any person by sentence of a court of justice.
4. Any agreement made between one trade union and another; or
5. Any bond to secure the performance of any of the above mentioned agreements.

But nothing in this section shall be deemed to constitute any of the above mentioned agreements unlawful."

This is a clear limitation on the power of the judiciary to enforce certain contractual incidents of the union-member relationship,[58] though its importance may have been diminished by the development of the social welfare system which superseded union schemes for benefits for members, which schemes gave rise to most of the litigation involving section 4.

---

[57] [1985] I.R.L.R. at 107–108.
[58] For cases illustrating the application of s. 4, see *McKernan* v. *United Operative Masons Association of Scotland* (1874) 1 R. (Ct. of Sess.) 453; *Shanks* v. *United Operative Masons' Association of Scotland* (1874) 1 R. (Ct. of Sess.) 823; *Rigby* v. *Connol* (1880) 14 Ch. D. 482; *Aitken* v. *Association of Carpenters and Joiners of Scotland* (1885) 12 R. (Ct. of Sess.) 1206; *Winder* v. *Kingston-Upon-Hull Corporation for the Poor* (1888) 20 Q.B.D. 412; *Mineral Water Bottle Exchange, etc. Society* v. *Booth* (1887) 36 Ch. D. 465; *Sayer* v. *Amalgamated Society of Carpenters and Joiners* (1902) 19 T.L.R. 122; *Mullett* v. *United French Polishers' London Society* (1904) 20 T.L.R. 595; *Steele* v. *South Wales Miners' Federation* [1907] 1 K.B. 361; *Cox* v. *National Union of Foundry Workers* (1928) 44 T.L.R. 345.

The Irish courts have applied section 4 in five cases. In *General Union Society of Operative Carpenters and Joiners (Belfast Branch)* v. *O'Donnell and Todd*,[59] the trustees of the union sought an absolute order of *certiorari* in order to have a decision of a Resident Magistrate (O'Donnell), ordering them to pay benefit to Todd, quashed, on the grounds that it violated section 4 (3) (*a*) of the 1871 Act. Neither O'Donnell nor Todd showed cause, so the order was made absolute. In *O'Bryan* v. *National Amalgamated Society of Operative House Decorators*,[60] Johnson J. granted a conditional order of *certiorari* to quash a decree of the Recorder of Londonderry awarding a trade union member £4 against his union for unemployment benefit. In a case decided the following year, *R. (Webster)* v. *Recorder of Londonderry*,[61] the Recorder had issued a decree awarding a sum of "unemployed benefit money" to a member of a registered trade union. On appeal a writ of prohibition was granted restraining the issue of process of execution under the decree, again on the grounds that the original decision infringed section 4 of the 1871 Act. The fourth Irish decision in this area was that in *Rooney* v. *Trustees of Textiles Operatives' Society of Ireland.*[62] Here, Dodd J. held that the representatives or nearest relatives of a deceased trade union member could not maintain an action against a union to recover death benefit under that union's rules on the death of a member.[63] A similar decision was given in *Burnside* v. *Amalgamated Society of Tailors and Tailoresses.*[64]

The intention behind section 4 was to minimise judicial supervision of internal union affairs. However, the section does not attempt to exclude all union contracts from the jurisdiction of the courts and this fact, coupled with a restrictive interpretation of section 4 on the part of the judiciary, ensures that the courts can exert some control over the contractual incidents of the union-member relationship.

This control can be exercised in the following situations:

1. Where the action is based on contracts which are lawful *dehors* the statute.
2. Where the action does not entail the direct enforcement, or recovery of damages for the breach, of any of the agreements specified in section 4.
3. Where the action is based on a contract other than those specified in section 4.
4. Where non-members of the union seek to enforce union contracts.
5. Where the action is indirectly based on a specified contract.

---

[59] (1877) 11 *I.L.T.S.J.* 282.
[60] (1900) 1 N.I.J.R. 160.
[61] (1901) 2 N.I.J.R. 26.
[62] (1913) 47 I.L.T.R. 303.
[63] But see now s. 8 of the Married Women's Status Act 1957. See *infra*, p. 130.
[64] (1917) 51 I.L.T.R. 47.

Contracts which are lawful dehors the statute[65]

Section 4 of the 1871 Act begins by stating that "nothing in this Act shall enable any court to entertain any legal proceeding." By implication, an action which could have been brought on a union contract prior to 1871 was unaffected by the Act. The legal status of trade unions at common law was not very clear, but the view that section 4 of the 1871 Act did not affect union contracts which might have been lawful at common law no doubt helped to swing the balance in favour of those who believed that unions were lawful at common law, as this increased the potential for judicial supervision of union contracts.

This possibility was first realised in *Swaine* v. *Wilson*,[66] where the plaintiff brought an action against the officials of a society in order to recover a sum of £50 to which it was agreed he was entitled under the rules of the Society. The defendants relied on section 4 of the 1871 Act, arguing that, if the funds of the society were applicable to illegal as well as legal objects or if they were derived from illegal sources such as fines under illegal rules, the society was altogether illegal. Mr. Swaine, on the other hand, argued that this could only be the case if the general object of the society was in restraint of trade. If the general object was lawful at common law, then the fact that one or two of the rules might be objectionable as being in restraint of trade would not render the society an illegal society and make it impossible to enforce such rules as might be unobjectionable. The Court of Appeal held for the plaintiff. Lindley L.J. pointed out that illegality had to be established by those who rely on it – in other words, the burden of proof rested on the defendants. Furthermore, on the authority of *Collins* v. *Locke*,[67] if the main objects of the society were legal, then the fact that some of the rules of the society were objectionable would at most only render those particular rules invalid. In any event, the rules in the instant case were held not to be in restraint of trade – they satisfied the rather nebulous test outlined by both Lord Esher M.R. and Lindley L.J., *viz.*, they were reasonable having regard to the real and legitimate objects of the society.[68] Consequently the plaintiff was entitled to succeed. This line of reasoning was followed in *Gozney* v. *Bristol Trade and Provident Society*,[69] where the Court of Appeal ruled that the objects of the union, which included the maintenance and support of striking members, were not illegal at common law. Consequently the

---

[65] The leading article here is still Kahn-Freund's "The Illegality of a Trade Union" (1944) 7 *M.L.R.* 192. See also Anon., "Can a trade union be sued on foot of rules providing benefits to members?" (1909) 43 *I.L.T.S.J.* 215; Anon., "Legality of Trade Union rules at Common law" (1911–12) 25 *Harv. L.R.* 465; Anon., "Actions against trade unions for the recovery of benefits by members" (1941) 75 *I.L.T.S.J.* 71.
[66] (1890) 24 Q.B.D. 252.
[67] (1879) 4 App. Cas. 674.
[68] Though on this see the views of Kahn-Freund, *loc. cit.*, at p. 197.
[69] [1909] 1 K.B. 901.

plaintiff was not precluded by section 4 from contesting the imposition of a fine for an alleged breach of union rules. In *Osborne* v. *Amalgamated Society of Railway Servants*,[70] the Court of Appeal held that union rules authorising the sanctioning of a strike voluntarily undertaken by union members were lawful at common law and went on to hold that, as a consequence, it had jurisdiction to entertain a claim of wrongful expulsion from the union.

This last case has been described as "the high water mark of the judicial tendency to control the internal management of trade union affairs by raising its 'legality' at common law."[71] In the subsequent House of Lords' decision in *Russell* v. *Amalgamated Society of Carpenters and Joiners*,[72] a majority of the House[73] took a more restrained view of the sort of rules which might be lawful at common law. In the instant case, they ruled that the provident purposes of the society could not be severed from its militant purposes because both objectives were financed by a common fund and also because the powers of the union to discipline and expel members, which would be used in furtherance of the militant purpose, would also affect the members' rights to benefits. Consequently, the courts could not entertain an action for the payment of such benefits. According to Kahn-Freund, the decision in *Russell* marked a "deliberate departure" from the policy adopted in the three earlier cases.[74] Certainly since *Russell*, there have been no reported decisions in the U.K. in which the common law legality of a trade union has been established. The more restrictive approach taken in *Russell* was reflected in subsequent Irish cases such as *Rooney* v. *Trustees of Textile Operatives' Society of Ireland*,[75] where Dodd J. stated that members of trade unions only acquired any rights they had against their unions by virtue of the Trade Union Acts and they could succeed under those Acts or not at all; *Burnside* v. *Amalgamated Society of Tailors and Tailoresses*;[76] and *Doyle* v. *Trustees of Irish Glaziers' and Glass Workers' Trade Union*.[77] In *McDona* v. *Croker and Power*,[78] however, Judge Davitt allowed an action to recover death benefit from a trade union, despite section 4, on the ground that the union was a lawful association at common law and that, even if some of its rules were in restraint of trade, those relating to the payment of benefits to members or their dependants were not. These were severable and consequently enforceable.

[70] [1911] 1 Ch. 540.
[71] Kahn-Freund, *loc. cit.*, pp. 201–202.
[72] [1912] A.C. 421.
[73] Lords MacNaghten, Mersey and Shaw of Dunfermline. Lord Atkinson and Earl Loreburn decided the case on the technical grounds that the defendant society could not be sued in its registered name in a common law action for breach of contract.
[74] *Loc. cit.*, at p. 203.
[75] (1913) 47 I.L.T.R. 303.
[76] (1917) 51 I.L.T.R. 47.
[77] (1926) 60 I.L.T.R. 78.
[78] [1941] Ir. Jur. Rep. 63 (Circuit Court).

Remedies

Section 4 forbids the courts from entertaining "any legal proceeding instituted with the object of *directly enforcing or recovering damages for the breach of*" any of the specified agreements.[79] This wording gives rise to the argument that section 4 does not affect any action instituted with an object other than the direct enforcement, or recovery of damages for breach, of any of the agreements there specified. This would enable union members to obtain an injunction to prevent union officials contravening the rules affecting the various agreements even though they could not get a decree of specific performance to have such contracts *directly* enforced.

The earlier authorities conflicted on the validity of this argument.[80] Then the matter came before the House of Lords in *Yorkshire Miners' Association* v. *Howden*.[81] The defendant union had misapplied part of the union funds by payments of strike money in cases not authorised by the rules. The plaintiff sought an injunction restraining the union from making the payments and the issue which finally presented itself to the House of Lords was whether this amounted to a direct enforcement of an agreement to provide benefits to members contrary to section 4 (3) (*a*) of the 1871 Act.

A majority[82] of the House held that it did not, on the ground that section 4 of the 1871 Act did not affect an action brought to restrain trustees from applying trust funds to purposes other than those contained in the trust, an action which sounds in property and not in contract. *Yorkshire Miners' Association* v. *Howden* was cited in a number of subsequent cases as authority for the proposition that once an action does not entail distribution of union funds then it is not prohibited by section 4 (3) (*a*) of the 1871 Act.[83] But doubts still lingered in some judicial minds. In *Smith* v. *Scottish Typographical Association*,[84] the court refused to grant the plaintiff either a declaration that the resolution expelling him from the union was *ultra vires* or an injunction restraining the defendants from enforcing the resolution on the grounds that this was a proceeding instituted with the object of directly enforcing an agreement between members of a trade union concerning the conditions on which they should be employed and as such was

---

[79] Emphasis added.
[80] It succeeded in *McLaren* v. *Miller* (1880) 7 R. 867; *Wolfe* v. *Matthews* (1882) 21 Ch. D 194; *In re Durham Miners' Association* (1900) 17 T.L.R. 39; *Alfin* v. *Hewlett* (1902) 18 T.L.R. 664. It failed in *Rigby* v. *Connol* (1880) 14 Ch. D 482; *Duke* v. *Littleboy* (1880) 43 L.T. 216; *Aitken* v. *A.C.J.S.* (1885) 22 S.L.R. 796; *Chamberlain's Wharf Ltd.* v. *Smith* [1900] 2 Ch. 605; *Mullett* v. *United French Polishers' London Society* (1904) 20 T.L.R. 595.
[81] [1905] A.C. 256.
[82] Earl of Halsbury L.C. and Lords Lindley, MacNaghten and Robertson. Lords Davey and James dissented.
[83] See *Cope* v. *Crossingham* [1902] 2 Ch. 148; *Osborne* v. *A.S.R.S.* [1911] 1 Ch. 540; *Kelly* v. *Nat. S.O.P.A.* (1914) 31 T.L.R. 32; *Joseph Evans & Co.* v. *Heathcote* [1918] 1 K.B. 418; *Sansom* v. *London and Provincial Union of Licensed Vehicle Workers* (1920) 36 T.L.R. 666; *Brodie* v. *Bevan* (1921) 38 T.L.R. 172.
[84] 1919 S.C. 43.

covered by section 4 (1). In *McLuskey* v. *Cole*,[85] the Court of Appeal refused to grant the union represented by the plaintiffs either a declaration that its expulsion from the union represented by the defendants was invalid or an injunction to restrain the defendants from enforcing that expulsion, because of the provisions of section 4 (4) of the 1871 Act. Similarly, in *Rae* v. *Plate Glass Merchants' Association*,[86] it was held that an action for an injunction to restrain the imposition of a fine was barred by section 4 (2). The matter was finally clarified by a unanimous House of Lords in *Amalgamated Society of Carpenters* v. *Braithwaite*.[87] This action in fact involved two different pieces of litigation in which the plaintiffs sought injunctions to restrain their threatened expulsion from their respective unions. The defendant unions had threatened to expel them for alleged breach of union rules insofar as they were both participants in a profit sharing scheme instituted by the company for whom they worked. In granting the injunctions, the House of Lords acceded to the contention that the plaintiffs were not seeking directly to enforce any of the contracts listed in section 4 and so were not barred by it.

The law as stated in *A.S.C.* v. *Braithwaite* has been applied in a number of subsequent U.K. decisions,[88] but has been considered in only one Irish case. In *Doyle* v. *Trustees of Irish Glaziers' and Glass Workers' Trade Union*,[89] the plaintiff sought an injunction to restrain the union from suspending or excluding him and he also claimed damages for breach of contract, the breach consisting in his wrongful suspension from the union. Judge Pigot held that, as a result of the decision in *A.S.C.* v. *Braithwaite*, it was impossible to argue that an injunction might not lie, though he also pointed out that the granting of an injunction was discretionary and that if the plaintiff had wilfully or recklessly contravened any regulation of the society he would not be entitled to relief. Furthermore, the court had jurisdiction to construe any agreement between a union and its members.[90] In the instant case, the plaintiff had not violated the union rule book and so he was entitled to an injunction.

Subject matter

It is clear from a perusal of the opening provisions of the 1871 Act that there are some union contracts which are legally enforceable in the courts. Section 3 of the 1871 Act excepted *all* union agreements and

[85] [1922] 1 Ch. 7.
[86] (1919) 56 S.L.R. 315.
[87] [1922] 2 A.C. 440. For comment, see (1922) 56 *I.L.T.S.J.* 221.
[88] *Blackall* v. *N.U.F.W.* (1923) 39 T.L.R. 431; *Miller* v. *A.E.U.* [1938] Ch. 669; *Bonsor* v. *Musicians' Union* [1956] A.C. 104. Admittedly, in *Cox* v. *N.U.F.W.* (1928) 44 T.L.R 345, Astbury J. refused to grant the plaintiff an injunction to prevent the union from enforcing resolutions reducing the amount of certain benefits on the grounds, *inter alia*, that such an action was barred by s. 4. It appears from the report that *A.S.C.* v. *Braithwaite* was not cited before the court and therefore it is submitted that the decision cannot be regarded as sound.
[89] (1926) 60 I.L.T.R. 78.   [90] See further *infra*, p. 133.

trusts from the doctrine of restraint of trade but section 4 specified only five types of union contracts which could not be enforced by the courts. By implication, the residual body of contracts are legally enforceable. For example, the wording of section 4 does not extend to proceedings for the re-distribution of assets following on the dissolution of a trade union.[91] Nor does it affect an action by a union official to recover salary or superannuation benefit under his contract of employment with a union.[92] Since 1913, unions can enter into contracts for purposes other than those listed in the statutory definition of trade unions contained in the 1871 Act, as amended by the 1876 Act, and those contracts are also unaffected by section 4 of the 1871 Act. Proceedings based on rules governing the election of union officers are also outside the scope of the section.[93]

Perhaps the most important point to note in this context is that section 4 does not deny the court's jurisdiction to enforce the union-member relationship, but rather only certain specified incidents thereof. Thus in *Osborne* v. *Amalgamated Society of Railway Servants*,[94] the plaintiff had been expelled from the defendant union "for resorting to the courts of this country to enforce the law applicable to the society of which he was a member."[95] He subsequently brought an action against the defendant union for reinstatement as a member, on the grounds that his expulsion was *ultra vires* and void. The defendants took the preliminary objection that the action could not be maintained because of, *inter alia*, the provisions of section 4 (3) of the 1871 Act. The Court of Appeal rejected this contention. Cozens-Hardy M.R. said:

> "The statement of claim asks a declaration in several forms to the effect that the resolution purporting to expel the plaintiff is *ultra vires* and void, and an injunction to restrain the society from acting upon and enforcing the resolution. It does not claim the payment of any sum of money out of the funds of the union. . . . If a member is threatened with expulsion on grounds not justified by the rules there is nothing in s. 4 which prevents him from maintaining an action to restrain the contemplated wrong. . . .
>
> The language of s. 4 is narrow and it ought not to be construed so as to cover every agreement under s. 3."[96]

---

[91] See *Re Printers' and Transferrers' Amalgamated Trades Protection Society* [1899] 2 Ch. 184; *Osborne* v. *A.S.R.S.* [1911] 1 Ch. 540, 554, *per* Cozens-Hardy M.R.
[92] *Telling* v. *N.A.O.P., The Times*, July 4, 1953. See Grunfeld, *Modern Trade Union Law* (London, 1966), at p. 164. See also *N.E.E.T.U.* v. *McConnell* (1983) 2 *J.I.S.L.L.* 97; *Connolly* v. *McConnell* [1983] I.R. 172.
[93] *Watson* v. *Smith* [1941] 2 All E.R. 725.
[94] [1911] 1 Ch. 540. See also *Kelly* v. *Nat. S.O.P.A.* [1914] 31 T.L.R. 32.
[95] *Per* Buckley L.J., [1911] 1 Ch. 540 at 569. The earlier piece of litigation to which Osborne was a party is reported at [1910] A.C. 87.
[96] *Ibid.*, at 554.

That the courts had jurisdiction to grant injunctions to restrain wrongful expulsion was firmly established by the House of Lords in *A.S.C.* v. *Braithwaite*.[97] The House of Lords subsequently decided that a member who is wrongfully expelled from his union can recover damages for breach of contract – *Bonsor* v. *Musicians' Union*[98] – counsel for the defendants conceding that section 4 was inapplicable. Irish courts have also entertained actions enforcing the contract of membership[99] though they have yet to award damages for wrongful expulsion.

Third Parties

Section 4 (3) (*a*) of the 1871 Act prevents the courts from enforcing or awarding damages for the breach of any agreement for the application of the funds of a trade union to provide benefits *to members*. The inclusion of the words "to members" in the statutory paragraph was relied upon in the Scottish case of *Love* v. *Amalgamated Society of Lithographic Printers of Gt. Britain and Ireland*[1] to enable the wife of a sick member of the defendant union to maintain an action for sick benefit for members' dependants provided for in the union rule book.

There does not appear to be any other case in Britain or Ireland in which a third party was permitted to enforce a contract for his benefit contained in the union rule book, no doubt because of the difficulties posed by the doctrine of privity of contract.[2] So in *Rooney* v. *Trustees of the Textile Operatives' Society of Ireland*,[3] the plaintiff, the mother of a deceased trade union member, brought an action against the union to recover death benefit under the union rules. Dodd J. held that the action was not maintainable because, *inter alia*, the plaintiff did not sue as representative of her deceased daughter and consequently there was no privity of contract between herself and the defendants.

The doctrine of privity of contract, therefore, was a serious obstacle to any person who wished to sue on a contract for his benefit contained in the union rule book. However, that doctrine has been qualified to a certain extent in Irish law by section 8 of the Married Women's Status Act 1957, which provides:

---

[97] [1905] A.C. 256. See also *Blackall* v. *N.U.F.W.* (1923) 39 T.L.R. 431; *Clarke* v. *Ferrie* [1926] N.I. 1; *Brodie* v. *Bevan* (1921) 38 T.L.R. 172.

[98] [1956] A.C. 104. For the implications of this decision on s. 4 of the 1871 Act, see Wedderburn, "The Bonsor Affair: A Post Script" (1957) 20 *M.L.R.* 105 at pp. 120, 121. See also *Santer* v. *N.G.A.* [1973] I.C.R. 60.

[99] See, *e.g., O'Neill* v. *T.G.W.U.* [1934] I.R. 633; *Moran* v. *W.U.I.* [1943] I.R. 485; *Kilkenny* v. *I.E.F.U.* [1939] Ir. Jur. Rep. 52. See *infra*, pp. 113–117.

[1] 1912 S.C. 1078.

[2] See, for instance, *Whellan* v. *Rodgers* (1887) 3 T.L.R. 450, where it was held that s. 4 barred a claim brought by the representatives of a deceased member against the union for funeral benefit.

[3] (1913) 47 I.L.T.R. 303.

Internal Trade Union Affairs 131

(1) When a contract . . . is expressed to be for the benefit of, or by its express terms purports to confer a benefit upon, a third person being the wife, husband or child of one of the contracting parties, it shall be enforceable by the third person in his or her own name as if he or she were a party to it.

(2) The right conferred on a third person by this section shall be subject to any defence that would have been valid between parties to the contract.

(3) Unless the contract otherwise provides, it may be rescinded by agreement of the contracting parties at any time before the third person has adopted it either expressly or by conduct.

Therefore it is submitted that if a union rule book provides expressly for the payment of a benefit to members' dependants, those dependants can enforce that contract against the union in their own names. It is further submitted that section 4 of the 1871 Act cannot be pleaded in defence if, as was accepted in *Love*, that section does not affect contracts to provide benefits to persons other than members.[4]

Actions based indirectly on contracts specified in section 4

In a number of cases the courts have entertained actions which had their source in one or other of the contracts listed in section 4. The justification used was that such actions were not based on the original agreement but rather on some intermediate agreement which arose between the conclusion of the first unenforceable agreement and the bringing of the action.[5]

In the Scottish case of *Wilkie* v. *King*,[6] the union sought to recover £100 paid out in benefit to the defendant. The union rule book provided that a member who became permanently disabled should receive the sum of £100 but that if he should resume work he must refund the £100 and that at the time of receiving the benefit he must sign a contract to that effect. The defendant had been paid the sum of £100 but subsequently resumed work and the union brought an action for the recovery of the money based on the contract signed by the defendant. He argued that the action could not be maintained because of section 4 of the Act of 1871. The Court of Session, by a majority of 3 to 1[7] however, decided against him, taking the view that section 4 of the

---

[4] Where the contract provides for a benefit *for members*, however, and a member assigns his interest to a third party, that third party is precluded by s. 4 from enforcing the contract – *Winder* v. *Kingston-Upon-Hull Corporation for the Poor* (1888) 20 Q.B.D. 412.

[5] A variation on this theme can be seen in *Strick* v. *Swansea Tin Plate Co.* (1887) 36 Ch. D. 588 where the basis of the Court's jurisdiction was not a subsequent agreement negotiated between the parties but rather an earlier judicial decree which arguably violated s. 4. However, s. 4 was not pleaded at the initial enquiry and North J. held that it was too late to raise it now. In his opinion, he was not enforcing an agreement which came within the scope of s. 4 – rather he was following out a court inquiry to its legitimate result.

[6] 1911 S.C. 1310.

[7] The Lord President, Lord Dunedin and Lord Kinnear, with Lord MacKenzie concurring.

1871 Act should be construed strictly. In the instant case, they felt that the action was based on the agreement signed by the defendant to return the money, and not on the agreement in the rule book to pay out benefit to members who were permanently disabled. Since the former agreement was not one for the payment of benefit to members, it was not covered by section 4 and so was enforceable. Lord Johnston dissented, albeit reluctantly, on the ground that this case involved, not two separate agreements, but rather one composite contract to pay benefits to members. Consequently, in his opinion, the action was barred by section 4.

At the same time as *Wilkie* v. *King* was decided in Scotland, a case with almost identical facts was going through the English courts. This was *Baker* v. *Ingall*,[8] in which the union sought to recover £100 paid out as disablement benefit to the defendant on the ground that he had since returned to work. Phillimore and Bankes JJ. decided (at Divisional level) that the action was based on an agreement signed by the defendant to return the money if he resumed work and as a result was not covered by section 4 of the 1871 Act. The Court of Appeal, by a majority, disagreed. Vaughan Williams and Buckley L.JJ. were of the opinion that the action was based on one entire agreement to provide benefits to members contained in the union rule book. Consequently it was not enforceable. Kennedy L.J., dissenting, took the view that the agreement signed by the defendant, in which he had agreed to return the money if he resumed work, was separate and independent from that contained in the union rule book. The mere fact that the deed in its recital referred to an earlier agreement did not mean that it formed part of that agreement. He was anxious to give effect to the intention of the parties to the deed and that meant allowing him to enforce the agreement at law. Furthermore, he was also in favour of giving section 4 a rather strict interpretation.

The situation, therefore, after *Baker* v. *Ingall* was rather confused, with the Scottish courts enforcing the agreement to repay, while the English courts did not.[9]

The approach taken in *Wilkie* v. *King* was adopted in a subsequent Scottish case, *Edinburgh Master Plumbers' Association* v. *Munro*.[10] The rules of the plaintiff association provided that members should pay a percentage on contracts received by them to the funds of the association, and the association tried to enforce this rule against the defendant. He disputed the claim and both parties agreed to refer the matter to arbitration. The arbitrator decided in favour of the plaintiff association and it brought an action against the defendant based on this

---

[8] [1912] 3 K.B. 106.
[9] Of the nine judges involved in the two cases, six of them favoured the Scottish approach – indeed a majority of the English judges, two in the Divisional Court and one in the Court of Appeal, disagreed with the ultimate line taken by the Court of Appeal.
[10] 1928 S.C. 565.

decree. The court held that they were merely seeking to enforce the agreement to arbitrate and "to obtemper any decree arbitral which was subsequently pronounced." Consequently the action was not barred by section 4. The case is slightly confusing insofar as the Court cited both *Wilkie* and *Baker* in favour of this conclusion. It would appear that the Court of Appeal decision in *Baker* was not cited to them and therefore the issue cannot be regarded as having been resolved by *Munro*.

Judicial interpretation of union rule books

The courts also have jurisdiction to give authoritative decisions as to the interpretation of the provisions of the rule book.

> "If the limitations to the actions of the courts contained in s. 4 be closely looked at, it will be found that they leave untouched the jurisdiction of the courts to pronounce on the meaning or validity of any contract whatever . . . [s. 4] affords no ban to any party who claims to be interested in contracts which are legally valid coming to the courts to obtain a pronouncement as to his rights thereunder."[11]

While the principles of construction to be applied to a union rule book are the same as those applied to any other contract,[12] it is necessary to bear in mind that trade union rule books are not drafted by parliamentary draftsmen. "Courts of law must resist the temptation to construe them as if they were, for that is not how they would be understood by the members. . . ."[13] It is the court's task to construe them so as to give them a reasonable interpretation which accords with what must have been intended, but the more imprecise the language used the greater the difficulty in deciding what was actually intended.

TRADE UNION OFFICIALS

The legal position of trade union officials resembles that of trade union members insofar as it consists of rights and obligations arising at common law, under statute, and by virtue of both the Constitution and E.E.C. law, but since there has been even less direct legislative regulation of the position of trade union officials,[14] the common law, or more specifically the contract between the official and the union, is

---

[11] *Per* Fletcher Moulton L.J. in *Osborne* v. *A.S.R.S.* [1911] 1 Ch. 540 at 560–561. See also his decision in *Gozney* v. *Bristol Trade and Provident Society* [1909] 1 K.B. 901, 918. Not every member of the judiciary took this view of the law. See *Smith* v. *S.T.A.* 1919 S.C. 43; also the remarks of Buckley L.J. in *Osborne* [1911] 1 Ch. 540 at 569. However, the House of Lords in *A.S.C.* v. *Braithwaite* [1905] A.C. 256 clearly asserted the right of the courts to interpret provisions of union rule books.

[12] *British Actors' Equity Association* v. *Goring* [1978] I.C.R. 791.

[13] *Per* Lord Wilberforce in *Heaton's Transport (St. Helens) Ltd.* v. *T.G.W.U.* [1973] A.C. 15.

[14] There is, for instance, no statutory definition of "trade union official", although the statutory definition of "employees' representative" in s. 1 of the Protection of Employment Act 1977 refers to trade union officials as including "shop stewards".

the primary source of the official's rights and obligations. The terms of this contract are to be found not only in any documentation or arrangements relating to the specific appointment but also in the union rule book, together, of course, with such terms as may be implied by law. It may be, for instance, that the particular official is, in law, an "office-holder" and, as such, entitled to whatever additional rights that status confers.[15] Although the legislation requires registered trade unions to establish a committee of management[16] and have certain other officers,[17] the overall structure and the method of appointment is for the union to decide, with the courts' role being "to extract from the contract of membership the form of government that has been chosen and then endeavour[ing] to safeguard that choice."[18]

Candidacy and appointment

If a person wishes to be a candidate in an election for union office he must comply with the rule book.[19] As the right to be nominated or stand for election to a union office is undoubtedly one of the benefits of trade union membership, the rule book cannot discriminate against members on the basis of sex or marital status[20] or because they do not contribute to the union's political fund.[21] Furthermore E.E.C. Regulations[22] guarantee Community "migrant workers" equality as regards eligibility to posts in the management and administration of trade unions. If a person's nomination is to be disallowed a clear authority so to do must be found in the rule book. In *Leigh* v. *National Union of Railwaymen*,[23] the union's general secretary refused to accept the plaintiff's nomination for office as President of the union on the ground that, as a member of the Communist party, the plaintiff would not be able to attend T.U.C. or Labour Party conferences. Non-membership of the Communist Party was not, however, one of the qualifications laid down by the rules which a candidate for the office of president was required to possess or observe, and the court refused to infer from a rule which provided that "no circular will be authorised for distribution until the nomination has been received and approved" that the general secretary was empowered to consider the wider issue of suitability. The general secretary's function under the rules was the

---

[15] See Napier's essay on the concept of an office holder in Gamillscheg ed., *In Memoriam Sir Otto Kahn-Freund* (Munich, 1980). See also *infra*, p. 140.
[16] Trade Union Act 1871, Sch. 1, para. 4.
[17] Such as a treasurer and trustees.
[18] *Rideout's Principles of Labour Law* 4th ed. (London, 1983), p. 440.
[19] See *Nelson* v. *N.U.S.* (1978) 128 *N.L.J.* 24. See also Trade Union Act Amendment Act 1876, s. 9.
[20] Employment Equality Act 1977, s. 5.
[21] Except in relation to the control or management of the political fund, – Trade Union Act 1913, s. 3 (1) (*b*). See *Birch* v. *N.U.R.* [1950] Ch. 602.
[22] Regulation 1612/68 as amended by Regulation 312/76.
[23] [1970] Ch. 326.

purely administrative duty of checking that the nomination was correct on the face of it and that the candidate had the qualifications prescribed by the rules. Furthermore, it is arguable, on the authority of *Glover* v. *BLN Ltd.*,[24] that, if the rules do confer a discretion to review generally the suitability of a candidate, the body exercising this discretion must adopt fair procedures[25] and, if necessary, give the nominee an opportunity to be heard.[26]

The one reported case in which the Irish courts have had to consider the nomination process of a union election – *Branigan* v. *Keady*[27] – is unusual inasmuch as it involved the effect of a Labour Court ruling, rather than a provision of the union's rule book or a decision of any union authority, on the plaintiff's eligibility. Here the plaintiff had been expelled from the Marine Port and General Workers' Union on September 11, 1957. Subsequently a dispute between the M.P.G.W.U. and the Irish Seamen's Union was resolved by the Labour Court which recommended that a new union to represent seamen be established and that all persons who were members of the No. 1 Branch of the M.P.G.W.U. on November 14, 1957 would be eligible to participate in elections for the new union's executive. At a general meeting of the M.P.G.W.U. on March 30, 1958, a resolution was passed revoking the plaintiff's expulsion order. However, a number of members were not afforded an opportunity to vote on this resolution. Consequently, a question arose as to the plaintiff's eligibility to vote in, or stand for, the election, and this question was referred to the Labour Court which ruled against the plaintiff. The plaintiff then brought proceedings seeking to establish his right to participate in the election. The Supreme Court found that, as the resolution purporting to revoke the expulsion order and restore the plaintiff to membership had not been passed in accordance with the rule book, he was not a member of the union on November 14, 1957 and thus was not eligible under the terms of the Labour Court recommendation to participate in the election.

Since there is no statutory regulation of the conduct of union elections there can only be judicial intervention if the election is not held or conducted in accordance with the rule book. So, on an application by six members of the Automobile, General Engineering and Mechanical Operatives' Union, McWilliam J. granted an interim injunction restraining the union from holding a postal ballot vote among provincial members for the post of treasurer as the rule book

---

[24] [1973] I.R. 388.
[25] *Craddock* v. *Davidson* [1929] S.R. Qd. 328, 336.
[26] In *Breen* v. *A.E.U.* [1971] 2 Q.B. 175, the Court of Appeal agreed that, in exercising their powers to approve the plaintiff's candidature for office, the members of the union's district committee were under a duty to act fairly. The Court disagreed, however, as to whether this meant, in this particular case, that the plaintiff should have been given a hearing.
[27] [1959] I.R. 283.

136 Irish Trade Union Law

made no provision for a postal vote.[28] Very minor irregularities will not result, however, in an election being declared invalid.[29]

Statutory regulation of the appointment of union officials

Registered trade unions must provide, in their rule books, both for the appointment and removal of a general committee of management, trustees, treasurer and other union officers.[30] A union applying to the Registrar of Friendly Societies for registration must submit, with its application, a list of the titles and names of the union officers[31] and such union must also notify the Registrar, in its annual returns, of any changes of officers in the preceding year.[32] An unregistered authorised trade union must notify the Minister for Labour of, *inter alia*, every change in its controlling authority, or trustees, or of its secretary or other principal officer within 21 days of the making of the change.[33]

In addition to being subject to the provisions of the Employment Equality Act 1977 and the Trade Union Act 1913,[34] the rule book must also comply with section 9 of the Trade Union Act Amendment Act 1876, as amended by the Age of Majority Act 1985, which prohibits members under the age of 18 from being a trustee, treasurer or on the committee of management of any registered trade union. Furthermore, section 17 of the Trade Union Act 1975[35] makes it a pre-condition both to the granting of a negotiation licence to, and the retention of such licence by, a foreign based union with Irish membership that the union have a committee of management, the members of which are all resident in the State or Northern Ireland, which is empowered by the union rule book to make decisions in "matters of an industrial or political nature which arise out of and in connection with the economic or political condition of the State or Northern Ireland, are of direct concern to members of the trade union resident in the State or Northern Ireland and do not affect members not so resident."

Powers and duties of union officials

The powers of union officials are conferred, in large part, by the union rule book and, possibly, where the rule book is silent on a specific point, by industrial custom and practice.[36] In addition, powers and rights may be conferred, particularly on shop stewards, by

---

[28] See *Irish Times*, March 28, 1980.
[29] *Brown* v. *A.U.E.W.* [1976] I.C.R. 147.
[30] Trade Union Act 1871, Sch. 1, para. 4.
[31] Trade Union Act 1871, s. 13, para. 1.
[32] Trade Union Act 1871, s. 16.
[33] Trade Union Act 1941, s. 13 (1) (*f*). Failure to do so is an offence punishable by a fine of up to £5, together with a further fine not exceeding £1 for every day during which the offence is continued – s. 13 (2).
[34] See *supra*, pp. 89–95.
[35] S. 17, so far as relates to existing holders of a negotiation licence, came into operation on July 1, 1983 – Trade Union Act 1975 (section 17) (Commencement) Order 1983 (S.I. No. 177 of 1983).
[36] *Heaton's Transport (St. Helens) Ltd.* v. *T.G.W.U.* [1973] A.C. 15.

collective agreements. Union officials have been invested with certain statutory powers. Thus the powers of trustees of registered trade unions in relation to the acquisition and protection of union property are provided for under the Trade Union Acts 1871 and 1876.[37] Union trustees also have statutory powers of investment under the Trustee Act 1893 as amended by the Trustee (Authorised Investment) Act 1958.[38] Finally, union officials have considerable statutory powers in relation to the amalgamation, or transfer of engagements, of unions.[39]

Liability for the acts of officials

Personal liability of the individuals

The personal liability of union officials arising out of their activities as officials has been modified in a number of ways by statute. In the area of tort, officials of authorised trade unions holding negotiation licences, in common with the members of such trade unions, enjoy the benefit of the immunities conferred by sections 1, 2 and 3 of the Trade Disputes Act 1906 from certain torts committed in contemplation or furtherance of a trade dispute.[40] Otherwise they are personally liable in respect of any tortious action in which they might engage.[41] Officials of trade unions which do not hold negotiation licences enjoy only an immunity from the tort of civil conspiracy, in respect of acts done in contemplation or furtherance of a trade dispute, by virtue of section 1 of the 1906 Act.

With regard to the liability of union officials in respect of union property, section 10 of the Trade Union Act 1871 limits the responsibility of trustees of registered unions for union funds to those funds actually received by them on account of such trade union. This must be read in the light of section 24 of the Trustee Act 1893 which applies to all trustees and which provides that a trustee is chargeable only for money and securities actually received by him notwithstanding his signing any receipt for the sake of conformity, and that he is answerable and accountable for his own acts and defaults and not for those of any other trustees, nor for any other loss, unless this is due to his own wilful default. Section 11 of the 1871 Act imposes an obligation on the treasurer or such other appropriate union official of a registered union to render an account to trustees, or to union members at a union meeting, of all money received and paid by him on behalf of the union and of all bonds and securities of the union. The account shall be given in accordance with the union rule book or whenever the appropriate

---

[37] See *supra*, pp. 82–83, 84–85.
[38] See *supra*, p. 85.
[39] Trade Union Act 1975, s. 8. See *supra*, p. 74.
[40] On this area generally, see *infra* pp. 249–281, 297–311.
[41] *Bussy* v. *A.S.R.S.* (1908) 24 T.L.R. 437; *Hardie & Lane Ltd.* v. *Chiltern* [1928] 1 K.B. 663; *Eglantine Inn Ltd.* v. *Smith* [1948] N.I. 29.

officer is asked to give an account. The trustees must have the account audited and may call on the treasurer to hand over the balance of money due from him and also any books, papers, property, *etc.* of the union which he has in his possession. Failure to do so can result in him being sued by the union trustees. Unregistered unions, not coming within the scope of section 11, must rely on the ordinary legal and equitable remedies for protection of their trust fund. Section 12 makes it a criminal offence, punishable by a fine of up to £20, for any person fraudently to obtain possession of any "money, securities, books, papers, or other effects, of such trade union" or wilfully to withhold or fraudulently to misapply the same or wilfully to apply any part of the same to purposes other than those in the rule book. Upon complaint being made to a court of summary jurisdiction, an order may be made directing such person to deliver up the property of the union or to repay the amount of money wrongfully applied, and the court may, if it thinks fit, impose a fine of up to £20. Failure to do this, or failure to pay the fine, can result in imprisonment for up to 3 months. Fraud or misrepresentation is an essential element of an offence under section 12 – mere inability to pay is not sufficient to constitute the offence.[42] It is not necessary to prove that the money was in the possession of the accused on the date when the charge was brought against him, provided there is evidence that money belonging to the union had been in his possession and was still being withheld.[43]

So in the case of a registered trade union, remedies are available against dishonest officials under sections 9,[44] 11 and 12 of the Trade Union Act 1871 or under general law. Conviction and imprisonment under section 12 constitutes a bar to further civil proceedings in respect of the same wrong.[45] Unregistered trade unions must rely on the general law to protect themselves from dishonest officials.

Finally in this context, it should be noted that the criminal law imposes certain obligations on union officials, although inflation has seriously affected the sanctions imposed. We have already seen how the criminal law may be used against union officials to protect union property. In addition, every official of a registered trade union incurs a penalty of £5 per day for the eighth and every subsequent day of operation of such a union without a registered office.[46] Failure to make annual returns to the Registrar renders every officer of the defaulting union liable to a penalty of £5.[47] Furthermore, any person who wilfully makes or orders to be made any false entry in or any omission from

---

[42] *Barrett* v. *Markham* (1872) L.R. 7 C.P. 405, a case which arose under an almost identical provision of the Friendly Societies Act 1875.
[43] *Best* v. *Butler* [1932] 2 K.B. 108.
[44] *Madden* v. *Rhodes* [1906] 1 K.B. 534.
[45] *Knight* v. *Whitmore* (1885) 1 T.L.R. 550.
[46] Trade Union Act 1871, s. 15.
[47] 1871 Act, s. 16.

such returns is liable to a penalty not exceeding £50 for each offence.[48] Circulating false copies of the rules with intent to mislead or defraud is a misdemeanour under the 1871 Act.[49] Failure to send in notice of dissolution of a trade union to the Registrar of Friendly Societies may also result in the imposition of a penalty on the defaulting official.[50] The Trade Union Act 1941 makes it an offence for the members of the committee of management of a body, not holding a negotiation licence and not being an excepted body, and the officers of such body, to consent or to facilitate such body in carrying on negotiations for the fixing of wages or other conditions of employment.[51] Any official of an authorised trade union, who consents to or facilitates such union in failing to comply with the statutory obligations of an authorised trade union under sections 12 and 13 of the 1941 Act, is guilty of an offence and liable, on summary conviction, to a fine not exceeding £5 together with a further fine not exceeding £1 for every day during which the offence is continued.[52]

Finally, failure on the part of an authorised union to make triennial returns of the number of its members to the Department of Labour results in the imposition of criminal liability on such of the members and officials of the union as consent to or facilitate such failure or the sending of a false statement.[53]

Liability of the union for the acts of its officials

A union may also be liable for the acts of its officials by virtue of the doctrines of agency and vicarious liability, except where the union is given a statutory immunity from suit.

By virtue of the doctrine of agency,[54] a union is liable in contract for the authorised act of an official acting on its behalf. The scope of the official's authority would be determined by reference to his contract of employment and the union rule book. Even where an official exceeds his authority, the union may still be liable if it subsequently ratifies his unauthorised act.[55] A union will be vicariously liable in tort for the actions of officials taken within the scope of their employment[56] unless the union can avail of the statutory immunity from suit afforded by section 4 of the Trade Disputes Act 1906, as amended.[57] Again the

---

[48] 1871 Act, s. 16.
[49] S. 18.
[50] Trade Union Act Amendment Act 1876, s. 15.
[51] S. 6 (2).
[52] Trade Union Act 1941, ss. 12 (2) and 13 (2).
[53] Trade Union Act 1941, s. 15 (2).
[54] As to which, in the Irish context, see O'Malley, *Business Law* (London, 1982), pp. 112-121.
[55] *Bonsor* v. *Musicians' Union* [1956] A.C. 104.
[56] *Giblan* v. *National Amalgamated Labourers' Union* [1903] 2 K.B. 600; *Nolan* v. *South Australian Laborers' Union* [1910] S.A.L.R. 85. As to the doctrine of vicarious liability in this context in Irish law, see McMahon and Binchy, *Irish Law of Torts* (Oxon., 1981), pp. 101-109.
[57] As to which see *infra*, pp. 250-257.

principle of ratification may make a union liable for the *ultra vires* activities of its officials.

Discipline and termination of appointment

Union officials enjoy the same legal protection as union members in relation to disciplinary proceedings. Thus any sanctions imposed by the union must be clearly provided for in the rule book.[58] If the union official is regarded as an office holder then the official is entitled at common law, *qua* office holder, to the protection of the rules of natural justice before any decision to remove from office is taken and, in the event of non-compliance with such rules, the decision will be invalid and the official concerned will be entitled to be reinstated in his office.[59] If the union official is an employee of the union he may be able to avail of the protection of the Unfair Dismissals Act 1977[60] as an alternative to a common law action for damages for wrongful dismissal.[61]

Difficult questions, and ones that have yet to come squarely before the Irish courts, arise where the dismissed person is an officer as well as an employee[62] or where the person's conditions of employment, particularly as regards dismissal, are to be found in the union rule book.[63] Will the courts grant an order such as a declaration or injunction which has the effect of restoring a union official to his position if he has been dismissed without a hearing or otherwise than in accordance with the rules of natural or constitutional justice or the union rule book? Normally the only remedy for an employee who has been dismissed is to bring an action for wrongful dismissal claiming damages or, alternatively, to claim redress under the Unfair Dismissals Act 1977. In *Shanks* v. *Plumbing Trades Union*,[64] Buckley J. drew a distinction between an elected officer, whom somebody other than those who elected him is seeking to remove from office, and an officer employed under a contract of employment. An injunction would be granted to prevent removal of the former class, but not the latter, if the removal from office would be in violation of the provisions of the rule book or the principles of natural justice.[65] More recently however, the courts appear more ready both to grant declarations that a purported dismissal is a nullity and to grant injunctions restraining dismissal where the contract of employment expressly limits the employer's

---

[58] *O'Neill* v. *T.G.W.U.* [1934] I.R. 634.
[59] Thus, arising out of the decision in *Connolly* v. *McConnell* [1983] I.R. 172, the official concerned obtained judgment for £31,577.44 being the net loss of salary suffered by him during his period of suspension.
[60] *Dalton* v. *Irish Pharmaceutical Union* UD137/1984.
[61] Unfair Dismissals Act 1977, s. 15.
[62] See, *e.g.* *Barthorpe* v. *Exeter Diocesan Board of Finance* [1979] I.C.R. 900.
[63] See, for example, rules 33 and 54 of the I.T.G.W.U.
[64] Unreported, November 15, 1967; considered in *Stevenson* v. *U.R.T.U.* [1977] I.C.R. 893.
[65] See, *e.g.*, *O'Neill* v. *T.G.W.U.* [1934] I.R. 633.

ability to dismiss otherwise than in accordance with particular procedures or upon limited grounds.[66]

So, in *Stevenson* v. *United Road Transport Union*,[67] the union's executive committee purported to remove the plaintiff, a member of the union, from his position as Regional Officer without giving the plaintiff an adequate opportunity of being heard. The plaintiff sought a declaration that the dismissal was in breach of the union's rules, or breach of natural justice, *ultra vires*, null and void. The plaintiff's conditions of employment as regional officer were stated to be as printed in the union rule book. The rules stated that officials, such as the plaintiff, held office so long as they gave satisfaction to the executive committee. The Court of Appeal said that it followed that, under the rules, the executive committee could only dismiss officials if they failed to give satisfaction to the executive committee. So to be competent to dismiss the plaintiff, the executive committee had, first, to reach a conclusion that the plaintiff's performance had been unsatisfactory. The court said that this was "clearly" a decision of a judicial kind and "one which the committee could not fairly reach without letting the plaintiff know in what respects his conduct was considered to have been unsatisfactory, giving him an opportunity to explain his conduct and to put his case."[68] As this had not been done, the court granted a declaration that the decision to dismiss the plaintiff was void *ab initio*.[69] Significantly, the court did not grant a declaration that the plaintiff's contract of employment was still outstanding or that it had remained in operation. In a more recent non-trade union case, however, the Court of Appeal has held[70] that where provisions relating to a disciplinary procedure had been incorporated into an employee's contract of employment, this prevented the employer from dismissing the employee on disciplinary grounds until the procedure had been carried out and it now seems clear that the courts can grant an injunction restraining dismissal until the procedure has been followed.

This does not mean that the old rule,[71] that specific performance will never be ordered in respect of an employee with a contract of personal service, has been completely abrogated. An injunction is a discretionary remedy and the courts do recognise that "if one party has no faith in

---

[66] For examples see *McClelland* v. *Northern Ireland General Health Services Board* [1957] 1 W.L.R. 594; *Hill* v. *C.A. Parsons & Co. Ltd.* [1972] Ch. 305; *Gunton* v. *Richmond upon Thames London Borough Council* [1980] I.C.R. 755; *R.* v. *B.B.C., ex parte Lavelle* [1983] 1 W.L.R. 23; *Irani* v. *Southampton and South-West Hampshire Health Authority* [1985] I.R.L.R. 203; *Fennely* v. *Assicurazioni Generali SPA* High Court, unreported, 12 March 1985 and Supreme Court, unreported, 16 April 1985 (see *Irish Times*, March 13 and April 17, 1985 respectively).
[67] [1977] I.C.R. 893.
[68] *Per* Buckley, Orr and Goff L.JJ. at 902.
[69] *Cf. Brophy* v. *Mapstone* (1985) 56 A.L.R. 135 where the power of the Branch Council to dismiss employees of the union was in no way conditional. See also Spicer C.J. in *McKay* v. *Oliver* (1967) 15 F.L.R. 39, 42.
[70] In *Gunton* v. *Richmond upon Thames London Borough Council* [1980] I.C.R. 755.
[71] See *de Francesco* v. *Barnum* (1890) 45 Ch. D. 430.

the honesty or integrity or the loyalty of the other, to force him to employ that other is a plain recipe for disaster".[72] This is well illustrated by *Leary* v. *National Union of Vehicle Builders*.[73] Here Megarry J. declined to grant an order, at the interlocutory stage, reinstating the plaintiff to his position as an area organiser because, first, the executive committee of the union did not believe it could depend on the loyalty or reliability of the plaintiff and, secondly, because the plaintiff would suffer no real hardship from his exclusion from his position continuing until the trial because the union had guaranteed that his take home pay as area organiser would continue to be paid until the trial.

---

[72] *Per* Geoffrey Lane L.J. in *Chappell* v. *Times Newspapers Ltd.* [1975] I.C.R. 145, 178.
[73] [1971] Ch. 34.

Chapter 6

COLLECTIVE BARGAINING

Introduction

The Trade Union Act 1941 identifies the primary function of a trade union as the carrying on of negotiations for the fixing of wages and other conditions of employment.[1] The carrying on of such negotiations with employers is known as collective bargaining. Since the foundation of the State, with the exception of the period 1941-1946[2] and the temporary legislation with respect to the banks in 1973, 1975 and 1976,[3] trade unions and employers have been free to bargain over wages and other conditions of employment without the intervention of the law.

Collective bargaining is thus a principal source of the terms governing the individual employment relationship; statutory machinery regulating terms and conditions of employment having always been regarded as a second best alternative. Since the 1960s however there has been a steady trend towards legislative regulation of areas that were traditionally the preserve of collective bargaining. Some regulatory legislation had long been a feature of Irish law. Health and safety at work and the payment of wages in cash were early examples,[4] followed more recently by holidays and hours of work, but in general the policy had been not to regulate the employment relationship by statute where it could effectively be done through collective bargaining. The Redundancy Payments Act 1967, which provided for the making of lump sum and periodic payments when employees were dismissed on account of redundancy, broke new ground and began a still continuing process of regulatory legislation in such areas as equal pay, maternity pay, notice, time off and unfair dismissal.

The legislation still permits "freedom of contract" at the collective level[5] because the provisions are merely a minimum, a floor of

---

[1] In the long title to the Act.
[2] A wages standstill was imposed by the Emergency Powers (No. 83) Order 1941 (S.R.O. No. 195 of 1941). This Order was revoked by S.R.O. No. 303 of 1946.
[3] Regulation of Banks (Remuneration and Conditions of Employment) (Temporary Provisions) Acts 1973, 1975 and 1976 which permitted the Minister for Labour to prohibit such increases of remuneration as were determined to be at variance with the provisions or purposes of the then current National Wage Agreements. The validity of this legislation was upheld by McWilliam J. in *Condon* v. *Minister for Labour* High Court, unreported, 11 June 1980. Though *cf.* McCormack (1982) 17 *Ir. Jur. (n.s)* 340.
[4] Areas which "did not lend themselves well to collective bargaining", *per* Kahn Freund, *Labour and the Law* (London, 1977) p. 24. .
[5] However, it should be noted that s. 5 of the Anti-Discrimination (Pay) Act, 1974 renders null and void any provision in a collective agreement in which differences in rates of remuneration are based on or related to the sex of employees.

statutory rights below which no employee, irrespective of trade union membership, may fall; they are also a platform upon which trade unions can seek to build in negotiations with employers. The centrality of collective bargaining is not preserved however. There is no exemption from the statutory framework, as there is in Northern Ireland, for employers whose employees are covered by a collective agreement where that agreement offers protection and benefits comparable with those provided by the legislation.[6]

Nor has collective bargaining itself been much affected by legal rules. The parties are not required by law to bargain, nor, if they do bargain, are they required to bargain in good faith. Solutions are not imposed, the parties are free to enter into disputes and they are not required to go through any particular procedure. What legislation there is, is designed to remove obstacles to the functioning and development of collective bargaining, *viz.* the legal status of trade unions and the lawfulness of industrial action, and to provide support mechanisms, *viz.* consultation and mediation machinery. More recently, however, membership of the E.E.C. has necessitated the enactment of legislation which tends more to positive encouragement of collective bargaining.[7]

The nature of collective bargaining

The Webbs described it thus, "instead of an employer making a series of separate contracts with isolated workmen he meets with a collective will and settles in a single agreement the principles upon which, for the time being, all workers of a particular class, group or grade will be engaged."[8] The Webbs dealt with collective bargaining as one of several methods[9] used by trade unions to further their basic purpose of maintaining or improving the conditions of their members' working lives. Whilst this is true, the Webbs' overall view of collective bargaining was deficient. For them collective bargaining was simply the collective equivalent of individual bargaining. As Allan Flanders has pointed out this is inadequate because there is hardly any consideration given to the employers' interest in collective bargaining: "After all employers could hardly be expected to welcome a strengthening of the bargaining position of their employees unless it brought them some compensating advantages."[10]

---

[6] See Contract of Employment and Redundancy Payments Act 1965, s. 21 (redundancy pay agreements); Industrial Relations (Northern Ireland) Order 1976, art. 26 (dismissals procedure agreement); Industrial Relations (Northern Ireland) Order 1976, art. 57 (collective redundancies); Industrial Relations (No. 2) (Northern Ireland) Order 1976, art. 8 (guaranteed pay agreements). See generally Bourn, "Statutory Exemptions for Collective Agreements" (1979) 8 *I.L.J.* 85.
[7] Such as the Protection of Employment Act 1977, discussed *infra* at pp. 167–179.
[8] *Industrial Democracy* (London, 1898), p. 178.
[9] The others being mutual insurance and legal enactment.
[10] In "Collective Bargaining: a theoretical analysis" (1969) 6 *B.J.I.R.* at p. 1.

Flanders offered an even more substantial theoretical objection to the Webbs' view. The individual contract of employment concluded between an employer and an employee provides for an exchange of work for wages and the conditions of the exchange. A collective agreement, however, does not commit anyone to buy or sell labour. "It ensures that when labour is bought and sold its price will accord with the provisions of the agreement. These provisions are in fact a body of rules intended to regulate amongst other things the terms of the employment contracts. Thus collective bargaining is itself essentially a rule making process and this is a feature which has no proper counterpart in individual bargaining."[11] In other words it was more correct to refer to collective bargaining as regulating, rather than replacing, individual bargaining. Speaking for the majority of the Supreme Court of Canada, Judson J. has said: "The collective agreement tells the employer on what terms he must, in the future, conduct his master and servant relations."[12] He went on to state that to regard a collective agreement as "the equivalent of a bundle of individual contracts between employer and employee" was a "complete misapprehension" of the nature of the juridical relation involved in a collective agreement.[13] Peter Pain J., writing extra-judicially,[14] has commented that the courts, in the United Kingdom at least, regard a collective agreement as "the price list by reference to which the individual contract is determined."

Flanders also queried the use of the word "bargaining" and felt that the Webbs had confused the economic concept of bargain with the political concept. In Flanders' view the result of negotiations between a trade union and employer were, in reality, compromise settlements of power conflicts. "What is known as collective bargaining is primarily a political institution because of [these] two features . . . it is a rule making process and involves a power relationship between organisations."[15] This is why Kahn Freund defined a collective agreement as "an industrial peace treaty and at the same time a source of rules for terms and conditions of employment for the distribution of work and the stability of jobs."[16] What distinguishes collective bargaining from the other rule making processes of industrial relations is what Flanders described as "the authorship of the rules" – the fact that they are jointly determined by representatives of employers and employees who consequently share responsibility for their content and observance.

---

[11] *Ibid.* at p. 4. Flanders' views are criticised by McCarthy, *Elements in a Theory of Industrial Relations* (Dublin, 1984) at pp. 27-30.
[12] *Syndicat Catholique des Employes de Magasin de Quebec Inc.* v. *Compagnie Pacquet Ltee.* [1959] S.C.R. 206, 212.
[13] At 214.
[14] (1981) 10 *I.L.J.* 137 at p. 139.
[15] *Loc. cit.*, at p. 6.
[16] *Labour and the Law* (London, 1977), p. 124.

This is of considerable importance. Collective bargaining is not limited to rule making, the parties to a collective agreement must also regulate their own relationship – their behaviour in settling disputes for example. The machinery of negotiation is as important as the product of negotiation.

As the Commission of Inquiry on Industrial Relations observed,[17] a major feature of Irish industrial relations is our system of centralised wage bargaining, which began in 1948 with the first of a series of wage rounds. From 1970–1982, wage trends were determined by successive National Wage Agreements,[18] which, in 1979 and 1980, had metamorphosed into National Understandings for Economic and Social Development.[19]

The National Understandings of 1979 and 1980 provided not only for maximum percentage increases in pay and the observance of certain procedures before initiating industrial action but also general areas such as employment legislation, taxation, education and health. As McCarthy put it:

> "While an essentially bi-partite bargain was struck by the employers and trade unions on pay and conditions in the traditional manner, the bargain was placed in the context of a tri-partite understanding, covering a programme, exceptionally explicit in character, designed to increase employment, to remedy taxation difficulties, to improve education and health and to promote further the objective of industrial democracy."[20]

The negotiations, so far as they provided for increases in pay, *etc.*, can be regarded as collective bargaining at national level, but the resultant agreement or understanding did no more than to provide norms which could not be exceeded by subsidiary local agreements. The norms nevertheless had to be implemented at local level by industry, district or plant agreements.

Registration of collective agreements

Under Part III of the Industrial Relations Act 1946 the Labour Court may register an "employment agreement", the primary effect of registration being to extend the coverage of the agreement to employers and workmen who were not parties to the negotiations.[21]

---

[17] At para. 20.
[18] See McCarthy, "A Review of the Objectives of the National Pay Agreements 1970–1977" (1977) 25 *Administration* 120.
[19] The parties being the Government, the Irish Congress of Trade Unions and employer associations.
[20] "Worker Participation in Decisions within the Enterprise", National Report (Ireland) to the International Society for Labour Law and Social Security (1982), para 1.31.
[21] See 1946 Act, s. 30. The registration provisions contained in the 1946 Act replaced and improved those contained in s. 50 of the Conditions of Employment Act 1936. The registration provisions of both the 1936 and the 1946 Acts were designed to deal with the situation where a majority of employers and a majority of employees in a particular industry

Employment agreement is defined[22] as an agreement "relating to the remuneration or the conditions of employment of workers of any class, type or group made between a trade union of workers and an employer or trade union of employers." Such trade union must hold a negotiating licence.[23]

It is not necessary that an agreement should be drawn up in any particular form. The agreement, however, must show who are the parties to it and what they have agreed on. So far as the form and wording of the agreement are concerned all that is necessary is that the agreement should be clear and that the wording used should leave no doubt about its meaning in the minds of persons acquainted with the trade or employment concerned.

Any party to the agreement may apply for the registration of it by sending a copy to the Labour Court with a letter asking for registration and giving the information the Court requires.[24] The agreement can only be registered if both parties consent, but if there is more than one party on either side there need not be complete unanimity.[25] Provided there is "substantial agreement" the opposition of some of the parties will not prevent registration. The application must also give enough information to enable the Labour Court to satisfy itself that the parties to the agreement are substantially representative of the employers and workers who will be affected by the agreement if it is registered.[26] Information should be given to show what proportion of the workers who are or may be affected are represented by the union or unions making the agreement. On the employers' side information should be given to show how far the employers who have made the agreement are representative of all the employers who will be affected. The Court will have to decide what information it needs to satisfy itself about the representative capacity of the parties and it may call for more information than is given when the application is made. But some definite information must be supplied when the application is made; the parties must not rely on common knowledge or assume that the Court knows as much about the trade concerned as they do. In particular the applicant should call attention to any substantial employers, for example, who are not represented by the parties to the agreement.

After the application has been processed the Court will give

---

were prepared to make an agreement providing for rates of wages *etc.* but could not make the agreement effective because a small number of employers refused to conform to it. It was hoped that the statutory provisions would facilitate the enforcement of such agreements without resort to industrial action. See the comments of the Minister for Industry and Commerce at 56 *Dáil Debates* at cc. 1273–1274 (17 May 1935).

[22] In the 1946 Act, s. 25.
[23] By virtue of the definition of trade union in s. 3 of the 1946 Act.
[24] S. 27.
[25] S. 27(3)(*a*).
[26] S. 27(3)(*c*).

directions about publication. Employers and workers who will be affected by it, if it is registered, *must* be informed of the application and given an opportunity of making representations or objections. The Court will therefore direct the parties to provide the necessary publicity at their own expense, such as placing advertisements in at least one daily newspaper circulating in the district in which the persons affected reside or work giving an indication of the contents of the agreement and indicating where copies of it can be obtained.[27]

A period of fourteen days must elapse between the publication of particulars of the agreement and the final stage of the registration procedure.[28] If, by the end of that period, no objection has been received the Court may proceed to register the agreement forthwith, although the Court generally arranges a sitting to consider each application for registration even where no objections are raised within the statutory period. If an objection is received then the Court, unless it considers the objection frivolous, must hold a sitting to hear the objections and any other persons concerned (including the parties to the agreement) who wish to give their views.[29] The only ground on which the Court can refuse registration is that the agreement fails to comply with one or more of the statutory requirements; objections as to its content – such as the level of wages – are irrelevant.

The agreement must define clearly the "class, type or group of workers" to whom it applies. The definition, therefore, must be appropriate to the purpose the parties have in mind in applying for registration of the agreement. Whatever the class, type or grade may be the Court has to be satisfied either that "it is a normal and desirable practice" or that "it is expedient to have a separate agreement" for that class, type or group.[30]

The agreement can deal with any matter which comes under the general heading of remuneration or conditions of employment. It does not, of course, have to deal with all such matters. Separate agreements can be registered, each dealing with separate matters if the parties so wish. Otherwise the Court is not concerned with the substance of the mutual rights and obligations which an agreement provides, subject to four important points:

1. Every agreement submitted for registration must provide that there shall be no strike or lockout, until the dispute has been submitted for settlement by negotiation in some way which is set out in the agreement.[31] The settlement procedure can be of any kind that the parties think suitable in the circumstances of their

---

[27] S. 27(4).
[28] S. 27(5)(*a*).
[29] S. 27(5)(*b*).
[30] S. 27(3)(*b*).
[31] S. 27(3)(*e*).

particular case, such as reference to a joint union-management committee or to the Labour Court. Only after the procedure has been followed will it be in order for industrial action to be taken.
2. The Court will also have to satisfy itself that the agreement is not intended to restrict unduly employment generally or the employment of workers of a particular class, type or group.[32] Exactly what those words mean in relation to a particular agreement will be a matter for the Court to decide, having regard to the provisions of the agreement and all the circumstances of the case. No general rule can be laid down in advance.
3. The Court has also to be satisfied that an agreement is not intended "to ensure or protect the retention in use of inefficient or unduly costly machinery or methods of working".[33] Here again each case must be considered on its merits and no general rule can be laid down in advance.
4. By virtue of section 5 of the Anti-Discrimination (Pay) Act 1974 any provision in which differences in remuneration are based on or related to the sex of employees shall be null and void. Section 9 of the Employment Equality Act 1977 has a similar effect in respect of provisions governing access to employment, training or promotion.

Duration and termination of registered employment agreement

The parties can include in their agreement whatever provisions they think proper concerning the length of time for which it is to operate and the method by which it is to be terminated. If it is for a specified period and notice to terminate it has not been given as provided in the agreement so that it is still in force, the Act provides that it shall continue in force even after the end of the period until the registration is cancelled.[34] This may be done in a number of ways:

1. All the parties can jointly notify the Court that they want it cancelled. The Court, if satisfied that all the parties have given their consent voluntarily, can cancel the registration.[35]
2. Any party on either side can apply to the Court for cancellation. The Court may cancel the registration if two conditions are met: (a) three months' notice must be given to the Court; (b) all the parties on one or other side must agree.[36]
3. The Court itself may cancel registration if it is satisfied that, since the agreement was registered, there has been such substantial

---

[32] S. 27(3)(*d*).
[33] S. 27(3)(*d*).
[34] S. 29(4)(*a*).
[35] S. 29(1).
[36] S. 29(4)(*b*).

change in the circumstances of the particular trade or business concerned that maintenance of registration is undesirable.[37]

If the agreement is of indefinite duration and does not include any provision stating how it is to be brought to an end the registration can be cancelled and the agreement deprived of any force under the Act in one of three ways:

1. All the parties on both sides can jointly notify the Court that they want it cancelled. The Court, if satisfied that all the parties have given their consent voluntarily, can cancel the registration.[38]
2. All the parties on one side or the other can apply to the Court for cancellation. The application must be made by all the parties on one side and they must give six months' notice to the Court. In this case cancellation cannot take place until twelve months after registration.[39]
3. The Court itself may cancel registration if it is satisfied that, since the agreement was registered, there has been such substantial change in the circumstances of the particular trade or business concerned that maintenance of registration is undesirable.[40]

Alteration of registered employment agreement

The effecting of changes to a registered employment agreement may be achieved, without having to terminate the agreement, cancelling its registration and submitting a new agreement for registration, by including in the original agreement a provision that it may be varied in accordance with section 28 of the 1946 Act. If this is done, any party to the agreement can apply to the Court for an order varying the agreement.[41] The Court will then consider the application and hear any person who appears to be concerned.[42] The Court is not bound to make the order sought, nor to make it in exactly the terms proposed in the application.[43] If the Court does make a variation order then the agreement has effect as varied by the order.[44]

---

[37] S. 29(2).
[38] S. 29(1).
[39] S. 29(3).
[40] S. 29(2).
[41] S. 28(1). S. 31(2) provides that when a registered employment agreement is varied the Court shall publish, in such manner as it thinks fit, notice of the variation, together with such particulars of the variation as the Court considers necessary.
[42] S. 28(2)(*a*).
[43] S. 28(2)(*b*) provides that the Court may, as it thinks fit, refuse the application or make an order varying the agreement in such manner as it thinks proper.
[44] S. 28(2)(*c*) provides that if the Court makes an order varying the agreement, the agreement shall, as from such date not being earlier than the date of the order as the Court specifies in the order, have effect as so varied.

Effect of registration

Contracts of employment are deemed, by virtue of section 30(2) and (3) of the 1946 Act, to have been amended to comply with the agreement so that if an employer pays lower wages or provides less favourable conditions of employment than the agreement requires, his employees would have the ordinary civil remedies for breach of contract. The 1946 Act also provides for enforcement through the Labour Court. A trade union or, since 1969, an employer may complain to the Court that an employer has failed to comply.[45] If the Court is satisfied, after hearing all persons interested, that the complaint is well founded the Court may direct the employer to comply.[46] If the employer fails to obey the Court's direction he is guilty of an offence and renders himself liable on summary conviction to a fine of up to £100 with a further fine of up to £10 for every day during which the offence is continued.[47] This offence is prosecuted by the Minister for Labour.

The registration of the agreement also places certain limitations on the freedom of action of the trade unions affected. If the Court is satisfied, on a complaint by an employer affected by a registered employment agreement,[48] that a union, representative of workers affected by the agreement, is providing or assisting out of its funds a strike which, to the knowledge of the committee of management, is in contravention of the agreement and which has for its object the enforcement of a demand on an employer to grant to a worker remuneration or conditions other than those fixed by the agreement, the Court may make an order directing the union to refrain from continuing to use its funds in maintaining the strike.[49] If a person to whom this direction is given fails to obey, he is guilty of an offence and is liable, on summary prosecution by the the Minister and conviction, to the same fines as an offending employer.[50] It should be noted that the offence can only be committed by a union which is representative of the workers affected by the agreement. Sympathetic assistance by unions which are not so representative could not be prevented. Moreover the strike which is being promoted or assisted must be both in breach of the agreement and one which has for its object the enforcement of a demand for remuneration or conditions other than

---

[45] 1969 Act, s. 10(1).

[46] 1969 Act, s. 10(1)(*b*). So, in *Construction Industry Federation* v. *Barry Brothers* REA Order No. 2 of 1985, the Court directed the employers (i) to become forthwith and remain party to a pension scheme the main purpose of which is the provision of pension and mortality benefits not less favourable than those set out in the registered agreement and to pay all arrears in respect of serving and past employees; (ii) to operate a sick pay scheme on conditions not less favourable than those set out in the registered agreement and to pay all arrears in respect of serving and past employees.

[47] 1969 Act, s. 10(2).

[48] Or a trade union representative of employers affected.

[49] S. 32(2)(*b*)(i). Alternatively the Court may cancel the registration of the agreement, see s. 32 (2)(*b*)(ii).

[50] S. 32(4).

those fixed by the agreement. It follows that this section neither applies to strike action in support of a demand for the remuneration or conditions set out in the agreement nor such action after the disputes procedure has been properly followed. Moreover the section only applies to a strike, not to any other form of industrial action. It should be noted that, by virtue of section 32(2), where a strike continues after the Court has made an order and members of an authorised trade union holding a negotiation licence, whose rates of remuneration or conditions of employment are not the subject of the strike, are unable or decline to work while the strike continues, then the payment to those members of strike benefit in accordance with the rules of the union shall not be regarded as assisting in the maintenance of the strike.

In 1984, there were 61 employment agreements on the Register, the most significant of these being the agreement for the construction industry. Many of the agreements have not been revised for many years and in consequence the rates of pay and conditions of employment therein are out of date.[51] The Commission of Inquiry on Industrial Relations were of the opinion that the provisions were under-utilised, the lack of interest being due primarily to the unwillingness of both unions and employers "to bind themselves to a rigid formula".[52] It should also be noted that since 1971 only nine agreements have been registered, the most recent being one for the security industry.[53] The Commission of Inquiry recommended no changes in the existing statutory provisions.[54]

Interpretation of agreements

Section 33(1) of the 1946 Act provides that the Court may give at any time, on the application of any person, its decision on any question as to the interpretation of a registered employment agreement or its application to a particular person and section 33(2) provides that a court of law, in determining any question arising in proceedings before it as to the interpretation of a registered employment agreement or its application to any person, "shall have regard to any decision of the Court on the said agreement referred to it in the course of the proceedings." If any question arises in proceedings before a court of law as to the interpretation of a registered employment agreement or its application to a particular person, the court of law, if it thinks proper, may refer the question to the Labour Court for its decision, and the Court's decision thereon is stated to be "final".[55]

---

[51] See the comments in the Court's *Thirty-Seventh Annual Report* at para. 40.
[52] See para. 769.
[53] The agreement was registered on May 1, 1984. For a full list of registered agreements see Appendix V to the Labour Court's *Thirty-Seventh Annual Report*. For an assessment of the registration system see Horgan, (1970) *Ind. Rel. Journal* 30.
[54] See para. 770.
[55] 1946 Act, s. 33(3). *Quaere* whether this provision is constitutionally valid in the light of Article 34 of the Constitution, particularly having regard to the possibility that the Labour

By virtue of section 7 of the 1969 Act, the Court is empowered to give its decision as to the interpretation of any collective agreement or its application to a particular person provided all the parties to the agreement have requested the Court to do so.

Legal status of collective agreements
Collective agreement is defined in section 1 of the Anti-Discrimination (Pay) Act 1974 as:

> "an agreement relating to terms and conditions of employment made between parties who are or represent employers and parties who are or represent employees."

When the legal status of such agreements was first considered in the late nineteenth century it was believed that collective agreements were not legally enforceable.[56] In the first place, the most common type of agreement then was an agreement between a trade union and a federation of employers. The combined effect of various statutory provisions[57] was to define a trade union in terms that covered associations of employers, and section 4 of the Trade Union Act 1871 provides that nothing in the Act would enable any court to entertain any proceedings "instituted with the object of directly enforcing or recovering damages for the breach" of a number of agreements, including any agreement between one trade union and another. In other words federated agreements could not be enforced by law.[58] The second reason given for the non-enforceability of collective agreements was that, even if one was not dealing with a federated agreement, trade unions lacked the capacity to make contracts.[59]

Of course, once it was accepted that a union did possess the legal capacity to enter into contracts[60] and the pattern of collective bargaining changed, the issue of the non-enforceability of collective agreements had to be reconsidered.[61] In 1954, however, Kahn Freund

---

Court's decision might be relied upon in criminal prosecutions. For a consideration of this argument in relation to comparable statutory provisions affecting the Registrar of Friendly Societies, see *supra*, pp. 45–48.

[56] See the Fifth and Final Report of the Royal Commission on Labour, Cd. 7241 (1894).

[57] Trade Union Act 1871, s. 23; Trade Union Amendment Act 1876, s. 16; Trade Union Act 1913, ss. 1 and 2. For the resultant definition see, *supra*, p. 89.

[58] See *Holland* v. *London Society of Compositors* (1924) 40 T.L.R. 440.

[59] See para. 149 of the Fifth and Final Report of the Royal Commission on Labour, Cd. 7241 (1894) and *Pitman* v. *Typographical Association, The Times*, September 26, 1949 (included in Wedderburn, *Cases and Materials on Labour Law* (Cambridge, 1966) at p. 279) where the contractual incapacity of an unincorporated employers' association was put to the Court as a reason for preventing the enforcement of a collective agreement.

[60] Following *Taff Vale Railway Co.* v. *Amalgamated Society of Railway Servants* [1901] A.C. 426.

[61] See Lewis, "Collective Agreements: The Kahn Freund Legacy" (1979) 42 *M.L.R.* 613, citing Tillyard and Robson, "The Enforcement of the Collective Bargain in the United Kingdom" (1938) 48 *Economic Journal* 15.

articulated[62] a new theory of the non-contractual nature of a collective agreement. The true reason for the "complete absence of any attempt to enforce the mutual obligations created by collective agreements" could only be found in the intention of the parties themselves. He continued:

> "An agreement is a contract in the legal sense only if the parties look upon it as something capable of yielding legal rights and obligations. Agreements expressly or implicitly intended to exist in the social sphere only are not enforced as contracts by the courts. This appears to be the case of collective agreements. They are intended to yield 'rights and duties' but not in the legal sense; they are intended, as it is sometimes put, 'to be binding in honour only' or 'to be enforceable through social but not through legal sanctions'."[63]

Kahn Freund also believed that the concepts of private contract law were inappropriate to collective bargaining and that non-enforceability was consistent with an informal and open-ended system of collective bargaining.[64] Therefore the lack of contractual intent was not due to the caprice of the parties. "It is rooted in the history and more importantly in the structure of collective bargaining and especially in the institutional or dynamic method of bargaining . . . and also the multiplicity of bargaining levels."[65]

It has also been judicially observed that, given the flexible and informal nature of many collective agreements, they will often be too vague and imprecise to be legally enforceable. So in *Baldwin* v. *Lett*[66] Kenny J. held that an agreement between the South and East Coast Fishermen's Association and the Herring Merchants' Association, expressing the terms on which a strike would be settled, was phrased in such wide terms that in a court of law many of its provisions would be void for uncertainty. Similarly, in *Ardmore Studios Ltd.* v. *Lynch*,[67] McLoughlin J. commented that, "having regard to its uncertain executory nature", he found it difficult to see how the provisions of a collective agreement relating to the hiring of replacement staff could be held to be legally enforceable. In an unreserved *ex tempore* judgment[68] McWilliam J. refused to grant an injunction, on the application of the Amalgamated Transport and General Workers'

---

[62] In "Legal Framework" in Flanders and Clegg eds., *The System of Industrial Relations in Great Britain* (Oxford, 1954).
[63] *Ibid.* at p. 57.
[64] In "Intergroup Conflicts and their Settlement" (1954) 5 *Brit. J. of Sociology* 153, reprinted in Chap. 2, Kahn Freund, *Selected Writings* (London, 1978).
[65] *Labour and the Law* (London, 1977), p. 127. This thesis was subsequently accepted by the courts in Britain. See *infra*, p. 155.
[66] High Court, unreported, 1 February 1971. See also *Kenny* v. *Vauxhall Motors Ltd.* Court of Appeal, unreported, 19 February 1985 (noted IRLIB 283).
[67] [1965] I.R. 1.
[68] Delivered on February 27, 1981. See *Irish Times*, February 28, 1981.

Union, restraining a company from breaking a provision in a collective agreement relating to the phasing out of staff. On the other hand Murphy J., in *Inspector of Taxes Association* v. *Minister for the Public Service*,[69] said that he agreed with the decision of Kenny J. in *McMahon* v. *Minister for Finance*[70] that the scheme of conciliation and arbitration in the civil service, which takes the form of an agreement between the Minister and a number of staff associations which represent groups in the civil service, was not a "statutory scheme" but a contract.

The most thorough analysis of the legal status of a collective agreement took place in *Ford Motor Co. Ltd* v. *Amalgamated Union of Engineering and Foundry Workers*[71] where Geoffrey Lane J. held that a collective agreement between the plaintiff company and nineteen trade unions was not a legally enforceable agreement. The agreement covered wage rates and hours and a clause provided that the parties would make every attempt to resolve the issues raised and that until every stage of a certain procedure had been carried through there should be no stoppage of work. Members of the defendant union were dissatisfied with a pay offer and went on strike without observing the procedures set out in the agreement. The strike was subsequently made official. The company thereupon sought an injunction contending that the agreement was a commercial one designed to regulate wages and conditions of employment and, as such, was legally enforceable. The union contended that the agreement was not legally enforceable in that it had been negotiated against a background of industrial opinion known to the parties which was adverse to collective agreements being legally enforceable and that the no-strike clause in particular was aspirational in content and too vaguely worded as to be enforceable in law.

Geoffrey Lane J. held that the parties had not intended to create a legally binding contract, and therefore refused to grant an injunction. Furthermore, he observed that collective bargaining "was not a series of easily distinguishable transactions comparable to the making of a number of contracts by two commercial parties." He cited the views of the Royal Commission on Trade Unions and Employers' Associations to the effect that collective bargaining was a "continuous process" in which "differences concerning the interpretation of an agreement merge imperceptibly into differences concerning claims to change its effect . . . such bargaining does not fit into the categories of the law of contract."[72]

---

[69] High Court, unreported, 24 March 1983.
[70] High Court, unreported, 1962.
[71] [1969] 2 Q.B. 303. On which decision see Lewis, "The Legal Enforceability of Collective Agreements" (1970) 8 *B.J.I.R.* 313; Selwyn, "Collective Agreements and the Law" (1969) 32 *M.L.R.* 777; Hepple, "Intention to Create Legal Relations" (1970) 28 *C.L.J.* 122; Clark (1970) 33 *M.L.R.* 117; Selwyn (1970) 33 *M.L.R.* 238.
[72] Para. 470.

In *Goulding Chemicals Ltd.* v. *Bolger*[73] Kenny J. doubted the correctness of the *Ford Motor Co.* decision, but, with respect, his doubts can only apply to the *presumption*, which Geoffrey Lane J. believed to be "deeply rooted in the structure of industrial relations", that collective agreements are not intended to create legal relations, not to the actual decision.[74] The case[75] he relies on as being incompatible with Geoffrey Lane J.'s decision is, with respect, irrelevant. It was a clear case of the agreement being enforced by an individual employee on the basis that the term in question had been incorporated into the employee's contract of employment. It had nothing to do with the enforceability of the agreement at the collective level. Kenny J. believed, however, that a contrary presumption existed, namely that an agreement capable of taking effect as a contractual arrangement should be presumed to be intended to create legal relations unless the agreement itself or the surrounding circumstances show that the parties did not intend to enter into legal relations. In fact Kenny J. and O'Higgins C.J. both expressed the view, *obiter*, that a short six point agreement between the plaintiff company and the trade union of which the defendants were members was intended to create legal relations and was intended to be a legally enforceable contract.[76] The point of departure between Kenny J. and Geoffrey Lane J. is therefore the onus of rebutting a presumption. Whichever view is adopted, it must be remembered that it is only a presumption. If the agreement contains a provision that expresses an intention that the agreement should or should not be binding in law then effect must be given to that intention.

The question of legal enforceability has yet to be definitively considered in this jurisdiction, but an important case is *O'Rourke* v. *Talbot Ireland Ltd.*,[77] where a collective agreement was enforced at the level of the individual contract of employment. The plaintiffs were foremen formerly employed by the defendants in their assembly business. They had been made redundant in 1980 and in their proceedings they claimed a declaration that the company was bound by an agreement made in 1979 whereby they alleged the company gave a guarantee that they would not be made redundant prior to 1984. The background to the case was as follows. From time to time the No. 2 branch of the I.T.G.W.U. entered into productivity agreements with management. "Generally speaking" Barrington J. was satisfied that these arrangements did not contemplate legal relations but were meant

---

[73] [1977] I.R. 211.
[74] Which was that the collective agreement in question was not legally enforceable. Moreover, as McCarthy J. has pointed out, in *Sinnott* v. *Quinnsworth Ltd.* [1984] I.L.R.M. 523, 537, it is not for the Irish Courts to express a view as to whether foreign cases were correctly decided, but merely to express agreement or otherwise with a legal principle stated in such decisions.
[75] *Edwards* v. *Skyways Ltd.* [1964] 1 W.L.R. 349.
[76] Per O'Higgins C.J. at 231, Kenny J. at 237.
[77] [1984] I.L.R.M. 587.

to be binding in honour on management and the union.[78] Apart from their trade union representatives, the foremen at the Santry plant elected a committee of three men which, from time to time, negotiated with management and discussed problems of common interest. In 1979 the company was running into difficulties and management were anxious to secure the plaintiffs' agreement to certain redeployment proposals. A meeting took place and the foremen, through their committee and in return for agreeing to and co-operating with management proposals, asked for a guarantee that their jobs would be secure. Furthermore they asked to have this in writing on company notepaper. The minutes of the meeting record that the management committee did give a guarantee of no compulsory redundancies until 1984. Nevertheless they were dismissed on account of redundancy in 1980.

Barrington J. accepted that the foremen were looking for something which was legally binding and pointed out that the guarantee of job security influenced the plaintiffs' attitude to the management proposals. He was also satisfied that management knew that the plaintiffs were looking for an alteration in their contracts of employment. Nevertheless the company submitted that the agreement was not legally enforceable, and relied strongly on Geoffrey Lane J.'s decision in *Ford Motor Co. Ltd.* v. *Amalgamated Union of Engineering and Foundry Workers*.[79] The I.T.G.W.U.'s branch secretary, on giving evidence, acknowledged that many agreements negotiated between employers and unions were binding in honour only but stated that the agreement which the plaintiffs had secured was unique in his experience as a trade union official. He regarded it as giving "cast iron and personal guarantees to each of the men concerned."

Barrington J. did not consider it necessary to express agreement or otherwise with the principle contained in Geoffrey Lane J.'s decision, for three reasons.

> "Firstly, we are not here dealing with a trade union or a group of trade unions negotiating on behalf of all the men employed in a vast concern or a particular industry but with three foremen negotiating on behalf of not more than seventeen of their peers and referring back to their peers and getting authority from time to time. Secondly, a productivity agreement which might not be legally enforceable in all its terms can still amend particular provisions in a worker's contract of employment *e.g.* his rate of pay. In the present case I have no doubt that the foremen made quite clear that they were looking for an alteration in their terms of employment. Finally, the plaintiffs in the present case carried out their side of the bargain

---

[78] At 589.
[79] [1969] 2 Q.B. 303.

and are standing over the authority of the agents who negotiated the agreement on their behalf."[80]

He accepted management's evidence that they did not intend to enter into legal relations, but pointed out that "unfortunately" this was never expressed or communicated to the plaintiffs who had made it clear that they were not looking for "some pious aspiration or commitment in honour." He was satisfied that when the negotiations were completed the plaintiffs thought that they had received a guarantee against being made redundant prior to 1984 and, on the basis that they had done so, co-operated in the implementation of management's proposals. He was also satisfied that the company, through its managers, knew that the workers had received such a guarantee and did not disabuse them of the position.

"Under these circumstances it appears to me that the company was in breach of its agreement with the plaintiffs in making them redundant in September 1980 and that the plaintiffs are, accordingly, entitled to relief."[81]

The question of legally binding collective agreements was considered by the Commission of Inquiry on Industrial Relations. The Commission accepted that "probably all trade unions and many employers would be opposed to any legislative step to give collective agreements the status of legally binding contracts" and recommended against making such agreements legally binding by statute.[82] The Commission did point out,[83] however, that there was nothing to stop employers and trade unions from giving agreements legal effect either by an explicit provision to that effect or by means of the facility for registration contained in the Industrial Relations Act 1946.[84]

Automatic transfer

It follows from the nature of collective bargaining and the general non-enforceability of collective agreements that only with difficulty can one create *legal* safeguards against repudiation of a collective agreement by either a trade union or an employer. The European Communities (Safeguarding of Employees' Rights on Transfer of

---

[80] [1984] I.L.R.M. at 594.
[81] At 594–5. A similar case was *Cummins* v. *B.L. Cars Ltd.* (1982 no. 4326P). Here the 27 plaintiffs, who had been dismissed for redundancy in December 1979, claimed that an agreement negotiated on their behalf by A.T.G.W.U. and A.G.E.M.O.U. gave them security in employment up to 1984 and they sued for breach of contract and wrongful dismissal. In an *ex tempore* judgment delivered July 18, 1984, McMahon J. dismissed their claim, and he is reported (*Irish Times,* July 19, 1984) as having said that the 1979 agreement was not legally enforceable.
[82] At para. 764.
[83] At para. 763.
[84] *Supra,* pp. 146–152.

Undertakings) Regulations 1980[85] introduce, however, the principle of automatic transfer of collective agreements upon a transfer of undertakings. Regulation 4(1) provides that, following a transfer, "the transferee shall continue to observe the terms and conditions agreed in any collective agreement on the same terms applicable to the transferor under that agreement, until the date of termination or expiry of the collective agreement or the entry into force or application of another collective agreement."

Incorporation

The individual contract of employment is the main point of contact between the legal process and the collective bargaining process. "Collective agreements are not by themselves of any legal significance unless they are translated into a contractual relationship between employer and employee."[86] The translation of collectively agreed provisions into the contract of employment is called *Incorporation* and it is thus at the *individual* level that a collective agreement may be enforced. So in *O'Rourke* v. *Talbot Ireland Ltd.*[87] Barrington J. accepted that a productivity agreement negotiated by a company with a trade union which was not legally enforceable in all its terms could still amend particular provisions in a worker's contract of employment, "*e.g.* his rate of pay." And, as we have just seen, Barrington J., in this case, accepted that the plaintiffs' contracts of employment had been altered as a result of the agreement entered into between the foremen's committee and the management committee. It is not the case (*pace* Murphy J. in *Allied Irish Banks Ltd.* v. *Lupton*[88]) that incorporation is conditional on the collective agreement itself being intended to create legal relations. The agreement does not *confer* contractual rights on the parties to the agreement. It is merely the *source* of the contractual rights of the employees. How then does this occur?

The simplest way is to provide expressly in the contract of employment that the terms as to pay and other conditions of employment will depend on the terms of agreements made from time to time between the employer and the employee's trade union. This has been facilitated to some extent by section 9 of the Minimum Notice and Terms of Employment Act 1973. This section provides that an employee may require the employer to furnish him with a written statement containing a number of particulars, including the rate and method of calculation of the remuneration. Subsection (4) of section 9 provides however that such a statement may refer the employee to a "document" containing these particulars which the employee has

---

[85] S.I. No. 303 of 1980. See further *infra*, pp. 179–181.
[86] *Per* Kilner Brown J. in *Land* v. *West Yorkshire Metropolitan County Council* [1979] I.C.R. 452, 458.
[87] [1984] I.L.R.M. 587.
[88] (1984) 3 *J.I.S.L.L.* 107, 113.

reasonable opportunities of reading during the course of his employment, or which is reasonably accessible to him in some other way. So it is quite permissible for such a statement to refer to the relevant collective agreement.[89]

Incorporation by statute: Occasionally statute may provide that the provisions of a collective agreement are to be incorporated into employees' contracts of employment. A general example of this is Part III of the Industrial Relations Act 1946 under which the provisions of registered employment agreements are incorporated into the contracts of employment of all the employees of the relevant group, class or grade.[90] A more specific example is provided by the Transport Acts 1924–1950 which provide[91] that the rates of pay, hours of work and other conditions of service are to be regulated in accordance with agreements made from time to time between Córas Iompair Éireann and trade unions representative of the employees.

In *Transport Salaried Staffs' Association* v. *Córas Iompair Éireann*[92] Walsh J. said that the object of these provisions was not to have

"agreements negotiated on behalf of employees in the sense that the trade unions might be taken to be the negotiating agents with the power to contract on behalf of each individual member, but rather to set up a uniform standard of wages, conditions of service, hours of duties, *etc.*, which would, by virtue of the statutory provisions, be required to be contained in each individual contract of employment."[93]

The Court rejected C.I.E.'s claim that the statutory provisions sought only a minimum requirement for each individual employee's contract of employment and granted a declaration to the effect that an agreement made in 1947 did not allow special recruitment into the clerical officer grade at salaries in *excess* of these fixed under the agreement.

Incorporation by agency: at first glance the use of the doctrine of agency to explain the process of incorporation in the absence of any express provision to that effect in the contract of employment appears attractive. The individual contracts are shaped by the collective bargaining process because the union bargains as agent for the employees. It is wholly unrealistic however to treat a trade union in negotiating a collective agreement as anything other than a principal. The union will act in and for the interest of its members, but it will also

---

[89] Care must be taken, of course, to ensure reference to the correct collective agreement. See *Gascol Conversions Ltd.* v. *Mercer* [1974] I.C.R. 420.
[90] See *supra*, p. 151.
[91] Railways Act 1925, s. 55 as extended by Railways Act 1933, s. 10 and further applied by the Transport Act 1950, s. 46.
[92] [1965] I.R. 180.
[93] At 200.

act in its own interest. Nor can the agency doctrine explain how the terms of the collective agreement are incorporated into the contracts of employment of non-members, employees who were not members at the time of concluding the agreement, members who opposed the conclusion of the agreement, and infants.

More pertinently the Supreme Court has denied that the terms of a collective agreement are incorporated simply by virtue of the fact of union membership. In *Gouldings Chemicals Ltd.* v. *Bolger*[94] O'Higgins C.J. said he would find it "very difficult to accept that membership of an association like a union could bind all members individually in respect of union contracts merely because such had been made by the union."[95] Kenny J. was more emphatic. He said that the contention was wrong in principle and continued:

> "Membership of . . . an association does not have the consequence that every agreement made by that association binds every member of it."[96]

Agency might be more appropriately used where the group of alleged principals (*i.e.* the employees) is small and definite and the matters dealt with are confined solely to that group. A good example is *Pattison* v. *Institute for Industrial Research and Standards*,[97] where the trade union official negotiating improvements for a small group of employees was treated by McWilliam J. as their legal agent. So there is no reason at all why, in a particular case, a union official should not be the legal agent of an employee or a group of employees.[98] An agency to effect binding transactions however does not stem from the mere fact that the alleged agent is a trade union representative and the alleged principals are trade union members. It must be supported by the creation of some specific agency and that can only arise if the evidence supports the conclusion that there was such an agency.[99]

---

[94] [1977] I.R. 211.
[95] At 231.
[96] At 237. See also *National Union of Gold, Silver and Allied Trades* v. *Albury Bros. Ltd.* [1979] I.C.R. 84. Here the British Jewellers' Association had negotiated a succession of agreements with the union relating to terms and conditions of employment. The question arose as to whether an individual member of the Association could be said to have "recognised" the union for collective bargaining purposes. The Court of Appeal held that the company could not be said to have recognised the union. Despite the Memorandum of Association of the B.J.A. containing as one of its objects a clause empowering it to negotiate terms and conditions and to enter into binding a agreements with any trade unions on behalf of any members of the B.J.A. for or concerning the employment of any such member's employees, Eveleigh L.J. and Sir David Cairns denied that any question of agency arose. Lord Denning M.R. said that an agreement between an employers' association and a trade union did not bind the individual employers "unless they have made separate agreements of their own in regard to it."
[97] High Court, unreported, 31 May 1979. Other examples include *Deane* v. *Craik, The Times*, March 16, 1962 and *Allen* v. *Thorn Electrical Industries Ltd.* [1968] 1 Q.B. 417.
[98] See the contrasting E.A.T. decisions on this: *Carroll* v. *Irish Biscuits Ltd.* (1982) 1 *J.I.S.L.L.* 63 and *McHugh* v. *Kileen Paper Mills* (1982) 1 *J.I.S.L.L.* 91.
[99] *Burton Group Ltd.* v. *Smith* [1977] I.R.L.R. 351.

Incorporation by conduct (or implied incorporation): Kahn Freund once referred to collective agreements as "crystallised custom" which were *automatically* incorporated into every employee's contract of employment, regardless of whether the employee was a member of the union, or whether the person objected to the terms of the agreement or was even an employee at the time of conclusion of the agreement. He argued that employees enter and remain in employment on the same terms as all the other employees and will be deemed therefore to have subjected themselves to those terms whatever they may turn out to be.[1] This view however does not accord with judicial or tribunal practice, and in *Gouldings Chemicals Ltd.* v. *Bolger*[2] O'Higgins C.J. spoke of the need for "acceptance"[3] on the part of the employee.

In *Joel* v. *Cammell Laird (Ship Repairers) Ltd.*,[4] the point at issue turned on whether a term in a collective agreement relating to transfers of employees between shipbuilding work and repair work had been incorporated into the employee's contract of employment. The Industrial Tribunal made it clear that, *absent* any express provision in the contract of employment, incorporation was not automatic. The tribunal stressed that a collective agreement entered into by a trade union on behalf of its members did not bind these members *proprio vigore*. The tribunal therefore considered the extent of the particular employee's knowledge of and participation in the bargaining process. On finding that the employee was aware of the relevant term and had accepted the benefits of the other provisions of the agreement the tribunal concluded that the mobility provision had been incorporated.

In *Singh* v. *British Steel Corporation*,[5] the claimant had been a member of a trade union which held the sole negotiating rights for manual workers at B.S.C. Swindon. The claimant, and others, having become dissatisfied with their representation, left the union in May 1973. In July 1973 the company and the union negotiated a new collective agreement which modified the shift system, and the claimant was informed that the new shift system would come into operation on a particular day. On that day the claimant turned up for work at his old starting time and, when attempts to persuade him to adopt the new system failed, he was dismissed.

---

[1] In Flanders and Clegg eds., *The System of Industrial Relations in Great Britain* (Oxford, 1954), pp. 58-59.
[2] [1977] I.R. 211.
[3] At 231. See too the decision of Barron J. in *Carpendale* v. *Barry* (1984) 3 *J.I.S.L.L.* 116. Here the issue was whether a term in an agreement between the Catholic Primary School Managers' Association and the Irish National Teachers' Organisation (of which the plaintiff was a member) had been incorporated into the plaintiff's contract of employment. The term concerned the procedure to be followed in the event of a vacancy in a "post of responsibility". The point was not conceded by the defendants but Barron J. said, at p. 119, that "since the evidence shows that they accepted its provisions, I accept the plaintiff's contention for the purposes of this application."
[4] [1969] I.T.R. 206. See also *Dudfield* v. *Ministry of Works, The Times*, January 4, 1964. *Cf*, however, *Brand* v. *London County Council, The Times*, October 28, 1967.
[5] [1974] I.R.L.R. 131. Noted by Hepple (1974) 3 *I.L.J.* 166.

It was held that he had not been unfairly dismissed but it was also stated that the claimant had not repudiated his contract of employment by refusing to work the new system. His contract of employment had not been varied by the collective agreement and it was held that neither expressly nor by custom nor by any implication of law was it part of the claimant's contract of employment that its terms could be varied, without reference to him, by an agreement between a union and the company. The claimant in fact had clearly rescinded any authority the union might have had to negotiate for and bind him by agreement.

Davies and Freedland suggest a general theory of incorporation of the results of collective bargaining in these terms:

"As far as the incorporation of the results of collective bargaining into the individual contracts of employment is concerned, the courts have in effect created a *presumption* of more or less systematic translation of the results of collective bargaining into individual contracts where those results are in practice operative and effective in controlling the terms in which employment takes place. There is probably a contrary *presumption* where the results of collective bargaining are not manifestly operative in practice."[6]

Once the terms have been incorporated the termination of the collective agreement from which they are derived will not affect the terms of the individual contracts of employment. This is clearly illustrated by the decision of the English Court of Appeal in *Morris* v. *C.H. Bailey Ltd.*[7] where Salmon L.J. said it was irrelevant that the collective agreements between the plaintiff's trade union and the employers' association to which the defendant company belonged had come to an end; "terms of those agreements were incorporated into the contract of service, but they remained . . . in that contract whether or not the agreements between the union and the association continued."[8] Similarly in *Burroughs Machines Ltd.* v. *Timmoney*[9] the Court of Session held that the act of the company in resigning from the federation of employers which had negotiated a collective agreement "had and could have had no effect whatever" upon the contracts of

---

[6] *Labour Law: Text and Materials* (London, 1984), pp. 295–6. But this is really no more than what Kahn Freund said 30 years earlier. Davies and Freedland cite *Howman & Son* v. *Blyth* [1983] I.C.R. 416 as an example of "linking the collective agreement to the individual contract of employment, in a way which comes right back to Kahn Freund's notion of crystallised custom." Here the issue was the duration of the employers' obligation to pay sick pay. It was accepted that the national agreement for the industry concerned did not form, in any formal sense, part of the plaintiff's contract of employment but the E.A.T. nevertheless accepted it as the guide to what would be a reasonable term to imply. Browne-Wilkinson J. added, at 421, that the E.A.T. considered itself entitled "to come to the conclusion which industrial relations common sense demands."

[7] [1969] 2 Lloyd's Rep. 215. See also *Gibbons* v. *Associated British Ports, The Times*, February 27, 1985.

[8] At 219–220.

[9] [1977] I.R.L.R. 404.

employment between the company and its employees into which the terms of the agreement had been incorporated.

Appropriateness of the terms for incorporation

Whatever link is used for the incorporation of the terms of the agreement into the individual contracts of employment, there still remains the further question of the suitability of the particular term for incorporation.[10] The substantive terms should present no problem in this respect but procedural terms, especially those collective in nature, are not so appropriate and may require the formulation of an individual version of the contractual obligation.[11] The incorporation of a "no strike" clause is the classic example since it is a term that is essentially collective in character.[12]

This aspect of the process of incorporation is well illustrated by the decision of the English Court of Appeal in *Camden Exhibition and Display Ltd.* v. *Lynott*.[13] Here the collective agreement provided that "overtime required to ensure the due and proper performance of contracts shall not be subject to restriction but may be worked by mutual agreement and direct arrangement between the employer and the operatives concerned", and the Court of Appeal had to decide whether a call for an overtime ban amounted to an inducement of breach of contract. Russell L.J. was of the opinion that this clause had no substantive effect at the individual level. He saw the clause as a procedural stipulation to the effect that the union would impose no maximum level for overtime working. He did not see it as a normative provision whereby each employee agreed not to limit or refuse to work overtime.[14] In his opinion therefore an overtime ban would not be a breach of contract. A majority of the Court of Appeal ruled otherwise. Lord Denning M.R.[15] said that this clause meant that the *employees* would not impose an embargo on overtime and that, if the defendant induced the employees to place an embargo on overtime, he was inducing them to break their contracts of employment.[16] The clause, in the majority's opinion, did take effect at the individual level.

This concept of appropriateness therefore determines the extent to which the provisions of the collective agreement may be enforced at the individual level. So, in *British Leyland (U.K.) Ltd.* v. *McQuilken*,[17] a col-

---

[10] See Wedderburn, *The Worker and the Law* (London, 1971) p. 193.
[11] See *Partington* v. *National and Local Government Officers' Association* [1981] I.R.L.R. 537.
[12] Such a term was conceded by counsel for the defendants in *Rookes* v. *Barnard* [1964] A.C. 1129 to have been incorporated into the employees' contracts of employment. This was, in the event, a most unfortunate concession.
[13] [1966] 1 Q.B. 555.
[14] At 568.
[15] Davies L.J. concurring.
[16] At 563.
[17] [1978] I.R.L.R. 245. See also *Tadd* v. *Eastwood* [1983] I.R.L.R. 320, cited by Davies and Freedland, *op. cit.*, at p. 294.

lective agreement provided that employees affected by the discontinuation of a department would be interviewed by a member of the personnel department with the object of establishing a list of employees who wished to be retrained, such list to be drawn up before a certain date. This had not happened and the E.A.T. had to consider whether these provisions had been incorporated into the claimant's contract of employment. They held that these provisions were not appropriate for incorporation since the agreement was "a long term plan dealing with policy rather than the rights of individual employees under their contracts of employment." Failure to interview the claimant was not therefore a breach of his employment contract.

Chapter 7

LEGAL SUPPORT FOR COLLECTIVE BARGAINING

As is pointed out in the Department of Labour's *Discussion Document on Industrial Relations Reform* (1983), the State's role in the free collective bargaining system has been, in the main, an auxiliary one – assisting the parties to resolve their differences voluntarily through the provision of industrial relations machinery which is representative of both sides of industry. As we have seen, the law plays no role in requiring employers to bargain with representative trade unions;[1] it plays no role in requiring employers to disclose information to representative trade unions;[2] it plays no role in requiring employers to grant time off (paid or unpaid) to enable employees to carry out trade union duties or take part in trade union activities.[3] Only to a very limited extent, dictated in the main by international obligations, does the law actively encourage and support collective bargaining. First, the law protects actual and potential trade unionists from certain discriminatory acts by their employers designed to discourage them from joining, or taking part in the activities of, a trade union.[4] Secondly, an employer proposing to dismiss a number of his employees for redundancy is required to consult in advance with any relevant recognised trade union.[5] Thirdly, where a transfer of business is contemplated, both the transferor and the transferee must consult with recognised trade unions.[6] Fourthly, by means of Joint Labour Committees, the State provides in certain industries a substitute for collective bargaining.[7] Fifthly, legislation provides for a limited amount of industrial democracy through the election of employees to the boards of certain State enterprises.[8]

With regard to the question of information disclosure certain developments can be anticipated, but before we look to the future the present scheme of legal support for collective bargaining will be examined.

---

[1] *Supra*, pp. 15–23.
[2] As it does in Northern Ireland through Article 50 of the Industrial Relations (No. 2) (Northern Ireland) Order 1976. See Wood (ed.), *Encyclopaedia of Northern Ireland Labour Law and Practice* (Belfast, 1983) Volume One, Section 6D.
[3] As it does in Northern Ireland through Articles 37 and 38 of the Industrial Relations (No. 2) (Northern Ireland) Order 1976.
[4] Unfair Dismissals Act 1977, s. 6(2)(*a*).
[5] Protection of Employment Act 1977.
[6] European Communities (Safeguarding of Employees' Rights on Transfer of Ownership) Regulations 1980 (S.I. No. 306 of 1980).
[7] Industrial Relations Act 1946, Part IV.
[8] Worker Participation (State Enterprises) Act 1977 and Postal and Telecommunications Services Act 1983, s. 34.

OBLIGATORY CONSULTATION ON REDUNDANCIES

The Protection of Employment Act 1977[9] imposes an obligation on an employer to consult with employee representatives in the event of collective redundancies. Time limits within which the consultation must take place are established and details which must be disclosed are specified. The clear intent behind the Act is to encourage employers and unions jointly to seek ways to minimise the impact of redundancy. In theory the Act is of immense significance in the context of collective bargaining, but in practice it has not had the impact similar legislation has had in Britain and Northern Ireland.

The Act is designed to satisfy Ireland's obligations under EEC Council Directive 75/129 on the approximation of the law of Member States relating to collective redundancies.[10] The recitals in the preamble to the Directive state that it is important that greater protection should be afforded to employees in the event of collective redundancies whilst taking into account the need for balanced economic and social development within the Community; that, despite increasing convergence, differences still remain between the provisions in force in the Member States of the Community concerning the practical arrangements and procedures for such redundancies and the measures designed to alleviate the consequences of redundancy for employees; that these differences may have a direct effect on the functioning of the common market; that the Council Resolution[11] of January 21, 1974 makes provision for a directive on the approximation of Member States' legislation on collective redundancies, and that it is therefore necessary to promote that approximation within the meaning of Article 117 of the Treaty which is intended to promote improved working conditions and an improved standard of living for employees, so as to make possible their harmonization while the improvement is being maintained.

With this in view the Directive determines the scope of the concept of "collective redundancies" and establishes a common body of rules applicable in all the Member States whilst leaving to the Member States power to apply or introduce provisions which are more favourable to employees.

Article 1 of the Directive gives a precise definition of the meaning of "collective redundancies", namely dismissals effected by an employer for one or more reasons not related to the individual employees concerned, involving a fixed number of dismissals within a fixed period. Article 2 of the Directive provides that where an employer is

---

[9] There are certain similarities between this Act and the legislation in the United Kingdom. See Part IV of the Industrial Relations (Northern Ireland) Order 1976 and Part IV of the Employment Protection Act 1975.

[10] O.J. L. 48/29, 22.2.1975. See Hepple, "Community Measures for the Protection of Workers against Dismissals" (1977) 14 *C.M.L. Rev.* 489; Freedland, "Employment Protection: Redundancy Provisions and the E.E.C." (1976) 5 *I.L.J.* 24.

[11] O.J. C. 13/1, 12.2.1974.

contemplating collective redundancies, he must begin consultations with the employees' representatives with a view to reaching an agreement. He is required to supply them with all relevant information and in any event to give in writing the reasons for the redundancies, the number of employees to be made redundant, the number of employees normally employed and the period over which the redundancies are to be effected. He is required to forward to the competent public authority a copy of that written communication.

Articles 3 and 4 of the Directive contain provisions concerning the measures to be taken by the competent public authority. The employer is required to notify that authority in writing of any projected collective redundancies. The notification must contain all relevant information on the matters specified in Article 2 and, in addition, on the consultations with the employees' representatives. A copy of that notification must be forwarded to those representatives. As a general rule collective redundancies may not take effect earlier than 30 days after notification. The competent public authority must use this period to seek solutions to the problems raised by the collective redundancies and the above-mentioned period may be extended for that purpose.

It has been observed that the Directive is primarily concerned with "the positive control of public authorities over the labour market",[12] and less with strengthening the collective bargaining process. In this respect the decision of the Court of Justice of the European Communities in *Commission* v. *Italy*[13] is interesting. The European Commission instituted proceedings claiming that the Italian Republic had failed to fulfil its Treaty obligation by not adopting within the prescribed period the measures needed to comply with Directive 75/129. The Italian government submitted that there was no need to introduce domestic legislation because, having regard to the whole of the system of protection in the case of dismissals established by existing legislation and collective agreements, the organisation of Italian industrial relations produced results similar to those referred to in the Directive. In short no collective redundancies take place in Italy unless the employer has begun consultation with workers' representatives "in order to keep redundancies within the limits of what is strictly indispensable and to mitigate the consequences thereof." The Italian system, however, did not provide, as is required by the Directive, that a competent public authority be notified of collective redundancies, nor did it compel that authority to intervene in order to seek solutions to the problems raised by the proposed redundancies. In any event the Court was of the opinion that certain sectors, especially agriculture and commerce, were not covered as comprehensively as the Directive required. Accordingly the Court declared that the Italian Republic had failed to fulfil its Treaty obligations.

[12] Freedland, *loc. cit.*, p. 34.
[13] Case 91/81, [1982] E.C.R. 2133.

As the 1977 Act is the domestic implementation of obligations under the Directive it must be interpreted accordingly. Where there is any ambiguity the Act should be construed so as to give effect to the principles enshrined in the Directive. A more difficult issue arises where the Act is unambiguously narrower than the Directive. To the extent that the Act falls short of the Directive it will be necessary to decide whether the Directive confers legal rights upon individuals and, if so, whether it can be invoked, not only against the State, but also against private individuals and companies. On the face of it the Directive has no direct application of its own force in Ireland. By virtue of Article 189 of the Treaty, Directives are declared to be binding, as to the result to be achieved, upon each Member State to which they are addressed and it is left to the national authorities to choose the form and method of implementation. The Court of Justice of the European Communities has ruled, however, that Directives can have direct effect. In *S.A.C.E.* v. *Ministry for Finance of the Italian Republic*[14] the Court stated that a Directive concerned not only the relations between the Community and the Member States but also entailed "legal consequences on which individuals may, in particular, rely whenever, by its very nature, the provision enacting that obligation is directly applicable." It has been argued[15] that the test for direct effectiveness of Directives is the same as that for Treaty provisions, namely that the provision should be clear, precise, unconditional and leave no real discretion to the Member State with regard to its application.[16] Many of the obligations in Directive 75/129 do appear sufficiently precise and unconditional to be relied on by individuals, but even if the Directive is capable of giving rise to directly enforceable rights against a member State or its institutions and its authorities, it is impossible, otherwise than in exceptional circumstances, to attribute to it such an effect in horizontal relationships between persons in private law.[17]

Meaning of collective redundancies

The term "collective redundancies" is defined in section 6 as

---

[14] Case 33/70, [1970] E.C.R. 1213. See also, Case 9/70, *Grad* v. *Finanzamt Traunstein* [1970] E.C.R. 825; Case 20/70, *Transports Lesage et Cie* v. *Hauptzollamt Freiburg* [1970] E.C.R. 861; Case 23/70, *Haselhorst* v. *Finanzamt Düsseldorf-Altstadt* [1970] E.C.R. 881; Case 41/74, *Van Duyn* v. *Home Office* [1974] E.C.R. 1337. Generally, see Bebr, "Directly Applicable Provisions of Community Law" (1970) 19 *I.C.L.Q.* 257; Winter, "Direct Applicability and Direct Effects" (1972) 9 *C.M.L. Rev.* 625; Steiner, "Direct Applicability in E.E.C. Law – A Chameleon Concept" (1982) 98 *L.Q.R.* 229.

[15] By Advocate General Mayras in Case 148/78, *Publico Ministerio* v. *Tullio Ratti* [1979] E.C.R. 1629.

[16] As stated in Case 26/62, *Van Gend en Loos* v. *Nederslandse Administratie der Belastingen* [1963] E.C.R. 1.

[17] Case 14/83, *von Colson* v. *Land Nortrhein-Westfalen* [1984] E.C.R. 1891. See also Easson, "Can Directives Impose Obligations on Individuals?" (1979) 4 *E.L. Rev.* 67.

meaning dismissals[18] which are effected for any one of five specified reasons where in any period of thirty consecutive days, the number of such dismissals is:

(a) at least five in an establishment normally employing[19] more than 20 and less than 50 employees;
(b) at least ten in an establishment normally employing at least 50 but less than 100 employees;
(c) at least 10% of the number of employees in an establishment normally employing at least 100 but less than 300 employees, and
(d) at least 30 in an establishment normally employing 300 or more employees.

The five specified reasons are:

(a) that the employer concerned has ceased, or intends to cease, to carry on the business[20] for the purposes of which the employees concerned were employed by him, or has ceased or intends to cease, to carry on that business in the place where those employees were so employed;
(b) that the requirements of the business for employees to carry out work of a particular kind in the place where the employees concerned were so employed have ceased or diminished or are expected to cease or diminish;
(c) that the employer concerned has decided to carry on the business with fewer or no employees, whether by requiring the work for which the employees concerned had been employed (or had been doing before their dismissal) to be done by other employees or otherwise;
(d) that the employer concerned has decided that the work for which the employees concerned had been employed (or had been doing before their dismissal) should henceforward be done in a different manner for which those employees are not sufficiently qualified or trained;
(e) that the employer concerned has decided that the work for which the employees concerned had been employed (or had been

---

[18] The word "dismissal" is not defined in the Act. The wording of the Directive provides that collective redundancies mean dismissals by an employer. In Case 284/83, *Dansk Metalarbejderforbund and Specialarbejderforbund I Denmark v. Nielsen*, the Court of Justice of the European Communities, in a judgment delivered on February 12, 1985, held that there was no provision in the Directive capable of extending the scope of dismissal to termination of employment by workers, in other words its scope does not extend to what are known as "constructive dismissals".

[19] Section 8 provides that the number of employees normally employed in an establishment shall be taken to be the average of the number so employed in each of the twelve months preceding the date on which the first dismissal takes effect.

[20] Business is defined for the purpose of s. 6 as including a trade, industry, profession or undertaking, or any activity carried on by a person or body of persons, whether corporate or unincorporate, or by a public or local authority or a Department of State, and the performance of its functions by a public or local authority or a Department of State.

doing before their dismissal) should henceforward be done by persons who are also capable of doing other work for which those employees are not sufficiently qualified or trained.

Establishment is defined in section 6(3)(*a*) as meaning, where an employer carries on business at a particular location, that location, or, where an employer carried on business at more than one location, each such location. For the purposes of this definition

> "each workplace, factory, mine, quarry, dockyard, wharf, quay, warehouse, building site, engineering construction site, electricity station, gas works, water works, sewage disposal works, office, wholesale or retail shop, hotel, restaurant, cafe, farm, garden or forest plantation shall be taken to be a separate location."

Section 6(3)(*c*) goes on to provide that in ascertaining for the purposes of this section the total number of employees employed in an establishment, account shall be taken of those employees who are based at the establishment but who also perform some of their duties elsewhere.

The drawbacks of this definition can be illustrated by the example of a building company operating on ten sites with a head office whose total workforce is 150. On each site there are 14 employees and 10 in head office. On each site is a temporary shed linked by telephone to the head office. The definition of "establishment" in section 6(3) means that the sites and head office are not to be regarded as one establishment. Since no establishment normally employs more than 20 persons, the Act does not apply.[21] In contrast the approach taken by the Directive is to focus on the relative numbers of employees to be dismissed.

Section 7(2) provides that the Act is not to apply to:[22]

(a) dismissals of employees engaged under a contract of employment for a fixed term or for a specified purpose (being a purpose of such a kind that the duration of the contract was limited but was, at the time of its making, incapable of precise ascertainment) where the dismissals occurred only because of the expiry of the term or the cesser of the purpose;

(b) a person employed by or under the State other than persons standing designated for the time being under section 17 of the Industrial Relations Act 1969;

(c) officers of a body which is a local authority within the meaning of the Local Government Act 1941;

---

[21] Section 7(1) provides that the Act applies, subject to s. 7(2), to all persons in employment in an establishment normally employing more than twenty persons.

[22] These exclusions follow closely the wording of Art. 2 of the Directive, on which see Case 215/83, *Commission* v. *Belgium*; Judgment of the Court of Justice of the European Communities delivered March 28, 1985.

(d) employment under an employment agreement pursuant to Part II or IV of the Merchant Shipping Act 1894.
(e) employees in an establishment the business carried on in which is being terminated following bankruptcy or winding-up proceedings or for any other reason as a result of a decision of a court of competent jurisdiction.

Consultation and notification

Section 9 provides that, where an employer proposes to create collective redundancies, "he shall, with a view to reaching an agreement, initiate consultations with employees' representatives representing the employees affected by the proposed redundancies". The consultations are to include (a) the possibility of avoiding the proposed redundancies, reducing the number of employees affected by them or otherwise mitigating their consequences, and (b) the basis on which it will be decided which particular employees will be made redundant. Section 9(3) goes on to provide that consultation shall be initiated "at the earliest opportunity and in any event at least 30 days before the first dismissal takes effect."

For the purpose of these consultations the employer must supply the employees' representatives with "all relevant information relating to the proposed redundancies." Section 10(2) then provides that, without prejudice to the generality of this obligation, the information supplied must include the following:

(a) the reasons for the proposed redundancies;
(b) the number, and descriptions or categories, of employees whom it is proposed to make redundant;
(c) the number of employees normally employed; and
(d) the period during which it is proposed to effect the proposed redundancies.

These details must be supplied in writing, and section 10(3) provides that the employer must supply the Minister for Labour, as soon as possible, with copies of all information supplied in writing under section 10(2). An employer who fails to initiate consultations under section 9 or fails to comply with section 10 is guilty of an offence and is liable, on summary conviction, to a fine not exceeding £500. What is the degree of particularity as to the reasons? All that can usefully be said is that there should be sufficient information to enable the trade union to make constructive proposals.[23] Of course, during the consultations, the employer must consider any representations made by the trade union and reply to them.

The term "employees' representatives" is defined in section 1 as meaning "officials (including shop stewards) of a trade union or of a

---

[23] See *General and Municipal Workers Union v. British Uralite Ltd.* [1979] I.R.L.R. 405.

Legal Support for Collective Bargaining 173

staff association with which it has been the practice of the employer to conduct collective bargaining negotiations." In other words the employer is only obliged to initiate consultations with recognised trade unions and, since the obligation is to consult with the representatives of those affected by the proposed redundancies rather than with the employees themselves, it is likely that non-unionists, as well as members of unrecognised trade unions, are not protected.[24] Assuming, however, that at least one union is recognised then, even in a situation where the employer is preparing to dismiss a number of non-unionists, some consultation with that union must take place since those who are not to be dismissed can still be said to be "affected by the proposed redundancies".

The question of whether it has been the practice of the employer to conduct collective bargaining negotiations has been considered on a number of occasions in Britain. Those cases demonstrate that there is a heavy burden of proof on the trade union.

The relevant law in this matter was laid down in *National Union of Gold, Silver and Allied Trades* v. *Albury Brothers Ltd.*[25]

> "First, the question of recognition is a mixed question of fact and law. Secondly, recognition requires mutuality, that is to say that the employer acknowledges the role of the union for the relevant purposes and the union assents to that acknowledgement. Thirdly, such a process requires agreement, which may be express or implied. Fourthly, if it is said to be implied, the acts relied on must be clear and unequivocal, and (usually) involve a course of conduct over a period of time."[26]

The E.A.T. went on to observe that the agreement, express or implied, between the employer and the trade union need not be legally enforceable in order to constitute recognition.

Here the employers made some of their employees redundant without consulting N.U.G.S.A.T. There was no formal recognition agreement between the company and the union. The company, however, was a member of the North Area Goldsmiths' and Jewellers' trade section of the British Jewellers' Association which had negotiated a succession of agreements relating to terms and conditions of employment with N.U.G.S.A.T. Eight of the employees were union members and the union's district secretary had met once with the company representative to discuss the wages of one employee but no agreement had been reached. An industrial tribunal, the E.A.T. and the Court of Appeal all held that the employers had not recognised the trade union and therefore were not obliged to consult on the

---

[24] The Directive does not require that the union be "recognised".
[25] [1978] I.C.R. 62. The decision of the E.A.T. was upheld on appeal by the Court of Appeal, [1979] I.C.R. 84.
[26] [1978] I.C.R. at 65.

redundancies. Lord Denning M.R. said that an agreement between an employers' association and a trade union "does not bind the individual employers unless they have made separate agreements of their own in regard to it: The terms can be used as guidelines, but that is all."[27] The Court of Appeal stressed that recognition was a most important matter for industry and that an employer was not to be held to have recognised a trade union unless the evidence was clear.[28]

A contrasting decision is *National Union of Tailors and Garment Workers* v. *Charles Ingram & Co. Ltd.*[29] where the E.A.T. held that the union had been recognised. The employers' association, of which Charles Ingram & Co. Ltd. was a member, had negotiated a number of collective agreements with N.U.T.G.W., but, in addition, the company had discussed matters of pay and conditions with N.U.T.G.W. representatives on a number of occasions and had even admitted on a questionnaire that they recognised N.U.T.G.W.

Another relevant British decision is *Union of Shop Distributive and Allied Workers* v. *Sketchley Ltd.*[30] where the company had afforded the union limited rights to represent their members in grievance procedures, together with facilities for appointing shop stewards and collecting union dues. The E.A.T. held that there is a distinction between recognition for representational purposes and recognition for negotiation purposes. The union was entitled to make representations but was not entitled, under the agreement, to negotiate over what the procedures themselves should be. In fact the agreement specifically provided that it did not confer "recognition for negotiation of terms and conditions". The E.A.T. said that, if it were to treat a representation agreement as tantamount to recognition for the purposes of collective bargaining, it would be contrary to "sound industrial relations practice".

In addition to the obligation in section 10 to supply the Minister with a copy of the written details given to the employees' representatives, section 12 imposes an obligation on an employer who proposes to create collective redundancies to notify the Minister in writing of his proposals at the earliest possible opportunity and in any event at least 30 days before the first dismissal takes effect.[31] A copy of any such

---

[27] [1979] I.C.R. at 88.
[28] See *Transport and General Workers Union* v. *Dyer* [1979] I.R.L.R. 93.
[29] [1977] I.C.R. 530.
[30] [1981] I.C.R. 644. See also *R* v. *Central Arbitration Committee, ex parte BTP Tioxide Ltd.* [1981] I.C.R. 843, 857.
[31] Regulation 2 of S.I. No. 140 of 1977 sets out the particulars which must be specified by an employer in a notification to the Minister under s. 12:
    (a) the name and address of the employer, indicating whether he is a sole trader, or a partnership or a company;
    (b) the address of the establishment where the collective redundancies are proposed;
    (c) the total number of persons normally employed at that establishment;
    (d) the number and descriptions or categories of employees whom it is proposed to make redundant;

notification is to be supplied by the employer, as soon as possible, to the employees' representatives who may forward to the Minister in writing any observations they have relating to the notification. An employer who fails to comply with these obligations is guilty of an offence and is liable on summary conviction to a fine not exceeding £500.[32]

Section 15(1) further provides that "for the purpose of seeking solutions to the problems caused by the proposed redundancies, the employer concerned shall, at the Minister's request, enter into consultations with him" and for the purpose of such consultations an employer must supply the Minister with such information relating to the proposed redundancies as the Minister "may reasonably require".

The meaning of the phrase "proposes to create collective redundancies" was considered in *Association of Patternmakers and Allied Craftsmen* v. *Kirvin Ltd.*[33] Here it was held that a proposal to create redundancies went beyond the mere contemplation of a possible event. Consultation could not take place until the employer had formed some view of how many employees are to be dismissed, when this is to take place and how it is to be arranged. The phrase therefore connotes a state of mind directed to a planned course of events. The obligation to consult and notify is imposed upon employers who have reached some decision, though not necessarily a final one. It is not imposed upon employers in whose minds the thought of redundancy exists only as a remote possibility.

The U.K. cases[34] also suggest that until the information outlined in section 10 is supplied to the employees' representatives there is no point in consulting, so that in effect the 30-day period will run from the time the information is given and effective consultation can begin. In *Irish National Teachers' Organisation* v. *St. Olcan's Maintained School Committee*,[35] a Northern Ireland industrial tribunal accepted that the mere giving of information did not amount to consultation.

The consultations must be meaningful. They should be real and substantial, not a nominal effort paying mere lip service to the

---

(e) the period during which the collective redundancies are proposed to be effected, stating the dates on which the first and final dismissals are expected to take effect:
(f) the reasons for the proposed collective redundancies;
(g) the names and addresses of the trade unions or staff associations representing employees affected by the proposed redundancies and with which it has been the practice of the employer to conduct collective bargaining negotiations;
(h) the date on which consultations with each such trade union or staff association commenced and the progress achieved in those consultations to the date of the notification.

[32] 1977 Act, ss. 11 and 13.
[33] [1978] I.R.L.R. 318. See also *National Union of Public Employees* v. *General Cleaning Contractors Ltd.* [1976] I.R.L.R. 362.
[34] Such as *Electrical and Engineering Staff Association* v. *Ashwell Scott Ltd.* [1976] I.R.L.R. 391; *General and Municipal Workers' Union* v. *British Uralite Ltd.* [1979] I.R.L.R. 409.
[35] No. 1/79 F.T.C.

statutory requirements. They should allow a reasonable time for proper discussions and for the employees' representatives to consider the situation and prepare a reply. It follows that, if notice of dismissal is given before consultations begin or so shortly afterwards that there is no time for discussion and reply, it is not really consultation at all, let alone "meaningful" consultation.[36] While the process of consultation must begin before notice of dismissal is given, the Act does not require that the process of consultation be completed before notice of dismissal is given.

Section 14(1) provides that collective redundancies shall not "take effect" before the expiry of the period of 30 days beginning on the date of the notification to the Minister under section 12. Section 14(2) provides that employers who effect collective redundancies before the expiry of the 30-day period are guilty of an offence and are liable on conviction or indictment to a fine not exceeding £3,000.

Particularly in view of the fact that there is no provision for compensating employees who are collectively dismissed for redundancy without the employer having initiated meaningful consultations with their representatives, the authors see no reason why an employee could not secure an injunction to restrain his dismissal, where that dismissal would be in violation of section 14. Subsection 1 quite emphatically states that the collective redundancies "shall not take effect" before the expiry of the 30-day period. Furthermore section 19 provides that any provision in any agreement, whether a contract of employment or otherwise, purporting to exclude or limit the operation of any provision of the 1977 Act is "null and void".

Where an employer is convicted of an offence under sections 11 or 14, section 22 provides that he may plead "in mitigation of the penalty for that offence" that there were "substantial reasons related to his business" which made it "impracticable" for him to comply with the section under which the offence was committed. It should be noted that this plea is not allowed in relation to an offence under section 12 (*i.e.* notification to the Minister). The burden of proof is on the employer.

There are two relevant stages to this plea. There must be substantial reasons related to the employer's business and these must render it impracticable for him to comply.[37] Examples would be destruction of the plant, a general trading boycott, the sudden withdrawal of supplies by the main supplier or a sudden, as distinct from a gradual, financial deterioration, such as where the employer has to close down after a bank suddenly stops further credit and appoints a receiver. Employers however, who are in the process of going into liquidation cannot avoid the obligations imposed by the Act simply by being unreasonably late in coming to a decision or negligently failing to foresee the obvious.

---

[36] See *National Union of Teachers* v. *Avon County Council* [1978] I.C.R. 626.
[37] See *Electrical and Engineering Staff Association* v. *Ashwell Scott Ltd.* [1976] I.R.L.R. 319.

This can be illustrated by reference to a company which is in serious financial difficulties. The directors believe that it can carry on by selling some assets. When they discover they are unable to do so, the company ceases trading and all its employees are made redundant without there being any consultation at all. Is the insolvency a substantial reason which makes it impracticable to consult? It is clear that, while insolvency *per se* cannot amount to a "substantial reason", a particular insolvency might, depending on the circumstances.[38] These circumstances, however, must be uncommon or out of the ordinary. If the cause of the insolvency is the gradual running down of the business, that is not something uncommon, exceptional or extraordinary. If the directors have failed to face up to the financial reality of the situation, if more experienced and astute business men would have responded earlier and anticipated the events that occurred, then the plea is not made out. A company in this position could easily say to the employees' representatives: "The writing is on the wall, we may have to close down unless somebody bails us out."

This does not mean, however, that there is any general requirement of consultation between an ailing company and a recognised trade union prior to any proposal for dismissals on account of redundancy. There is nothing requiring an employer to do anything about consultation unless and until a proposal to dismiss some of its employees on the ground of redundancy is, at least, in the mind of the employer. This is reinforced by reference to the Directive which the Court of Justice of the European Communities has held does not apply where by reason of the financial situation of the undertaking the employer ought to have contemplated collective redundancies but did not do so.[39] It is only when the employer contemplates collective redundancies that the obligation to consult arises. Kilner Brown J. has commented[40] that the legislation does not require a trade union to be involved "in preliminary policy considerations which are a managerial responsibility."

Armour (Receiver of Barry Staines Ltd.) v. *Association of Scientific, Technical and Managerial Staffs*[41] is illustrative of this, since the decisions to cease trading and to dismiss the workforce were arrived at virtually simultaneously. The company was in financial difficulty and applied for assistance from the British government. It was given a substantial loan but this proved to be "too late and not enough". The directors applied for a second loan but were refused. Four days after

---

[38] *Clarks of Hove Ltd.* v. *Bakers' Union* [1978] I.C.R. 1076. See also *Union of Shop, Distributive and Allied Workers* v. *Leancut Bacon Ltd.* [1981] I.R.L.R. 295.
[39] Case 284/83, *Dansk Metalarbejderforbund and Specialarbejderforbund I Denmark* v. *Nielsen*; Judgment delivered February 12, 1985.
[40] In *National and Local Government Officers' Association* v. *National Travel (Midlands) Ltd.* [1978] I.C.R. 598, 601.
[41] [1979] I.R.L.R. 24.

this the workforce were dismissed. The company should have appreciated that if the second loan were refused it would be obliged to cease trading immediately. The E.A.T. said that the need for the loan and the consequences of failing to receive it should have been explained to the union, but they held that an application for a government loan by a company which had already received substantial financial help from government sources was a circumstance sufficiently special to make it not reasonably practicable to give the final written details required until the outcome of the application was known. The E.A.T. went on to point out that a substantial measure of consultation could have occurred before the redundancies were declared. "The position of the company, the importance of the loan and the consequences of refusal were matters which should have been disclosed to responsible trade union officials . . . that would have complied with the spirit if not the letter of the [Act]."[42]

Miscellaneous matters
The Minister's authorised officers are empowered by section 17(1) to:

(a) enter at all reasonable times any premises or place where they have reasonable grounds for supposing that any employee is employed;[43]
(b) there make any examination or enquiry necessary for ascertaining whether this Act has been or is being complied with:
(c) require an employer or his representative to produce any records which the employer is required by this Act to keep, and inspect and take copies of entries in the records;
(d) examine with regard to any matters under this Act any person whom they have reasonable cause to believe to be or to have been an employer or employee and require him to answer any questions (other than questions tending to incriminate him) which the officers may put relating to those matters and to sign a declaration of the truth of the answers.

Any person who –

(a) obstructs or impedes an authorised officer in the exercise of any power conferred by this section;
(b) refuses to produce any record which an authorised officer lawfully requires him to produce;

---

[42] At 27.
[43] S. 17(2) provides that this power shall not be exercisable in respect of a private dwelling house unless the Minister (or an Officer of the Minister approved by the Minister for the purpose) certifies that he has reasonable grounds for believing that an offence under s. 17 in relation to an employee employed in the house has been committed by the employer, and the authorised officer in applying for admission to the house produces the certificate.

(c) produces, or causes to be produced or knowingly allows to be produced, to an authorised officer any record which is false in any material respect knowing it to be false;
(d) prevents or attempts to prevent any person from appearing before or being questioned by an authorised officer; or
(e) wilfully fails or refuses to comply with any lawful requirement of an authorised officer under subsection (1)(*d*)

shall be guilty of an offence and shall be liable on summary conviction to a fine not exceeding £500.[44]

Section 18 provides that the employer must keep such records as may be necessary to enable the Minister or an authorised officer to ascertain whether the provisions of the 1977 Act are being or have been complied with. These records must be retained by the employer for a period of "not less than three years from the date on which they were made."[45]

Offences under the Act may be prosecuted by the Minister for Labour.[46] At the time of writing, the authors are not aware of any prosecutions under the 1977 Act having been initiated. In the case of a company in liquidation, the authors can appreciate that the Department of Labour may feel that no useful purpose can be served by prosecuting the company for failure to consult or notify. In general, however, the authors feel as did the English E.A.T. in *Talke Fashions Ltd v. Amalgamated Society of Textile Workers and Kindred Trades*[47] that the imposition of penalties for "bad behaviour" is a retrograde step in the field of legislation dealing with good industrial relations. Far more appropriate would be an award of compensation commensurate with the loss suffered by an employee who has been given "short shrift" in a redundancy situation.

TRANSFER OF UNDERTAKINGS

A further duty to inform and consult trade union representatives is imposed by regulation 7 of the European Communities (Safeguarding of Employees' Rights on Transfer of Undertakings) Regulations 1980.[48] These regulations are designed to satisfy our obligations under EEC Council Directive 77/187, commonly referred to as the Acquired Rights Directive, which safeguards employees' rights in the event of a

---

[44] S. 17(3).
[45] Failure to keep and/or retain such records is an offence and the employer shall be liable on summary conviction to a fine not exceeding £500. S. 18(4) provides that, where the employer fails to keep or retain records, the onus of proving that he has complied or is complying with the Act shall be on him.
[46] S. 21(1).
[47] [1977] I.C.R. 833.
[48] S.I. No. 306 of 1980. For analyses of the U.K. equivalent, see Hepple, "The Transfer of Undertakings (Protection of Employment) Regulations" (1982) 11 *I.L.J.* 29 and Rideout, "The Great Transfer of Employee Rights Hoax" (1982) *Current Legal Problems* 233.

transfer of the business in which they are employed.[49] Regulation 7 provides that both parties concerned in a transfer must inform the representatives[50] of their respective employees affected by the transfer of –

(a) the reasons for the transfer;
(b) the legal, economic and social implications of the transfer for the employees; and
(c) the measures envisaged in relation to the employees.

If the "transferor" or the "transferee" envisages measures in relation to the employees, regulation 7(2) provides that he must consult the representatives of the employees "in good time" on such measures, and this consultation must be "with a view to seeking agreement". The information must be given "in good time before the transfer is carried out" and in any event before the employees are directly affected by the transfer as regards their conditions of work and employment. The information should be given long enough before a relevant transfer to enable consultations to take place. It does not seem however that there is a requirement to inform as to when the transfer is to take place.[51]

If there are no employee representatives, a statement in writing, containing the three particulars set out above, must be given "in good time before the transfer is carried out" to each employee in the business or undertaking. Furthermore, notices containing the aforesaid particulars must be displayed "at positions in the workplaces of the employees where they can be read conveniently by the employees."

The duty to inform and consult only applies when there is a transfer, by sale or other disposition or operation of law, of a business or a self contained part of a business, as a going concern. Transfers of share capital, a common form of takeover in Ireland, are excluded, as are dispositions of physical assets. In this respect Professor Rideout's words are apt:

> "The failure to include such transfers will have a substantial effect upon the benefits which would otherwise have been derived from prior consultation with and information to employees concerning the effects of the change. These are just as likely to be far reaching in a share transfer as they are in any other form of takeover. Usually employees are wholly unaware that the share transfer is pending until after it occurs. By that time the plans of the transferee are normally well advanced. The employee lacks both the opportunity

---

[49] OJ L. 61/26, 5.3.1977. See Hepple, "Workers' Rights in Mergers and Takeovers: The E.E.C. Proposals" (1976) 5 *I.L.J.* 197 and Bartlett, "Employees' Rights in Mergers and Takeovers – E.E.C. Proposals and the American Approach" (1976) 25 *I.C.L.Q.* 621.
[50] Unlike the Protection of Employment Act 1977, employee representatives are not required to be officials of a trade union or staff association with which it has been the practice to conduct collective bargaining negotiations.
[51] See Rideout, *loc. cit.*, at p. 245.

to influence them and the advance warning to make alternative arrangements for his own future."[52]

A person who fails to inform or consult is guilty of an offence and is liable on summary conviction to a fine not exceeding £500. Offences may be prosecuted by the Minister. It should be noted that the obligations to inform and consult are absolute. There is no dispensation where the person can show that it was not reasonably practicable for him to comply with such a duty.

CONSULTATION OVER HEALTH AND SAFETY

Sections 35-39 of the Safety in Industry Act 1980 not only provide for consultation over matters of health and safety between employers and employees' representatives but also provide the structure within which the consultation shall take place. The creation of plant level institutions for the handling of a particular problem is a significant development. It was hoped that the creation of specific bodies would avoid an adversarial approach to health and safety issues. By not locating these issues within the machinery and the climate of day-to-day worker/management relations, co-operation, not confrontation, would be fostered. The rationale is aptly described in the Minister's second stage speech on the 1980 Bill:

> "I believe that worker participation in the vital area of occupational health and safety is deserving of every encouragement. While the main responsibility for ensuring safety at work rests, as it should, on the occupier, workers have a positive contribution to make as well. Indeed, it would be impossible to devise safety legislation which would decrease, or even eliminate, accidents at work, if at the same time, workers did not have due regard for their own safety and for that of their fellow workers. So, what I am hoping to achieve with the sections on safety representatives and safety committees is a coming together, in a spirit of co-operation and co-responsibility, of occupiers and workers in the common interest of securing a safe and healthy workplace."[53]

In factories where up to twenty workers are employed the persons employed can appoint from among themselves a Safety Representative. In larger factories the persons employed may select and appoint from amongst their numbers members of a Safety Committee. The number of members of a Safety Committee shall not be less than three and shall not exceed one for every twenty persons employed in the relevant premises at the time when the committee is appointed, or ten, whichever is the less.

---

[52] Ibid., at pp. 235-6.
[53] 94 Seanad Debates cc. 395-396.

The selection and appointment of the committee is at the option of the persons employed, not their trade unions, but the employer has the right to appoint one member where the number of members of which the committee is to be composed is four or less; two members where the number is not more than eight and not less than five; and three members where the number is more than eight.

It is important to note that the Act contains no formal recognition of the role of trade unions in the matter,[54] although it should be noted that before the Minister can make regulations under the Act he must consult "such organisations or other bodies of persons representative of trade unions or bodies analogous to trade unions as he considers appropriate."

In the endeavour to avoid confrontation, the topic of health and safety was kept out of the trade unions' negotiation sphere and entrusted to management and the workers directly. Nevertheless, in practice, the trade unions have a considerable role to play. They are as entitled to negotiate on safety and health issues, as they are on other conditions of employment.

The system introduced by the 1980 Act is mandatory. If the workers do not exercise the option the employer is obliged to appoint the Safety Representative or Safety Committee, as appropriate. Section 37(2) provides however that before making such an appointment the occupier must afford to the persons employed on the premises an opportunity for consultation regarding the appointment.

The function of a Safety Representative is set out in section 35. Subsection (3) provides that the occupier shall hold consultations with the representative for the purpose of ensuring co-operation on the premises in relation to the provision of (i) the Safety in Industry Acts 1955 and 1980; (ii) regulations under the Acts relating to safety, health and welfare and applicable to or in respect of the person with whose safety, health and welfare he is concerned; and (iii) such other enactments applying to the premises or to such persons or to both as may be prescribed. Subsection (5) further provides that the occupier "shall consider any representations made to him by the Safety Representative or any matter affecting the safety, health and welfare of the persons employed."

The function of a Safety Committee is set out in section 36. Subsection (4)(*a*) provides that it shall be a function of the committee to assist the occupier concerned and the persons employed in the relevant premises in relation to the provision of the Acts and of regulations under the Acts and to perform or exercise such other functions (if any), relating to the safety or health of such persons, as may stand for the time being specified in regulations made by the

---

[54] See the *Report of the Commission of Inquiry on Safety, Health and Welfare at Work* (1983) (Pl. 1868) at para. 9.16.

Minister. Subsection (4)(*g*) provides that the occupier shall consider any representations made to him by the Safety Committee on matters affecting the safety, health and welfare of persons employed in the relevant premises, and subsection (4)(*a*) imposes a similar obligation on the committee in respect of such representations made by the occupier. Subsection (6) provides that, on a request being made by a Safety Committee, the occupier shall consult with the committee with the object of reaching agreement concerning the facilities for holding meetings of the committee, and the frequency, duration and times of meetings of the Safety Committee. Subsection (7) provides that, subject to the terms of any agreement between the occupier and the committee, meetings of the committee shall be held from time to time on such days as the committee shall decide and such meetings may be held during normal working hours without loss of remuneration to the members if certain conditions are satisfied, namely:

(a) except in the case of an emergency, such meetings shall not be held more frequently than once every two months;
(b) the duration of each such meeting shall not exceed two hours, and
(c) the number of members attending shall be at least such as is required to form a quorum, and
(d) the times at which the meetings are held shall be compatible with the efficient operation of the premises concerned.

JOINT LABOUR COMMITTEES

Low pay is said to be a characteristic feature in industries in which voluntary collective bargaining is non-existent and prospects for collective organisation are poor.[55] In these conditions, some form of minimum wage regulation is essential in order to prevent the worst extremes of exploitation which arise from competitive wage undercutting.

Prior to the enactment of the Industrial Relations Act 1946, the Minister for Industry and Commerce could establish Trade Boards which were to set legally enforceable minimum rates of pay in trades "where the rate of wages prevailing in any branch of the trade is exceptionally low, as compared with that in other employments."[56] Under the 1946 Act, these bodies were renamed Joint Labour Committees (J.L.C.) and the power of establishment was transferred to the Labour Court. There are currently 17 J.L.C.s covering approximately 30,000 employees in areas such as catering, hotels and

---

[55] Low Pay Unit *Who Needs the Wages Councils?* Pamphlet No. 24(1983), p. 15. See also Pond, "Wages Councils, the Unorganised, and the Low Paid" in Bain ed., *Industrial Relations in Britain* (Oxford, 1983), pp. 179–208.
[56] Trade Boards Act 1909, s. 1(2), as amended by Trade Boards Act 1918.

clothing manufacture.[57] The most recently established[58] is the Contract Cleaning (City and County of Dublin) J.L.C. which came into operation on April 30, 1984 following an application by the I.C.T.U. and a Labour Court investigation which satisfied the Court that the existing machinery for effective regulation of remuneration and other conditions of employment of certain workers employed by contract cleaning firms in the City and County of Dublin was inadequate.

The workers covered by J.L.C.s are generally poorly unionised and poorly paid; the great majority are women.[59] The industries covered contain a high proportion of small firms using labour intensive techniques and operating in a restricted and highly competitive product market.

The philosophy behind the creation of bodies such as J.L.C.s is that "they should provide workers with an institutional bridge towards the establishment of full voluntary collective bargaining, while in the meantime ensuring a legally enforceable minimum wage in those industries, set at an adequate level."[60] Nevertheless, the trade unions have found it difficult to penetrate the J.L.C. industries since there are a number of characteristics which tend to frustrate attempts to increase the level of organisation. These include the industrial structure, but the characteristics of the labour force also make the establishment of collective bargaining difficult. The very nature of the jobs offered in these industries means that staff turnover is high. The recruitment and retention of members in these circumstances is an expensive job for trade unions. Even where they are able to obtain and maintain membership, their bargaining strength is severely weakened by the vulnerability of the people they represent.[61]

The J.L.C. system is also designed to satisfy Ireland's international obligations with regard to the maintenance of adequate wage levels. I.L.O. Convention No. 26 requires signatory states "to create or maintain machinery whereby minimum rates of wages can be fixed for

---

[57] The full list is as follows: Aerated Waters and Wholesale Bottling; Agricultural Workers; Boot and Shoe Repairing; Brush and Broom; Catering; Contract Cleaning (Dublin); General Waste Materials Reclamation; Hairdressing (Dublin); Hairdressing (Cork); Handkerchief and Household Piece Goods; Hotels; Law Clerks; Messengers (Dublin); Provender Milling; Shirtmaking; Tailoring; Womens' Clothing and Millinery.
[58] S.I. No. 105 of 1984.
[59] Figures in the Department of Labour's Annual Report for 1984 show that there were 9,081 male workers and 20,046 female workers covered by J.L.C.s.
[60] Low Pay Unit Pamphlet No. 24, *op. cit.*, p. 15. The weight of opinion within the trade union movement, however, is that bodies such as J.L.C.s have inhibited, rather than stimulated, the development of voluntary collective bargaining. It should be noted, however, that when the British Department of Employment commissioned research on the effects of abolition of wages councils the researchers found that voluntary collective bargaining had not developed following abolition and that, in the main, low pay remained a problem. See Department of Employment Research Papers nos. 12, 15 and 18; Craig *et al, Labour Market Structure, Industrial Organisation and Low Pay* (Cambridge, 1982); ACAS Annual Report (1980), p. 58.
[61] See Pond in Bain ed., *op. cit.*, at pp. 200–204.

workers employed in certain trades . . . where no arrangements exist for the effective regulation of wages by collective agreement or otherwise and wages are exceptionally low." Article 4 of the European Social Charter includes the right to a "fair remuneration" and requires that this right "be achieved by freely concluded collective agreements, by statutory wage-fixing machinery, or by other means appropriate to national conditions."

The specific function of a J.L.C. is to submit to the Labour Court proposals for fixing the minimum rates of remuneration or for regulating the conditions of employment of workers covered by the J.L.C.[62] When proposals submitted by a J.L.C. are confirmed by the Labour Court, through the making of an Employment Regulation Order (E.R.O.), they become statutory minimum remuneration and statutory conditions of employment and employers are bound under penalty to pay rates of wages and to grant conditions of employment not less favourable than those prescribed in the E.R.O.[63]

Establishment of a J.L.C.

Section 36 of the 1946 Act provides that an application for the establishment of a J.L.C. may be made to the Court by (a) the Minister, (b) a trade union, or (c) any organisation or group of persons claiming to be representative of the workers and employers in respect of whom the application is made. Where an application is duly made to the Court for an establishment order the Court must consider the application and must be satisfied, in the case of an application made by an organisation or group claiming to be representative, that the claim is well founded.[64] In any case, the Court must be satisfied that either–

(i) there is substantial agreement between the workers and their employers to the establishment of a J.L.C.; or
(ii) the existing machinery for effective regulation of remuneration and other conditions of employment of the workers is inadequate or is likely to cease to be adequate; or
(iii) having regard to the existing rate of remuneration or conditions of employment of any of the workers, it is expedient that a J.L.C. should be established.[65]

---

[62] 1946 Act, s. 42. It should be noted that a J.L.C. is an excepted body for the purposes of the Trade Union Act 1941 (see 1941 Act, s. 6(3)(f), as amended by 1946 Act, s. 56). Similarly bodies which negotiate on a J.L.C. are not, by reason only of so negotiating, required to have a negotiation licence (see Trade Union Act 1942, s. 3(1), as amended by 1946 Act, s. 56).
[63] 1946 Act, s. 44.
[64] S. 37(a).
[65] S. 37(b). So, in respect of the I.C.T.U.'s application for the establishment of a J.L.C. to operate in relation to workers employed by Consultant Engineers and Consultant Architects, the Court, in a decision communicated to the parties on January 10, 1985, declined to make an establishment order because it was not satisfied that the existing machinery for effective regulation of remuneration and other conditions of employment was inadequate.

Where an application is made and the Court is satisfied of any of the above, section 38 of the 1946 Act provides that the Court, after consulting with such parties as it thinks necessary, should prepare a draft establishment order and should publish in the prescribed manner a notice setting out that the Court proposes to hold an inquiry into the application, the day and time and place at which the inquiry will be held, and the place where copies of the draft establishment order may be obtained. Objections to the draft order may be submitted to the Court before the date for the holding of the inquiry.[66] Every such objection must be in writing and must set out the grounds for the objection and the omissions, additions or modifications asked for.[67] The Court must hold the inquiry on the day specified in the notice and the Court must consider any objections to the draft which have been duly submitted.[68]

Where the Court has duly held such an inquiry, the Court "if it thinks fit" may make the order either in terms of the draft order or with such modifications as "it considers necessary".[69] Where an establishment order is made the Court must publish the order and the order shall come into operation on the date on which it is published or such other date, not being later than fourteen days after the date on which it is so published, as is specified therein.[70] The Court is also empowered[71] to abolish or vary the field of operation of an existing J.L.C. Applications to amend an establishment order or abolish a J.L.C. may be made to the Court by (a) the Minister, (b) any trade union, or (c) any organisation or group of persons which claims to be and is, in the Court's opinion, representative of the workers and employers in respect of whom the establishment order is in force. As with the making of an establishment order, the Court must hold an inquiry before making an abolition or amending order. In 1984, four J.L.C.s – Button Making, Messengers (Cork City), Messengers (Limerick City) and Messengers (Waterford City) – were abolished[72] following an application by the Minister for Labour.

Composition and proceedings of a J.L.C.

The provisions with respect to the constitution, officers and proceedings of a J.L.C. are found in the Second Schedule to the 1946 Act. A J.L.C. is to consist of such number of employers' representatives as the Labour Court thinks fit, an equal number of workers' representatives, together with an independent chairman and not more than two other independent persons. The independent members are

---

[66] S. 38(c).
[67] Ibid.
[68] S. 38(d).
[69] S. 39(1).
[70] S. 39(2).
[71] By s. 40.
[72] See S.I. Nos. 39, 40, 41, 42 of 1984.

appointed by the Minister for Labour, the employer and worker representatives by the Labour Court, although paragraph 2(2) of the Schedule provides that before appointing a representative member the Labour Court "so far as it reasonably practicable" must consult any organisation of employers or workers concerned. The independent members hold office "during the pleasure of the Minister", and the Labour Court is empowered "at its discretion" to terminate the membership of a representative member. The Court must terminate the membership of a representative person, when that person ceases, in the opinion of the Court, to be representative of the employers or workers whom he was appointed to represent. Similar provisions apply to the membership of the agricultural workers' J.L.C. except that here section 5 of the Industrial Relations Act 1976 provides that the chairman and independent members are to be appointed by the Minister with the consent of the Minister for Agriculture and the representative members are to be appointed by the Court from a panel prepared and presented to the Court by the Minister after consulting with organisations representative of agricultural employers and agricultural workers and with the consent of the Minister for Agriculture.

In order to constitute a meeting of a J.L.C. at least one independent member and at least one-third of the whole number of the representative members must be present. Every member has one vote, but if at any meeting of a J.L.C. the group of employers' members does not equal in number the group of worker members, whichever of the said groups is in the majority may arrange that any one or more of its number shall refrain from voting so as to preserve equality. If no such arrangement is arrived at, the chairman of the J.L.C. may adjourn the voting to another meeting of the J.L.C. The use of the word "may" suggests that the J.L.C. has a discretion in this matter but, as the Supreme Court decision in *Burke* v. *Minister for Labour*[73] demonstrates, this discretion is considerably qualified by notions of justice and fairness. That there may be votes where the employer and worker members are not equal in number is foreseen by paragraph 6(3) which provides that the chairman has a second or casting vote on any question in which the voting is otherwise equal. Paragraph 9 further provides that any member of the Labour Court may be present at a meeting of a J.L.C. and has the right to take part in the proceedings but does not have the right to vote.

Paragraph 7 provides that a J.L.C. shall meet at such times and places as it may from time to time determine to be suitable for the discharge of its functions. Save otherwise than is provided by the 1946 Act, a J.L.C. can adopt such procedure at its meetings and otherwise,

---

[73] [1979] I.R. 354.
[74] See Henchy J. at 361.

as it may determine to be suitable. Although the Supreme Court made it clear in *Burke* v. *Minister for Labour* that this discretion was considerably fettered, they did indicate that it was well within the competence of a J.L.C. to decide that motions did not require formal votes of acceptance or rejection.[74]

Employment regulation orders

The function of a J.L.C. is to submit proposals to the Labour Court for Orders, known as Employment Regulation Orders, fixing rates of pay and conditions of employment for all or any of the employees covered. Sections 42–44 of the 1946 Act set out the procedure which must be followed. The initiative for the making of an E.R.O. is set in motion when the J.L.C. submits proposals to the Labour Court.

When the Labour Court receives the proposals, it may, if it thinks fit, refer the proposals back to the J.L.C. with such observations thereon as the Labour Court thinks proper, and in that case the J.L.C. shall reconsider the proposals having regard to such observations and may, if it thinks fit, re-submit the proposals to the Labour Court either without amendment or with such amendments as it thinks fit having regard to those observations. If the Labour Court does not so refer the proposals back to the J.L.C. or, having so referred them back, the J.L.C. re-submit them to the Labour Court with or without amendment, the Labour Court must then publish a notice as to the proposals and stating that representations may be made within twenty-one days. If representations are made within the twenty-one days, the J.L.C. must consider them and may, if it thinks fit, re-submit the proposals with or without amendment to the Labour Court. Where the notice is published and either no representations are made or the J.L.C. re-submit the proposals, the Labour Court, as it thinks fit, may either make an order giving effect to the proposals as from such date (subsequent to the date of the order) as the Court thinks proper and specifies in the order, or refuse to make an order. The Commission of Inquiry on Industrial Relations estimated that it normally takes "about six weeks" before proposals emanating from a J.L.C. could be embodied in an E.R.O.[75]

In *Burke* v. *Minister for Labour*[76] Henchy J., with whom the other members of the Supreme Court[77] agreed, said that the power to make an E.R.O. was "a delegated power of a most fundamental, permissive and far-reaching kind."[78] He continued:

"By the above provisions of the Act of 1946 Parliament, without reserving to itself a power of supervision or a power of revocation or

---

[75] At para. 573 of its *Report* (Pl. 114).
[76] [1979] I.R. 354.
[77] O'Higgins C.J., Griffin, Kenny and Parke JJ.
[78] At 358.

cancellation (which would apply if the order had to be laid on the table of either House before it could have statutory effect) has vested in a joint labour committee and the Labour Court the conjoint power to fix minimum rates of remuneration so that non-payment thereof will render employers liable to conviction and fine and (in the case of conviction) to being made compellable by court order to pay the amount fixed by the order of the Labour Court. Not alone is this power given irrevocably and without parliamentary, or even ministerial, control, but once such an order is made (no matter how erroneous, ill-judged or unfair it may be) a joint labour committee is debarred from submitting proposals for revoking or amending it until it has been in force for at least six months. While the parent statute may be amended or repealed at any time, the order, whose authors are not even the direct delegates of Parliament, must stand irrevocably in force for well over six months."[79]

In this case, an E.R.O., in respect of those employed in the hotel industry, was impugned by two of the employer representatives on the J.L.C. They did not challenge the order on constitutional grounds but merely submitted that the J.L.C. had not exercised its powers justly and fairly and that therefore the order was tainted by illegality. The core of the complaint was that, whilst the J.L.C. took into account the increases to which the employees were entitled under the national wage agreement of 1977, they left out of the reckoning completely the case which the employer representatives tried to make for increases in the values which the E.R.O. should attribute to board and lodgings supplied to employees and deductible from gross earnings. The employer representatives had proposed that the values of board and lodgings should be fixed having regard to their cost to the employer. It was manifest from the minutes of meetings held that a majority of the members repeatedly set their face against such a proposal.

The Supreme Court unanimously took the view that the J.L.C. were not entitled to make an E.R.O. without paying some regard to the real cost to the employers of board and lodging supplied. Henchy J. said:

"As I have earlier observed, the delegated power that was vested in the Committee was of the most extensive nature. It enabled the Committee to formulate the proposals for an order fixing minimum rates of remuneration. All the Labour Court could do was to refer the proposals back to the Committee with observations. The Labour Court is given no power of initiation or amendment. It could but make or refuse to make the Order. Essentially, therefore, the order-making body was the Committee. Apart from the skeletal provisions in the second schedule to the Act of 1946 as to its constitution,

[79] At 358–359.

officers and proceedings, the Act of 1946 is silent as to how a committee are to carry out their functions in making orders.

Where Parliament has delegated functions of that nature, it is to be be necessarily inferred as part of the legislative intention that the body which makes the orders will exercise its functions, not only wish constitutional propriety and due regard to natural justice, but also within the framework of the terms and objects of the relevant Act and with basic fairness, reasonableness and good faith. The absoluteness of the delegation is susceptible of unjust and tyrannous abuse unless its operation is thus confined; so it is entirely proper to ascribe to the Oireachtas (being the Parliament of a State which is constitutionally bound to protect, by its laws, its citizens from unjust attack) an intention that the delegated functions must be exercised within those limitations.

Here the Committee undertook the task of making a statutory instrument fixing minimum rates of remuneration for certain workers in the hotel industry. The representatives of employers in the hotel industry, as members of the Committee, wished the Committee to give consideration, before such an order was made, to the actual cost to employers of board and lodging supplied to workers. That was an eminently reasonable proposal. It was not possible to assess a fair and reasonable figure for minimum remuneration until a fair and reasonable assessment was made of the gross value of cash remuneration plus board and lodging. By the self-denying restraint by which the Committee debarred themselves from looking at the data necessary to determine the true cost to the employer of board and lodging, the Committee left themselves open to the charge that the consequent minimum-remuneration order may be unjust and unfair.

It is no answer to that charge to say that the Committee were following the practice adopted previously before such orders were made. Two wrongs do not make a right; but in this case there was the difference that the Committee were specifically and repeatedly asked to receive and have regard to evidence as to the cost of the benefits which the workers were getting in the form of board and lodging. Nor is it a good answer to say that, if the Committee had taken into account the true, rather than the estimated, cost of board and lodging, the figures fixed as minimum rates of remuneration would not have been materially affected. As the Committee did not hear such evidence, it is impossible to say what effect such evidence would have had on them. Even if such evidence would have made no difference, the Committee, by rejecting it unheard and unconsidered, left themselves open to the imputation of bias, unfairness and prejudice. Such accusations, if made, would be unmerited; the members of the Committee were, no doubt, all acting in good faith and to the best of their abilities.

However, the fact is that the Committee, in formulating the proposals for the order of 1978, was acting as an unelected body, functioning behind closed doors, to produce a statutory order fixing minimum rates of remuneration which could not be varied for at least six months, and non-compliance with it could lead to criminal responsibility and civil compellability. Elementary fairness required that the employers as well as the employees, both of whom were represented on the Committee, should have been allowed to preent and to see consideration given to material which was crucially relevant to the question of minimum rates of remuneration.

By failing to receive and consider that evidence, the Committee failed to keep within the confines of their statutory terms of reference as those must necessarily be inferred. In other words, the order of 1978 was made in excess of jurisdiction to that extent."[80]

Under section 43(1)(*d*) an E.R.O. has effect only from a date *subsequent* to the date of its making. The Commission of Inquiry on Industrial Relations accepted suggestions that J.L.C.s should have the power to make E.R.O.s retrospective and recommended the introduction of amending legislation.[81] Such a change was introduced in Northern Ireland in 1981 where the legislation now provides that the operative date may be earlier than the date on which the prescribed period for receipt of written representations to the proposals ended. Opposition to such a change could be anticipated on the ground that to permit the issue of retrospective E.R.O.s would cause problems for smaller employers who would be faced with increased expenditure which they had not foreseen.

When an order is made fixing a statutory minimum remuneration an employer must pay at least that remuneration and in case the order fixes conditions of employment, grant conditions of employment at least as favourable. If an employer fails to do so, he is guilty of an offence and is liable on summary conviction thereof to a fine not exceeding £50.[82] Furthermore, on conviction, the employer may be ordered by the court to pay the employee the difference between the statutory minimum remuneration and the remuneration actually paid and, where the employer has not complied with the statutory conditions, the court may order the employer to pay such compensation as it considers fair and reasonable in respect of such non compliance.[83] Remuneration, for the purpose of the relevant statutory provisions, is to be construed as the amount obtained or to be obtained in cash clear of all deductions in respect of any matter whatsoever, except for deductions lawfully made under any enactment.[84] This, however, is

[80] At 361–363.
[81] At para. 576 of its *Report* (Pl. 114).
[82] S. 65(1) and (3).
[83] S. 45(2) and (3)(*b*).
[84] S. 47(1).

subject to the proviso that, subject to any enactment for the time being in force, the order may authorise specified benefits or advantages to be reckoned as payment of remuneration in lieu of payment in cash and the order shall define the monetary value of such benefit of advantage.[85]

Moreover, section 44(2) provides that if the contract of employment of an employee to whom an E.R.O. applies provides for the payment of less remuneration than the statutory minimum remuneration, or for less favourable conditions of employment, then that contract shall have effect as if the statutory minimum remuneration and the statutory conditions of employment were substituted for the contract remuneration or conditions. This enables the employee to enforce his statutory entitlement in the civil courts, and section 45(7) provides that the powers given by the section to the court to order compensation in criminal proceedings "shall not be in derogation of any right of the worker to recover such sums in court proceedings."

A limited provision exists for exemption in respect of special circumstances concerning employees suffering from infirmity or physical incapacity.[86] If the appropriate J.L.C. is satisfied, on application being made to it, that an employee is affected by infirmity or physical incapacity such that it renders him incapable of earning the statutory minimum remuneration, it may, if it thinks fit, grant, subject to such conditions (if any) as it may determine, a permit authorising his employment at less than the statutory minimum remuneration. While such permit is in force the remuneration authorised to be said to him by the permit shall be deemed, if the conditions are complied with, to be the statutory minimum remuneration.

Section 57 gives the Labour Court jurisdiction to determine, on the application of any person,[87] at any time,[88] whether a particular J.L.C. operates as respects a particular person or whether a particular E.R.O. applies to a particular person. Subsection (2) of section 57 provides that a court of law, in determining any question arising in proceedings before it as to whether a particular E.R.O. applies to a particular person, or a particular J.L.C. operates as respects a particular person, "shall have regard" to any decision of the Labour Court referred to it in the course of the proceedings. Subsection (3) provides that if any question arises in proceedings before a court of law as to whether a J.L.C. operates, or a particular E.R.O. applies, to a particular person, that court may, if it thinks proper, refer the question

---

[85] S. 47(2).
[86] S. 46.
[87] Including a trade union, see Determination 1/1982, *Fletchers Killeshandra Ltd.* and *Irish Transport and General Workers' Union*.
[88] Either in the course of pay negotiations – see Determination 2/1983, *John Brady & Son Ltd. and Two Workers* – or redundancy – see Determination 1/1983, *Robert J. Crane and One Worker*.

to the Labour Court for its decision and the decision of the Labour Court thereon is stated to be "final".[89]

An employer to whom an E.R.O. applies is obliged by section 49 to keep "such records as are necessary" to show whether he had complied with the E.R.O., and must retain these records for three years. The employer is also obliged to put up notices in the place of work setting out particulars of the statutory rates of remuneration and conditions of employment.[90] Failure to keep or retain the required records or to put up the prescribed notices is an offence punishable on summary conviction by a fine not exceeding £20.

E.R.O.s are enforced by inspectors appointed for this purpose by the Minister. These inspectors are empowered by section 52 to enter premises, inspect wage sheets and other records, examine the employers and employees concerned and institute proceedings. The obstruction or impeding of inspectors, refusal to produce records and wilfully failing or refusing to comply with any lawful requirement of an inspector is an offence punishable on summary conviction by a fine not exceeding £20.[91]

WORKER PARTICIPATION

A large measure of employee participation in company decision making can be achieved through collective bargaining. There is a range of issues however which collective bargaining alone cannot reach. Decisions on investment, location or product specialisation, for example, are taken at levels where collective bargaining does not take place. Many would doubt, indeed, that such issues are suited to the collective bargaining process which is, by nature, adversarial. Nevertheless major decisions about the nature of a company's organisation can affect closely the persons they employ and, indeed, the community in which they operate. Under present company law directors of a company must act *bona fide* in what they consider is in the interests of the company. They are only entitled to have regard to the interests of the present and future members of the company – its shareholders. The interests of their employees, the consumers of its product or the community as a whole are legally irrelevant.[92] Nevertheless most directors implicitly accept that they must take account of the interests of their employees.

Over the past fifteen years, considerable attention has been given to the establishment of mechanisms which could provide a greater degree

---

[89] On the constitutionality of such provision see *supra*, pp. 47–48.
[90] Industrial Relations Act 1976, s. 7, provides that s. 49(2) of the 1946 Act, which relates to the posting of notices, shall not apply to agricultural employers.
[91] In Northern Ireland the maximum fine for obstructing an Inspector is £100 (sterling). Furthermore the maximum fine for keeping false records is £400 and for not keeping records £100.
[92] See *Parke* v. *Daily News* [1962] Ch. 927.

of employee involvement in decisions affecting their working lives.[93] Much of the impetus for this is derived from the social, industrial and economic changes that have occurred over the last two decades. Of considerable importance also has been the experience of our European partners, most of whom have recognised what the Commission of the European Communities has dubbed[94] "the democratic imperative" that "those who will be substantially affected by decisions made by social and political institutions must be involved in the making of these decisions" and have implemented measures which make possible the representation of employees on company boards.[95]

Of particular significance are the European Commission's controversial proposals for a Fifth Directive on company law providing for worker participation in the decision making process.[96] After a long series of delays, amendments and revisions, the Commission's proposals were finalised in 1984 and formally submitted to the Council of Ministers. The revised proposals take into account the diversity of company structure in Europe, while at the same time preserving the fundamental concept that there should be a clear division between the function of management and the function of supervision. It is proposed that national laws may either impose a two tier system, *i.e.* a supervisory board and a management board each with carefully defined powers, or may permit the company itself to choose either a two tier system or a one tier system, *i.e.* a single administrative board in which a distinction is drawn between the executive board members, who exercise the function of management, and the non-executive board members who exercise the function of supervision.

The revised proposals adopt a flexible approach with four possible options for participation. Participation in one of these forms will be mandatory for undertakings which, directly or indirectly, employ over 1,000 people in the E.E.C. The four participation options are as follows:

(1) Employee participation by employee representation on the supervisory board or on the unitary administrative board. The number of employee representatives must be between one-third and one-half of the supervisory members or of the non-executive directors;

---

[93] See the I.C.T.U. *Annual Reports* of 1967 and 1968 at pp. 165 and 221 respectively; the interim and final Reports of the Committee on Industrial Relations on the Electricity Supply Board (1968 and 1969); the Department of Labour's White Paper *Election of Employees to the Boards of State Enterprises* (1975); the Department of Labour's Discussion Paper on *Worker Participation* (1980).

[94] In their Green Paper *Employee Participation and Company Structure*, Bulletin of the E.C., Supplement 8/75 at p. 9.

[95] See Batstone and Davies, *Industrial Democracy: European Experience*. Two reports prepared for the Committee of Inquiry on Industrial Democracy (H.M.S.O., 1976)

[96] First published in 1972, Bulletin of the E.C., Supplement 10/72, modified in 1975, Bulletin of the E.C., Supplement 8/75, and subsequently considerably revised. For the current text see O.J. C240/2, 9.9.83.

(2) Employee participation on a supervisory board appointed by co-option;
(3) Employee participation by the creation at company level of separate body comprised solely of employee representatives. Such a body will be limited to rights of consultation and information analogous to those of a supervisory board.
(4) Participation by means of systems agreed by collective bargaining. The results of such collective agreements must correspond to the minimum common principles of the other three options.

The Worker Participation (State Enterprises) Act 1977 marked a significant initiative in this matter. The Act provides for the election of employees to the boards of directors of seven designated State enterprises.[97] The then Minister for Labour was insistent that this was the beginning of a much more comprehensive strategy which would be extended to other state enterprises and then to the private sector and which would also create a new climate of participation.[98] Subsequently, in the Postal and Telecommunications Services Act 1983,[99] provision was made for the election of worker directors to the Boards of An Post and Bord Telecom Éireann;[1] and speaking in the Dáil in June 1984, the Minister for Labour announced[2] that the Government had decided to improve and extend the 1977 Act to a further six State enterprises.[3] Moreover, the Minister also announced that legislation will be introduced requiring State enterprises to establish sub-board structures on a request by a majority of the employees. Such sub-board structures would help worker directors communicate back with those who elected them and would allow them to raise issues with executive management. The Minister envisaged that this would be an enabling measure giving support to employee influence but not regulating in detail how decisions should be made or what decisions should be reached. These issues could be developed through complementary collective agreements. Subsequently, in March 1985, the Minister announced the establishment of an Advisory Committee on Worker Participation.[4] The Committee is composed of representatives of employers, trade unions and government and persons with practical experience of

---

[97] Bord na Móna, Córas Iompair Éireann, Electricity Supply Board, Aer Lingus Teo. British & Irish Steam Packet Co. Ltd., Comhlucht Siuicre Éireann Teo., Nitrigin Éireann Teo.
[98] In an address to the I.C.T.U. annual summer school, July 14, 1974. Cited by McCarthy, "Worker Participation in Decisions Within the Enterprise", National Report (Ireland) to the International Society for Labour Law and Social Security (1982), para. 1.41.
[99] In s. 34.
[1] The polling days for the first elections in Bord Telecom Éireann and An Post are September 20, and September 25, 1985 respectively.
[2] 352 Dáil Debates c. 430.
[3] Aer Rianta, Bord Gáis Éireann, An Foras Forbatha, the National Rehabilitation Board, Irish Steel Ltd., and the Voluntary Health Insurance Board.
[4] The Committee is to report by February 1986.

implementing worker participation programmes at company level. The purpose of the Committee is to advise the Minister on the scope of the development of employee participation at sub-board level in different types of work organisation; promote interest in practical experimentation in workplace participation; identify research need and make recommendations.

The 1977 Act provides[5] that one-third of the board members should be worker representatives and that, while trade unions would have the right to nominate the candidates for election,[6] the electorate would consist of all the workers in the enterprise (provided they were over 18 and had been continuously employed for at least a year).[7] All seven enterprises have now twice elected four representatives of workers to their boards (with five having had three elections) and a report published in 1980 by the European Foundations for the Improvement of Living and Working Conditions indicated that the practice has worked "reasonably well".[8] The worker directors themselves are satisfied that they have been accepted at board level and have been able to influence decisions by providing the board with constructive proposals and information about the aspirations and frustrations of the employees.

Elections under the 1977 Act are held every three years.[9] The first election for the E.S.B., Bord na Móna and the B. & I. Steam Packet Co. Ltd. was in December 1978, for Nitrogen Éireann Teo. in April 1979, for the Irish Sugar Company in July 1979, for C.I.E. in October 1980 and for Aer Lingus in April 1981.[10] Where an election is contested, the poll is taken by secret ballot and according to the principle of proportional representation.[11] Section 10 provides that, where an election is contested, every person whose name is on the relevant list of electors and who is, on the day fixed for the taking of the poll at the election, an employee[12] of the enterprise to which the election relates shall be entitled to one vote.

---

[5] S. 23(2).
[6] S. 11.
[7] S. 10.
[8] Murphy and Walsh, *The Worker Director and his Impact on the Enterprise – Expectations, Experience and Effectiveness in Seven Irish Companies* (Dublin, 1980).
[9] S. 6(1)(*b*). At the time of writing there have been three elections in B. & I., E.S.B., Bord na Móna, N.E.T., C.S.E.T., and two in C.I.E. and Aer Lingus.
[10] The percentage poll in the first elections ranged between 97% (N.E.T.) to 54% (E.S.B.), in the second between 96% (N.E.T.) and 72% (C.I.E.) and in the third between 97% (N.E.T.) to 70% (E.S.B.). For full details see the Department of Labour's Annual Report for 1984 at pp. 59–61.
[11] S. 9(3). The system used is that of the single transferable vote.
[12] Defined in s. 1 as a person employed in a whole-time capacity under a contract of service or apprenticeship. For the purpose of s. 10 a person employed in such a capacity by Aerlinte Teo. under such a contract shall be regarded as being an employee of Aer Lingus Teo. Furthermore s. 10(4) specifically provides that the fact that an employee is on secondment to another body or person shall neither disentitle him to vote, nor have his name entered on the list of electors.

The list of electors is prepared and maintained by the "returning officer" of the enterprise in question. Section 7(1) provides that the "returning officer" shall be:

"(a) the secretary of the body, or in case there is no such secretary, the officer of the body who performs the functions of secretary of the body, or

(b) in lieu of such secretary or officer, any other person who in the opinion of such secretary or officer is both competent to perform the functions of returning officer and acceptable to –

(i) a trade union or other body of persons which the secretary or officer is satisfied is both recognised by the designated body for the purposes of collective bargaining and representative of a majority of the employees of the body, or

(ii) two or more trade unions or other bodies of persons which the secretary or officer is satisfied between them collectively represent a majority of such employees and as regards each of which the secretary or officer is satisfied that the body is so recognised."

Section 7(3) provides that the returning officer shall not be entitled to be nominated as, or to nominate, a candidate, at the election.

The returning officer, not later than seventy days before the day fixed for the receipt of nominations, must fix a day which is referred to in the Act as the "stated day", being a day which is neither earlier than the fifty-sixth nor later than the forty-second day before the nomination day.[13] Every person who on the "stated day" is a full-time employee of the relevant enterprise and who, on that day, is not less than eighteen years of age and has, for a continuous period of not less than one year before that day, been such an employee, is entitled to have his name entered on the list of electors.[14] The age, status and continuous service requirements are the only matters of which the returning officer has to be satisfied.[15]

As well as fixing the "stated day", the returning officer must also fix the period or periods during which nominations will be received on the nomination day.[16] This period, or the aggregate of the periods, must not be less than three hours.[17] At any time during the period or periods so fixed, any trade union or other body of persons which is a "qualified body" may propose for nomination as candidates at the election persons each of whom must be a full time employee, aged between 18

---

[13] S. 8(a).
[14] S. 10(2).
[15] Ibid.
[16] S. 8(b).
[17] Ibid.

and 65, who has been continuously employed for three years.[18] Such persons can be jointly proposed for nomination by two or more qualified bodies with the proviso that a qualified body is not entitled both to nominate one or more candidates of its own accord and to nominate one or more candidates jointly with another qualified body.[19] Furthermore a qualified body, other than a qualified body by whom a candidate of an election is jointly or otherwise nominated, may, with the agreement of the body or bodies by whom the candidate is nominated, notify the returning officer that the body supports the candidate and the fact of that support shall be indicated in the prescribed manner on the relevant ballot papers.[20]

When the period for receiving nominations expires, the returning officer must rule, "as soon as may be", on the validity of each nomination received.[21] Only if he is satisfied that the nominated person is not qualified for nomination, or that the nomination is not properly made out or subscribed, or that the afore-mentioned proviso has been contravened, is the returning officer entitled to rule that the nomination is invalid, and his ruling is stated to be final and unappealable.[22]

The returning officer of C.I.E. had to make such a ruling during the second election there. One of the candidates nominated for election was on strike on the nomination day. Despite objections, his nomination was accepted as valid. Subsequently, however, and before the polling day, he was dismissed. The returning officer took the view that, although the person was required to be an employee on the "stated day" and the nomination day[23] nothing in the Act required that he be an employee on the polling day and ruled that, notwithstanding his dismissal, the candidate was to be allowed to go forward for election. It should be noted, however, that section 16 provides that where between the ascertainment of the result and the day on which the board next meets, a candidate elected at an election ceases to be an employee, the appointment of that candidate as a worker director shall not be made, and, in case such appointment has been made, the appointment shall cease to have effect.

Section 11(6) provides that a trade union or any other body of persons shall be deemed a "qualified body" if, and only if, the returning

---

[18] S. 11(1). Nominations must be made in writing and be on the prescribed form and be sent to the returning officer in the prescribed manner, s. 11(3).

[19] S. 11(2). In the second election of Aer Lingus in April 1984 one of the candidates was jointly nominated by N.E.E.T.U., A.G.E.M.O.U., A.U.E.W., E.E.T.P.U., N.U.S.M.W.I. and N.U.W.W.M.

[20] S. 11(5). In the second election at Aer Lingus in April 1984 one of the candidates nominated by the F.W.U.I. was supported by the N.U.J.

[21] S. 11(4).

[22] *Ibid.* It may of course be reviewed in the High Court by way of *certiorari*. For consideration of the constitutionality of comparable statutory provisions, see *supra*, pp. 47–48.

[23] S. 11(1) provides that a qualified body may nominate a person who *is* an employee . . . *etc.*

officer is satisfied that, on the nomination day, the trade union or other body is recognised for the purposes of collective bargaining negotiations by the enterprise to which the election relates. If there is any dispute as to whether a trade union or other body is a "qualified body" the dispute shall be determined by the returning officer "whose decision shall be final and shall not be appealable".[24]

During the second election at Aer Lingus such a dispute arose. One of the candidates for election was employed by Aer Lingus in Britain and was nominated by A.S.T.M.S. Other nominating bodies objected to a British union nominating a British employee but the returning officer was satisfied that A.S.T.M.S. was a qualified body and that the candidate was qualified for nomination, there being nothing in the Act preventing the nomination of aliens nor restricting the meaning of "qualified body" to the exclusion of foreign unions.

If, at the end of the period during which nominations are to be received, the number of duly nominated candidates does not exceed the number which, as regards the enterprise concerned, is appropriate, the returning officer shall forthwith declare each of such candidates to be elected.[25] If there are less candidates than there are places to be filled the vacancy may be filled by a person appointed by the Minister.[26] If, however, the number standing does exceed the appropriate number the returning officer must fix a "polling day", which must not be earlier than the seventh day after the nomination day.[27] Alternatively, if it is decided to use postal votes, the returning officer shall fix a polling period of more than one but not more than five days, the first of which must not be earlier than the seventh day after the nomination day.[28] It is important to note that, if a "polling day" is fixed, votes, other than postal votes, may only be cast during the period on the particular day which the polling officer has fixed for that purpose.[29]

If there is to be a poll the returning officer must give notice, in such a manner as he considers appropriate, of —

(a) the polling day in the polling period, as may be appropriate;
(b) the place or places at which, the day or days on which and the hours during which votes, other than postal votes, may be cast;
(c) in case a polling period is fixed, the place at which and the period during which and before the expiration of which postal ballot papers are to be received by or on behalf of the returning officer, and

---

[24] S. 11(7). See fn. 22 *supra*.
[25] S. 12(1).
[26] S. 22(1).
[27] S. 12(1).
[28] *Ibid.*
[29] S. 12(3). If a "polling day" is fixed, postal votes cannot be used. They can only be used if a "polling period" is fixed.

(d) the names and descriptions of the candidates as entered on their nomination forms, and of the proposers.[30]

It is also the duty of the returning officer to provide such ballot boxes, ballot papers and other things and appoint such persons and do such other acts and things as may be necessary for effectively taking the poll.[31]

Section 13 provides a procedure where one or more "qualified bodies", *i.e.* trade unions or other bodies recognised for collective bargaining purposes, representing, individually or collectively, not less than 15% of the employees of the enterprise in question, may object to the holding of an election. If the returning officer receives, during the period of seven days beginning on the "stated day", an application in writing requesting him not to proceed with the election, he must arrange forthwith for the taking of a preliminary poll to ascertain whether a majority of those entitled to vote[32] is in favour of proceeding with the election.[33] If the majority of the votes at this preliminary poll is against proceeding further with the election the returning officer shall not proceed further with the election.[34] If not less than half of the votes at the poll are in favour of proceeding with the election, the returning officer shall proceed with the election.[35]

Once the relevant Minister has been informed of the names of the candidates elected or declared to have been elected at the election, he must make, "as soon as may be", an appointment in respect of each of these candidates in relation to the enterprise as regards which the election was held.[36] The term of office of elected directors is effectively three years, unless they sooner die, resign or become disqualified.[37] Section 17(3) provides that the elected directors are eligible for renomination and re-election. Where a vacancy occurs by reason of death, resignation or disqualification the vacancy may be filled by a person appointed by the appropriate Minister[38] and that person, unless he sooner dies, resigns or is disqualified, holds the office for the remainder of the period for which the person occasioning the vacancy would have held office if he had continued.[39] Section 22(2) provides however, that in appointing a person to fill a vacancy, the appropriate Minister must have regard to the poll at the last election.

As regards the remuneration of worker directors, section 18(2)

---

[30] S. 12(4).
[31] *Ibid.*
[32] To vote at the preliminary poll one must be on the relevant list of electors.
[33] A preliminary poll was held in B. and I. in October 1978. 80% of poll voted in favour of proceeding with the main election.
[34] S. 13(5). Spoilt, blank or marked ballot papers are not counted, s. 13(3)(*e*).
[35] S. 13(6). The returning officer is also empowered to fix a new "nomination day".
[36] S. 16(1).
[37] S. 17.
[38] S. 22(1).
[39] S. 22(3).

provides that such persons shall not suffer any reduction in the remuneration and allowances which, as an employee, he would, if he were not a director, normally expect to receive. Worker directors are not to be treated any differently than other directors and the usual rules of company law as to disclosure of interests, voting and confidentiality apply.

DISCLOSURE OF INFORMATION

Collective bargaining is not simply about negotiating increases in wages and improvements of working conditions. It is also a means whereby trade unions can extend the area of their involvement and influence over factors which affect their members' working lives. If trade unions are to negotiate effectively with management they need an adequate informational base to allow them to form an independent judgment on management proposals and policies. Some companies do provide information, recognising that it constitutes a key resource for the conduct of constructive bargaining and negotiation. Others however, prefer to operate on the basis of concealment viewing with distaste the idea of even giving unions information which in fact is freely available in the company's annual return.[40] There can be no doubt that part of good industrial relations practice is the disclosure of information by employers to assist trade union representatives in collective bargaining. Indeed the I.L.O. in 1981 adopted a recommendation concerning the promotion of collective bargaining which contains a provision that employers, at the request of a trade union representative, "should make available such information as is necessary in the economic and social situation of the negotiation unit and the undertaking as a whole, to the extent to which its disclosure is not prejudicial to the undertaking."[41]

In most member states of the E.E.C., employers are required to provide employee representatives with information which is needed for meaningful negotiation on conditions of employment. At present, in Ireland, there is no general legal obligation on an employer to disclose

---

[40] Every registered company is required to give the public information relating to its constitution, the officials and its capital structure by filing these matters with the registrar of companies (Companies Act 1963, ss. 17, 195, 47). In addition the 1963 Act provides in s. 125 for an annual return to be made to the registrar. On payment of such fee as may be fixed by the Minister (currently 50p.) *any person* may inspect the documents kept by the registrar of companies (s. 370). The particulars required to be shown in the annual return are set out in the Fifth Schedule to the 1963 Act with minor additions made by the Companies Acts 1982 and 1983. They include the balance sheet, the auditors' report and the directors' report. The belated implementation of the E.E.C. Fourth Directive on Company Law (No. 78/660) by means of the Companies (Amendment) Bill 1985 (on which see Kelleher, (1985) 3 *I.L.T. (n.s.)* 164) will considerably affect the public disclosure requirements. The Bill was presented on May 29, 1985. Companies which are quoted on the Stock Exchange must also comply with the European Communities (Stock Exchange) Regulations 1984 (S.I. No. 282 of 1984) and register certain information with the registrar of companies (reg. 13).

[41] This recommendation was adopted at the I.L.O.'s 67th Session.

any information to his employees or their trade union representatives. The Second National Understanding on Economic and Social Development provided for the drafting of a voluntary code of practice on disclosure designed to improve employee knowledge of company affairs and facilitate responsible collective bargaining.[42] A draft code of practice was prepared by the Department of Labour and was circulated in June 1981 to the I.C.T.U. and F.U.E. for their comments. Further progress has not been spectacular and in the 1983 Discussion Document on Industrial Relations Reform the Minister has indicated that it would be "useful to discuss the possibility of the *mandatory* provision of certain information to employees in firms of a certain size."[43]

Regardless of what emerges from those discussions, some legislation on information disclosure will have to be introduced to comply with the proposed E.E.C. Council Directive on procedures for informing and consulting employees.[44] The Commission's original proposal[45] on procedures for informing and consulting employees of undertakings with complex structures aroused considerable debate and lobbying and an amended proposal was adopted by the Commission and submitted to the Council in July 1983[46] which incorporates the Opinions delivered by the European Parliament[47] and the Economic and Social Committee.[48] According to the amended proposal, the directive would apply both to groups of companies and to single undertakings operating through geographically distinct plants which employ as a whole at least 1,000 workers in the E.E.C. Management of a parent undertaking would be obliged to provide general but explicit information[49] to the management of each of its subsidiaries in the E.E.C., with a view to the communication of this information to the employees' representatives. Additionally management of the parent undertaking would be obliged to forward precise information[50] to the management of each of the subsidiaries where it proposed to take a decision concerning the whole or a major part of the parent undertaking, or a subsidiary, liable to have serious consequences for

---

[42] (1980), para. 19.
[43] At p. 52.
[44] Popularly known as the Vredeling proposal, after Mr. H. Vredeling the Social Affairs Commissioner of the E.E.C. at the time the draft was initially accepted by the Commission in November 1980. For a detailed account of the progress of the draft directive up to June 1983 see Blanpain, Blanquet, Herman and Mouty, *The Vredeling Proposal* (Kluwer, 1983).
[45] O. J. C297/3, 15.11.1980 (Bulletin of the E.C., Supplement 3/80).
[46] O.J. C217/3, 12.8.1983.
[47] O.J. C292/33, 8.11.1982; O.J. C13/25, 17.1.1983.
[48] O.J. C77/6, 29.3.1982.
[49] Relating in particular to the undertaking's structure; its economic and financial situation; the probable development of the business and of production and sales; the employment situation and probable trends; and investment prospects.
[50] Giving details of the reasons for the decision; its legal, economic and social consequences; and the measures planned for the employees.

the interests of the employees of its subsidiaries in the E.E.C.[51] This information would have to be forwarded in good time so that consultation could take place with the employees' representatives, such consultation being "with a view to reaching agreement".

The amended proposals continued to attract controversy and a number of anomalies were identified, the most serious being that while the draft applied to enterprises with a complex, and in particular a multinational structure, it did not apply to large-scale enterprises operating as one unit. While a number of member states, such as the United Kingdom, already have legislation on information disclosure,[52] others, such as Ireland, do not. Logically the directive should cover all E.E.C. based undertakings above a certain size. On the initiative of the Minister for Labour, as President of the Council of Ministers for Social Affairs, a decision was taken in July 1984 to set up a Working Group on the draft directive. This Working Group met on a number of occasions and submitted a report which was forwarded to the Permanent Representatives Committee for examination by the Social Affairs Council, in December 1984.

Under a suggested revised draft[53] the Directive will cover all E.E.C. based undertakings of a certain size and uniform information and consultation arrangements are to be introduced for national and transnational undertakings whatever their structure. One important feature of the revised draft is that it permits the implementation of information and consultation procedures through collective agreements, provided the collectively agreed procedures assure a similar standard of performance to those laid down in the Directive. The revised draft avoids the lack of equivalence in terms and conditions of employment as between workers within and without complex structure enterprises. The starting point is now the right of an employee to receive information, not a duty on a particular undertaking to give information. It is now a Directive much more clearly concerned with social policy.

---

[51] Examples of such a decision would be the closure of an establishment or a major part thereof; major modification with regard to organisation, working practices or production methods; and the introduction of long-term co-operation with other undertakings.

[52] In Northern Ireland by virtue of articles 50–54 of the Industrial Relations (no. 2) Order 1976, and in Britain by virtue of ss. 17–21 of the Employment Protection Act 1975. Generally, see Gospel, "Disclosure of Information to Trade Unions" (1976) 5 *I.L.J.* 223.

[53] See (1985) 133 *European Industrial Relations Review* 6.

Chapter 8

LIABILITY IN RESPECT OF INDUSTRIAL ACTION

Introduction

Industrial action, in whichever of its many forms, invariably causes damage or inconvenience both to the employees involved in or laid off as a result of industrial action[1] and the employer in dispute and, occasionally, other employers and the general public. In all liberal democratic societies, however, the ability of employees to combine and withdraw their labour is considered to be a fundamental freedom alongside the freedom to organise, assemble and express one's opinion.[2] Moreover the development of an autonomous system of collective bargaining presupposes the access of both sides to autonomous social sanctions if the bargaining process fails to result in agreement. The ability of employees to engage in industrial action is an essential part of the collective bargaining process.

The extent to which the law can and should exercise control over this ability is a matter of vital political and social concern. Arguments about the ability to strike and the extent to which the law should restrict or permit it are invariably based on the assumption that some freedom to strike is desirable and the further assumption that this freedom is to be used responsibly. It is not the authors' intention to enter into this debate here. Our purpose is to set out the extent to which the law does exercise control over this ability and to provide the material for judging the appropriateness of the existing law and understanding how it has come to take its present form. In the next chapter we will deal with the meant by which statute has attempted to prevent the common law from rendering the freedom to strike illusory. In this chapter we are concerned with three main areas: the effect of industrial action on the contract of employment, including the power of the employer to dismiss; the criminal liability of those who organise or participate in industrial action; and the civil liability of those who organise or participate in industrial action. Consideration is also given to the constitutional dimension of industrial action. Before turning to these specific areas however it is necessary to define more precisely what we mean by industrial action.

---

[1] The F.U.E. has estimated that married persons on average industrial earnings of £150 gross per week would see, in the most favourable circumstances (*i.e.* strike pay, tax rebate and social welfare assistance), their earnings fall by £42 per week during a strike. See F.U.E. *Bulletin*, November 1984.

[2] See Kahn-Freund and Hepple, *Laws against Strikes* (Fabian Research Series 305) (London, 1972), pp. 5–6.

Definition

The most obvious and well documented[3] form of industrial action is the strike. It is defined in section 6 of the Redundancy Payments Act 1967, for the purposes of that legislation and the Minimum Notice and Terms of Employment Act 1973, as follows:

> "'strike' means the cessation of work by a body of persons employed acting in combination, or a concerted refusal or a refusal under a common understanding of any number of persons employed to continue to work for an employer in consequence of a dispute, done as a means of compelling their employer or any person or body of persons employed, or to aid other employees in compelling their employer or any persons or body of persons employed to accept or not to accept terms or conditions of or affecting employment."

This definition, which is almost identical to that contained in the Unfair Dismissals Act 1977, contains two essential elements – a cessation of work and concerted action. Other forms of industrial action not amounting to a concerted stoppage of work do not come within its ambit. It is also defined in terms of ends, based on a purpose of compelling employers or others to accept or not to accept terms or conditions of employment. In its popular sense strike is only defined in terms of means, and employees may withdraw their labour to protest about the taxation structure or the conviction of persons who fail to pay ground rent. The response of the law, however, will vary according to the ends and means of industrial action.

Barring work place occupations, a strike is the most extreme form of industrial action. Industrial action, however, is a much broader concept than the concerted withdrawal of labour. Since a strike has the built-in disincentive that the employer usually ceases the payment of wages, resort to other forms of industrial action is common. Examples are overtime bans, go-slows and working to rule. There are also many other forms of action open to employees which receive little or no publicity such as withdrawal of enthusiasm and co-operation.

The distinction between strikes and other forms of industrial action is potentially very important. In those jurisdictions, such as Italy, where there is a constitutional right to strike, the right does not encompass any type of industrial action short of a concerted stoppage of work.

Another distinction which should be noted, although it is of little legal significance, is that industrial action may be described as official or unofficial. This distinction depends on whether the industrial action has been taken in accordance with the rules of the trade union. A further distinction is between constitutional and unconstitutional

---

[3] See Kelly and Brannick, "The Pattern of Strike Activity in Ireland, 1960–1979: Some Preliminary Observations" (1983) 5 *I.B.A.R.* 65.

action. This somewhat misleading distinction turns on whether the action is in violation of procedures agreed between the employer and the trade union.[4]

INDUSTRIAL ACTION AND THE INDIVIDUAL EMPLOYEE

The effect of industrial action on the individual contract of employment raises various questions – Can the employer dismiss? What effect does it have on continuity of service? Does it break the contract? Does it establish liability in tort? The attitude of the common law was very simple. Employees who participated in strikes had either broken or terminated their contracts of employment depending on whether notice of the appropriate length had been given.[5] This, of course, has further implications for the liability of those who participate in or organise industrial action. If the industrial action is in breach of contract then the organiser may be liable for the tort of inducement of breach of contract and those who participate in it might be liable for the torts of intimidation or conspiracy. Furthermore some breaches of the employment contract are criminal offences.[6] If it is a breach of contract then the employer could sue for damages or dismiss. Most employers, however, do not sue striking employees for breach of contract. Quite apart from the effect that this would have on industrial relations, the level of damages would be small.[7] Nevertheless a third party damaged by the industrial action may wish to sue in tort and liability will depend, in part, on the unlawfulness of the conduct that caused the loss. It should also be noted that, for some persons, participation in industrial action might be viewed as unprofessional conduct, resulting in disciplinary proceedings being taken by their professional association.[8]

As far as the effect on continuity of employment is concerned one need only look to the First Schedule to the Minimum Notice and Terms of Employment Act 1973. This provides that participation in a strike (as defined) does not break continuity of service. Paragraph 11 goes on to provide, however, that if, in any week or part of a week, an employee is absent from his employment because he is taking part in a strike in relation to the trade or business in which he is employed, that week shall not count as a period of service. Presumably, participation in strikes that do not fall within the statutory definition do not affect continuity of service unless the strike terminates the contract. If a strike takes place without any prior notice it seems clear that it must almost

---

[4] See Brannick and Kelly, "Unofficial Strike Action" (1984) 3 *J.I.S.L.L.* 27.
[5] See *Bowes and Partners Ltd.* v. *Press* [1894] 1 Q.B. 202; *Parker* v. *South Helton Coal Co. Ltd* (1907) 97 L.T. 98.
[6] Conspiracy and Protection of Property Act 1875, ss. 4 and 5.
[7] See *National Coal Board* v. *Galley* [1958] 1 W.L.R. 16.
[8] See, for example, the Code of Ethics for Nurses issued by An Bord Altranais which, *inter alia*, enjoins nurses to provide the best possible care of patients. This could be invoked against nurses where industrial action was seen as putting patients at risk.

always be in breach of the employees' contracts since it involves their disregarding one of their essential obligations, *viz.* to do the work they are employed to do. It would follow that the employer at common law would be quite entitled to accept the breach and terminate the contract by dismissing with or without notice or to sue for damages. Every employee has, however, the right to withdraw his labour, alone or in combination, upon giving to the employer the notice called for by the contract of employment. In practice strike notices, when given, rarely take the form of notice to terminate.[9] Strike notices as notices to terminate would not reflect the daily experience, understanding and practice of those engaged in industrial relations. The belief that no one engaged in industrial relations supposes that the effect of a strike is to terminate *ipso facto* the contract of employment led Lord Denning M.R. to suggest, in *Morgan* v. *Fry*,[10] that strike notice was neither notice of breach nor notice of termination. It was a notice to *suspend* the contract, or at least, to suspend certain provisions of the contract. Lord Denning M.R. said:

> "The truth is that neither employer nor workmen wish to take the drastic action of termination if it can be avoided. The men do not wish to leave their work for ever. The employers do not wish to scatter their labour force to the four winds. Each side is, therefore, content to accept a 'strike notice' of proper length as lawful. It is an implication read into the contract by the modern law as to trade disputes. If a strike takes place, the contract of employment is not terminated. It is suspended during the strike: and revives again when the strike is over."[11]

Neither of Lord Denning's colleagues in *Morgan* v. *Fry* agreed with this conclusion. Davies L.J. said that strike notice amounted to notice to terminate the existing contract and an offer to continue on different terms. Russell L.J. said that since a strike was a breach of contract, strike notice amounted to a threatened breach. The English E.A.T. subsequently held, in *Simmons* v. *Hoover Ltd.*,[12] that they were not bound by *Morgan* v. *Fry* to hold that the effect of a strike, even if preceded by due notice, suspended the contract. Phillips J. reiterated the traditional common law view that participation in a strike was a repudiatory breach of the contract of employment and that strike notice was merely notice to the employer that the employees are going to break their contracts by going on strike.

Lord Denning's "suspension" theory was approved, however, by a majority of the Supreme Court in *Becton Dickinson & Co. Ltd.* v. *Lee*.[13]

---

[9] See Lowry J., in *Sherrard* v. *Ulster Pension Trustees Ltd.* Northern Ireland High Court, unreported, 22 February 1971, who said it was "hard" to construe something which on its face looked like a strike notice as if it were a notice to terminate a contract of service.
[10] [1968] 2 Q.B. 710.
[11] At 728. On strike notices see O'Higgins, (1973) 2 *I.L.J.* 152.
[12] [1977] I.C.R. 61. [13] [1973] I.R. 1, 35.

Walsh J., with whom Ó Dálaigh C.J. and Butler J. agreed, asserted that there was.

> "to be read into every contract of employment an implied term that the service of a strike notice of a length not shorter than would be required for notice to terminate the contract would not in itself amount to notice to terminate the contract and would not in itself constitute a breach of the contract and that to take action on foot of the strike notice would likewise not be a breach of the contract."

The majority of the Supreme Court agreed with Lord Denning that it was to be implied into every contract of employment that if a strike takes place, after due notice, the contract is suspended. Walsh J. observed that such an implied term would not be read into a contract where there was an express provision to the contrary or where by necessary implication a provision to the contrary must be read into the contract. He added however:

> "An express no-strike clause in a contract is itself such an unusual feature of a contract of employment and is such an apparent departure from the long-established right to strike that a court would be slow to imply it where it is not expressly included in the contract or where it is not a necessary implication; a court would probably only do so in cases where there was some particular provision for machinery to deal with disputes, the provision being so phrased as to give rise to the implication that it had been agreed between the parties that no other course would be adopted during the currency of the contract."[14]

The authors accept that the suspension theory is not in total harmony with the traditional common law view. This reflects in part the fact that the suspension theory was first developed in those jurisdictions where there is a *right* to strike. The analysis that a strike is a breach of contract does not sit well with such a right. If the employees have a right to withdraw their labour to put pressure on their employer, that right is rendered meaningless if participation in a strike exposes the employee to a sanction for breach of contract.[15]

Nevertheless the adoption of the suspension theory leaves a number of legal problems in its wake, which are well summarised in the *Report of the Royal Commission on Trade Unions and Employers' Associations*.[16]

> "The concept is not as simple as it sounds: and before any such new law could be formulated problems of some difficulty would have to be faced and solved. They include the following: (a) To what strikes

---

[14] At 38.
[15] See Blanc-Jouvan in Aaron and Wedderburn eds, *Industrial Conflict* (London, 1972) at pp. 176 *et seq.*
[16] At para. 943.

would it apply? To unofficial and unconstitutional as well as to official strikes? How would strikes be defined for this purpose? (b) Would it also apply to other industrial action such as a ban on overtime in breach of contract or to a 'go-slow'? (c) Would it apply to 'lightning strikes' or only to strikes where at least some notice was given, though less than the notice required for termination of the contract? If so, what length of notice should be required? (d) Would the new law apply to the gas, water, and electricity industries, which at present are subject to the special provisions of section 4 of the Conspiracy and Protection of Property Act 1875? What also would be the position under section 5 of the same Act? (e) Would the employer still be allowed instantly to dismiss an employee for grave misconduct during the course of the strike? If so, what kind of acts would constitute 'grave misconduct'? (f) Would 'contracting out' of the new law be permissible, *e.g.* in collective bargains, or in individual contracts of employment? (g) Would strikers be free to take up other employment while the contract was suspended? If so, would any obligations of secrecy in the suspended contract be suspended too? (h) If all efforts to end the strike failed, upon what event would the suspension of the contract cease and be replaced by termination?"

With the exception of the last question, all these can be satisfactorily answered. Walsh J. in *Becton Dickinson & Co. Ltd.* v. *Lee* made it quite clear that only strikes preceded by due notice would suspend the contract and that "contracting out" would be permissible.[17] As the suspension theory is a reflection of the existence of a right to strike, then it would seem to follow that it would only apply to concerted stoppages of work and not to other less extreme forms of industrial action. It would also seem to be more accurate to describe the effect of a strike as suspending certain terms of the contract – namely the obligations to work and to pay wages – leaving the rest of the contract alive. The employer would then be free to dismiss for grave misconduct during the course of a strike.

A specific example of this is presented by the decision of the E.A.T. in *McDonagh* v. *Turmec Teo.*[18] where, in the course of a trade dispute, the claimant assaulted a driver and threatened the General Manager by using abusive language and swinging a hurley. He was summarily dismissed and the E.A.T. said that they were satisfied that the respondent had shown substantial grounds justifying the dismissal. The principal effect of suspension therefore is to excuse each party from the execution of the main obligation that is imposed upon him by the contract. It releases the employee from his duty to perform work and it releases the employer from his duty to pay wages.

---

[17] See his comments at [1973] I.R. 35 and 38.
[18] U.D. 104/1982. See also *Gibson* v. *British Transport Docks Board* [1982] I.R.L.R. 228.

There appears no reason why the taking of alternative employment should not be permitted, provided of course the striking employee did not put himself in a position whereby he would not be able to resume work immediately upon cessation of the strike. Admittedly counsel for the employee in *Simmons* v. *Hoover Ltd.* said that there would be a fundamental breach of the contract if the employee took another job,[19] but there seems no reason in principle why, subject to the above mentioned proviso, this should be the case.

A more difficult question to answer is the last. If all efforts to end the strike failed, upon what event would the suspension cease? One answer would be to apply the doctrine of frustration, another would be to imply a term that the employer is free to take on other staff in an attempt to keep the business going. This would certainly be a corollary to the ability of the striking employee to take on alternative employment. More pertinently, the Unfair Dismissals Act 1977 deals specifically with the dismissal of strikers and to this we now turn.

Dismissal of strikers

Section 5(2) of the Unfair Dismissals Act 1977 provides that

> "the dismissal of an employee for taking part in a strike or other industrial action shall be deemed, for the purposes of this Act, to be an unfair dismissal, if –
> (a) one or more employees of the same employer who took part in the strike or other industrial action were not dismissed for so taking part, or
> (b) one or more of such employees who were dismissed for so taking part are subsequently offered reinstatement or re-engagement and the employee is not."

The wording of section 5(2) is significantly different to that of the comparable Northern Irish provision[20] which provides that, unless there is discrimination in dismissal or in the re-employment of strikers, the industrial tribunal shall not determine whether the dismissal was fair or unfair. The intention was twofold – to prevent victimisation of strikers and to permit the employer to dismiss all the strikers and take on new employees.[21] The intention behind section 5(2) is not so clear. True, the Minister explained the intention behind the subsection as being to ensure that "no individual victimisation would result from a return to work after a trade dispute"[22] and to this end the subsection effects a conclusive presumption that selective dismissals for taking part in a strike or other industrial action are *automatically* unfair.[23] But

---

[19] See [1977] I.C.R. at 64.
[20] Industrial Relations (Northern Ireland) Order 1976, Article 23.
[21] See *Heath* v. *J.F. Longman (Meat Salesmen) Ltd.* [1973] 2 All E.R. 1228, 1230.
[22] 296 *Dáil Debates* c. 59.
[23] See *Butler* v. *M. B. Ireland Ltd.* U.D. 1058/1982; *Duffy* v. *Tara Mines Ltd.* U.D. 50/1980.

it does not go on to say that non-selective dismissals are *automatically* fair. Redmond has persuasively argued that, despite the obscure wording of the subsection, non-selective dismissals can give rise to claims of unfair dismissal.[24] Of course the E.A.T. will then be in the invidious position of having to consider whether there were substantial grounds justifying the dismissal. This will inevitably involve some consideration of the merits of the dispute which led to the strike.

In *Jordan* v. *Walter D. McKenna Ltd.*,[25] all the employees who had participated in a strike were dismissed and three subsequently claimed that they had been unfairly dismissed. The E.A.T. accepted that it had jurisdiction to hear the claims and required the company to show that there were substantial grounds for the action taken. The E.A.T. accepted that management were faced with the prospect of industrial action by employees who had not joined the strike if the claimants had been re-employed and that they did not feel obliged to work at reconciling the "loyal" staff to the taking back of the claimants. In these circumstances the E.A.T. found that there were substantial grounds for the action of the respondent company.

In *Power* v. *National Corrugated Products*,[26] the claimants had all participated in a "sit in" and had been dismissed. The "sit in" was prompted by management's handling of the re-instatement of three employees. The E.A.T. were unanimous that in the circumstances the dismissals were unfair. In reaching its decision the E.A.T. took into account the fact that management made no serious effort to contact the claimants' union during the "sit in" and said that the issuing of dismissal notices was inconsiderate and irresponsible.

While the employer may not discriminate as between those of the strikers to be re-employed, section 5(2)(*b*) seems to permit the employer to discriminate between the strikers by offering some re-engagement and others re-instatement.

"Strike" and "industrial action" are specifically defined in section 1 of the 1977 Act as follows:

> "'strike' means the cessation of work by any number or body of employees acting in combination, or a concerted refusal or a refusal under a common understanding of any number of employees to continue to work for an employer, in consequence of a dispute, done as a means of compelling their employer or any employee or body of employees, or to aid other employees in compelling their employer or any employee or body of employees, to accept or not to accept terms or conditions of or affecting employment;

---

[24] "Dismissal for taking part in a strike or other industrial action" (1980) 74 *Gazette of the Incorporated Law Society of Ireland* 101 and 119.
[25] U.D. 577/1982. See also *Boyne* v. *British American Optical Co.* U.D. 951/1982.
[26] U.D. 336/1980.

'industrial action' means lawful action taken by any number or body of employees acting in combination or under a common understanding, in consequence of a dispute, as a means of compelling their employers or any employee or body of employees, or to aid other employees in compelling their employer or any employee or body of employees, to accept or not to accept terms or conditions of or affecting employment;"

It will be noted that the statute roots the meaning of "strike" strictly in a industrial relations context. Cessation of work in protest at the jailing of persons who refuse to pay ground rent or at the visit of a foreign head of state would not be included and any resulting dismissals would presumably be treated as dismissals for misconduct. It will also be noted that it encompasses cessations of work which are not in breach of contract.[27] The interaction between this and the Supreme Court decision in *Becton Dickinson & Co. Ltd.* v. *Lee*[28] has yet to be judicially or tribunally explored. All that can be said at this stage is that, if there is a constitutional right to withdraw one's labour, which right is vindicated by the suspension theory, that right would be completely frustrated if employers were able lawfully to dismiss employees for participating in a strike.[29]

The meaning of "taking part in a strike" has given rise to some disagreement amongst the British judiciary. In *McCormick* v. *Horsepower Ltd.*,[30] Lawton and Templeman L.JJ. stressed the element of common purpose or concerted interest. Mere refusal to pass a picket line was not enough to prove participation in a strike. In *Coates and Venables* v. *Modern Methods and Materials Ltd.*,[31] Stephenson L.J. was of a contrary opinion.

> "Participation in a strike must be judged by what the employee does and not by what he thinks or why he does it. If he stops work when his workmates came out on strike and does not say or do anything to make plain his disagreement, or which could amount to a refusal to join them, he takes part in their strike. The line between unwilling participation and not taking part may be difficult to draw, but those who stay away from work with the strikers without protest for whatever reason are to be regarded as having crossed that line to take part in the strike."[32]

Kerr L.J. agreed that it would not be correct to differentiate between those who chose not to work by reference to their reasons for doing

---

[27] See *Tramp Shipping Corp.* v. *Greenwich Marine Inc.* [1975] I.C.R. 261.
[28] [1973] I.R. 1.
[29] See Blanc-Jouvan, *op. cit.*, at pp. 182 and 184. On the constitutional dimension of industrial action see *infra*, pp. 247–248.
[30] [1981] I.C.R. 535.
[31] [1982] I.C.R. 763.
[32] At 777.

so.³³ Eveleigh L.J. dissented however. He said that for a person to take part in a strike "he must be acting jointly or in concert with others who withdrew their labour, and this means that he must withdraw his labour in support of their claim."³⁴ He concluded that a person, whose reason for not going into work was unwillingness to expose himself to abuse, could not be said to be taking part in a strike.

On balance the authors believe the interpretation of Stephenson and Kerr L.JJ. to be correct. Withdrawal of labour when or after others do so, even if the employee does not share the common purpose of the strikers, will usually contribute to achieving the object of the strike. As Stephenson L.J. said: "In the field of industrial action those who are not openly against it are presumably for it."³⁵

The definition of "strike" clearly includes what has been described as a "sympathetic strike" but it must be stressed that it only includes a complete cessation of work. A mere refusal to handle goods produced by a particular employer whilst continuing to work normally in all other respects would not be a strike. It would be other industrial action. But, as can be seen from the above cited definition, "industrial action" for the purpose of the Unfair Dismissals Act 1977 is defined as "lawful action . . ." and refusal to handle certain goods, if required to do so by the employer, would be a breach of contract.³⁶

Much industrial action short of a strike is "unlawful" at least in the sense that it involves a breach of contract. "Works to rule" and "go-slows" are good examples of such "unlawful" industrial action short of a strike.³⁷ The exclusion of dismissals for participating in unlawful industrial action from the ambit of section 5(2) presents no real problems because the fairness or unfairness of such dismissals will still be considered by the E.A.T. under section 6. Again, however, the E.A.T. will be required to consider the merits of the dispute.

---

³³ At 783.
³⁴ At 778–779.
³⁵ At 777. See *Williams* v. *Western Mail & Echo Ltd.* [1980] I.C.R. 366. In this context it is interesting to note that the Social Welfare Tribunal (on which see *infra*, pp. 371–376) stated in *Harris* v. *I.S. Varian & Co. Ltd.* A2/1984, at p. 6 of its adjudication, that it was not of major significance whether the withdrawal of labour resulted from a direct participation in the strike or from a refusal to pass the official picket line.
³⁶ As was recognised by Hamilton J. in *Reg Armstrong Motors* v. *C.I.E.* High Court, unreported, 2 December 1975. See also the Report to the Minister for Labour under s. 24 of the Industrial Relations Act 1946 (Labour Court, 21 May 1985) on the dispute over the handling of South African produce in Dunnes Stores' Henry Street branch. At p. 6 of the report, the Labour Court states that "by refusing to handle South African goods the workers were probably in breach of their contracts of employment." This conclusion was disputed by Asmal, "Implications for Apartheid of Dunne's Strike" *Irish Times*, June 3, 1985.
³⁷ See *Secretary of State for Employment* v. *Amalgamated Society of Railway Servants* [1972] 2 Q.B. 455; *Seaboard World Airlines Inc.* v. *Transport and General Workers' Union* [1978] I.C.R. 458. See also Napier, (1972) 1 *I.L.J.* 125. On whether an employer is entitled to withhold part of the wages or salary from an employee who, as part of industrial action, remains at work but refuses to carry out some of his contractual duties, see Parker L.J. in *Miles* v. *Wakefield Metropolitan District Council* [1985] I.C.R. 363, 373.

CRIMINAL LIABILITY

Until 1875[38] the principal impediment to trade union activity was the criminal law. Workers had to contend not only with a myriad of statutory prohibitions,[39] predominant being the Combination Laws Repeal Act Amendment Act 1825 which created vague crimes of intimidation, obstruction and molestation and which frequently formed the basis of criminal prosecutions of workers engaged in industrial action, but also with common law crimes such as conspiracy. For example in 1851 Erle J. held, in *R. v. Duffield*,[40] that it was unlawful for persons to combine to induce others, even by peaceful persuasion, to leave their employment with the object of forcing their employer to improve conditions. Such conduct was regarded as criminal obstruction or molestation of the employer not only under the 1825 Act but also at common law. Moreover the Master and Servant Acts made simple breach of contract on the part of the worker a criminal offence punishable by imprisonment.[41]

An attempt was made to provide some measure of legality with the Molestation of Workmen Act 1859 which provided that no person was to be deemed guilty of molestation or obstruction or liable for criminal conspiracy by reason merely of his agreeing with others to fix wages or hours of work or by endeavouring in a peaceable and reasonable manner to persuade others to cease or abstain from work for that purpose. Nothing in the Act however authorised the procurement or commission of a breach of contract and in practice it did nothing to enlarge the sphere of lawful industrial action.[42]

The Criminal Law Amendment Act 1871 was much more ambitious. It repealed the 1825 and 1859 Acts and supposedly dealt with criminal liabilities at large. In this it was ineffective. The 1871 Act made it an offence for any person to use violence, threats, intimidation, molestation or obstruction with a view to coercing an employer or workman to act in certain specified ways, but explicitly restricted the meaning of "threats" and "intimidation" to such acts as would justify a Justice of the Peace in binding over the defendant to keep the peace. A mere threat to strike was therefore no longer a statutory offence. In *R. v. Bunn*[43] however, Brett J. held that at common law the existence of

---

[38] With the enactment of the Conspiracy and Protection of Property Act 1875 (38 & 39 Vict., c. 86).
[39] Between 1447 and 1824 approximately 40 statutes were passed in Ireland dealing with conspiracies among the working classes. See Park, "The Combination Acts in Ireland, 1727–1825" (1979) 14 *Ir. Jur. (n.s.)* 340.
[40] (1851) 5 Cox 404.
[41] Repealed in 1875 by s. 17 of the Conspiracy and Protection of Property Act.
[42] See, *inter alia, Skinner* v. *Kitch* (1867) L.R. 2 Q.B. 393; *Shelbourne* v. *Oliver* (1866) 13 L.T. 630; *Springhead Spinning Co.* v. *Riley* (1868) L.R. 6 Eq. 551.
[43] (1872) 12 Cox 316.

a combination might convert an otherwise non-criminal act into a crime, and that this doctrine was not affected by the 1871 Act. Workers had threatened to go on strike unless a fellow worker, who had been dismissed, was reinstated. Brett J. held this to be a criminal conspiracy, even though the acts threatened were not themselves independently illegal or unlawful. He commented that the threatened strike amounted to an "unjustifiable annoyance and interference with the masters in the course of their business."

Conspiracy and Protection of Property

Following a successful campaign to change the law the ambit of the criminal law was considerably restricted by the Conspiracy and Protection of Property Act 1875. Section 3 deals with common law conspiracy and provides in relevant part:

> "An agreement or combination by two or more persons to do or procure to be done any act in contemplation or furtherance of a trade dispute . . . shall not be indictable as a conspiracy if such act committed by one person would not be punishable as a crime."

This section thus reverses *R.* v. *Bunn*, but only in so far as the action is taken "in contemplation or furtherance of a trade dispute". The common law crime of conspiracy itself is unaffected by section 3. *Bunn* remains therefore, albeit as a shadowy presence in the wings.[44]

Section 7 prohibits, *inter alia,* violence, intimidation, persistent following, hiding tools and "watching or besetting". The two principal offences are "watching or besetting" and intimidation. The former will be discussed in detail in the chapter on *Picketing.*[45] The latter was considered relatively recently in *R.* v. *Jones.*[46] Here, it was argued on behalf of the defendants that, for there to be intimidation, there had to be conduct amounting to, or implying a threat of, violence to the person, and that damage to plant, buildings or equipment, or threats of such damage, would not suffice. In *Gibson* v. *Lawson,*[47] Lord Coleridge C.J. had stated that there was much to be said for the view that to constitute intimidation a threat of personal violence was necessary. In *Jones*, however, the Court of Appeal upheld the direction of the trial judge to the jury in which he had said that intimidation did not necessarily involve personal violence. James L.J., whilst not seeking to define "intimidation" exhaustively, said that it included:

---

[44] Elias, Napier and Wellington, *Labour Law; Cases and Materials* (London, 1980) p. 281.
[45] Chapter 10.
[46] [1974] I.C.R. 310. See also *The Garda Síochána Guide* 5th ed. (Dublin, 1981) pp. 1188-1191.
[47] [1891] 2 Q.B. 545. *Cf. Curran* v. *Treleaven* [1891] 2 Q.B. 560.

"putting persons in fear by the exhibition of force or violence, or the threat of force or violence, and there is no limitation restricting the meaning to cases of violence or threats of violence to the person."[48]

Nor is it necessary to prove that someone has been intimidated in fact. It is the intention and character of the threats that are relevant.

R. v. Jones also demonstrates that the common law crime of conspiracy is still extremely relevant, notwithstanding section 3 of the 1875 Act. The maximum penalty for offences under section 7 is three months imprisonment. The defendants, as well as having been charged with the substantive offence of intimidation, were also charged with conspiracy to intimidate. If the charge of conspiracy were allowed the maximum penalty for conspiracy to commit an offence under section 7 would be the same as that for all common law conspiracies, namely life imprisonment. One of the defendants was in fact sentenced to three years imprisonment.[49] It was argued that the conspiracy charge was bad for duplicity. The Court of Appeal upheld the trial judge's decision not to quash the conspiracy charge. They said that, whilst it was not desirable to include a charge of conspiracy which adds nothing to an effective charge of a substantive offence, in the circumstances of the instant case where the charge of the substantive offence did not "adequately reflect the overall criminality" it was appropriate and right to include the conspiracy charge.[50]

In the same year, 1974, the House of Lords reviewed the extent of criminal liability for conspiracy to commit acts not in themselves illegal in *R. v. Kamara*.[51] The speeches re-define the nature of criminal liability for conspiracy to trespass in terms equally applicable to conspiracy to commit other torts and clearly raises, if it were to be followed in this jurisdiction, the possibility of wide liability for conspiracy to commit an economic tort such as unlawful interference with trade or business.[52]

Although the general criminal liability for breach of the contract of employment was abolished by the Employers and Workmen Act 1875, sections 4 and 5 of the Conspiracy and Protection of Property Act 1875 do provide that breaches of contracts of employment will be illegal in two situations. First, where the breach is by persons employed in certain public utilities. Secondly, in any case where the breach is likely to involve serious injury to any person or property.

---

[48] [1974] I.C.R. at 318.
[49] Two other defendants received two years and nine months respectively.
[50] [1974] I.C.R. at 316.
[51] [1974] A.C. 104.
[52] Wallington in his article "Criminal Conspiracy and Industrial Conflict" (1975) 4 *I.L.J.* 69, refers, at p. 72, to a prosecution of five building workers in England in 1973 for conspiracy to trespass when they occupied an employment bureau alleged to be supplying "scab labour". The five, and the three members of a TV crew who had been arrested with them, were acquitted, however, because of s. 3 of the 1875 Act.

Section 4 provides:

"Where a person employed by a municipal authority or by any company or contractor upon whom is imposed by Act of Parliament the duty, or who have otherwise assumed the duty of supplying any city, borough, town, or place, or any part thereof, with gas or water, wilfully and maliciously breaks a contract of service with that authority or company or contractor, knowing or having reasonable cause to believe that the probable consequences of his so doing, either alone or in combination with others, will be to deprive the inhabitants of that city, borough, town, place, or part, wholly or to a great extent of their supply of gas or water, he shall on conviction thereof by a court of summary jurisdiction, or on indictment as herein-after mentioned, be liable either to pay a penalty not exceeding twenty pounds or to be imprisoned for a term not exceeding three months, with or without hard labour."

This section, which makes it a criminal offence for a person employed in the supply of gas or water to the public to break his contract of employment, in circumstances which make it probable that the public will be deprived of their supply, was extended to electricity workers by section 110 of the Electricity Supply Act 1927.[53]

Section 5 provides:

"Where any person wilfully and maliciously breaks a contract of service or of hiring, knowing or having reasonable cause to believe that the probable consequences of his so doing, either alone or in combination with others, will be to endanger human life, or cause serious bodily injury, or to expose valuable property whether real or personal to destruction or serious injury, he shall on conviction thereof by a court of summary jurisdiction, or on indictment as herein-after mentioned, be liable either to pay a penalty not exceeding twenty pounds, or to be imprisoned for a term not exceeding three months, with or without hard labour."

A number of points need to be noted about these two sections.[54] First, they speak of wilful and malicious breaches of contract. Citrine argued that the word "maliciously" was redundant since it means "knowing that the act will injure the person or property of another" and the *mens rea* required to constitute the crime is expressly provided for in the words "knowing or having reasonable cause to believe".[55] It

---

[53] For an account of the since repealed Electricity (Temporary Provisions) Act 1961 and Electricity (Special Provisions) Act 1966, see Asmal, "The Fairy Wand or the Big Stick?" (1969) 1 *D.U.L.R.* 63.

[54] It should also be noted that s. 4 requires the employer, on pain of financial penalty (£2), to post up a printed copy of this section in some conspicuous place where the same can be conveniently read by the employees and "as often as such copy becomes defaced, obliterated or destroyed, shall cause it to be renewed with all reasonable dispatch". Failure to exhibit the notice does not excuse an employee who breaches his contract.

[55] *Citrine's Trade Union Law* (London, 1967) p. 525.

could be argued, however, that the word "maliciously" applies only to those consequences which the employee desires to produce and not to those which are merely likely to flow directly from his wilful conduct. Whichever interpretation is preferred, it is clear that the act or omission constituting the breach of contract must be deliberate and intentional. Secondly, the actual consequences are not material, except in so far as they are evidence of what was probable. So Citrine argued that it would be immaterial that the particular consequences were avoided by prompt action on the part of the employer or someone else and that there was in fact no deprivation to the public.[56] Thirdly, section 5 is of much wider application than section 4. The words "serious" and "valuable" for example are capable of wide interpretation. Hospital personnel, fire brigade staff, security guards, *etc.*, could all be affected. Finally they are not limited to strikes; any wilful breach of contract is a criminal offence if the consequences are within the section.

Miscellaneous

While the 1875 Act is of principal concern in respect of criminal liability there are a number of other statutory provisions of potential significance as far as industrial action is concerned. Industrial action which is designed to put pressure on an employer to "do in relation to employment anything which constitutes discrimination" is prohibited by section 9 of the Employment Equality Act 1977. Section 20(c) of this Act empowers the Employment Equality Agency, where it is of the opinion that this is being done, to refer the matter to the Labour Court. So where a trade union threatened industrial action if a new non-discriminatory system of recruitment was implemented, an Equality Officer ruled that, while nothing in the 1977 Act precluded negotiations on the introduction of non-discriminatory practices, any attempt to procure the re-introduction of the previous discriminatory practice would contravene the Act. Furthermore she ruled that the Act is contravened whenever an act takes place which is contrary to its terms whether there was a deliberate intention to discriminate or not. Therefore, even though the union was convinced that the course of action it took was not an attempt to procure the employer to discriminate, it had contravened section 9.[57]

Of significance to industrial action in the public sector is section 9(2) of the Offences Against the State Act 1939 which provides:

> "Every person who shall incite or encourage any person employed in any capacity by the State to refuse, neglect, or omit (in a manner or to an extent calculated to dislocate the public service or a branch

---

[56] *Ibid.* at p. 527.
[57] *Employment Equality Agency* v. *Irish Transport and General Workers' Union* EE14/1984.

thereof) to perform his duty or shall incite or encourage any person so employed to be negligent or insubordinate (in such manner or to such extent as aforesaid) in the performance of his duty shall be guilty of a misdemeanour and shall be liable on conviction thereof to imprisonment for a term not exceeding two years."

Subsection (3) goes on to provide that every person who attempts to do anything prohibited by subsection (2), or who acts or abets or conspires with another person to do any such thing or advocates or encourages the doing of any such thing, "shall be guilty of a misdemeanour and shall be liable on conviction thereof to imprisonment for a term not exceeding twelve months."

Similarly it is a misdemeanour both to induce any member of the Garda Síochána to withhold his services or to commit a breach of discipline and to incite any person subject to military law to refuse to obey lawful orders from a superior officer or to refuse or omit to perform any if his duties or to commit any other act in dereliction of his duty.[58]

An Post employees engaged in industrial action run the risk of violating section 84 of the Postal and Telecommunications Services Act 1983 which provides in relevant part that a person who "delays or detains any . . . postal packet or does anything to prevent its due delivery" shall be guilty of an offence and Bord Telecom Éireann employees run the risk of violating section 45 of the Telegraph Act 1863 which provides, so far as is material, that any person in the employment of the company who "by any wilful or negligent act or omission prevents or delays the transmission or delivery of any message" shall be guilty of an offence.[59]

Seamen, for historical reasons no longer relevant, were always regarded by the British Parliament as a case apart and they were specifically excluded from the Conspiracy and Protection of Property Act 1875.[60] Their employment is governed by the Merchant Shipping Acts, in particular the Act of 1894. This Act, *inter alia*, makes it an offence for a seaman to neglect or refuse without reasonable cause to join his ship, and also makes it an offence for anyone to persuade a seaman to neglect his duty. In *Cunard SS Co.* v. *Stacey*[61] the Court of Appeal granted an interlocutory injunction to restrain union officials

---

[58] Garda Síochána Act 1924, s. 13(3) and Constabulary and Police (Ireland) Act 1919, s. 3; Defence Act 1954, ss. 254, 255.

[59] The penalties for these offences are, on summary conviction, a fine not exceeding £800 or imprisonment for a term not exceeding 12 months or both or, on indictment, a fine not exceeding £50,000 or imprisonment for a term not exceeding 5 years or both. For a case arising out of similar provisions in Britain see *Gouriet* v. *Union of Post Office Workers* [1978] A.C. 435.

[60] S. 16. This exemption means that seamen cannot be made liable to punishment under the 1875 Act, see *R.* v. *Wall* (1890) 112 C.C.C. Sess. Cas. 880 and *R.* v. *Cole* (1891) 113 C.C.C. Sess. Cas. 622 cited in *Citrine's Trade Union Law* (London, 1967) p. 548, fn. 64. As is also pointed out in *Citrine*, the section does not exempt persons who are not seamen from prosecution for offences against seamen under the 1875 Act. See *Kennedy* v. *Cowie* [1891] 1 Q.B. 771.

[61] [1955] 2 Lloyd's Rep. 247.

from breaking the latter provision and inducing seamen to break the former.

This last mentioned case demonstrates that, even if these statutory provisions are not used to base prosecutions against those participating in or organising industrial action, persons affected by illegal industrial action might bring a civil action based upon the breach of a penal statute. Could a customer of the E.S.B., whose business is likely to be affected by threatened industrial action on the part of E.S.B. employees which appears to violate section 110 of the Electricity Supply Act 1927, obtain an injunction to restrain the industrial action?

The authorities on this point are not particularly clear and it has been asserted that this branch of the law is "unpredictable in its operation and difficult to state with any degree of clarity."[62] On the one hand there is a common law principle that generally speaking a statute which imposes a criminal penalty is not to be read as providing a private right of action unless there is an indication in the statute that this was intended.[63] Since sections 4 and 5 of the 1875 Act do not expressly provide for a civil action, the availability of a civil remedy depends "on the purview of the legislature" and "the language which they have there employed." On this view the basis of liability is "legislative intention" but since the immediate purpose of the legislature was to create a criminal offence the availability of an additional civil remedy is a matter to which the legislature may well have given no attention. The question therefore falls to the courts as a matter of construction. In *Lonhro Ltd.* v. *Shell Petroleum Ltd.*,[65] the House of Lords, in applying this principle, said that where a statute provides for a criminal penalty and is silent on civil liability a plaintiff could bring no action for damages unless he proves either that the statute was passed for the benefit of a particular class of which he forms one, or that a public right has been infringed and he has suffered special damage.[66]

This approach has not found favour with Lord Denning M.R. He regarded it as a "guesswork puzzle" and declined to indulge in "such a game of chance". In *Ex parte Island Records*,[67] he expressed the view that a person who is carrying on a lawful trade or calling had a right to be protected from any *unlawful* interference with it, adding that this

---

[62] Buckley, "Liability in Tort for Breach of Statutory Duty (1984) 100 *L.Q.R.* 204, citing Lord Denning in *Ex parte Island Records* [1978] Ch. 122, 135.

[63] *Doe d. Rochester* v. *Bridges* (1831) 1 B. & Ad. 847, 859; *Monk* v. *Warbey* [1935] 1 K.B. 75, 85 (a passage approved by Gannon J. in *Walsh* v. *Kilkenny County Council* High Court, unreported, 23 January 1978);

[64] *Per* Lord Cairns L.C., *Atkinson* v. *Newcastle and Gateshead Waterworks Co.* (1877) 2 Ex. D. 441, 448. See also *Bligh* v. *Rathangan Drainage Board* [1898] 2 I.R. 205, 224–225.

[65] [1982] A.C. 173. Hereafter referred to as *Lonrho*.

[66] *Per* Lord Diplock, in whose speech Lords Edmund-Davies, Keith, Scarman and Bridge concurred, at 185.

[67] [1978] Ch. 122, 135. See also *The Queen in Right of Canada* v. *Saskatchewan Wheat Pool* (1983) 143 D.L.R. (3d) 9.

was a right in the nature of a property right. Interference with this right as a consequence of criminal activities was actionable. In expressing the matter this way, Lord Denning M.R., was relying in great measure on the equitable principle that the courts may grant an injunction to a person who claims that he will suffer special damage to a property interest of his by a crime.[68] This principle could also be said to underlie the much criticised decision of the High Court of Australia in *Beaudesert Shire Council* v. *Smith*[69] where it was asserted that –

> "independently of trespass, nuisance or negligence but by an action for damages in the case, a person who suffers harm or loss as the inevitable consequences of the unlawful intentional or positive acts of another is entitled to recover damages from that other."[70]

In *Lonhro*, however, the House of Lords expressly rejected the proposition that "whenever a lawful business carried on by one individual in fact suffers damage as the consequence of contravention by another individual of any statutory probition the former has a civil right of action against the latter for such damage."[71] They stressed that an essential element of liability for unlawful interference with trade or business was an intention to injure the plaintiff.

A position mid-way between *Lonhro* and *Island Records* was adopted by the Supreme Court of Canada in *Canada Cement La Farge Ltd.* v. *British Columbia Lightweight Aggregate Ltd.*[72] where Estey J., speaking for the Court, said that where the conduct of the defendant is illegal and is directed towards the plaintiff and where the defendant "should know in the circumstances that injury to the plaintiff is likely to" and does in fact result in injury then it was not necessary that the predominant purpose of the defendant was to cause injury to the plaintiff.[73]

In summary therefore, the position may be stated as follows. There is both a "narrow" and a more "general" proposition the ambit of both being unclear. The former proposition may be expressed as follows: interference with a private right by criminal means will be actionable if, on construction of the legislation a civil remedy is intended. There is a presumption against liability where the Act provides for a sanction and a presumption in favour of liability where it does not. Moreover the statute must have been intended for the benefit of a certain "class" of person as distinct from the public at large. The more general proposition is that there is a civil cause of action where a person suffers

---

[68] See Malins V.-C. in *Springhead Spinning Co.* v. *Riley* (1868) L.R.6 Eq. 551, 558–559.
[69] (1966) 120 C.L.R. 145. Much criticised by Dworkin and Harari (1967) 40 *A.L.J.* 296. On whither *Beaudesert*, see Sadler, (1984) 58 *A.L.J.* 38 and the cases cited therein.
[70] Per Taylor, Menzies and Owen JJ. at 155–156. Described by Heuston in the *Child & Co. Oxford Lecture* 1982 as "three members of a strong appellate tribunal."
[71] [1982] A.C. at 187.
[72] (1983) 145 D.L.R. (3d) 385.
[73] At 399.

harm through either (i) the inevitable, or (ii) the foreseeable, or (iii) the intended consequence of the unlawful acts of another. In the case of the narrow proposition liability is strict, as it is under the first alternative general proposition. Many commentators have called for the cessation of the quest for a fictitious legislative intent.[74] The Oireachtas should make it a rule to state explicitly what its intention is in this important matter and not leave it to the courts to discover what that intention may be supposed to be.[75] The problem is further exacerbated when one has to deal with legislation from a very different era. The legislation imposes a penalty on a strictly admonitory basis and there seems little justification in adding civil liability when such liability would tend to produce liability without fault. If there is to be liability then it should be founded on negligence or intention, and the House of Lords in *Lonhro* opted for the latter basis of liability. If this approach were to be followed here, then this would mean that, if the consumer is the target of industrial action by E.S.B. workers and the means employed are unlawful, there will be liability whereas, if the employer is the target and the consumer only the incidental victim, there will be no liability. But, as Lord Wedderburn has observed, *Lonhro* was decided entirely without regard to liability for negligence.[76] *Lonhro* was concerned with liability for *foreseeable* injury caused by an act which is unlawful on some ground not providing a clear cause of action to the claimant and in *Junior Books Ltd.* v. *Veitchi Co. Ltd.*[77] the House of Lords have opened up the whole question of recoverability of pure economic loss in negligence.

As early as 1914 Thayer[78] argued that civil claims arising out of breach of statute should be confined to situations in which the existing law of negligence already recognised that the defendant owed a duty of care at common law. The statutory provision should then be regarded as determining that failure to take the measures required by it automatically constituted breach of that duty. This approach has been adopted by some of the courts in North America although with the important qualification that contravention of the statute is not conclusive; it is merely *evidence* of negligence.[79] This approach, if it were to be adopted in this jurisdiction, would involve asking whether an E.S.B. employee owes a common law duty to all consumers to take reasonable care so as not to interrupt their supply and cause consequential economic loss. This duty is predicated, *per* Lord Roskill in *Junior Books*, upon foresight of the damage on the part of the

---

[74] See Glanville Williams, "The Effect of Penal Legislation in the Law of Tort" (1960) 23 *M.L.R.* 233.

[75] See Law Commission Report No. 21, *The Interpretation of Statutes* (1969), para. 38.

[76] (1983) 46 *M.L.R.* 224 at p. 230.

[77] [1983] A.C. 520.

[78] (1914) 24 *Harv. L.R.* 317.

[79] See *Restatement (Second), Torts,* paras. 286–288. See also *R.* v. *Saskatchewan Wheat Pool* (1983) 143 D.L.R. (3d) 9 (noted by Mathews, (1984) 4 *Oxford Journal of Legal Studies* 429).

employees and reliance on the employees by the customer.[80] It is therefore submitted that there would not be liability in such circumstances. The relevant relationship is that between the customer and the E.S.B. It is governed by a contract which contains numerous exception clauses, in particular by reference to interruptions in supply consequent upon industrial disputes. The customer relies, not on the employees, but on the E.S.B. to behave in such a way so as not to cause economic loss. The mere fact that the employees can foresee that, if they go on strike, regardless of whether it is a breach of contract, they will cause economic loss to customers of their employer does not impose a duty to take care to avoid such loss.[81]

CIVIL LIABILITY

We have seen how the Conspiracy and Protection of Property Act 1875 virtually excluded common law criminal liabilities from the field of trade disputes. The reaction of employers and the courts, denied the use of criminal liabilities, was to turn to the law of tort, which provided remedies against conduct deliberately aimed at causing financial loss. The ability of employees to take effective industrial action was thus placed in jeopardy by the threat, not of criminal prosecutions, but of awards of damages and orders for injunctions. Tortious liability for conspiracy replaced criminal liability, a process which culminated in the decision of the House of Lords, on appeal from the Irish Court of Appeal, in *Quinn* v. *Leathem*[82] that trade union officials who threatened an employer with a strike if he did not dismiss non-unionists and who persuaded customers not to deal with him were liable for the tort of conspiracy to injure.

An equally significant development was the decision of the House of Lords the same year (1901) in *Taff Vale Railway Co.* v. *Amalgamated Society of Railway Servants*[83] that a trade union, registered under the Trade Union Act 1871, was a legal entity capable of being sued in its registered name for the tortious actions of its members and officials. This decision exposed union funds to legal actions by employers, and in 1903 was extended, in *Giblan* v. *National Amalgamated Labourers Union of Great Britain*,[84] to render a union liable if the act of the union

---

[80] [1983] 1 A.C. at 545–547.
[81] This conclusion is strengthened by reference to *Clegg Parkinson & Co.* v. *Early Gas Co.* [1896] 1 Q.B. 592 where a customer was refused redress when the defendant gas company failed to supply him with a supply of gas in the quantity and of the purity required by Statute.
[82] [1901] A.C. 495.
[83] [1901] A.C. 426. On which, see *supra*, p. 64.
[84] [1903] 2 K.B. 600. See also *Nolan* v. *South Australian Laborers' Union* [1910] S.A.L.R. 85 where Gordon J. held, at 89, that a trade union was answerable for the wrongs of its officials, "whether authorised or ratified or not," which are done in the course of their employment and generally for the union's benefit. He did add however that, unless special authorisation were proved, a trade union would not be liable for the consequences of threats by its officials to do something which, according to its constitution, the union could not itself do. See further *Heaton's Transport (St. Helens)* v. *Transport and General Workers' Union* [1973] A.C. 15; *General Aviation Services Ltd.* v. *T.G.W.U.* [1976] I.R.L.R. 224.

official was done in the service of and for the benefit of the union even though his action was *ultra vires*.

Added to these developments was the emergence of the view that picketing was a common law nuisance and the realisation that union officials who organised a strike or who persuaded customers and suppliers not to deal with the employer could be sued for the tort of inducement of breach of contract.

The issue was, therefore, how the unions could counter the combined effects of civil liability and the exposure of union funds to legal action. Pragmatic demands were again made – immunity from the common law civil liabilities and reversal of *Taff Vale*. The Trade Disputes Act 1906 provided this. The Act gave unions immunity by prohibiting actions in tort against them and, for persons acting in contemplation or furtherance of a trade dispute (the golden formula), it gave immunities from liability for the torts of conspiracy to injure and inducement of breach of contract, although here the immunity was limited to inducement of breach of a contract of employment. The only element of a positive nature was the section on picketing which provides that "it shall be lawful for one or more persons" to picket peacefully. This apart, the Act confers no positive rights to strike or to organise industrial action. It merely immunises against civil liability. The economic torts still remain, held back only by the "golden formula". It is necessary, therefore, to examine the nature of the relevant liabilities, before turning our attention, in the next chapter, to the 1906 Act. This is a complex area because the law of tort does not provide a remedy against all forms of deliberate interference with trade or business.

Interference with trade or business

During the nineteenth century the courts were faced with the fundamental question of whether, and to what extent, it was unlawful deliberately to harm the interests of another. In *Wilkinson* v. *Downton*,[85] Wright J. held that where a person wilfully did an act calculated to cause *physical harm* to another person, that person had a good cause of action if physical loss resulted. Less than one month later, the same judge advised the House of Lords in *Allen* v. *Flood*[86] that, where a person wilfully did an act calculated to cause *economic harm* to another person, that person did not have a good cause of

---

[85] [1897] 2 Q.B. 57.
[86] [1898] A.C. 1. Eight High Court Judges advised the House of Lords which, for this case, consisted of nine law Lords. Six of the High Court judges advised that the Lords should find in favour of the plaintiffs with Wright and Mathew JJ. advising for the defendant. The House of Lords by a majority of six to three accepted Wright and Mathew JJ.'s advice. The authors are grateful to Professor Heuston for informing them that Wright J. was an "ardent radical" and legal adviser to the T.U.C. for twenty years. More than any other of the twenty-one judges who heard the case he would have appreciated what the real issues were and seen how important the case was for the unions.

action if economic loss resulted. A majority of the House of Lords agreed[87] and held that, in the absence of additional factors such as the use of unlawful means, deliberate interference with trade did not give rise to liability. According to Fleming,[88] this was done for the sake "of ensuring some elbow-room for the aggressive pursuit of self-interest in a society dedicated to free enterprise" and was influenced by "a desire to reduce judicial intervention in labour disputes and the market place."

Allen v. *Flood* is also taken as laying down an equally fundamental proposition that an act, otherwise lawful, is not rendered unlawful because of malice on the part of the actor.[89] Holmes argued that the case was not one which on the facts entailed the denial of liability for wrongfully motivated behaviour.[90] He pointed out that the jury were instructed so as to make their findings of malice mean only that the defendant had acted with foresight of the harm he would achieve, rather than actual spite. Holmes defined "malice" as a malevolent motive for action without reference to any hope of a remoter benefit to oneself to be accomplished by the intended harm to another, *i.e.* disinterested malevolence.[91] Nevertheless *Allen* v. *Flood*, and the earlier decision in *Mayor of Bradford* v. *Pickles*,[92] are regarded as laying down that motive is essentially irrelevant to the determination of liability in tort. According to Lord Dunedin in *Sorrell* v. *Smith*,[93] these cases "settle beyond dispute that in an action against an individual for injury he has caused by his action, the whole question is whether the act complained of was legal and motive or interest is immaterial."

It is worth considering this question further for a number of reasons. First, Lord Shand, who was in the majority in *Allen* v. *Flood*, subsequently denied that the decision was authority for the proposition that malicious intention on the part of one was not actionable.[94] He said that "the purpose of the defendant [in *Allen* v. *Flood*] was, by the acts complained of, to promote his own trade interest, which it was

---

[87] See Lord Watson at 96, Lord Herschell at 118 and 126, Lord MacNaghten at 151, Lord Shand at 163-164, Lord Davey at 172, Lord James at 180. Of the dissenters – Lord Halsbury, Ashbourne and Morris – Lord Ashbourne was the Lord Chancellor of Ireland and Lord Morris its former Lord Chief Justice.

[88] *The Law of Torts* 6th ed. (Sydney, 1983), p. 658.

[89] See for instance *Clerk and Lindsell on Torts*, 15th ed. (London, 1982), p. 749 when talking of the principle enunciated in *Allen* v. *Flood*: "the exercise of a right will not be rendered unlawful only because of the evil nature of the person who exercises it." Further, on p. 750, "it is now recognised to be a 'leading heresy' to believe that spiteful interference with another's trade is in itself actionable when no unlawful means have been threatened or employed." The phrase "leading heresy" is taken from Lord Dunedin's speech in *Sorrell* v. *Smith* [1926] A.C. 700, 719. The decision of Dixon J. in *Hawkins* v. *Rogers* [1951] I.R. 48, however, proceeds on the basis that there is a cause of action in tort for economic loss wilfully inflicted.

[90] *Aikens* v. *Wisconsin* (1904) 195 U.S. 194, 204.

[91] "Privilege, Malice and Intent" (1894) 8 *Harv. L.R.* 1, 2. See also Fridman, "Malice in the Law of Torts" (1958) 21 *M.L.R.* 484.

[92] [1895] A.C. 587.

[93] [1925] A.C. 700, 724.

[94] In *Quinn* v. *Leathem* [1901] A.C. 495.

held he was entitled to do, although injurious to the plaintiff."[95] If, however, the purpose of the defendant was to injure the plaintiff in his trade as distinguished from the intention of legitimately advancing his own interest, he would have been liable.

Secondly, as is pointed out in *Salmond and Heuston on the Law of Torts*,[96] it is clear that the House of Lords in *Bradford* v. *Pickles* did not regard the defendant as having been motivated by spite or malice. As Professor Heuston puts it:

> "[Pickles'] position was simple. He had something to sell and he did not see why the Corporation should not pay the price he wanted. It was an attitude with which they, as representatives of one of the great commercial communities of Yorkshire, must have been perfectly familiar. His motive was simply one that the common law did not regard as improper. The common law has never recognised as an illegal motive the instinct of self advancement which is the very incentive to all trade."

Thirdly, the courts in the United States have not accepted the validity of the proposition. In *Tuttle* v. *Buck*,[97] for example, the Supreme Court of Minnesota held that the common law did not permit a person to be damaged in his trade or business for the mere gratification of malice. In other words "the state of a man's consciousness always is material to his liability."[98]

Fourthly, three years after the decision in *Allen* v. *Flood*, a slightly differently constituted House of Lords[99] held, in *Quinn* v. *Leathem*,[1] that, even though an act which caused economic loss to A might not be actionable if done by B alone, it was actionable if B did it precisely for the same motive pursuant to an agreement between B and C. *Allen* v. *Flood* was distinguished on the basis that there was no combination. Plurality of defendants made all the difference. The distinction is said to be based on the "sound reasoning" that a combination may make oppressive or dangerous that which if preceded only from a single person would be otherwise. But, as Lord Diplock has said:

> "To suggest today that acts done by one street-corner grocer in concert with a second are more oppressive and dangerous to a competitor than the same acts done by a string of supermarkets

---

[95] At 515. The authors concede, however, that Lord Watson devoted much of his speech to the "annihilation" of the *dictum* of Lord Esher's in *Temperton* v. *Russell* [1893] 1 Q.B. 715 that "an act otherwise lawful may become unlawful if done with a spiteful or malevolent motive."

[96] 18th ed. (London, 1981) at pp. 17–18.

[97] (1909) 119 N.W. 946 (Sup. Ct., Minnesota).

[98] Holmes, (1894) 8 *Harv. L.R.* 1, 5. See also *Burke* v. *Smith* (1888) 37 N.W. 838 (Sup. Ct., Michigan); *Racich* v. *Mastrovich* (1937) 273 N.W. 660 (Sup. Ct., Sth. Dakota), and the dissenting judgment of Madden C.J. in *Martell* v. *Victorian Miners Association* (1903) 29 V.L.R. 475.

[99] Lords Halsbury, MacNaghten, Shand, Brampton, Robertson and Lindley.

[1] [1901] A.C. 495.

under a single ownership or that a multinational conglomerate . . . does not exercise greater economic power than any combination of small businesses, is to shut one's eyes to what has been happening in the business and industrial world since the turn of the century."[2]

Logically therefore, as Lord Diplock conceded, either motive conspiracy should not be a tort or *Allen* v. *Flood* should not be regarded as laying down that malevolent action by one alone is not tortious.[3]

Conspiracy

The tort of civil conspiracy has been described as "a judicial weapon designed to check what were perceived to be socially dangerous activities by organised labour."[4] The dubious nature of this tort is evident from the early editions of *Salmond on Torts* where *Quinn* v. *Leathem* is treated as a case of intimidation.[5] Nor was it favoured by earlier Irish judges. In *Sweeney* v. *Coote*,[6] Lord Ashbourne said that, if the agreement was to do what was lawful and to do it by lawful means, the motives of the parties could not expose them to an action and did not require any justification. Fitzgibbon L.J. was of like mind. He said that it was absurd to say that an act may be done by each of two people without incurring any legal liability for loss consequent thereon and yet that same act done in the same way with the same intent and with the same consequence would be actionable if it was done in pursuance of an agreement made between them before they did it.

Nowadays, however, the case is regarded as establishing an independent tort called conspiracy.[7] It is sometimes said that there are two kinds of civil conspiracy – motive conspiracy and conspiracy to injure using unlawful means.[8] In respect of the latter, Lord Dunedin, in *Sorrell* v. *Smith*,[9] said that an averment of conspiracy in the case of a combination involving tortious acts was mere surplusage and this was the view taken by the Supreme Court in *Dillon* v. *Dunne's Stores*,[10] where it was held that where a tort had been committed by two or more persons an allegation of prior agreement to commit the tort added nothing; the prior agreement merged in the tort.[11] It has been pointed out, however,

---

[2] In *Lonrho Ltd.* v. *Shell Petroleum Co. Ltd.* [1982] A.C. at 189.
[3] See also Heydon *Economic Torts* 2nd ed. (London, 1978) at pp. 27–28.
[4] Burns, "Civil Conspiracy; An Unwieldy Vessel Rides a Judicial Tempest" (1982) 16 *U.B.C.L.R.* 229, citing Whitson, "Civil Conspiracy – A Substantive Tort?" (1979) 59 *Boston Univ. L.R.* 921, 923. See also Redmond (writing *sub nom.* Mathews), "The Tort of Conspiracy in Irish Labour Law" (1973) 8 *Ir. Jur. (n.s.)* 252.
[5] See the 6th ed. (London, 1924) at pp. 576–578.
[6] [1906] I.R. 428; See also Palles C.B. in *Kearney* v. *Lloyd* (1890) 26 L.R. Ir. 268.
[7] See the comments of Lord Diplock in *Lonhro* [1982] A.C. at 189: "The civil tort of conspiracy to injure . . . must I think be accepted by this House as too well established to be discarded, however anomalous it may seem today."
[8] See *Salmond on Torts* 17th ed. (London, 1977), p. 379.
[9] [1925] A.C. 700, 716.
[10] Supreme Court, unreported, 20 December 1968.
[11] See also *Galland* v. *Mineral Underwriters Ltd.* [1977–78] W.A.R. 116, 120.

that there may be a procedural advantage in framing the action in conspiracy in that it might be easier on the ground of conspiracy, as opposed to that of joint tortfeasorship, to find liable instigators who do not actually participate in the commission of the substantive tort.[12] Additionally, the conduct comprising the unlawful means might not be actionable in itself as a tort, such as breach of contract and breach of a statute which does not grant a private right of action. The distinction between the two types has always been said to be that in the case of motive conspiracy everything turns on proof of a specific intention to injure the plaintiff on the part of those combining. Since "intent to injure" as opposed to "legitimate self-interest" is an element of the tort itself, the burden falls on the plaintiff to establish it. Whereas in the case of conspiracy to injure by unlawful means, no such specific intent need be shown.

As a result of the decision of the House of Lords in *Lonhro Ltd.* v. *Shell Petroleum Co. Ltd.*[13] it is now clear, at least in Britain, that there is only one type of conspiracy, since irrespective of the lawfulness of the means employed, the defendants must intend to injure the plaintiff. The House of Lords denied that, if two or more persons combined to do an act in contravention of a penal statute and, in the carrying out of the act, damage results to another person, that person automatically had a cause of action in conspiracy.[14] Liability for the tort of conspiracy arose only where the defendants acted "for the purpose, not of protecting their own interests, but of injuring the interests of the plaintiff." As put more fully by Dixon J. in *McKernan* v. *Fraser*,[15] when talking of a combination whose end was not in itself unlawful, where the means were not unlawful and where no threat of an illegality was made.

> "... for a combination ... to be actionable in such circumstances, the parties to the alleged conspiracy must have been impelled to combine and to act in pursuance of the combination, by a desire to harm the plaintiff, and ... this must have been the sole, the true, or the dominating, or main purpose of their conspiracy ... To adopt a course which necessarily interferes with the plaintiff in the exercise of his calling, and thus injures him, is not enough."

The essence of the tort, therefore, is intention to injure, mere forseeability of injury is not enough even if the acts are unlawful.

Motive conspiracy
Here the authors are concerned with combinations which give rise to civil liability where the end was brought about by conduct or acts which by themselves, and apart from the element of combination or concerted action, would not be regarded as a legal wrong.

---
[12] See Burns, *loc. cit.*, at p. 245.
[13] [1982] A.C. 173.
[14] See Lord Diplock at 189.
[15] (1931) 46 C.L.R. 343, 362.

The most comprehensive analysis of this tort took place in *Crofter Hand Woven Harris Tweed Co.* v. *Veitch.*[16] Lord Simon said that, as a tort, conspiracy arose from a combination the real purpose of which was the infliction of damage on the plaintiff as distinguished from a combination serving the *bona fide* and legitimate interests of those who so combine.[17] Here the plaintiff company marketed cloth woven by crofters on the Isle of Lewis in the Outer Hebrides, using yarn imported from the mainland of Scotland. Yarn was also produced in mills on the island and the majority of yarn spinners on the island were members of a union. The union put in a claim for higher wages which was refused by the spinners' employers on the ground that it would lead to an increase in costs which would prevent them from competing with the plaintiff company. The union thereupon instructed their members at the principal port on the island to refuse to handle imported yarn consigned to the plaintiff company which then sought an injunction restraining the embargo claiming that the defendants were involved in an unlawful conspiracy to injure. The House of Lords refused to grant an injunction. Lord Wright said that the sole object of the defendants was to promote their union's interests by promoting the interests of the industry on which their members' wages depended.[18] Lord Simon spoke in the same vein.

> "The predominant object of the [defendant trade union officials] in getting the embargo imposed was to benefit their trade union members by preventing undercutting and unregulated competition, and so helping to secure the economic stability of the island industry. The result they aimed at achieving was to create a better basis for collective bargaining, and thus directly to improve wage prospects. A combination with such an object is not unlawful."[19]

The tort requires an agreement, combination, undertaking, or concert to injure involving two or more persons. All that is needed is a combination and a common intention. The conspirators need not all join in at the same time, nor need they have exactly the same aim in mind. Questions may arise, however, as to whether a particular defendant, who perhaps attended a meeting but who played no active role, having regard to his knowledge, utterances and actions, was sufficiently a party to the combination and the common design.

Intention to injure is an essential element of conspiracy, as is the actual injury itself. Where the defendants act in combination with mixed purposes, it is the predominant purpose that is important. If the predominant purpose is to damage another and damage results, that is

---

[16] [1942] A.C. 435. See also *McGowan* v. *Murphy* Supreme Court, unreported, 10 April 1967, where Walsh J. said that if "the real purpose of the combination was not to injure the plaintiff but to defend the interests of the trade union by maintaining discipline then no wrong was committed and no action will be even though damage to the plaintiff resulted provided that the means used were not in themselves unlawful."
[17] At 443. [18] At 478–479. [19] At 447.

tortious conspiracy; if the predominant purpose is the lawful protection or promotion of any lawful interests of the combiners it is not a tortious conspiracy, even though it causes damage to another. As Dixon J. put it in *McKernan* v. *Fraser*,[20] when denying that the adoption of a course which necessarily interferes with the plaintiff was actionable:

> "Nor is it enough that this result should be intended [*i.e.* interference with the plaintiff] if the motive which actuates the defendants is not the desire to inflict injury but that of compelling the plaintiff to act in a way required for the advancement or for the defence of the defendants' trade or vocational interests."

It also seems that if one member of the combination acts, not out of a desire to protect the standards of the trade union, but because he wishes to revenge himself on the plaintiff, the others will not be infected by this malice and it will not convert the combination into an unlawful conspiracy.[21] It must be remembered that strong feelings are always present when a trade union enters a struggle with an employer. There is of course the desire to protect and advance its members' economic interests but there may also be the desire to inflict harm. As Evatt J. put it, this latter desire, before it can be dubbed malice, must be much more than a sign of the reality and persistence of the struggle between the plaintiff and the defendants.[22]

The burden of proving both the combination and the purpose of damaging the plaintiff lies on the plaintiff. In most cases of conspiracy the plaintiff seeks to prove the case by the inferences available from the defendants' acts. In the words of Isaacs J.:[23]

> "Community of purpose may be proved by independent facts, but it need not be. If the other defendant is shown to be committing other acts tending to the same end, then though primarily each set of acts is attributable to the person whose acts they are and to him alone, there may be such a concurrence of time, character, direction and result as naturally to lead to the inference that these separate acts were the outcome of pre-concert, or some mutual contemporaneous engagement, or that they were themselves the manifestation of mutual consent to carry out a common purpose, thus forming as well as evidencing a combination to effect the one object towards which the separate acts are found to converge."

Inducement of breach of contract

Knowingly to induce or, as it is sometimes put, to procure a third

---

[20] (1931) 46 C.L.R. 343, 362.   [21] *Per* Evatt J., *McKernan* v. *Fraser* (1931) 46 C.L.R. 343, 401.
[22] *Ibid.* at 404. See also Gordon J. in *Nolan* v. *South Australian Laborers' Union* [1910] S.A.L.R. 85, 94.
[23] *R. and Attorney General of the Commonwealth* v. *Associated Northern Collieries* (1911) 14 C.L.R. 387, 400.

party to breach his contract to the detriment of the other contracting party without justification or excuse is a tort. It extends to intentionally causing breaches of any type of contract and is regarded as encompassing two separate methods of achieving such interference. The defendant may have acted either by directly inducing one of the contracting parties to break the contract – which is properly called inducement of breach of contract – or by inducing someone else to act in such a way as to cause one of the contracting parties to breach the contract – which might more properly be regarded as falling within the sphere of "unlawful interference with trade".

The modern basis of the tort of inducement of breach of contract is found in the majority judgments of the Court of Queen's Bench in *Lumley* v. *Gye*[24] in 1853, although its origins go back to ancient times.[25] The majority of the court held that a cause of action lay for the intentional and malicious inducement of a breach of a contract for personal service. Both Compton and Erle JJ. stressed the malicious violation of contractual rights. Although there was some initial doubt as to the correctness of the decision, due in no small part to the powerful dissent of Coleridge J., it was approved by a majority of the Court of Appeal in *Bowen* v. *Hall*,[26] and was extended to commercial contracts in *Temperton* v. *Hughes*.[27] Here builders had contracted with the plaintiff to purchase their building materials from him. The plaintiff was in a dispute with a trade union and the defendants, officials of the union, induced the builders to refuse to take further supplies from the plaintiff, in breach of their contracts. The Court of Appeal rejected the defendants' contention that the doctrine enunciated in *Lumley* v. *Gye* was confined to contracts of personal service. The relevance of malice was also stressed. In *Quinn* v. *Leathem*,[28] however, Lord MacNaghten said that the decision in *Lumley* v. *Gye* was not based on malice but violation of a legal right.

> "A violation of a legal right committed knowingly is a cause of action . . . and it is a violation of a legal right to interfere with contractual relations recognised by law if there be no sufficient justification for the interference."[29]

Lord MacNaghten's judgment was regarded by the House of Lords in *South Wales Miners' Federation* v. *Glamorgan Coal Co.*[30] as correctly setting out the juristic basis of the tort. Here the Federation had called its members out on strike, in breach of their contracts of employment. At first instance, Bigham J. held that in so doing the Federation had

---

[24] 2 E. & B. 216.
[25] Bracton, writing in the 13th century and drawing on Roman law ideas, stated that "*actio indirecta*" lies for the lord in so far as it was to his interest not to be deprived of the services of his household servants nor of the labour of his slaves and of such like". 3 *Bracton*, Tr. 1, f. 115.
[26] (1881) 6 Q.B.D. 333. [27] [1893] 1 Q.B. 715. [28] [1901] A.C. 495. [29] At 510.
[30] [1905] A.C. 239.

been actuated by an honest desire to forward the interests of its members and not by any malicious intention to injure the plaintiff company. He therefore found for the defendant union. In the House of Lords it was confirmed that to support an action for procuring or inducing a breach of contract it was not essential to prove actual malice.

To Sayre writing in 1922[31] the most remarkable feature of this form of tortious liability was "the surprising rapidity with which courts have adopted it, broadened it, and pared away restricting limitations." He continued –

> "Conceived originally as a doctrine applicable to cases of malice, and applied to a contract of purely personal services, the doctrine was first broadened to include *all* contracts, and then widened to include cases where no malevolence could be shown."[32]

There are five essential elements that must be present to constitute liability.

(1) There must be a contract. At the outset it must be stressed that there is a fundamental distinction[33] between intentionally inducing a person to breach a contract and intentionally inducing a person not to enter into a contract.[34] In *Temperton* v. *Russell*,[35] Lord Esher criticised this distinction but only because liability, in his opinion, was predicated upon malice.

> "It seems rather a fine distinction to say that, where a defendant maliciously induces a person not to carry out a contract already made with the plaintiff and so injures the plaintiff, it is actionable, but where he injures the plaintiff by maliciously preventing a person from entering into a contract with the plaintiff, which he could otherwise have entered into, it is not actionable."[36]

He did not believe the distinction could prevail because there was the same type of injury and the same wrongful intent. Following *Quinn* v. *Leathem*,[37] however, it is clear that this distinction is fundamental, because as we have seen, *Allen* v. *Flood* is regarded as having closed the door against liability in respect of loss suffered as a consequence of a person, even though motivated by malice, persuading another person not to enter into a contract. In other words the tort vindicates a person's right to be protected from interference with his rights under a contract already made; it does not seek to vindicate a

---

[31] 36 *Harv. L.R.* 663.
[32] *Ibid.* at p. 674.
[33] Described by Lord Herschell, in *Allen* v. *Flood* [1898] A.C. 1, 121, as a "chasm".
[34] See *Midland Cold Storage Ltd* v. *Steer* [1972] Ch. 630, 644–5.
[35] [1893] 1 Q.B. 715.   [36] At 728.   [37] [1901] A.C. 495.

person's right to carry on business, that is to make contracts without interference.[38]

The tort is said to consist in the intentional inducement of the breach of an existing and valid contractual obligation.[39] If the contract is void on grounds of incapacity or illegality, no tort is committed[40] but the tort has been held to extend to contracts which are unenforceable because, for instance, they are not evidenced in writing.[41] More difficulty arises where the contract is determinable and the defendant induces the contracting party to determine the contract lawfully. Here there is no breach, therefore there should be no liability—unless the defendant has used unlawful means.[42] There are, however, a number of English decisions which appear to hold that there is liability. *Emerald Construction Co.* v. *Lowthian*[43] is a good example. Here the main contractors responded to trade union pressure by exercising their option, granted under the sub-contract with Emerald Construction Ltd., lawfully to terminate the contract. Emerald Construction Ltd. had no cause of action for breach of contract against the main contractors, nevertheless the defendant was held liable for inducement of breach. In part the decision is based on the defendant's lack of knowledge of the option to terminate clause – he acted with the intention of procuring a breach of contract even though the contract was not in fact broken.[44] Three years later, in *Torquay Hotel Co. Ltd.* v. *Cousins*,[45] Lord Denning M.R. declared that the time had come when the principle in *Lumley* v. *Gye* should be "further extended to cover deliberate and direct interference with the execution of a contract without that causing any breach."[46] He stated that if a person intentionally prevented or hindered performance of a contract there would be liability even though there was no breach. If Lord Denning is correct in this, then it is only a "small step" to holding that to intentionally induce a person not to enter into a contract is also tortious. As Elias and Ewing have pointed out,[47] Lord Denning's formulation involves a change in the underlying principle of *Lumley* v. *Gye*.

---

[38] *Per* Loring J., *Beekman* v. *Masters* (1907) 80 N.E. 817, 819.
[39] *Clark and Lindsell on Torts* 15th ed. (London, 1982), p. 705.
[40] *Ibid.*
[41] *Unident Ltd.* v. *Delong* (1982) 131 D.L.R. (3d) 225, 231.
[42] *Per* Slesser L.J., *McManus* v. *Bowes* [1938] 1 K.B. 98, 127; and *per* Morris L.J., *Thomson (D.C.) & Co. Ltd.* v. *Deakin* [1952] Ch. 646, 702.
[43] [1966] 1 W.L.R. 691.
[44] See Lord Denning at 700–701.
[45] [1969] 2 Ch. 106.
[46] At 137–138.
[47] "Economic Torts and Labour Law: Old Principles and New Liabilities" (1982) 41 *C.L.J.* 321, 329.

"It also shifts the boundary line between *Lumley* v. *Gye* and *Allen* v. *Flood* and stakes a larger claim for the former by protecting contractual expectations as well as contractual rights. Although the shift may appear a small one, its ramifications are very far reaching. For once contractual expectations are protected how can it be lawful to persuade a party to a contract to terminate it lawfully, at least where the other party has a reasonable expectation that the contract will continue in force? . . . And logically why should the protection of expectations not extend, at least in some circumstances, to rendering it unlawful to persuade a man not to enter into a contract?"[48]

The scope of this liability is extremely uncertain. What if the defendant's action does not prevent performance of the contract but merely makes it more onerous? Wedderburn has warned that any extension into this area will threaten commercial competition or legitimate economic or industrial activity, and has argued convincingly that Lord Denning's *dicta* should be confined to cases where there is interference, short of breach, brought about deliberately by *unlawful* means.[49]

Torquay Hotel is also authority for a related proposition to the one just discussed, namely that the tort is not confined to the procuring of such non-performance of primary obligations under a contract as would necessarily give rise to secondary obligations to make monetary compensation by way of damages. In *Torquay Hotel* an injunction was granted against defendants who had induced a company to cease supplies of oil under a standing contract which provided that neither party would be liable for any failure to fulfil any term of the agreement if fulfilment was delayed, hindered, or prevented by any circumstance whatever which was not within their immediate control, including labour disputes. This *force majeure* clause meant that the hotel would not have been able to recover damages against the oil company for breach of contract. Although the Court of Appeal regarded the clause as excepting the oil company from liability for non-performance, Lord Denning made it clear that it would not have made any difference, in his opinion, if the clause excepted the oil company from its obligation to perform.

(2) There must be an act of inducing the breach of contract. There are two distinct forms of wrongful interference which give rise to liability. The interference may be effected directly or indirectly. It may be effected directly, by an inducement or procurement operating immediately on one of the parties to the contract or on

---
[48] *Ibid.*
[49] In *Clerk and Lindell on Torts* 15th ed. (London, 1982), at para. 15-05.

things or states of affairs that are in themselves essential to the performance of the contract, or indirectly, by inducing those upon whom one of the parties to the contract relies for the performance of his contract with another to break their contracts of employment so as to render performance of the principal contract either impossible or substantially more onerous.

The more obvious form is direct inducement where the defendant actively persuades one of the contracting parties to break the contract.[50] A direct communication from one person to another will suffice and it will make no difference that this communication is made through the instrumentality of a third person.[51]

There is difficulty, however, in attempting to define precisely what is inducement. The textbooks state that persuasion must be distinguished from the mere communication of information and advice, and that the transmission of information must contain some element of pressure or persuasion before it will be considered an inducement.[52] But the cases show that it is practically impossible to draw such a line.[53] Advice which is intended to have persuasive effects is not distinguishable from an inducement[54] and the courts, certainly in England, have tended in recent years to find more readily a persuasive element in the transmission of information from a union to an employer.[55] It is thus very difficult for those involved to know exactly when they have crossed the line between transmission of information and inducement.

One case where it was held that the defendants had not crossed the line was *Reg Armstrong Motors Ltd.* v. *C.I.E.*[56] A number of trade unions were engaged in a campaign to prevent the continued importation of fully built-up (FBU) vehicles into the Republic, and thus to save jobs in the Irish car assembly industry. The I.C.T.U. approved a call for a complete ban on the importation of such vehicles. The plaintiff company had entered

---

[50] As in *Lumley* v. *Gye* (1853) 2 E. & B. 216.
[51] See *Cattle Express Shipping Corp. of Liberia* v. *Cheasty* High Court, unreported, 19 April 1983. The *ex tempore* judgment of Barrington J. is noted at (1983) 2 *J.I.S.L.L.* at pp. 62–63.
[52] See *Clerk and Lindsell on Torts* 15th ed. (London, 1982), p. 715, citing Evershed M.R. in *Thomson (D.C.) & Co. Ltd.* v. *Deakin* [1952] Ch. 646, 686.
[53] Coleridge J. described this as a task for a casuist rather than a jurist, let alone a juryman; *Lumley* v. *Gye* (1853) 2 E. & B. 216, 252.
[54] *Per* Simonds J., *Camden Nominees Ltd.* v. *Forcey* [1940] Ch. 352, 366.
[55] See, *inter alia*, Winn L.J. in *Torquay Hotel Co. Ltd.* v. *Cousins* [1969] 2 Ch. 106, 147. "It was one of counsel for the defendants' main submissions that mere advice, warning or information cannot amount to tortious procurement of breach of contract. Whilst granting *arguendi causa* that a communication which went no further would, in general, not, in the absence of circumstances giving a particular significance, amount to a threat or intimidation, I am unable to understand why it may not amount to an inducement."
[56] High Court, unreported, 2 December 1975. Hereafter referred to as *Reg Armstrong.*

into contracts with British Rail and C.I.E. for the transportation of FBU vehicles from Fishguard to Rosslare to Dublin. C.I.E. did not fulfil their part of the contract and the plaintiff company claimed that C.I.E. were in breach of their contract and that this breach had been induced by the acts of the defendant trade union officials. Hamilton J. held that the defendants had merely informed C.I.E. of the position, namely that there was an I.C.T.U. approved embargo. C.I.E., having been so informed, "prudently" decided that they would not require any of their employees to handle the vehicles. There was no element of pressure or procuration; the fact that C.I.E. might be described as "chicken hearted" was irrelevant – "the ease with which a person may be persuaded is not a relevant consideration"; the advice was not of the "or else" variety. There was, therefore, in Hamilton J.'s opinion, no *direct* inducement of the breach of contract between C.I.E and the plaintiff company.

The second form of inducement is where the defendant, without directly inducing one of the parties to break the contract, contrives a situation which will result in a breach of contract. This often occurs when the defendant induces a third party to do something so as to prevent performance of a contract.[57] So in *Reg Armstrong* the defendants might have instructed their members in Rosslare to refuse to handle FBU vehicles thus causing C.I.E. to break the contract of delivery. But, as Hamilton J. emphasised in this case, indirect inducement is only actionable if unlawful means are used. As C.I.E. had not required their employees to handle FBU vehicles, there was no breach of the employees' contracts of employment and thus no unlawful means. No actionable wrong is committed by a person who, by acts not in themselves unlawful, prevents another person from obtaining the performance of a contract by a third person or who induces others so to prevent that person by lawful means.

The most comprehensive analysis of this form of the tort, where the unlawful means consists of inducing employees to break their contracts of employment, is that of Jenkins L.J. in *Thomson & Co. Ltd.* v. *Deakin*;[58] an analysis that was "gratefully accepted" by Hamilton J. in *Reg Armstrong.*[59] For liability to exist it must be shown:

(i) that the defendant knew of the contract;
(ii) that he intended its breach and with this object in mind definitely and unequivocally persuaded, induced, or pro-

---

[57] Similarly, wrongfully to remove the only means of performing the contract is also actionable.
[58] [1952] Ch. 646, 697.
[59] At p. 15 of his unreported judgment.

cured the employees to break their contracts of employment;
(iii) that the employees so procured did break their contracts of employment;
(iv) that the breach of the contract forming the alleged subject matter of interference ensued as a necessary consequence of the breaches by the employees concerned of their contracts of employment.

While there must be knowledge of the contract it is not necessary that the defendant knows the precise terms of the contract. As Lord Pearce said in *J.T. Stratford Ltd.* v. *Lindley*:[60]

"It is no answer to a claim based on wrongfully inducing a breach of contract to assert that the respondents did not know with exactitude all the terms of the contract. The relevant question is whether they had sufficient knowledge to know that they were inducing a breach."

The Court of Appeal subsequently went further and held, in *Emerald Construction Co. Ltd.* v. *Lowthian*,[61] that "even if the defendants did not know of the actual terms of the contract but had the means of knowledge which they deliberately disregarded that would be enough."

The second requirement would suggest that general exhortations during a trade dispute such as "Stop Supplies to X" are not inducements of any consequential breaches of contract if that object could be attained by lawful means.[62] As for the fourth requirement Lord Diplock in *Merkur Island Shipping Corpn.* v. *Laughton*[63] was of the opinion that Jenkins L.J. intended to include all prevention of due performance of a primary obligation under a contract.

Indirect interference in the execution of a contract is therefore actionable provided unlawful means are used. This is the crucial distinction between the two forms of the tort. Direct persuasion to breach a contract is unlawful in itself. The intentional bringing about of breach or non-performance by indirect methods requires unlawful means for there to be liability. Another distinction between the direct and indirect forms is that, in the latter, the breach of the contract forming the subject matter of the dispute must ensue as a *necessary* consequence of

---

[60] [1965] A.C. 269, 332.
[61] [1966] 1 W.L.R. 691, 700, *per* Lord Denning M.R. See also *Wooley* v. *Dunford* (1972) 3 S.A.S.R. 243.
[62] See Jenkins L.J. in *Thomson* v. *Deakin* [1952] Ch. 646 at 698, where he said that it was not actionable to advocate objects which can be achieved by lawful means merely because they can also be achieved by unlawful means.
[63] [1983] 2 A.C. 570, 608.

the unlawful acts. In the former, the breach need only be a *reasonable* consequence of the defendant's action.[64]

(3) The action must be intentional. The plaintiff must show that there was an intentional invasion of his contractual rights. It is not enough that the breach of contract was the natural or foreseeable consequence of the defendant's conduct. Unless the defendant has actually expressed an intent, his intent can only be ascertained from a consideration of his actions and the surrounding circumstances. A general principle, at least in the criminal law, with regard to establishing intent has regularly been stated as being that every person is taken to intend the natural and probable consequences of his own act. Yet this is only an inference, belonging to the law of evidence.[65] If a person is able to foresee the natural consequences of his acts, it is usually reasonable to infer that he did foresee them and intend them. But, as Byrne J. once pointed out, "while this is an inference which may be drawn, and on the facts in certain circumstances must inevitably be drawn, yet if on all the facts in a particular case it is not the correct inference, then it should not be drawn."[66] The fundamental question is whether the defendant actually intended the natural and probable consequences of his act. A useful interpretation of "intention" was offered by Asquith L.J. in *Cunliffe* v. *Goodman*:[67]

> "An 'intention' to my mind connotes a state of affairs which the party 'intending' . . . does more than merely contemplate: it connotes a state of affairs which, on the contrary, he decides, so far as in him lies, to bring about, and which, in point of possibility, he has a reasonable prospect of being able to bring about, by his own act of volition."

(4) The action must be without lawful justification.[68] It is clear from what has been said above that to procure a breach of contract intentionally is actionable regardless of the motive or reason for so doing, since the action is based upon violation of the plaintiff's right and is not based on the defendant's malice or spite. Yet it is equally clear that there is a defence of justification.[69] There are no reported Irish cases however, and only one reported English case, in which the defence has

---

[64] Per Lord Pearce in *Stratford* v. *Lindley* [1965] A.C. at 333.
[65] See Lord Bridge in *R.* v. *Moloney* [1985] 1 All E.R. 1025, 1033–1039. See also McWilliam J. delivering the judgment of the Court of Criminal Appeal in *People (D.P.P.)* v. *Douglas and Hayes* [1985] I.L.R.M. 25, 28.
[66] *Director of Public Prosecutions* v. *Smith* [1961] A.C. 290, 300.
[67] [1950] 2 K.B. 237, 253.
[68] See Heydon, "The Defence of Justification" (1970) 20 *Univ. Toronto L.J.* 139.
[69] *Posluns* v. *Toronto Stock Exchange* (1964) 46 D.L.R. (2d) 210, (1966) 53 D.L.R. (2d) 193; and, in a trade union context, see *Pete's Towing Services Ltd.* v. *North Industrial Union of Workers* [1970] N.Z.L.R. 32 and *Latham* v. *Singleton* [1981] 2 N.S.W.L.R. 843 at 867–840.

succeeded, and so its scope is incapable of precise definition. The only conclusion that one can draw from *Brimelow* v. *Casson*[70] – the isolated case where the defence was successful – is that it lies only within extremely narrow limits and in most cases a defendant will not be able to rely upon it.[71] Here the representatives of an actors' association were held justified in inducing theatrical proprietors to break their contracts with the plaintiff, because the plaintiff's chorus girls received so little remuneration that they were forced to resort to prostitution.

(5) Damage must be caused as a result of the commission of the tort. The plaintiff must prove not only the wrongful interference but also that he has been damaged by the breach of contract. When damage can be proved, or inferred, the plaintiff is entitled to recover, in respect of that damage, which is not too remote a consequence of the breach. Doubt exists however as to the operation of the doctrine of remoteness. In *Clerk and Lindsell on Torts*[72] it is asserted that the plaintiff cannot recover for losses which were not foreseeable but there is Canadian authority for the proposition that the doctrine of foreseeability, while appropriate to actions of negligence, is not suitable for intentional torts.[73]

In summary, therefore, the juristic basis of the tort is that there has been a knowing and intentional interference with the plaintiff's contractual rights without justification. It must be proved that, when the alleged interference took place, a contract, not discharged and not yet finally performed, was in existence. The alleged interference will consist of procuring or causing a breach of the contract (it may also consist of preventing or hindering the performance of a contract). The actionable interference may be effected directly or indirectly; where the interference is direct the persuasion or inducement is regarded by the law as wrongful in itself, where it is indirect the means by which the interference is effected must be unlawful.

Intimidation

The essential ingredients of the tort of intimidation are that (i) there must be a threat by one person to use unlawful means so as to compel

[70] [1924] 1 Ch. 302.
[71] The common law position is probably best summed up in *Read* v. *Friendly Society of Operative Stonemasons* [1902] 2 K.B. 732 where the Court of Appeal denied that a trade union could be under a moral or social duty to act *bona fide* in the interests of its members sufficient to provide a justification for the trade union inducing breaches of employment contracts. See also *Slade and Stewart Ltd.* v. *Haynes* (1969) 5 D.L.R. (3d) 736. That the common law may have taken, in time, a different view is a distinct possibility (*vide* the change of attitude to conspiracy evidenced by *Crofter Hand Woven Harris Tweed Co.* v. *Veitch* [1942] A.C. 435) but the power to develop a defence of justification was taken out of the Irish and British judiciary's hands by s. 3 of the Trade Disputes Act 1906.
[72] 15th ed. (London, 1982), p. 724.
[73] *Bettel* v. *Yim* (1979) 88 D.L.R. (3d) 543.

another to obey his wishes and (ii) the person so threatened must comply with the demand. In such circumstances the person damnified by the compliance can sue for intimidation. It is clear then that the potential plaintiff can either be the person threatened (two-party intimidation) or a third person (three-party intimidation). Although there is little authority the editors of *Salmond and Heuston on Torts* do not doubt that it is an actionable wrong intentionally to compel a person by means of a threat of an illegal act to do some act whereby loss accrues to him.[74] So an action will lie at the suit of an employer who has been compelled to shut down his business because of threats of personal violence made against him.[75]

It is essential that the threat is to do something unlawful. It was never challenged that it covered threats of violence or threats of a tortious or criminal nature. In *Riordan* v. *Butler*[76] however, the plaintiff had been wrongfully dismissed by his employer because of threats made by the defendants to cease work immediately if the plaintiff was allowed to continue to work. The threat that they would "walk off the job" was viewed by O'Byrne J. as a threat to break their contracts. This was held to be sufficient unlawful means for the purposes of the tort of intimidation.[77] This judgment was subsequently approved by the House of Lords in *Rookes* v. *Barnard*.[78] Here the defendants had threatened their employer with a strike unless the plaintiff was dismissed. It was conceded that a no-strike clause contained in a collective agreement between the employer and the defendants' trade union had been incorporated into the defendants' contracts of employment. The threatened strike was, therefore, a threat to break their contracts and the plaintiff successfully contended before the House of Lords that a threat to break a contract constituted unlawful means. Lord Devlin said that he found nothing to differentiate a threat of a breach of contract from a threat of physical violence or any other illegal act.[79]

The decision that breach of contract could amount to unlawful means for the purpose of this tort was strongly criticised by Wedderburn[80] on the ground that it denied "the most basic distinctions

---

[74] 18th ed. at p. 356.
[75] See *Huljich* v. *Hall* [1973] 2 N.Z.L.R. 279.
[76] [1940] I.R. 347.
[77] Following a *dictum* of Gavan Duffy J. in *Cooper* v. *Millea* [1938] I.R. 749, a decision which Walsh J. believes to have been wrongly decided on its facts, see *Becton Dickinson Ltd.* v. *Lee* [1973] I.R. 1, 30. *Cf* O'Higgins J. in *Kire Manufacturing Co. Ltd.* v. *O'Leary* High Court, unreported, 29 April 1974 who, at p. 22 of his judgment, could not accept that *Cooper* v. *Millea* was incorrectly decided. In O'Higgins J.'s view *Cooper* v. *Millea* was no different to *Rookes* v. *Barnard* in that the defendants were not merely threatening to induce a breach of contract by others which would be protected by s. 3 but were in addition threatening to break their own contracts of employment which would not.
[78] [1964] A.C. 1129.
[79] At 1209. See also Lord Evershed at 1118, Lord Hodson at 1201, Lord Pearce at 1234 and Lord Reid at 1169.
[80] (1964) 27 *M.L.R.* 257 especially pp. 263–267.

between tort and contract," but he has subsequently conceded that, whatever the merits of these arguments, it is now established that breach of contract constitutes unlawful means.[81] The Supreme Court of Canada, however, in *Central Canada Potash Co. Ltd.* v. *Government of Saskatchewan*[82] refused to apply the reasoning in *Rookes* v. *Barnard* to a case of two-party intimidation. Maitland J. was in agreement with the view expressed in *Winfield and Jolowicz on Tort*.[83]

> "It is submitted, therefore, that the two-party situation is properly distinguishable from the three-party situation and that it does not necessarily follow from *Rookes* v. *Barnard* that whenever A threatens B with an unlawful act, including a breach of his contract with B, he thereby commits the tort of intimidation. In fact the balance of advantage seems to lie in holding that where A threatens B with a breach of his contract with B, B should be restricted to his contractual remedies. The law should not encourage B to yield to the threat but should seek to persuade him to resist it. If he suffers damage in consequence he will be adequately compensated by his remedy in damages for breach of contract, as his damage can scarcely be other than financial. Where, however, what is threatened is a tort, and especially if the threat is of violence, it is both unrealistic to insist that proceedings for a *quia timet* injunction afford him adequate protection against the consequences of resistance and unreasonable to insist that if violence is actually inflicted upon him he is adequately compensated by an award of damages thereafter. The view is preferred, therefore, that although A commits the tort of intimidation against B where he threatens B with violence or perhaps with any other tort, no independent tort is committed when all that is threatened is a breach of contract."

The position surely is different if A threatens B not with a breach of the contract between A and B but with breach of that between A and C. The writers have in mind here a situation where the threatened strike is not in breach of the employment contracts but is in breach of the union's rules.

A threat is an "intimation by one to another that unless the latter does or does not do something the former will do something which the latter will not like."[84] In other words the threat must be coercive, of the "or else" variety.[85] A trade union official would not, therefore, be liable if he merely informed the employer of the possibility of a strike.[86]

---

[81] In *Clerk and Lindsell on Torts* 15th ed. at p. 741.
[82] (1978) 88 D.L.R. (3d) 609.   [83] 10th ed., p. 458.
[84] *Per* Peterson J., *Hodges* v. *Webb* [1920] 2 Ch. 70, 89.
[85] See Walsh J. in *Becton Dickinson Ltd* v. *Lee* [1973] I.R. 1, 31.
[86] "A man cannot have an action brought against him if he makes a statement as to something injurious which might occur, if afterwards it does happen to occur." *Per* A'Beckett J., *Martell* v. *Victorian Coal Miners' Association* (1903) 29 V.L.R. 475, 484. See also Lord Donovan in *Stratford* v. *Lindley* [1985] A.C. 269, 340.

There is nothing unlawful, in Lord Wright's words, "in giving a warning or intimation that if the party addressed pursues a certain line of conduct, others may act in a manner which he will not like or which will be prejudicial to his interests so long as nothing unlawful is threatened or done."[87]

It is "abundantly clear" that the tort of intimidation cannot be committed if the threat is ineffective. "If the threat is carried out and the desired result is not procured, there has been no tort of intimidation."[88]

Lord Denning M.R. on two occasions[89] has suggested that there is a defence of justification whereby a defendant who has committed the tort of intimidation can excuse himself from liability. What has been said about the defence of justification, in the case of inducement of breach of contract, applies with more force here, since, unlike direct contractual interference where no independent illegality need be shown, the method of intervention here is *per se* unlawful.

Unlawful interference with trade or business

If threatening unlawful action against an employer with intent to harm someone else is tortious, then it would seem to follow that committing such unlawful action with the same intent is equally tortious. It now seems clear that, in addition to the three nominate torts of conspiracy, inducement of breach of contract and intimidation, there is a tort "of uncertain ambit" which consists in one person using unlawful means with the object and effect of interfering in someone else's trade or business.[90] The modern formulation of this species of liability derives from decisions of Lord Denning M.R., particularly *Torquay Hotel Co. Ltd.* v. *Cousins*.[91] Its existence, however, was recognised by Gavan Duffy P. in *Sheriff* v. *McMullen*[92] and can be traced back to *Allen* v. *Flood*,[93] if not beyond that to *dicta* of Holt C.J. in *Keeble* v. *Hickeringill*.[94]

Here liability is based on the proposition stated by Lord Dunedin in

---

[87] *Crofter Hand-Woven Harris Tweed Co.* v. *Veitch* [1942] A.C. 435, 467.
[88] *Per* Walsh J., *Becton Dickinson Ltd.* v. *Lee* [1973] I.R. 1, 31.
[89] *Morgan* v. *Fry* [1968] 2 Q.B. 710, 729 and *Cory Lighterage Ltd.* v. *Transport and General Workers' Union* [1973] I.C.R. 339, 356-357.
[90] *Clerk and Lindsell on Torts* 15th ed., p. 747. See Carty, "Unlawful Interference with Trade" (1983) 3 *Legal Studies* 193.
[91] [1969] 2 Ch. 106. See also *Daily Mirror Newspapers Ltd* v. *Gardner* [1968] 2 Q.B. 762; *Acrow (Automation) Ltd.* v. *Rex Chainbelt Inc.* [1971] 1 W.L.R. 1676; *Carlin Music Corp.* v. *Collins* [1979] F.S.R. 348. Lord Denning's formulation has also been approved in Canada and New Zealand, see, *inter alia, Mark Fishing Ltd.* v. *United Fishermen and Allied Workers' Union* (1972) 24 *D.L.R.* (3d) 385, although see O'Sullivan J.A. in *Mintuck* v. *Valley River Band No. 63A* (1977) 75 D.L.R. (3d) 589, 605, and *Coleman* v. *Myers* [1977] 2 N.Z.L.R. 225.
[92] [1952] I.R. 236 at 256-8.
[93] [1898] A.C.1, 138 and 180. The tort was recognised as long ago as 1914 by the New Zealand Court of Appeal in *Fairbairn, Wright & Co.* v. *Levin & Co. Ltd* (1914) 34 N.Z.L.R. 1. See now *Van Camp Chocolates Ltd.* v. *Aulsebrooks Ltd.* [1984] 1 N.Z.L.R. 354.
[94] (1705) 11 East 547n.

Sorrell v. *Smith*[95] that one is not entitled to interfere by illegal means with another's method of gaining a living, and restated by Lord Denning M.R. in *Ex parte Island Records* that "a man who is carrying on a lawful trade or calling has a right to be protected from any unlawful interference with it."[96] Damage is essential and it is fundamental that the damage must be shown to have been caused by *unlawful* interference. It is crucial to distinguish interference by unlawful means from interference with economic interests where the means are lawful. The latter is only tortious where conspiracy is made out.

It is clear that indirect inducement of breach of contract and intimidation can be regarded as part of this wider form of liability since the common feature is unlawful means. The tort of unlawful interference, however, does not require proof that existing contracts have been broken or interfered with. It protects, as Elias and Ewing have pointed out in a valuable article,[97] not merely the plaintiff's legal rights but also his other interests such as the business expectations of an employer and the expectation of continued employment by an employee. It matters not that a contract between the plaintiff and someone else is lawfully terminated nor whether a contract is not entered into, provided the defendant has used unlawful means with the intention of causing harm to the plaintiff's trade, business or employment interests.

The crucial question here, as with intimidation and indirect inducement of breach of contract, is what constitutes unlawful means. It would obviously make for "brevity, logic and elegance" if the scope of unlawful means was the same for all forms of liability, howsoever named, which require unlawful means.[98]

Unfortunately no such clear principle emerges from the cases. All agree that crimes and torts are sufficient to create liability. Breach of trust is also favoured as being sufficient.[99] In this jurisdiction, infringement of a person's constitutional rights would certainly be sufficient.[1] In *Rookes* v. *Barnard*,[2] however, Lord Devlin, while holding that breach of contract was unlawful means for the purpose of intimidation, left open the question of whether it would be so for the purpose of conspiracy. Logically there is no reason for drawing a

---

[95] [1925] A.C. 700, 769.
[96] [1978] Ch. 122, 136.
[97] "Economic Torts and Labour Law: Old Principles and New Liabilities" (1982) 41 *C.L.J.* 321.
[98] Wedderburn in *Clerk and Lindsell on Torts* 15th ed., p. 751.
[99] So when directors of a company, at the behest of a franchisor, notified a bank of a change in the cheque signing authority without the required directors' resolution to that effect, it was held by the Appeal Division of the Nova Scotia Supreme Court in *Volkswagen Canada Ltd.* v. *Spicer* (1978) 91 D.L.R. (3d) 42, that this amounted to unlawful means for the purpose of establishing liability for interfering with the economic interests of the shareholders. (At 61-62, *per* Cooper J.A.).
[1] See Henchy J. in *Talbot (Ireland) Ltd.* v. *Merrigan* Supreme Court, unreported, 30 April 1981.
[2] [1964] A.C. 1129, 1210.

distinction of this kind since the reason for the requirement of unlawful means is the same in both cases and in principle it is scarcely reasonable that a defendant should be liable when he intentionally causes damage by means of a coercive threat but should escape liability when he causes the same damage deliberately by doing that very act or employing those very means. Lord Denning M.R. has also suggested that behaviour contrary to the public interest or which interferes with the freedom of the Press would be enough.³ The authors would agree with those who have stated that this appears to be an "idiosyncratic" view and one which was rightly not relied upon by Lord Denning's colleagues. "In effect, it is simply dubbing what the judge considers unacceptable to be unlawful."⁴ Much more doubt, however, attaches to the question of breach of statute. The narrow view favoured by most academic commentators is that only wrongs which are independently actionable can constitute unlawful means.⁵ This involves asking whether a civil action for breach of statutory duty would arise.⁶ A wider view is that there is no reason in principle why the breach of statute should be independently actionable, since the basis of liability is the use of unlawful means specifically directed to damage the plaintiff. So in *Acrow (Automation) Ltd.* v. *Rex Chainbelt Inc.*,⁷ Lord Denning M.R. held that an act in contempt of court constituted unlawful means.

Although this issue appears similar to that of whether a civil action based on breach of statute has been created, the similarity is only superficial. The issue here is not whether breach of statute gives rise to a civil action; it is whether there is any good reason for holding that an act which the defendant is not at liberty to commit does not amount to 'unlawful' means. The authors note, however, that Lord Devlin "tentatively" expressed the opinion in *Rookes* v. *Barnard*⁸ that if the illegality is merely technical it might not be sufficient to constitute unlawful means. Elias and Ewing have commented that this is a "sensible and important" exception.⁹

"The essence of liability is the imposition of unlawful coercion, or the threat of it. Where the illegality is incidental to the pressure and not an integral part of it, there is good reason to ignore it. Admittedly this distinction between illegalities which are incidental and those which are essential to the pressure imposed will not always be easy to draw. But difficulty of application is not a good reason for rejecting the distinction. By refusing to treat incidental illegalities as

---

³ In *Associated Newspapers Group Ltd.* v. *Wade* [1979] I.C.R. 664.
⁴ Elias and Ewing, *loc. cit.*, p. 338.
⁵ See *Clerk and Lindsell on Torts* 15th ed., pp. 753–759; Elias and Ewing, *loc. cit.* pp. 339–341.
⁶ See *supra*, pp. 220–223.
⁷ [1971] 1 W.L.R. 1676.
⁸ [1964] A.C. at 1218–1219.
⁹ *loc. cit.*, p. 341.

sufficient to ground liability, the courts could be countering what is perhaps the strongest criticism of the view that any unlawful act might constitute unlawful means, namely that the commission of irrelevant and possibly fortuitous illegalities could then provide an arbitrary justification for departing from *Allen* v. *Flood*."

Before concluding it should be pointed out that the economic torts do not cover the whole range of civil liabilities potentially applicable to those who organise industrial action. *Prudential Assurance Co. Ltd.* v. *Lorenz*[10] is often cited as demonstrating that the inducement of a breach of an employee's duty which owes its existence to equity rather than contract is not protected by the Trade Disputes Act 1906. Here Plowman J. granted an interlocutory injunction to stop a union call to insurance agents instructing them to withhold the submission of their weekly accounts to their employer. This instruction was regarded as an inducement to the agents to default on their duty to account to their principal, a duty independent of contract.

Breach of statutory duty is another form of liability. If industrial action compels an employer to act in breach of his statutory duties does he, or the persons to whom the duty is owed, have any legal recourse against those who have organised or participated in the industrial action? In *Meade* v. *London Borough of Haringey*,[11] Lord Denning M.R. expressed the opinion, *obiter*, that a call to take strike action which had the effect of closing local authority schools would be unlawful because it amounted to an inducement of breach of the local authority's statutory duties. Lord Denning M.R. was of the view that an injunction could have been obtained to restrain the leaders of the relevant trade unions from interfering with the opening of the schools and, further, that an injunction could have been obtained not only by the local authority but also by parents whose children were prevented from attending school. In *Associated Newspapers Group Ltd.* v. *Wade*,[12] Lord Denning M.R. repeated these views, this time in the context of industrial action by a print union which had the effect of preventing various public authorities from complying with their statutory duty to publish formal notice of certain proposed actions.

While the authors would accept that the local authority has a cause of action if its statutory duties are interfered with, they do not accept that a third party who is an incidental victim of industrial action has a remedy, especially if that person cannot even enforce the duty against the local authority.[13] The position would of course be different if there

---

[10] (1971) 11 K.I.R. 78.
[11] [1979] 1 W.L.R. 637.
[12] [1979] I.C.R. 664.
[13] See *O'Byrne* v. *Eastern Health Board* High Court, unreported, 14 May 1980 where Keane J., in an *ex tempore* judgment, refused to grant an injunction to the father of an eight year old autistic boy who had been discharged from hospital following a strike at the hospital involving a number of psychiatric supervisory nurses. The father had submitted that the E.H.B. had a statutory obligation to provide the necessary in-patient treatment for the boy.

was a deliberate intention to interfere with that person's trade or business by means of the breach of statutory duty.[14]

INDUSTRIAL ACTION AND THE CONSTITUTION

The constitutional dimension of industrial action can be viewed from two different perspectives. From the point of view of those who take industrial action, to what extent can they rely on the Constitution? Conversely, from the point of view of those affected by industrial action, does the Constitution afford them any legal protection, and if so, to what extent?

A right to take industrial action?

Those seeking to engage in industrial action arguably can rely on three different aspects of the Constitution. First, it could be contended that the constitutional guarantee of freedom of association encompasses the right to take industrial action in furtherance of the lawful objects of the association.[15] Secondly, the constitutional rights of the citizen to assemble peaceably and to express freely his or her opinion could be regarded as conferring a right to picket.[16] Thirdly, there are *dicta* suggesting that the implicit rights guaranteed in Article 40.3 of the Constitution include the right to withdraw labour. In *Brendan Dunne Ltd.* v. *Fitzpatrick*,[17] Budd J. indicated that the Constitution protected, *inter alia*, the right of the employer and employee respectively "to deal with and dispose of their property and labour as they will without interference unless such interference be made legitimate by law".[18] In the subsequent case of *Educational Co. of Ireland Ltd.* v. *Fitzpatrick (No. 2)*,[19] Kingsmill Moore J. referred to the right to dispose of one's labour and to withdraw it as a "fundamental personal right".[20] Moreover, it should be noted that the majority of the Supreme Court in *Becton Dickinson & Co.* v. *Lee*[21] adopted the "suspension theory" view of strike action, which view is consistent with a constitutional right to strike.[22]

If there is a constitutional right to take industrial action, a number of implications follow. In the first place, any legislation restricting the

---

[14] See *supra*, p. 222.
[15] See *supra*, pp. 23–24.
[16] See *infra*, p. 284.
[17] [1958] I.R. 29.
[18] *Ibid.*, at p. 34.
[19] [1961] I.R. 345.
[20] *Ibid.*, at p. 397. It would appear that he did not view the right to picket in the same light, as this quote immediately follows on from a sentence reading ". . . as at present advised, the claim to picket and the claim to strike seem to me to involve very different considerations."
[21] [1973] I.R. 1. See pp. 207–209.
[22] For further on this, see Kerr, "Trade Disputes, Economic Torts and the Constitution" (1981) 16 *Ir. Jur. (n.s.)* 241 at pp. 253 *et seq.*

right to take industrial action must be capable of being justified by reference to the common good.[23] Secondly, "no strike" clauses in contracts of employment or collective agreements can only be legally valid if it can be shown that the parties bound by such clauses knowingly and voluntarily waived their right to strike.[24] Thirdly, one cannot regard the terms of the Trade Disputes Act 1906, as amended, as being necessarily conclusive of the issue as to whether particular industrial action is lawful or unlawful, as citizens, *prima facie*, may invoke the wider terms of the Constitution in support of such action. Finally, this view must affect the interpretation of section 5(2) of the Unfair Dismissals Act 1977 which deals with dismissal for taking industrial action.[25]

Constitutional limitations on industrial action

Though it has yet to be definitively ascertained that the Constitution may be invoked in support of industrial action, it is well settled that it imposes limitations on such action by reference to the constitutional rights of others. In *Educational Co. of Ireland Ltd.* v. *Fitzpatrick (No. 2)*[26] the Supreme Court restrained industrial action which had the effect of infringing the right to dissociate of certain of the plaintiffs' employees. More recently, in *Talbot (Ireland) Ltd.* v. *Merrigan*[27] the Supreme Court gave notice of the potential of constitutional rights generally to restrict freedom to take industrial action. This case arose out of a dispute concerning redundancies in the motor trade industry. The union involved, the A.T.G.W.U., sought the support of other trade unions and announced an embargo on the products of Talbot (Ireland) Ltd. This move was endorsed by the executive council of the I.C.T.U., whereupon the company successfully applied in the High Court[28] for an interlocutory injunction restraining the general secretary of the A.T.G.W.U., and the I.C.T.U., from imposing the embargo. An appeal was taken to the Supreme Court against this order but was dismissed. In the course of his judgment, Henchy J. is reported as saying that "whether there was a trade dispute or not, a body or bodies must operate within the constitutional framework and the constitutional guarantees in Article 40, and it would have to be borne

---

[23] See Kenny J. in *Ryan* v. *Attorney General* [1965] I.R. 294, 312-313.
[24] On the question of waiver, see *G.* v. *An Bord Uchtála* [1980] I.R. 32. See also *supra*, pp. 31-32.
[25] See *supra*, pp. 210-213.
[26] [1961] I.R. 345. See *supra*, pp. 8-11.
[27] Judgment in this case was handed down *ex tempore* in the Supreme Court on April 30, 1981. A summary of Henchy J.'s decision, together with a one-sentence summary of Kenny J.'s decision, appeared in the *Irish Times* of May 1, 1981 and has now been reproduced in McMahon and Binchy, *Cases and Materials on the Law of Torts* (Oxon, 1983) at p. 450. No written version of the judgment has ever been produced by the Supreme Court office, a factor which seriously affects the precedential status of the decision, though in what must be an unprecedented step, Henchy J. did comment extra-judicially on the decision in a subsequent newspaper feature – see the *Sunday Tribune*, August 2, 1981 at p. 2.
[28] On April 10, 1981, reported in the *Irish Times*, April 11, 1981.

in mind that innocent persons could not be damnified". Such innocent persons included "persons such as dealers who had no dispute with anybody, or the owners of vehicles who had no dispute with anybody but who, because of this embargo, could not get their vehicles serviced – a service they were entitled to under contract." That incidental interference with contractual rights would appear to be an infringement of Article 40 of the Constitution (presumably Art. 40.3),[29] and that a plaintiff may rely on the infringement or threatened infringement of a third party's constitutional rights in an application for an injunction.[30] Such a view would have very far reaching implications for the legal protection afforded to parties to industrial action, if one takes the traditional view that such protection is conferred solely by the 1906 Act, because the statutory protection of the 1906 Act would have to submit to the constitutional rights of an injured party in the event of a conflict. However, if one takes the view that those who participate in industrial action may themselves be able to look to the Constitution for protection, the situation is transformed. Viewed in this light, the conflicting constitutional rights of the various parties would have to be resolved by the courts in the light of all the circumstances of the case and, in the absence of proof that one side was exercising its constitutional rights for the purpose of infringing the constitutional rights of the other,[31] the outcome could by no means be a foregone conclusion. There is even a suggestion of this type of approach to be found in the judgment of Henchy J. as reported, for he does describe (albeit indirectly) picketing and striking as "legitimate industrial action."[32] It is certainly arguable that the Constitution is capable of protecting picketing and the withdrawal of labour; it is not so easy to make out a similar argument for a trade embargo. Perhaps this forms the conceptual basis for the distinction between legitimate industrial action and the embargo used in the Talbot case. In the absence of such a balanced development of the Constitution in relation to industrial action, the courts will inevitably come to play a highly interventionist role in trade disputes, a role for which many would consider they are not suited and which may ultimately do more harm than good.

---

[29] *Cf.* the decision of McWilliam J. in *Gannon* v. *Duffy*, High Court, unreported, 4 March, 1983, on an application for an interlocutory injunction, where he appears to suggest that the incidental infringement of constitutional rights in the course of the exercise of other lawful rights is not actionable. This case is considered by the authors in (1984) 6 *D.U.L.J. (n.s.)* 187.
[30] This point was decided *sub silentio* in *Educational Co. of Ireland Ltd.* v. *Fitzpatrick (No. 2)* [1961] I.R. 345 where the plaintiff company succeeded in getting an injunction to restrain the defendant's activities because these activities infringed the constitutional right of third parties.
[31] *Crowley* v. *Ireland* [1980] I.R. 102 at 109–110. See Kerr and Whyte, *loc. cit.*
[32] In response to the suggestion that the embargo was nothing more than an all-out strike, Henchy J. is reported to have said, "But what had happened had gone far beyond that – far beyond any picket; far beyond any strike; far beyond any legitimate industrial action."

Chapter 9

STATUTORY PROTECTION IN TRADE DISPUTES

Introduction

After the enactment of the Conspiracy and Protection of Property Act 1875 tortious liability replaced criminal liability as the principal sanction against industrial action. Although the 1875 Act had provided that a combination to do acts not in themselves unlawful was not a crime when it was in contemplation or furtherance of a trade dispute, it said nothing about its status as a tort. Those who took part in industrial action left themselves open therefore to a civil action for conspiracy.[1] In addition those who organised the strike could be held liable for the tort of inducing a breach of the contracts of employment of those involved[2] and picketing could be restrained on the ground that it constituted a nuisance.[3] Moreover, following the decision in *Taff Vale Railway Co.* v. *Amalgamated Society of Railway Servants*,[4] a union's funds could be attacked by damage actions in respect of the tortious acts of its members and officials.

The unions campaigned vigorously for changes in the law but, as Wedderburn[5] has convincingly argued, they made "pragmatic not ideological demands". They opposed the enactment of a comprehensive labour law code with positive rights and obligations[6] and in March 1906, three months after the election of the Liberal government, a Bill was introduced[7] granting immunity from the tort of conspiracy, affirming the decision in *Allen* v. *Flood*,[8] legalising peaceful picketing and relieving trade unions of liability for the unauthorised tortious acts of their members and officials. After a remarkable parliamentary career, during which a number of important amendments were made, the Trade Disputes Act was enacted on 20 December 1906.[9] Kidner described the 1906 Act as "a legislative coup of the greatest proportion for the trade union movement [which] went much further than they

---

[1] See *supra*, pp. 227–230.
[2] See *supra*, pp. 230–239.
[3] See *infra*, pp. 283–288.
[4] [1901] A.C. 426.
[5] "Labour Law and Labour Relations in Britain" (1972) 10 *B.J.I.R.* 270, 272–276.
[6] As recommended by the Royal Commission appointed by the Conservative government in 1903. *Report of the Royal Commission on Trade Disputes and Trade Combinations, 1903–1906* Cd. 2825 (1906). The Commission consisted of Lord Dunedin, Sir Godfrey Lushington, Sir William Lewis, Arthur Cohen and Sidney Webb.
[7] By the Attorney General, Sir John Walton. On the origins and passage of the Bill, see Kidner's valuable article, "Lessons in Trade Union Law Reform" (1982) 2 *Legal Studies* 34.
[8] [1898] A.C. 1. *Allen* v. *Flood* decided that there was no tort of interference with trade by *lawful means*. See *supra*, pp. 224–227.
[9] 6 Edw VII, c.47.

could have hoped in 1902",[10] because the amendments conferred a *blanket* immunity on trade unions by prohibiting actions in tort against them in their registered name and an additional immunity to persons who induced a breach of a contract of employment.

The immunities conferred by sections 1, 2 and 3 of the 1906 Act, *i.e.* in respect of conspiracy, picketing, and inducement of breach of contract, are restricted to persons "acting in contemplation or furtherance of a trade dispute",[11] and it is by the interpretation of this formula[12] that the boundaries of lawful industrial action are defined. The judiciary therefore play a central role in determining the legality of industrial action, and the Irish courts have always taken the view that the 1906 Act, since it abrogates or curtails common law rights, ought to be construed with reasonable strictness and given "no wider scope" than is clearly marked out in it.[13] Moreover the Act itself was described by Parke J. in *Gouldings Chemicals Ltd.* v. *Bolger*[14] as "a child of political expediency, hastily conceived and prematurely delivered" with many "inbred imperfections". Kenny J., in the same case, said it was introduced to redeem an election pledge of the Liberal Party and that there were "many indications in it that it was hurriedly drafted and that its wording did not receive adequate consideration."[15]

In this chapter we will begin by examining the general immunity afforded to trade unions by section 4 and will then turn to consider the more specific immunities conferred by sections 1 and 3 before concluding with an analysis of the phrase "in contemplation or furtherance of a trade dispute". Section 2 is reserved for consideration until the next chapter.

SECTION 4

Section 4 provides that actions against a trade union in respect of any *tortious* act alleged to have been committed by or on behalf of the trade union "shall not be entertained by any court".[16] Whilst the

---

[10] *Loc. cit.* at p. 52.
[11] Note that ss. 2 and 3 now apply only in relation to members and officials of an authorised trade union which is the holder of a negotiation licence, Trade Union Act 1941, s. 11. In *Goulding Chemicals Ltd.* v. *Bolger* [1977] I.R. 211, the Supreme Court ruled that s. 11 was not so restricted in application as to apply only to members and officials of such unions acting with the authority, or pursuant to a decision, of their trade union.
[12] Dubbed the "golden formula" by Wedderburn in *The Worker and the Law* (London, 1965) p. 222.
[13] *Per* Ó Dálaigh J. in *Esplanade Pharmacy Ltd.* v. *Larkin* [1957] I.R. 285, 298. See also Lord Parker in *Larkin* v. *Long* [1915] A.C. 814, 832-833.
[14] [1977] I.R. 211, 242.
[15] At 235-236.
[16] The section is limited to actions *against* a trade union; it does not prevent the trade union from bringing actions for torts committed against it. See the large number of cases in which trade unions have sued for defamation cited in *Citrine's Trade Union Law*, 3rd ed. p. 174, n. 29 of which *National Union of General and Municipal Workers* v. *Gillian* [1946] K.B. 81 is best known. See also *Irish Transport and General Workers' Union* v. *Green and the Transport and General Workers' Union* [1936] I.R. 471.

Statutory Protection in Trade Disputes 251

section originally provided immunity to registered and unregistered trade unions alike, whether of workers or employers, it now applies, following the Trade Union Act 1941, *only* to authorised trade unions holding a negotiating licence and to members and officials sued in a representative action on behalf of such a union.[17] All other registered unions can be sued in their registered names.[18] Nor does the immunity extend to individuals sued in their personal capacity as wrongdoers or joint tortfeasors.[19]

Section 4 specifically restricts the immunity to "tortious acts". It has been held not to apply to actions based on breach of contract, thus allowing actions arising out of wrongful expulsions to be brought against trade unions,[20] or breach of trust, thus allowing actions to restrain the mis-application of union funds, or for an account of union funds.[21] Similarly it would not apply to an action for money had and received which may be described as an action for restitution.[22] In *Universe Tankships Inc. of Monrovia* v. *International Transport Workers Federation*[23], the action was the repayment of money obtained by duress. An I.T.F. representative had threatened to "black" the plaintiff shipowners' vessel unless, *inter alia*, the plaintiffs paid a sum of money to the I.T.F. Most of this sum represented the difference between the actual rates of pay of the crew members and what they would have received under the I.T.F. collective agreement had it been in force when they signed on. Part of it, however, was paid to as a contribution to a seafarer's benevolent fund. Having paid the money the blacking was lifted and the ship sailed. The shipowners then claimed that the money was recoverable as money paid under duress.

In the Court of Appeal, Megaw L.J. said that the equivalent British provision to section 4[24] appeared to be wholly irrelevant since this was not a claim in tort and he referred to the "difficult questions" which would arise if a trade union was liable to refund moneys paid to it where it had obtained these moneys by the use of duress.[25] Neither the

---

[17] Trade Union Act 1941, s. 11.
[18] As has been shown, *supra* at pp. 62–63, it is procedurally impossible to sue unregistered trade unions in tort because of the difficulties involved in bringing a representative action against a body with a fluctuating membership.
[19] *Eglantine Inn* v. *Smith* [1948] N.I. 29.
[20] See, for instance, *O'Neill* v. *Transport and General Workers' Union* [1934] I.R. 633. Although in *Orchard* v. *Tunney* (1957) 8 D.L.R. (2d) 273 Rand and Locke JJ. said that a wrongful expulsion from a trade union was a tort (at 284 and 289 respectively).
[21] *Parr* v. *Lancashire and Cheshire Miners' Federation* [1913] 1 Ch. 366.
[22] See Goff and Jones, *The Law of Restitution* (London, 1978) pp. 176.
[23] [1982] I.C.R. 262, H.L.; [1980] I.R.L.R. 363, C.A.: see Sterling, "Actions for Duress, Seafarers and Industrial Disputes" (1982) 11 *I.L.J.* 156. See also Wedderburn's invaluable note, (1982) 45 *M.L.R.* 556.
[24] Trade Union and Labour Relations Act 1974, s. 14(1), which provided that no action in tort shall lie against a trade union in respect of any act done by or on behalf of, or threatened so to be done by it. The section has now been replaced by the Employment Act 1982, s. 15(1).
[25] The authors would submit that, although the immunities provided by the 1906 Act are not directly applicable to an action for money had and received, they do afford an indication of

Court of Appeal nor the House of Lords had to decide this point as the shipowners conceded that the relevant British legislation was effective to deprive them of the right to recover any part of the moneys save the portion paid to the seafarer's benevolent fund. Nevertheless, as this was a restitution action it was allowed to proceed against the union in its registered name.

Similarly it could be contended that section 4 would not apply to actions in respect of bailment although Parker J. held, in *American Express Co.* v. *British Airways Board*,[26] that the immunity granted to the Post Office[27] in respect of actions in tort was effective to prevent an action founded on bailment nor to interference with one's constitutional rights, on the basis that the liability here is *sui generis* and that such an action is not an action in tort.

After a period of initial hesitation it was confirmed by the House of Lords, in *Vacher* v. *London Society of Compositors*[28], that the immunity in section 4(1) was total, and was not confined to tortious acts committed in contemplation or furtherance of a trade dispute. This decision was approved and applied by the Supreme Court in *Corry* v. *N.U.V.G.A.T.A.*[29] The "golden formula" does not appear at all in section 4(1) and the words "any tortious act" must be read without qualification. As Lord Shaw said in *Vacher*:

> "To limit the words to tortious acts of a particular character or in respect of particular things, such as trade disputes, is to imply an addition to the language, and to impart a limit to the comprehensiveness of the section, and so *pro tanto* to defeat the statute".[30]

This interpretation is strengthened by the inclusion of the "golden formula" in section 4(2).

Section 4(2) provides that nothing in section 4 should affect the liability of the trustees of a trade union to be sued in the events provided for by section 9 of the Trade Union Act 1871, except in

---

where public policy requires that the line should be drawn between what kind of pressure by a trade union on an employer in the field of industrial relations ought to be treated as legitimised despite the fact that the will of the employer is thereby coerced, and what kind of pressure does amount to economic duress entitling the employer to restitutionary remedies. If the acts relied on as constituting the economic redress were tortious – such as inducing breaches of contracts of employment – and are rendered not actionable in tort by the 1906 Act, then it would be inconsistent with legislative policy to say that when the cause of action is economic duress, not tort, the acts become unlawful. See Lord Diplock, [1982] I.C.R. at 274.

[26] [1983] 1 W.L.R. 701.

[27] S. 29(1) of the Post Office Act 1969 provides that "no proceedings in tort shall lie against the Post Office in respect of any loss or damage suffered by any person by reason of . . . anything . . . omitted to be done in relation to anything in the post. . . .". In this jurisdiction, s. 64, of the Postal and Telecommunications Services Act 1983 provides that An Post is immune "for all liability in respect of any loss or damage suffered by a person in the use of a postal service by reason of [*inter alia*] failure or delay in providing, operating or maintaining a postal service."

[28] [1913] A.C. 107.

[29] [1950] I.R. 315.

[30] [1913] A.C. 107, 126.

respect of any tortious act committed by or on behalf of the union in contemplation or furtherance of a trade dispute. Section 9[31] empowers trustees of registered trade unions, or other officials authorised by the rules of such unions,

> "to bring or defend or cause to be brought or defended, any action, suit, prosecution or complaint in any court of law and equity, touching and conceiving the property, right or claim to property of the trade union."

The extent to which the liability of union trustees is preserved by section 4(2) is unclear because of conflicting interpretations of section 9 of the 1871 Act. In *Linaker* v. *Pilcher*[32] Mathew J. interpreted section 9 as meaning that trustees could be made parties to *any* action which endangered the funds of the union. The other interpretation is that favoured by the Northern Ireland Court of Appeal in *Drennan* v. *Beechey*,[33] namely that trustees could only be sued if the cause of action arose out of the use of, or claim to, some specific property of the union.

As section 9 of the 1871 Act only applies to trustees of registered trade unions, the position of trustees of unregistered trade unions is unclear. In the second edition of *Citrine's Trade Union Law* it was asserted that their immunity from suit was absolute.[34] In the third edition, however, it was suggested that the trustees of unregistered unions might be sued "in those limited circumstances in which trustees in general could be held liable in relation to torts arising out of property vested in them, such as nuisance, if they were held at law also to be the occupiers and responsible for it."[35] This was because the wording of section 4(1) was not appropriate to cover proceedings against union trustees,[36] and R.S.C. O.15 r.8 provides that the trustees are deemed to represent all persons beneficially entitled to the trust property.

That section 4(1) prohibits actions for damages in respect of tortious acts "alleged to have been committed" is clear. That it prohibits injunctive relief in respect of tortious acts that have not yet been committed is less clear.[37] The use of the past tense, it could be argued, means that the section has no application to actions brought to restrain an apprehended tort.[38] Nor would union funds be *directly* attacked as a

---

[31] See *supra*, pp. 86–88.
[32] (1901) 17 T.L.R. 256. See also *Curle* v. *Lester* (1893) 9 T.L.R. 480.
[33] [1935] N.I. 74.
[34] (1960), pp. 159, 490.
[35] (1967), p. 596.
[36] *Ibid.*, p. 595.
[37] Kidner, *loc. cit.*, points out, at p. 51, that both Sir Charles Dilke and Mr. Herbert moved amendments to clear up this point but the Attorney General refused on the grounds that the amendments were unnecessary.
[38] See Upjohn and Diplock L. JJ. in *Boulting* v. *Association of Cinematograph, Television and Allied Technicians* [1963] 2 Q.B. 606, 643 and 649; Fenton Atkinson J. in *F. Bowles and Sons Ltd.* v. *Lindley* [1965] 1 Lloyd's Rep. 207.

result of this interpretation. Union funds would however be depleted by fines for contempt of court if the union disregarded the injunction.

Prior to legislation on this point in 1974[39] the position in Britain was unclear, although the weight of authority was in favour of the view that section 4(1) precluded the courts from granting injunctions to restrain trade unions from committing tortious acts, in respect of which no damages could be claimed if actually committed. This was the view of Scrutton and Atkin L.JJ. in *Ware and de Freville Ltd.* v. *Motor Trade Association*,[40] Lord Denning M.R. in *Camden Exhibition and Display Ltd.* v. *Lynnott*[41] and Lord Denning M.R. and Winn L.J. in *Torquay Hotel Ltd.* v. *Cousins*.[42]

This was also the view of Meredith J. in *I.T.G.W.U.* v. *Green*,[43] where he said that:

> "That the action is brought in the form of a Chancery suit and that an injunction, as well as damages, is sought is clearly immaterial. On this point I have no hesitation in acting on the *dictum* of Scrutton L.J., approved by Atkin L.J. in *Ware and de Freville Ltd.* v. *Motor Trade Association*."[44]

In *Torquay Hotel Ltd.* v. *Cousins*[45] the point was fully argued and Winn L.J. said:

> "Having heard the issue fully argued in the present appeal I myself think that s. 4 does protect trade unions against actions being brought against them in which any form of injunction, including a *quia timet* injunction, is sought. It seems to me relevant and impressive (*a*) that any action in which it could be effectively contended that future tortious conduct is so probable as to require that it be restrained by an injunction without also alleging and proving that tortious conduct has occurred, would be so relatively rare in that it is improbable either that Parliament intended to leave the remedy open for use in such a case, or that had it so intended it would not have expressed that intention more plainly than by the adoption of the aorist tense in referring to a tort 'alleged to have been committed'; (*b*) that were an injunction to be granted against a trade union and disobeyed the only processes of enforcement would be monetary *viz.* sequestration of assets of the union or a fine. In 1906 . . . unions needed, and I think Parliament intended to grant, protection for their comparatively slender funds to avoid depletion

---

[39] Trade Union and Labour Relations Act 1974, s. 14.
[40] [1921] 3 K.B. 40, 75 and 92. See also *Shinwell* v. *National Sailors' and Firemens' Union* (1913) 2 S.L.T. 83.
[41] [1966] 1 Q.B. 555, 564, reiterating his opinion in *Boulting* v. *A.C.T.A.T.* [1963] 2 Q.B. 606, 629.
[42] [1969] 2 Ch. 106.
[43] [1936] I.R. 471. See also *Corry* v. *N.U.V.G.A.T.A.* [1950] I.R. 315.
[44] At 480.
[45] [1969] 2 Ch. 106.

of the resources from which members and their families could be assisted."[46]

Lord Denning M.R. agreed adding:

"It would be strange if a trade union could *not* be sued for the wrong done before the writ but *could* be sued for the self same wrong to be done in the future."[47]

Finally the question of whether section 4(1) is consistent with the provisions of the Constitution needs to be considered. The immunity conferred by this provision on authorised trade unions holding a negotiation licence appears *prima facie*, to conflict with at least two aspects of the Constitution, viz. the right of an individual to litigate[48] and, to the extent that it is not possible to sue such a union in its registered name for defamation, more specifically the right of an individual to a good name.[49]

A preliminary issue here is whether section 4(1) enjoys the benefit of the presumption of constitutionality.[50] Since the 1906 Act was enacted before the passing of the Constitution it would appear, at first glance, that it does not. This was indeed the view of Budd J. in *Educational Co. of Ireland Ltd* v. *Fitzpatrick (No. 2)*.[51] Should, however, weight be given to the fact that the Oireachtas has, since 1937 amended, adapted and made use of the 1906 Act? Where Acts passed since the coming into force of the Constitution expressly re-enact pre-Constitution statutes the Supreme Court has held on a number of occasions[52] that such re-enactment gives to them the status of having been passed since the coming into force of the Constitution, thus applying the presumption. In *Electricity Supply Board* v. *Gormley*[53] however, the Supreme Court emphasised that the mere fact of an amendment of a pre-Constitution

---

[46] At 145–146.
[47] At 140. Emphasis in the original.
[48] In *Macauley* v. *Minister for Posts and Telegraphs* [1966] I.R. 345 Kenny J. held that one of the personal rights of the citizen included in the general guarantee in Article 40.3 was a right to have recourse to the High Court to defend and vindicate a legal right. The view that the right to litigate was a personal right within Article 40.3 was confirmed by the Supreme Court in *O'Brien* v. *Keogh* [1972] I.R. 144 and *O'Brien* v. *Manufacturing Engineering Co. Ltd.* [1973] I.R. 334 although the Court did view the right as a form of property right. Subsequently in *Moynihan* v. *Greensmyth* [1977] I.R. 55, O'Higgins C.J. reserved the question of whether the right to litigate was a property right protected by Art. 40.3. That it is so protected is now clear from the decisions in *Blake* v. *Attorney General* [1982] I.R. 117 and *Re Housing (Private Rented Dwellings) Bill 1981* [1983] I.R. 181.
[49] Article 40.3.2°. See Kelly, *The Irish Constitution* 2nd ed. (Dublin, 1984) pp. 471–473.
[50] Namely that it must be assumed that the Oireachtas did not intend to violate the constitutional provisions referred to unless the statutory provision leads to no other possible conclusion; see *McDonald* v. *Bord na gCon* [1965] I.R. 217, 239; *East Donegal Co-operative Livestock Marts Ltd.* v. *Attorney General* [1970] I.R. 317, 341. For an interesting analysis of this area of the law, see Kelly, *The Irish Constitution* 2nd ed. (Dublin, 1984) at pp. 284–299.
[51] [1961] I.R. 345, though *cf. O Monacháin* v. *An Taoiseach* Supreme Court, unreported, 16 July 1982.
[52] Such as *People (Attorney General)* v. *Conmey* [1975] I.R. 341.
[53] Supreme Court, unreported, 21 March 1985.

statute contained in a statute passed after the coming into force of the Constitution did not of itself give to the pre-Constitution statute a presumption of validity.[54] Barrington J. put it well when he said in *Brennan v. Attorney General*:[55]

> "A statute cannot be presumed to conform to the provisions of a Constitution which was not in existence at the date of its enactment. In particular, a statute of the Sovereign British Parliament must be read as having the meaning it had on the date of its enactment. . . . The issue is whether the statute, bearing the meaning it then had, is or is not consistent with the Constitution of 1937 and was or was not carried forward by Art. 50. . . . If the statute, as so interpreted, was not carried forward by Art. 50 it is immaterial that the Oireachtas tried to amend or adapt it because there was nothing for them to amend or adapt."

If however, by virtue of section 4's implicit re-enactment by section 11 of the Trade Union Act 1941, the provision does enjoy the presumption of constitutionality, then its interpretation is governed by the "double construction" rule. If, in respect of a statutory provision, two or more constructions are reasonably open, one of which is consistent with the Constitution, the other not, it must be presumed that the Oireachtas intended only the constitutionally consistent construction.[56]

Two interpretations of section 4 are reasonably open. Because of the reference to section 9 of the Trade Union Act 1871 in section 4(2) it may be that, whereas one cannot sue a union in tort, one can sue the union's trustees.[57] What is the trustees' liability in tort? Does it extend to any action, the outcome of which may affect the union's property or is it restricted to actions which arise directly out of the union's property or its use of or claim to such property, subject of course to the proviso that one cannot sue the trustees in respect of tortious acts committed by or on behalf of the union which are in contemplation or furtherance of a trade dispute?

The adoption of the former interpretation would nullify any argument that section 4(1) was constitutionally over-broad, extending as it does to tortious acts where no trade dispute arises,[58] and the more restricted immunity in section 4(2) could be defended on the basis that it is simply a regulation in the interests of the common good of the

---

[54] At p. 7 of the unreported judgment delivered by Finlay C.J. for the Supreme Court (Finlay C.J., Walsh, Henchy, Griffin and McCarthy JJ.)
[55] [1983] I.L.R.M. 449, 479.
[56] See *Morgan v. Park Developments Ltd.* [1983] I.L.R.M. 156.
[57] See *supra*, pp. 86–88.
[58] See *supra*, p. 252.

Statutory Protection in Trade Disputes 257

constitutional right to litigate.[59] In this respect the comments and conclusions of the *Royal Commission on Trade Unions and Employers' Associations 1965-1968*[60] are apposite. The Commission were not convinced that the position of trade unions would be "seriously prejudiced" if their immunity were confined to torts committed in contemplation or furtherance of a trade dispute.

"Whatever may happen in a trade dispute, it is not the case that trade unions frequently commit torts when no trade dispute is involved, or that they need to do so. The officials remain liable at all times to be sued for any torts they commit: and when these are committed while acting in the course of their employment as trade union officials the union sometimes pays any damages which may be awarded out of its own funds. To that extent the immunity conferred by section 4(1) is waived. Again when no trade dispute is involved, and the tort touches or concerns the union's property (a phrase of wide potential import), the trustees of the union may be sued and the funds of the union made answerable for any damages awarded."[61]

SECTION 1
Section 1 provides that:

"An act done in pursuance of an agreement or contribution by two or more persons shall, if done in contemplation or furtherance of a trade dispute, not be actionable unless the act, if done without any such agreement or combination, would be actionable."[62]

The section alters the law of conspiracy where there is a trade dispute but leaves it intact in every other case. It provides immunity from actions in conspiracy in respect of acts done in combination which would not be actionable if done by one person alone. It does not affect the liability of combinations which, although aiming at a lawful end, employ unlawful means.[63] The section, in its original form, provided that persons would only be liable if the conspiracy was to do an act otherwise actionable *in tort*, rather than actionable in some other way. Following an objection at the committee stage[64] the words "in tort" were deleted, the effect of which is to restrict the immunity. Since a

---

[59] "None of the personal rights of the citizen are unlimited; their exercise may be regulated by the Oireachtas when the common good requires this." *Per* Kenny J., *Ryan v. Attorney General* [1965] I.R. 294, 312.
[60] Cmnd. 3623.
[61] Para. 908.
[62] The section actually provides that this paragraph should be added as a new paragraph after the first paragraph of s. 3 of the Conspiracy and Protection of Property Act 1875. Since that section does not apply to seamen, s. 1, unlike the remainder of the 1906 Act, is also inapplicable to such persons.
[63] See *Rookes* v. *Barnard* [1964] A.C. 1129.
[64] By Lord Robert Cecil, see Kidner, *loc. cit.*, p. 49 and *Citrine's Trade Union Law* 3rd ed., p. 555, n. 30.

breach of contract is *actionable* if done by one person alone a conspiracy to break contracts of employment would be actionable, despite section 1.[65] This would not be the case however, if the words "in tort" had remained, since breach of contract is not actionable as a tort.

The practical value of the section has diminished considerably because of the radical change in judicial attitudes to trade unions since 1906, which change is reflected in a number of decisions which recognised as legitimate the aspirations of the trade union movement.[66] Conduct which before 1906 might have been condemned as a conspiracy is now recognised as incurring no liability. The section, however, does make it crystal clear that, once it is established that a trade dispute exists, or is contemplated, and that the acts complained of were done in contemplation or furtherance of that dispute, the court is relieved of the necessity of deciding whether the combination was for the purpose of injuring the plaintiff, or of furthering the interests of the defendants.

SECTION 3

Section 3 provides that:

> "An act done by a person in contemplation or furtherance of a trade dispute shall not be actionable on the ground only that it induces some other person to break a contract of employment or that it is an interference with the trade, business, or employment of some other person, or with the right of some other person to dispose of his capital or labour as he wills."

The section has two limbs. The first provides an immunity for inducing a breach of a contract of employment; the second was explained as giving legislative effect to *Allen* v. *Flood*.[67] In 1906 the constituent elements of the economic torts were still unclear, and the second limb was inserted to ensure that, if the judiciary changed their mind as to the actionability of mere interference with trade,[68] there would be an immunity if the act was done in contemplation or furtherance of a trade dispute.[69]

The immunity in the first limb of section 3 is limited to inducement of breaches of contracts of employment and does not extend to other contracts, such as commercial contracts of supply or hiring, contracts to supply labour and contracts for services.[70] Nor does it extend to

---

[65] *Per* Walsh J., *Becton Dickinson & Co. Ltd.* v. *Lee* [1973] I.R. 1, 28.
[66] Such as *Crofter Hand Woven Harris Tweed Co.* v. *Veitch* [1942] A.C. 435; *Scala Ballroom (Wolverhampton) Ltd.* v. *Ratcliffe* [1958] 1 W.L.R. W57. See *supra*, pp. 229–230.
[67] See the comments of Sir John Walton in 162 H.C. Deb. (4th Ser.) c. 1675.
[68] *I.e.* where no unlawful means were used. See *supra*, pp. 224–225.
[69] See Lords Reid, Evershed and Pearce in *Rookes* v. *Barnard* [1964] A.C. 1129, at 1177, 1192, 1236.
[70] See, *e.g. Sheriff* v. *McMullen* [1952] I.R. 236; *J.T. Stratford & Son Ltd.* v. *Lindley* [1965] A.C. 269; *Emerald Construction Co. Ltd.* v. *Lowthian* [1906] 1 W.L.R. 691.

inducement of breaches of fiduciary duty.[71] It is important to note also that the immunity does not apply to the actual breach of contract of employment, it applies only to the person who induces the breach.[72] The House of Lords in *Rookes* v. *Barnard*[73] had no difficulty therefore in holding that section 3 could not apply to a threat to break a contract of employment, and thus did not apply to the tort of intimidation that was there committed.[74] But, since the immunity in section 3 applies to a person who threatens to induce a breach of contract of employment, it would seem to follow that if the inducement itself is not actionable a threat to induce a breach must also be not actionable, at least by the employer. The result would appear to be that:

> "a workman can be guilty of the tort of intimidation by threatening to break his contract of employment where the employer gives in to some demand, but that a union official . . . will not be guilty of the tort of intimidation by demanding the very same result from the employer by threatening to induce the employer's workmen to break their contracts."[75]

Is the position different if the action is brought by someone other than the employer? This question depends on the meaning of the phrase "not actionable". Lord Pearce, in *J.T. Stratford and Son Ltd.* v. *Lindley*,[76] said that the inducement of a breach of a contract of employment, though rendered "not actionable" by the employer, was still an unlawful act which could be used by third parties for the purpose of establishing liability in tort. The first limb of section 3 dealt only with the position between the employer and the person who had induced the breach of the employment contracts. The words used were not, in his opinion, apt to extinguish the unlawfulness of the conduct. The words "shall not be actionable" were to be read as "shall not be actionable by the employer". Lord Diplock in *Hadmor Productions Ltd.* v. *Hamilton*,[77] said that this was wrong "even in relation to section 3 of the Trade Disputes Act 1906." Lord Diplock stated emphatically,

---

[71] *Prudential Assurance Co. Ltd.* v. *Lorenz* (1971) 11 K.I.R. 78, by virtue of the word "only". See also *Royal London Mutual Insurance Society Ltd.* v. *Williamson* (1921) 37 T.L.R. 742.
[72] *Per* Walsh J., *Becton Dickinson & Co. Ltd.* v. *Lee* [1973] I.R. 1, 28.
[73] [1964] A.C. 1129.
[74] See *supra*, p. 240.
[75] *Per* Walsh J., *Becton Dickinson & Co. Ltd.* v. *Lee* [1973] I.R. 1, 31. See also Lord Denning in *Camden Exhibition and Display Ltd.* v. *Lynnott* [1966] 1 Q.B. 555, 564: "If it is not actionable to induce a breach, I cannot see that it is actionable to threaten to induce it."
[76] [1965] A.C. 269, 336. This was also the view of Lord Evershed M.R. in *Thomson (D.C.) & Co. Ltd.* v. *Deakin* [1952] Ch. 646, 657; Widgery J. in *Morgan* v. *Fry* [1968] 1 Q.B. 521, 547; Winn L.J. in *Torquay Hotel Ltd.* v. *Cousins* [1969] 2 Ch. 106, 147; Templeman J. in *Camellia Tanker Ltd. S.A.* v. *International Transport Workers' Federation* [1976] I.C.R. 274, 288–289; Lord Denning M.R. in *Hadmor Productions Ltd.* v. *Hamilton* [1981] I.C.R. 690, 710 (recanting his previously expressed view in *Stratford* v. *Lindley* [1965] A.C. 269, 285; *Morgan* v. *Fry* [1968] 2 Q.B. 710, 728–729; *Torquay Hotel Ltd.* v. *Cousins* [1969] 2 Ch. 106, 139–140).
[77] [1983] 1 A.C. 191, 231.

albeit in the context of the legislation in Britain subsequent to the 1906 Act,[78] that acts rendered "not actionable" were not available to third parties as "unlawful means" for the purpose of establishing liability in tort.

The point is not an academic one. The facts of *Sheriff* v. *McMullen*[79] and *Talbot (Ireland) Ltd.* v. *Merrigan*[80] and the decision of the Supreme Court in the latter case[81] illustrate that if an act rendered "not actionable" is held to amount to unlawful means it would imperil "over a wide area . . . the legality of ordinary wage dispute strikes between an employer and his workforce."[82]

In *Sheriff* v. *McMullen*,[83] there was a dispute between a timber company and a trade union. The company's product was "blacked" and a purchaser refused to take delivery of a quantity of timber because its employees refused to handle it. This is a classic instance of interference with a commercial contract by unlawful means, the unlawful means being the inducement of the employees to break their contracts of employment. Kingsmill Moore J., in the High Court, held that, even if the defendants were acting in contemplation or furtherance of a trade dispute, they were still liable because "procurement of the breach of any contract other than a contract of employment is not protected, even if the acts which procure the breach are done in pursuance or contemplation of a trade dispute."[84] On appeal to the Supreme Court it was held that there was no trade dispute and therefore the immunity in section 3 could not apply but Murnaghan J., with whom Maguire C.J. agreed, said that he was not convinced that Kingsmill Moore J.'s interpretation was "sound" and expressly reserved his opinion on the point.[85] He did say that if Kingsmill Moore J. was correct it would mean that if "a dispute exists between a building contractor and his men about wages, any inducement to the men to strike will be illegal, because the building contractor will be unable to carry out his contract with a third party, the owner of the land."[86]

In *Talbot (Ireland) Ltd.* v. *Merrigan*,[87] the Supreme Court granted an

---

[78] Trade Union and Labour Relations Act 1974, s. 13(3), which provided that neither inducement of a breach of contract, nor the breach of contract itself, should be regarded as the doing of an unlawful act or as the user of unlawful means for the purpose of establishing liability in tort, if it was done in contemplation or furtherance of a trade dispute; Employment Act 1980, s. 17(8), which provides that s. 13(3) "shall cease to have effect."
[79] [1952] I.R. 236.
[80] Supreme Court, unreported, 30 April 1981. See the report in the *Irish Times* May 1, 1981, reproduced in McMahon and Binchy, *A Casebook on the Irish Law of Torts* (Oxon, 1983), p. 450.
[81] On which see Kerr, "Trade Disputes, Economic Torts and the Constitution: The Legacy of *Talbot*" (1981) 16 Ir. Jur. (n.s.) 241.
[82] 410 H.L. Deb. (5th Ser.) c.690.
[83] [1952] I.R. 236.
[84] At 248.
[85] At 263.
[86] At 262–263.
[87] Supreme Court, unreported, 30 April 1981.

interlocutory injunction restraining a boycott of the plaintiff company. In so doing they proceeded, apparently, on the basis that inducements to employees to break their contracts of employment which resulted in commercial contracts of the company being broken were still unlawful means despite the inducements being "in contemplation or furtherance of a trade dispute".[88] The most controversial aspect of this decision is that the injunction was granted, not to a third party affected by the boycott, but to the employer who was party to the dispute. This goes even further than Lord Pearce in *Stratford* v. *Lindley*,[89] who said that the words "not actionable" did apply to the employer whose contract of employment was broken, but not to third parties. The authors would submit that the views originally expressed by Lord Denning M.R.,[90] and subsequently confirmed by Lord Diplock,[91] should be approved in this jurisdiction, if not by judicial decision, then by a legislative amendment to the effect that an act rendered 'not actionable' by section 3 shall not be regarded as the doing of an unlawful act or the use of unlawful means for the purpose of establishing liability in tort. For the law to be otherwise would mean that the ability of a trade union to order industrial action would be severely constrained.

IN CONTEMPLATION OR FURTHERANCE OF A TRADE DISPUTE[92]

In order for the formula to apply the following criteria must be met:

(i) there must be a dispute, actual or imminent;
(ii) it must be between the proper parties;
(iii) it must be "connected with" one or more of a number of specific matters;
(iv) the action must be taken in contemplation or furtherance of the dispute.

Dispute

The need for a dispute seems self evident but an important procedural limitation was introduced by the decision of the Court of Appeal in *British Broadcasting Corporation* v. *Hearn*.[93] Here Lord Denning M.R. seems to insist that an employer must at least have an opportunity to respond to a demand before a dispute can be said to

---

[88] See Kerr, *loc. cit.*, pp. 248–250.
[89] [1965] A.C. 269, 336.
[90] In *Stratford* v. *Lindley*, *Morgan* v. *Fry* and *Torquay Hotel* (*supra*, n. 76). See also Salmon L.J. in *Stratford* v. *Lindley* [1965] A.C. 269, 303–305.
[91] In *Hadmor Productions Ltd.* v. *Hamilton* [1983] 1 A.C. 191, 231.
[92] See, generally, Simpson, "Trade Dispute and Industrial Dispute in British Labour Law" (1977) 40 *M.L.R.* 16; Ewing, "The Golden Formula: Some Recent Developments" (1979) 8 *I.L.J.* 133; Kerr, "In Contemplation or Furtherance of a Trade Dispute" (1979–80) *D.U.L.J.* 59; Simpson, "A Not-so Golden Formula: In Contemplation or Furtherance of a Trade Dispute after 1982" (1983) 46 *M.L.R.* 463.
[93] [1977] I.C.R. 685.

have arisen between the parties. This approach is supported to a certain extent by the decision of McWilliam J. in *Córas Iompair Éireann* v. *Darby*[94] to the effect that, as there had been no claim for, and refusal of, recognition, there was no dispute between the company and the union. In *Hearn*, the union involved had a policy of opposing racial discrimination in broadcasting. In pursuance of this policy the defendant announced that the union of which he was general secretary would take whatever steps were necessary to ensure that the 1977 F.A. Cup Final[95] would not be relayed live by satellite to South Africa. The B.B.C. sought an interlocutory injunction to restrain the defendant from asking those members concerned in covering the cup final not to work on the programme. This was refused by Peter Pain J.[96] but granted by the Court of Appeal. One ground for their decision was that, if a dispute did exist, it was not a trade dispute because of the lack of the required connection with the appropriate subject matter. Lord Denning M.R. went on to say however:

> "To become a trade dispute, there would have to be something of the kind which was discussed in the course of argument before us: 'We would like you [the Director General of the B.B.C.] to consider putting a clause in the contract by which our members are not bound to take part in any broadcast which may be viewed in South Africa because we feel that is obnoxious to their views and to the views of a great multitude of people. We would like that clause to be put in, or a condition of that kind to be understood.' If the B.B.C. refused to put in such a condition, or refused to negotiate about it, that might be a trade dispute."[97]

While this suggests that there should be a demand and a refusal before a dispute can be said to have come into existence, it ignores the fact that there need not be an actual dispute in being at the time of the action.

The use of the phrase "in contemplation *or* furtherance of a dispute" necessarily implies that the dispute need not yet be in existence.[98] This is well illustrated by the differing decisions of the Court of Appeal and the House of Lords in *J.T. Stratford & Sons Ltd.* v. *Lindley*.[99] Here a trade union had twice been refused recognition and when the union's officials discovered that another trade union had been accorded recognition they took immediate industrial action. In the Court of Appeal, Lord Denning M.R. and Salmon L.J. took the view that the action was in contemplation of a dispute, despite the union's failure to

---

[94] High Court, unreported, 16 January 1980.
[95] Between Liverpool and Manchester United.
[96] *The Times*, May 20, 1977.
[97] [1977] I.C.R. 685, 693.
[98] See *infra*, p. 276.
[99] [1965] A.C. 269.

make a fresh recognition request, since it was a "reasonable inference" that the employer would refuse to recognise the union.[1] Lord Pearce, however, and Viscount Radcliffe and Lord Donovan, all concentrated on the fact that there had been no fresh approach to the employer. Lord Pearce said:

> "When a union makes a genuine claim on the employers . . . and the employers reject the claim, a trade dispute is in contemplation even though no active dispute has yet arisen. . . . Here it would seem that at the material time there was no such claim and refusal."[2]

With all respect it would seem that once the employers rejected the claim, a dispute would have come into existence and any action taken would have been in "furtherance" of that dispute not in "contemplation" of it. Once the dispute is over, the immunities cease to apply.[3]

A more difficult question to answer is whether "dispute" encompasses disputes occurring outside the State, thereby enabling Irish workers to take industrial action, for example, in support of a claim for improved conditions for crews of foreign registered ships. The growth of multi-national and transnational enterprises makes it unrealistic to limit the legitimacy of industrial action by reference to whether acts or omissions of employers giving rise to disputes occurred inside or outside the State[4] but the authors would accept that difficulties could arise in interpreting the 1906 Act so as to include within the golden formula what might be described as overseas trade disputes.[5]

Parties to the dispute

The dispute must be between employers and workmen or between workmen and workmen. A dispute between two employers is therefore not a "trade dispute".[6] Workman is defined as "all persons employed, whether or not in the employment of the employer with whom a trade dispute arises, but does not include a Member of the Defence Forces or of the Garda Síochána."[7] The fact that a person's contract of

---

[1] [1965] A.C. at 281 and 299.
[2] [1965] A.C. at 335. See also Viscount Radcliffe at 327 and Lord Donovan at 341.
[3] *Hutchinson* v. *Aitchison* (1970) 9 K.I.R. 69.
[4] See Wedderburn, "Multi-National Enterprise and National Labour Law" (1972) 1 *I.L.J.* 12.
[5] See *infra*, pp. 275–276.
[6] *Larkin* v. *Long* [1915[A.C. 814; *Kantoher Co-Operative Agricultural and Dairy Society Ltd.* v. *Costello* High Court, unreported, 23 and 24 August 1984 (where the picketing which was restrained was in furtherance of a dispute between the plaintiffs and Golden Vale Co-Op.).
[7] This definition derives from the Trade Disputes (Amendment) Act 1982 which deleted the "trade or industry requirement"; on which see *Smith* v. *Beirne* (1965) 89 I.L.T.R. 24 and *B. and I. Steampacket Co.* v. *Branigan* [1958] I.R. 128. These decisions meant that any worker in the employment of Dublin Corporation, the County Councils, persons employed as teachers, nurses and doctors *etc.* could not claim the protection of the 1906 Act. See subsequently *University College Galway* v. *Conlon* High Court, unreported, 17 January 1977; *Jervis St. Hospital* v. *Fagan* High Court, unreported, 20 January 1977; *South Eastern Health Board* v. *Murphy* High Court, unreported, 3 March 1980; *Western Health Board* v. *Greaney* High Court, unreported, 9 June 1982.

employment has been lawfully terminated will not make that person cease to be a workman within the meaning of the Act.[8]

The word "employer" is not defined in the Act and its meaning was considered in *Roundabout Ltd.* v. *Beirne*.[9] Here the owners of a pub were in dispute with a union over the dismissal of union members. The pub closed and five days later the plaintiff company was incorporated. Its directors were the owner of the pub, his wife, his brother, his accountant and three former employees. This company then took a yearly tenancy of the pub, the licence was transferred and the premises reopened. On reopening, the company sought an injunction to restrain the picketing of the pub. Dixon J. granted an injunction on the ground that, as the plaintiff company was a legal entity distinct from the owner of the pub and so far employed no employees, it could not be held to be an employer within the meaning of the Act.

The decision can hardly be described as satisfactory. The formation of the plaintiff company and the letting to it of the pub was clearly a sham transaction entered into with the principal object of defeating the trade dispute. In contrast the English Court of Appeal were prepared, in *Examite Ltd.* v. *Whitaker*[10] to 'pierce the corporate veil' and look to see who in reality were the parties to the dispute. Moreover the mere fact that the bar staff were directors of the company need not have prevented them from being treated as workmen. Similarly, just as a person does not cease to be a "workman" merely because he is, for instance, between jobs, an employer does not cease to be an "employer" merely because for the time being he employs no-one. The plaintiff company was clearly a potential or prospective employer.

An equally unsatisfactory decision is *Lamb Bros. (Dublin) Ltd.* v. *Davidson*.[11] Here, Costello J. held that, as the contract between the plaintiff company and the defendant was a contract for services, the company was not an "employer" and thus the defendant was not entitled to the immunities in the 1906 Act. The writers would respectfully submit that the company, though perhaps not the defendant's employer, were still employers, since they clearly employed other persons. The defendant, though not the company's employee, was a "workman" for the purposes of the 1906 Act. The dispute was thus between an employer and a workman.

Another difficult question is the status of a dispute between an

---

[8] *Ferguson* v. *O'Gorman* [1937] I.R. 620, 634; *Quigley* v. *Beirne* [1955] I.R. 62; *Silver Tassie Co. Ltd.* v. *Cleary* (1958) 92 I.L.T.R. 27; *Goulding Chemicals Ltd.* v. *Bolger* [1977] I.R. 211 (where O'Higgins C.J. said that the word "employed" did not mean a person in actual present employment but rather referred to the occupation or way of life of those who are to be regarded as "workmen"). The *dictum* of Overend J. to the contrary in *Doran* v. *Lennon* [1945] I.R. 315, 326 is clearly erroneous and should not be followed. See also Lord Tucker in *Bird* v. *O'Neal* [1960] A.C. 907, 925.
[9] [1959] I.R. 423. Noted by Hudson, (1964) 24 *M.L.R.* 276.
[10] [1977] I.R.L.R. 312.
[11] High Court, unreported, 4 December 1978.

employer and a trade union. Lord Diplock in *NWL Ltd.* v. *Woods*[12] was clearly of the opinion that under the 1906 Act a trade union could not be a party to a trade dispute. In his view it was only since the 1974 legislation in Britain that trade unions could "with impunity intermeddle with relationships between employers and workers" initiating their own disputes with an employer as to the terms and conditions of employment even where "perfect peace prevailed".[13] Lord Scarman in the same case, however, was of the opposite view.[14]

It can be stated with some certainty that a dispute connected with the matters specified in section 5(3) between an employer and a trade union representing workmen will be regarded as a "trade dispute".[15] It is where none of the persons, whose employment forms the subject matter of the dispute, are members of the union concerned that clarification is required. In *Ryan* v. *Cooke and Quinn*[16] and *Doran* v. *Lennon*[17] the High Court held that, since none of the union members were employees of the employer with whom the union was in dispute, there could be no trade dispute. The unions involved were regarded as "mere intermeddlers". This approach was subsequently approved by McLoughlin J. in *Crowley* v. *Cleary*.[18] In *Sheriff* v. *McMullen*,[19] however, Murnaghan J., with whom Maguire C.J. agreed, said that there *might* be occasions on which members of a trade union *might* have a dispute with an employer even though none of the employer's employees was a member of the union, but he hastened to add that "not every dispute with a trade union was a trade dispute."[20] Lord Parker, in *Larkin* v. *Long*,[21] had also admitted that there were situations where a dispute between an employer and a trade union which had "chosen to interfere" would be a trade dispute. The union might well be acting on behalf of its members in the trade in which the employer is employed or on behalf of those who might become employees of the employer.[22]

It is significant that there is nothing in the Act which limits the

---

[12] [1979] I.C.R. 867, 877.
[13] Using Lord Atkinson's phrase in *Conway* v. *Wade* [1909] A.C. 506, 518.
[14] [1979] I.C.R. at 887.
[15] *Brendan Dunne Ltd.* v. *Fitzpatrick* [1958] I.R. 29; *Smith* v. *Beirne* (1952) 89 I.L.T.R. 24, 38 (per Ó Dálaigh J.). See the *Report of the Royal Commission on Trade Unions and Employers' Associations 1965-1968* (Cmnd. 3623) at para. 822, stating that under the 1906 Act a dispute over the matters specified in s. 5(3) between an employers' association representing employers and a trade union representing workmen was regarded as a dispute between employers and workmen "so as to qualify as a trade dispute". See also Lord Wright in *National Association of of Local Government Officers* v. *Bolton Corporation* [1943] A.C. 166, 189; Viscount Radcliffe in *Stratford* v. *Lindley* [1965] A.C. 269, 326.
[16] [1938] I.R. 512.
[17] [1945] I.R. 315.
[18] [1968] I.R. 261, 267.
[19] [1952] I.R. 236.
[20] At 252.
[21] [1915] A.C. 814, 833.
[22] See *Bird* v. *O'Neal* [1960] A.C. 907; *Health Computing Ltd.* v. *Meek* [1981] I.C.R. 24, 32.

immunity to disputes between an employer and his workmen. Indeed it is clear, from the presence of the phrase "whether or not in the employment of the employer with whom a trade dispute arises", that a trade dispute is not confined to disputes between an employer and his workmen. There can be a dispute between an employer and persons employed elsewhere. This enables workmen to strike against their own employer to bring pressure to bear upon another employer to maintain, say, recognised terms of employment. Here, there is no dispute between the workmen and their employer, nevertheless, there is a trade dispute. Similarly, where there is a trade dispute between workmen and their employer, the definition permits other workmen to join in the dispute in sympathy. That sympathetic action was immune, provided the required connection with employment, non-employment, terms of employment or conditions of labour was established, was recognised by Lord Loreburn in *Conway* v. *Wade*.[23]

> "A dispute may have arisen in a single colliery of which the subject matter is so important to the whole industry that either employers or workmen may think a general lockout or a general strike is necessary to gain their point. Few are parties to but all are interested in the dispute."

This was confirmed three years later by the Court of Appeal in *Dallimore* v. *Williams*[24] and was accepted as correct by Dixon J. in *Roundabout Ltd.* v. *Beirne*.[25] Furthermore, since the dispute can be connected with the employment *etc.* "of any person", it is also clear that the persons concerned in a trade dispute fall into two categories: the parties to the dispute and the persons whose position, rights or obligations constitute the subject matter of the dispute. The latter are frequently the parties to the dispute, but this is not necessarily so and is not required before the dispute qualifies as a trade dispute.[26]

This is illustrated by the decision of the former Supreme Court in *Esplanade Pharmacy Ltd.* v. *Larkin*.[27] Here the Court, whilst granting an injunction, accepted that the parties to a trade dispute could be an employer and a trade union which acted on behalf of its members in the trade in which the employer was employed even where there was no actual dispute between the employer and his workmen, provided the union was merely voicing its members' objections and acting on their behalf.

A powerful argument against making the existence of a trade dispute

---

[23] [1909] A.C. 506, 512.
[24] [1913] 29 T.L.R. 67.
[25] [1959] I.R. 423.
[26] The definition extends to disputes between employers and workmen which are connected with, *inter alia*, the employment of any person. The significance of the phrase "of any person" is considered *infra* at pp. 275–276.
[27] [1957] I.R. 285. See also *Brendan Dunne Ltd.* v. *Fitzpatrick* [1958] I.R. 29.

dependent on members of the union involved having employment with the employer in dispute is that this would give positive encouragement to the employer who sought to prevent union organisation developing in his firm. As long as the employer was successful in preventing union members being employed in his firm the union would be deprived of any lawful redress against him.

Connection

The dispute must be "connected with the employment or non-employment on the terms of employment, or the conditions of labour of any person." This raises three issues, namely the meaning of "connected with", the ambit of the specified subject matter and the significance of the phrase "of any person."

Connected with

The phrase suggests that any connection is sufficient, and indeed the House of Lords in *NWL Ltd.* v. *Woods*[28] gave the identical phrase in the 1974 British legislation a broad interpretation. There the dispute was "connected with" the terms and conditions of employment of the plaintiff shipowners' crew but it was contended that the real object of the defendants was to drive flags of convenience off the seas. Lord Diplock said that even if this were so it would not prevent the immediate dispute over the wages and conditions of employment of the crew being a trade dispute. He specifically said that it would not matter that the demand was made and the dispute pursued with more than one object in mind and "that of these objects the predominant one was not the improvement of the terms and conditions of employment" of the persons to whom the demand relates.[29] Lord Scarman stated that all that was required for the golden formula to operate was that the dispute be connected with one or more of the specified matters and continued:

> "Predominance of subject matter is an irrelevance, provided always there is a real connection between the dispute and one or other of the matters mentioned in the subsection. A dispute may be political or personal in character and yet be connected with, for example, the terms and conditions of employment of workers."[30]

These *dicta* led the Northern Ireland Court of Appeal to say, in *Crazy Prices (Northern Ireland) Ltd.* v. *Hewitt*,[31] that, as long as there was a connection, albeit a tenuous one, with the required subject

---

[28] [1979] I.C.R. 867. See also *White* v. *Riley* [1921] 1 Ch. 1 where the Court of Appeal were critical of Astbury J.'s decision in *Valentine* v. *Hyde* [1919] 2 Ch. 129 requiring that a dispute be directly connected with employment or non-employment.
[29] *Ibid.* at 878.
[30] *Ibid.* at 889.
[31] [1980] N.I. 150, 169. Noted by Kerr, (1981) 32 *N.I.L.Q.* 343.

matter, the immunity applied. The connection did not have to be "immediate or proximate".

Lord Scarman has warned,[32] however, that if the alleged connection was only "ostensible", or a "pretext or cover" for another dispute which was in no way connected with any of the required subject matter, the immunity would not apply. A good example of this is provided by *Huntley* v. *Thornton*.[33] Here the plaintiff had incurred the wrath of some members of a union's district committee and to assuage their "ruffled dignity" they took steps to ensure that he did not secure employment in the district. They were held liable in conspiracy because the only connection with the plaintiff's employment or non-employment was ostensible, a "cloak" beneath which they furthered their own designs.

Great care must be taken with the motive limitation because it may very well be that the immediate cause of action is anger against the employer and a desire to injure him but nevertheless it may also be in contemplation or furtherance of a trade dispute. Trade disputes invariably give rise to strong and passionate feelings on each side. This was indeed recognised by Kingsmill Moore J. in *Sheriff* v. *McMullen*[34] when he said "malice, anger or hatred may inspire a course of action, but, nevertheless, if it is in furtherance of a trade dispute the Act gives protection." Nevertheless Gavan Duffy P., in the same case, said:

> "The outstanding fact is that the plaintiff's machinations [influencing his employees to leave a union], as alleged, tended directly to undermine the authority and lower the prestige of a nation-wide trade union and that conduct could not be tolerated by any union strong enough to hit back. The real purpose of the defendants . . . was to teach Sheriff (and other employers who might be tempted to emulate him) the lesson that *nemo impune me lacessit* by giving him cogent, practical proof that a costly and disastrous *eric* could and would be exacted by the . . . Union from an antagonist daring to use the seductive methods open to an employer to cast discredit upon the union."[35]

That the Irish courts would take the same broad view on the meaning of "connected with" as that taken by the House of Lords in *NWL Ltd.* v. *Woods*[36] is therefore open to question. Indeed, the general trend is to give the expression a restricted interpretation, and require

---

[32] In *NWL Ltd.* v. *Woods* [1979] I.C.R. 867, 888.
[33] [1957] 1 W.L.R. 321.
[34] [1952] I.R. 236, 241. See also *Norbrook Laboratories Ltd.* v. *King* [1984] I.R.L.R. 200, 208, where Gibson L.J., recognising that hostility towards an employer was often present in most trade disputes, said that such hostility could only be relevant where it was so extreme as to negative any genuine intention to promote the dispute.
[35] [1952] I.R. 236, 255.
[36] [1979] I.C.R. 867.

that the dispute be *directly* or *immediately* connected with the required subject matter.[37] It must be pointed out however that the Act does not require, as it might have done, that the dispute be "wholly or mainly" related to the required subject matter; moreover there would be more justification for invoking a predominant purpose test if the words had been "concerning" or "about" and not "connected with."[38]

It is also important to note that if the dispute is connected with, say, terms of employment the fact that it appears to the Court to be unreasonable, because compliance with it is commercially impracticable, does not prevent its being a dispute connected with terms of employment.[39] The immunity is not forfeited by being "stubborn or pig-headed".[40]

Employment or non-employment[41]

This term is wide enough to cover any dispute arising out of the employment or dismissal of any person. It covers future termination as well as an immediate dismissal and it does not matter whether the dismissal was lawful or fair, since a trade dispute is not confined to disputes over the legal rights of the parties.[42] As Lavery J. said in *Quigley* v. *Beirne*:[43]

> "The Trade Disputes Act is designed to permit, within limits, certain actions to secure recognition of extra legal claims of a particular nature and to bring pressure to bear on employers to observe certain principles and standards which the law does not impose. Trade disputes may involve matters of legal right but ordinarily they are concerned with other matters."

This was confirmed when the Supreme Court, in *Gouldings Chemicals Ltd.* v. *Bolger*,[44] rejected the argument that, as the Redundancy Payments Acts (1967–1979) recognised that employers might be compelled to dismiss employees as a result of economic pressure, they must be taken as having impliedly amended the 1906 Act so as to

---

[37] See, for instance, *Esplanade Pharmacy Ltd.* v. *Larkin* [1957] I.R. 285.
[38] The amended "golden formula" in Britain now provides that the dispute must "relate wholly or mainly" to one or more of the relevant matters, the effect of which is to give the concept of a trade dispute a "substantially more restricted meaning" (per May L.J., *Mercury Communications Ltd.* v. *Scott-Garner* [1984] Ch. 37, 87) and to clearly exclude disputes where the primary motive of the defendants is political rather than industrial (Employment Act 1982, s. 18).
[39] "A dispute does not cease to be a trade dispute within the meaning of the Trade Disputes Act 1906 merely because the claim by the employees appears to be unreasonable." Per McWilliam J., *Cleary* v. *Coffey* High Court, unreported, 30 October 1979.
[40] Per Lord Diplock, *NWL Ltd* v. *Woods* [1979] I.C.R. 867, 878.
[41] See Kerr, "Trade Disputes Act 1906 – Employment or Non-Employment" (1980) 74 *Gazette of the Incorporated Law Society of Ireland* 191.
[42] *Gouldings Chemicals Ltd.* v. *Bolger* [1977] I.R. 211. See also *Myerscough & Co. Ltd.* v. *Kenny* High Court, unreported, 18 April 1974.
[43] [1955] I.R. 66.
[44] [1977] I.R. 211.

withdraw from its protection employees who were entitled to redundancy payments under the legislation. Kenny J. said that the statutory entitlement to redundancy pay was a minimum which the employer had to pay and employees were quite entitled to demand a sum greater than that and take industrial action which would be protected if the claim was refused.[45] So McWilliam J. held, in *Cleary* v. *Coffey*,[46] that a dispute over a payment of a higher redundancy payment than that provided by the Redundancy Payments Acts was nevertheless a trade dispute.

"Non-employment" is a much wider concept than dismissal and, as Hamilton J. has confirmed in *McHenry Bros.* v. *Carey*,[47] there can be no logical distinction between the case of a dismissed employee and that of a person seeking initial employment.[48] A dispute over the hiring policies of an employer or his refusal to hire a particular person will thus be a trade dispute. Subsequently, however, McWilliam J. has said, in *J. Bradbury Ltd.* v. *Duffy*,[49] that there had to be some restriction on "the universality of the application of the term 'non-employment'."[50] He took the "extreme case" of a person starting a new business for which ten employees were required, and he received fifty applications. McWilliam J. could not accept that the forty unsuccessful applicants were entitled to take any sort of industrial action simply because they had not been given jobs.[51] Similarly, in *Barton* v. *Harten*,[52] the High Court held that there was no trade dispute in the case of a publican's assistant who, having been arrested by government forces in October 1922, was released in September 1923 and came looking for his job but was told it was no longer available. Malony C.J. said that this was no dispute at all,

> "but only an attempt on the part of an organisation to compel an employer to give employment to one who has been out of his employment for a long time and whose position has been filled in the ordinary course."[53]

This language suggests that the true basis for this decision was that the dispute was not between an employer and a workman, although, as has been noted the fact that a person's contract of employment has been

---

[45] At 238. See also *Newbridge Industries Ltd.* v. *Bateson* High Court, unreported, 7 July 1975; *Cunningham Bros. Ltd.* v. *Kelly* High Court, unreported, 18 November 1974.
[46] High Court, unreported, 30 October 1979.
[47] (1984) 3 *J.I.S.L.L.* 82 (judgment delivered 19 November 1976).
[48] At p. 85.
[49] (1984) 3 *J.I.S.L.L.* 86 (judgment delivered 26 March 1979).
[50] At p. 90.
[51] *Id.* The language used suggests that McWilliam J. was of the view that where the demand was impossible of fulfilment there could be no trade dispute. This point is considered in more detail *infra*, pp. 276–280.
[52] [1925] 2 I.R. 37.
[53] At 41. See also *Stephen Geraghty & Co. Ltd.* v. *Whelan* High Court, unreported, 19 September 1979.

lawfully terminated will not cause that person to cease to be a workman within the meaning of the Act.

Dicta of Lord Denning M.R. in *Cory Lighterage Ltd.* v. *Transport and General Workers' Union*,[54] albeit in relation to the differently worded provision in the Industrial Relations Act 1971,[55] indicate doubts as to whether disputes over suspension from employment, or the duties of employment, are covered. The dispute in that case was over, *inter alia*, the suspension of an employee on full pay. As no express reference is made to suspension in the 1906 Act a restrictive approach would exclude such a dispute. A dispute over the disciplinary suspension of a person clearly falls within the definition as it would be connected with "terms of employment".[56]

Terms of employment or conditions of labour

In *Brendan Dunne Ltd.* v. *Fitzpatrick*,[57] Budd J. interpreted "terms of employment" to mean "all matters covered by the contract of employment either express or implied" and interpreted "conditions of labour" to mean "the physical conditions under which a workman works".[58] Thus disputes over substantive terms, such as pay, hours of work, overtime, holidays and sick leave, are covered by the first term, as are procedural matters such as recognition of the employee's trade union for collective bargaining purposes. A trade union's principal function is to negotiate terms and conditions of employment and a dispute as to whether it should be recognised for this purpose by an employer is clearly connected with such terms. Despite doubts expressed in *E.I. Co. Ltd.* v. *Kennedy*,[59] this was confirmed by the Supreme Court in *Becton Dickinson & Co. Ltd.* v. *Lee*.[60] Furthermore it is submitted that any dispute over machinery for negotiation or consultation, including facilities for trade union officials, will also be a trade dispute.

The second term is wide enough to include the physical environment and the stress under which work is performed, and there is nothing in the expression to exclude such matters as the circumstances under which an employee carries out his or her employment.[61] In other

---

[54] [1973] I.C.R. 339, 355–356.
[55] S. 167(1).
[56] Simpson, "Trade Dispute and Industrial Dispute in British Labour Law" (1977) 40 *M.L.R.* 16, 20.
[57] [1958] I.R. 29.
[58] At 37. He said that, since the legislature had made a distinction between the expressions by using both disjunctively, it appeared that it was intended that the words "conditions of labour" should mean something different or additional to the words "terms of employment". See also *Cory Lighterage Ltd.* v. *T.G.W.U.* [1973] I.C.R. 339 at 355 and 364, *per* Lord Denning M.R. and Orr L.J.
[59] [1968] I.R. 69, 83.
[60] [1973] I.R. 1, 24–25, *per* Walsh J.
[61] *Elston* v. *State Services Commission (No. 3)* [1979] 1 N.Z.L.R. 218 234–235, *per* Barker J.

words, it extends beyond purely physical conditions to include the psychological environment.[62] In *B.B.C. v. Hearn*,[63] both Peter Pain J., at first instance, and Roskill L.J., on appeal, said that the equivalent phrase in the then British legislation[64] was to be given a wide meaning. Peter Pain J. concluded that a dispute over a condition which derived from the employee's conscientious objection to the effect his work will have was a trade dispute, and, although the Court of Appeal overruled Peter Pain J. and granted an injunction, Roskill L.J. in fact agreed that disputes over matters of conscience could properly be said to be trade disputes, although he did recognise that "problems of great difficulty and delicacy" might arise.[65]

Disputes over allocation of work – demarcation disputes – or allocation of the duties of employment[66] are clearly trade disputes[67] but disputes over the employer's trading hours are more problematic. In both *Esplanade Pharmacy Ltd. v. Larkin*[68] and *Brendan Dunne Ltd. v. Fitzpatrick*[69] there was industrial action following breakdown of an agreement between the employers in the industries concerned as to trading hours. In the former case, none of the employees were required to work the longer hours, the directors doing the work themselves. In the latter case, the employees voluntarily worked the extended hours. Whereas Budd J. was able to say, in the latter case, that the dispute was between workmen and workmen and was connected with one of the specified matters, the Supreme Court held, in the former case, that there was no trade dispute. The fact that the employer's act, in staying open longer, might lead to other firms departing from the agreement and requiring their employees to work the longer hours was regarded as irrelevant. The Supreme Court recognised that a trade dispute might arise in the future with other employers but, in their view, what had

---

[62] Thus Simpson, *loc. cit.*, submits that the dispute in *Scala Ballroom (Wolverhampton) Ltd. v. Ratcliffe* [1958] 1 W.L.R. 1057, where, because of their large coloured membership, the Musicians' Union boycotted a ballroom which operated a colour bar on the dance floor, "probably fell" within the 1906 definition. The dispute between members of I.D.A.T.U. and Dunnes Stores over the handling of South African produce would also appear to come within the definition.

[63] [1977] I.C.R. 685.

[64] S. 29(1)(a) of the Trade Union and Labour Relations Act 1974 defined trade dispute as a dispute "connected [*inter alia*] with the terms and conditions of employment or the physical conditions in which any workers are required to work."

[65] Note, however, that Lord Cross, in *Universe Tankship Inc. of Monrovia v. International Transport Workers Federation* [1982] I.C.R. 262 at 280–281, stressed that a trade union could not "turn a dispute which in reality has no connection with terms and conditions of employment" into a trade dispute "by insisting that the employer inserts appropriate terms into the contracts of employment." Lord Brandon, dissenting, said, at 296, that "any arrangement which affects, directly or indirectly, the benefits which a worker enjoys in connection with his employment, can properly be treated as a condition of such worker's employment."

[66] Such as the allocation of shifts between workmen.

[67] Even if the employer is not a party to the dispute, if it is between "workmen and workmen."

[68] [1957] I.R. 285.

[69] [1958] I.R. 29.

happened so far was not a trade dispute. The decision of the plaintiff company to keep the shop open beyond an agreed two hour period did not affect the conditions of employment of their employees and did not affect or interfere with the working conditions of any person employed by any other firm.[70]

Another situation illustrating the restrictive approach to the interpretation of the Act is *Sheriff* v. *McMullen*.[71] Subject to what is said in Chapter 1 in relation to freedom of association,[72] a dispute over the insertion into a contract of employment of a term requiring the employee either to join or not to join a trade union is a "trade dispute", being clearly connected with "terms of employment." Yet in *Sheriff*, Kingsmill Moore J. was of the opinion that a dispute over the right of an employer to influence his employees to leave a trade union by paying them a bonus if they resigned was not a trade dispute. The defendants had maintained that this was a trade dispute, being connected with the employment of the men who had resigned from the union. Kingsmill Moore J., however, took the view that there had been a dispute in the past over wages which was settled when the employees resigned from the union. The plaintiff had not made it a condition of employment that his employees cease to be members of the union, nor had the union insisted, in its subsequent dealings with the plaintiff, that he only employ union labour. Kingsmill Moore J. said:

> "It was suggested, though not very emphatically, that a dispute as to whether employees should be in or out of a trade union was a dispute as to the terms of their employment. In itself membership or non-membership of a union seems to me to be a question of status, and not a question of the terms of employment or conditions of labour."[73]

He went on to say that a dispute as to whether a person is or is not to belong to a trade union might become a trade dispute if the employer refused to employ union members, but here the dispute was over the use, by the employer, of arguments and inducements to get his employees to leave the union.

> "I cannot think that a dispute as to whether an employer was entitled to behave in this way could, without more, come within the definition. Such a dispute is one about the behaviour of the employer, not about the employment or terms or conditions of employment of the men."[74]

---

[70] See Lavery and Ó Dálaigh JJ. at [1957] I.R. at 293 and 298 respectively.
[71] [1952] I.R. 236.
[72] *Supra*, pp. 8–14.
[73] [1952] I.R. 236, 245.
[74] *Ibid*. Similarly where a union is in dispute with an employer because he will not bring pressure to bear on the employees to join a trade union. See *Ryan* v. *Cooke and Quinn* [1938] I.R. 512.

On appeal, Gavan Duffy P. said that he would need further argument to determine the question of whether this was a trade dispute and commented that authority was "scanty", but was prepared to assume, without so deciding, that it was a trade dispute. Murnaghan J., with whom Maguire C.J. agreed, was not satisfied, however, that a trade dispute existed.

The definition of a trade dispute as a dispute between employers and workmen, or between workmen and workmen, connected with employment, non-employment, terms of employment or conditions of labour suggests that a distinction may legitimately be drawn between "economic disputes" and "political disputes", and that those who pursue political goals by industrial action are not immunised from liability in tort. Thus, in the British case of *Associated Newspapers Group Ltd.* v. *Flynn*,[75] it was held that a one-day strike organised by the defendants in protest against proposed legislation in the sphere of industrial relations was not entitled to any immunity, and similarly, in *Beaverbrook Newspapers Ltd.* v. *Keys*,[76] it was accepted by all concerned that a proposed "Day of Action" against the U.K. government's economic policy did not attract any immunity either. These cases indicate that a purely political strike will fall outside the golden formula either because the dispute is not between the proper parties or because the connection with the required subject matter is not established. But, as Roskill L.J. observed in *Sherard* v. *Amalgamated Union of Engineering Workers*,[77] the phrase "political dispute" is one which should be used with "considerable caution", particularly in a court of law, because it does not lend itself to precise or accurate definition.

> "It is all too easy for someone to talk of a strike as being a 'political strike' when what that person really means is that the object of the strike is something of which he as an individual subjectively disapproves."[78]

On the face of it, the industrial action complained of in *Sherard* was purely political, being a demonstration against the enactment of legislation implementing a wages freeze.[79] The Court of Appeal, however, endorsed the view expressed by Phillips J. that, since the effect of the legislation was to freeze wage claims already in the pipeline, the infrastructure of the demonstration would consist of action which was entitled to the immunities because of the necessary connection with the required subject matter, in this case terms of employment, and it was irrelevant that the dispute contained a "political element".

---

[75] (1970) 10 K.I.R. 17.
[76] [1978] I.C.R. 582.
[77] [1973] I.C.R. 421.
[78] *Ibid.*, at 435.
[79] Counter-Inflation (Temporary Provisions) Act 1972.

Of any person

The presence of these words in the golden formula[80] indicates that the persons who are the subject matter of the dispute need not be employed by the employer who is party to the dispute.[81]

The use of the word "person" and not "workman" raises a number of difficult questions. Provided the dispute is between an employer and workmen, can the dispute be connected with the employment *etc.* of persons who are not workmen? Need the persons whose employment *etc.* is the subject matter of the dispute even be employed in Ireland? This latter question raises, of course, the legality of transnational sympathetic industrial action.[82]

The words "of any person" were considered by the former Supreme Court in *Smith* v. *Beirne*.[83] At that time, "workman" was defined as "any person employed in trade or industry", and this meant that barmen employed by a private club were not "workmen" and thus could not be parties to a trade dispute. Their union argued that since it was comprised largely of "workmen", it could be in dispute with the club over the terms of employment of the barmen, the barmen being "persons". This argument was rejected by a majority of the Supreme Court but their reasons for so doing are not clear. Kingsmill Moore J.[84] said that if workers could not legitimately take industrial action on their own behalf they could not have others do it for them. He thus equated "workman" and "person", and concluded that if the union's argument was accepted it meant that unions could espouse the cause of footmen, maids, grooms, gardeners, private secretaries and domestic chaplains.[85] Ó Dálaigh J., however, accepted the argument. He said that while "workman" was defined, "person" was not and that this must be deliberate and that therefore the Act did allow workmen a field wider than trade or industry for the exercise of the privileges conferred upon them by the Act.[86] Now that the "trade or industry" requirement has been repealed,[87] it is likely that the significance of the word "person" would only be relevant if the action was taken in sympathy with

---

[80] A study of the legislative history of the Act shows that the Trade Disputes Bill contained no definition of trade dispute until the Report stage. When it was introduced it read as follow: "any dispute which is connected with the employment or non-employment or terms of employment or conditions of labour of any person." It was subsequently amended by the insertion of the words "between employers and workmen or between workmen and workmen" after "dispute", but the words "of any person" were left untouched. See Hickling, "Restoring the Protection of the Trade Disputes Act: Some Forgotten Aspects" (1966) 29 *M.L.R.* 32, 37; Kidner, "Lessons in Trade Union Law Reform: the origins and passage of the Trade Disputes Act 1906" (1982) 2 *Legal Studies* 34, 51.

[81] See *supra*, pp. 265–266.

[82] See Wedderburn, "Multi-National Enterprise and National Labour Law" (1972) 1 *I.L.J.* 12.

[83] (1954) 89 I.L.T.R. 24. See Delany, (1955) 18 *M.L.R.* 338.

[84] Affirming Dixon J. on this point. Maguire C.J., with whom Lavery J. agreed, merely endorsed Dixon J. without adverting to the significance of the words.

[85] (1954) 89 I.L.T.R. 24, 34.

[86] *Ibid.*, at 36–38.

[87] By the Trade Disputes (Amendment) Act 1982.

persons employed outside the State. Most British commentators assumed that the 1906 Act had no transnational effect[88] and the authors would submit that a legislative amendment[89] should be enacted that recognises (i) our membership of the European Community; (ii) that the growth of multi-national corporations makes it unrealistic to limit the legitimacy of industrial action by reference to whether acts of employers giving rise to disputes occurred inside or outside the State; and (iv) that trade unionism transcends national frontiers.

In contemplation or furtherance

The final criterion is that the action be taken in contemplation or furtherance of the trade dispute. The use of the word "contemplation" indicates that it is not necessary that there be a dispute in existence; as long as the action is taken in contemplation of a dispute it is protected.[90] The mere anticipation of a possible dispute at some time in the future is not enough, however, as is illustrated by the decision of the Supreme Court in *Esplanade Pharmacy Ltd.* v. *Larkin*.[91] Groundless fears of remotely possible events will not suffice.[92] In this respect the words of Lord Shaw in *Conway* v. *Wade*[93] are apposite:

> "To 'contemplate a trade dispute' is to have before the mind some objective event or situation but does not mean a contemplation in regard to something as yet wholly within the mind and of a subjective character."

The word "furtherance" was the subject of considerable judicial debate in Britain in the mid-1970s and the Court of Appeal, spearheaded by Lord Denning M.R., took the view that a "totally unlimited construction" of the word was "a recipe for anarchy".[94] The Court of Appeal was able to do this because interpretation of the word "furtherance" is not clear cut. It could be interpreted as requiring only

---

[88] See Wedderburn, (1972) 1 *I.L.J.* 12, 16. Simpson (1977) 49 M.L.R. 16, 22. *Cf.* however the statement in *Citrine's Trade Union Law* (3rd ed.) p. 614, n. 43 where it is stated: "The 1906 Act applies to an act of a trade union in furtherance of a trade dispute outside the country – see *Winter* v. *United Soc. of Boilermakers* (1909) 26 Sh. Ct. Rep. 320."

[89] Similar to that in art. 3(3) of the Industrial Relations (Nothern Ireland) Order 1976 – "There is a trade dispute for the purposes of this Order even though it relates to matters occuring outside Northern Ireland."

[90] *Per* Lord Loreburn, *Conway* v. *Wade* [1909] A.C. 506, 512. See also *Crazy Prices (N.I.) Ltd.* v. *Hewitt* [1980] N.I. 150 and *Health Computing Ltd.* v. *Meek* [1980] I.C.R. 24.

[91] [1957] I.R. 285. *Supra*, p. 266.

[92] See Lynsky J. in *Bents Brewery Co. Ltd.* v. *Hogan* [1945] 2 All E.R. 570.

[93] [1909] A.C. 506, 522. This *dictum* was approved by the Supreme Court in *Esplanade Pharmacy Ltd.* v. *Larkin* [1957] I.R. 285, 294. In *Crazy Prices*, Lord Lowry C.J. said, at [1980] N.I. 150, 165, that a defendant could not claim to be acting in contemplation of a dispute "just because his act would be likely, or even certain, to cause a dispute" and Gibson L.J. added, at 167, that it was necessary for the court to conclude, before considering whether the defendant's action was in contemplation of a dispute, that the dispute be "either imminent or actual".

[94] *Per* Ackner J., *United Biscuits (U.K.) Ltd.* v. *Fall* [1979] I.R.L.R. 110, 113.

an intention to further; in other words the immunity merely depends on the *bona fides* of the defendant. Was the act done in the course of a trade dispute and for the purpose of promoting the interests of either party? Alternatively, it could be interpreted as requiring, as well as an intention to further, an actual furtherance or the capability of furtherance; in other words the matter was to be looked at objectively. Just how far did Parliament intend to go? The matter is further complicated because it is by no means certain that the legislative purpose of the 1906 Act is identical to that of the subsequent British legislation which repeated the formula and in relation to which all of the relevant British decisions were given. When this issue of interpretation first came before the Court of Appeal, it was held that, for an act to be in furtherance of a trade dispute, it had to be "directly" in furtherance of it.[95] A more sophisticated interpretation was later adopted, namely that anyone seeking the protection of the statute had to establish not only that he had a genuine intention to further a trade dispute but also that the acts done pursuant to that intention "were reasonably capable of achieving the end". In *Express Newspapers Ltd.* v. *MacShane*,[96] Brandon L.J. said that in order to obtain the immunity a defendant had to show that the action taken was in fact reasonably capable, or had a reasonable prospect, of achieving such furtherance.[97] As stated subsequently by Lord Denning M.R. in *Associated Newspapers Group Ltd.* v. *Wade*:[98] "It is the fact of 'furtherance' that matters, not the belief in it." So if the dispute was over demands that were quite impossible to fulfill, or were indeed "wholly extortionate", immunity was not provided because the action could not further the dispute.[99]

This objective interpretation of furtherance was not accepted by the House of Lords. In *MacShane*,[1] Lord Diplock made it quite clear that the test was subjective:

"If the party who does the act honestly thinks at the time he does it that it may help one of the parties to the trade dispute to achieve their objectives and does it for that reason, he is protected by the section."[2]

Nor was there anything that required that there be any proportionality between the extent to which the act was likely to increase the bargaining strength of one side and the damage caused to the victim.

---

[95] *Beaverbrook Newspapers Ltd.* v. *Keys* [1978] I.C.R. 582. Noted by Simpson (1978) 41 *M.L.R.* 430.
[96] [1979] I.C.R. 210.
[97] At 222.
[98] [1979] I.C.R. 664, 695. Noted by Simpson, (1979) 42 *M.L.R.* 701.
[99] See *Star Sea Transport Corp.* v. *Slater* [1978] I.R.L.R. 507; *Publishers Book Delivery Service* v. *Filkins* [1979] I.R.L.R. 356.
[1] [1980] A.C. 672 (where it is incorrectly spelt *McShane*). See Wedderburn, (1980) 43 *M.L.R.* 319.
[2] At 686. Echoing Lord Shaw in *Conway* v. *Wade* [1909] A.C. 506.

> "The doer of the act may know full well that it cannot have more than a minor effect in bringing the trade dispute to the successful outcome that he favours, but nevertheless is bound to cause disastrous loss to the victim, who may be a stranger to the dispute and with no interest in its outcome. The act is nonetheless entitled to immunity."[3]

Lord Scarman agreed, saying that once it was shown that a trade dispute exists the person who acts, but not the court, is the judge of whether his acts will further the dispute. "If he is acting honestly, Parliament leaves to him the choice of what to do."[4] Lord Scarman confessed to being "relieved" at this conclusion.

> "It would be a strange and embarrassing task for a judge to be called upon to review the tactics of a party to a trade dispute and to determine whether in the view of the court the tactic employed was likely to further, or advance, that party's side of the dispute. . . . It would need very clear statutory language to persuade me that Parliament intended to allow the courts to act as some sort of backseat driver in trade disputes."[5]

Despite confirmation in *Duport Steel Ltd.* v. *Sirs*[6] that a subjective interpretation was to be applied to the word "furtherance", it is by no means certain that this interpretation would be adopted by the Irish courts. Indeed it is arguable that the Irish courts have already adopted, *sub silentio*, an objective interpretation. Moreover, closer analysis of the speeches in *MacShane* reveals that, in practice, there may be no difference between the interpretations. Only Lord Diplock was unequivocal as to the defendant's state of mind being the sole determinant.

Lords Keith and Scarman, whilst agreeing with Lord Diplock, said that the defendant's evidence as to his state of mind would be tested by the application of the usual criteria for credibility, namely by asking "whether a reasonable man could have thought that what he was doing would support his side of the dispute."[7] Lord Salmon was even more equivocal. He said the natural and ordinary meaning of the words "in furtherance of a trade dispute" was that the person doing the act must "honestly and reasonably believe that it may further the trade dispute." If the person honestly but wholly unreasonably believed his act was in furtherance of the trade dispute, he would not be entitled to the immunity.[8]

Lord Wilberforce expressly dissented. He thought the conclusions of

---
[3] At 687.
[4] At 694.
[5] *Id.*
[6] [1908] I.C.R. 161.
[7] Lord Keith at 692, Lord Scarman at 693.
[8] At 689–690.

Lords Keith and Scarman "emasculated" the subjective test, "because a man may perfectly well have a genuine belief that something is practicable which is in fact not practicable – or more exactly what a judge thinks is not practicable."[9] He could not accept, however, the pure subjective test put forward by Lord Diplock.

> "To accept it would mean that immunity from civil suit, as regards all those persons who may now be affected by industrial action, would depend on an assertion by the person(s) taking the action as to his or their state of mind, subject only to some qualification as to *bona fides* or genuine belief, a safeguard of obvious weakness. Given the strong feelings which usually accompany the taking of industrial action, this would give no protection to such persons against action by enthusiasts, extremists and fanatics, so long as the action was accompanied by a statement that those taking it had the necessary belief."[10]

Whilst Lord Wilberforce believed that an objective interpretation of furtherance was required, he could not accept that the test should be one of "practical effect". This, he felt, went too far and involved judging the matter by results. The act had to be appraised when it was done. He preferred to hold that the acts must be reasonably capable of furthering the trade dispute, and it was not necessary to prove that what is done would in fact further the trade dispute. This conclusion he tempered with the statement:

> "In applying [this test] the court must take into account the belief of the initiators of the action as to the capability of that action to achieve the objective. If these are, as in most but not all cases they will be, experienced trade union officials; if they express a clear opinion as to the 'capability' of the action; and if there is no evidence the other way, the court will or should be very reluctant to substitute its own judgment for theirs. The court may have to form its own judgment, either if there is no such clear expression of opinion or if it comes from a source less fitted to form a judgment, or, rarely, if the conclusion suggested is so implausible, or the connection between the action called for and the objective is so remote and tenuous that the court feels justified in disregarding it."[11]

In this jurisdiction, although Ó Dálaigh J., in *Silver Tassie Ltd.* v. *Cleary*,[12] did speak of the immunity depending "on the *bona fides* of the parties", the High Court appears to have adopted an objective interpretation. The decision of Butler J. in *Ellis* v. *Wright*[13] is evidence

[9] At 683.
[10] At 682–683.
[11] At 684.
[12] (1958) 92 I.L.T.R. 27, 31.
[13] [1976] I.R. 8.

of this. Butler J. was not prepared to accept that the 1906 Act legalised the most "disruptive and indiscriminate" industrial action. He said that before picketing could be said to further a trade dispute, there must be a "clearly discernible connection between the premises picketed and the dispute" in the sense that "the employer or workman affected by the picket is directly concerned with the dispute."[14] More recently, Carroll J. has applied this reasoning in rejecting a claim by former employees of Navan Carpets (Yarns) Ltd. that they were entitled to picket an associated company, Youghal Carpets (Yarns) Ltd., because the latter company were in no position to concede or negotiate in the dispute.[15] Moreover, in *Goulding Chemicals Ltd.* v. *Bolger*,[16] O'Higgins C.J. confessed[17] to having a great deal of sympathy for the argument that for the immunity to apply there had to be "some reality" in the question of possible employment if the dispute was over "non-employment".

Unofficial Action

Industrial action by members of a trade union which is either contrary to union policy or contrary to the union rules is termed "unofficial". Whilst the Supreme Court has confirmed, in *Goulding Chemicals Ltd.* v. *Bolger*,[18] that unofficial picketing is protected by section 2, there is some authority for the proposition that the protection of section 3 is not available if the action of inducing a breach of a contract of employment is "unofficial". In *McCobb* v. *Doyle*,[19] the defendants, the President of the Dundalk branch of the National Union of Boot and Shoe Operatives and the members of the executive committee, had asked all the employers in Dundalk not to employ anyone who resided more than three miles away from the centre of Dundalk or who had left employment for the purpose of taking up other employment. This was done with the stated aim of safeguarding the interests of the local unemployed. The plaintiff fell into the latter category and was dismissed after representations concerning his continued employment had been made to his employer by the defendants. Murnaghan J. held that section 3 of the 1906 Act afforded no immunity to the action for inducement of breach of contract brought by the plaintiff, because the defendants had acted without the approval of their members. Murnaghan J. was of the opinion that, since the principles in pursuance of which the defendants had acted were not "generally recognised as trade union principles", it was necessary, for there to be a trade dispute, to show that the Dundalk

---

[14] At 13.
[15] See the report in the *Irish Times*, May 4, 1982. See also *J. Bradbury Ltd.* v. *Duffy* (1984) 3 J.I.S.L.L. 86, *per* McWilliam J. at p. 90.
[16] [1977] I.R. 211.
[17] At 228.
[18] [1977] I.R. 211.
[19] [1938] I.R. 444. See also *O'Connor* v. *Martin* [1949] Ir. Jur. Rep. 9.

branch had accepted, approved or adopted those principles. The defendants' failure to have this done was fatal, because Murnaghan J. concluded that the principles were merely the personal views of the defendants and that they could not "make a dispute in connection with their personal views a 'trade dispute' because the dispute must be, not one that concerned them individually, but one that concerned the trade union of which they were members and officials."[20]

The decision is not, however, authority for the proposition that an *employer* can secure an injunction, restraining union officials from calling a strike, on the grounds that either the union rules have not been complied with[21] or that the approval of the members has not been specifically obtained by ballot. Murnaghan J.'s decision is based upon his finding that there was no trade dispute. Since there was a dispute and it was clearly connected with the plaintiff's employment, it follows that Murnaghan J. merely decided that it was not between the proper parties. The defendants were not "workmen" since they were not acting as representatives of workmen. They were "intermeddlers" pursuing a private grievance. If the defendants had been acting in pursuance of "generally recognised trade union principles" then it would have been immaterial whether the action was in accordance with the union rule book, particularly so in the case of employers, since they are not party to the contract of membership constituted by the rule book. If unofficial action is to be restrained it can only be at the suit of other members of the union,[22] and it should be noted that inducement of breach of the contract of membership is not protected by section 3, of the 1906 Act.

---

[20] At 448–449.
[21] See *Kenny* v. *O'Reilly* (1927) 61 I.L.T.R. 137.
[22] As in *Brennan* v. *Glennon* Supreme Court, unreported, 26 November 1975.

Chapter 10

PICKETING

Picketing, a predominant feature of industrial action in Ireland,[1] raises additional issues to those discussed in relation to strikes. Those on strike who also picket are seeking to persuade others to take their side. Whoever these others might be, the pickets are seeking to persuade them to do something which they would not have done otherwise and this of course raises the issue of protection of individual liberty. Picketing is also a very public form of industrial action and as such raises the issue of public order.

The reasons for picketing are easy to state. It is intended first to persuade other workers not to work for the employer in dispute and second to persuade third parties, such as suppliers and customers, not to have dealings with him. Where a strike occurs it is obviously in the interests of the strikers to persuade other employees to join in the withdrawal of labour, to dissuade other workers recruited by the employer during the strike from entering the premises and to dissuade customers and suppliers from dealing with the employer while the strike continues. This requires such other workers and such customers and suppliers knowing both that a strike is taking place and the strikers' side of the case. Picketing is the means to which workers have traditionally resorted to communicate their grievances since they are often denied access to more conventional methods. In this respect the words of Douglas J. of the U.S. Supreme Court are pertinent:

> "Conventional methods of petitioning may be, and often have been, shut off to a large group of our citizens. Legislators may turn deaf ears, formal complaints may be routed endlessly through a bureaucratic maze; courts may let the wheels of justice grind very slowly. Those who do not control television and radio, those who cannot afford to advertise in newspapers or circulate elaborate pamphlets may have only a limited type of access to public officials. Their methods should not be condemned as tactics of obstruction and harrassment as long as the assembly and petition are peaceful . . ."[2]

On the other hand, in the words of Budd J. in *Brendan Dunne Ltd.* v. *Fitzpatrick*:[3]

---

[1] And one that has attracted considerable judicial criticism in the past. See, *e.g. per* Kingsmill Moore J. in *Educational Co. of Ireland Ltd.* v. *Fitzpatrick (No. 2)* [1961] I.R. 345, 390–391.
[2] In *Adderly* v. *Florida* (1966) 385 U.S. 39.
[3] [1958] I.R. 29.

"The right to picket is a powerful weapon. There can be few who do not view the prospect of being picketed without grave disquiet. Just as trade unionists would claim that this hard won right ought not to be unreasonably curtailed, as likewise the rights of the public and those who may be affected by the exercise of this right must be considered. The exercise of the right must not be allowed to exceed what the law permits."[4]

In this jurisdiction, picketing is regulated by the law both directly – in relation to the manner of picketing – and indirectly – in relation to its economic consequences. Consideration is therefore given to both the criminal and civil liabilities of pickets. Nor is sight lost of the fact that picketing is a particular type of public demonstration, not unique to trade disputes, which raises important considerations of freedom of assembly and expression. Attention is therefore paid to the constitutional dimension of picketing. Also considered will be the legality of an even more physical manifestation of industrial action, namely "workplace occupations". At the outset it should be noted that the law on picketing is unduly complex creating, as Kidner once observed, the "regrettable situation" that "the lay view of the law differs substantially from the law itself" and where "the consequent over-simplification of the law in the minds of those whom it affects causes an inevitable conflict with the rule of law."[5]

THE LEGAL STATUS OF PICKETING

The Irish judiciary have stated on many occasions that picketing is only lawful on the conditions set out in section 2(1) of the Trade Disputes Act 1906.[6] Section 2(1), which is considered in detail below, provides:

> "It shall be lawful for one or more persons, acting on their own behalf or on behalf of a trade union or of an individual employer or firm in contemplation or furtherance of a trade dispute, to attend at or near a house or place where a person resides or works or carries on business or happens to be, if they so attend merely for the purpose of peacefully obtaining or communicating information, or of peacefully persuading any person to work or abstain from working."

Since the protection conferred by section 2 is now confined to members and officials of authorised trade unions holding a negotiation licence,[7] it seems to follow that persons who are not members or

---

[4] At 43.
[5] "Picketing and the Criminal Law" [1975] *Crim L.R.* 256 at p. 256.
[6] See for instance Ó Dálaigh J. (as he then was) in *Esplanade Pharmacy Ltd.* v. *Larkin* [1957] I.R. 285, 298.
[7] By virtue of Trade Union Act 1941, s. 11.

officials of such trade unions cannot lawfully picket.[8] The authors do not share this view. They believe that it is based on a misconception as to both the effect of section 2 and the status of picketing at common law, an examination of which reveals that peaceful picketing in contemplation or furtherance of a trade dispute by members or officials of authorised trade unions with a negotiation licence is not in any privileged position.[9] It is the authors' view that such members or officials have no more protection than any other person.

Moreover any other interpretation would be inconsistent with the fact that the 1937 Constitution expressly guarantees liberty, in Article 40.6.1°(ii), for the exercise of the right of citizens to assemble peacefully and without arms. Indeed, since picketing is primarily a form of communication, the ability to picket could also be viewed as falling within the ambit of Article 40.6.1°(i), which guarantees liberty for the exercise of the right of citizens to express freely their convictions and opinions.[10] Both those rights, however, are subject to public order and morality and the Constitution expressly permits provisions to prevent or control meetings which are determined in accordance with law to be calculated to cause a breach of the peace or to be a danger or nuisance to the general public and to prevent or control meetings in the vicinity of either House of the Oireachtas. One such provision is section 28(1) of the Offences Against the State Act 1939 which provides:

"It shall not be lawful for any public meeting to be held in, or any procession to pass along or through, any public street or unenclosed place which or any part of which is situate within one-half of a mile from any building in which both Houses or either House of the Oireachtas are or is sitting or about to sit if either –
(a) an officer of the Gárda Síochána not below the rank of chief superintendent has, by notice given to a person concerned in the holding or organisation of such meeting or procession or published in a manner reasonably calculated to come to the knowledge of the persons so concerned, prohibited the holding of such meeting in or the passing of such procession along or

---

[8] See *Ballymun Inns Ltd.* v. *Fagan* High Court, unreported, 11 January 1980 where D'Arcy J. granted an injunction restraining the picketing of the Seven Towers public house by disgruntled customers; *Artane Service Station Ltd.* v. *O'Byrne* High Court, unreported, 13 June 1984; *Leadmore Ice Cream Ltd.* v. *Cummins* High Court, unreported, 9 July 1984; *Penney's Ltd.* v. *Kerrigan* High Court, unreported, 7 February 1977.

[9] Although it is true to say that one must be a member or official of an authorised trade union holding a negotiation licence in order to obtain the protection of s. 2(1) of the 1906 Act, the authors' argument is that s. 2 does not confer more protection than the common law, and that it is irrelevant that one is not protected by the express words of s. 2(1). See *infra* pp. 000–000.

[10] In *Thornhill* v. *Alabama* (1940) 310 U.S. 88, the U.S. Supreme Court declared that peaceful picketing to publicise the fact of a labour dispute was constitutionally protected free speech. Subsequently however, the Court took the view that picketing was "speech plus" and that a State could regulate the "plus": see *International Brotherhood of Teamsters, Local 695* v. *Vogt Inc.* (1957) 354 U.S. 284 and *Cox* v. *Louisiana* (1965) 379 U.S. 559.

through any such public street or unenclosed place as aforesaid, or

(b) a member of the Gárda Síochána calls on the persons taking part in such meeting or procession to disperse."

To confine the exercise of the right to assemble and the right to express freely one's convictions and opinions by reference to membership of a particular trade union does not, we submit, come within the proviso.

In the absence of protection under section 2, the prevalent judicial view is that picketing is an unlawful watching and besetting contrary to section 7 of the Conspiracy and Protection of Property Act 1875 which provides, in relevant part, that a criminal offence, prosecutable summarily, is committed by

> "every person who, with a view to compel any other person to abstain from doing or to do any act which such other person has a legal right to do or abstain from doing, wrongfully and without legal authority, . . . watches or besets the house or other place where such other person resides, or works, or carries on business, or happens to be, or the approach to such house or place; . . . ."

A rider to section 7 provided that attendance in order merely to obtain or communicate information should not be deemed a "watching or besetting" within the meaning of the section. This rider was repealed however by section 2(2) of the 1906 Act. Thus it is easy to see why the Irish judiciary have inclined to the view that persons, who are not entitled to the protection of section 2 and who attend for the purpose of obtaining or communicating information or peacefully persuading people not to work, commit a criminal offence.

It has been strongly argued, however, that peaceful picketing confined to persuasion or the communication of information is not unlawful either at common law or under section 7. Citrine cites four nineteenth century cases[11] – *Selsby*,[12] *Druitt*,[13] *Shepherd*[14] and *Hibbert*[15] – and a Canadian case[16] in support. Of these *R.* v. *Hibbert*[17] is perhaps the most important, since it was heard at a time when neither peacefully obtaining or communicating information nor peaceful persuasion was expressly declared by statute to be lawful. In his charge to the Grand Jury in that case[17] the Recorder of London[18] said:

---

[11] *Citrine's Trade Union Law*, 3rd ed. (London, 1967), p. 558.
[12] *R.* v. *Selsby* (1847) 5 Cox 495n.
[13] *R.* v. *Druitt* (1867) 10 Cox 592.
[14] *R.* v. *Shepherd* (1869) 11 Cox 325.
[15] *R.* v. *Hibbert* (1875) 13 Cox 82.
[16] *Lupovich* v. *Shane* [1944] 3 D.L.R. 193.
[17] Parl. Papers (1875), Vol. 61, p. 233, Ref. No. 273. It is noted in *Citrine's Trade Union Law* 3rd ed. (London, 1967) p. 559, n. 52 that the charge was referred to with approval by Lord Cairns L.C. in the House of Lords debates on the 1875 Act, *Hansard*, 3rd Ser., Vol. 226, pp. 37–38.
[18] Mr. Russell Gurney.

"That they did watch the place of business, probably, there is no doubt, but there are some purposes for which they had a perfect right to watch . . . the more important object, no doubt, that the workers had in view was to inform all of the existence of the strike, and endeavour to persuade them to join them. All this is lawful so long as it is done peaceably. . . ."

The most authoritative decision cited in support of Citrine's argument that peaceful picketing is not *per se* unlawful at common law is that in *Ward, Lock & Co* v. *Operative Printers' Assistants' Society*[19] where the effect of section 7 was fully considered by a strong Court of Appeal.[20] It was there held that the words "wrongfully and without legal authority" in the first clause of section 7 were not "mere surplusage" as they had been described earlier in *Lyons* v. *Wilkins*.[21] Section 7 only covered acts which were in some way wrongful in themselves and the section merely provided, in addition to the existing civil remedy, a summary remedy by summons before a magistrate. As Fletcher Moulton L.J. said,[22] the section "legalises nothing and it renders nothing wrongful that was not so before." Its object was "solely to visit certain selected classes of acts which were previously wrongful, *i.e.* were at least civil torts, with penal consequences capable of being summarily inflicted." It was accordingly held that since the picket in question did not constitute a common law nuisance, no offence had been committed under section 7. Further support can be obtained from Lord Denning M.R.'s judgment in *Hubbard* v. *Pitt*[23] where he strongly expressed the opinion that picketing was not necessarily unlawful at common law. Here members of a tenants' association "picketed" the office of an estate agent. Lord Denning said that their attendance at or near the plaintiff's premises in order to obtain and communicate information was not a nuisance.

"It does not become a nuisance unless it is associated with obstruction, violence, intimidation, molestation or threats. Here there was no such obstruction *etc*. Nothing except a group of people standing about with placards and leaflets outside the plaintiff's premises. All quite orderly and well behaved. That cannot be a common law nuisance."[24]

The decision in *Ward Lock* is inconsistent with the earlier decision in

---

[19] (1906) 22 T.L.R. 327.
[20] Vaughan Williams, Fletcher Moulton and Stirling L.JJ.
[21] [1899] 1 Ch. 255, *per* Lindley M.R. and Chitty L.J. at 267 and 272 respectively.
[22] (1906) 22 T.L.R. at 329. His conclusion was accepted as correct by a subsequent Court of Appeal in *Fowler* v. *Kibble* [1922] 1 Ch. 487.
[23] [1976] 1 Q.B. 142.
[24] *Ibid.* at 176.

Lyons v. *Wilkins* where a differently constituted Court of Appeal[25] held that all picketing, however peacefully carried on, was a common law nuisance on the ground that it seriously interfered with the ordinary comfort of human existence and the ordinary enjoyment of the premises picketed.[26] This case, however, demonstrates "a confusion of thought" which was only clarified in *Ward Lock*, namely that the tort of nuisance was not committed merely by persuading workmen, through lawful means, to abstain from work.[27] At common law therefore, picketing may or may not be so conducted as to amount to a nuisance, and thus it will depend on the particular facts of each case as to whether an offence under section 7 of the 1875 Act is committed.[28] The question of whether it is actionable must be considered apart from the section altogether and if what is done is not actionable apart from the section it is not made so by reason of it. Of great importance in this respect will be the defendant's intention and state of mind, as the decision in *Mersey Dock & Harbour Co.* v. *Verrinder*[29] illustrates. Here a small number of pickets attended at or near the entrance to two terminals owned and operated by the plaintiff company – the Port Authority of the Port of Liverpool. The company sought an injunction to restrain the picketing. No complaint or criticism was made with regard to the manner in which the pickets had conducted themselves personally. In particular, there were no allegations of violence or threats or intimidation. "The personal conduct of the individual pickets appears to have been exemplary."[30] Nevertheless the company argued that the pickets constituted a nuisance and that the British equivalent to section 2[31] did not apply. Judge Fitzhugh, in granting the injunction sought (though not against the first defendant), came to the conclusion that, even though there was no violence or intimidation, the pickets did constitute a nuisance. Violence and intimidation were not the only factors to which regard was to be had. The defendants' intentions and states of mind were also crucial.

> "From the evidence at present before me, it seems that the intention of the pickets is not merely to obtain or communicate information; it is to compel the company to ensure that at the terminals only haulage contractors preferred by the defendants are employed, to the exclusion of others not acceptable to them. In other words, the intention is to force the company to take some action against shipowners who employ [cheap transport]. It is tantamount, in my

---

[25] Lindley M.R., and Chitty L.J., Vaughan Williams L.J. (dissenting).
[26] See Lindley M.R. at [1899] 1 Ch. 255, 267. See also *Charnock* v. *Court* [1899] 2 Ch. 35.
[27] *Citrine's Trade Union Law* 3rd ed. (London, 1967), p. 560.
[28] See Vaughan Williams L.J. in *Lyons* v. *Williams* [1899] 1 Ch. 265, 273-274.
[29] [1982] I.R.L.R. 152.
[30] *Per* Judge Fitzhugh at 153.
[31] Trade Union and Labour Relations Act 1974, s. 15, as amended by the Employment Act 1980.

view, to an attempt on the part of the defendants to regulate and control the container traffic to and from the company's terminals. If that is right, the conduct of the pickets is, in my view, capable of constituting a private nuisance."[32]

The authors concede, however, that the tendency of the Irish courts has been to persist in the "confusion of thought" rampant in *Lyons* v. *Wilkins*. In *Educational Co. of Ireland Ltd.* v. *Fitzpatrick*[33] for instance, Kingsmill Moore J. said that picketing, as "ordinarily conducted", was a "murderous weapon" and that, even if carried on with scrupulous avoidance of any express threats, its inevitable effect was to intimidate customers and to cause such a conditioned reflex on all trade unionists as inevitably to interfere with the business of the party picketed and with the ordinary user and enjoyment of his property in such a way as to constitute a common law nuisance.[34] Kingsmill Moore J.'s conclusion, with the greatest of respect, does not accurately or satisfactorily set out the true legal position. Liability is made to turn simply on the fact that the picketing carries with it a good chance of securing the ends for which it is employed, and not on the unlawfulness of the means employed.

Nuisance is not the only aspect of the potential civil (and criminal) liability of pickets which needs be considered. Trespass is another. Picketing invariably involves a gathering of persons outside a premises on a highway. At common law, a highway is a strip of privately owned land dedicated to the use of the public for passing and repassing. The highway is the whole of the geographical area over which the dedication extends, including footpaths and pavements. Any use of the highway outside the dedication is a trespass against the owner, unless that use has been permitted by the owner.[35] There is a presumption that the owner of property bordering a street owns also the soil of the street opposite to his premises up to the middle line. That, however, is only a presumption and it may be rebutted by evidence, such as that the top spit and the subsoil are vested in the highway authority.

The question of whether peaceful picketing could be a trespass against the owner of the subsoil was considered by Meredith J. in *Ferguson Ltd.* v. *O'Gorman*.[36] The crucial question for the judge was what use of the highway was within the scope of the fictitious dedication to the public. Was it strictly confined to passing and repassing? Meredith J. cited *Harrison* v. *Duke of Rutland*[37] and *Hickman* v. *Massey*[38] as evidence that the fictitious dedication included

---

[32] [1982] I.R.L.R. at 155.
[33] [1961] I.R. 345.
[34] At 390–391.
[35] See *Harrison* v. *Duke of Rutland* [1893] 1 Q.B. 142 and *Hickman* v. *Massey* [1900] 1 Ch. 752.
[36] [1937] I.R. 620.
[37] [1893] 1 Q.B. 142.
[38] [1900] 1 Ch. 752.

"reasonable extensions" of the bare right to pass and repass.[39] In the former case, Lord Esher M.R. stated that highways were dedicated *prima facie* for the purpose of passage and added that this was subject to the qualification that things were done upon them which were recognised by everybody as being rightly done and as constituting a reasonable and usual mode of using a highway as such.[40] Meredith J. confirmed that other "reasonable and usual" uses of the highway were lawful so long as the primary purpose of the dedication, passage, was kept in mind. He went on to describe section 2 of the 1906 Act as being statutory recognition that the acts therein described were not necessarily a trespass and that the reasonable user of the highway included user by acts of the kind these described.

> "Peaceful picketing has been going on ever since the Act of 1906 and for a good while before, and it would seem rather late in the day to discover that, no matter how it is conducted, it is a trespass on the rights of the owner of the soil. It is a form of traffic on the highway, concentrated on a limited portion for the purpose of conveying information to persons who are unquestionably using the highway in the normal manner, and it is coincident with their user for the purpose of reaching particular premises."[41]

Picketing on private property is undeniably a trespass, which causes problems when the premises of the employer in dispute is located inside a shopping centre or industrial estate. This issue and the related question of "workplace occupations" are considered in more detail below.[42]

PICKETING AND THE CRIMINAL LAW

Conspiracy and Protection of Property Act 1875

Section 7 of the 1875 Act provides:

> "Every person[43] who, *with a view to compel* any other person to abstain from doing or to do any act which *such other person* has a legal right to do or abstain from doing, *wrongfully and without legal authority*, –

---

[39] [1937] I.R. at 631.
[40] [1893] 1 Q.B. 142, 146.
[41] [1937] I.R. at 632.
[42] See *infra*, pp. 303–305 and 311–315.
[43] Note that s. 16 of the 1875 Act provides that nothing in the Act shall apply to seamen or to apprentices to the sea service. "Seamen" was defined by the Court for Crown Cases Reserved in *R. v. Lynch* [1898] 1 Q.B. 61 as meaning persons employed or engaged on board ship, so that the section did not exempt persons whose calling or occupation is the sea but who were not actually so employed or engaged. Note also that in *Kennedy* v. *Cowie* [1891] 1 Q.B. 771 it was held that s. 16 meant only that the punishments prescribed by the 1875 Act were not to fall on seamen. The case of an offence against a seaman by a person who was not a seaman was therefore not excluded.

(1) *Uses violence to or intimidates*[44] such other person or his wife or children, or injures his property; or,
(2) *Persistently follows* such other person about from place to place; or,
(3) *Hides* any tools, clothes, or other property owned or used by such other person, or deprives him of or hinders him in the use thereof; or,
(4) *Watches or besets* the house or other place where such other person resides, or works, or carries on business or happens to be, or the approach to such house or place; or,
(5) *Follows* such other person with two or more other persons in a disorderly manner in or through any street or road,
shall, on conviction thereof by a court of summary jurisdiction or on indictment as hereinafter mentioned, be liable either to pay a penalty not exceeding twenty pounds, or to be imprisoned for a term not exceeding three months."[45]

The five subheads are each governed by the opening words of the section and in *Attorney General* v. *O'Brien*[46] the Court of Criminal Appeal confirmed that the section creates only one offence, the five subheads merely indicating various methods of committing the offence. In *O'Brien,* the particulars of the offence stated that the accused "with a view to compelling T.H. to do an act, namely to close his business premises . . . , which the said T.H. had a legal right to abstain from doing, did wrongfully and without legal authority watch *and* beset the said premises where the said T.H. carries on business." The accused contended unsuccessfully that watching and besetting were two separate and distinct offences which could not be included in the one count.

A prosecution under the section may be brought by either the person aggrieved or the gardaí without such person's leave, or by the Director of Public Prosecutions.[47] The person aggrieved is not limited to bringing a prosecution. He may bring a civil action either alternatively or in addition.[48]

"With a view to compel"
These words contain the "gist and pith" of the offence each of the

---

[44] On which see *supra*, pp. 215–216.
[45] The words in italics are considered separately below.
[46] (1936) 70 I.L.T.R. 101, following *Stuart* v. *Clarkson* (1894) 32 S.L.R. 4. See also *State (Hardy)* v. *O'Flynn* [1948] I.R. 343.
[47] By virtue of S.I. No. 282 of 1972, offences under s. 7 are "scheduled offences" under s. 36 of the Offences against the State Act 1939. This means that, if summary proceedings are instituted, the D.P.P. can order the transfer of these proceedings to the Special Criminal Court and, if proceedings on indictment are instituted, the return for trial must be to the Special Criminal Court unless the D.P.P. directs otherwise, see 1939 Act, ss. 45–47.
[48] *Citrine's Trade Union Law* 3rd ed. (London, 1967), p. 534.

subheads is governed by them.[49] The word "view" does not import motive, but purpose.[50] The defendant's motive is immaterial.[51] "With a view to compel" means with intent to compel. Whether the compulsion is effective or not is also immaterial.

"Such other person"
These words, which appear in the opening words of the section and in the subsequent paragraphs, were considered by the Court of Appeal in *Lyons* v. *Wilkins*.[52] It was submitted there that to watch or beset one person's house with a view to compel someone else was not within the section. Lindley M.R.'s "direct answer" to this argument was that "such other" meant "any other", saying that to interpret the section otherwise would render the Act nugatory "in a great number of cases clearly within the mischief intended to be remedied."[53] The decision was criticised in *Citrine*[54] and the authors set out, in full, the relevant passage which we respectfully endorse.

> "It . . . disregards entirely the use by the legislature of the word 'such', which clearly indicates an intention that, in order to constitute the crime, the subject of the acts of intimidation set out in the various paragraphs and the subject of the view to compel must be one and the same person or persons. The section refers to compelling 'any other person' to abstain from doing or to do any act which 'such other person' has a legal right to do, *etc.* Here it is patent that the words 'such other' refer to the person whom it is sought to compel. The subsequent paragraphs, which are the continuation of the same sentence, each refer to 'such other person', *e.g.*, '(5) Follows such other person,' *etc.* It is this following a person with intent to compel *him* that is aimed at. Had the legislature intended the meaning of 'intimidation' to include persons remote from the scene of operations, it would have been easy enough to have used the words 'any person' in the paragraphs, instead of laboriously repeating the phrase 'such other person'. Moreover, paragraph (1) expressly refers to 'such other person or his wife or children', clearly showing that the legislature could not have intended 'such other person' to mean 'any other person'; otherwise, the mention of 'his wife or children' would be superfluous."

"Wrongfully and without legal authority"
As pointed out above[55] these words are not mere surplusage, and the

---

[49] *Per* the Court of Criminal Appeal in *Attorney General* v. *O'Brien* (1936) 70 I.L.T.R. at 103.
[50] *Per* Chitty L.J., *Lyons* v. *Wilkins* [1899] 1 Ch. 255, 270. Approved by Kennedy C.J. in *Attorney General* v. *O'Brien* (1936) 70 I.L.T.R. 101, 103.
[51] See *Allied Amusements* v. *Reaney* (1936) 3 W.W.R. 129.
[52] [1899] 1 Ch. 255.
[53] At 268.
[54] *Citrine's Trade Union Law* 3rd ed. (London, 1967), p. 537.
[55] *Supra*, p. 286.

authors do not share the view expressed in *Citrine*[56] that they are intended to modify the word "compel" and not the various acts mentioned in the various subheads. In our view, each of the subheads is governed by them.

"Persistently follows"
As is pointed out in *Citrine*,[57] the offence here is constituted without violence or threats of violence. Nor is it necessary that the "following" should be done in a disorderly manner. Unlike the offence of "disorderly following" in paragraph 5, there is no requirement that more than one person should be engaged in the act of following.[58]

"Watches or besets"
These words are not defined in the Act and have been the subject of some judicial refinement. In *R.* v. *Wall*,[59] it was suggested by Palles C.B. that "watching" involved some element of persistence. In *Attorney General* v. *O'Brien*,[60] however, Kennedy C.J. said that the Chief Baron meant the word "persistent" to be understood in the sense of "insistent". Kennedy C.J. continued:

> "The opinion of this Court [the Court of Criminal Appeal] is that, as regards time in any particular case, it is a matter of degree in relation to the circumstances and facts proved in evidence . . . I am of the opinion that 'watching' does not necessarily connote or involve long duration, or, in fact, any specific duration of time."[61]

In *Larkin* v. *Belfast Harbour Commissioners*,[62] O'Brien L.C.J. said that the words "watching or besetting" "plainly" meant an external operation – "something not within a house or place, but without it."[63] Wright J., in the same case said that the words referred to the action of someone outside, in the approach to, or neighbourhood of some house or other place.[64] In *Galt* v. *Philp*,[65] however, the High Court of Justiciary in Scotland held that the offence was not limited to the maintenance of an external watch. Here a number of staff, who were involved in a trade dispute with their employers, staged a "work-in" at their place of work. They locked the premises, barricaded themselves inside and prevented access. Lord Cameron said:

---

[56] 3rd ed., p. 535.
[57] *Ibid.*, p. 540, citing *Wilson* v. *Renton* (1909) 47 S.L.R. 209.
[58] *Smith* v. *Thomasson* (1890) 16 Cox 470.
[59] (1907) 21 Cox 401.
[60] (1936) 70 I.L.T.R. 101.
[61] At 103. See also Stirling J. in *Charnock* v. *Court* [1899] 2 Ch. 35, 38: "There is nothing in the statute which defines the meaning of watching. It may be . . . for a short time, and as to that I refer to the words of the proviso itself which speaks of attending at or near a house or place [*etc.*] . . . The word 'attending' does not necessarily imply any lengthened attendance upon the spot."
[62] [1908] 2 I.R. 214.
[63] At 220.
[64] At 228.
[65] 1984 S.L.T. 28.

"It would . . . be manifestly absurd, having regard to the evil which the statute seeks to suppress, so to construe the statute that the external watcher should be held guilty of an offence, but scatheless if he were to force his way in and occupy the house or place concerned, for precisely the same purpose and objective."[66]

Miscellaneous offences

Besides section 7, persons engaged in picketing have to contend with a number of other possible offences. Of course, pickets may indulge in criminal activities unconnected with the act of picketing such as using threatening behaviour,[67] making use of threatening, abusive and insulting words to provoke a breach of the peace,[68] possession of offensive weapons and assault occasioning actual bodily harm. In the main, however, the authors are concerned here with the potential criminal liability of picketing *per se*.

The picket may amount to a statutory obstruction of the highway[69] and as such it would be unlawful, despite section 2 of the 1906 Act. In addition, the picket may constitute a public nuisance. In *Cunningham v. McGrath Brothers*[70] Kingsmill Moore J., speaking generally, said that any obstruction of the public highway was a public nuisance prosecutable on indictment and a tort sounding in damages if any member of the public should suffer particular injury thereby.[71] Similar sentiments were expressed by Forbes J. at first instance in *Hubbard v. Pitt*.[72] He said: "The public has a right to go on every part of the highway, and any act which makes it less commodious is a public nuisance unless it can be said to be so fleeting and so unappreciable as to fall within the *de minimis* rule."[73] The Court of Appeal refused to endorse this proposition. Lord Denning M.R. rejected it outright[74] and Stamp L.J. said that he could not regard Forbes J.'s conclusion, that the picket in question was a public nuisance, as a satisfactory application of the law to the facts which he found.[75] Orr L.J. was content to assume that certain criticisms of the trial judge's judgment "may turn out to be well founded".[76] The leading authority here is the

---

[66] At 39. See also Lord Emslie at 38 denying that the words "watching or besetting" were only apt to cover actions outside the relevant place.
[67] This would be in addition to the offence of intimidation contained in s. 7. Note that intimidation does not necessarily involve threats of personal violence; threats of damage to property will be sufficient. See *supra* pp. 215–216.
[68] Contrary, for instance, to the Dublin Police Act 1842, s. 14(13). On which see Law Reform Commission Report on Offences under the Dublin Police Acts (L.R.C. 14–1985), pp. 45–51.
[69] Contrary to Road Traffic Act 1961, s. 98 and Road Traffic Act 1968, s. 60. See *Tynan v. Balmer* [1967] 1 Q.B. 91.
[70] [1964] I.R. 209.
[71] At 213.
[72] [1976] 1 Q.B. 142.
[73] At 152.
[74] At 175.
[75] At 180.
[76] At 189.

decision of the Supreme Court in *Wall* v. *Morrissey*[77] where it was held that it was not the law that every obstruction of the highway amounted to a public nuisance. The right of the public to pass and repass along the highway had to be considered in relation to the rights of other members of the public who could create temporary obstructions in the course of their normal user of the highway.[78] So in *Lowdens* v. *Keaveney*[79] Gibson J. said that a procession, moving along a thoroughfare in a peaceful manner, would not amount to a public nuisance.

Pickets which are not in themselves of a peaceable nature may fall foul of the common law crimes of unlawful assembly, rout, riot and affray. "Unlawful assembly" was judicially defined by McLoughlin J. as –

> "an assembly of three or more persons (a) for purposes forbidden by law, such as that of committing a crime by open force; or (b) with intent to carry out any common purpose, lawful or unlawful, in such a manner as to endanger the public peace, or to give firm and courageous persons in the neighbourhood of such assembly reasonable grounds to apprehend a breach of the peace or consequence of it."[80]

McLoughlin J. added that he had never come across a case in which unlawful assembly was held to exist where there was not "some evidence of force or violence in the commission of an offence or of some show of force or violence or of some breach of the peace or of some conduct tending to excite alarm in the mind of a person of firm and reasonable courage."[81] An unlawful assembly becomes a rout as soon as the assembled persons do any act towards carrying out the illegal purpose which has made their assembly unlawful[82] and a rout becomes a riot as soon as this illegal purpose is put into effect forcibly by persons mutually intending to resist any opposition.[83] In order to establish the offence of affray in a public place the prosecution must establish that (i) there was unlawful fighting or unlawful violence used by one or more than one persons against another or others, or there was an unlawful display of force by one or more than one person and (ii) the unlawful fighting, violence or display or force was such that a bystander of reasonable firmness and courage, whether present or not, might reasonably be expected to be terrified.[84]

---

[77] [1969] I.R. 10.
[78] *Per* Fitzgerald J., [1969] I.R. 10, 20.
[79] [1903] 2 I.R. 82.
[80] In *Barrett* v. *Tipperary (N.R.) County Council* [1964] I.R. 22, 28.
[81] *Id*. There is also the offence of tumultuous assembly under the Tumultuous Risings Act 1775, s. 2.
[82] *R.* v. *McNaughten* (1881) 14 Cox 576.
[83] *Id*.
[84] *Per* Lord Lane C.J., Boreham and Tudor JJ. in *Attorney General's Reference (No. 3 of 1983)* [1985] 1 All E.R. 501, 505–506.

Finally it should be noted that the Canadian courts have held that the establishment of a picket line at the entrance of a court house constitutes criminal contempt in that it is designed to induce officers of the court to refrain from carrying out their duties and it obstructs or tends to obstruct the open administration of justice.[85]

Control of pickets

Two English cases, *Piddington* v. *Bates*[86] and *Kavanagh* v. *Hiscock*,[87] vividly illustrate the power of the gardaí to limit and control the activities of pickets through the law relating to breaches of the peace. In the former case, two persons were picketing at each entrance to a factory and P. attempted to join the picket. He was told by a policeman that two pickets were quite sufficient but nevertheless "gently pushed past the policeman." He was arrested and charged with obstructing a police constable in the execution of his duty, and the question arose as to whether the policeman was justified in limiting the number of pickets by reference to an apprehended breach of the peace. The Divisional Court upheld P.'s conviction but Lord Parker C.J. stressed that the mere statement by a policeman that he did anticipate that there might be a breach of the peace was not enough. There had to exist proven facts from which a policeman could reasonably anticipate such a breach. Moreover he added that it was not enough that his contemplation is that there is a remote possibility, there must be a real possibility of such a breach.[88] The imminence or immediacy of the threat to the peace determines what action is reasonable.[89]

The latter case involved a person who had tried to push through a police cordon which had been formed to clear the roadway to allow a coach to drive in. The Divisional Court upheld his conviction noting that the police had reasonable apprehension that the rights of the coach driver would be interfered with by being forced to stop and that the police had a general duty to regulate the use of the highway.[90] It would seem to follow that a garda would be justified in dispersing a lawful picket where he had reasonable grounds for fearing that it would lead to a breach of the peace.[91] It is important to realise that the

---

[85] *Re British Columbia Government Employees Union and Attorney General for British Columbia* (1984) 2 D.L.R. (4th) 705; *Newfoundland Association of Public Employees* v. *Attorney General for Newfoundland* (1984) 14 D.L.R. (4th) 323.
[86] [1961] 1 W.L.R. 162. [87] [1974] I.C.R. 282.
[88] [1961] 1 W.L.R. 162, 169. As to what constitutes a breach of the peace see *Attorney General* v. *Cunningham* [1932] I.R. 28, 33.
[89] *Per* Skinner J. delivering the judgment of the Queen's Bench Divisional Court in *Moss* v. *McLachlan* [1985] I.R.L.R. 76, 78.
[90] [1974] I.C.R. 282, 288.
[91] See *Humphries* v. *Connor* (1867) 17 I.C.L.R. 1; *O'Kelly* v. *Harvey* (1882) 10 L.R. Ir. 285; (1883) 14 L.R. Ir. 105; *Coyne* v. *Tweedy* [1898] 2 I.R. 167. Kelly asserts that the Constitution acknowledges this principle when it speaks in Article 40.6.1°(ii) of the right to assemble peacefully being subject to prevention or control if the meeting is determined, in accordance with law, to be calculated to cause a breach of the peace or to be a danger or nuisance to the general public. *The Irish Constitution* 2nd ed. (Dublin, 1984), p. 590.

powers of the gardaí are extensive. They have considerable discretion to take whatever measures may reasonably be considered necessary to ensure that pickets remain peaceful and orderly. As May J. has said:

> "Where a police officer reasonably anticipates that in the circumstances obtaining in the particular case the consequence of any peaceful picketing may well be a breach of the peace, either by the pickets or by spectators, whether supporters of the pickets or not, then it is the duty of that police officer to take such steps as are reasonably necessary to prevent that anticipated breach of the peace. These steps may include requiring would-be pickets to desist, for so long as the police officer may reasonably deem necessary to prevent the breach of that peace, from any attempt to picket at that place."[92]

These powers could even extend to stopping cars carrying persons who appeared to be on their way to join a picket. In *Moss* v. *McLachlan*[93] police stationed in Nottingham stopped cars, carrying persons who appeared to be striking miners from outside the county, some miles away from a number of working collieries, and ordered them to turn back. The issue arose as to whether the police were acting in the execution of their duty to take reasonable steps to prevent an apprehended breach of the peace. Skinner J. said:

> "If the police feared that a convoy of cars travelling towards a working coal field bearing banners and broadcasting, by sight or sound, hostility and threats towards working miners might cause a violent episode, they would be justified in halting the convoy to enquire into its destination and purpose. If on stopping the vehicles, the police were satisfied that there was a real possibility of the occupants causing a breach of the peace one-and-a-half miles away, a journey of less than five minutes by car, then in our judgment it would be their duty to prevent the convoy from proceeding further and they have the power to do so."[94]

He added that, in reaching their conclusion, the police were bound to take into account all they had heard and read and to exercise their judgment and common sense on that material as well as on the events which are taking place before their eyes.

The way in which the gardaí exercise their power is as important as the power itself.[95] If picketing is to be effective and yet be perceived as

---

[92] In *Kavanagh* v. *Hiscock* [1974] I.C.R. 282, 292.
[93] [1985] I.R.L.R. 76. Noted by Morris, (1985) 14 *I.L.J.* 109.
[94] At 79.
[95] See Kahn, Lewis, Livock and Wiles, *Picketing* (London, 1983), pp. 86-99 for an excellent examination of policing industrial disputes in Britain. See also the evidence of senior policemen to the House of Commons Select Committee on Employment 1979-1980, *Minutes of Evidence*, 462 (ii), 27 February 1980. For the amount of force allowed – no more than the purpose necessitates – see *Lynch* v. *Fitzgerald (No. 2)* [1938] I.R. 382.

peaceful it must be properly organised, otherwise the gardaí may apprehend a breach of the peace or the courts may draw the inference that it is not merely for the purposes stated in section 2, namely the communication of information or peaceful persuasion. The words of Walter Citrine are still apposite.

"Much of the trouble that has occurred with picketing in the past has resulted from the unnecessary presence of strikers, outsiders and even deliberate mischief makers. Picketing has sometimes been rendered completely nugatory by the action of such people. It is therefore essential that not only should the presence of such people be discouraged but that the pickets themselves should be clearly identified. Wherever possible, pickets should wear official badges and their number should never be greater than is reasonably necessary having regard to the number of persons to be picketed and the area in which the picketing is to be carried out. They should also be given comprehensive written instructions with a view to ensuring that wrongful acts should not be committed. . . ."[96]

PICKETING AND CIVIL LIABILITY

Trade Disputes

Section 2(1) of the Trade Disputes Act 1906 provides that:

"It shall be lawful for one or more persons, acting on their own behalf or on behalf of a trade union or of an individual employer or firm in contemplation or furtherance of a trade dispute, to attend at or near a house or place where a person resides or works or carries on business or happens to be, if they so attend merely for the purpose of peacefully obtaining or communicating information, or of peacefully persuading any person to work or abstain from working."

What is the effect of section 2? The answer to that question depends, in part, upon the view taken of the legality of picketing at common law. One view is that the section is declaratory of the common law; that it merely clears up the doubt created by the contradictory decisions of *Lyons* v. *Wilkins* and *Ward Lock* v. *O.P.A.S.* and establishes quite clearly that attending for the purposes set out in the section does not constitute a trespass to the highway or a common law nuisance. In other words section 2 does not confer any extra protection to that which the common law already confers.[97] This would explain why alone of all the sections in the 1906 Act it commences: "It shall be lawful. . . .".

The majority of judicial *dicta* in this jurisdiction, however, favour the view that section 2 does alter the existing common law, albeit only

---
[96] *Citrine's Trade Union Law* 3rd ed. (London, 1967), p. 565.
[97] This view is expressed in *Citrine, op. cit.*, at p. 561.

to a very limited extent. Madden J., in *Larkin* v. *Belfast Harbour Commissioners*,[98] best sums this up.

> "The effect of this section is perfectly clear. It legalised, for the first time by positive enactment, a course of action which might otherwise, *if carried out in a certain manner*, have amounted to a nuisance at common law, provided such a course of action is resorted to merely for effecting certain specified peaceful purposes. To this extent only does the Act affect the enjoyment of private property."[99]

In other words, the section grants immunity against certain forms of nuisance. It legalises such acts as are reasonably necessary to the carrying out of peaceful picketing which would constitute a degree of annoyance which would otherwise be sufficient to support an action at common law. The fallacy inherent in this view is that it supposes that the common law is that set out in *Lyons* v. *Wilkins*, whereas the authors would submit that the common law is that set out in *Ward Lock* v. *O.P.A.S.*, namely that many forms of peaceful picketing are not, as such, trespasses to the highway or nuisances.[1]

Moreover, if the pickets do in fact constitute a nuisance, in that their actions amount to an unreasonable interference with, disturbance of, or annoyance to another person in the exercise of his rights relating to the ownership or occupation of land or of some easement, profit or other right enjoyed in connection with land, the section provides no immunity. So if a picket violently bangs on a door, shouts or interferes seriously with the enjoyment of the premises the picket's common law right ceases, as does his section 2 right, and neither will protect him from civil or criminal liability for any of these acts.[2]

"For one or more persons"

Most picket lines are composed of a reasonably small number of pickets. Is there anything different about a large number of pickets? If each individual picket is entitled to attend, does this become unlawful because a large number of others do the same? It could be said that if large numbers are involved the police may reasonably apprehend a breach of the peace, and it has been judicially observed that it should not be difficult to infer that pickets who assemble in unreasonably large numbers do have the purpose of preventing free passage.[3] But is mass picketing illegal *per se*?

In *Broome* v. *D.P.P.*,[4] Lord Salmon expressed his doubts as to this. He said that it would depend on the facts in each case.

---

[98] [1908] 2 I.R. 214.
[99] At 225. Emphasis added.
[1] See *supra*, pp. 285–289.
[2] *Citrine, op. cit.*, p. 563.
[3] *Per* Lord Reid in *Broome* v. *D.P.P.* [1974] A.C. 587, 598.
[4] [1974] A.C. 587. But see *Thomas* v. *National Union of Mineworkers (South Wales Area)* [1985] I.R.L.R. 136.

"The fact that the pickets were physically preventing people from entering would, I suppose, be some evidence that one of their purposes was to prevent entry. Men are usually presumed to intend the natural consequences of their acts. It may be, however, that justices could be persuaded that the crowd of pickets around the entrance of a factory was there solely for the purpose of peaceful persuasion or peacefully imparting information and not at all for the purpose which in fact they achieved, namely, prevention of entry."[5]

In *E.I. Co. Ltd.* v. *Kennedy*,[6] Walsh J. commented:

"Excessive numbers in pickets may also go beyond what is reasonably permissible for the communication of information or for the obtaining of information and may amount to obstruction or nuisance or give rise to a reasonable apprehension of a breach of the peace."[7]

Further consideration was given to this question in *Brendan Dunne Ltd.* v. *Fitzpatrick*,[8] where Budd J. said that picketing would not be lawful if the methods adopted were "such as to overcome those who happen to be on the premises being picketed or the members of the public who might be minded to have business dealings with them, to the extent that people of ordinary nerve and courage may be prevented from doing what they have a lawful right to do." He continued:

"The method of picketing must be reasonable having regard to all the circumstances. It would not be justifiable I feel to place a picket consisting of a hundred or so persons on a small suburban business premises with one or two of a staff. On the other hand, it might be quite reasonable to place several quite large pickets on a large factory with several entrances. It is a matter of degree according to the circumstances. . . ."[9]

He concluded that "the number of the picket should bear reasonable relations to the nature of the premises and the number of persons with whom the dispute arises."[10] In his view, sixty persons parading outside the plaintiff company's premises in Dawson Street, Dublin 2, was an "unduly large" picket and was one which was "calculated to frighten and overcome those picketed and members of the public wishing to do business with them."

A novel approach to "mass picketing" was taken by Scott J. in *Thomas* v. *National Union of Mineworkers (South Wales Area)*.[11] Here

---

[5] At 604.
[6] [1968] I.R. 69.
[7] At 91.
[8] [1958] I.R. 29.
[9] At 44.
[10] *Id.*
[11] [1985] I.R.L.R. 136.

the gist of the plaintiffs' evidence was that on a regular daily basis there had been on average sixty pickets placed on their place of employment. The pickets' conduct was abusive but fell short of constituting an assault. Scott J. considered that the pickets constituted an unreasonable interferance with the plaintiffs' right to use the public highway for the purpose of entering and leaving their place of work and held that this "plainly unreasonable harassment" was actionable in tort.

If more are employed than are reasonably required for the purposes mentioned in the section the court may infer that it is not *bona fide* and merely for the purposes set out in the section and hence not protected by the section. What is reasonable is a question of degree and depends on the circumstances of the particular case – the size of the premises, the number of persons working or calling at them, the number of entrances, the confines and user of the area in which the picketing takes place *etc*.[12] Any attempt to lay down a specific figure appropriate to all situations is obviously impracticable, although in particular cases it is not uncommon for the High Court to limit by order the number of persons allowed to picket.[13]

"Acting on their own behalf or on behalf of a trade union"

In *Darby* v. *Leonard*,[14] Walsh J. said that it would be lawful for a dismissed employee to picket the premises of his ex-employer and "for other persons acting on his behalf to do likewise" in furtherance of the dispute.[15] This *dictum*, however, has not been applied in subsequent cases. In *Penney's Ltd.* v. *Kerrigan*,[16] the first-named defendant had been dismissed by the plaintiff company. She began to picket the premises and was assisted by her father and her sister-in-law, neither of whom were employed by the plaintiff company. McWilliam J. granted an interlocutory injunction against the father and sister-in-law and is reported[17] as having said that it was not open to a relative of a dismissed employee to engage in picketing. Of course, it may have been that her relatives were not members of an authorised trade union holding a negotiation licence. A similar case is *Allied Irish Banks* v.

---

[12] In *Ferguson Ltd.* v. *O'Gorman* [1937] I.R. 620 the Supreme Court viewed four to six pickets engaging in a continuous patrol up and down the twenty foot wide frontage of a shop a reasonable number. In *Silver Tassie Co. Ltd.* v. *Cleary* (1958) 92 I.L.T.R. 27 five persons picketing a public house was also viewed as reasonable.

[13] See the order made by Hamilton J. on July 6, 1979 in the McDonalds dispute directing that a roster of picketers be drawn up and a copy supplied to the restaurant owners, Pantry Franchise (Ireland) Ltd., "so that there should be no doubt who should be entitled to picket and who should not." In addition he declared that not more than three persons at any one time could picket the company's premises in O'Connell St. and Grafton St., Dublin. See also the order made by Barrington J. on April 5, 1984 in the Moracrete dispute limiting the number on the picket line to four.

[14] (1973) 107 I.L.T.R. 82.

[15] At 86.

[16] High Court, unreported, 7 February 1977.

[17] *Irish Times*, February 8, 1977.

Tuite and Kirwan.[18] Here the bank were in dispute with an employee who commenced picketing the bank's premises at West Street, Drogheda after an injunction had been granted restraining him from being on the bank's premises. He was joined in the picket by four employees of Becton Dickinson & Co. Ltd. and an injunction was granted against two of these restraining them from picketing. McWilliam J. appears to have accepted the argument that they must be picketing on their own behalf or on behalf of a trade union in order to enjoy the protection of section 2. If they were merely there on behalf of a friend they were not entitled to picket.

Provided the persons picketing are members or officials of an authorised trade union possessing a negotiation licence it does not matter if they are acting without, or contrary to, the authority of that union. Section 2 applies equally to unofficial and official action. This was confirmed by the Supreme Court in *Goulding Chemicals Ltd.* v. *Bolger*.[19] There it was submitted that the effect of section 11 of the Trade Union Act 1941 was to confine the protection given by section 2 to such authorised trade unions holding negotiation licences and to members and officials of such unions *acting with the authority, or pursuant to a decision, of their union*. The defendants, former employees of the company, were picketing in defiance of a settlement reached by their union on behalf of all its members who had been dismissed for redundancy. They were acting, therefore, in opposition to the views of their colleagues and without the approval of their union. The Supreme Court, however, on construing the relevant provisions, came to the conclusion that the protection given by section 2 applied to members and officials of an authorised trade-union with a negotiation licence whether such members and officials were acting on behalf of the union or on their own behalf. Since the defendants were members of such a trade union they were entitled to the protection, such as it was, of section 2.[20]

Any discussion of unofficial picketing would be incomplete without reference to the policy adopted by the I.C.T.U. in 1970 which was designed to "identify pickets which have been placed as a result of democratic decisions of the trade union movement and to secure that these pickets, and only these, have the support of trade union members."

---

[18] High Court, unreported, 2 February 1981. See the report in the *Irish Times*, February 3, 1981. See also the report in the *Irish Times*, November 27, 1981 of an injunction granted by Carroll J. restraining eleven named defendants from picketing Castleisland Co-Op Livestock Mart. The judge is reported as having said that the person whose employment formed the subject matter of the dispute was not a member of a trade union and only two of those picketing were, and there was no evidence that the two who were members were acting on behalf of a trade union. The judge said she interpreted s. 2(1) to mean that the protection was given only to the person acting in respect of his or her own employment and to persons acting on behalf of a trade union.
[19] [1977] I.R. 211.
[20] See O'Higgins C.J. at 227 (Henchy and Griffin JJ. concurring) and Kenny J. at 240.

As a result of this picketing policy, there are now two types of "official picket" – a union picket and an all-out picket.[21] With the former, the union does not involve the members of other unions. It places pickets on places where its own members are employed and calls upon them to respect the picket. The union is not entitled to call on the members of other unions, who have not been involved in the strike decision, to stop doing their work. It follows that it is not entitled under this policy to place pickets at places where none of its own members are employed.

The policy recognises, however, that in most cases a trade union in dispute with an employer will want the support of other trade unions. Where a union wishes to seek the support of other unions it submits a request for an all-out strike to I.C.T.U. This request is circulated to all affiliated unions, and the unions, whose members will be directly concerned, meet with the Industrial Relations Committee of the I.C.T.U. If the Committee considers that an all-out strike is justified, permission will be granted for the use of all-out pickets. The present practice is to grant permission whenever the Committee believes that there has been a breach of agreement or that trade union principles are at stake. The Committee, while giving permission for an all-out picket, is also empowered to defer its implementation.

Two riders to this policy need to be mentioned. First, the policy permits postmen to pass all pickets, except in cases where the business can be carried on by post. Secondly, nothing in the policy prevents another union deciding to support the union in dispute, even where an all-out strike has not been approved by the Committee.

The question of strike pay was not dealt with in the 1970 policy but in 1973 the Executive Council of I.C.T.U. made a recommendation to the Annual Congress which was debated and approved. It states that no union should pay strike pay to members who refuse to pass either an unofficial picket or a picket placed by another union where no all-out strike has been approved.

"To attend at or near".

The word "attend" was considered by the Supreme Court in *Ferguson Ltd.* v. *O'Gorman*[22] where it was submitted that the action of four to six persons patrolling in front of the plaintiff's premises was not attendance within the meaning of the section. Sullivan C.J. said that there was nothing in the act to limit the meaning of the word attend and make it inapplicable to prolonged and continuous action.[23]

---

[21] In May 1985, it was announced (see *Irish Times*, May 20, 1985) that the I.C.T.U. had begun a review of the all-out picket policy, following complaints about its operation. Some unions want to see the policy considerably tightened up, with union members disciplined for passing an all-out picket and sanctions imposed on unions who fail to discipline their members.
[22] [1937] I.R. 620.
[23] At 644–645.

The meaning of the words "at or near" and the general scope of the section, were considered in *Larkin* v. *Belfast Harbour Commissioners*[24] and *McCusker* v. *Smith*.[25] In the former case, Jim Larkin had addressed a crowd of workmen on a quay, the property of the Belfast Harbour Commissioners, without the permission of their Secretary, in breach of a by-law made by them. He was prosecuted by the Commissioners, and was convicted of an offence against the by-law. On a case stated, the Court of King's Bench[26] held that the conviction was right. It was argued on Larkin's behalf that he was entitled, under section 2(1) of the 1906 Act, to enter upon the quay for the purposes mentioned in the section, but that argument was rejected by every member of the Court. O'Brien L.C.J. in his judgment stated the question at issue as follows:–

"Do the words 'to attend at or near a house or place where a person resides or works' authorise a person of the specified class, that is to say, one or more persons acting on their own behalf, or on behalf of a trade union, or of an individual employer or firm, in contemplation or furtherance of a trade dispute, to attend not only in the immediate proximity of a house or place where a person resides or works, but in – within – the house or place itself? Does, in fact, the Act of Parliament authorise an entry into a house or place, against the will of the owner, for the purpose mentioned in the clause of the section which I have read? If this be so, the Legislature has, indeed, conferred on the specified class a right which I think neither trade unions nor anyone connected with them has ever before claimed – a right to invade the privacy of a man's house, or the factory or place of business where a man's work is carried on."[27]

The Court emphatically answered this question in the negative. Madden J. said that the idea of trespass on or upon private property was "wholly absent" from that of peaceful picketing.[28] The section was not available as a justification for trespass. In *McCusker* v. *Smith*,[29] it was held by the Court of King's Bench in a case stated that section 2(1) did not authorise the defendant's entry into the hall of the complainant's licensed premises for the purposes specified in the section. Sir James Campbell C.J. concluded his judgment, in which Kenny J. concurred, as follows:

"Again, 'at or near' does not include entering on the premises of the complainant. This Court has already decided in *Larkin's Case* that

---

[24] [1908] 2 I.R. 214.
[25] [1918] 2 I.R. 432.
[26] O'Brien L.C.J., Madden, Wright and Dodd JJ.
[27] [1908] 2 I.R. 214, 219–220.
[28] *Ibid.* at 225. See also Wright J. at 228 and Dodd J. at 230. The decision has been approved and applied by a Queen's Bench Divisional Court in *British Airports Authority* v. *Ashton* [1983] I.C.R. 696 in respect of picketing on Heathrow Airport aerodrome.
[29] [1918] 2 I.R. 432.

'at or near' must be construed so as to exclude the premises themselves. 'At' does not mean 'in' or 'upon'. This being settled law, there was evidence that some acts of the defendant were committed in or upon the premises, and therefore he could not justify his conduct under the section."[30]

Gibson J. concurred, stating that the defendant had lost the protection of the 1906 Act, as he had invaded the complainant's premises.

The section therefore confers no right to attend *on* land for the purposes of peaceful picketing. As can be appreciated difficulties will arise therefore in the case of industrial estates and shopping centres. If an employee in dispute with an employer pickets outside the employer's unit, the employee is subject to liability for trespass at the suit of the owner of the centre. If the employee pickets outside the shopping centre, the other tenants might then complain that their business is being affected by the picketing and move for an injunction. This is precisely what was happening in a case before Barrington J. in April 1982.[31] The Irish National Union of Vintners, Grocers and Allied Trades Assistants were in dispute with Powers Supermarkets who traded in one of the 27 units in Rathmines Town Hall Shopping Centre. All entrances were picketed and the owners – the New Ireland Assurance Co. Ltd. – and one of the tenants sought an injunction restraining picketing of the entrances to the shopping complex. Counsel alleged that business in all the units had been "decimated". An injunction was granted but only on the basis of an undertaking by the owners to permit reasonable picketing of the Powers Supermarkets unit within the complex.

What if the owner is not prepared to consent to picketing inside the complex or estate? The question was considered at some length by the Supreme Court of Canada in *Harrison* v. *Carswell*.[32] The factual setting was as follows. The location was a shopping centre, in which a large number of tenants carried on a wide variety of business. The centre had the usual amenities such as access road, parking lists and sidewalks which were open for use by members of the public who might or might not be buyers at the time they came to the centre. An employee of a tenant in the shopping centre participated in a strike and then

---

[30] At 440.
[31] The proceedings are noted at (1982) 1 *J.I.S.L.L.* at p. 21. See also *Intacta Investments Ltd.* v. *Power* (1974 no. 1438P) where a motion by the owners of a shopping centre for interlocutory relief to restrain picketing by the employees of a tenant (trading as Londis) was adjourned generally on the defendants' undertaking to picket only at the entrance to Londis and to carry placards indicating that the trade dispute was only with Londis.
[32] (1975) 62 D.L.R. (3d) 68. The question has also been considered in the United States of America, see *Schwartz-Torrence Investment Corp.* v. *Bakery and Confectionery Workers' Union, Local 31* (1964) 394 P 2d 921; *Amalgamated Food Employees' Union, Local 590* v. *Logan Valley Plaza Inc.* (1968) 391 U.S. 308; *Lloyd Corp. Ltd.* v. *Tanner* (1972) 407 U.S. 551.

proceeded to picket peacefully on the sidewalk in front of his employer's premises. The employer, the tenant, took no action against the picketing but the owner of the shopping centre told the employee that picketing was not permitted in any area of the centre. She refused to leave and criminal charges of trespass followed. She was convicted and a majority of the Supreme Court upheld her conviction on the ground that:

> "an owner who has granted a right of entry to a particular class of the public [employees of his tenants] has not thereby relinquished his or her right to withdraw its invitation to the general public or any particular member thereof, and that if a member of the public whose invitation to enter has been withdrawn refuses to leave, he thereby becomes a trespasser . . ."

Laskin C.J.C. dissented and his judgment appears to the authors to be the more persuasive in the Irish context. The Chief Justice of Canada concluded that the right of a person to picket peacefully in support of a lawful strike was of greater social significance than the proprietary rights of an owner of a shopping centre. The public interest served by permitting union members to bring economic pressure to bear upon their respective employers through peaceful pickets outweighed in this situation the right of the individual to the enjoyment of private property.[33]

"A house or place where a person resides or works or carries on business or happens to be"

These words are deliberately wide.[34] There is no condition that the place picketed must be the picket's place of work, and thus on its face the section would permit secondary picketing[35] even of "innocent" third parties not involved in the dispute. In the past the Irish courts have accepted that the section is wide enough to cover such action. In *Roundabout Ltd. v. Beirne*,[36] Dixon J. said that the effect of the

---

[33] See his judgment at 73–77. The U.S. Supreme Court has also concluded (see cases in fn. 32 *supra*) that to apply the rules against trespass to private property in those situations would be at variance with the goal of free expression and communication "that is the heart of the First Amendment" (*per* Marshall J. in *Amalgamated Food Employees Union, Local 590 v. Logan Valley Plaza Inc.* (1968) 391 U.S. 308, 325).

[34] The High Court, however, has granted injunctions restraining the picketing of the homes of company officials, see *Irish Dunlop Ltd. v. Power* High Court, unreported, 10 September and 23 September 1981 (Barrington J. and Finlay P. respectively); *Datsun Ltd. v. O'Loughlin* High Court, unreported, 20 December 1983. In this latter case 29 employees were restrained from picketing the homes, or such other places as directors or members of management or staff might be found. Barrington J. is reported (*Irish Times*, December 21, 1983) has having told the defendants that while they were perfectly entitled to picket their place of work in a peaceful manner, they were not entitled to picket the homes of directors or staff or any place they might be attending on social visits.

[35] *I.e.*, picketing of someone other than the employer with whom the pickets are in dispute.

[36] [1959] I.R. 423.

definition in section 5(3) was that once there was a trade dispute it would be permissible for the workman to picket entirely different premises owned or occupied by a totally different employer.[37] In more recent years, the High Court, at least at the interlocutory stage, has adopted a more restrictive attitude.[38] In *Ellis* v. *Wright*,[39] Butler J. said he was not prepared to accept that the section legalised the most "disruptive and indiscriminate" industrial action. He continued:

> "the fundamental requirement to render a picket lawful is that it must be in contemplation or furtherance of a trade dispute. That necessitates a clearly discernible connection between the premises picketed and the dispute in the sense that the employer or workman affected by the picket is directly concerned with the dispute."[40]

What exactly is meant by "connection" is not entirely clear. Butler J. said that it would be found in the fact that the employer in dispute had a controlling interest in the company which was picketed[41] or in the fact that one or more employees of the employer in dispute visited or attended the premises picketed in the course of their employment. Although Butler J. did not expressly refer to this situation, it is submitted that where the employer, with whom there is a dispute, arranges for another company to complete the work, which in the absence of the strike would have been done by that employer, the second company should be subject to all the pressures to which the primary employer is subjected just as if its employees were replacements put to work in the primary employer's premises. Beyond this the position is unclear. The insistence on a "clearly discernible connection" and the requirement of "direct concern" suggests that Butler J. was following a parallel line of reasoning to that of Lord Denning M.R. and some other members of the Court of Appeal in Britain, in a series of cases in the late 1970s, where it was held that for an act to be in furtherance of a trade dispute it had to be "directly" in furtherance of it and that in general secondary action was too remote.[42] Anyone seeking the protection of the Act had to establish not only that they had a genuine intention to achieve the objective of a trade dispute but also

---

[37] At 428–429.
[38] In *Córas Iompair Éireann* v. *Hennessy* High Court, unreported, 13 June 1983, Murphy J. is reported (*Irish Times*, June 14, 1983) as having told the defendants (members of the M.P.G.W.U.) who were picketing Plunkett Station, Waterford, that they could certainly picket their own employers but when they sought to picket any other employer's property they were in a difficult area and likely to be stopped.
[39] [1978] I.R. 6.
[40] At 13.
[41] See *P.M.P.A. Insurance Co. Ltd.* v. *Walsh* High Court, unreported, 4 August 1977 where D'Arcy J. refused to grant an interlocutory injunction restraining picketing.
[42] See *Beaverbrook Newspapers Ltd.* v. *Keys* [1978] I.C.R. 582; *Express Newspapers Ltd.* v. *MacShane* [1979] I.C.R. 210; *Associated Newspapers Group Ltd.* v. *Wade* [1979] I.C.R. 664; *Publishers Book Delivery Service* v. *Filkins* [1979] I.R.L.R. 356.

that the acts were reasonably capable of achieving that end.[43] In Lord Denning's words,[44] for the immunity to apply the picketing "must help one side or the other in a practical way." Butler J.'s reasoning in *Ellis* v. *Wright* appears consistent with this, since to picket someone not directly concerned in the dispute would not, in most cases, *further* the dispute.[45] So, in May 1982, Carroll J. rejected a claim by former employees of Navan Carpets (Yarns) Ltd. that they were entitled to picket an associated company, Youghal Carpet Yarns Ltd. Carroll J. indicated that the employers picketed would have to be in a position to concede or negotiate in the dispute.[46]

There are decisions, however, which appear to go even further in delimiting the ambit of lawful secondary picketing. In *Crosspan Developments Ltd.* v. *Bridgman*,[47] three painters were restrained from picketing any houses on a Dublin building site other than those on which their employer, a subcontractor to the main builder, was engaged. In another case, twelve members of A.G.E.M.O.U., who were in dispute with Massey Ferguson Ltd., were restrained from picketing the premises of Datsun Ltd., 25% of whose issued share capital was owned by TMG Ltd. who owned the entire share capital of Massey Ferguson Ltd. The same defendants were also restrained from picketing the premises of A.H. Masser Ltd. which occupied a single-complex premises owned by TMG Ltd.[48] In neither of these cases, however, were written judgments delivered so it is difficult to ascertain the principles on which the injunctions were granted.[49] A written judgment was delivered in *Cleary* v. *Coffey*,[50] where the plaintiff sought an injunction restraining the defendants from picketing her licensed premises. The defendants had been employed by the plaintiff's aunt, who had recently died. The plaintiff was one of the executors of

---

[43] *Per* Lawton L.J. in *MacShane* [1979] I.C.R. 210, 220.
[44] In *Express Newspapers Ltd.* v. *MacShane* [1979] I.C.R. 210, 218.
[45] It must not be forgotten, however, that the House of Lords overruled the Court of Appeal in *MacShane* (see [1980] A.C. 672). The remoteness test in all its guises was strongly criticised. The decision of the House of Lords in *MacShane* and in the subsequent case of *Duport Steel Ltd.* v. *Sirs* [1980] I.C.R. 161 made it clear that the test of furtherance was subjective, not objective. "If the party who does the act honestly thinks at the time he does it that it may help one of the parties to the trade to achieve their objectives and does it for that reason, he is protected." *Per* Lord Diplock in *MacShane* at p. 686. See *supra*, pp. 276–280.
[46] Reported in the *Irish Times*, May 4, 1982. See also the reports of the interim injunction granted by Barrington J. (*Irish Times*, May 24, 1985); the interlocutory injunctions granted by Finlay P. (*Irish Times*, May 29, 1982), and Costello J. (*Irish Times*, March 14, 1984); and the permanent injunction granted in *Guinness and Mahon Ltd.* v. *Cunningham and Whelan* High Court, unreported, 22 May 1984 (noted (1984) 3 *J.I.S.L.L.* at p. 40).
[47] High Court, unreported, 23 October 1979.
[48] Reported in the *Irish Times*, June 29, 1977.
[49] Similarly with respect to the decisions in *Brittain Smith Manufacturing Ltd.* v. *Fitzpatrick* High Court, unreported, 13 March 1969; *Doyle* v. *Beirne* High Court, unreported, 22 August 1977; *Waterford Co-Op Society Ltd.* v. *Griffin* High Court, unreported, 8 May 1979; and *Datsun Ltd.* v. *Mooney* High Court, unreported, 25 June 1979. Generally see Kerr, "In contemplation or furtherance of a trade dispute" (1979–80) *D.U.L.J.* at pp. 82–87.
[50] High Court, unreported, 30 October 1979.

the aunt's will and was also one of the residuary legatees. The executors had decided to sell the licensed premises where the defendants were employed. The defendants were given notice and were paid the full redundancy payments to which they were entitled under statute. The defendants claimed, however, that they were entitled to further payments over and above the statutory payments as was customary in the licensed trade. In furtherance of this dispute, the defendants picketed the plaintiff's premises. McWilliam J., whilst holding that there was a trade dispute between the defendants and their deceased employer's successors in title and that this dispute did not cease to be a trade dispute merely because the claim appeared to him to be unreasonable, pointed out that there was not, and never had been, any "business association" between the premises picketed and the premises where they had been employed. He went on to hold that employees of a deceased person were not entitled to picket the premises of the executors, personal representatives or residuary legatees. They were not "directly concerned" in the dispute, and the fact that the plaintiff was engaged in the same kind of business was irrelevant. "Although there is a clearly discernible connection between the plaintiff and the dispute it seems to be that the connection is not sufficiently close to justify picketing of her premises. . . ."[51]

The legal status of 'secondary picketing' is therefore uncertain. Despite the plain wording of section 2(1), the Irish courts tend to regard it as unlawful. The ability of employees to take secondary action, however, may be essential in certain circumstances. The application of pressure on a third party, with whom the union has no dispute, to induce that person to cease doing business with an employer with whom the union does have a dispute is a very effective way of furthering a dispute if the primary action has not been totally successful. No matter how widely the union spreads the dispute, the purpose remains the same. All the union seeks to achieve is the equivalent of a fully effective strike of the primary employer. All the union asks is that others act as if the employer were in fact closed by the strike. To curtail secondary action, therefore, is to deprive workers of an element of their strength, "to make them enter the economic struggle with one hand tied."[52]

"If they so attend merely for the purpose of peacefully obtaining or communicating information, or of peacefully persuading any person to work or abstain from working"
Full effect is given to the word "merely".[53] Attendance for other

---

[51] At p. 6 of his unreported judgment.
[52] Summers and Wellington, *Cases and Materials on Labor Law* (New York, 1968), p. 279.
[53] "If the picketing is done for a purpose other than peacefully obtaining or communicating information or of peacefully persuading any person to work or abstain from working the section cannot be relied on." *Per* Henchy J. in *Becton Dickinson & Co. Ltd.* v. *Lee* [1973] I.R. 1, 44.

purposes is not permitted, such as picketing a shop or a theatre with the object of persuading customers to boycott it and frequent another.[54] So in *Newbridge Industries Ltd.* v. *Bateson*,[55] Kenny J. was satisfied that the evidence showed that the picket was not put on for the purpose of obtaining or communicating information or of peacefully persuading any person to work or abstain from working but to prevent the material in the factory from being taken out and so he granted the injunction sought. On appeal, the Supreme Court upheld the order but limited its terms to prohibit picketing save for the purpose of communicating information and peacefully persuading persons to work or not to work.[56]

The object may, in effect, be accomplished through the communication of information. As is pointed out in *Citrine*:

"The section does not require that the information should have reference to the question of working or abstaining from working. Thus, if pickets confine themselves to publishing, by word of mouth or by means of placards or handbills, accurate information as to the nature of the dispute, the section will cover them in the normal way."[57]

This means that pickets may seek to 'invite' rather than persuade customers not to shop. Citrine submitted that the mere exhibition of a notice setting out the facts and saying "In view of these facts we invite you not to deal here" would not amount to persuasion.[58]

The section does not authorise the dissemination of false or inaccurate information. So in *Ryan* v. *Cooke and Quinn*,[59] an injunction was granted when pickets carried placards outside the plaintiff's shops stating untruth-fully that she refused to employ trade union labour. Johnston J. held that the dissemination of a falsehood could not be described as a "peaceful" way of "communicating information".

In *Goulding Chemicals Ltd.* v. *Bolger*,[60] particular emphasis was laid, in the course of the argument, on the use of the word "merely" and it was suggested that in this case the motive behind the picketing was to prevent the winding up of the plaintiff's operations and the consequent mothballing of the machinery. O'Higgins C.J. said that this argument

---

[54] *Toppin* v. *Feron* (1909) 43 I.L.T.R. 190; *Ryan* v. *Cook and Quinn* [1938] I.R. 512; *Brendan Dunne Ltd.* v. *Fitzpatrick* [1958] I.R. 29. In the United States of America, the Supreme Court has drawn a distinction between picketing employed only to persuade customers not to buy the struck product, which is lawful, and picketing employed to persuade customers not to trade at all with the person picketed, which is unlawful. See *National Labour Relations Board* v. *Fruit and Vegetable Packers, Local 760* (1964) 377 U.S. 58.
[55] High Court, unreported, 15 July 1975.
[56] In an *ex tempore* judgment delivered July 31, 1975.
[57] *Citrine's Trade Union Law* 3rd Ed. (London, 1967), p. 577.
[58] *Id.*
[59] [1938] I.R. 512.
[60] [1977] I.R. 211.

confused the motive or reason for an action and the purpose or object to be obtained from that action. The motive inspiring the picketing was irrelevant.[61] Kenny J. was of the same mind when he said, in the same case, that section 2 was not dealing with the predominant motive of those picketing but with the aim or purpose to be achieved by the picketing.[62]

Attendance for the purpose of peaceful permission includes the right to ttalk to him but only for so long as the person is willing to listen; he cannot be compelled to stay.

Picketing in breach of procedure

A question which often arises in practice is whether an employer can obtain an injunction to restrain picketing in furtherance of a trade dispute when the picketing is contrary to the procedure set put in a collective agreement. If the requirement to follow procedure before taking industrial action has been incorporated into the pickets' contracts of employment, then the picketing will be in breach of contract and, in *Becton Dickinson & Co. Ltd.* v. *Lee*,[64] Walsh J. expressly reserved his opinion on the question of whether a withdrawal of labour in breach of contract constituted a "trade dispute" within the meaning of section 5(3) of the 1906 Act and whether picketing in furtherance of it was lawful within the meaning of section 2. Kenny J. has held on a number of occasions that one cannot picket in breach of contract[65] but O'Higgins J. (as he then was) ruled emphatically, in *Kire Manufacturing Co. Ltd.* v. *O'Leary*,[66] that the fact that the defendants were picketing, having broken their own contracts of employment, was "wholly irrelevant" once it was found that they were picketing in furtherance of a *bona fide* trade dispute. The authors would submit that O'Higgins J.'s reasoning is to be preferred. However desirable it may be that procedures set out in a collective agreement should be exhausted before picketing takes place, the plain wording of section 2 does not warrant the implication of such a requirement.

More recently, however, the High Court appears to have adopted the view that picketing in violation of a disputes procedure is unlawful, regardless of whether the procedures have been incorporated into the individual contracts of employment. In *Kayfoam Woolfson Ltd.* v. *Woods*,[67] a shopsteward had been dismissed and a picket placed on the

---

[61] At 232.
[62] At 239.
[63] *Broome* v. *Director of Public Prosecutions* [1974] A.C. 587, 597, *per* Lord Reid who went on to liken a picket with a hitch-hiker.
[64] [1973] I.R. 1, 39.
[65] *Irish Biscuits Ltd.* v. *Miley* High Court, unreported, 3 April 1972; *Merchants Warehousing Co. Ltd.* v. *McGrath* High Court, unreported, 22 April 1974; *Waltham Electronics (Ireland) Ltd.* v. *Doyle* High Court, unreported, 15 November, 1974.
[66] High Court, unreported, 29 April 1974.
[67] High Court, unreported, 4 June 1980.

plaintiff employer's premises. Keane J. admitted that it was not "seriously in issue" that there was a trade dispute. Nevertheless he granted an injunction restraining the picketing. Keane J. is reported[68] as having said that he accepted the plaintiff's argument that the picketing was unlawful as being in breach of a collective agreement which provided for the referral of disputes to the Labour Court's conciliation machinery and which further provided that there would be no industrial action until the Labour Court had issued a recommendation.

A similar decision was reached in *Acton and Jordon Ltd.* v. *Duff,*[69] where the primary reason given for the granting of interim and interlocutory injunctions was reported[70] as having been that the picketers were in breach of the disputes procedure set out in the registered employment agreement for the construction industry. The authors find it difficult to reconcile these cases with the wording of the 1906 Act, and indeed with that of the Industrial Relations Act 1946. The 1946 Act stipulates that one of the conditions for registration of an employment agreement is the inclusion of a disputes procedure. Furthermore it imposes penalties on a trade union which initiates or supports a strike in breach of a registered agreement.[71] What the 1946 Act does not provide, as it might have done, is that industrial action taken in violation of the agreement, was not entitled to the immunities contained in the 1906 Act. The authors would, therefore, respectfully submit that both *Woods* and *Duff* were wrongly decided.[72]

Occupations

Section 2 of the 1906 Act merely permits persons to attend "at or near" not "in or on" premises. It does not confer a licence on trade union officials to enter upon property for the purpose of addressing the employees,[73] even at the request of the employees, nor are the employees protected if they go beyond picketing and occupy or seize control of either the whole or part of the premises. The occasions on which a trade union official actually trespasses on an employer's premises may well be rare but workplace occupations are a more frequent form of industrial action, often in response to proposals by management to declare redundancies.

"From the employees' point of view it has the advantages that it is a much more dramatic assertion of their desire to retain their jobs, it is

---

[68] *Irish Times*, June 5, 1980.
[69] High Court, unreported, 12 July 1982.
[70] *Irish Times*, July 13, 1982. The case is criticised by Asmal, *Irish Times*, July 17, 1982.
[71] See *supra*, pp. 151–152.
[72] See also *Dunnes Stores (Clonmel) Ltd.* v. *Butler* High Court, unreported, 7 November 1972; *Dublin Glass and Paint Co. Ltd.* v. *Collinge* High Court, unreported, 22 July 1977.
[73] See *Larkin* v. *Belfast Harbour Commissioners* [1908] 2 I.R. 214; *Norbrook Laboratories Ltd.* v. *King* [1982] I.R.L.R. 456 and [1984] I.R.L.R. 200. The latter case is noted by Simpson (1982) 4 *D.U.L.J. (n.s.)* 124 and (1984) 6 *D.U.L.J. (n.s.)* 192.

easier for the employees to maintain their morale than during a strike when the employees merely stay at home, and it may be more effective than a strike plus picket lines in preventing management from removing machinery and stocks of finished goods, control of which is the employees' strongest bargaining counter."[74]

The occupation may in itself be extremely peaceful and cause no actual damage but nevertheless it is a clear interference with the property rights of the employer, and possibly others. It constitutes a trespass and may involve those concerned in both civil and criminal liability. It has been recently confirmed, both by Lynch J. in *B.H.S. Ltd.* v. *Mitchell*[75] and Hamilton J. in *F.W. Woolworth Ltd.* v. *Haynes*,[76] that despite the existence of a *bona fide* trade dispute, the 1906 Act provided no immunity to the unlawful occupation of the plaintiff companies' premises in Dublin. The government has also made it clear that there can be "no question of extending the definition of legal strike action to include sit-ins."[77]

In the first place an occupation is actionable at the suit of the employer or some other person entitled to possession of the premises, such as a liquidator. Trespass is actionable *per se*; this means that the plaintiff need show no damage in order to succeed.[78] The tort of trespass to land is defined[79] as consisting of entering or remaining on land in the possession of another without lawful justification. Although the employees are lawfully present when they perform their duties, their presence in this situation will almost certainly take them outside the scope of their licence to be on the premises.

The employer may either seek an injunction or an order of possession directed to the Sheriff to deliver up possession of the premises.[80] This latter procedure was invoked to terminate the occupation of Ranks (Ireland) Ltd.'s Dublin flour mills. The Sheriff experienced considerable difficulty in carrying out the order and a garda superintendent told Carroll J.[81] that members of the gardai would accompany the Sheriff's employees, would protect them from being assaulted or molested in any fashion but would not break down doors or cut bolts or locks. That would have to be done by the Sheriff

---

[74] Davies and Freedland, *Labour Law: Text and Materials* 2nd ed. (London, 1984) p. 887.
[75] High Court, unreported, 18 April 1984.
[76] High Court, unreported, 19 July 1984.
[77] Department of Labour *Discussion Document on Industrial Relations Reform* (1983) para. 3.13. Moreover the Government announced in February 1984 that no replacement industries would be sought for those factories where the workforce were engaged in a sit-in.
[78] On the tort of trespass to land generally, see McMahon and Binchy *Irish Law of Torts* (Oxon, 1981), pp. 463–473.
[79] *Salmond and Heuston on the Law of Torts* 18th ed. (London, 1981), p. 36.
[80] R.S.C. O.47 r.2. Apart from Dublin City, the County Borough of Dublin, Cork City and the County Borough of Cork, which have their own Sheriffs, the relevant person would be the County Registrar who acts as Under-Sheriff.
[81] See the report in the *Irish Times*, May 22, 1984.

and his employees. The gardai's role therefore was perceived by them as one of protection not assistance. In *Attorney General* v. *Kissane*[82] it was held that the Sheriff, in his sole discretion, has the right to require "the protection and assistance of the constabulary" in the execution of such an order[83] and a refusal to give that protection and assistance will be punished as a contempt of the court whence the order issued. Johnson J. added[84] that the Sheriff is bound to be provided with "a force sufficient to overcome any degree of resistance that may be offered to him."

The occupiers may also be sued by some third party whose property is being wrongfully detained. So in *Roadstone Ltd.* v. *Bailie*[85] O'Hanlon J. directed the defendants, who were engaged in a sit in at the premises of A.H. Masser Ltd., to release a crane belonging to the plaintiff company, which had been taken to A.H. Masser Ltd. for repair, and to cease from wrongfully detaining it.

The occupation may also attract a criminal prosecution under the Prohibition of Forcible Entry and Occupation Act 1971.[86] Sections 2 and 3 of this Act provide that a person who forcibly enters land or who remains in forcible occupation of land shall be guilty of an offence, although section 4 provides that an offence is not committed if the person does not interfere with the use and enjoyment of the land by the owner and, if requested to leave by the owner or a member of the Garda Síochána in uniform, he does so with all reasonable speed and in a peaceable manner. Section 4 provides that a person who encourages or advocates the commission of an offence under sections 2 or 3 is guilty of an offence. Moreover, if the encouragement *etc.* is made by or on behalf of a group of persons, every person who is a member of the group and who consented to the making of the statement is also guilty of an offence. Land is defined as including houses or other buildings or structures whatever, such as a mobile home, and parts of such buildings or structures. "Forcibly" is defined as using or threatening to use force in relation to person or property, and for this purpose participation in action or conduct with others in numbers or circumstances calculated to prevent by intimidation the exercise by any person of his rights in relation to any property is deemed to constitute a threat to use force. Forcible occupation of land is described as including the act of locking, obstructing or barring any window, door

---

[82] (1893) 32 L.R. Ir. 220.

[83] Although such order may not be executed in the interval between the commencement of two hours before sunset and sunrise or 6 a.m., whichever is later.

[84] (1893) 32 L.R. Ir. 220, 248.

[85] High Court, unreported, 10 November 1982. See also *Pantry Franchise (Ireland) Ltd.* v. *Castlemahon Frozen Foods Ltd.* High Court, unreported, 27 March 1979.

[86] Submissions made in support of the contention that ss. 2 and 3 of the Act were invalid having regard to the provisions of the Constitution were rejected by the Supreme Court in *Dooley* v. *Attorney General* [1977] I.R. 205.

or other entry or means of exit from land, with a view to preventing or resisting a lawful attempt to enter the land; or the act of erecting a physical obstacle to an entry or means of exit from land with a view to preventing or resisting a lawful attempt to enter; or the act of physically resisting a lawful attempt at ejection from land. In other words, the erection of barricades will only constitute forcible occupation contrary to section 3 if the action is calculated to prevent or obstruct the entry of any person lawfully entitled to enter. Section 7 provides that every person who commits an offence under the Act shall be liable:

(a) on summary convinction in the case of a first offence, to a fine not exceeding £50 or to imprisonment for a term not exceeding 6 months or to both such fine and such imprisonment;
(b) on summary conviction in the case of a second or subsequent offence, to a fine not exceeding £100 or to imprisonment for a term not exceeding 12 months or to both such fine and such imprisonment;
(c) on conviction on indictment, to a fine not exceeding £500 or to imprisonment for a term not exceeding 3 years or to both such fine and such imprisonment.

Section 6 directs the court, in coming to a decision as to the penalty for an offence under sections 2 or 3, to take the damage to property into account, including damage "reasonably and unavoidably" caused by the owner or a member of the Garda Síochána in the course of lawfully entering or taking possession of the premises. Section 9 confers a power of arrest without warrant if (i) the garda knows or has reasonable cause for suspecting that a person is committing an offence under section 3; (ii) the owner represents, and the garda reasonably believes, that serious damage to the land or serious interference with the owner's lawful rights or serious inconvenience to the public is being or will be caused; (iii) the garda reasonably believes that an arrest is necessary to prevent such damage, interference or inconvenience; and (iv) it is not reasonably practicable to apply for a warrant.

Section 1(4) provides that nothing in this Act shall affect the law relating to acts done in contemplation or furtherance of a trade dispute within the meaning of the 1906 Act. The view of the Garda Commissioner, as revealed to Carroll J. during the Ranks dispute,[87] is that the Act does not apply to occupations during a trade dispute. This is clearly erroneous and, in June 1982, the Supreme Court actually directed the Gardaí to operate the Act against six employees who were occupying the premises of British American Optical Co. Ltd. during a trade dispute.[88] Moreover O'Hanlon J. in *Ross Co. Ltd.* v. *Swan*[89]

---

[87] See the report in the *Irish Times*, May 22, 1984.
[88] See the report in the *Irish Times*, June 24, 1982.
[89] [1981] I.L.R.M. 416.

refused to grant orders of attachment or committal against defendants who were deliberately disobeying a court order restraining the occupation of the plaintiff company's premises because there was some "reasonable alternative course" available instead. This alternative course was for the Gardaí to use their powers under the 1971 Act within whose scope "the case appears to fall squarely."[90]

In addition to committing offences under the 1971 Act, the occupiers may also be guilty of an offence under section 7 of the Conspiracy and Protection of Property Act 1875.[91] In *Galt* v. *Philp*[92] the High Court of Justiciary in Scotland unanimously ruled that the words "watching and besetting" were not restricted to the maintenace of an *external* watch on premises and could include sit-ins. The Lord Justice-General[93] said:

"The mischief to which s. 7 head 4 is directed is action designed to prevent persons from going into or coming out of a relevant place, and it would be contrary to common sense to hold that control of access or egress from a position immediately outside the main door of a building is within the ambit of s. 7 whereas exercise of the same control from a position immediately on the inner side of the main door is not."[94]

Finally it should be noted that section 10(1) of the Criminal Law (Jurisdiction) Act 1976 provides that a person who unlawfully, by force or threat thereof, or by any other form of intimidation, seizes or exercises control of or otherwise interferes with the control of, or compels or induces some other person to use for an unlawful purpose, any vehicle (whether mechanically propelled or not) or any ship or hovercraft shall be guilty of an offence and shall be liable on conviction on indictment to imprisonment for a term not exceeding fifteen years.

---

[90] At 417.
[91] See Coleman, "Sit-Ins and the Conspiracy and Protection of Property Act 1875" [1970] *Crim. L.R.* 608.
[92] 1982 S.L.T. 28.
[93] Lord Emslie.
[94] At p. 38.

Chapter 11

THE LABOUR INJUNCTION[1]

In virtually all trade dispute cases the remedy sought is not damages but an injunction to prevent the commission of tortious injuries which are threatened or anticipated, or in the case of a continuing injury, to restrain its continuance. Most employers are little interested in bringing a civil action for damages in respect of injuries inflicted by their employees in the course of a dispute. For the employer, his interest "is most likely to be in the maintenance of good industrial relations with his employees, which would of course be jeopardised by the institution of legal action."[2] Such considerations would not, however, apply to third parties affected detrimentally by the dispute in question. In Britain these considerations have, in the main, resulted in relatively few civil actions for damages or, until recently, for injunctions. In Ireland however, for reasons which no research has adequately explained, employers have been much more ready to resort to injunctions as a way of processing trade disputes. The 'labour injunction', as it is popularly known, is perceived by many employers as an effective means of relieving the pressure and enabling them to negotiate from a position of strength. Much of the dissatisfaction and frustration which has manifested itself in non-compliance with court orders and the jailing of trade unionists for contempt of court[3] can be traced to the frequency with which injunctions are sought and granted in trade disputes, coupled with the wholly unsatisfactory nature of such proceedings.

The power to grant an injunction is possessed by the High Court and is derived from the Judicature (Ireland) Act 1877, section 28(8) of which provides that an injunction "may be granted by interlocutory order of the court in all cases in which it appears to the court to be just

---

[1] See generally Frankfurter and Greene, *The Labor Injunction* (New York, 1930); Davies and Anderman, "Injunction Procedure in Labour Disputes" (1973) 2 *I.L.J.* 213 and (1974) 3 *I.L.J.* 30; Casey, "The Injunction in Labour Disputes in Eire" (1969) 18 *I.C.L.Q.* 347; Stewart, "Injunctions and the right to strike" (1975) 109 *I.L.T.S.J.* 289, 295, 305; von Prondzynski, "Trade Disputes and the Courts: The Problem of the Labour Injunction" (1981) 16 *Ir. Jur. (n.s.)* 228; Kerr, "The Problem of the Labour Injunction Revisited" (1983) 18 *Ir. Jur. (n.s.)* 3; Evans, "The Labour Injunction Revisited" (1983) 12 *I.L.J.* 129.

[2] Davies and Freedland, *Labour Law: Text and Materials* 1st ed. (London, 1979), p. 630.

[3] On November 9, 1981 Carroll J. committed eight Dublin factory workers to prison for refusing to obey a court order restraining them from picketing and trespassing at their place of work. On July 12, 1982 the same judge committed a I.N.P.D.T.U. shop steward, and on July 14, 1982 two other members of the same union were committed. In February 1983 fourteen former employees of Ranks (Ireland) Ltd were committed (ten by Barrington J. and four by O'Hanlon J.). In May 1984 nine former employees of Moracrete Ltd. were committed (five by Barrington J. and four by Carroll J.).

and convenient that such order shall be made."[4] Although the subsection refers only to the granting of injunctions by interlocutory order, Sir George Jessel M.R. held, in *Beddow* v. *Beddow*,[5] that it extended to the grant of an injunction at the trial of the action. Injunctions may be granted in all cases in which it appears to the court to be "just and convenient" to do so. The words "just and convenient" do not confer an arbitrary discretion on the court; their effect, it has been said, is to enable the court to grant such injunctions as could formerly have been granted by a court of equity.[6] This discretion, however, confers great flexibility as to the terms of the injunction.

Injunctions are of three main types – interim, interlocutory and perpetual – and may be either prohibitory or mandatory. The former are much more common than the latter, although it is not unknown for the High Court, in addition to restraining defendants from issuing unlawful instructions, to require them to withdraw any instructions already given.[7] Interim and interlocutory injunctions are also much more significant than perpetual injunctions since the grant or refusal of interlocutory relief generally disposes of the matter in trade dispute cases.[8] As McCarthy J., speaking extra-judicially, has observed, actions for injunctive relief in trade disputes seldom come to actual trial.

> "The effect . . . of the granting of an interim injunction has been and, I think, remains virtually decisive in determining any particular case. . . . [T]he granting of the interim injunction, since it nullifies the most effective weapon the union has, the instant, continuing picket, will generally produce some form of solution – reluctant, possible[sic], resented and incomplete but lacking in finality."[9]

Prohibitory injunctions

The mere proof of a legal wrong done in the past is insufficient to

---

[4] Applied to the present High Court by ss. 8(2) and 48(3) of the Courts (Supplemental Provisions) Act 1961.

[5] (1878) 9 Ch. D. 89, 93.

[6] *North London Railway* v. *Great Northern Railway* (1883) 11 Q.B.D. 30.

[7] See, for example, *Cattle Express Shipping Corp. of Liberia* v. *Cheasty and the International Transport Workers' Federation* High Court, unreported, 19 April 1983, noted (1983) 2 *J.I.S.L.L.* at pp. 62–63.

[8] Apart from those cases where the parties agree to treat the interlocutory application as the trial of the action (such as *Corry* v. *N.U.V.G.A.T.A.* [1950] I.R. 315, *Quigley* v. *Beirne* [1955] I.R. 62 and *Darby* v. *Leonard* (1973) 107 I.L.T.R. 82) there have been only seven cases since 1950, where a "labour injunction" case went on for full trial (all but one involving appeals to the Supreme Court) – *Smith* v. *Beirne* (1955) 89 I.L.T.R. 24; *Esplanade Pharmacy Ltd.* v. *Larkin* [1959] I.R. 285; *Silver Tassie Co. Ltd.* v. *Cleary* (1958) 92 I.L.T.R. 29; *Educational Company of Ireland* v. *Fitzpatrick* [1961] I.R. 345; *Crowley* v. *Cleary* [1968] I.R. 261; *Becton Dickinson & Co. Ltd.* v. *Lee* [1973] I.R. 1; *Gouldings Chemicals Ltd.* v. *Bolger* [1976] I.R. 211.

[9] "A Review of the Law on Trade Disputes" SYS Lecture 147 (1983) at p. 4. See also Lord Diplock in *NWL Ltd.* v. *Woods* [1979] I.C.R. 867, 879: "It is in the nature of industrial action that it can be promoted effectively only so long as it is possible to strike while the iron is hot; once postponed it is unlikely that it can be revived."

entitle the plaintiff to an injunction. The court must be satisfied that the interference is continuing or that it is likely to be repeated unless restrained. This is not to say that it is premature for a plaintiff to come to the court before any damage has occurred. The court has jurisdiction to issue an injunction *quia timet* to restrain conduct which if allowed to go ahead would almost certainly lead to substantial damage to the plaintiff.[10]

Interim injunctions

An interim injunction may be sought by a plaintiff in a matter of urgency. Normally the application is made *ex parte* to a judge of the High Court sitting in chambers as soon as the plaintiff has issued his summons. In matters of extreme urgency the plaintiff may apply for an injunction before the issue of the summons and the judge may grant an injunction on terms providing for the issue of the summons. If there is no judge sitting in chambers, an application may be made to a judge in his own home.[11] Such application may be made at any time, including weekends and public holidays. There is no requirement that any steps be taken with a view to securing that notice of the application and an opportunity of being heard be given to the defendants.[12] The application, however, must be supported by an affidavit setting out the grounds on which the application is based. In these cases therefore, only the plaintiff's legal representative will be heard and only the plaintiff's affidavits will be read. If the interim injunction is granted, the first the defendant will hear about it will be when the summons is served informing him of this fact. Although an undertaking by the plaintiff as to damages must be given, the procedures governing the grant of interim injunctions are much criticised by the trade unions, and cases where an interim injunction has been granted but an interlocutory injunction refused are not infrequent.[13] The Commission of Inquiry accepted that there were valid grounds for objecting to the use of *ex parte* injunctions in trade disputes. They said:

---

[10] See Spry, *Equitable Remedies* (London, 1980), pp. 350-355.

[11] See for instance the interim order prohibiting picketing at the premises of Talbot (Ireland) Ltd. granted by Barrington J. at a special sitting of the High Court at his home on Saturday, April 18, 1981.

[12] As there is in Britain, Trade Union and Labour Relations Act 1974, s. 17 (as amended by Employment Protection Act 1975, Schedule 16, part III, para. 6). Section 17 provides in relevant part:
(1) Where an application for an injunction is made to the court in the absence of the party against whom the injunction is sought or any representative of his and that party claims, or in the opinion of the court would be likely to claim, that he acted in contemplation or furtherance of a trade dispute, the court shall not grant the injunction unless satisfied that all steps which in the circumstances have been reasonable have been taken with a view to securing that notice of the application and an opportunity of being heard with respect to the application have been given to that party.

[13] As in *McCormick MacNaughton Ltd.* v. *Brangan* where Ellis J. granted an interim injunction on June 26, 1980 but an interlocutory injunction was refused by McMahon J. on July 18, 1980.

"The grant of an injunction can halt legitimate picketing and can confer an important strategic advantage on an employer in a dispute. We believe that, in view of these possible consequences of the injunction, it would be obviously desirable to allow both sides to state their side of the case before an interim injunction is granted. *We recommend, therefore, that consideration should be given by the relevant authorities to ending, as far as possible, the grant of interim injunctions in trade disputes on an ex parte basis.* We understand that to do so might involve certain legal difficulties. We suggest that, in view of the importance of the proposal, every effort be made to overcome any obstacles that might exist in attempting to give effect to it."[14]

An interim injunction, if granted, is usually for a 48-72 hour period. If the application is refused the judge invariably gives liberty to serve short notice on the defendants informing them of the application for an interlocutory injunction.

Interlocutory injunctions

Applications for interlocutory injunctions are heard on notice to the defendant and, if granted, continue to the full hearing of the action, which may be, if the matter goes that far, a period of at least one year. The object of an interlocutory injunction is to prevent further injury to the plaintiff until the legality of the defendant's actions have been finally pronounced upon. As Lord Diplock said in *American Cyanamid Co. v. Ethicon Ltd*:[15]

"It was to mitigate the risk of injustice to the plaintiff during the period before that uncertainty [of the legal validity of the plaintiff's claim] could be resolved that the practice arose of granting him relief by way of interlocutory injunction. . . . The object of the interlocutory injunction is to protect the plaintiff against injury by violation of his right for which he could not be adequately compensated in damages recoverable in the action if the uncertainty were resolved in his favour."

In 1983 the Supreme Court, twice within the space of a month, restated the principles to be applied by High Court judges when exercising their discretion whether to grant or refuse interlocutory relief and these decisions are considered below.[16] Prior to the 1983 restatement the leading case was *Educational Company of Ireland Ltd. v. Fitzpatrick*.[17] The generally accepted interpretation of this case at the

---

[14] *Report of the Commission of Inquiry on Industrial Relations* (Pl. 114) at para. 752.
[15] [1975] A.C. 396, 406.
[16] At pp. 323–325.
[17] [1961] I.R. 323. Hereafter referred to as *Fitzpatrick*.

time[18] was that the former Supreme Court endorsed the proposition that a person seeking interlocutory relief must be able to show a fair *prima facie* case that his legal rights would be violated by the defendant's activity. As stated more fully in *Kerr on Injunctions,*[19] the plaintiff was not required

> "to make out a clear legal title, but he must satisfy the court that he has a fair question to raise as to the existence of the legal right which he sets up and that there are substantial grounds for doubting the existence of the alleged legal right, the exercise of which he seeks to prevent. The Court must, before disturbing any man's right, or stripping him of any of the rights with which the law has clothed him, be satisfied that the probability is in favour of his case ultimately failing in the final issue of the suit."

In *E.I. Co. Ltd.* v. *Kennedy*[20] the Supreme Court, therefore, refused to grant an interlocutory injunction because the plaintiff company had not shown a *prima facie* case that the dispute raised as to the terms of employment and conditions of labour was specious. Walsh J. further stated that, if it should turn out upon a full trial of the facts that the dispute was indeed specious, the consequences would be grave for the defendants but that was "not a matter which need be considered at this stage." He continued:

> "When I am of opinion there is a *prima facie* case in favour of the existence of a trade dispute, I could not at the same time support an injunction to restrain the exercise of the rights conferred by s. 2 of the Act of 1906."[21]

Other cases however, including *Fitzpatrick* itself, demonstrate that the courts, in addition to considering whether the plaintiff had made out *prima facie* case, also considered the balance of convenience. Lavery J. in his judgment in *Fitzpatrick* referred approvingly to this passage from the second edition of *Halsbury's Laws of England:*[22]

> "Where any doubt exists as to the plaintiff's right, or if his right is not disputed, but its violation is denied, the court, in determining whether an interlocutory injunction should be granted, takes into consideration the balance of convenience to the parties and the nature of the injury which the defendant, on the one hand, would

---

[18] See *Esso Petroleum Co. (Ireland) Ltd.* v. *Fogarty* [1965] I.R. 531, 538 where Ó Dálaigh C.J. said that the principles of law to be applied by the High Court in an application for an interlocutory injunction were "well summarised" in the judgment of Lavery J. in *Fitzpatrick* and insisted that the plaintiff had to show a "fair *prima facie* case".
[19] 6th ed., (London, 1927) at p. 15.
[20] [1968] I.R. 69.
[21] At 90. See also *Keenan Bros. Ltd.* v. *Córas Iompair Éireann* (1963) 97 I.L.T.R. 34.
[22] (London, 1935) vol. 18, p. 33, para. 49.

suffer if the injunction was granted and he should ultimately turn out to be right and that which the plaintiff on the other hand might sustain if the injunction was refused and he should ultimately turn out to be right."

But what role did it play? If the plaintiff could show a fair *prima facie* case might the balance of convenience then be examined to deny the grant of interlocutory relief? Or, if the plaintiff was unable to show a fair *prima facie* case, might the balance of convenience then be examined to justify the grant of interlocutory relief? Consideration of the balance of convenience, even in a subsidiary role, clearly emasculated the *prima facie* test, especially when decisions as to whether the evidence disclosed a fair *prima facie* case were made without any comment as to what exactly was meant by this.

In this respect the decision of the Supreme Court in *Brennan* v. *Glennon*[23] is instructive. Here it was "common case" that there was a trade dispute within the meaning of the 1906 Act. A strike had been called by the District Committee of the Amalgamated Union of Engineering Workers and a picket mounted, but without any vote being taken by the union members in the plant involved. The District Committee's right to do this was called in question by the plaintiffs, who claimed that the decision was not in accordance with the rules of the union. O'Higgins C.J.[24] said that it was essential for the proper assertion of the plaintiffs' rights that the *status quo* be restored by the grant of an injunction to restrain the picketing.

> "The desirability of restoring the *status quo* existing before the Union picket began, rests on the fact that this factory is likely to close down in a matter of days if that picketing continues. The plaintiffs are Union members who work in the factory and have brought these proceedings in an effort to safeguard their livelihood. It is crucial to them that the legal points taken by them should not be decided when the factory has ceased production and they have lost their jobs. This litigation would then have become a dead letter for their purposes. If they were successful in the action they could not be properly compensated by damages. The loss would be irreparable."[25]

E.I. Co. Ltd. v. *Kennedy* and *Brennan* v. *Glennon* illustrate the difference between what has been called the "multi-requisite test" and the "multi-factor test".[26] In the former the questions of a *prima facie* case and the balance of convenience are regarded as separate hurdles which have to be sequentially cleared, whereas with the latter the

---

[23] Supreme Court, unreported, 26 November 1975.
[24] Henchy and Kenny JJ. concurring.
[25] At pp. 4–5 of his unreported judgment.
[26] See *Yule Inc.* v. *Atlantic Pizza Delight Franchise (1968) Ltd.* (1979) 80 D.L.R. (3d) 725, 730.

enquiry as to whether the plaintiff has made out a *prima facie* case is not undertaken separately from the Court's consideration of other matters which may be relevant to the exercise of the discretion.

More detailed analysis of the principles involved was inevitable following the decision of the House of Lords in *American Cyanamid Co. v. Ethicon Ltd.*,[27] where it was held that the English Court of Appeal had been wrong to apply a rule that an interlocutory injunction should only be granted if the applicant could satisfy the court that, on the balance of probabilities, his legal rights would be violated by the defendant's activity. Lord Diplock said that no such rule existed. The only thing of which the trial judge must be satisfied was that the claim was not frivolous or vexatious; "in other words, that there is a serious issue to be tried." He continued:

> "unless the material available to the court at the hearing of the application for an interlocutory injunction fails to disclose that the plaintiff has any real prospect of succeeding in his claim for a permanent injunction at the trial, the court should go on to consider whether the balance of convenience lies in favour of granting or refusing the interlocutory relief that is sought."[28]

In other words the likelihood of a permanent injunction being obtained at trial is merely a factor, albeit a weighty factor, to be taken into account rather than a factor which, as a matter of law, precludes or demands its grant. Lord Diplock's formulation is similar to the above mentioned "multi-requisite" test, in that he sets out a series of hurdles which have to be sequentially cleared, but differs in that the threshold requirement has been lowered from the plaintiff's need to make out a *prima facie* case to a need merely to raise a serious issue to be tried.

American Cyanamid had a mixed reception in this jurisdiction.[29] Some judges considered that Lord Diplock's speech contained the "true test" to be applied in applications for interlocutory injunctions.[30] Others took the view that the principles laid down by the former Supreme Court in *Fitzpatrick* were clearly binding on the High Court and in so far as the decision in *American Cyanamid* suggested the application of different principles it did not represent the law in Ireland.[31] Others were of the opinion that the decisions in *Fitzpatrick* and *American Cyanamid* did not differ but "to some extent each

---

[27] [1975] A.C. 396. Hereafter referred to as *American Cyanamid*.
[28] At 408.
[29] It has had an equally mixed reception in other common law jurisdictions. See the cases in Kerr, "The Problem of the Labour Injunction Revisited" (1983) 18 *Ir. Jur. (n.s.)* 34, 39, n. 25.
[30] See McWilliam J.'s judgments in *Aksjeselskapet Jotul v. Waterford Ironfounders Ltd.* High Court, unreported, 8 November 1977; *Griffin v. Kelly's Strand Hotel* High Court, unreported, 24 January 1980; *Irish Shell Ltd. v. Burrell* High Court, unreported, 17 June 1981; *Córas Iompair Éireann v. Darby* High Court unreported, 16 January 1980.
[31] See Keane J. in *TMG Group Ltd. v. Al Babtain Trading and Contracting Co.* [1982] I.L.R.M. 349.

complement[ed] the other in certain aspects of the questions raised."[32] Murphy J. for instance said that while certain distinctions might be drawn between the two decisions the distinctions were "more apparent than real". In *Campus Oil Ltd. v. Minister for Industry and Energy (No. 1)*[33] he referred approvingly to Lord Diplock's comment in *American Cyanamid*[34] that the purpose sought to be achieved by giving the court a *discretion* to grant an interlocutory injunction would be "stultified" if the discretion were "clogged by a technical rule" forbidding its exercise if, upon incomplete untested evidence, the court evaluated the chances of the plaintiff's ultimate success at 50% or less. Murphy J. believed Lord Diplock's comment echoed Kingsmill Moore J.'s comment in *Fitzpatrick*[35] that "it would be undesirable in the absence of consent to decide a legal question of this magnitude merely on the affidavits filed for the purpose of the interlocutory motion."

Murphy J. concluded that, as the defendants had made a case which could not be even evaluated, let alone determined, without the investigation of disputed facts covering a complex area, it did not seem that

> "it would be possible or necessary at this stage to decide whether the case made out by the plaintiffs would properly be described as a strong case or a *prima facie* case . . . the only issue which I can decide as to the legal rights of the parties is whether the plaintiffs have established that 'there is a fair question raised to be decided at the trial'."[36]

Given this confusion in the High Court it was inevitable that the Supreme Court would be called on to resolve the question and the opportunity arose in *Campus Oil Ltd. v. Minister for Industry and Energy (No. 2)*[37] and *Irish Shell Ltd. v. Elm Motors Ltd.*[38]

In the former case the ground of appeal against Keane J.'s decision to grant an interlocutory injunction was that he had failed to have regard to the correct criteria. O'Higgins C.J., with whom Hederman J. concurred, rejected the argument that an applicant for interlocutory relief is required to establish a probability of success at the trial. He said that the judgments in *Fitzpatrick* supported no such argument, and that the reference to "probability" contained in the extract from *Kerr on Injunctions* cited by Lavery J. was, "in its context", of "doubtful significance". O'Higgins C.J. said that Lavery J. "clearly

---

[32] *Per* Finlay P. in *Rex Pet Foods Ltd. v. Lamb Bros. (Dublin) Ltd.* High Court, unreported, 26 August 1982, at p. 2 of his judgment.
[33] [1983] I.L.R.M. 258.
[34] [1975] A.C. 396, 406.
[35] [1961] I.R. 323, 342.
[36] [1983] I.L.R.M. 258, 264.
[37] [1983] I.R. 88. Hereafter referred to as *Campus Oil*.
[38] [1984] I.L.R.M. 595.

laid down" the proper test to be applied at page 337 of the Irish Reports for 1961, namely that the plaintiffs would have to establish "that there is a fair question raised to be decided at the trial" and continued that any other test would be "contrary to principle".[39] O'Higgins C.J. went on to state that he "entirely agreed" with the following *dicta* of Lord Diplock from *American Cyanamid*:[40]

> "It is no part of the Court's function at this stage of the litigation to try to resolve conflicts of evidence on affidavit as to facts on which the claims of either party may ultimately depend nor to decide difficult questions of law which call for detailed argument and mature considerations. These are matters to be dealt with at the trial. . . . So unless the material available to the Court at the hearing of the application for an interlocutory injunction fails to disclose that the plaintiff has any real prospect of succeeding in his claim for a permanent injunction at the trial, the Court should go on to consider whether the balance of convenience lies in favour of granting or refusing the interlocutory relief that is sought."

The other judgment was delivered by Griffin J., and his comments were also adopted by Hederman J. In it he comprehensively analysed the four judgments in *Fitzpatrick* and the two judgments in *Esso Petroleum* v. *Fogarty*.[41] He concluded that only Maguire C.J. in *Fitzpatrick* applied a "probability of success" requirement. Lavery J. stated the requirement but did not apply it, and Kingsmill Moore and O Dalaigh JJ. were satisfied that there was a serious question to be tried. In *Esso Petroleum* v. *Fogarty*, O Dalaigh C.J., with whom Lavery J. agreed, stated[42] that the Court must be satisfied that the probability was in favour of the defendant's case ultimately failing in the final issue of the suit. Walsh J. however spoke of the need to make out a substantial issue to be tried.[43]

Griffin J. then referred to Lord Diplock's speech in *American Cyanamid*, indicated that he believed that the differences between *Fitzpatrick* and *American Cyanamid* were "more apparent than real", concluded that Lord Diplock's formulation had "much to recommend it in logic, common sense and principle" and said he would "respectfully adopt it as being a correct statement of the law in cases of this kind." He went on to say that in a number of cases, in none of which was judgment reserved, the Supreme Court had applied as the true test:

---

[39] [1983] I.R. 88, 106.
[40] [1975] A.C. 396, 407.
[41] [1965] I.R. 531.
[42] [1965] I.R. 531, 539.
[43] [1965] I.R. 531, 541.

"whether a fair or serious question has been raised to be decided at the trial, and, if so, whether the balance of convenience was in favour of granting or refusing the interlocutory injunction sought."[44]

In *Irish Shell Ltd.* v. *Elm Motors Ltd.*[45] the Supreme Court heard an appeal from a judgment and order of Costello J.[46] in effect directing the defendant to comply in detail with the relevant provisions of a lease made between the plaintiff and defendant whereby the defendant, *inter alia*, agreed to sell the plaintiff's products. McCarthy J. was of the opinion that the case, dealing as it did with the applicability of the doctrine of restraint of trade to restrictive covenants in leases, raised many "complex legal issues" and required "mature consideration".[47] In the instant appeal Costello J. had taken a "very decided view" of the legal issues raised, and had in fact concluded that the common law doctrine of restraint of trade did not apply to restraints on the use of a particular piece of land when imposed by a conveyance or lease of the land in question. This finding, as McCarthy J. recognised, in effect determined the issue and rendered a trial superfluous, and explains perhaps why Costello J. ordered the defendant to pay the plaintiff's costs of the motion and failed to recite the standard form of undertaking given by a moving party in applications of this kind.

McCarthy J., with whom O'Higgins C.J. and Griffin J. agreed on this point, was critical of this. He said that it was "unnecessary" and "undesirable" to have come to such a firm conclusion.

"In my judgment, whilst reserving the question as to whether or not there are cases in which it is proper for the Court to express a concluded view as to factual or legal issues arising at the interlocutory stage, ordinarily the determination of whether or not to grant an interlocutory injunction lies and lies only in answer to the two material questions as to there being a fair case to be made and where the balance of convenience lies."[48]

Following *Campus Oil* and *Elm Motors* it is now clear that the classical *prima facie* test has been rejected by the Supreme Court. What has replaced it, however, is less clear. First, what did Griffin J. mean by saying in the former case that Lord Diplock's formulation was a correct statement of the law "in cases of this kind"? Did he mean cases of interlocutory applications in general or did he mean cases where "rights are disputed and challenged and where a significant period must elapse before the trial"? Secondly, in what sort of case would it be proper for the Court to express a concluded view as to factual or legal

---
[44] [1983] I.R. 88, 111.
[45] [1984] I.L.R.M. 595. Hereafter referred to as *Elm Motors*.
[46] [1982] I.L.R.M. 519.
[47] [1984] I.L.R.M. 595, 601.
[48] *Id.*

issues? McCarthy J. merely commented that they would be "most exceptional". Similar doubts as to the ambit of *American Cyanamid* arose in Britain and Lord Denning M.R., in particular, sought to cut down its potential application on the basis that one set of standards was not appropriate to every class of case.[49] Thirdly, the imprecision of language employed, particularly in Griffin J.'s judgment in *Campus Oil*, is to be regretted. A "fair question" is not necessarily a "serious question". Still less is a "fair question" the same as a "substantial question".[50]

Despite the lengthy and elaborate reconsideration in *Campus Oil* and *Elm Motors* the threshold criterion remains unclear. Given the nature of the interlocutory injunction, the wide variety of situations in which it may be used and the consequent need for flexibility, it may be that the criteria should not be over-strictly scrutinised.[51] The authors would submit, however, that a certain criterion and strict scrutiny are required in the case of the 'labour injunction', if only because applicants do not perceive the injunction, if granted, as merely maintaining the *status quo ante* until the trial of the action. For employers it is a simple and relatively inexpensive way of bringing the dispute to a head by depriving the employees of a bargaining counter. Furthermore, since the interlocutory hearing is in reality the final trial of the action, a more stringent and more certain threshold criterion is appropriate in cases of this kind.

The reality, however, is that whatever approach is used applications for interlocutory injunctions in labour disputes will invariably be successful.[52] The facts are often in dispute between the parties and the judge will face considerable difficulty in resolving conflict through reading the affidavits and will thus be reluctant to predict the probable outcome of the proceedings were they to go to plenary hearing.

Whatever verbal formula is used there are still two hurdles to clear, namely likelihood of success at the trial and the balance of convenience. The increasing irrelevance of the Trade Disputes Act 1906[53] and the unpredictable nature of the common law[54] virtually

---

[49] See *Hubbard* v. *Pitt* [1976] Q.B. 142; *Fellowes & Son* v. *Fisher* [1976] Q.B. 122; *Bryanston Finance Ltd.* v. *de Vries (No. 2)* [1976] Ch. 63; *Lewis* v. *Heffer* [1978] 1 W.L.R. 1061. The cases subsequent to *American Cyanamid* are comprehensively considered by Gray, "Interlocutory Injunctions since Cyanamid" (1981) 40 *C.L.J.* 307.

[50] The meaning of Lord Diplock's phrase "a serious question to be tried" was considered in *Mothercare Ltd.* v. *Robson Books Ltd.* [1979] F.S.R. 466.

[51] See Lord Cottenham L.C. in *Saunders* v. *Smith* (1837) 3 My. & Cr. 710 at 728.

[52] The most recent recorded or reported example of an application *by an employer* for an interlocutory injunction being refused by the High Court is *Coal Distributors Ltd.* v. *McDaid* High Court, unreported, 13 October 1980. An application *by employees* was refused by McWilliam J. in *Gannon* v. *Duffy* High Court, unreported, 4 March 1983 and an application by a property developer was refused by Barron J. in *Deerpark Ltd.* v. *Leonard* High Court, unreported, 10 June 1983.

[53] See *supra*, pp. 249–281.

[54] See *supra*, pp. 223–246.

guarantees a clear passage over the first hurdle and what goes into the scales of the balance of convenience invariably guarantees a clear passage over the second.

There are, as has been pointed out in a previous chapter,[55] a considerable number of "serious questions" concerning the Trade Disputes Act 1906 that await judicial or legislative clarification in this jurisdiction.[56] This means that in all but the most clear-cut of cases the plaintiff will have a smooth ride over the first hurdle. *Vide* Henchy J.'s decision in *E.I. Co. Ltd.* v. *Kennedy*[57] that the then doubt about whether a recognition dispute qualified as a trade dispute raised a "fair question to be decided at the trial", and was, furthermore, a question of "such magnitude" that it would be undesirable *in the absence of consent* to decide it merely on the affidavits filed for the purpose of the interlocutory motion.[58]

Secondly, when weighing the balance of convenience in trade dispute cases the Irish courts have invariably repeated the formula that the effect of the granting of the injunction will be merely to delay the picketing for a while whereas the employer will suffer irreparable loss if the injunction is not granted.[59] If due weight is not given to the "temporary" loss of a bargaining counter, judgment will inevitably be given against the defendant. This was recognised by Lord Diplock in *NWL Ltd.* v. *Woods*.[60] He said:

> "In the normal case of threatened industrial action against an employer, the damage that he will sustain if the action is carried out is likely to be large, difficult to assess in money and may well be irreparable. Furthermore damage is likely to be caused to customers of the employer's business who are not parties to the action, and to the public at large. On the other hand the defendant is not the trade union but an individual officer of the union who, although he is acting on its behalf, can be sued in his personal capacity only. In that personal capacity he will suffer virtually no damage if the injunction is granted, whereas if it is not granted and the action against him ultimately succeeds it is most improbable that damages on the scale that are likely to be awarded against him will prove to be recoverable

---

[55] Chapter 9.
[56] Such as whether the statutory immunity in s. 1 applies to conspiracy to break a contract; whether the protection in s. 2 extends to secondary picketing; whether picketing in contravention of a disputes procedure is entitled to the protection of s. 2; whether the expression "in furtherance of a trade dispute" in s. 5(3) is to be given an objective or a subjective interpretation; and whether a trade union can be a party to a trade dispute.
[57] [1969] I.R. 69.
[58] This matter was resolved by the decision of the Supreme Court in *Becton Dickinson & Co. Ltd.* v. *Lee* [1973] I.R. 1, where it was held that such disputes do come within the statutory protection of the 1906 Act. See *supra*, p. 271.
[59] See Teevan J. in *Educational Co. of Ireland Ltd.* v. *Fitzpatrick* [1961] I.R. 323, 326 and Henchy J. in *E.I. Co. Ltd.* v. *Kennedy* [1969] I.R. 69, 74.
[60] [1979] I.C.R. 867.

from him. Again, to grant the injunction will maintain the *status quo* until the trial; and this too is a factor which in evenly balanced cases generally operates in favour of granting an interlocutory injunction. So on the face of the proceedings in an action of this kind the balance of convenience as to the grant of an interlocutory injunction would appear to be heavily weighted in favour of the employer."[61]

He continued:

"To take this view, however, would be to blind oneself to the practical realities (1) that the real dispute is not between the employer and the nominal defendant but between the employer and the trade union that is threatening industrial action, (2) that the threat of "blacking" or other industrial action is being used as a bargaining counter in negotiations either existing or anticipated to obtain agreement by the employer to do whatever it is the union requires of him, (3) that it is the nature of industrial action that it can be promoted effectively only so long as it is possible to strike while the iron is hot; once postponed it is unlikely that it can be revived, and (4) that, in consequence of these three characteristics, the grant or refusal of an interlocutory injunction generally disposes finally of the action...."[62]

Nor must it be forgotten that the harm that will be caused to the defendant by the grant of the injunction is of a kind for which money cannot constitute any worthwhile recompense, if it turns out at the trial that the injunction should not have been granted. Lord Diplock admitted that, where the grant or refusal of the interlocutory relief would have the practical effect of putting an end to the action, the degree of likelihood, that the defendant would have succeeded in establishing that what was done was done in contemplation or furtherance of a trade dispute, was a factor "to be brought into the balance by the judge in weighing the risks that injustice may result from his deciding the application one way rather than the other."[63] One can only agree with the Master of the Rolls when, as Donaldson J., he said, in *NWL Ltd.* v. *Nelson*,[64] that "it is very unsatisfactory for trade unions in particular ... that this should be decided on the balance of convenience; it ought to be decided on the basis of real rights." The court, therefore, should not be permitted the luxury of saying that, since there may be a substantial argument on a question of law, the matter should go on for full trial when it knows that the matter will not in fact go on for full trial. Trade dispute cases are ones where both

---

[61] At 879.
[62] At 879.
[63] At 881.
[64] [1979] I.C.R. 755, 766.

justice and the needs of the parties justify a more extensive type of interlocutory hearing than is currently employed.

Since an interlocutory injunction freezes the situation and prevents the defendant from taking action which, at the trial, may prove to be lawful, its grant may cause the defendant to suffer loss. Accordingly the injunction will not normally be granted unless it is accompanied by an undertaking given by the plaintiff to the defendant to pay to the defendant such damages as it is just the defendant should receive if the issue of the interlocutory injunction should turn out to have been unjustified. Again this is of little practical use as the matter will almost certainly not come on for trial if an injunction has been granted at the interlocutory stage, and if it does it will be very difficult to estimate the pecuniary loss the defendants have suffered by being prevented from carrying on the dispute in the way injuncted.

Perpetual injunction

A perpetual injunction in trade dispute cases is a rare sight[65] since the matter hardly ever comes on for full trial, but if granted it lasts forever unless a further different order is subsequently granted.

Mandatory injunctions

The granting of a mandatory injunction, which is an injunction in positive terms requiring the defendant to take some specific action,[66] depends upon a number of factors in addition to those which may affect the grant of prohibitory injunctions. A mandatory injunction may be granted at the interlocutory stage, but only in exceptional circumstances.[67] The relevant authorities were comprehensively considered by Megarry V.-C. in *Shepherd Homes Ltd.* v. *Sandham*[68] and the Vice-Chancellor there concluded that the matter was tempered by a judicial discretion which would be exercised so as to withhold an injunction more readily if it is mandatory than if it is prohibitory. The language of the case and the instances the Vice-Chancellor gives are not particularly analogous to trade disputes but he did say that the case had to be "unusually strong and clear" before a mandatory injunction would be granted.

---

[65] Although a permanent injunction was granted by Keane J. restraining the picketing of the bankers, Guinness and Mahon Ltd., in *Guinness and Mahon Ltd.* v. *Cunningham and Sheehan* High Court, unreported, 22 May 1984.

[66] Note the necessity of the Court making it clear exactly what is required of the defendant when a mandatory injunction is granted, *per* Lord Upjohn, *Morris* v. *Redland Bricks Ltd.* [1970] A.C. 652, 663 *et seq.*

[67] *Per* Barrington J., *Carty* v. *Dublin County Council* High Court, unreported, 6 April 1984 at pp. 11–12 of his judgment. See also Costello J. in *Irish Shell Ltd.* v. *Elm Motors Ltd.* [1982] I.L.R.M. 519 at 532–533; Sir John Donaldson M.R., Browne-Wilkinson and Mustill L.JJ. in *Parker* v. *Camden London Borough Council* [1985] 2 All E.R. 141 at 146, 149 and 150 respectively.

[68] [1971] Ch. 340. See also *Hounslow London Borough Council* v. *Twickenham Garden Developments Ltd.* [1971] Ch. 233.

"By granting a prohibitory injunction the court does no more than prevent for the future the continuance or repetition of the conduct of which the plaintiff complains. The injunction does not attempt to deal with what has happened in the past, that is left for the trial to be dealt with by damages or otherwise. On the other hand a mandatory injunction tends at least in part to look to the past, in that it is often a means of undoing what has already been done so far as that is possible. Furthermore, whereas a prohibitory injunction merely requires abstention from acting, a mandatory injunction requires the taking of positive steps. . . . Most importantly if it is granted on motion there will normally be no question of granting a further mandatory injunction at the trial, what is done is done and the plaintiff has on motion obtained once and for all that which he seeks."[69]

More pertinently Geoffrey Lane L.J. has said, in *Harold Stephen & Co. Ltd.* v. *Post Office*,[70] that it could only be "in very rare circumstances and in the most extreme circumstances that this court should interfere by way of mandatory injunction in the delicate mechanism of industrial disputes and industrial negotiations."

Denial of injunction

No complete list of "special circumstances" depriving the plaintiff of his right to an injunction can be compiled since the grant of an injunction is discretionary. The plaintiff's own conduct however is an obvious factor as is any unreasonable delay in prosecuting the claim.[71]

Terms of the injunction

It is important to note that, in applications to restrain picketing, it does not follow from the fact that the picketing is unlawful that an injunction will be granted to restrain the picket completely. The injunction may be granted on such conditions as will prevent only the unlawful aspects of the picket. Thus, in *Newbridge Industries Ltd.* v. *Bateson*,[72] the Supreme Court varied the interlocutory injunction restraining picketing granted by Kenny J. to apply only to non-peaceful picketing. Moreover the court has a wide discretion as to the terms on which the injunction is granted. Thus in the MacDonalds dispute in 1979, Costello J. granted injunctions on terms that prohibited unauthorised persons from joining the picket line and that picketing cease each evening at 10 p.m.[73] The injunctions stated that

---

[69] At 348.
[70] [1977] 1 W.L.R. 1172, 1180.
[71] On this generally, see *Clerk and Lindsell on Torts* 15th ed. (London, 1982), pp. 281–284. For laches, see Brady and Kerr, *The Limitation of Actions in the Republic of Ireland* (Dublin, 1984), pp. 97–99.
[72] Supreme Court, unreported, 31 July 1975.
[73] See the report in the *Irish Times*, April 19, 1979.

the picket be restricted to reasonable numbers, namely three, and restrained the pickets from obstructing the premises, from using abusive language against employees and customers, and further ordered that the defendants, and those associated with them, be restrained from calling at the homes of employees of the plaintiff company in relation to matters connected with the dispute. Subsequently Hamilton J. directed that a roster of pickets be drawn up and a copy supplied to the plaintiffs "so that there should be no doubt who should be entitled to picket and who should not."[74]

It is also to be noted that injunctions granted by the Irish courts in recent years are often stated to apply to the defendants and any persons having notice of the making of the order.[75]

Appeals

While it is rare that a trade dispute case will go to a full trial it is not uncommon for the losing party at the interlocutory stage to appeal to the Supreme Court.[76] It is therefore necessary to set out the criteria to be applied by the Supreme Court when hearing an appeal against the grant or refusal of interlocutory relief. In *Hadmor Productions Ltd.* v. *Hamilton*,[77] Lord Diplock stressed that an appellate court had only a limited function in such appeals.

> "An interlocutory injunction is a discretionary relief and the discretion whether or not to grant it is vested in the High Court judge by whom the application for it is heard. Upon an appeal from the judges' grant or refusal of an interlocutory injunction the function of an appellate court, whether it be the Court of Appeal or your Lordship's house, is not to exercise an independent discretion of its own. It must defer to the judge's exercise of his discretion and must not interfere with it merely upon the ground that the members of the appellate court would have exercised the discretion differently."[78]

The very idea of discretion involves a latitude of individual choice and leaves room for differences of opinion and Lord Diplock continued by stressing that the appellate court's function was initially one of review only.

---

[74] See the report in the *Irish Times*, July 5, 1979.
[75] This practice has been approved by the Supreme Court in *John Paul & Co. Ltd.* v. *Martin*, unreported, 21 June 1979.
[76] See for example, *E.I. Co. Ltd.* v. *Kennedy* [1968] I.R. 69; *Pye Ireland Ltd.* v. *Tuamley*, unreported, 23 March 1969; *Brennan* v. *Glennon*, unreported, 31 July 1975; *Reg Armstrong Motors Ltd.* v. *Córas Iompair Éireann*, unreported, 16 December 1975; *Talbot Ireland Ltd.* v. *Merrigan* unreported, 30 April 1981. See also *Pantry Franchise Ireland Ltd.* v. *Macken*, unreported, 5 April 1979 (an appeal to the Supreme Court to vary an *interim* injunction); *Intacta Investments Ltd.* v. *Power*, unreported, 7 April 1974 (where Gannon J. refused an interim injunction but it was granted by the Supreme Court on an *ex parte* application).
[77] [1983] A.C. 191.
[78] At 220.

"It may set aside the judge's exercise of his discretion on the ground only that it was based upon a misunderstanding of the law or of the evidence before him or upon an inference that particular facts existed or did not exist, which, although it was one that might legitimately have been drawn upon the evidence that was before the judge, can be demonstrated to be wrong by further evidence that has become available by the time of the appeal; or upon the ground that there has been a change of circumstances after the judge made his order that would have justified his acceding to an application to vary it.[79] Since reasons given by judges for granting or refusing interlocutory injunctions may sometimes be sketchy, there may also be cases where even though no erroneous assumption of law and fact can be identified the judge's decision to grant or refuse the injunction is so aberrant that it must be set aside upon the ground that no reasonable judge regardful of his duty to act judicially could have reached it."[80]

It was only when the appellate court had reached the conclusion that the judge's exercise of his discretion had to be set aside for one of these five reasons that it became entitled to exercise an original discretion of its own; and to these five there might be added two more – where the judge had failed altogether to exercise his discretion and where the judge had taken irrelevant matters into account. As Lord Lowry L.C.J. said in *Boyd* v. *Sinnamen*,[81] "it is important for the proper functioning of our legal process that the deference due to the exercise of the judge's discretion should not descend into mere lip service."

This "restatement" of established law in Britain[82] was prompted mainly by the increasing tendency of Lord Denning M.R. to completely disregard the trial judge's decision and to exercise an original discretion of his own.[83] In so doing Lord Denning M.R. was merely echoing Lord Atkin who, in *Evans* v. *Bartham*,[84] said that, while an appellate court would not normally interfere with the exercise of the judge's discretion unless it was clearly satisfied that he was wrong, it did have the power, "nay the duty", to intervene if the judge's decision resulted in injustice.

In what circumstances will the Supreme Court interfere with the discretion of the High Court judge? It seems the Supreme Court need not even pay lip service to the trial judge's discretion. In *Vella* v.

---

[79] As for instance in *McDonald* v. *Feely* Supreme Court, unreported, 23 July 1980.
[80] [1983] A.C. 191, 220.
[81] Northern Ireland Court of Appeal, unreported, 17 June 1974.
[82] See the cases cited in Kerr, *loc. cit.* at p. 53, n. 113.
[83] See his disregard of Peter Pain J.'s reasons in *B.B.C.* v. *Hearn* [1977] I.C.R. 685; those of Dillon J. in *Hadmor Productions* v. *Hamilton* [1981] I.C.R. 690; those of Donaldson J. in *N.W.L. Ltd.* v. *Woods* [1979] I.C.R. 744 and those of Kenneth Jones J. in *Duport Steel Ltd.* v. *Sirs* [1980] I.C.R. 161.
[84] [1937] A.C. 473.

Morelli,⁸⁵ Walsh J. said that under the provisions of Article 34.4.3° of the 1937 Constitution all decisions of the High Court whether of a discretionary nature or not are subject to an appeal to the Supreme Court "unrestricted and unfettered by any previously existing rule of practice of a restrictive nature". The jurisdiction of the Supreme Court could only be restricted within the limits permitted by the Constitution by a law enacted subsequent to the coming into force of the Constitution.⁸⁶

In *H. Wigoder & Co. Ltd.* v. *Moran*,⁸⁷ Kenny J. referred to the supposed rule that when the judge in a lower court makes a discretionary order, the appeal court should not interfere with the exercise of his discretion unless it is shown that he acted on a wrong principle of law. He continued:

> "The origin of this rule is unknown. I deny that it exists. When the case is heard on affidavit only, the appellate court is in the same position as the trial judge to exercise its discretion and if the members of that court think that the discretion was wrongly exercised they should not, in my view, hesitate to reverse it."⁸⁸

Parke and Henchy JJ. agreed, the latter adding:

> "Where all the necessary primary facts are admitted, or have been found by the judge of first instance, the court of appeal is no less qualified than he to exercise the requisite discretion on the basis of the facts so found or admitted."⁸⁹

Injunctions to restrain breaches of the criminal law

So far the authors have been examining the availability of injunctive relief in the context of restraining civil wrongs. A related question is whether a private individual can apply to the courts for an injunction to restrain a breach of the criminal law. In *Gouriet* v. *Union of Post Office Workers*,⁹⁰ the House of Lords ruled that a private individual could not so apply without the consent of the Attorney General.⁹¹ This was qualified however by their Lordships' admission that an injunction would lie at the suit of a private individual when the criminal action

---

⁸⁵ [1968] I.R. 11.
⁸⁶ At 21.
⁸⁷ (1977) 111 I.L.T.R. 105.
⁸⁸ At 113. Both Parke J. and himself thought that the passage of Davitt J. in *Hayes, Conyngham and Robinson Ltd.* v. *Kilbride* [1963] I.R. 185, 191, to the effect that the discretion of the trial judge should not be interfered with unless he erred in principle, was "plainly wrong" and should not be followed.
⁸⁹ At 108.
⁹⁰ [1978] A.C. 435.
⁹¹ See Casey, *The Office of the Attorney General in Ireland* (Dublin, 1980) at pp. 148–150.

threatened to interfere with some private right of the plaintiff or where it was anticipated that he would suffer special damage as a consequence of the defendant's action.[92] This is highly significant because, as has been shown in a previous chapter,[93] for damages to be available to a person who has suffered loss as a result of the defendant's criminal acts that person must be the target of the defendant's actions. In *Gouriet* however it seems to have been assumed that, had the plaintiff's private rights been infringed, an injunction would have been granted, even though the plaintiff was not the target of the defendant's actions.

Non-observance of injunctions

Non-compliance with court orders amounts to a civil contempt of court.[94] The person who has obtained the order may seek, in cases of non-compliance, an order of attachment directing that the person or persons against whom the order is directed shall be brought before the court to answer the contempt in respect of which the order is issued.[95] The Rules of the Superior Courts[96] provide that every order of attachment shall be directed to the Commissioner and members of the Garda Síochána. R.S.C. O.44 r.3 provides that no order of attachment shall be issued except by the leave of the court to be applied for by motion on notice to the party against whom the order of attachment is to be directed. When the person against whom an order for attachment is directed is brought before the High Court, the Court may either discharge him on such terms and conditions as to costs or otherwise as the Court thinks fit or commit him to prison for his contempt either for a definite period to be specified in the order or until he purges his contempt and be discharged by further order of the Court. If the person, against whom an order of attachment is directed, is not arrested and brought to Court, the Court is empowered to issue an order of committal directing that upon his arrest the person shall be lodged in prison until he purge his contempt and is discharged pursuant to further orders of the court. The jurisdiction which the Court exercises in such cases is summary.

There is often dissatisfaction expressed when court orders are openly flouted and nothing appears to be done. In these cases, however, the Court acts at the instance of the party whose rights are being infringed and who, in the first instance, has obtained from the Court the order

---

[92] See Lord Denning M.R. in *Ex parte Island Records Ltd.* [1978] Ch. 122, 135 building on *dicta* in *Gouriet* [1978] A.C. 435 at 492, 499, 506, 513 and 518.
[93] Chapter 8.
[94] Where an injunction is granted by the Court to restrain picketing, the order does not confer any power of arrest if the order is broken. A separate application must be made to the Court authorising the arrest.
[95] R.S.C., O.44, r.1.
[96] R.S.C., O.44, r.7.

which he seeks to have enforced. If that person is content that it should not be enforced, the Court, generally speaking, has no interest in interfering so as to enforce what the litigant does not want enforced. "The order is made so as to assist the litigant in obtaining his rights and he may consult his own interests in deciding whether or not to enforce it."[97] This is why the purpose of committal proceedings is described as coercive not punitive, and why the imprisonment is usually in the form of an indefinite imprisonment which may be terminated either when the court, upon application by the person imprisoned, is satisfied that he is prepared to abide by the order, or when the party seeking to enforce that order shall for any reason waive his rights and agrees, or consents, to the release of the imprisoned party.[98]

The Rules of the Superior Courts do provide however that the Court has power to commit the person in contempt for a fixed period. This order is necessarily punitive. Indeed O'Hanlon J., in *Ross Co. Ltd.* v. *Swan*,[99] indicated expressly that he was prepared to exercise the High Court's undoubted jurisdiction to commit for contempt not merely for the purpose of compelling obedience to its orders but also to vindicate the authority of the court whose order has been disobeyed.[1]

Whether the Court has, or should have, the power to act of its own volition and make a punitive order are much more delicate issues. Megarry V.-C. has surely voiced the thoughts of many judges when he said, in *Clarke* v. *Chadburn*,[2] that there was a case for considering whether there should be some "relaxation" by the courts of their "present restraint upon themselves in enforcing their orders in cases where these are being openly flouted and the administration of justice is being brought into disrespect." What must not be forgotten is that the Attorney General undoubtedly has the right to institute committal proceedings in the public interest.[3] It would be a very rare case indeed, where both the party who has obtained the order and the Attorney General had decided not to institute committal proceedings, that the Court would feel it necessary to act on its own volition.

In *Ross Co. Ltd.* v. *Swan*,[4] O'Hanlon J. approved a *dictum* of Lord Denning M.R.[5] to the effect that the power to commit to prison for contempt of court in civil proceedings, for disobedience to the court's orders, was a jurisdiction that should not be exercised when it is unlikely to produce the desired result and when there is some

---

[97] *Per* Megarry V.-C., *Clarke* v. *Chadburn* [1985] 1 W.L.R. 78, 82.
[98] See Finlay P., *State (Commins)* v. *McRann* [1977] I.R. 78, 89. As happened in the Ranks dispute in February 1983.
[99] [1981] I.L.R.M. 416.
[1] At 417.
[2] [1985] 1 W.L.R. 78, 83.
[3] See Casey, *op. cit.*, chapter 10. See also Edwards, *The Attorney General, Politics and the Public Interest* (London, 1984) p. 165.
[4] [1981] I.L.R.M. 416.
[5] In *Danchevsky* v. *Danchevsky* [1975] Fam. 17, 22.

reasonable and alternative course available instead of committal. O'Hanlon J. continued:

> "It is undesirable that the High Court should commit to prison for an indefinite period a person who has no intention of obeying the order of the court, and who may even welcome the publicity he gains by the making of such an order as a means of furthering his own cause. If no other reasonable course is open, then the order may have to be made to vindicate the authority of the court. If some other reasonable course is open, then it is preferable that it should be adopted."[6]

In that case it seemed to O'Hanlon J. that there was an alternative course available. On the evidence before him the case appeared to fall squarely within the scope of the Prohibition of Forcible Entry and Occupation Act 1971[7] and he declined to make an order committing the defendants to prison for contempt. However, he did award the costs of the application to the plaintiff against the defendants.

---

[6] [1981] I.L.R.M. 416, 417.
[7] See *supra*, pp. 313–315.

Chapter 12

DISPUTES RESOLUTION

In our system of collective bargaining the parties are free to settle their disputes directly by negotiation and compromise. In the event of their failing to resolve any differences, the law does not impose a settlement or require resort to certain procedures. The parties are free, within certain limits, to take industrial action whether by way of strike or lockout.[1] Alternatively, they can go, if they wish, to the Labour Court for conciliation, mediation or even arbitration. Official conciliation machinery has been in operation in Ireland since 1896.[2] Before this, the State had attempted to legislate for the settlement of trade disputes by the setting up of arbitration machinery. For instance, the Arbitration Act 1824 provided that when workmen and masters could not agree as to the price to be paid for work actually done, then either side could demand arbitration, the arbitrator being the J.P. of the district. This Act was "a complete dead letter from its passage to its repeal in 1896."[3] The Royal Commission[4] which was set up after the 1889 dock strike to report on whether legislation could be directed "to the remedy of any of the problems that might be disclosed" rejected, by a majority, any idea of compulsory reference of disputes to state boards of arbitration whose decisions would be legally binding. They felt that less faith should be placed in legal sanctions and more emphasis placed on the development of voluntary institutions. They did recommend, however, that the Board of Trade should be bestowed with discretionary powers to enable it to take the initiative in aiding with advice and to conciliate on the application of both parties. The outcome was the enactment of the Conciliation Act 1896, which applied to both Britain and Ireland.

With the war-time state of emergency, a wages standstill had been imposed.[5] The Government of the day was naturally concerned that, when the emergency restrictions were lifted, there would be an orderly release of the pent-up pressures, not only in the private sector, but also in the civil and public services. The Government did not consider the

---

[1] Within the limits set out in Chapter 10.
[2] Conciliation Act 1896; on this and the earlier arbitration legislation of 1824 and 1872, see Sharp, *Industrial Conciliation and Arbitration in Great Britain* (London, 1950).
[3] Sharp, *op. cit.*, p. 281.
[4] The proceedings of the Royal Commission are contained in 67 publications including five reports: Cd. 6708 (1892); Cd. 6795 (1892); Cd. 6894 (1893/4); Cd. 7063 (1893/4); Cd. 7421 (1894).
[5] By the Emergency Powers (No. 83) Order 1941 (S.R. & O. No. 95 of 1941). This was one of a series of measure which the Government put into force during the war with a view to limiting the inflationary effects of an expanding supply of money in a time of reduced supplies of goods. Complementary measures included price control, limitations on company dividends and directors' remuneration, and a special tax on company profits in excess of pre-war profits.

pre-war machinery to be suitable for this. It was not that the 1896 Act was inherently defective, but simply that it had been designed for very different conditions. New means by which differences could be more smoothly adjusted were required.[6] Therefore the 1896 was repealed by the Industrial Relations Act 1946,[7] the aim of which Act was "to make further and better provision for promoting harmonious relations between workers and their employers and for this purpose to establish machinery . . . for the prevention and settlement of trade disputes."[8] The 1946 Act established the Labour Court, an independent adjudicating body charged, *inter alia*, with the task of promoting harmonious industrial relations. Its principal function lies in the promotion of good industrial relations by assisting the parties to settle their disputes in accordance with procedures laid down in the Act (as amended).[9] It fulfils this in two ways, namely, (i) the provision of an industrial relations service, and (ii) the investigation of disputes and the making of recommendations towards settlement. The Labour Court has been judicially described as a "highly responsible board of conciliation charged with the duty of promoting harmony between workers and employers and it investigates a trade dispute with a view to making not an order, but a recommendation . . . The object is to bring about peace by persuasion instead of submission by coercion."[10]

The Court at present consists of a Chairman, three deputy chairmen and eight ordinary members, all of whom are appointed by the Minister for Labour. The appointment of further deputy chairmen and ordinary members is provided for in section 8 of the Industrial Relations Act 1976 if the Minister considers it expedient for the speedy dispatch of the business of the Court. The ordinary members are nominated for appointment by "organisations representative of workers' and employers' trade unions," the former being the I.C.T.U. and the latter the F.U.E. Ordinary members may not hold office for more than five years and may be removed by the Minister only for stated reasons and only with the consent of the organisation that nominated the member in question.[11] It is further provided that an ordinary member shall not hold the office of trustee, treasurer, secretary or any other office in, or be a member of any committee of a trade union or hold any office or employment which would prevent him from being at all times available for the work of the Court.[12] There

---

[6] See the remarks of Deputy Lemass at 101 *Dáil Debates* cc. 2281-2282.
[7] On which, see Mortished, "The Industrial Relations Act 1946" (1942-47) 17 *J.S.S.I.S.I.* 671, reprinted in King (ed), *Public Administration in Ireland* Vol.2 (Dublin, 1949) at pp. 75-89.
[8] See the long title to the Act.
[9] In 1955, 1956, 1969 and 1975 (although the 1955 Amendment Act was repealed in its entirety by the 1969 Act).
[10] *Per* Gavan Duffy P., *McElroy* v. *Mortished* High Court, unreported, 17 June 1949. The full text of the judgment is included as an Appendix to the *Third Annual Report* of the Labour Court.
[11] 1946 Act, s. 10(8).
[12] 1946 Act, s. 10(11).

is nothing in the legislation requiring the Minister to consult trade unions or employers' associations before appointing the Chairman or any deputy chairmen, although normally there will be consultation.[13] The Chairman and deputy chairmen hold office on such terms as are fixed by the Minister and are required to devote their full time to the work of the Court.[14] All members must be ordinarily resident in the State.[15] None are required to be lawyers,[16] indeed a suggested amendment that the Chairman be a practising barrister or solicitor of not less than five years' standing was defeated.[17]

It was suggested in the Dáil, during the committee stage of the Bill, that the Chairman be given the tenure of a High Court or Circuit Court Judge since that status would enable him to be free from pressure and free from the suspicion that pressure could be applied, but the Government felt it unwise to do this as it could mean making a permanent choice and having no power to rectify the position if they found that the Chairman was neither suitable nor satisfactory.[18]

Section 3 of the 1969 Act provides that whenever the Chairman is of the opinion that it is expedient, for the speedy dispatch of business, that the Court should act by divisions, he may direct accordingly and, until he revokes this direction, the court shall be grouped into divisions. The Chairman then assigns to each division the business to be transacted by it and, for the purpose of the business so assigned to it, each division shall have the powers of the Court and the chairman of the division (being one of the deputy chairmen) shall have all the powers of the Chairman.

The members are paid out of public funds but they are not civil servants nor do they act under instruction from the Minister. In fact, when the Minister for Labour performed the official opening ceremony of the Court's new headquarters[19] in 1984, he expressly rejected doubts about the Court's independence and stressed that the Government in which he participated was committed to maintaining the Court's unbiased role.[20] At the same ceremony the then Chairman of the Court stressed his determination that the Court would remain a wholly independent forum for the settlement of disputes, which would not act as an arm of government economic policy.

---

[13] The failure of the Minister to consult in 1977 over changes in the Chairmanship and Deputy Chairmanship was severely criticised by both sides of industry. See the comments of the President of the Workers' Union of Ireland as reported in the *Irish Times* March 7, 1977 and those of the F.U.E. in its February 1977 *Bulletin*.
[14] 1946 Act, s. 10(10), as amended by 1969 Act, s. 4(2), and 1976 Act, s. 8(3).
[15] 1946 Act, s. 10(12) and 1969 Act, s. 4(5).
[16] Although the first Deputy Chairman of the Court was a Senior Counsel.
[17] 102 *Dáil Debates* cc. 871–879.
[18] 102 *Dáil Debates* cc. 861–871 and cc. 896–897.
[19] Tom Johnson House. The new building is situated in the old Beggars Bush barracks on Haddington Road, Dublin 4, and is named after Tom Johnson, leader of the Labour Party from 1918 to 1927 and a member of the Labour Court from 1946 to 1956.
[20] See the *Irish Times* May 2, 1984.

This same point was forcefully made by R.J.P. Mortished, the first Chairman of the Court, at the Court's inaugural meeting on September 23, 1946.

> "By the passage of the Industrial Relations Act the Oireachtas effected a very noteworthy change. It has transferred from a government department to a specially constituted court the responsibility for securing a reasonable adjustment and settlement of differences between employers and workers by negotiation, discussion and agreement between the parties. This court is an independent body, independent of the government and of every other body. It is so constructed that representatives of employers and workers may take part on a basis of equality under its work. The Act may be regarded as an expression of industrial self government."[21]

The Court, despite its name, is not a body concerned with the determination of legal questions, except when it is exercising its functions under the 1974 and 1977 equality legislation.[22] It is concerned rather with the responsibility of promoting good industrial relations and is thus a court of reasonableness and fair dealing. It is enhanced with the spirit of co-operation not compulsion and as such its decisions are not binding on the parties. They are merely recommendations which may be accepted or rejected by the parties. McCarthy put it well when he said that a recommendation of the Labour Court was "essentially a third view"[23] not a judgment, and that the court was established "as a body whose purpose was to promote accommodation . . . to act as an honest broker, neither to apply law nor to create it."[24]

Conciliation

The Court's most basic, and some would say its most important, role is the provision of a conciliation service.

Conciliation is the participation of a third party in the negotiation of the settlement to the dispute. The conciliator's role is to aid the parties to reach an agreement. The conciliator has no power to compel the parties to participate and reach an agreement, that is something for the disputing parties themselves. Here no "third view" is offered.

> "The function here is to facilitate the making of a bargain or to provide a solution for a dispute of a non-bargaining kind. . . . The process is one of mutual clarification and a more exact method of

---

[21] Published as an appendix to the Court's *First Annual Report*.
[22] Disputes arising under the Anti-Discrimination (Pay) Act 1974 and the Employment Equality Act 1977 are referred to the Labour Court. See the Employment Equality Agency's policy statement *The Role of the Labour Court in Enforcement Procedures under Equality Legislation – Recommendations for Change* (Dublin, 1984), noted by Curtin (1984) 3 *J.I.S.L.L.* 156.
[23] *Elements in a Theory of Industrial Relations* (Dublin, 1984), p. 37.
[24] *Ibid.*, p. 52.

communication since the conciliator (often moving from one party to another in separate rooms) may be able to communicate impressions and non committal views which allow exploration of positions that would otherwise be impossible. The conciliator is a skilful instrument in the negotiation, not, in these circumstances, a determiner of the result."[25]

The first annual report of the British Advisory Conciliation and Arbitration Service contains an excellent description of the conciliation process which the authors believe is worth citing in full.

"The conciliation officer aims to provide a calm and informal atmosphere, a patient understanding of difficulties and a knowledge and experience of industrial relations. He probes and identifies the areas of agreement and disagreement and acts as an intermediary between the parties in dispute, conveying proposals without the formal committment that direct negotiations sometimes require."

Although the conciliator may make suggestions on how to make progress towards a settlement, responsibility for the settlement lies with the parties and the conciliator should never exert pressure on either party in order to achieve a settlement. From this it is apparent that conciliation will only be effective if both parties are willing to accept the intervention and assistance of the conciliator. The conditions for conciliation are best in cases where both parties are interested in having the dispute resolved. When conciliation does take place, it is therefore in effect a continuation of the process of collective bargaining, albeit with outside assistance.

The Labour Court's conciliation functions are to be found in section 6 of the Industrial Relations Act 1969. Conciliators are known as Industrial Relations Officers and they are required to perform any duties assigned to them by the Court or its Chairman, but in particular they are required "to assist in the prevention and settlement of trade disputes and in the establishment and maintenance of means for conducting voluntary negotiations between employers and workers."[26]

In fact, the Labour Court is precluded from investigating a dispute before it has received a report from an Industrial Relations Officer stating that the parties to the dispute have failed to arrive at a settlement through conciliation, unless there are exceptional circumstances.[27]

In 1983 the number of disputes in which the Industrial Relations Officers acted as conciliators was 2,090 and the percentage of cases

---

[25] *Ibid.*, p. 53.
[26] S. 6(2).
[27] 1946 Act, s. 67(1A) and (1B) as amended by 1969 Act, s. 18.

settled at conciliation conferences was 53.3% compared with 49.8% in 1982, 47.8% in 1981 and 50.4% in 1980. In the great majority of disputes not settled the parties agreed to proceed to either the Court or a Rights Commissioner for a recommendation on terms of settlement.[28]

Industrial Relations Officers are not, however, solely concerned with helping the parties find an acceptable basis for the settlement of industrial disputes. They are also concerned with helping to bring about a permanent improvement in the relations between the parties which will enable them more easily to settle future differences without outside assistance. Conciliation therefore "oils the wheels of industry far more than the statistics tell",[29] and its importance in our industrial relations system cannot be overestimated.[30]

The powers of the Court regarding conciliation are limited to conciliating in existing or apprehended trade disputes.[31] A more severe limitation is that it cannot conciliate in certain sectors – the civil service for example.[32] The Industrial Relations Officers, however, are available to act as mediators on the Conciliation Councils of a number of conciliation and arbitration schemes in the public service.

Mediation

Section 69 of the 1946 Act enables the Labour Court, before it undertakes the investigation of a trade dispute, to appoint an Industrial Relations Officer to act as a mediator in the dispute "for the purposes of effecting the permanent settlement thereof or such temporary settlement as will ensure that no stoppage of work shall occur pending the investigation of the dispute."[33] A mediator has a slightly different role to that of a conciliator, in that he plays a more active role, making recommendations as to a possible solution whilst still leaving it to the parties to negotiate the actual settlement.

Investigation of trade disputes

The Labour Court's most public function is the investigation of

---

[28] Figures taken from the Annual Reports of the Labour Court.
[29] Wedderburn and Davies, *Employment Grievances and Disputes Procedure in Britain* (University of California, 1969) pp. 222–3.
[30] Settlements voluntarily entered into by the parties involved are qualitatively superior to those imposed on them. See Marsh, *Disputes Procedure in British Industry* Research Paper 2 for the Royal Commission on Trade Unions and Employers' Associations (HMSO 1966).
[31] 1946 Act, s. 67.
[32] By virtue of the definition of worker in the Acts. Note that, while by virtue of s. 17 of the 1969 Act the Minister for Finance is empowered to designate any persons employed by or under the State as workers, this power expressly does not extend to established civil servants within the meaning of the Civil Service Regulation Act 1956. S. 17(3) provides, however, that the Government may by order amend the definition of "worker" in Part VI of the 1946 Act.
[33] S. 69(2) empowers the Chairman of the Court to give a "general authority" to an Industrial Relations Officer to act as mediator in relation to trade disputes generally or trade disputes of a particular character.

trade disputes and the issue of recommendations for their settlement. Trade dispute is given a similar definition to that in the Trade Disputes Act 1906, namely, "any dispute or difference between employers and workers, or between workers and workers, connected with the employment or non employment or the terms of employment or with the conditions of employment of any person." Worker, however, is given a slightly different definition to that of workman in the 1906 Act,[34] namely, "any person aged fifteen or more who has entered into, or works under, a contract with an employer, whether the contract be for manual labour, clerical work or otherwise, whether it be express or implied, oral or in writing and whether it be a contract of service or of apprenticeship or a contract personally to execute any work or labour", but does not include (a) a person who is employed by or under the State; (b) a teacher in a national or a secondary school; or (c) an officer of a local authority, a vocational education committee, a committee of agriculture or a school attendance committee.[35] Before it was amended in 1956 and 1969 the definition also excluded employees of a local authority, and until 1976 agricultural workers were excluded from all but Part VI of the Act.

Section 67 of the 1946 Act, which empowers the Court to investigate trade disputes, also sets out certain disputes which the Court should not investigate, namely

(i) a trade dispute between persons who are represented on a registered Joint Industrial Council[36] unless (a) the Council so requests or (b) the Court is of the opinion that the dispute is likely to lead to a stoppage of work;

(ii) a trade dispute in which a trade union is concerned if the trade union establishes to the Court's satisfaction that there is an agreement in force between the trade union and the other parties to the dispute which provides another method of determining the dispute, unless the Court is of the opinion that the dispute is likely to lead to a stoppage of work; and,

(iii) a dispute between persons to whom a registered employment agreement[37] applies concerning matters to which the agreement relates unless (a) a party to the agreement so requests or (b) the Court is of the opinion that the dispute is likely to lead to a stoppage of work.

---

[34] In *State (St. Stephen's Green Club)* v. *The Labour Court* [1961] I.R. 85, Walsh J. observed that the omission of the words "employed in trade or industry" from the definition of "worker" was intended to give "worker" a much wider definition in the 1946 Act than the expression "workman" had in the 1906 Act. Since the trade or industry requirement was deleted by the Trade Disputes (Amendment) Act 1982, the definitions are once again similar in scope.
[35] 1969 Act, s. 4(1) as amended by 1976 Act, s. 2.
[36] On which see *infra*, pp. 357–358.
[37] On which see *supra*, pp. 146–153.

The 1946 Act provides[38] that, unless there are exceptional circumstances which warrant it intervening, the Court is not to investigate a trade dispute unless the parties to the dispute request it to do so and then only if it receives a report from an Industrial Relations Officer that conciliation has failed to settle the dispute. It is important to note that section 67 of the 1946 Act only empowers the Court to investigate a trade dispute; it does not impose any obligation on the Court to investigate. The Court is only obliged to investigate in the circumstances set out in section 20(1) of the 1969 Act, *i.e.* where the workers concerned in the dispute, or their trade union, undertakes before the investigation to accept the Court's recommendation. A section 20(1) investigation is to be given priority over the other business of the Court.

Under section 8 of the 1969 Act, Court investigations must be held in private unless one of the parties concerned requests a public hearing. In public investigations, however, the Court does have the power to hear any part of the case in private if it is satisfied that that part of the investigation concerns a matter that should, in the interests of any party to the dispute, be treated as confidential.[39]

When investigating a trade dispute, the Court may consist of the Chairman and all the ordinary members or a Chairman (who may be one of the deputy chairmen) and two ordinary members being one employers' representative and one workers' representative. In practice the Court always sits in divisions for the investigation of trade disputes.

The procedure and general atmosphere prevailing at a Labour Court hearing for the purpose of investigating a dispute bear little resemblance to the formalities of a court of law, and are best described by the Court itself.

> "Formalities are reduced to a minimum. Written submissions are normally made by both parties before the Court investigation commences. These written submissions are read at the Court hearing by the main spokesman for each side but the fact that certain aspects of the dispute are not covered in the written submission does not prevent a party from covering these additional aspects by way of supplementary oral submission. Any points on which clarification or elaboration is required will be dealt with by way of questions by members of the Court. The more fully facts and arguments are given in the written and oral submissions the less need there will be for members of the Court to put questions. Written submissions are required to be in the hands of the Court some days before the hearing."[40]

---

[38] 1946 Act, s. 67 as amended by 1969 Act, s. 18.
[39] S. 8(2).
[40] Taken from the Labour Court's explanatory handout.

A certain amount of formality is, however, indispensable to the orderly conduct of proceedings, which must be conducted with due dignity and decorum.

The Court is empowered by section 21 of the 1946 Act to summon witnesses before it, to examine on oath the witnesses standing before it and require any such witness to produce to the Court any document in his power or control. In *State (Casey)* v. *Labour Court*,[41] O'Hanlon J. pointed out that since the 1946 Act conferred a discretion on the Court to regulate its own procedures in this respect – *i.e.* to allow testimony to be given on oath or as unsworn testimony as the Court thinks fit – neither the parties nor the High Court could dictate to the Labour Court as to the manner in which it conducts its own procedures "once it exercises its powers in accordance with the statute from which it derives its authority to act."[42] He did observe, however, that the Labour Court should not allow itself to be deterred by considerations of difficulty or inconvenience from taking evidence on oath where it would otherwise be proper or desirable to do so.[43]

The Court then is the judge of what information it needs and it is empowered to insist on getting that information if it is not voluntarily submitted. Needless to say, the Court would always prefer not to have to make use of that power.

Any information which the Court secures, whether voluntarily or by compulsion, is for the Court and not for anybody else. The extent to which information may be disclosed in Court or otherwise was dealt with in a public statement by the Court in December 1946.[44] If spokesmen at a hearing have information which they think would be useful for the Court to have but which they do not wish to make known to the general public, they should submit this information by way of a written statement and ask the Court to consider it in private sitting. The spokesmen, however, may have information of such a nature that they would be reluctant to make it known even in private sitting with the Press and Public excluded. In such a case the Court indicated that it might be prepared to receive and examine the information in private. The Court noted, however, that it could well be hampered in its examination of the information if it was deprived of the assistance of the other side, but stated that it would be "slow to invite the assistance of the other side against the wishes of those who had supplied the information." It would do so only "for reasons which it felt to be compelling". It would communicate to the other side only so much of the information as it considered absolutely necessary and would communicate it in such a form as would ensure so far as possible that confidential information was not divulged to the other side.

---

[41] (1984) 3 *J.I.S.L.L.* 135.
[42] At p. 138.
[43] *Ibid.*
[44] Published as an appendix to the Court's *First Annual Report.*

This practice[45] is now reinforced by section 8(2) of the 1969 Act which provides that where an investigation of a trade dispute is being carried out in public, the Court if it is satisfied that any part of the investigation concerns a matter that should, in the interests of any party to the dispute, be treated as confidential, may conduct that part of the investigation in private.

Section 20(6) of the 1946 Act provides that no person shall be entitled to appear by counsel or solicitor before the Court unless the rules made by the Court for the regulation of its proceedings so provide.[46] The relevant rule, rule 6(2), provides that a party may apply to the Court for leave to appear by counsel or solicitor and the Court "may grant such leave if it is of the opinion that the matter in issue is of such a nature that the applicant ought to be assisted by counsel or solicitor." The validity of this rule was challenged in *McElroy* v. *Mortished*.[47] The plaintiffs, Co. Monaghan employers, and the I.T.G.W.U. were in dispute. Before the Labour Court had an opportunity to investigate the dispute, it received a letter from the plaintiffs' solicitor stating that counsel[48] was to be briefed to appear for the plaintiffs. The secretary of the Court replied, warning the plaintiffs that the case did not look like one in which counsel would be allowed to appear and drawing their attention to the relevant rule. This reply indicated, however, that the Court would have no objection to counsel appearing *purely* in the capacity of spokesman. This was not acceptable to the plaintiffs who refused to appear before the Court unless counsel could appear *qua* counsel and sought an injunction to restrain the Court from proceeding with the matter and a declaration that rule 6(2) was contrary to natural justice.

Gavan Duffy P. considered the case to be "ill-advised, irresponsible and mischievous", and was swift to dismiss all but one of the plaintiffs' arguments. He said that there was no support, even from Aristotle and Maritain, for the novel proposition that a man is entitled as a matter of natural justice to be represented by a barrister before a non-judicial tribunal.[49] Some consideration was given, however, to the argument

---

[45] Which is unlikely to be altered by the decision of Barron J. in *State (Cole)* v. *The Labour Court* (1984) 3 *J.I.S.L.L.* 128 since the decision not to divulge information to the other side cannot be judicially reviewed where, as here, the Court is not making a binding decision which affects the legal rights of the persons appearing before it. See further *infra*, pp. 354–355.

[46] See the comments of Deputy Lemass at 102 *Dáil Debates* c. 922. Generally lawyers are only allowed to appear before the Labour Court when it is exercising its jurisdiction in respect of equal pay and employment equality cases. In this context, the present Chairman of the Court has assured the I.C.T.U. that lawyers who do appear in the Labour Court would not be granted any special privileges because of their qualifications and would not normally be allowed to cross examine witnesses or make lengthy legalistic submissions (see *Irish Times*, June 25, 1985.)

[47] *Supra*, fn. 10.

[48] Mr. Vaughan Buckley, S.C., who had previously been the first Deputy Chairman of the Court. One might speculate that the union's objection was not to the use of counsel as such but to the use of this particular counsel.

[49] This matter was subsequently considered in *State (Smullen)* v. *Duffy* High Court, unreported, 21 March 1980. See also *Pett* v. *Greyhound Racing Assoc* [1969] 1 Q.B. 125; *Enderby Town F.C.* v. *Football Association Ltd.* [1971] Ch. 591; *Fraser* v. *Mudge* [1975] 1 W.L.R. 1132.

concerning section 20(6) which authorises the Labour Court to provide for the cases in which counsel or a solicitor may appear. Rule 6(2), however, does not so define the cases; it leaves the decision on each occasion to the Labour Court. Gavan Duffy P. said:

> "If this were a court of law, one would be inclined to construe the Act as requiring a definition or description of the cases in which counsel should be allowed to appear; but the tribunal is a board of laymen and it is engaged upon an experiment of the highest public importance; and if, in such a matter as representation by counsel, it considers that it must feel its way by practical experience, in the novel field which it is exploring, I think that this judicial tribunal would be wrong if it applied a curial standard to the board, alien to its peculiar constitution and purpose; a statute governing the rules of a body of this kind is most aptly interpreted in a broad and liberal spirit. If, as I am entitled to assume, the Labour Court believed, when it made the rules, that the best it could do was entrust the allowance of counsel to the particular tribunals, I do not think the High Court of Justice, when construing the Act, can fairly say that the Labour Court was wrong, by reading into the section a judicial standard for a non-judicial tribunal. For these reasons, I must uphold the rule."

The making of recommendations

The Court, having investigated a trade dispute, *may* make a recommendation.[50] It invariably does but it is not obliged to. The Court is only obliged to make a recommendation where the workers concerned in the dispute, or their trade union, request the court to investigate under section 20(1) of the 1969 Act, *i.e.* where they undertake before the investigation to accept the recommendation of the Court. In its annual reports for 1981 and 1982[51] the Court has commented on the noteable increase in the number of cases being referred for investigation under section 20(1). In its 1983 report the Court referred to the "substantial" increase on the previous two years.[52] The Court noted that recourse to this section arose out of the reluctance of some employers to join in a referral of the matters at issue to either the Conciliation Service of the Court or to a Rights Commissioner. In a "small number" of these cases, after many attempts to persuade employers to attend, including the issuing of witness summonses in accordance with its powers under section 21 of the 1946 Act, the Court was obliged to carry out its investigations in the absence of employers.

---

[50] 1946 Act, s. 68(1) as inserted by 1969 Act, s. 19.
[51] The *Thirty-Fifth* and *Thirty-Sixth Annual Reports*, paras. 13 and 20 respectively.
[52] *Thirty-Seventh Annual Report*, para. 19.

If the Court decides to issue a recommendation, it must set forth its opinions on the merits of the dispute and the terms on which it should be settled.

Before 1969 the Court was obliged[53] to have regard to the public interest, the promotion of industrial peace, the fairness of the terms to the parties concerned and the prospects of the terms being acceptable to them. These criteria were somewhat confusing and R.J.P. Mortished, the first Chairman of the Court, observed, very shortly after the Court was established, that "unfortunately" it was not easy to reconcile all four of these criteria.

> "A settlement acceptable to the parties might be against the public interest and one which was not acceptable to the parties would hardly promote industrial peace."[54]

This problem became particularly acute in the 1960's when, as McCarthy has pointed out, the Court had to resist strongly the idea that it should be the "promoter or implementer" of national pay agreements.

> "It took the view instead . . . that the Court should be free to seek a settlement as best it could in all the circumstances of the case, taking account of course of the need for consistency and taking account of the national interest whether expressed in national bargains or not, but ultimately being free to pursue, in common sense, what seemed to be appropriate for a solution of the dispute actually under examination."[55]

The requirement to have regard to the four above-stated criteria was deleted by section 19 of the 1969 Act though, of course, the Court is still entitled, if it wishes, to have regard to any or all of them.

The parties are under no obligation to accept the recommendation and nothing can be done if they fail to implement it. The Court's duty is simply to make a recommendation, the responsibility for the settlement rests at all times with the parties themselves. The principle is guidance not compulsion. It was hoped that, in the course of time, respect for the Court's intelligence and integrity and the common sense basis of its recommendations would create a climate in which the recommendations would ordinarily be accepted,[56] particularly since, except under section 20(1), the Court is normally precluded from investigating unless both parties request it to do so. As Mortished put it:

---

[53] By virtue of s. 68(1) as originally worded.
[54] *Third Annual Report*, p. 3.
[55] *Op. cit.*, p. 38.
[56] See the comments of Deputy Lemass at 102 *Dáil Debates* c. 724.

"All that the Court can do is help [the parties] reach agreement, by clarifying the issues, creating an atmosphere of reasonableness and goodwill, reminding them if need be of their obligations to each other and to the community, endeavouring to establish certain standards of common sense and good conduct and on occasion providing for one or other party a means of dignified retreat from an awkward or untenable situation. But if the Court's efforts should prove unsuccessful, the parties are quite free to decide their future course of action, and the Court cannot compel them to do what it thinks right or impose any penalty on them if they decline to take its advice."[57]

In 1983 the Court issued 1,045 recommendations compared with 975 in 1982, 326 in 1973 and 162 in 1971.[58] This is not to say that the number of industrial disputes has risen that dramatically over the last decade. In too many cases full and meaningful negotiations between the parties has not taken place and the Court is ceasing to be a place of last resort. This tendency was commented on in the *Thirty-First Annual Report*, where the Court pointed out that the responsibility for promoting harmonious relations between employers and workers did not rest on the Court alone; it also rested "on all those who are concerned with industrial relations on whose co-operation, in working towards this end, the Court must rely." This co-operation embraced, *inter alia*, "full and exhaustive negotiations at local and conciliation level before, where necessary, referring a case to the Court for investigation and also the making, at the investigation, of full detailed submissions to the Court on all relevant matters." The Court said that it was evident that:

"parties often use negotiation procedures at local and conciliation level merely as stepping stones to arrive at a Court investigation – this despite the efforts of Industrial Relations Officers to get the parties to make full and proper use of negotiation procedures. Whatever the reason, a situation of this kind denotes an overdependence on the Court to have work done through the Court investigation which should have been done by the parties themselves before an investigation was sought.

Failure to negotiate fully leads, in turn, to the making of inadequate and, to an extent, irrelevant submissions at investigations because sufficient home work on the matters at issue has not been done. This means that the Court has to request further information or, on some occasions, further submissions and the other party must be afforded an opportunity to comment on the additional infor-

---

[57] In King ed., *Public Administration in Ireland* Volume 2 (Dublin, 1949), p. 75.
[58] Figures taken from the Labour Court's *Annual Reports*.

mation received. Because of this the Court has, at times, no option but to refer the parties back for further negotiations. Situations of this kind seriously hinder the Court in the effective and expeditious discharge of its functions."[59]

There has been some criticism of the way in which the Court issues its recommendations.[60] Normally, the recommendations take the form of a summary of the case submitted by each party to the dispute, followed by the Court's recommendation with regard to a basis for settlement. Occasionally the Court also makes oral recommendations at the end of a hearing or issues its recommendations by letter. The recommendation neither sets out fully the Court's opinion on the merits of the dispute nor the reasons for coming to the particular decision. There is a conscious attempt to avoid building up a system of precedent. The F.U.E. has argued that if the reasons and the merits were in every case fully stated it would encourage and stimulate a more intelligent consideration of the Court's recommendations by both sides of industry. The Court's own opinion, as set out in its *Third Annual Report*, is that it issues the recommendation for consideration by the parties to the dispute and not as findings set out in a formal instrument to be interpreted by lawyers. Indeed the High Court has stated that even when the Labour Court is exercising its appellate function under the 1974 and 1977 equality legislation it is not obliged to state its reasons for upholding or dismissing an appeal.[61]

There is one situation where the Court's recommendations may be given legal force and that is where it acts under section 71 of the 1946 Act. The Minister responsible for the Act, Sean Lemass T.D., saw this as the solution to the problem of the unofficial strike.[62] The section, however, has hardly been used. It allows the Court, on its own initiative, to investigate any trade dispute which has resulted in a stoppage of work provided it is satisfied that no trade union is promoting or assisting the dispute. Once it has completed its investigation it may either decide not to take any action in regard to the dispute or make a recommendation setting forth its opinion on the merits of the dispute and the manner in which it should be settled, or alternatively it may make an award setting forth the conditions on which the dispute should be settled.

Section 72 provides that if the Court makes an award under section 71 the award is to be "in force" for a three month period and if an employer employs or agrees to employ a worker on conditions inconsistent with those of the award, that employer is liable, on summary conviction, to a fine not exceeding £100. Only on one

---

[59] Paras. 15 and 17.
[60] See the comments of the F.U.E. in their February 1977 *Bulletin.*
[61] *State (Cole)* v. *The Labour Court* (1984) 3 *J.I.S.L.L.* 128 at p. 135.
[62] 101 *Dáil Debates* c. 2290.

occasion has the Court ever issued an award under section 71, and that was in 1948 in relation to an unofficial strike in the Cork bakery trade.

Issue of recommendations

The usual practice is to communicate the recommendation in the first place to the parties concerned and then to other interested parties. In special cases, however, where the Court feels that general publication of details of the dispute would tend to exacerbate feelings on both sides or to render a situation of the dispute more difficult, the Court does not issue the recommendation to any but the parties directly affected.[63]

Arbitration

Section 70 provides that where a trade dispute has occurred or is apprehended, the Court, with the consent of the parties concerned in the dispute, may refer the dispute to the arbitration of one or more persons or may itself arbitrate upon the dispute. The arbitrator's decision binds the parties only so far as they have agreed to accept it, and the 1946 Act provides no sanctions in the case of non-observance.[64]

Section 24 references

Section 24 of the 1946 Act provides that the Court "shall consider any matter referred to it by the Minister concerning the employment conditions prevailing as regards the workers of any class and their employers and shall furnish a report thereon to the Minister together with recommendations (if any) as it thinks proper." The section is not infrequently utilised.[65] The Department of Labour, however, submitted to the Commission of Inquiry on Industrial Relations[66] that the Minister's powers in this respect were "seriously inadequate". The Department pointed out that:

(i) the section did not specifically apply to dispute situations;
(ii) it did not apply to workers in the public service; and
(iii) under the section, the Court could comply with a Ministerial

---

[63] 1946 Act, s. 68(2), provides that the Court "shall communicate a recommendation under this section to all the parties to the dispute and to such other persons as the Court thinks fit, and the Court may also publish the recommendation in such manner as it thinks fit."

[64] *Quaere* whether a party who had reneged on the award could be required by a mandatory injunction to observe the award? Deputy Lemass did comment in the Dáil, however, that in practice compulsory arbitration decisions are not, in fact, enforceable against a body of workers who are opposed to their terms. See 102 *Dáil Debates* c. 681.

[65] For example, in 1974 the Court made thirteen s. 24 reports. See *Twenty-Fifth Annual Report*, para. 20. In 1985 the dispute over the handling of South African produce in the Henry Street branch of Dunnes Stores was also the subject of a s. 24 reference.

[66] See the Report of the Commission of Inquiry on Industrial Relations (Pl. 114) at paras. 526-529.

request merely by "furnishing a report" which could, in fact, simply consist of a statement of its unwillingness or inability to take any direct action. In addition, any report or recommendations by the Court under the section were sent, not to the parties, but to the Minister.

The Department proposed, accordingly, that the Minister for Labour should have power to request the Labour Court to investigate particular disputes.

The Labour Court were opposed to a change of this kind stating that the Court should not intervene against its better judgement merely for the sake of being seen to be doing something, and the Commission agreed. The members of the Commission believed that the Court would be involved in any dispute of sufficient importance to warrant the Minister's intervention. Were it not involved at the request of the parties, it had the power, under section 18(1)(b) of the 1969 Act, to intervene on its own initiative when satisfied that "exceptional circumstances" exist. If the Labour Court "did not consider the circumstances to be right for direct intervention or where it believed that it could not contribute to the settlement of a dispute, matters would be unlikely to be improved – and might well be exacerbated – by Ministerial intervention." Moreover, the intervention of the Court at the direct request of the Minister might lead many employers and workers to doubt the Court's independence in other matters.

The Commission, while opposed to granting the Minister the power to request an investigation in a particular dispute, did recommend, however, that it should be made clear that the Minister's existing power under section 24 could be used to request the Court to make a report, with recommendations, in a particular dispute and that it would be of value if this report were sent to all interested parties not just the Minister. The authors can see little difference between a power to request the Court to investigate and a power to request the Court to make a report. The Court can hardly make a report without investigating. What the Commission may have intended to recommend was a power to request the Court *to consider* making a report. The Labour Court, in fact, had submitted that if section 24 were to be amended it should be on the following lines – "In ordering its business the Court shall consider any representations by the Minister concerning any dispute."

Ministerial Intervention

Every year, pressure is put on Ministers and other public figures to intervene in trade disputes, especially in cases where essential services are affected. There is nothing, beyond the principle of ministerial non-intervention, to prevent this but the Labour Court has forcefully stated its view that:

"such ad hoc intervention tends to have weakened the structure of industrial relations and could undermine seriously the national dispute settling machinery provided by the legislature."[67]

Miscellaneous matters

Section 7 of the 1969 Act empowers the Court, on the application of the parties to a collective agreement, to give its decision as to the interpretation of the agreement or its application to a particular person.

Section 11 of the 1969 Act empowers the Court, after consulting with organisations representative of workers and employers, to make "fair employment rules". These rules, however, must be approved by organisations representing a substantial number of workers and employers. A person who contravenes a fair employment rule is guilty of an offence and is liable on summary conviction to a fine not exceeding £100 and, in the case of a continuing offence, a further fine not exceeding £10 for every day during which the offence is continued. The Court has yet to make any such rules although consideration was given to the making of rules governing the employment of the disabled.

Decision making process

Section 20(3) of the 1946 Act provides that where any question arises under the Act at a meeting or sitting of the Court and the members are unable to agree on the determination of the question the following provisions shall have effect:

(i) if the majority of the *ordinary* members agree the question shall be determined accordingly;
(ii) if the majority of the ordinary members do not agree, but a majority of all the members agree, the question shall be determined accordingly;
(iii) otherwise the question shall be determined in accordance with the opinion of the Chairman.

Section 20(4) provides that the decision of the Court shall be pronounced by the Chairman or such other member as the Chairman shall authorise for this purpose, and no other opinion whether assenting or dissenting, shall be pronounced nor shall the existence of any such other opinion be disclosed.

Appeals and judicial review

Section 17 of the 1946 Act provides that no appeals should lie from the decision of the Court on any matter within its jurisdiction to a court of law.[68] This section was considered by the Supreme Court in

---

[67] *Thirty-Fourth Annual Report*, para. 11.
[68] See the comments of Deputy Lemass at 102 *Dáil Debates* c. 1231.

Branigan v. *Keady*.[69] In 1958, the Irish Seamen's Union (I.S.U.) concluded an agreement with the Irish Shipowners' Association (I.S.A.) under which the I.S.A. agreed to employ only I.S.U. members. Another union which represented seamen, the M.P.G.W.U., took industrial action when this agreement was implemented. The Labour Court intervened and issued a recomendation which was accepted by all the parties to the dispute. The recommendation provided that one union be created for all seamen. Steps were taken to elect the new union's executives but disagreement arose between the I.S.U. and the M.P.G.W.U. as to the plaintiff's eligibility for election and his right to vote. The question of his eligibility was referred to the Labour Court who ruled that he was not eligible. The plaintiff then sought an injunction in the High Court to restrain the Labour Court, under whose auspices the election was taking place, until the High Court could determine the question of his eligibility. Haugh J. decided that the action was in effect an appeal from the decision of the Labour Court and that, therefore, he was precluded by section 17 from granting the injunction. The plaintiff appealed to the Supreme Court who disagreed with Haugh J. on this point and held, in ruling on the plaintiff's eligibility, that the Labour Court had not acted under any statutory power or in pursuance of any statutory jurisdiction but "in pursuance of the agreement of the parties to the dispute to accept the terms of the recommendation." Kingsmill Moore J. continued:

> "The only jurisdiction which the Court was exercising was a jurisdiction to act as an agreed arbitrator. I think s. 17 must be confined in its operation to a decision given in the exercise of a jurisdiction conferred by the Statute, and does not extend to a decision under an agreement to arbitrate, unless perhaps in a case under s. 70 where the Court undertakes to arbitrate on a *trade dispute* at the request of the parties."[70]

Section 17 is not, however, worded in a way which ousts the inherent jurisdiction which the High Court has over all inferior tribunals to ensure that they have not improperly exercised their discretion. To a certain extent, therefore, the Labour Court is subject to review by the High Court by way of *certiorari, mandamus* or prohibition.[71] The Court must act in good faith, listen fairly to both sides and obtain information in a way which would give a fair opportunity to the parties to correct or contradict any statement prejudicial to their case but otherwise the High Court will only intervene where the Labour Court has misdirected itself in law, has taken irrelevant considerations into account or has reached a decision to which no reasonable industrial

---

[69] [1959] I.R. 283.
[70] At 297.
[71] See Hogan, "Public Law Remedies and Judicial Review in the Context of Employment Law" (1985) 4 *J.I.S.L.L.* forthcoming.

relations agency, with a due appreciation of its statutory obligations, would have come.[72] The State Side orders will only lie, however, when the Labour Court's decision affects legal rights or imposes liability. Therefore, as Walsh J. held in *State (St. Stephen's Green Club)* v. *Labour Court*,[73] prohibition will not lie against the Labour Court when it is acting under section 68, as the 1946 Act does not provide any machinery for enforcing the recommendations nor for translating the recommendations into findings binding upon the parties. Prohibition would lie, however, when the Court acted under section 71, as it could, under that section, affect rights and impose liability.

Privilege

A question yet to be decided is whether statements made to, or in documents produced before, the Labour Court are protected by absolute privilege. If they are, they cannot under any circumstances give rise to an action for libel or slander. The general rule was laid down by Lopes L.J. in *Royal Aquarium* v. *Parkinson*:[74]

> "No action of libel or slander lies, whether against judges, counsel, witnesses or parties, for words written or spoken in the course of any proceedings before any Court recognised by law, and this though the words written or spoken were written or spoken maliciously, without any justification or excuse, and from personal ill-will and anger against the person defamed."

Absolute privilege also protects statements made or documents produced in other tribunals which have "similar attributes to a court of justice" and "act in a manner similar to that in which such courts act."[75] In *Trapp* v. *Mackie*[76] Lord Diplock referred to the undesirability of witnesses before tribunals being harassed by actions for libel and slander, especially when they are compellable to give evidence and to appear and punishable in case of refusal.

Is the Labour Court such a tribunal? Although it is recognised by law, its object could hardly be described as to arrive at a judicial law, its object could hardly be described as being to arrive at a judicial determination and it does not proceed in a manner that is similar to a court of justice. The true nature of the proceedings is nearer to conciliation or mediation than arbitration or adjudication. In this respect the decision of Hirst J. in *Tadd* v. *Eastwood*[77] is worthy of consideration. Here it was held that an allegedly defamatory document,

---

[72] See *Associated Provincial Picture Houses Ltd* v. *Wednesday Corporation* [1948] 1 K.B. 223; *United Kingdom Association of Professional Engineers* v. *Advisory, Conciliation and Arbitration Service* [1979] I.C.R. 205 (particularly Lord Scarman at 211).
[73] [1961] I.R. 85. Cf. *State (Shannon Atlantic Fisheries Ltd.)* v. *McPolin* [1976] I.R. 93.
[74] [1892] 1 Q.B. 431, 451.
[75] Per Lord Atkin, *O'Connor* v. *Waldron* [1935] A.C. 76, 81.
[76] [1979] 1 W.L.R. 377.
[77] [1983] I.R.L.R. 320.

presented by the first defendant to a joint committee of the Newspaper Publishers' Association and the Institute of Journalists set up under agreed conciliation procedures, was not protected by absolute privilege but only by qualified privilege. The object of the joint committee was to arrive at something other than a judicial determination and it did not proceed in a manner similar to a court of justice. What was decisive, however, was that this was a "mere conciliation proceeding" and not a process recognised by law.

The authors believe that this is sufficient to distinguish this case. The Labour Court is recognised by law. The Court is empowered to summon witnesses before it, to examine witnesses on oath and require any such witnesses to produce documents. The investigation can be held in public and witnesses can be cross-examined. The relative informality of procedure does not outweigh those factors, and the authors would submit that the general principle expressed by Lopes L.J. should be extended to Labour Court investigations but not to conciliation proceedings with an Industrial Relations Officer.

Rights Commissioners

The office of Rights Commissioner was created by the Industrial Relations Act 1969.[78] At present, there are four commissioners[79] whose function, in this context, is to investigate a trade dispute provided that:

(a) a party to the dispute does not object in writing to such an investigation;

(b) it is not a dispute connected with rates of pay, hours or times of work, or annual holidays of a *body of workers*;

(c) it is not a dispute involving persons who do not have access to the Labour Court;

(d) the Labour Court has not already made a recommendation about the same dispute.

A Rights Commissioner's investigation is conducted in private[80] and he determines his own procedures.[81] Parties to a dispute may not be represented at an investigation by counsel or solicitor unless the Rights Commissioner gives them permission beforehand to be so represented.

---

[78] S. 13.
[79] S. 13(4) provides that a Rights Commissioner shall hold office for such period as the Minister for Labour may determine and shall be paid such fees and expenses as the Minister for Labour, with the consent of the Minister for Finance, may determine from time to time and shall hold office upon and subject to such other terms and conditions as the Minister for Labour may determine from time to time. S. 13(5) provides that a Rights Commissioner may only be removed from office by the Minister for Labour for stated reasons and that neither the Civil Service Commissioners Act 1956 nor the Civil Service Regulation Acts 1956 and 1958 shall apply to the office of Rights Commissioner.
[80] S. 13(8).
[81] S. 13(6).

When a Rights Commissioner has investigated a dispute, he must issue a recommendation to the parties setting forth his opinion on the merits of the dispute unless, of course, the dispute has been settled in the meantime.

Where a Rights Commissioner has made a recommendation a party to the dispute may appeal to the Labour Court against the recommendation.[83] The parties will be bound by the decision of the Labour Court on appeal.[84] In 1983 the Rights Commissioners issued 583 recommendations and in 100 of these cases there were appeals to the Labour Court. McCarthy has described the Rights Commissioners as being "essentially industrial ombudsmen, not dealing with bargaining matters but with rights, although in practice the service is largely based on good sense and fair play, is very informal and has little legalism associated with it."[85]

Joint Industrial Councils

Joint Industrial Councils owe their development to the Whitley Committee[86] which recommended in 1917 "the establishment for each industry of an organisation representative of employers and workmen to have as its object the regular consideration of matters affecting the progress and well being of the trade from the point of view of all those engaged in it." Such bodies would be most beneficial in industries where there are a large number of employees and trade unions. Although these bodies are the voluntary creations of industry the 1946 Act does provide for their formal recognition and the Labour Court is empowered to assist in their establishment.[87] All the Court can do, however, is offer its assistance in any case in which it may be desired.

Provided the body fulfils certain conditions, it may apply to the Court for registration as a Joint Industrial Council and the Court, if satisfied, will place it on the register of registered councils. The conditions are as follows:

(1) it must be substantially representative of workers of a particular class, type or group and their employers;

---

[82] S. 13(3)(a)(ii) also requires the Rights Commissioner to notify the Labour Court of the recommendation.
[83] S. 13(9)(a).
[84] Ibid., although the Act provides no sanction if one of the parties does not adhere to the Labour Court's decision. This issue has yet to arise in practice since on the very few occasions in the past where the Court has heard that a party has not accepted a decision it has brought informal pressure to bear.
[85] Decade of Upheaval (Dublin, 1973), p. 31.
[86] See the Interim Report on Joint Standing Industrial Councils by the Sub-Committee on Relations between Employers and Employed of the Committee on Reconstruction (1917) Cd. 8606 and the Second Report on Joint Standing Industrial Councils by the Committee of the Ministry of Reconstruction on Relations between Employers and Employed (1918) Cd. 9002.
[87] See Part V of the 1946 Act. S. 64 provides that the Court, at the request of the J.I.C., may appoint the chairman and secretary of the J.I.C.

(2) its object must be the promotion of harmonious relations between such employers and such workers;
(3) its rules must provide that if a trade dispute arises between such workers and their employers a lock out or strike will not be undertaken in support of the dispute until the dispute has been referred to the body and considered by it.

At present, there are only three councils on the register, these being the Joint Board of Conciliation and Arbitration for the Footwear Industry, the Joint Industrial Council for the Dublin Wholesale Fruit and Vegetable Trade and the Joint Industrial Council for the Construction Industry. Unfortunately, the J.I.C. for the Construction Industry has been suspended since July 1982 due to unresolved differences between the employers and union representatives and that for the Footwear Industry since October 1983 for similar reasons. Mortished's prediction in 1949 that the registration of J.I.C.s would prove "eventually to have laid down the most useful line of future development"[88] in Irish industrial relations does not appear to have come true.

In addition to the three registered councils, there are 13 other J.I.C.s which have not applied for registration. They exist in respect of the following industries: Bacon Curing, Bakery and Confectionery Trades, Banks, Cleaning and Dyeing, Electrical Contracting, Flour Milling, Grocery Provision and Allied Trades, Hosiery and Knitted Garments Manufacture, Laundries (Dublin), Nursing Staff (District Mental Hospitals), Printing and Allied Trades (Dublin), State Industrial Employees, Woollen and Manufacture. Some 120,000 workers are represented on the 16 councils. There is also the E.S.B. Industrial Council which was set up in 1969.

Registration only confers marginal advantages and accommodation and secretarial facilities are made available by the Court, at the request of the parties, to registered and unregistered councils alike. Industrial Relations Officers act as chairmen of the three registered councils and eleven of the unregistered councils, the exceptions being Banks and Nursing Staff (District Mental Hospitals).

Public sector conciliation and arbitration schemes[89]

Public service and local authority employees were deliberately excluded from the Industrial Relations Act 1946, and although non-officers of local authorities and health boards were included in 1955 and industrial employees in the public service in 1969, negotiations on pay and conditions for most workers in the public service are concluded under agreed schemes of conciliation and arbitration. There

---

[88] In "The Industrial Relations Act 1946 – An outline" in King ed., *Public Administration in Ireland* Vol. 2 (Dublin, 1949), p. 89.
[89] See McGinley, "Pay Negotiation in the Public Service" (1976) 24 *Administration* 76.

are, in fact, nine separate schemes, the express purpose of which are "to provide means acceptable both to the State and to its employees for dealing with claims and proposals relating to the conditions of service." The schemes cover civil servants, teachers, gardaí, local authorities and health board officers, Vocational Education Committee staffs (two schemes), professional staffs of county committees of agriculture, postmasters and branch managers of unemployment exchanges. They number in total about 130,000. These schemes are not statutory schemes in the sense that they have been confirmed by statute or have in some way the force of a statute. According to Kenny J. in *McMahon* v. *Minister for Finance*,[90] they are merely contracts, an analysis accepted by Murphy J. in *Inspector of Taxes' Association* v. *Minister for the Public Service*.[91]

The first of these schemes covered the civil service. Negotiations were concluded in 1949 and the scheme came into operation on April 8, 1950 on a trial basis. Following a further trial period and agreement on some amendments, a permanent scheme was introduced on April 1, 1955. In its present form it represents a version revised as of March 31, 1976 with some incidental additions and alterations made subsequent to that date. The other schemes came into operation in the mid-1950s and early 1960s.

The schemes have two essential features. First, agreed procedures for discussion of claims between representatives of staff and management – the conciliation level – and arrangements for arbitration on major issues, including pay, if agreement is not reached at conciliation. In most schemes Industrial Relations Officers of the Labour Court act as mediators on the conciliation councils. The civil service conciliation scheme is divided between a General Council for matters of service wide concern and Departmental Councils for matters of local interest. The former consists of a Chairman, nominated by the Minister for the Public Service, with not more than five other official representatives as well as a principal staff representative and not more than three other staff representatives. These Councils discuss principles governing recruitment to, and promotion of members of, departmental classes; claims for grading of posts; and claims relating to departmental classes only, in relation to pay and allowances, overtime rates and subsistence, travelling, lodging and disturbance allowances. Other matters may be discussed by agreement of both sides.

As well as creating Conciliation Councils, the schemes also establish Arbitration Boards, comprised of a Chairman appointed by the Government in agreement with the staff side of the Conciliation Council, two representatives of the official side nominated by the Minister for the Public Service and two representatives of the staff side. In addition, either side can request the addition of two members of the

[90] High Court, unreported, 1962.
[91] High Court, unreported, 24 March 1983.

Labour Court for particular claims. The Chairman of the Arbitration Board is usually an eminent senior counsel.

Claims coming for arbitration must have been discussed at conciliation and have been disagreed but agreed claims are also capable of being arbitrated where the recommendation was not accepted by the Minister for the Public Service. The schemes do not expressly provide that the Arbitration Board's decision is conclusive. Normally it is, but the schemes do provide that the Government on receiving the decision can refer the matter to the Oireachtas with a recommendation that the award be varied or rejected.

Chapter 13

STRIKERS AND SOCIAL WELFARE

The Irish social welfare system can be broadly divided into two component parts – social insurance and social assistance. The basic principle of the former is that benefit is payable to those persons[1] who have an adequate contribution record on the occurrence of certain specified events[2] which affect their ability to sustain themselves. The basic principle of the latter is to provide assistance to persons who are without resources to meet basic living requirements or whose resources must be supplemented in order to meet such requirements. It follows that social assistance is means-tested, whereas social insurance is not.

Both of these component parts of the social welfare system are further sub-divided into smaller schemes, each of which is designed to deal with particular categories of claimant. In the present context, we need only concern ourselves with four of these individual schemes –

(i) unemployment benefit, which is payable to those unemployed individuals who have made a specified minimum contribution to the social insurance fund;

(ii) unemployment assistance, which is payable to those unemployed individuals who are not eligible for unemployment benefit;

(iii) supplementary welfare allowance, which is a residual social assistance allowance, payable to anyone whose income is insufficient to meet his or her needs or the needs of his or her dependants;

(iv) family income supplement, which is a means-tested payment designed to help families whose total earned income falls below specified limits.

The significant feature of these four schemes is that unemployment resulting directly from a trade dispute in which the claimant is "involved" disentitles him or her to benefit or assistance.[3]

The question of availability of benefit or assistance to strikers and their families is clearly a delicate one but the rationale behind the present position is not as obvious as may appear. First, this is said to be an instance of voluntary unemployment and, as such, does not come within the net of unemployment for which these schemes have been

---

[1] The vast majority of employees are required to be covered by social insurance and in addition limited provision exists for the self-employed to become contributors.
[2] Principally unemployment, sickness, retirement and old age and bereavement. For the full list of benefits, see Social Welfare (Consolidation) Act 1981, s. 17.
[3] See Social Welfare (Consolidation) Act 1981, ss. 35 (1), 142 (3), 203 (1) and Social Welfare (Family Income Supplement) Regulations 1984, art. 20 (1).

established. As Ogus and Barendt have observed,[4] this is not a complete justification because it would compel the law to distinguish between strikes and lockouts and this, as we shall see, it does not do. Moreover the disqualification extends beyond the strikers themselves and covers certain other persons who have been laid off as a result of the dispute.

Secondly, this is said to be an expression of a policy of neutrality in trade disputes. The State should not be involved in the financing of strikes, since a strike is economically wasteful. To allow strikers access to the social welfare system would be to influence directly the outcome of disputes. It would reduce the financial cost of striking and would result in strikes becoming longer. As Gennard has pointed out,[5] this is a strange kind of neutrality since the State is "obviously not a neutral element in strikes." A decision to deny even restricted access to the social welfare system for strikers in itself influences the outcome or even discourages the occurrence of strikes.

In this jurisdiction the principle of disqualifying strikers has been seriously modified by the Social Welfare (No. 2) Act 1982, which allows the payment of unemployment benefit or unemployment assistance to strikers whenever the Social Welfare Tribunal, established under the Act, considers it reasonable, having regard to all the circumstances of the case, so to do. It is to be noted that the 1982 Act does not extend to cases where supplementary welfare allowance or family income supplement is sought. This is difficult to justify in principle.

The general rule

Section 35 (1) of the Social Welfare (Consolidation) Act 1981 provides that:

"A person who has lost employment by reason of a stoppage of work which was due to a trade dispute at the factory, workshop, farm or other premises or place at which he was employed shall be disqualified for receiving unemployment benefit so long as the stoppage of work continues, except in a case where he has, during the stoppage of work, become *bona fide* employed elsewhere in the occupation which he usually follows or has become regularly engaged in some other occupation."

Section 203 (1) of the 1981 Act, which deals with supplementary welfare allowance provides that:

"In any case where, by reason of a stoppage of work due to a trade dispute at his place of employment, a person is without employment

---

[4] *The Law of Social Security* 2nd ed. (London, 1982), p. 119.
[5] *Financing Strikers* (London, 1977), p. 12.

for any period during which the stoppage continues, and such person has not, during that stoppage, become *bona fide* employed elsewhere in the occupation which he usually follows, or has not become regularly engaged in some other occupation, his needs for that period shall be disregarded for the purpose of ascertaining his entitlement to supplementary welfare allowance except insofar as such needs include the need to provide for his adult or child dependents."

and "place of employment" is defined in section 203 (3) as meaning "the factory, workshop, farm or other premises or place at which the person was employed." Similarly, article 20 (1) of the Social Welfare (Family Income Supplement) Regulations 1984[6] provides that family income supplement is not payable to a person who has lost employment by reason of a stoppage of work which was due to a trade dispute at the factory, workshop, farm or place at which he or she was employed.

Section 142 (3) of the 1981 Act provides a similar disqualification as regards the receipt of unemployment assistance. It should be noted, however, that there is a slight but significant difference in the wording. Section 142 (3) refers to a person who has lost employment by reason of a stoppage of work which was due to a trade dispute at "the factory, workshop or other premises" at which he was employed. The words "farm" and "place", present in the other provisions, have been omitted from section 142 (3). This leads to the conclusion that farm workers who lose employment by reason of a stoppage of work at the farm at which they were employed are not disqualified from receiving unemployment assistance.[7]

In relation to the above disqualifications, the onus is on the deciding officer of the Department of Social Welfare[8] to prove that (i) there was a trade dispute; (ii) it was at the claimant's place of employment; (iii) it resulted in a stoppage; and (iv) the claimant lost employment as a result of that stoppage. Trade dispute is defined in section 35 (6) of the 1981 Act as "any dispute between employers and employees, or between employees and employees, which is connected with the employment or non-employment or the terms of employment or the conditions of employment of any persons whether employees in

---

[6] S.I. No. 278 of 1984. Note that article 20 of the Regulations together with the Schedule thereto, provides for the application, *mutatis mutandis*, of s. 35 of the Social Welfare (Consolidation) Act 1981 to Family Income Supplement.

[7] Unless it is possible to construe the phrase "other premises" as including "farm" which in the light of its specific inclusion in ss. 35 (1) and 203 of the 1981 Act, would appear to fly in the face of the traditional principles of statutory interpretation.

[8] In the case of applications for supplementary welfare allowance, claims are heard by Community Welfare Officers of the various Regional Health Boards – Social Welfare (Consolidation) Act 1981, s. 204.

the employment of the employer with whom the dispute arises or not."[9]

The general rule, therefore, does not require that the claimant himself be actually involved in the dispute. It is sufficient that the dispute is at the claimant's place of employment, although it should be noted that sections 35 (2), 142 (4) and 203 (3) of the 1981 Act provide that where separate branches of work which are commonly carried on as separate businesses in separate premises are in any case carried on in separate departments of the same premises, each of those departments shall be deemed to be a separate factory, workshop, *etc.*[10]

While the onus of proving that the trade dispute was at the claimant's place of employment is on the deciding officer, the onus of proving that they constitute a separate business is on the claimant. As Ogus and Barendt observe,[11] this is a formidable hurdle because the claimant must show that (i) there are separate branches of work at his place of employment; (ii) typically elsewhere such branches are carried on as "separate businesses in separate premises or at a separate place"; and (iii) at his place of employment the branches are carried on in separate departments.

The claimant must have lost employment "by reason of a stoppage of work due to a trade dispute" for the disqualification to apply. This clearly covers the case where the stoppage of work occurs because of a strike but it also extends to cases where the claimant has been laid off or dismissed as a result of a trade dispute. This will be so even where the dispute is over but the lay off or dismissals are necessitated by a fall off in production caused by that dispute.[12] Nor is it necessary that any industrial action be taken or threatened. This is vividly illustrated by the facts of *State (Kearns)* v. *Minister for Social Welfare*.[13] A company plant had two separate factories, one processing beef and the other processing pigmeat. The company decided to close the beef factory and lay off the workers employed there. The union claimed that selection for lay off should depend on seniority regardless of which factory the employee worked in. The company refused to accept this and subsequently all the company's employees were dismissed. They were refused unemployment benefit because, in the view of the deciding and appeals officers, there was a trade dispute that had led to the stoppage

---

[9] This definition also applies to the unemployment assistance disqualification (Social Welfare (Amendment) Act 1981, s. 17) the supplementary welfare allowance disqualification (Social Welfare (Consolidation) Act 1981, s. 203 (3)) and the family income supplement disqualification (Social Welfare (Family Income Supplement) Regulations 1984, art. 20 and the Schedule thereto).

[10] Though note that ss. 35 (2) and 203 (3) are slightly more expansive on this than s. 142 (4), referring as they do to separate branches of work which are commonly carried on as separate businesses in separate premises "or at separate places".

[11] *Op. cit.* at p. 122.

[12] See *Sheridan* v. *Heritage Knitwear Ltd.* A6/1984.

[13] High Court, unreported, 10 February 1982; see *Irish Times*, February 11, 1982.

of work even though no industrial action was taken or threatened. In the High Court, McMahon J. refused to grant an order of *mandamus* directing the Minister to pay unemployment benefit.[14] In his view the dismissal of the employees was the result of a failure by the union to agree on a formula to decide who would be retained in the pigmeat processing factory. This failure to agree was a "trade dispute" as defined and this dispute led to the stoppage of work.

The disqualification, it should be noted, does not apply to a person, unemployed because of a trade dispute, who genuinely takes work elsewhere but becomes unemployed from that job while the dispute continues.

In summary therefore, the general rule is that a person who becomes unemployed by reason of a trade dispute will not be disqualified for receiving benefit unless the dispute occurs at his place of employment. If it occurs elsewhere it will not matter that he loses his employment in consequence. Moreover, if a person becomes unemployed by reason of a strike by other employees at his place of work, he will not be disqualified if his work, and the strikers' work, is normally carried out in separate premises.

The proviso
Even if the stoppage of work is due to a trade dispute at his place of employment, a person who loses work in consequence may still qualify for unemployment benefit, unemployment assistance, supplementary welfare allowance or family income supplement, if he proves that –

(a) he is neither participating in, financing nor directly interested in the dispute; and
(b) there are no members of the grade or class to which he belongs at the premises where the stoppage of work occurs who are participating in, financing or directly interested in the dispute.[15]

The principle underlying this "grade or class" provision has been stated as follows:

"The grade or class provision considers the position of workers in relation to a particular trade dispute, not according to whether they are personally involved in the dispute in the sense that they are individually participating in, financing or directly interested in the dispute, but according to whether they belong to a group of workers containing workers who are personally involved. It assumes that a group of workers doing much the same kind of work in the same

---

[14] The government subsequently agreed to pay all the company's workforce their respective social welfare "entitlements" from the date of dismissal until the resumption of work some ten weeks later. These payments were in fact made by the Department of Agriculture and did not come out of the Social Insurance Fund. See *Irish Times*, March 20, 1982.
[15] See ss. 35 (1), 142 (3) (b), 203 (2) of the 1981 Act.

place and under the same conditions and circumstances have a corporate identity and a special relationship one with another – a 'community of interest' – quite apart from their position in relation to any particular trade dispute. The argument runs that just as members of a particular grade or class are treated alike in so many other aspects of their working life in the factory so they should also be treated alike for purposes of the trade dispute disqualification. Thus if any member of the grade or class is personally involved in the dispute as participating, financing, or directly interested in it, all the other members of the grade or class are deemed to be involved by virtue of their corporate identity as members of the same grade or class, and cannot therefore escape disqualification. In some cases, a high proportion of the grade or class will be personally involved. In others this proportion will be small. The principle of treating the whole grade or class alike however applies irrespective of the proportion of members personally involved."[16]

The law, in other words, is based on the assumption that this 'community of interest' between a group of workers identified as a grade or class is a reality of sufficient importance to justify treating them all alike in the matter of entitlement to unemployment benefit where work is lost as a result of a trade dispute. The authors doubt whether this assumption is valid and concur in the conclusion of the Royal Commission on Trade Unions and Employers' Associations 1965-1968:[17]

"In our view the reasoning said to underlie the grade or class provision is fallacious. In order to ascertain whether a class of persons has a common interest simply because it is a class one needs to know what common attribute it is which marks such persons off as a class. This the law makes no attempt to do. It simply assumes, apparently, that if a group of workers in the same place of employment can by some means be identified as a 'class' or 'grade' then automatically they possess a common interest as such: and no investigation is required to disqualify them from receiving unemployment benefit beyond discovering whether there is at least one of the class participating in the trade dispute, or financing it, or directly interested in it. This seems to us not so much the recognition of an interest as the invention of it. The capricious results which the provision can and does produce are themselves some indication of the invalidity of the assumption which underlies it. If for example the process workers at a particular works go on strike on an issue

---

[16] Evidence of Ministry of Social Security to the Royal Commission on Trade Unions and Employers' Associations. See Minutes of Evidence 54, Ministry of Social Security, Seventh Memorandum, pp. 2334-5, reproduced in the Royal Commission's Report, Cmnd. 3623, paras. 975-976.
[17] Cmnd. 3623, paras. 975-976.

which concerns them alone and one member out of a total of 100 maintenance workers strikes in sympathy, the remaining 99 if laid off will all be disqualified from receiving unemployment benefit, though they have no interest in the strike and indeed are hostile to it.

Moreover the grade or class provision will operate if only one member of the grade or class is 'financing' the trade dispute. A member of a trade union which is paying the strikers their strike benefit is normally regarded as "financing" the dispute. Thus if 'A' were a storeman in a works comprising different departments and a dispute occurred in the foundry shop which led to a stoppage of work, during which the union concerned paid strike benefit, 'A' would be disqualified for receiving unemployment benefit if he happened to belong to the same union. So also would all the other storemen, although they might belong to a different union or unions."

The terms "grade" and "class" are not defined in the Act but they are well known industrial terms, determined by reference to some aspect of the work performed.[18]

Participating

Ogus and Barendt say that this term "connotes the idea of knowingly doing something or refraining from doing something which contributes to the continuance of the dispute."[19]

Financing

This has been consistently held to include membership of a trade union which is financially supporting those involved in the dispute, such as by paying strike pay.[20] It is immaterial whether the claimant is continuing, while unemployed, to pay his membership contributions. The act of the union in paying strike pay, and thus financing the dispute, is considered to be the act of each and every one of its members. As a member of an unincorporated association of individuals bound by a common contract providing financial support for fellow members on strike, all are regarded as involved in the act, individually as well as collectively. It would seem, by the use of the present tense, that if the claimant resigns from the trade union during the trade dispute, the fact that the funds from which strike pay is paid are funds to which the claimant has contributed in the past is irrelevant, and he would come within the proviso.[21]

There is some cause for concern that the financing provision could give a marginal advantage to unofficial action. Claimants may be

---

[18] *Ibid.*, para. 977.
[19] *Op. cit.*, at p. 126. See also Calvert, *Social Security Law* (London, 1974), pp. 138-139.
[20] See Calvert, *op. cit.*, at pp. 139-143.
[21] Report of the Royal Commission on Trade Unions and Employers' Associations 1965-1968, para. 988.

refused benefit if a strike by their fellow members is made official and strike pay paid. If the strike is unofficial, and no strike pay paid, they may be granted benefit.[22]

Directly interested

The use of the word "directly" suggests that, if the claimant is only "indirectly" interested in the dispute, such as where his terms or conditions of employment are not immediately in issue, then he will not be disqualified. Obviously, where the dispute concerns the claimant's terms and conditions of employment, the claimant is "directly interested". But what if the dispute concerns the terms and conditions of another grade or class of employees? Will the claimant be disqualified merely because the settlement of the dispute may lead to a relativity claim by the claimant's grade or class? This issue has been considered by the judiciary in Britain. In *Watt* v. *Lord Advocate*,[23] the Court of Session emphasised the need for a close relationship between those involved in the dispute and those who stand to be affected by it. If the outcome of the dispute was likely to have consequences "virtually immediate and automatic" for the claimant, then he was "directly interested".

But what if some act or event is interposed between the outcome of the dispute and the occurrence of a change in the claimant's terms and conditions, such as further negotiations between the employer and the claimant's group? This matter was considered in *Presho* v. *Department of Health and Social Security*.[24] The claimant was a production worker and a member of U.S.D.A.W. Also employed at her place of employment were members of A.U.E.W. This latter union put in a claim which, if conceded, would have represented a financial improvement for their members. The company did not concede the claim, a stoppage of work occurred and the production workers were temporarily laid off. The claimant applied for unemployment benefit and was refused. The insurance officer took the view that she was disqualified from receiving such benefit because she was "directly interested" in the dispute. She appealed to the social security commissioner who dismissed her appeal. The commissioner was of the opinion that, although her union had not even made a similar claim, it was "incontrovertible" that, if the claim by the A.U.E.W. were conceded, it would "automatically" be applied to U.S.D.A.W. members as well. The Court of Appeal disagreed, Kerr L.J. saying:

---

[22] *Ibid.*, para. 989. This was one of the reasons given by the Royal Commission for recommending that the "financing" provision be repealed. This proposal was ultimately implemented by s. 111 (1) of the Employment Protection Act 1975.
[23] 1979 S.L.T. 137.
[24] [1984] A.C. 310, noted by Troup (1985) 14 *I.L.J.* 112. See also *Punton* v. *Ministry of Pensions and National Insurance (No. 2)* [1964] 1 W.L.R. 226.

"The proper meaning of 'directly', I think . . . is that the circumstances are such that the probable outcome of the dispute will automatically affect the claimant by virtue of some pre-existing agreement whether legally binding or not. . . . To put the converse, I think that a claimant is not 'directly' interested in the dispute if its outcome, in relation to those who have stopped work, will only affect the claimant after and as the result of further separate and distinct negotiations, even if these are likely to lead to a similar or even to a substantially identical outcome, and whatever the eventual outcome may turn out to be."[25]

The insurance officer appealed to the House of Lords who unanimously allowed the appeal and restored the decision of the commissioner. The House of Lords, in a speech delivered by Lord Brandon, held that:

"where different groups of workers, belonging to different unions, are employed by the same employers at the same place of work, and there is a trade dispute between the common employers and one of the unions to which one of the groups of workers belong, those in the other groups of workers belonging to other unions are directly, and not merely indirectly, interested in that trade dispute provided that two conditions are fulfilled. The first condition is that, whatever may be the outcome of the trade dispute, it will be applied by the common employers not only to the group of workers belonging to the one union participating in the dispute, but also to the other groups of workers belonging to the other unions concerned. The second condition is that this application of the outcome of the dispute 'across the board', as it has been aptly described, should come about automatically as a result of one or other of three things: first, a collective agreement which is legally binding; or, secondly, a collective agreement which is not legally binding; or, thirdly, established industrial custom and practice at the place of work concerned."[26]

The House of Lords were emphatic that a person could be directly interested in a dispute, even though his own pay and conditions of work did not form the subject matter of the dispute. They could not accept the drawing of a distinction between a person ebing "interested in a trade dispute" and his being "interested in the outcome of a trade dispute." These two concepts, to Lord Brandon, amounted to "very much the same thing." Later on in his speech he comments that to accept such a distinction would leave the way "wide open for deliberate and calculated evasions" of the basic provision.[27]

---

[25] [1983] I.C.R. 595, 607.
[26] [1984] A.C. 310, 318.
[27] Ibid., at 319.

Deciding officers in this jurisdiction appear to take a similar view on the meaning of the phrase "directly interested". When the *Irish Press* laid off over 700 workers because of a strike by journalists, the workers were refused benefit or assistance by a deciding officer on the ground that part of the journalists' dispute was over the non-payment of the 1982 wage round and it seemed certain that any concession made to the strikers on this point would have to be extended to other *Irish Press* employees.[28]

Strikers' families

Although persons may be disqualified from receiving unemployment benefit or assistance because, for instance, they are participating in a strike, they may claim supplementary welfare allowance in respect of the needs of their dependants. Section 203 (1) of the Social Welfare (Consolidation) Act 1981 provides that if a person is unemployed by reason of a stoppage of work at that person's place of employment and he does not come within the terms of the proviso "his needs for that period shall be disregarded for the purpose of ascertaining his entitlement to supplementary welfare allowance except insofar as such needs include the need to provide for his adult and child dependants."

The general principle with regard to strikers' families is that they have a right to receive assistance because they are the dependants of an unemployed person who has insufficient income to support them. With regard to strikers themselves, or those financing or directly interested in the dispute, they can only claim assistance in cases of "severe immediate hardship" and even then any assistance given is discretionary.[29] Guidelines drawn up for the Health Boards by the Department of Social Welfare state that "urgent need" payments to strikers can be made –

> "in a disaster situation, *e.g.* fire or flood... Again in a prolonged strike situation a person may have used up any reserves of capital in meeting ordinary everyday needs and thus, if essential items of say, clothing or bedding require to be replaced, a payment of supplementary welfare allowance might be appropriate to meet such needs."[30]

The criteria to be applied are also identified in these Guidelines. In deciding whether a striker is in "urgent need", full account is to be taken of his particular circumstances. All resources, including, for a single person, assistance from parents and other relatives, and all income received or which could have been received since the beginning of the strike, such as supplementary welfare allowances paid to

---

[28] *Irish Times*, July 26, 1983. *Cp.* the subsequent dispute between the *Irish Press* and the Irish Print Union over the introduction of new technology, where all the *Irish Press* staff were laid off but only members of the I.P.U. were refused benefit or assistance. See *Irish Times*, May 29, 1985.
[29] See s. 213 (1) of the 1981 Act.
[30] *Guidelines for Health Boards on the Operation and Administration of the Supplementary Welfare Allowance Scheme* (1977), pp. 25-36.

dependants, strike pay and income tax refunds, must be taken into account along with the length of time the stoppage has continued and how long it is likely to last.

With regard to receipt of family income supplement,[31] the position is less clear. Certainly strikers themselves, and other persons caught by the provisions of section 35(1), are disqualified from receiving family income supplement. It is arguable, however, that the spouse of such a person could still apply provided he or she is engaged in remunerative full-time employment and the weekly family income falls short of the prescribed amount.[32] Weekly family income is calculated, insofar as it comprises earnings from employment by an employee, by reference to the weekly average of the gross amount of such earnings received in the period of two months immediately prior to the date on which the claim for family income supplement had been made, where such earnings are received at monthly intervals, or in the period of six weeks immediately prior to such date where such earnings are received at weekly or fortnightly intervals.[33] Thus, at any time up to six weeks or two months into the trade dispute, depending on the periodicity of wages, his normal earnings will be taken into account in computing family income, and in many cases this will effectively exclude the family from the scope of the family income supplement scheme. Thereafter it is at the discretion of the deciding officer or the appeals officer, as the case may be, as to whether regard will be had, in computing weekly family income, to the employee's normal pay as opposed to any strike pay he may be receiving from the union.

Social Welfare Tribunal[35]

Following the decision in *State (Kearns)* v. *Minister for Social Welfare*,[36] the law was amended to modify the effect of the trade disputes disqualification in relation to unemployment benefit and assistance. The Social Welfare (No. 2) Act 1982[37] created a new tribunal – the Social Welfare Tribunal (S.W.T.) – which is empowered to award unemployment benefit or assistance to persons refused same by a deciding officer and an appeals officer because of the trade dispute disqualification.

---

[31] The Government has announced its intention to replace, *inter alia*, family income supplement with a new Child Benefit Scheme – see *Building On Reality 1985–1987* (Pl. 2648), para. 5.58.

[32] Currently £100 in the case of a family with only one child, or in the case of a family with more than one child, £100 increased by £18 for each additional child up to and including the fifth child – Social Welfare (Consolidation) Act 1981, s.232B (as inserted by Social Welfare Act 1984, s. 13) as amended by Social Welfare Act 1985, s. 4.

[33] Art. 3(1) (a) of S.I. No. 278 of 1984.

[34] *Ibid.*, art. 3(2).

[35] See, generally, Clark, "Towards the 'Just' Strike" (1985) 48 *M.L.R.* forthcoming. For an explanation of the mode of citation see note to Table of S.W.T. adjudications.

[36] High Court, unreported, 10 February 1982. See *supra*, pp. 364–365.

[37] The Act passed all stages in the Dáil on July 15, 1982 and all stages in the Seanad on July 22, 1982. It was signed by the President on July 31 and came into effect on October 5, 1982. See 337 *Dáil Debates* cc. 2611–2642, 2883–2919, 2920–2929; 98 *Seanad Debates* cc. 1390–1411.

Section 1 of the Act inserts section 301A into the 1981 Act, and section 301A (1) provides:

> "Where, in relation to a stoppage of work, or a trade dispute, which was or is in existence on or after the 1st day of June, 1982,[38] a deciding officer and appeals officer have decided that a person is disqualified under section 35 (1) for receiving unemployment benefit or under section 142 (3) for receiving unemployment assistance, that person may, notwithstanding any other provision of this Act, apply to the Social Welfare Tribunal (in this section and in section 301B referred to as 'the Tribunal') for an adjudication under this section."

The S.W.T. has a limited and well defined function. It is in no way concerned with the correctness or reasonableness of the original decision to exclude a claimant under sections 35 (1) or 142 (3) of the 1981 Act.[39]

The only issue which the S.W.T. is to consider is whether, notwithstanding the decision to disqualify, the claimant was "unreasonably deprived of his employment." If the S.W.T. so determines, then the claimant will be entitled to receive unemployment benefit or assistance, notwithstanding that he is participating, financing or directly interested in the dispute. The S.W.T., it should be noted, is only concerned with claimants for unemployment benefit or assistance. Its jurisdiction does not extend to cases concerning denial of supplementary welfare allowances or family income supplement. The S.W.T., in coming to its decision as to whether the claimant has been "unreasonably deprived of his employment," is directed[40] to take into account "all the circumstances of the stoppage of work concerned and of the trade dispute which caused the stoppage of work" and is required to take particular cognisance of four factors:

> "(i) the question whether the applicant is or was available for work and willing to work, but is or was deprived of his employment through some act or omission on the part of the employer concerned which amounted to unfair or unjust treatment of the applicant;

---

[38] *Quaere* whether the S.W.T. can declare that a person is entitled to benefit or assistance in respect of a period before June 1, 1982. In *Galvin* v. *North Western Cattle Breeding Society Ltd.* A1/1985, the period of disqualification involved was January 1, 1982 to June 7, 1982, although the parties appear to have remained in dispute after the latter date. In the event, the S.W.T. decided that the claimant had not been unreasonably deprived of his employment, but the inference is that if he had been, the S.W.T. would have declared him entitled to benefit or assistance.

[39] This was emphasised by the S.W.T. in *Comer* v. *Clery & Co. (1941) Ltd.* A5/1983 and *Galvin* v. *North Western Cattle Breeding Society Ltd.* A1/1985. In fact, all the S.W.T. receives is a certificate from the Department of Social Welfare confirming that a Deciding Officer and an Appeals Officer has declared the claimant ineligible. It does not see the actual decision.

[40] By s. 301A (2) (*a*).

(ii) the question whether the applicant is or was prevented by the employer from attending for work at his place of employment or was temporarily laid off by the employer, without (in either case) any reasonable or adequate consultation by the employer with the applicant or with a trade union acting on his behalf, or without (in either case) the use by the employer or by anybody acting on his behalf of the services normally availed of by employers in the interests of good industrial relations,
(iii) the question whether any action or decision by the employer, amounting to a worsening of the terms or conditions of employment of the applicant and taken without any or any adequate consultation with, or any adequate notice to, the applicant, was a cause of the stoppage of work or of the trade dispute which caused the stoppage of work and was material grounds for such stoppage or such trade dispute,
(iv) the question whether the conduct of the applicant or of a trade union acting on his behalf was reasonable."

Although factors (i) and (iv) would suggest that the S.W.T. may concern itself with the merits of a dispute, in practice the S.W.T. has focussed on procedural rather than substantive issues, concentrating on the circumstances leading to the actual stoppage of work. From an analysis of the adjudications issued so far, certain trends can be discerned, although the Chairman has stressed that the S.W.T. is not in the business of creating new principles but in applying "well established industrial relations principles."[41]

The S.W.T. has stressed in a number of cases that the onus of ensuring that all normal negotiating procedures are used rests on the party who seeks a change in the *status quo*,[42] so for a company to decline to agree to a union's proposal that the issue be referred to the Labour Court would not be in keeping with good industrial relations practices.[43] *Donohue* v. *Whessoe (Ireland) Ltd.*[44] is particularly instructive in this respect. The company had sought to introduce new work practices. Redundancies were agreed but the union wanted agreement on payment for the new practices before they were introduced. No agreement had been reached when the company implemented the changes and following a refusal to commence the new practices, 22 employees were laid off. The S.W.T., while accepting that

---

[41] In a talk to the Irish Society for Labour Law on May 9, 1985.
[42] See *Donohue* v. *Whessoe (Ireland) Ltd.* A2/1983; *Saunders* v. *Cahir Meat Packers Ltd.* A5/1984. If, however, a union over-reacts to management's proposals and short-circuits the normal industrial relations procedures, such as by calling industrial action without notice, it is likely that the S.W.T. will find that there has been no unreasonable deprivation of employment. See *D'Alton* v. *Longford Printing and Publishing Co. Ltd.* A1/1984; *Harris* v. *I.S. Varian & Co. Ltd.* A2/1984; *Coveney* v. *Blackwater Ltd.* A8/1984; *Dunphy* v. *Nacanco (Ireland) Ltd.* A2/1985.
[43] *Loughnane* v. *Roscrea Meat Products Ltd.* A4/1983; *Collins* v. *European Printing Corp. Ltd.* A10/1984.
[44] A2/1983.

the company needed to introduce the changes, noted that the dispute was not about whether these changes would be introduced. It was about the terms on which these changes would be introduced. The S.W.T. stressed that, since it was the employer who was seeking a change in the *status quo*, the onus rested on the company to ensure that all normal negotiating procedures were exhausted before laying off the workers and the S.W.T. said that it was "forced to the conclusion" that the lay offs were effected "without the use by the employer or by anybody acting on his behalf of the services normally availed of by employers in the interests of good industrial relations." Moreover undue delay in entering into negotiations could result in a finding of unreasonable behaviour.[45]

Similarly, whoever is responding to proposed changes is entitled to know precisely what is involved before being expected to agree.[46] Conversely, any party who proposes to take action to resolve a dispute must take reasonable steps to ascertain the true position.[47]

Where the issue between the parties has been referred to the Labour Court, the proposed changes should not be implemented by management until the Court's recommendation becomes available, unless postponement of the changes would seriously damage the company's business or its viability.[48] A difficult issue is whether the S.W.T. will pass judgment on the failure of a party to implement a Labour Court recommendation, particularly in the light of the fact that the only obligation mentioned in the statutory guidelines is to *avail* of the services of a body like the Labour Court. In *O'Neill* v. *Alfa Cavan Rubber Manufacturing Co. Ltd.*,[49] there was a dispute over the reinstatement of employees who had been made redundant in 1981. The matter had been referred to the Labour Court and the Court had recommended that the company was under no obligation to re-employ these workers. This recommendation was not accepted by the union and strike notice was issued and implemented. The S.W.T., while recognising that the union was free to reject the Court's findings, pointed out that if the union decided to take strike action in support of that claim, it must accept responsibility for the consequences of such decision and therefore the strikers were not "unreasonably deprived of their employment".

The S.W.T. has also taken the view that it would be unreasonable for the employer to make acceptance of new terms unconnected with the dispute a pre-condition to returning to work;[50] however, an employer

---

[45] *Cox* v. *Hanley Meats Group* A3/1985.
[46] *D'Alton* v. *Longford Printing and Publishing Co. Ltd.* A1/1984.
[47] *Ibid.*
[48] *Hannon* v. *Becton Dickinson & Co. Ltd.* A3/1984. See also *Brennan* v. *Comer International Ltd.* A1/1982.
[49] A3/1983.
[50] *Enright* v. *Trust House Forte (Ireland) Ltd.* A2/1983; *Collins* v. *European Printing Corp. Ltd.* A10/1984.

is under no obligation to resume business immediately upon resolution of the dispute where there is no work available as a result of the dispute.[51]

The adjudication which will probably have the most far reaching ramifications is *McNamara v. Nissan Datsun Ltd.*[52] Here the S.W.T. said that a person could not be said to have been reasonably deprived of his or her employment unless he or she –

(i) has abandoned the employment; or
(ii) was participating in a strike; or
(iii) was fairly dismissed on grounds of redundancy or for other reasons; or
(iv) was laid off for good and sufficient cause.

The S.W.T. consists of five persons: the Chairman,[53] appointed by the Minister for Social Welfare, and four others,[54] two nominated by the I.C.T.U. and two nominated by the F.U.E. The procedures governing applications and the powers of the S.W.T. are set out in the Social Welfare (Social Welfare Tribunal) Regulations 1982.[55] Applications must be made, on a form approved by the S.W.T., within 21 days after receipt of the appeals officer's decision disqualifying the applicant from unemployment benefit or assistance.[56] The application should contain a statement of the facts and the contention on which the claimant intends to rely.[57] A copy of the application must also be given to the employer, who, within fourteen days of receipt, must enter an appearance by sending to the S.W.T.'s secretary a statement indicating the extent to which the facts and contentions are admitted or disputed.[58] A right to representation is given to all persons summoned to the hearing, either through counsel, solicitor, trade union or employers' association representative, or, with the leave of the S.W.T., by any other person.[59]

The procedure during the course of the hearing is in marked contrast to social welfare appeals, where the procedure is at the discretion of the appeals officer.[60] Parties may make an opening statement, call witnesses, cross-examine and give evidence on their own behalf, and make a final address. The decision is recorded and a copy sent to the

---

[51] *Sheridan v. Heritage Knitwear Ltd.* A6/1984.
[52] A7/1984.
[53] W.J. Farrell, a former Rights Commissioner.
[54] At present T. McGrath and P. Murphy (I.C.T.U.) and J. Doherty and R. de Zaayer (F.U.E.).
[55] S.I. No. 309 of 1982.
[56] Art. 4. Late applications may be entertained however – art. 17. See *Kelly v. Becton Dickinson & Co. Ltd.* A8/1984 and *McGuigan v. Trust House Forte (Ireland) Ltd.* A9/1984.
[57] Art. 4.
[58] Art. 6(1). An extension may be granted, the Chairman deciding what period of time should be granted – art. 6(2).
[59] Art. 7. To date lawyers have only appeared in three cases.
[60] See Clark, "Social Welfare Insurance Appeals in the Republic of Ireland" (1978) 13 *Ir. Jur. (n.s.)* 265.

parties and any other interested person. As Clark puts it: "This is a great improvement on all other social welfare appeals where the decision is not recorded in detail, the applicant being entitled to notice of the decision and not a copy of the decision itself."[61] Decisions may be taken by a majority of the members,[62] but no dissenting views are expressed.[63] Appeals from the S.W.T.'s adjudications may be made to the High Court on a point of law only.[64] The S.W.T. itself is also given extensive powers for reviewing its own decisions.[65]

In virtually all the cases that have come before the S.W.T. to date, the dispute has been resolved and the claimants are back at work when the hearing takes place. In part this is due to the relative shortness of the period of disqualification – in some cases only four to five days – but it also reflects the difficulties encountered by the S.W.T. in convening a meeting at which the parties and all five members of the tribunal can be present. The fact that the dispute is over when the hearing takes place present. The fact that the dispute is over when the position since he may be tempted, out of a desire not to "re-open old wounds", not to dispute the submission that he acted unreasonably, and this in turn may make the S.W.T.'s task of adjudicating on the question of whether the claimants have been reasonably deprived of their employment that much more difficult.

---

[61] (1985) 48 *M.L.R.* forthcoming.
[62] Art. 12 (1).
[63] Although this is not laid down in the legislation.
[64] Social Welfare (Consolidation) Act 1981, s. 301A (2)(*c*), inserted by Social Welfare (No. 2) Act 1982, s. 1.
[65] Art. 19.

INDEX

AMALGAMATION *see also* TRANSFER OF ENGAGEMENTS
  ballot on, 73-74
  complaints procedure, 74-77, 110
    constitutionality of, 76
  conditions necessary for, 72-74
  foreign-based union, involving, 71-72, 80
  grants, in support of, 77
  instrument of, 72-73
    effect of registration, 79
  legislative history, 70
  negotiation licence, effect on, 53, 54, 57, 79
  political fund, position of, on, 78-79, 80
  powers of Registrar in relation to, 46, 47, 110
  property, position of, on, 77
  union rule book, modification of, on, 74, 108, 110
ARBITRATION
  Labour Court and, 351
  public sector, in, 358-360
ASSOCIATION, FREEDOM OF *see also* CLOSED SHOP
  international obligations, 2, 13-15
  qualifications on, 26-33
    legislative regulation, 27-29
    constitutional rights of others, 29-31
  right to form trade union, 4, 12-13
  right to join trade union, 4-5, 12-13
  right to participate in decision-making processes, 24-26
  right to take industrial action, 23-24
  statutory protection of, 33-37
  voluntary restrictions on, 102-103

BOYCOTT
  liability for, 260-261

CHECK OFF
  generally, 96-98
  Truck Acts and, 96-97
CLOSED SHOP
  admission to union, right of, 4, 6, 12-13
  internationsl restrictions on, 13-15
  legality of, generally, 7-12, 31
  meaning of, 7
  post-entry, legality of, 8-12
  pre-entry, legality of, 7-8
  trade dispute concerning, 7-12
COMMISSION OF INQUIRY ON INDUSTRIAL RELATIONS
  recommendations, 1, 2, 56, 77, 99, 146, 152, 158, 188, 191, 318-319, 351-352
COLLECTIVE AGREEMENT *see also* REGISTERED EMPLOYMENT AGREEMENT
  binding effect of, 153-165

  contract of employment, incorporation in, 159-165
  discriminatory provisions in, 143, 149
  enforceability of, 153-158
  interpretation of, 152-153
  nature of, 153-154
  non-union members, effect on, 162-164
  registration of, 146-153
  termination of, 163
COLLECTIVE BARGAINING
  agency of union, 139-140, 160-161
  consultation on health and safety, 181-183
  consultation on collective redundancies, 20, 167-179
  consultation on transfer of undertakings, 179-181
  disclosure of information, 201-203
  generally, 143-165
  legal rules and, 144
  legislative support for, 166-203
  minimum wage legislation and, 183-193
  National Wage Agreements, 146
  National Understanding, 146
  nature of, 144-146, 153-158
  positive encouragement of, 144
  recognition, 15-23
  State's role in relation to, 166
COLLECTIVE REDUNDANCIES
  consultation, exemption from, 170, 171-172
  consultation on, generally, 167-179
  consultation, meaning of, 172-178
  consultation, requirements for, 172-178
  employees' representatives, definition of, 172-173
  failure to consult or notify, criminal proceedings in respect of, 172, 175-179
  meaning of, 167-168, 169-172
  Minister's powers, in relation to, 178-179
  proposal to create, meaning of, 175
CONCILIATION
  industrial relations officers, 341-342
  machinery, legislative history of, 337-338
  public sector, in, 358-360
  trade disputes, in, 341-342
CONDITIONS OF EMPLOYMENT
  collective bargaining as source, 143
  registered employment agreement as source, 146, 151-152
  statutory regulation of, 12
CONSPIRACY *see also* TORT
  civil, 227-230
  criminal, 215-216
  immunity from, in trade dispute, 257-258
  unlawful means, infringement of constitutional rights as, 12

CONSTITUTION
  conditions of entitlement for negotiation licence, compatibility with, 54
  constitutional rights, balancing of, 29–31
  constitutional rights, forfeiture of, 32–33
  constitutional rights, vindication of, 10, 11–12
  constitutional rights, waiver of, 26, 31–32
  dissociate, right to, 7–15
  equality under, 102
  fair procedures, right to, 26, 111–112, 115–121
  form trade union, right to, 4–7, 12–13
  freedom of belief, 9, 90, 102
  industrial action, constitutional limitations on, 247–248
  industrial action, right to take, 23–24, 205, 246–247
  join trade union, right to, 4, 6 12–13, 24–26
  participate in decision-making process of trade union, right to, 24–26, 112
  picketing and, 284–285
  powers of Labour Court, constitutionality, 152–153
  powers of Registrar, constitutionality, 45–48
  recognition, right to, 15–20
  source of union rules, as, 111–112
CONTEMPT OF COURT *see also* INJUNCTIONS
  committal for, 334–336
  infringement of constitutional rights as, 30
  non-observance of injunctions, 334–336
  picketing as, 295
CONTRACT OF EMPLOYMENT
  breach of, criminal liability in respect of, 216–218
  suspension of, during strike, 207–210
CRIMINAL PROCEEDINGS
  collective redundancies, failure to consult or notify, for, 172, 175, 176–177, 178–179
  employment regulation order, failure to maintain records, for, 193
  employment regulation order, failure to observe, for, 191
  industrial action, in respect of, 214–233
  occupations, in respect of, 313–315
  picketing, in respect of, 289–295
  property of trade unions, concerning, 49, 89, 110–111
  register, failure to keep open, for, 59
  registered employment agreements, breach, for, 151–152
  returns, failure to make, for, 50, 60, 88, 111
  returns, false, for, 50, 88, 111
  trade union officials, against, 137–139
  transfer of undertakings, failure to consult, for, 181

DEFENCE FORCES
  freedom of association, restriction on, 29
  strikes, prohibition of, 219
DISMISSAL
  industrial action, for, 35–36, 210–213
  remedies for, adequacy of, 37
  trade dispute concerning, 269–270
  trade union activities, for, 35–37
  trade union membership, for, 34–35
  trade union officials, of, 140–142
DISCLOSURE OF INFORMATION
  collective redundancies, upon, 172–178
  E.E.C. proposals in relation to, 202–203
  generally, 201–203
  transfer of undertakings, upon, 179–180
DISCRIMINATION
  eligibility for union membership, 7, 101–102, 112
  eligibility for union office, 112–113
  industrial action to maintain, 218
  registered employment agreement, prohibition of, in relation to, 149
  regulating freedom of association, prohibition of, in relation to, 27, 28
  trade unionists, prohibition of, against, 166

EMPLOYMENT REGULATION ORDERS *see* JOINT LABOUR COMMITTEE
EMPLOYERS' ASSOCIATION
  recognition by, 161
  trade union as, 39
EUROPEAN CONVENTION ON HUMAN RIGHTS
  incorporation into domestic law, 3
  right to associate under, 13–14, 54
  right to dissociate under, 13–14
  right of recognition under, 18
EUROPEAN ECONOMIC COMMUNITY
  collective redundancies, Directive on, 167–169, 170, 171, 173, 177
  disclosure of information, Directive on, 202–203
  membership, effect of, 144
  migrant workers, equality of treatment, 100, 112–113
  source of union rules, as, 112–113
  transfer of undertakings, Directive on, 179–180
  worker participation, Directive on, 194–195
EUROPEAN SOCIAL CHARTER
  right to associate, regulation of, 53
  right to dissociate under, 14

FOSS v. HARBOTTLE
  rule in, 5, 67–69, 121–123

GARDA SÍOCHÁNA
  dissaffection among, causing, 219

obstruction of, 295–297
picketing, control by, 295–297
sit-ins, role in relation to, 312–315
union membership, restrictions on, 29

HEALTH AND SAFETY
consultation, generally, 181–183
safety committee, appointment of, 181–182
safety committee, functions of, 182–183
safety representative, appointment of, 181
safety representative, functions of, 182
trade unions, role in relation to, 182

INDUCEMENT OF BREACH OF CONTRACT *see* TORT
INDUSTRIAL ACTION *see also* STRIKE, PICKETING, TRADE DISPUTE
breach of contract, as, 206–210, 213
closed shop, over, 7–12
conspiracy, civil, as, 227–230
conspiracy, criminal, as, 214–215
constitutional limitations on, 247–248
constitutional right to take, 23–24, 205, 246–247
continuity of employment, effect on, 206
criminal sanctions against, 214–223
definition of, 205–206
dismissal for, 35–36, 210–213
immunity in respect of, 257–261
liability in respect of, generally, 204–248
picketing, 282–311
secondary action, 276–280
sit-ins, 311–315
sympathetic action, 265–266
unconstitutional action, 205–206, 310–311
unofficial action, 205–206, 280–281
INDUSTRIAL DEMOCRACY *see also* WORKER PARTICIPATION
INJUNCTIONS
balance of convenience, 320–321, 327–329
breaches of the criminal law, to restrain, 333–334
denial of, 330
dismissal of trade union official, to restrain, 140–142
generally, 316–336
interim, 317, 318–319
interlocutory, 317, 319–329
  appeals against grant or refusal, 331–333
  criteria for the granting of, 319–326
  discretion, 317
  object of, 319, 326
mandatory, 317, 329–330
permanent, 317, 329
power to grant, 316–317
terms of. 330–331

trade union, against, 253–255
INTERNATIONAL LABOUR ORGANISATION
Conventions
  Freedom of Association, 14–15, 54
  Minimum wages, 184–185
  Promotion of Collective Bargaining, 201
INTERFERENCE WITH CONTRACT *see* TORT
INTERFERENCE WITH TRADE *see* TORT
INTIMIDATION *see* TORT
IRISH CONGRESS OF TRADE UNIONS
Constitution of, 6–7
  enforceability of, 102
  cl. 47(d), constitutionality of, 103
Disputes Committee, 2, 6, 16–17, 30, 102–106
  natural justice before, 103–106
  ruling, implementation of, 106
picketing policy, 301–302

JOINT INDUSTRIAL COUNCIL
excepted body and, 52
purpose of, 357
registration of, 357–358
trade union as, 40
JOINT LABOUR COMMITTEE
abolition of, 186
composition of, 186–187
employment regulation orders, 188–193
  Constitution and, 189–191
  effect of, 191–193
  factors to be taken into account in making of, 188–191
  offences in connection with, 191, 193
  power of Minister, in respect of, 193
  submission of proposals for, 188
establishment of, 184, 185–186
excepted body, as, 51
function of, 185, 188
generally, 183–193
policy behind, 183–185
proceeding of, 187–188
role of Labour Court, 183–193

LABOUR COURT
administration of business of, 339, 353
appeals from, 353–354
composition of, 338–339
confidential information, 345
functions in relation to
  arbitration, 351
  conciliation, 340–342
  Fair Employment Rules, 353
  interpretation of agreements, 152–153, 353
  investigation of trade disputes, 342–351
  Joint Industrial Councils, 357–358
  mediation, 342

Index 379

Ministerial references, 351–352
minimum wage-fixing machinery,
   183–193
registered employment agreements,
   146–153
Rights Commissioners, 357
generally, 338–356
independence of, 339–340, 352–353
industrial relations officers, 341–342
judicial review of, 354–355
lawyers and, 346–347
privilege before, 355–356
procedures before, 344–347
recommendations, effect of, 348–349,
   350–351
recommendations, issue of, 351
recommendations, making of, 347–351
recognition disputes, and, 20–23
sittings in camera, 344–345
witnesses, powers in relation to, 345
MINIMUM WAGE LEGISLATION see
JOINT LABOUR COMMITTEE

NEGOTIATION LICENCE
advantages of, 60–62
amalgamation, effect of, on, 79
application procedure, 58
automaticity, principle of, 58
conditions of entitlement, 53–57
   compatibility with constitution, 54
foreign based unions, 56–57
   controlling authority, 57
High Court application and, 56
need for, 50–51, 139, 301
NATURAL JUSTICE see also
CONSTITUTION
admission to trade union, in, 106–107
dismissal of union officials, in, 140–142
expulsion from trade unions, in, 104–106,
   111–112, 115–121
union rules excluding, 117–118
NUISANCE see also TORT
picket as, 286–288, 298

OCCUPATIONS see SIT-IN

PICKETING
affray, as, 297
breach of the peace, as, 295–297
civil liability for, 297–311
Constitution and, 8, 10, 284–285
consumer picketing, 309
contempt of court, as, 295
control of, by gardaí, 295–297
criminal liability for, 289–295
generally, 282–311
Houses of the Oireachtas, in vicinity of,
   284–285
I.C.T.U. policy on, 301–302
immunity in respect of, 297–311
   statutory restrictions on, 300–301

injunction to restrain see
INJUNCTIONS
legal status of, 283–289
legality of, at common law, 8, 285–289
location of, 302–308
mass picketing, 298–300
non-unionists, by, 300–301
nuisance, as, 286–288, 298
obstruction of gardaí, as, 295–297
obstruction of highway, as, 293–294
place of work, whether limited to,
   305–308
procedure, breach of, in, 310–311
public nuisance, as, 293–294
purpose of, 308–310
reasons for, 282
riot, as, 294
rout, as, 294
secondary picketing, 305–308
trespass to highway, as, 288–289
unlawful assembly, as, 294
watching and besetting, 285, 289–293
POLITICAL FUND
alteration of union rules and, 92, 108
amalgamation affecting, 78–79, 80
ballot for, 92–93
Constitution and, 9
contracting out of, 93–94
discrimination concerning, 7, 93–94
generally, 89–95, 98, 99–100
jurisdiction of courts in relation to, 94,
   95
political objects, meaning of, 90–92
powers of Registrar in relation to, 46–47,
   94–95, 110
non-contributor to, position of, 93–94

RECOGNITION
consequence of, 19–20
constitutional right to, 15–20
employers' association, by, 161
industrial action to secure, 271
Labour Court, policy on, 20–23
meaning of, 15
statutory provision for securing, 1, 19
trade dispute concerning, 19, 271
REGISTERED EMPLOYMENT
AGREEMENT
alteration of, 150
definition of, 147
duration of, 149–150
interpretation of, 152
Labour Court and, 146–153
procedure concerning registration,
   147–149
registration, effect of, 151–152
termination of, 150
REGISTRAR OF FRIENDLY
SOCIETIES
amalgamations, powers in relation to, 46,
   47, 72–77

certification, powers in relation to, 41–42
decisions, right of appeal against, 45, 46, 47–48
political fund, powers in relation to, 46–47, 94–95, 110
powers, constitutionality of, 45–48
registration, powers in relation to, 43–44
trade union rules, powers in relation to, 46–47
withdrawal of certificate of status, powers in relation to 41–42
withdrawal of certificate of registration, powers in relation to, 44–45
RESTRAINT OF TRADE
purposes of trade union, as being in, 82
rules of trade union, as being in, 125–126
RIGHT TO WORK *see* CONSTITUTION
RIGHTS COMMISSIONER
functions of, 356
office of, 356–357
recommendations of, appeal against, 357

SCHREGLE
Memorandum, 1
SEAMEN
strike by, 219–220
SECONDARY ACTION *see also* TRADE DISPUTE
immunity in respect of, 276–280
picketing, 305–308
SOCIAL WELFARE
disqualification from, during trade dispute, 361–376
general rule, 362–365
policy behind, 361–362
proviso, 365–370
strikers' families, 370–371
Social Welfare Tribunal, 371–376
composition of, 375
function of, 372
procedure before, 375–376
"unreasonable deprivation of employment", 372–375
SOCIAL WELFARE TRIBUNAL *see* SOCIAL WELFARE
SIT-IN
civil liability, 311–313
criminal liability, 313–315
injunction to restrain *see* INJUNCTION
orders of possession, 312–313
STATUTORY DUTY
breach of, 220–223
STRIKE
breach of contract as, 206–210
conspiracy as, 215–216
contemplation or furtherance of a trade dispute in, 276–280
continuity of employment, effect on, 206
criminal sanctions against, 214–233
defence forces by, 219
defence forces, by, 219

dismissal for, 210–213
electricity workers, by, 217–218
gardaí, by, 219
gas workers, by, 217–218
no-strike clauses, 148–149, 208
organisers, liability of, 230–239
political strikes, 274
postal and telecommunications workers, by, 219
public sector employees, by, 218–219
registered employment agreement, in breach of, 151–152
right to, 9, 205, 208, 212
seamen, by, 219–220
social welfare payments during, 361–376
suspension of contract by, 207–210
taking part in, 212–213
tortious liability for, 223–246
water workers, by, 217–218

TORT
breach of statutory duty, 220–223, 245–246
conspiracy, 12, 227–230
immunity from, in trade dispute, 257–258
immunity from liability in, 224, 250–281
limitations on, 261–281
inducement of breach of contract, 230–239
direct, 234–236
immunity from, in trade dispute, 258–261
indirect, 235, 236–238
inducement, definition of, 235
justification, 238–239
interference with trade, 224–227, 242–246
immunity from in trade dispute, 258–261
intimidation, 239–242
nuisance, picketing as, 286–288, 298
picketing, liability in, 297–311
trespass, picketing as, 288–289
unlawful interference with trade, 242–246
TRADE DISPUTE
conciliation in, 340–342
contemplation of, in, 276
definition of, 263–276, 343
furtherance of, in, 276–280
"golden formula", 261–280
connection with required subject matter, 267–269
dispute, need for, 261–263
person, definition of, 275–276
workman, definition of, 263, 275–276
immunity in, effect of, 259
inter-union disputes, 263
Labour Court investigation into, 342–351
outside the State, 275–276
parties to, 263–267
political disputes, 274

resolution of, generally, 337–360
social welfare payments during, 361–376
statutory protection in, generally, 249–281
   immunity in respect of conspiracy, 257–258
   immunity in respect of inducement of breach of contract, 258–261
   immunity in respect of interference with trade, 258–261
   lack of immunity in respect of intimidation, 259
   legislative history of, 249–250
   tortious immunity of trade unions, constitutionality of, 255–257
subject matter of, generally, 269–276
   closed shop, 7–12
   conditions of labour, 271–274
   employment, 269–271
   non-employment, 269–271
   recognition, 19, 271
   terms of employment, 271–274
   trade union membership, 273–274
trade union as party to, 264–267

TRADE UNION FUNDS
annual returns, in respect of, 50, 58
books, inspection of, 88
immunity of, 137
investment of, 84–86
trustees and, 48–49, 85–86, 137

TRADE UNION MEMBERSHIP
cesser of, 5, 59
conditions of entry, 5, 7, 59
contract of, 107–109
disciplinary proceedings, 113–121
   exhaustion of internal remedies, need for, 119–120
   jurisdiction of courts, 119
discrimination, 101–102
dismissal for, 34–35
expulsion, 103–106, 113–121, 127–128, 129–130
formation of, 101–107
generally, 100–133
incidents of, 107–113
judicial attitude towards, 101–101, 121–133
participation in decision-making process, right to, 24–26
resignation from, 81, 113, 118–119
right to, 4–5
trade dispute concerning, 273–274

TRADE UNION OFFICIALS
appointment, 134–136
   statutory regulation, 136
candidacy, 134–136
dismissal of, 115–117, 140–142
generally, 133–142
liability, 137–139
powers and duties, 136–137
union liability for acts of, 139–140

TRADE UNION RULES
admission, 106–107
amendment of, 92, 108
automatic forfeiture clauses, 114–115, 118
contract, as, 107–109
elections, 134–136
enforceability of, 99, 120–133
expulsion, 103–106, 113–121, 127–130
implication of, 103–104, 107–108
industrial action and, 120–121
interpretation of, 107, 113–121, 133, 134–136
modification of, in amalgamation, 74, 100
natural justice and, 104–107
ousting jurisdiction of court, 119
powers of Registrar in relation to, 46–47
privity, doctrine of, in relation to, 130–131
restraint of trade as, 107, 125–126
sources of, 107–113
   Constitution, 111–112
   contract, 107–109
   E.E.C. law, 112–113
   statute, 109–111
statutory requirements in relation to 108–109

TRADE UNIONS
accounts, 88–89, 109
action in tort against, 61, 62–63, 250–257
activities of, dismissed for, 35–36
admission to, 29, 100–107
affairs of, right to participate in 24–26
agent as, 139–140, 160–161
amalgamation of, 2, 70–80
authorised union, 53–62
   condition of entitlement, 53–57
   High Court deposits, 53–57
   obligations of, 59–60
   see also NEGOTIATION LICENCE
branches of, 81, 81, 83
   recession, 81, 113
capacity to sue, 66
capacity to be sued, 63–69
certified union, 41–42
check off, 96–98
classification of, 38–62
companies as, 40
consultation with on collective redundancies, 167–179
consultation with on health and safety, 181–183
consultation with on transfer of undertakings, 179–181
definition of, 38–41
disputes between, 1–2, 5–6, 16–17, 263
dissolution of, 80–81, 109, 129
   distribution of assets, 80–81
doctrine of illegality and, 107

doctrine of restraint of trade and, 82, 107, 125–126
doctrine of *ultra vires*, 67, 89
employers associations as, 39
excepted bodies, 51–52
federations of, 40
formation of, 2
freedom of association *see* FREEDOM OF ASSOCIATION
inspection of books, 59, 109
internal affairs, judicial intervention into 121–133
internal government of, 99, 100, 109, 112–113, 136
Joint Industrial Councils as, 40
Joint Labour Committees as, 40
legal status of, 62–69
  registered, 63–66
  unregistered, 62–63
legality of, 38, 82, 125–126
membership of, dismissal for, 34–35
multiplicity of, 1
name, change of, 43, 78
objects of, 38–39
partnership as, 40–41
political fund, 85–95
property of, 48–49, 77, 82–83, 137–138
register, maintenance of, 59
registered union, 42–50
  advantages of registration, 48–50
  effect of registration, 44
  obligations incurred as a result of registration, 50
  process of registration, 42
representative action, 62–63
returns, 50, 60, 88–89, 109, 136, 138–139
rule in Foss v. Harbottle and, 67–69
taxation, 49
tort, immunity in, 224, 250–257
  constitutionality, 255–257
trade dispute, party to, 264–267
trustees, 48–49, 82–88, 137
  appointment of, 83–84
  duties of, 85–86, 89
  liability of, 86–88, 98
  powers of, 84–85

replacement, 84
unofficial strikers as, 40
TRANSFER OF ENGAGEMENTS *see also* AMALGAMATION
ballot on, 73–74
complaints procedure, 74–77
constitutionality of, 76
conditions necessary for, 72–74
foreign based unions, involving, 71–72, 80
grants in support of, 77
instrument of, 72–73
property, position of, on, 77
union rule book, modification on, 74, 108, 110
TRANSFER OF UNDERTAKINGS
consultation on, generally, 179–181
consultation, meaning of, 180
consultation, requirements for, 180–181
failure to consult, criminal proceedings in respect of, 181
meaning of, 180
TRESPASS
picketing as, 288–289
sit-in as, 303–304, 311–315

VICARIOUS LIABILITY
union, of, for acts of officials, 139–140

WORKER PARTICIPATION *see also* COLLECTIVE BARGAINING
Advisory Committee on, 195–196
appointment of directors, 200
E.E.C. proposals in relation to, 194–195
elections in respect of, 196–200
  entitlement to vote in, 196, 197
employee representation, 193–201
generally, 193–201
nomination of candidates, 20, 196, 197–199
policy behind, 193–194
provision of information, 201–203
qualified body, meaning of, 198–199
remuneration of directors, 200–201
returning officer, 197, 198, 199
State enterprises, affecting, 195